I0085672

Sioux City Western Publishing Company

HISTORY of WESTERN IOWA

its Settlement and Growth

Sioux City Western Publishing Company

HISTORY of WESTERN IOWA
its Settlement and Growth

ISBN/EAN: 9783741123429

Manufactured in Europe, USA, Canada, Australia, Japa

Cover: Foto ©Lupo / pixelio.de

Manufactured and distributed by brebook publishing software
(www.brebook.com)

Sioux City Western Publishing Company

HISTORY of WESTERN IOWA

Sioux City Western Publishing Company

HISTORY of WESTERN IOWA

OF

WESTERN IOWA

Its Settlement and Growth,

A COMPREHENSIVE COMPILATION OF PROGRESSIVE EVENTS CONCERNING
THE COUNTIES, CITIES, TOWNS AND VILLAGES—BIOGRAPH-
ICAL SKETCHES OF THE PIONEERS AND BUSI-
NESS MEN, WITH AN AUTHENTIC

HISTORY OF THE STATE OF IOWA.

SIOUX CITY:
WESTERN PUBLISHING COMPANY.
1882.

PREFACE.

FEW enterprises are more liable to misunderstanding than a work of this character. The main trouble arises from confounding it with books in general. A large, elegantly-bound volume—maybe a History of the World, or of some particular Nation, or embracing a scope of interest to a very considerable portion of mankind, in the gathering of material for which the continuous time and labor of but one person have been employed, and the sales of which are equally extensive and continuous with the very general and comprehensive nature of the whole—such a volume, we say, finds purchasers at so low a price as to make that asked for a work of the kind herewith presented seem disproportionately large.

Perhaps it is a work of fiction that is offered the purchasing public. Very well; the "Novel" is sumptuously bound, artistically illustrated, and contains a great number of closely printed pages; yet its price per copy is even less than that for which the Publishers offer their HISTORY OF WESTERN IOWA. Hence, not infrequently individuals leap unthinkingly to inadequate and necessarily hasty conclusions, such as, that the price asked is exorbitant, and so on, for quantity. Such a mode of overleaping reasonableness naturally leads to depreciation of the enterprise, and per consequence, many highly creditable works, having begun their career with a "damning by faint praise," have ended it in unthinking condemnation.

Now, it is not the intention to argue or philosophize. We herewith present the results of half a year's diligent labor, which has occupied the entire time and attention of a number of competent men—labor not of the most inviting kind, but of a sort akin to drudgery. . And not only time and work, but money also to a not inconsiderable amount, has been expended. The Publishers ask you to remember that the HISTORY OF WESTERN IOWA has been compiled for *you;* that its sales are limited almost wholly to that portion of country the facts concerning which it recounts; that, were it possible to send the books broadcast over the country, and sell them in every city, village and hamlet, the selling price could, and would, be proportionately reduced. The work is intended mainly for home consumption; the expense is large, the sales disproportionately small. In presenting this work to the citizens of Western Iowa, we do so at the very lowest possible margin of profit, and that, even, problematic.

With these remarks, we trust we have established relations of friendly understanding with every candid patron. The nature and plan of the work were fully explained in the PROSPECTUS, to the promises of which we have endeavored strictly to adhere. There are errors, of course; no book was ever published

that did not contain errors.   These are most likely, in this instance, to occur in
the Biographical Departments of the work.   The persons approached by a member of the Publishing Staff in many instances themselves unintentionally give
incorrect information; the historian has no other means of knowing, and so,
trusting to the accuracy of the informant—especially as the matter sought is of
personal concern to the informant himself—he "makes a note" of it, and transcribes it for the HISTORY.   Hence. patrons should judge leniently concerning
such errors as may appear; for, in both the matter of compiling and printing,
no pains have been spared to insure the strictest accuracy.

It goes without the saying. that it is not to the interest of either the Publishers or their employes to pervert the facts in any case to the help or hurt of
any one.

And so, asking only a recognition of the difficulties, risk and unavoidable
obstacles in the way of such an undertaking, we launch the HISTORY OF WESTERN IOWA upon the sea of popular favor, confident that it will meet with a
reception in some degree commensurate to its merits.

Very Respectfully,

THE PUBLISHERS.

March, 1882.

CONTENTS.

HISTORY OF IOWA.

DISCOVERY AND OCCUPATION.

The name Iowa is said to signify "The Beautiful Land," and was applied to this magnificent and fruitful region by its ancient owners, to express their appreciation of its superiority of climate, soil and location. Prior to 1803, the Mississippi River was the extreme western boundary of the United States. All the great empire lying west of the "Father of Waters," from the Gulf of Mexico on the south to British America on the north, and westward to the Pacific Ocean, was a Spanish province. A brief historical sketch of the discovery and occupation of this great empire by the Spanish and French governments will be a fitting introduction to the history of the young and thriving State of Iowa, which, until the commencement of the present century, was a part of the Spanish possessions in America.

Early in the Spring of 1542, Ferdinand DeSoto discovered the mouth of the Mississippi River at the mouth of the Washita. After the sudden death of DeSoto, in May of the same year, his followers built a small vessel, and in July, 1543, descended the great river to the Gulf of Mexico.

In accordance with the usage of nations, under which title to the soil was claimed by right of discovery, Spain, having conquered Florida and discovered the Mississippi, claimed all the territory bordering on that river and the Gulf of Mexico. But it was also held by the European nations that, while discovery gave title, that title must be perfected by actual possession and occupation. Although Spain claimed the territory by right of first discovery, she made no effort to occupy it; by no permanent settlement had she perfected and held her title, and therefore had forfeited it when, at a later period, the Lower Mississippi Valley was rediscovered and occupied by France.

The labors of the zealous French Jesuits of Canada in penetrating the unknown region of the West, commencing in 1611, form a history of no ordinary interest, but have no particular connection with the scope of the present work, until in the Fall of 1665. Pierre Claude Allouez, who had entered Lake Superior in September, and sailed along the southern coast in search of copper, had arrived at the great village of the Chippewas at Chegoimecegon. Here a grand council of some ten or twelve of the principal Indian nations was held. The Pottawatomies of Lake Michigan, the Sacs and Foxes of the West, the Hurons from the North, the

Illinois from the South, and the Sioux from the land of the prairie and wild rice, were all assembled there. The Illinois told the story of their ancient glory and about the noble river on the banks of which they dwelt. The Sioux also told their white brother of the same great river, and Allouez promised to the assembled tribes the protection of the French nation against all their enemies, native or foreign.

The purpose of discovering the great river about which the Indian nations had given such glowing accounts, appears to have originated with Marquette, in 1669. In the year previous, he and Claude Dablon had established the Mission of St. Mary's, the oldest white settlement within the present limits of the State of Michigan. Marquette was delayed in the execution of his great undertaking, and spent the interval in studying the language and habits of the Illinois Indians, among whom he expected to travel.

About this time the French Government had determined to extend the Dominion of France to the extreme western borders of Canada. Nicholas Perrot was sent as the agent of the government, to propose a grand council of the Indian nations, at St. Mary's.

When Perrot reached Green Bay, he extended the invitation far and near; and, escorted by Pottawatomies, repaired on a mission of peace and friendship to the Miamis, who occupied the region about the present location of Chicago.

In May 1671, a great council of Indians gathered at the Falls of St. Mary, from all parts of the northwest, from the head waters of the St. Lawrence, from the valley of the Mississippi and from the Red River of the North. Perrot met with them, and after grave consultation, formally announced to the assembled nations that their good French Father felt an abiding interest in their welfare, and had placed them all under the powerful protection of the French Government.

Marquette, during that same year, had gathered at Point St. Ignace the remnants of one branch of the Hurons. This station, for a long series of years, was considered the key to the unknown West.

The time was now auspicious for the consummation of Marquette's grand project. The successful termination of Perrot's mission, and the general friendliness of the native tribes, rendered the contemplated expedition much less perilous. But it was not until 1673 that the intrepid and enthusiastic priest was finally ready to depart on his daring and perilous journey to lands never trod by white men. Having implored the blessing of God upon his undertaking, on the 13th day of May, 1673, with Joliet and five Canadian-French voyageurs, or boatmen, he left the mission on his daring journey. Ascending Green Bay and Fox River, these bold and enthusiastic pioneers of religion and discovery proceeded until they reached a Miami and Kickapoo village, where Marquette was delighted to find "a beautiful cross planted in the middle of the town, ornamented with white skins, red girdles and bows and arrows, which these good people had offered to the Great Manitou, or God, to thank Him for the pity He had bestowed on them during the winter,in having given them abundant chase." This was the extreme point beyond which the explorations of the French missionaries had not then extended. He called together the principal men of the village, and informed them that his companion, Joliet, had been sent by the French Governor of Canada to discover new countries, to be added to the dominion of France; but that he, himself, had been sent by the Most High God, to carry the glorious religion of the Cross; and assured his wondering hearers that on this mission he had no fear of death, to which he knew he would be exposed on his perilous journeys.

Obtaining the services of two Miami guides, to conduct his little band to the Wisconsin River, he left the hospitable Indians on the 10th of June. Conducting them across the portage, their Indian guides returned to their village, and the little party descended the Wisconsin, to the great river which had so long been so anxiously looked for, and boldly floated down its unknown waters.

On the 25th of June, the explorers discovered indications of Indians on the west bank of the river, and landed a little above the mouth of the river now known as Des Moines, and for the first time Europeans trod the soil of Iowa. Leaving the Canadians to guard the canoes, Marquette and Joliet boldly followed the trail into the interior for fourteen miles (some authorities say six), to an Indian village situated on the banks of a river, and discovered two other villages, on the rising ground about half a league distant. Their visit, while it created much astonishment, did not seem to be entirely unexpected, for there was a tradition or prophecy among the Indians that white visitors were to come to them. They were, therefore, received with great respect and hospitality, and were cordially tendered the calumet or pipe of peace. They were informed that this band was a part of the Illini nation, and that their village was called Monin-gou-ma or Moingona, which was the name of the river on which it stood. This, from its similarity of sound, Marquette corrupted into Des Moines (Monk's River), its present name.

Here the voyagers remained six days, learning much of the manners and customs of their new friends. The new religion they boldly preached, and the authority of the King of France they proclaimed were received without hostility or remonstrance by their savage entertainers. On their departure, they were accompanied to their canoes by the chiefs and hundreds of warriors. Marquette received from them the sacred calumet, the emblem of peace and safeguard among the nations, and re-embarked for the rest of his journey.

In 1682, LaSalle descended the Mississippi to the Gulf of Mexico and in the name of the King of France took formal possession

of all the immense region watered by the great river and its
tributaries from its source to its mouth. and named it Louisiana,
in honor of his master, Louis XIV. At the close of the seventeenth century, France claimed, by right of discovery and occupancy, the whole valley of the Mississippi and its tributaries, including Texas, as far as the Rio del Norte.

In 1719, Phillipe Francis Renault arrived in Illinois with two
hundred miners and artisans. The war between France and Spain
at this time rendered it extremely probable that the Mississippi
Valley might become the theater of Spanish hostilities against the
French settlements; to prevent this, as well as to extend French
claims, a chain of forts was begun, to keep open the connection
between the mouth and the sources of the Mississippi. Fort Orleans, high up the Mississippi River, was erected as an outpost in
1720.

The Mississippi scheme was at the zenith of its power and glory
in January, 1720, but the gigantic bubble collapsed more suddenly
than it had been inflated, and the Company was declared hopelessly
bankrupt in May following. France was impoverished by it, both
private and public credit were overthrown, capitalists suddenly found
themselves paupers, and labor was left without employment. The
effect on the colony of Louisiana was disastrous.

While this was going on in Lower Louisiana the region about
the lakes was the theater of Indian hostilities,rendering the passage
from Canada to Louisiana extremely dangerous for many years. The
Englishhad not only extended their Indian trade into the vicinity of
the French settlements, but through their friends, the Iroquois, had
gained a marked ascendancy over the Foxes, a fierce and powerful
tribe, of Iroquois descent, whom they incited to hostilities against
the French. The Foxes began their hostilities with the siege of
Detroit in 1712, a siege which continued for nineteen consecutive
days, and although the expedition resulted in diminishing their numbers and humbling their pride, yet it was not until after several successive campaigns, embodying the best military resources of New
France, had been directed against them, that they were finally defeated at the great battles of Butte des Morts, and on the Wisconsin River, and driven west in 1746.

The Company, having found that the cost of defending Louisiana exceeded the returns from its commerce, solicited leave to surrender the Mississippi wilderness to the home government. Accordingly, on the 10th of April, 1732, the jurisdiction and control
over the commerce reverted to the Crown of France. The Company had held possession of Louisiana fourteen years. In 1735,
Bienville returned to assume command for the King.

A glance at a few of the old French settlements will show the
progress made in portions of Louisiana during the early part of
the eighteenth century. As early as 1705, traders and hunters had
penetrated the fertile regions of the Wabash, and from this region,

at that early date, fifteen thousand hides and skins had been collected and sent to Mobile for the European market.

In the year 1716, the French population on the Wabash kept up a lucrative commerce with Mobile by means of traders and voyageurs. The Ohio river was comparatively unknown.

In 1746, agriculture on the Wabash had attained to greater prosperity than in any of the French settlements besides, and in that year six hundred barrels of flour were manufactured and shipped to New Orleans, together with considerable quantities of hide, peltry, tallow and beeswax.

In the Illinois country, also, considerable settlements had been made, so that, in 1730, they embraced one hundred and forty French families, about six hundred "converted Indians," and many traders and voyageurs.

In 1753, the first actual conflict arose between Louisiana and the Atlantic colonies. From the earliest advent of the Jesuit fathers, up to the period of which we speak, the great ambition of the French had been, not alone to preserve their possessions in the West, but by every possible means to prevent the slightest attempt of the English, east of the mountains, to extend their settlements toward the Mississippi. France was resolved on retaining possession of the great territory which her missionaries had discovered and revealed to the world. French commandants had avowed their intention of seizing every Englishman within the Ohio Valley.

The colonies of Pennsylvania, New York and Virginia were most affected by the encroachments of France in the extension of her dominion; and particularly in the great scheme of uniting Canada with Louisiana. To carry out this purpose the French had taken possession of a tract of country claimed by Virginia, and had commenced a line of forts extending from the lakes to the Ohio River. Virginia was not only alive to her own interests, but attentive to the vast importance of an immediate and effectual resistance on the part of all the English colonies to the actual and contemplated encroachments of the French.

In 1753, Governor Dinwiddie, of Virginia, sent George Washington, then a young man just twenty-one, to demand of the French commandant "a reason for invading British dominions while a solid peace subsisted." Washington met the French commandant, Gardeur de St. Pierre, on the head waters of the Alleghany, and having communicated to him the object of his journey, received the insolent answer that the French would not discuss the matter of right, but would make prisoners of every Englishman found trading on the Ohio and its waters. The country, he said belonged to the French, by virtue of the discoveries of La Salle, and they would not withdraw from it.

In January, 1754, Washington returned to Virginia, and made his report to the Governor and Council. Forces were at once raised and Washington, as Lieutenant Colonel, was dispatched at the head of a hundred and fifty men, to the forks of the Ohio, with orders to "finish the fort already begun there by the Ohio Company, and to make prisoners, kill or destroy all who interrupted the English settlements."

On his march through the forests of Western Pennsylvania, Washington, through the aid of friendly Indians, discovered the French concealed among the rocks, and as they ran to seize their arms, ordered his men to fire upon them, at the same time, with his own musket, setting the example. An action lasting about a quarter of an hour ensued; ten of the Frenchmen were killed, among them Jumonville, the commander of the party, and twenty-one were made prisoners. The dead were scalped by the Indians, and the chief, bearing a tomahawk and a scalp, visited all the tribes of the Miamis, urging them to join the Six Nations and English against the French. The French, however, were soon re-enforced and Col. Washington was compelled to return to Fort Necessity. Here, on the 3d day of July, De Villiers invested the fort with 600 French troops and 100 Indians. On the 4th, Washington accepted terms of capitulation and the English garrison withdrew from the valley of the Ohio.

This attack of Washington upon Jumonville aroused the indignation of France, and war was formally declared in May, 1756, and the " French and Indian War " devastated the colonies for several years. Montreal, Detroit and all Canada were surrendered to the English, and on the 10th of February, 1763, by the treaty of Paris—which had been signed, though not formally ratified by the respective governments, on the 3d of November, 1762—France relinquished to Great Britain all that portion of the province of Louisiana lying on the east side of the Mississippi, except the island and town of New Orleans. On the same day that the treaty of Paris was signed France, by a secret treaty, ceded to Spain all her possessions on the west side of the Mississippi, including the whole country to the head waters of the Great River, and west to the Rocky Mountains, and the jurisdiction of France in America, which had lasted nearly a century, was ended.

At the close of the Revolutionary war, by the treaty of peace between Great Britain and the United States, the English Government ceded to the latter all the territory on the east side of the Mississippi River and north of the thirty-first parallel of north latitude. At the same time, Great Britain ceded to Spain all the Floridas, comprising all the territory east of the Mississippi and south of the southern limits of the United States.

At this time, therefore, the present State of Iowa was a part of the Spanish possessions in North America, as all the territory west of the Mississippi River was under the dominion of Spain. That government also possessed all the territory of the Floridas east of the great river and south of the thirty-first parallel of north latitude. The Mississippi, therefore, so essential to the prosperity of the western portion of the United States, for the last three hundred miles of its course flowed wholly within the Spanish dominions, and that government claimed the exclusive right to use and control it below the southern boundary of the United States.

The free navigation of the Mississippi was a very important question during all the time that Louisiana remained a dependency of the Spanish Crown, and as the final settlement intimately affected the status of the then future State of Iowa, it will be interesting to trace its progress.

The people of the United States occupied and exercised jurisdiction over the entire eastern valley of the Mississippi, embracing all the country drained by its eastern tributaries; they had a natural right, according to the accepted international law, to follow these rivers to the sea, and to the use of the Mississippi River accordingly, as the great natural channel of commerce. The river was not only necessary but absolutely indispensable to the prosperity and growth of the western settlements then rapidly rising into commercial and political importance. They were situated in the heart of the great valley, and with wonderful expansive energies and accumulating resources, it was very evident that no power on earth could deprive them of the free use of the river below them, only while their numbers were insufficient to enable them to maintain their right by force. Inevitably, therefore, immediately after the ratification of the treaty of 1783, the Western people began to demand the free navigation of the Mississippi—not as a favor, but as a right. In 1786, both banks of the river, below the mouth of the Ohio, were occupied by Spain, and military posts on the east bank enforced her power to exact heavy duties on all imports by way of the river for the Ohio region. Every boat decending the river was forced to land and submit to the arbitrary revenue exactions of the Spanish authorities. Under the administration of Governor Miro, these rigorous exactions were somewhat relaxed from 1787 to 1790: but Spain held it as her right to make them. Taking advantage of the claim of the American people, that the Mississippi should be opened to them, in 1791, the Spanish Government concocted a scheme for the dismemberment of the Union. The plan was to induce the Western people to separate from the Eastern States by liberal land grants and extraordinary commercial privileges.

Spanish emissaries, among the people of Ohio and Kentucky, informed them that the Spanish Government would grant them favorable commercial privileges, provided they would secede from the Federal Government east of the mountains. The Spanish Minister to the United States plainly declared to his confidential correspondent that, unless the Western people would declare their independence and refuse to remain in the Union, Spain was determined never to grant the free navigation of the Mississippi.

By the treaty of Madrid, October 20, 1795, however, Spain formally stipulated that the Mississippi River, from its source to the Gulf, for its entire width, should be free to American trade and commerce, and that the people of the United States should be permitted for three years, to use the port of New Orleans as a port of deposit for their merchandize and produce, duty free.

In November, 1801, the United States Government received, through Rufus King, its Minister at the Court of St. James, a copy of the treaty between Spain and France, signed at Madrid, March 21, 1801, by which the session of Louisiana to France, made the previous autumn, was confirmed.

The change offered a favorable opportunity to secure the just rights of the United States, in relation to the free navigation of the Mississippi, and ended the attempt to dismember the Union by an effort to secure an independent government west of the Alleghany Mountains. On the 7th day of January, 1803, the American House of Representatives adopted a resolution declaring their "unalterable determination to maintain the boundaries and the rights of navigation and commerce through the River Mississippi, as established by existing treaties."

In the same month, President Jefferson nominated and the Senate confirmed Robert R. Livingston and James Monroe as Envoys Plenipotentiary to the Court of France, and Charles Pinckney and James Monroe to the Court of Spain, with plenary power to negotiate treaties to effect the object enunciated by the popular branch of the National Legislature. These envoys were instructed to secure, if possible, the cession of Florida and New Orleans, but it does not appear that Mr. Jefferson and his cabinet had any idea of purchasing that part of Louisiana lying on the west side of the Mississippi. In fact, on the 2d of March following, the instructions were sent to our Ministers, containing a plan which expressly left to France "all her territory on the west side of the Mississippi." Had these instructions been followed, it might have been that there would not have been any State of Iowa or any other member of the glorious Union of States west of the "Father of Waters."

In obedience to his instructions, however, Mr. Livingston broached this plan to M. Talleyrand, Napoleon's Prime Minister, when that courtly diplomatist quietly suggested to the American Minister that France *might* be willing to cede the *whole French domain* in North America to the United States, and asked how much the Federal Government would be willing to give for it. Livingston intimated that twenty millions of francs might be a fair price. Talleyrand thought that not enough, but asked the Americans to "think of it." A few days later, Napoleon, in an interview with Mr. Livingston, in effect informed the American Envoy that he had secured Louisiana in a contract with Spain for the purpose of turning it over to the United States for a mere nominal sum. He had been compelled to provide for the safety of that province by the treaty, and he was "anxious to give the United States a magnificent bargain for a mere trifle." The price proposed was one hundred and twenty-five million francs. This was subsequently modified to fifteen million dollars, and on this basis a treaty was negotiated, and was signed on the 30th day of April, 1803.

This treaty was ratified by the Federal Government, and by act of Congress, approved October 31. 1803, the President of the United States was authorized to take possession of the territory and provide for it a temporary government. Accordingly, on the 20th day of September following, on behalf of the President, Gov. Clairborne and Gen. Wilkinson took possession of the Louisiana purchase, and raised the American flag over the newly acquired domain, at New Orleans. Spain, although it had by treaty ceded the province to France in 1801, still held *quasi* possession and at first objected to the transfer, but withdrew her opposition early in 1804.

By this treaty. thus successfully consummated, and the peaceable withdrawal of Spain, the then infant nation of the New World extended its dominion west of the Mississippi to the Pacific Ocean, and north from the Gulf of Mexico to British America.

If the original design of Jefferson's administration had been accomplished, the United States would have acequired only that portion of the French territory lying east of the Mississippi River, and while the American people would thus have acquired the free navigation of that great river, all of the vast and fertile empire on the west, so rich in its agricultural and inexhaustible mineral resources, would have remained under the dominion of a foreign power. To Napoleon's desire to sell the whole of his North American possessions, and Livingston's act transcending his instructions, which was acquiesced in after it was done, does Iowa owe her position as a part of the United States by the Louisiana purchase.

By authority of an act of Congress, approved March 26. 1804, the newly acquired territory was. on the 1st day of October following, divided: that part lying south of the 33d parallel of north latitute was called the Territory of Orleans, and all north of that parallel the District of Louisiana, which was placed under the authority of the officers of Indiana Territory, until July 4, 1805, when it was organized with territorial government of its own. and so remained until 1812, when the Territory of Orleans became the State of Louisiana, and the name of the Territory of Louisiana was changed to Missouri. On the 4th of July, 1814, that part of Missouri Territory comprising the present State of Arkansas, and the country to the westward, was organized into the Arkansas Territory.

On the 2d of March, 1821, the State of Missouri, being a part
of the territory of that name, was admitted to the Union. June
28, 1834, the territory west of the Mississippi River and north of
Missouri, was made a part of the Territory of Michigan; but two
years later, on the 4th of July, 1836, Wisconsin Territory was
erected, embracing within its limits the present States of Iowa,
Wisconsin and Minnesota.

By act of Congress, approved June 12, 1838, the

TERRITORY OF IOWA

was erected, comprising, in addition to the present State, much the
larger part of Minnesota, and extending north to the boundary of
the British possessions.

THE ORIGINAL OWNERS.

Having traced the early history of the great empire lying west
of the Mississippi, of which the State of Iowa constitutes a part,
from the earliest discovery to the organization of the Territory of
Iowa, it becomes necessary to give some history of the Indians of
Iowa.

According to the policy of the European nations, possession
perfected title to any territory. We have seen that the country
west of the Mississippi was first discovered by the Spaniards, but
afterward, was visited and occupied by the French. It was ceded
by France to Spain, and by Spain back to France again, and then
was purchased and occupied by the United States. During all that
time, it does not appear to have entered into the heads or hearts of
the high contracting parties that the country they bought, sold and
gave away was in the possession of a race of men who, although
savage, owned the vast domain before Columbus first crossed the
Atlantic. Having purchased the territory, the United States
found it still in the possession of its original owners, who had
never been dispossessed; and it became necessary to purchase
again what had already been bought before, or forcibly eject the
occupants; therefore, the history of the Indian nations who occupied Iowa prior to and during its early settlement by the whites,
becomes an important chapter in the history of the State, that
cannot be omitted.

For more than one hundred years after Marquette and Joliet
trod the virgin soil of Iowa, not a single settlement had been made
or attempted; not even a trading post had been established. The
whole country remained in the undisputed possession of the native
tribes, who roamed at will over her beautiful and fertile prairies,
hunted in her woods, fished in her streams, and often poured out
their life-blood in obstinately contested contests for supremacy.
That this State so aptly styled "The Beautiful Land," had been
the theater of numerous, fierce and bloody struggles between rival
nations, for possession of the favored region, long before its settlement by civilized man, there is no room for doubt. In these

savage wars, the weaker party, whether aggressive or defensive, was either exterminated or driven from their ancient hunting grounds.

In 1673, when Marquette discovered Iowa, the Illini were a very powerful people, occupying a large portion of the State; but when the country was again visited by the whites, not a remnant of that once powerful tribe remained on the west side of the Mississippi, and Iowa was principally in the possession of the Sacs and Foxes, a war-like tribe which, originally two distinct nations, residing in New York and on the waters of the St. Lawrence, had gradually fought their way westward, and united, probably, after the Foxes had been driven out of the Fox River country, in 1846, and crossed the Mississippi. The death of Pontiac, a famous Sac chieftain, was made the pretext for war against the Illini, and a fierce and bloody struggle ensued, which continued until the Illinois were nearly destroyed and their hunting grounds possessed by their victorious foes. The Iowas also occupied a portion of the State for a time, in common with the Sacs, but they, too, were nearly destroyed by the Sacs and Foxes, and, in "The Beautiful Land," these natives met their equally warlike foes, the Northern Sioux, with whom they maintained a constant warfare for the possession of the country for many years.

When the United States came in possession of the great valley of the Mississippi, by the Louisiana purchase, the Sacs and Foxes and Iowas possessed the entire territory now comprising the State of Iowa. The Sacs and Foxes, also, occupied the most of the State of Illinois.

The Sacs had four principal villages, where most of them resided, viz: Their largest and most important town—if an Indian village may be called such—and from which emanated most of the obstacles and difficulties encountered by the Government in the extinguishment of Indian titles to land in this region, was on Rock River, near Rock Island; another was on the east bank of the Mississippi, near the mouth of Henderson River; the third was at the head of the Des Moines Rapids, near the present site of Montrose, and the fourth was near the mouth of the Upper Iowa.

The Foxes had three principal villages, viz: One on the west side of the Mississippi, six miles above the rapids of Rock River; another about twelve miles from the river, in the rear of the Dubuque lead mines, and the third on Turkey River.

The Iowas, at one time identified with the Sacs, of Rock River, had withdrawn from them and become a separate tribe. Their principal village was on the Des Moines River, in Van Buren County, on the site where Iowaville now stands. Here the last great battle between the Sacs and Foxes and the Iowas was fought, in which Black Hawk, then a young man, commanded one division of the attacking forces.

The Sacs and Foxes, prior to the settlement of their village on Rock River, had a fierce conflict with the Winnebagoes, subdued them and took possession of their lands. Their village on Rock River, at one time, contained upward of sixty lodges, and was among the largest Indian villages on the continent. In 1825, the Secretary of War estimated the entire number of the Sacs and Foxes at 4,600 souls. Their village was situated in the immediate vicinity of the upper rapids of the Mississippi, where the beautiful and flourishing towns of Rock Island and Davenport are now situated. The beautiful scenery of the island, the extensive prairies, dotted over with groves; the picturesque bluffs along the river banks, the rich and fertile soil, producing large crops of corn, squash and other vegetables, with little labor; the abundance of wild fruit, game, fish, and almost everything calculated to make it a delightful spot for an Indian village, which was found there, had made this place a favorite home of the Sacs, and secured for it the strong attachment and veneration of the whole nation.

North of the hunting grounds of the Sacs and Foxes, were those of the Sioux, a fierce and warlike nation, who often disputed possession with their rivals in savage and bloody warfare. The possessions of these tribes were mostly located in Minnesota, but extended over a portion of Northern and Western Iowa to the Missouri River. Their descent from the north upon the hunting grounds of Iowa frequently brought them into collision with the Sacs and Foxes; and after many a conflict and bloody struggle, a boundary line was established between them by the Government of the United States, in a treaty held at Prairie du Chien, in 1825. But this, instead of settling the difficulties, caused them to quarrel all the more, in consequence of alleged trespasses upon each other's side of the line. These contests were kept up and became so unrelenting that, in 1830, Government bought of the respective tribes of the Sacs and Foxes, and the Sioux, a strip of land twenty miles in width, on both sides of the line, and thus throwing them forty miles apart by creating between them a "neutral ground," commanded them to cease their hostilities. Both the Sacs and Foxes and the Sioux, however, were allowed to fish and hunt on this ground unmolested, provided they did not interfere with each other on United States territory. The Sacs and Foxes and the Sioux were deadly enemies, and neither let an opportunity to punish the other pass unimproved.

In April, 1852, a fight occurred between the Musquaka band of Sacs and Foxes and a band of Sioux, about six miles above Algona, in Kossuth County, on the west side of the Des Moines River. The Sacs and Foxes were under the leadership of Ko-ko-wah, a subordinate chief, and had gone up from their home in Tama County, by way of Clear Lake, to what was then the "neutral ground." At Clear Lake, Ko-ko-wah was informed that a party of Sioux were encamped on the west side of the East Fork of the Des

Moines, and he determined to attack them. With sixty of his warriors, he started and arrived at a point on the east side of the river, about a mile above the Sioux encampment, in the night, and concealed themselves in a grove, where they were able to discover the position and strength of their hereditary foes. The next morning, after many of the Sioux braves had left their camp on hunting tours, the vindictive Sacs and Foxes crossed the river and suddenly attacked the camp. The conflict was desperate for a short time, but the advantage was with the assailants, and the Sioux were routed. Sixteen of them, including some of their women and children, were killed, and a boy 14 years old was captured. One of the Musquakas was shot in the breast by a squaw as they were rushing into the Sioux's camp. He started to run away, when the same brave squaw shot him through the body, at a distance of twenty rods, and he fell dead. Three other Sac braves were killed. But few of the Sioux escaped. The victorious party hurriedly buried their own dead, leaving the dead Sioux above ground, and made their way home, with their captive, with all possible expedition.

PIKE'S EXPEDITION.

Very soon after the acquisition of Louisiana the United States Government adopted measures for the exploration of the new territory, having in view the conciliation of the numerous tribes of Indians by whom it was possessed, and, also, the selection of proper sites for the establishment of military posts and trading stations. The Army of the West, Gen. James Wilkinson commanding, had its headquarters at St. Louis. From this post, Captains Lewis and Clarke, with a sufficient force, were detailed to explore the unknown sources of the Missouri, and Lieut. Zebulon M. Pike, to ascend to the head waters of the Mississippi, Lieut. Pike, with one Sergeant, two Corporals and seventeen privates, left the military camp, near St. Louis, in a keel-boat, with four month's rations, on the 9th day of August, 1805. On the 20th of the same month, the expedition arrived within the present limit of Iowa, at the foot of the Des Moines Rapids, where Pike met William Ewing, who had just been appointed Indian agent at this point, a French interpreter and four chiefs and fifteen Sac and Fox warriors.

At the head of the rapids, where Montrose is now situated, Pike held a council with the Indians, in which he addressed them substantially as follows: "Your great Father, the President of the United States wished to be more intimately acquainted with the situation and wants of the different nations of red people in our newly acquired territory of Louisiana, and has ordered the General to send a number of his warriors in different directions to take them by the hand and make such inquiries as might afford the satisfaction required." At the close of the council he presented the red men with some knives, whisky and tobacco.

Pursuing his way up the river, he arrived, on the 23d of August, at what is supposed, from his description, to be the site of the present city of Burlington, which he selected as the location of a military post. He describes the place as being "on a hill, about forty miles above the River de Moyne Rapids, on the west side of the river in latitude about 41 degrees 21 minutes north. The channel of the river runs on that shore; the hill in front is about sixty feet perpendicular; nearly level on top; four hundred yards in the rear is a small prairie fit for gardening, and immediately under the hill is a limestone spring, sufficient for the consumption of a whole regiment." In addition to this description, which corresponds to Burlington, the spot is laid down on his map at a bend in the river a short distance below the mouth of the Henderson, which pours its waters into the Mississippi from Illinois. The fort was built at Fort Madison, but from the distance, latitude, description and map furnished by Pike, it could not have been the place selected by him while all the circumstances corroborate the opinion that the place he selected was the spot where Burlington is now located, called by the early voyagers on the Mississippi, " Flint Hills."

On the 24th, with one of his men, he went on shore on a hunting expedition, and following a stream which they supposed to be a part of the Mississippi, they were led away from their course. Owing to the intense heat and tall grass, his two favorite dogs, which he had taken with him, became exhausted and he left them on the prairie, supposing that they would follow him as soon as they should get rested, and went on to overtake his boat. Reaching the river, he waited some time for his canine friends, but they did not come, and as he deemed it inexpedient to detain the boat longer, two of his men volunteered to go in pursuit of them, and he continued on his way up the river, expecting that the two men would soon overtake him. They lost their way, however, and for six days were without food, except a few morsels gathered from the stream, and might have perished had they not accidentally met a trader from St. Louis, who induced two Indians to take them up the river, and they overtook the boat at Dubuque.

At Dubuque Pike was cordially received by Julien Dubuque, a Frenchman, who held a mining claim under a grant from Spain. Dubuque had an old field piece and fired a salute in honor of the advent of the first Americans who had visited that part of the Territory. Dubuque, however, was not disposed to publish the wealth of his mines, and the young and apparently inquisitive officer could obtain but little information from him.

After leaving this place, Pike pursued his way up the river, but as he passed beyond the limits of the present State of Iowa, a detailed history of his explorations on the upper waters of the Mississippi more properly belongs to the history of another State.

It is sufficient to say that on the site of Fort Snelling, Minnesota, at the mouth of the Minnesota River, Pike held a council with the Sioux, September 23, and obtained from them a grant of one hundred thousand acres of land. On the 8th of January 1806,

Pike arrived at a trading post belonging to the Northwest Company, on Lake De Sable in latitude 47 °. At this time the then powerful Northwest Company carried on their immense operations from Hudson's Bay to the St. Lawrence; up that river on both sides, along the Great Lakes to the head of Lake Superior, thence to the sources of the Red River of the North, and west to the Rocky Mountains, embracing within the scope of their operations the entire Territory of Iowa. After successfully accomplishing his mission, and performing a valuable service to Iowa and the whole Northwest, Pike returned to St. Louis, arriving there on the 30th of April, 1806.

INDIAN WARS.

The Territory of Iowa, although it had been purchased by the United States, and was ostensibly in the possession of the Government, was still occupied by the Indians, who claimed title to the soil by right of ownership and possession. Before it could be open to settlement by the whites, it was indispensible that the Indian title should be extinguished and the original owners removed. The accomplishment of this purpose required the expenditure of large sums of money and blood, and for a long series of years the frontier was disturbed by Indian wars, terminated repeatedly by treaty, only to be renewed by some act of oppression on the part of the whites or some violation of treaty stipulation.

As previously shown, at the time when the United States assumed the control of the country by virtue of the Louisiana purchase, nearly the whole State was in possession of the Sacs and Foxes, a powerful and warlike nation, who were not disposed to submit without a struggle to what they considered the encroachments of the pale faces.

Among the most noted chiefs, and one whose reitlessness and hatred of the Americans occasioned more trouble to the Government than any others of his tribe, was Black Hawk, who was born at the Sac village, on Rock River, in 1767. He was simply the chief of his own band of Sac warriors, but by his energy and ambition he became the leading spirit of the united nation of Sacs and Foxes, and one of the prominent figures in the history of the country from 1804 until his death. In early manhood he attained some destinction as a fighting chief, having led campaigns against the Osages, and other neighboring tribes. About the beginning of the present century he began to appear prominent in affairs on the Mississippi. Some historians have added to the statement that " it does not appear that he was ever a great general, or possessed any of the qualifications of a successful leader." If this was so, his life was a marvel. How any man who had none of the qualifications of a leader became so prominent as such, as he did, indicates either that he had some ability, or that his cotemporaries, both Indian and Anglo-Saxon, had less than he. He is said to have been the "victim of a narrow prejudice and bitter ill-will against the Americans." but the impartial historian must admit that if he was the enemy of the Americans, it was certainly not without some reason.

It will be remembered that Spain did not give up possession of the country to France on its cession to the latter power, in 1801, but retained possession of it, and, by the authority of France, transferred it to the United States, in 1804. Black Hawk and his band were in St. Louis at the time, and were invited to be present and witness the ceremonies of the transfer, but he refused the invitation, and it is but just to say that this refusal was caused probably more from regret that the Indians were to be transferred from the jurisdiction of the Spanish authorities than from any special hatred toward the Americans. In his life he says: "I found many sad and gloomy faces because the United States were about to take possession of the town and country. Soon after the Americans came, I took my band and went to take leave of our Spanish father. The Americans came to see him also. Seeing them approach, we passed out of one door as they entered another, and immediately started in our canoes for our village, on Rock River, not liking the change any more than our friends appeared to at St. Louis. On arriving at our village, we gave the news that strange people had arrived at St. Louis, and that we should never see our Spanish father again. The information made all our people sorry."

On the 3d day of November, 1804, a treaty was concluded between William Henry Harrison, then Governor of Indiana Terrirory, on behalf of the United States, and five chiefs of the Sac and Fox nation, by which the latter, in consideration of two thousand two hundred and thirty-four dollars' worth of goods then delivered, and a yearly annuity of one thousand dollars to be paid in goods at just cost. ceded to the United States all that land on the east side of the Mississippi, extending from a point opposite the Jefferson, in Missouri, to the Wisconsin River, embracing an area of over fifty-one millions of acres.

To this treaty Black Hawk always objected and always refused to consider it binding upon his people. He asserted that the chiefs or braves who made it had no authority to relinquish the title of the nation to any of the lands they held or occupied; and, moreover, that they had been sent to St. Louis on quite a different errand, namely, to get one of their people released, who had been imprisoned at St. Louis for killing a white man.

The year following this treaty (1805), Lieutenant Zebulon M. Pike came up the river for the purpose of holding friendly councils with the Indians and selecting sites for forts within the territory recently acquired from France by the United States. Lieutenant Pike seems to have been the first American whom Black Hawk ever met or had a personal interview with; and he was very much prepossessed in Pike's favor. He gives the following account of his visit to Rock Island:

"A boat came up the river with a young American chief and a small party of soldiers. We heard of them soon after they passed Salt River. Some of our young braves watched them every day, to see what sort of people he had on board. The boat at length arrived at Rock River, and the young chief came on shore with his interpreter, and made a speech and gave us some presents. We in turn presented them with meat and such other provisions as we had to spare. We were well pleased with the young chief. He gave us good advice, and said our American father would treat us well."

The events which soon followed Pike's expedition were the erection of Fort Edwards, at what is now Warsaw, Illinois, and Fort Madison, on the site of the present town of that name, the latter being the first fort erected in Iowa. These movements occasioned great uneasiness among the Indians. When work was commenced on Fort Edwards, a delegation from their nation, headed by some of their chiefs, went down to see what the Americans were doing, and had an interview with the commander; after which they returned home apparently satisfied. In like manner, when Fort Madison was being erected, they sent down another delegation from a council of the nation held at Rock River. According to Black Hawk's account, the American chief told them that he was building a house for a trader who was coming to sell them goods cheap, and that the soldiers were coming to keep him company—a statement which Black Hawk says they distrusted at the time, believing that the fort was an encroachment upon their rights, and designed to aid in getting their lands away from them.

It has been held by good American authorities, that the erection of Fort Madison at the point where it was located *was* a violation of the treaty of 1804. By the eleventh article of that treaty, the United States had a right to build a fort near the mouth of the Wisconsin River; by article six they had bound themselves "that if any citizen of the United States or any other white persons should form a settlement upon their lands, such intruders should forthwith be removed." Probably the authorities of the United States did not regard the establishment of military posts as coming properly within the meaning of the term "settlement," as used in the treaty. At all events, they erected Fort Madison within the territory reserved to the Indians, who became very indignant. Not long after the fort was built, a party led by Black Hawk attempted its destruction. They sent spies to watch the movements of the garrison, who ascertained that the soldiers were in the habit of marching out of the fort every morning and evening for parade, and the plan of the party was to conceal themselves near the fort, and attack and surprise them when they were outside. On the morning of the proposed day of attack, five soldiers came out and were fired upon by the Indians, two of them being killed. The Indians were too hasty in their movement, for the regular drill had not yet commenced. However, they kept up the attack for several days, attempting the old Fox strategy of setting fire to the fort with blazing arrows; but finding their efforts unavailing, they soon gave up and returned to Rock River.

When war was declared between the United States and Great Britain, in 1812, Black Hawk and his band allied themselves with the British, partly because he was dazzled by their specious promises, and more probably because they had been deceived by the Americans. Black Hawk himself declared that they were "forced into the war by being deceived." He narrates the circumstances as follows: "Several of the chiefs and head men of the Sacs and Foxes were called upon to go to Washington to see their Great Father. On their return, they related what had been said and done. They said the Great Father wished them, in the event of a war taking place with England, not to interfere on either side, but to remain neutral. He did not want our help, but wished us to hunt and support our families, and live in peace. He said that British traders would not be permitted to come on the Mississippi to furnish us with goods, but that we should be supplied with an American trader. Our chiefs then told him that the British traders always gave them credit in the fall for guns, powder and goods, to enable us to hunt and clothe our families. He repeated that the traders at Fort Madison would have plenty of goods; that we should go there in the fall and he would supply us on credit, as the British traders had done."

Black Hawk seems to have accepted of this proposition, and he and his people were very much pleased. Acting in good faith, they fitted out for their winter's hunt, and went to Fort Madison in high spirits to receive from the trader their outfit of supplies. But, after waiting some time, they were told by the trader that he would not trust them. It was in vain that they pleaded the promise of their great father at Washington. The trader was inexorable; and, disappointed and crestfallen, they turned sadly toward their own village. "Few of us," says Black Hawk, "slept that night; all was gloom and discontent. In the morning a canoe was seen ascending the river; it soon arrived, bearing an express, who brought intelligence that a British trader had landed at Rock Island with two boats loaded with goods, and requested us to come up immediately, because he had good news for us, and a variety of presents. The express presented us with tobacco, pipes and wampum. The news ran through our camp like fire on a prairie. Our lodges were soon taken down, and all started for Rock Island. Here ended all hopes of our remaining at peace, having been forced into the war by being deceived."

He joined the British, who flattered him, styled him "General Black Hawk," decked him with medals, excited his jealousies against the Americans, and armed his band; but he met with defeat and disappointment, and soon abandoned the service and came home.

With all his skill and courage, Black Hawk was unable to lead all the Sacs and Foxes into hostilities to the United States. A portion of them, at the head of whom was Keokuk ("the Watchful Fox"), were disposed to abide by the treaty of 1804, and to cultivate friendly relations with the American people. Therefore, when Black Hawk and his band joined the fortunes of Great Britain, the rest of the nation remained neutral, and, for protection, organized, with Keokuk for their chief. This divided the nation into the "War and the Peace Party."

Black Hawk says he was informed, after he had gone to the war, that the nation, which had been reduced to so small a body of fighting men, were unable to defend themselves in case the Americans should attack them, and having all the old men and women and children belonging to the warriors who had joined the British on their hands to provide for, a council was held, and it was agreed that Quash-qua-me (the Lance) and other chiefs, together with the old men, women and children, and such others as chose to accompany them, should go to St. Louis and place themselves under the American chief stationed there. They accordingly went down, and were received as the "friendly band" of the Sacs and Foxes, and were provided for and sent up the Missouri River. On Black Hawk's return from the British army, he says Keokuk was introduced to him as the war chief of the braves then in the village. He inquired how he had become chief, and was informed that their spies had seen a large armed force going toward Peoria, and fears were entertained of an attack upon the village; whereupon a council was held, which concluded to leave the village and cross over to the west side of the Mississippi. Keokuk had been standing at the door of the lodge where the council was held, not being allowed to enter on account of never having killed an enemy, where he remained until Wa-co-me came out. Keokuk asked permission to speak in the council, which Wa-co-me obtained for him. Keokuk then addressed the chiefs; he remonstrated against the desertion of their village, their own homes and the graves of their fathers, and offered to defend the village. The council consented that he should be their war chief. He marshaled his braves, sent out spies, and advanced on the trail leading to Peoria, but returned without seeing the enemy. The Americans did not disturb the village, and all were satisfied with the appointment of Keokuk.

Keokuk, like Black Hawk, was a descendant of the Sac branch of the nation, and was born on Rock River, in 1780. He was of a pacific disposition, but possessed the elements of true courage, and could fight, when occasion required, with a cool judgment and heroic energy. In his first battle, he encountered and killed a

Sioux, which placed him in the rank of warriors, and he was honored with a public feast by his tribe in commemoration of the event.

Keokuk has been described as an orator, entitled to rank with the most gifted of his race. In person, he was tall and of portly bearing: in his public speeches, he displayed a commanding attitude and graceful gestures; he spoke rapidly, but his enunciation was clear, distinct and forcible; he culled his figures from the stores of nature. and based his arguments on skillful logic. Unfortunately for the reputation of Keokuk as an orator, among white people, he was never able to obtain an interpreter who could claim even a slight acquaintance with philosophy. With one exception only, his interpreters were unacquainted with the elements of their mother-tongue. Of this serious hindrance to his fame, Keokuk was well aware, and retained Frank Labershure, who had received a rudimental education in the French and English languages, until the latter broke down by dissipation and died. But during the meridian of his career among the white people, he was compelled to submit his speeches for translation to uneducated men, whose range of thought fell below the flights of a gifted mind, and the fine imagery drawn from nature was beyond their power of reproduction. He had sufficient knowledge of the English language to make him sensible of this bad rendering of his thoughts, and often a feeling of mortification at the bungling efforts was depicted on his countenance while speaking. The proper place to form a correct estimate of his ability as an orator was in the Indian council, where he addressed himself exclusively to those who understood his language, and witness the electrical effect of his eloquence upon his audience.

Keokuk seems to have possessed a more sober judgment, and to have had a more intelligent view of the great strength and resources of the United States, than his noted and restless cotemporary, Black Hawk. He knew from the first that the reckless war which Black Hawk and his band had determined to carry on could result in nothing but defeat and disaster, and used every argument against it. The large number of warriors whom he had dissuaded from following Black Hawk became, however, greatly excited with the war spirit after Stillman's defeat, and but for the signal tact displayed by Keokuk on that occasion, would have forced him to submit to their wishes in joining the rest of the warriors in the field. A war-dance was held, and Keokuk took part in it, seeming to be moved with the current of the rising storm. When the dance was over, he called the council to prepare for war. He made a speech, in which he admitted the justice of their complaints against the Americans. To seek redress was a noble aspiration of their nature. The blood of their brethren had been shed by the white man, and the spirits of their braves, slain in battle, called loudly for vengeance. " I am your chief," he said, " and it is my duty to lead you to battle, if, after fully considering the matter, you are determined to go. But before you decide on taking this important step, it is wise to inquire into the chances of success." He then portrayed to them the great power of the United States, against whom they would have to contend, that their chances of success was utterly hopeless. "But," said he, "if you do determine to go upon the war-path, I will agree to lead you, on one condition, viz: that before we go, we will kill all our old men and our wives and children, to save them from a lingering death of starvation, and that every one of us determine to leave our homes on the other side of the Mississippi.

This was a strong but truthful picture of the prospect before them, and was presented in such a forcible light as to cool their ardor, and cause them to abandon the rash undertaking.

But during the war of 1832, it is now considered certain that small bands of Indians, from the west side of the Mississippi, made incursions into the white settlements, in the lead mining region, and committed some murders and depredations.

When peace was declared between the United States and England, Black Hawk was required to make peace with the former, and entered into a treaty at Portage des Sioux, September 14, 1815, but did not "touch the goose-quill to it until May 13, 1816, when he smoked the pipe of peace with the great white chief," at St. Louis. This treaty was a renewal of the treaty of 1804, but Black Hawk declared he had been deceived; that he did not know that by signing the treaty he was giving away, his village. This weighed upon his mind, already soured by previous disappointment and the irresistible encroachments of the whites; and when a few years later, he and his people were driven from their possessions by the military, he determined to return to the home of his fathers.

It is also to be remarked that in 1816, by treaty with various tribes, the United States relinquished to the Indians all the lands lying north of a line drawn from a southernmost point of Lake Michigan west to the Mississippi, except a reservation five leagues square, on the Mississippi River, supposed then to be sufficient to include all the mineral lands on and adjacent to Fever River, and one league square at the mouth of the Wisconsin River.

THE BLACK HAWK WAR.

The immediate cause of the Indian outbreak in 1830 was the occupation of Black Hawk's village, on the Rock River, by the whites, during the absence of the chief and his braves on a hunting expedition, on the west side of the Mississippi. When they returned they found their wigwams occupied by white families, and their own women and children were shelterless on the banks of the river. The Indians were indignant, and determined to repossess their village at all hazards, and early in the spring of 1831 recrossed the Mississippi and menacingly took possession of their own cornfields and cabins. It may be well to remark here that it was expressly stipulated in the treaty of 1804, to which they attributed all their troubles, that the Indians should not be obliged to leave their lands until they were sold by the United States, and it does not appear that they occupied any lands other than those owned by the Government. If this was true, the Indians had good cause for indignation and complaint. But the whites, driven out in turn by the returning Indians, became so clamorous against what they termed the encroachments of the natives, that Gov. Reynolds, of Illinois, ordered Gen. Gaines to Rock Island with a military force to drive the Indians again from their homes to the west side of the Mississippi. Black Hawk says he did not intend to be provoked into war by anything less than the blood of some of his own people; in other words, that there would be no war unless it should be commenced by the pale faces. But it was said and probably thought by the military commanders along the frontier, that the Indians intended to unite in a general war against the whites, from Rock River to the Mexican borders. But it does not appear that the hardy frontiersmen themselves had any fears, for their experience had been that, when well treated, their Indian neighbors were not dangerous. Black Hawk and his band had done no more than to attempt to repossess the old homes of which they had been deprived in their absence. No blood had been shed. Black Hawk and his chiefs sent a flag of truce, and a new treaty was made, by which Black Hawk and his band agreed to remain forever on the Iowa side and never recross the river without the permission of the President or the Governor of Illinois. Whether the Indians clearly understood the terms of this treaty is uncertain. As was usual, the Indian traders had dictated terms on their behalf, and they had received a large amount of provisions, etc., from the Government, but it may well be doubted whether the Indians comprehended that they could never revisit the graves of their fathers without violating their treaty. They undoubtedly thought that they had agreed never to recross the Mississippi with hostile intent. However this may be, on the 6th day of April, 1832, Black Hawk and his entire band, with their women and children, again recrossed the Mississippi in plain view of the garrison of Fort Armstrong, and went up Rock River. Although this act was construed into an act of hostility by the military authorities, who declared that Black Hawk intended to recover his village, or the site where it stood, by force; yet it does not appear that he made any such attempt, nor did his appearance create any special alarm among the settlers. They knew that the Indians never went on the war path encumbered with the old men, their women and their children.

The *Galenian*, printed in Galena, of May 2d, 1832, says that Black Hawk was invited by the Prophet and had taken possession of a tract about forty miles up Rock River; but that he did not remain there long, but commenced his search up Rock River. Captain W. B. Green, who served in Captain Stevenson's company of mounted rangers, says that "Black Hawk and his band crossed the river with no hostile intent, but that his band had had bad luck in hunting during the previous winter, were actually in a starving condition, and had come over to spend the summer with a friendly tribe on the head waters of the Rock and Illinois Rivers, by invitation from their chief. Other old settlers who all agree that Black Hawk had no idea of fighting, say that he came back to the west side expecting to negotiate another treaty, and get a new supply of provisions. The most reasonable explanation of this movement, which resulted so disastrously to Black Hawk and his starving people, is that, during the fall and winter of 1831-2, his people became deeply indebted to their favorite trader at Fort Armstrong (Rock Island), they had not been fortunate in hunting, and he was likely to lose heavily, as an Indian debt was outlawed in one year. If, therefore, the Indians could be induced to come over, and the fears of the military could be sufficiently aroused to pursue them, another treaty could be negotiated, and from the payments from the Government the shrewd trader could get his pay. Just a week after Black Hawk crossed the river, on the 13th of April, 1832, George Davenport wrote to Gen. Atkinson: "I am informed that the British band of Sac Indians are determined to make war on the frontier settlements. * * * From every information that I have received, I am of the opinion that the intention of the British band of Sac Indians is to commit depredations on the inhabitants of the frontier." And yet, from the 6th day of April, until after Stillman's men commenced war by firing on a flag of truce from Black Hawk, no murders nor depredations were committed by the British band of Sac Indians.

It is not the purpose of this sketch to detail the incidents of the Black Hawk war of 1832, as it pertains rather to the history of the State of Illinois. It is sufficient to say that, after the disgraceful affair at Stillman's Run, Black Hawk, concluding that the whites, refusing to treat with him, were determined to exterminate his people, determined to return to the Iowa side of the Mississippi. He could not return by the way he came, for the army was behind him, an army, too, that would sternly refuse to recognize the white flag of peace. His only course was to make his way northward and reach the Mississippi, if possible, before the troops could overtake him, and this he did; but, before he could get his women and children across the Wisconsin, he was overtaken, and a battle ensued. Here, again, he sued for peace, and, through his trusty Lieutenant, "the Prophet," the whites were plainly informed that the starving Indians did not wish to fight, but would return to the west side of the Mississippi, peaceably, if they could be permitted to do so. No attention was paid to this second effort to negotiate peace, and, as soon as supplies could be obtained, the pursuit was resumed, the flying Indians were overtaken again eight miles before they reached the mouth of the Bad Axe, and the slaughter (it should not be dignified by the name of battle) commenced. Here, overcome by starvation and the victorious whites, his band was scattered, on the 2d day of August, 1832. Black Hawk escaped, but was brought into camp at Prairie du Chien by three Winnebagoes. He was confined in Jefferson Barracks until the spring of 1833, when he was sent to Washington, arriving there April 22. On the 26th of April, they were taken to Fortress Monroe, where they remained till the 4th of June, 1833, when orders were given for them to be liberated and returned to their own country. By order of the President, he was brought back to Iowa through the principal Eastern cities. Crowds flocked to see him all along his route, and he was very much flattered by the attentions he received. He lived among his people on the Iowa River till that reservation was sold, in 1836, when, with the rest of the Sacs and Foxes, he removed to the Des Moines Reservation, where he remained till his death, which occurred on the 3d of October, 1838.

INDIAN PURCHASES, RESERVES AND TREATIES.

At the close of the Black Hawk War, in 1832, a treaty was made at a council held on the west bank of the Mississippi, where now stands the thriving city of Davenport, on grounds now occupied by the Chicago, Rock Island & Pacific railroad company, on the 21st day of September, 1832. At this council, the United States were represented by Gen. Winfield Scott and Gov. Reynolds, of Illinois. Keokuk, Pash-a-pa-ho and some thirty other chiefs and warriors of the Sac and Fox nation were present. By this treaty, the Sacs and Foxes ceded to the United States a strip of land on the eastern border of Iowa, fifty miles wide, from the northern boundary of Missouri to the mouth of the Upper Iowa River, containing about six million acres. The western line of the purchase was parallel with the Mississippi. In consideration of this cession, the United States Government stipulated to pay annually to the confederated · tribes, for thirty consecutive years, twenty thousand dollars in specie, and to pay the debts of the Indians at Rock Island, which had been accumulating for seventeen years, and amounted to fifty thousand dollars, due to Davenport & Farnham, Indian traders. The Government also generously donated to the Sac and Fox women and children, whose husbands and fathers had fallen in the Black Hawk war, thirty-five beef cattle, twelve bushels of salt, thirty barrels of pork, fifty barrels of flour and six thousand bushels of corn.

This territory is known as the "Black Hawk Purchase," Although it was not the first portion of Iowa ceded to the United

States by the Sacs and Foxes, it was the first opened to actual settlement by the tide of emigration that flowed across the Mississippi as soon as the Indian title was extinguished. The treaty was ratified February 13, 1833, and took effect on the 1st of June following, when the Indians quietly removed from the ceded territory, and this fertile and beautiful region was opened to white settlers.

By the terms of the treaty, out of the Black Hawk Purchase was reserved for the Sacs and Foxes 400 square miles of land situated on the Iowa River, and including within its limits Keokuk's village, on the right bank of that river. This tract was known as "Keokuk's Reserve," and was occupied by the Indians until 1836. when, by a treaty made in September between them and Gov. Dodge. of Wisconsin Territory, it was ceded to the United States. The council was held on the banks of the Mississippi, above Davenport, and was the largest assemblage of the kind ever held by the Sacs and Foxes to treat for the sale of lands. About one thousand of their chiefs and braves were present, and Keokuk was their leading spirit and principal speaker on the occasion. By the terms of the treaty, the Sacs and Foxes were removed to another reservation on the Des Moines River, where an agency was established for them at what is now the town of Agency City.

Besides the Keokuk Reserve. the Government gave out of the Black Hawk Purchase to Antoine Le Claire, interpreter, in fee simple, one section of land opposite Rock Island, and another at the head of the first rapids above the island, on the Iowa side. This was the first land title granted by the United States to an individual in Iowa.

Soon after the removal of the Sacs and Foxes to their new reservation on the Des Moines River, Gen. Joseph M. Street was transferred from the agency of the Winnebagoes, at Prairie du Chien, to establish an agency among them. A farm was selected, on which the necessary buildings were erected, including a comfortable farm house for the agent and his family, at the expense of the Indian Fund. A salaried agent was employed to superintend the farm and dispose of the crops. Two mills were erected, one on Soap Creek, and the other on Sugar Creek. The latter was soon swept away by a flood, but the former remained and did good service for many years. Connected with the agency were Joseph Smart and John Goodell, interpreters. The latter was interpreter for Hard Fish's band. Three of the Indian chiefs, Keokuk, Wapello and Appanoose. had each a large field improved, the two former on the right bank of the Des Moines. back from the river, in what is now "Keokuk's Prairie," and the latter on the present site of the city of Ottumwa. Among the traders connected with the agency were the Messrs. Ewing. from Ohio. and Phelps & Co., from Illinois, and also Mr. J. P. Eddy, who established his post at what is now the site of Eddyville.

The Indians at this agency became idle and listless in the absence of their natural and wonted excitements, and many of them plunged into dissipation. Keokuk himself became dissipated in the latter years of his life, and it has been reported that he died of *delirium tremens* after his removal with his tribe to Kansas.

In May, 1843, most of the Indians were removed up the Des Moines River, above the temporary line of Red Rock, having ceded the remnant of their lands in Iowa to the United States on the 21st of September, 1837, and on the 11th of October, 1842. By the terms of the latter treaty, they held possession of the "New Purchase" till the Autumn of 1845, when the most of them were removed to their reservation in Kansas, the balance being removed in the Spring of 1846.

1. *Treaty with the Sioux*—Made July 19, 1815; ratified December 16, 1815. This treaty was made at Portage des Sioux, between the Sioux of Minnesota and Upper Iowa and the United States, by William Clark and Ninian Edwards. Commissioners, and was merely a treaty of peace and friendship on the part of those Indians toward the United States at the close of the war of 1812.

2. *Treaty with the Sacs.*—A similar treaty of peace was made at Portage des Sioux, between the United States and the Sacs, by William Clark, Ninian Edwards and Auguste Choteau, on the 13th of September, 1815, and ratified at the same date as the above. In this, the treaty of 1804 was re-affirmed, and the Sacs here represented promised for themselves and their bands to keep entirely separate from the Sacs of Rock River, who, under Black Hawk, had joined the British in the war just then closed.

3. *Treaty with the Foxes.*—A separate treaty of peace was made with the Foxes at Portage des Sioux, by the same Commissioners, on the 14th of September, 1815, and ratified the same as the above, wherein the Foxes re-affirmed the treaty of St. Louis, of November 3, 1804, and agreed to deliver up all their prisoners to the officer in command at Fort Clark, now Peoria, Illinois.

4. *Treaty with the Iowas.*—A treaty of peace and mutual good will was made between the United States and the Iowa tribe of Indians, at Portage des Sioux, by the same Commissioners as above, on the 16th of September, 1815, at the close of the war with Great Britain, and ratified at the same date as the others.

5. *Treaty with the Sacs of Rock River*—Made at St. Louis on the 13th of May, 1816, between the United States and the Sacs of Rock River, by the Commissioners, William Clark, Ninian Edwards and Auguste Choteau, and ratified December 30th, 1816. In this treaty, that of 1804 was re-established and confirmed by twenty-two chiefs and head men of the Sacs of Rock River, and Black Hawk himself attached to it his signature, or, as he said, "touched the goose quill."

6. *Treaty of 1824.*—On the 4th of August, 1824, a treaty was made between the United States and the Sacs and Foxes, in the city of Washington, by William Clark, Commissioner, wherein the Sac and Fox nation relinquished their title to all lands in Missouri and that portion of the southeast corner of Iowa known as the "Half-Breed Tract" was set off and reserved for the use of the half-breeds of the Sacs and Foxes, they holding title in the same manner as Indians. Ratified January 18, 1825.

7. *Treaty of August 19, 1825.*—At this date a treaty was made by William Clark and Lewis Cass, at Prairie du Chien, between the United States and the Chippewas, Sacs and Foxes, Menomonees, Winnebagoes and a portion of the Ottawas and Pottawatomies. In this treaty, in order to make peace between the contending tribes as to the limits of their respective hunting grounds in

Iowa, it was agreed that the United States Government should run a boundary line between the Sioux, on the north, and the Sacs and Foxes, on the south, as follows:

Commencing at the mouth of the Upper Iowa River, on the west bank of the Mississippi, and ascending said Iowa River to its west fork; thence up the fork to its source; thence crossing the fork of Red Cedar River in a direct line to the second or upper fork of the Des Moines River; thence in a direct line to the lower fork of the Calumet River, and down that river to its junction with the Missouri River.

8. *Treaty of 1830.*—On the 15th of July, 1830, the confederate tribes of the Sacs and Foxes ceded to the United States a strip of country lying south of the above line, twenty miles in width, and extending along the line aforesaid from the Mississippi to the Des Moines River. The Sioux also, whose possessions were north of the line, ceded to the Government, in the same treaty, a like strip on the north side of the boundary. Thus the United States, at the ratification of this treaty, February 24, 1831, came into possession of a portion of Iowa forty miles wide, extending along the Clark and Cass line of 1825, from the Mississippi to the Des Moines River. This territory was known as the "Neutral Ground," and the tribes on either side of the line were allowed to fish and hunt on it unmolested till it was made a Winnebago reservation, and the Winnebagoes were removed to it in 1841.

9. *Treaty with the Sacs and Foxes and other Tribes.*—At the same time of the above treaty respecting the "Neutral Ground" (July 15, 1830), the Sacs and Foxes, Western Sioux, Omahas, Iowas and Missouris ceded to the United States a portion of the western slope of Iowa, the boundaries of which were defined as follows: Beginning at the upper fork of the Des Moines River, and passing the sources of the Little Sioux and Floyd Rivers, to the fork of the first creek that falls into the Big Sioux, or Calumet, on the east side; thence down said creek and the Calumet River to the Missouri River; thence down said Missouri River to the Missouri State line above the Kansas; thence along said line to the northwest corner of said State; thence to the high lands between the waters falling into the Missouri and Des Moines, passing to said high lands along the dividing ridge between the forks of the Grand River; thence along said high lands or ridge separating the waters of the Missouri from those of the Des Moines, to a point opposite the source of the Boyer River, and thence in a direct line to the upper fork of the Des Moines, the place of beginning.

It was understood that the lands ceded and relinquished by this treaty were to be assigned and allotted, under the direction of the President of the United States, to the tribes then living thereon, or to such other tribes as the President might locate thereon for hunting and other purposes. In consideration of three tracts of land ceded in this treaty, the United States agreed to pay to the Sacs three thousand dollars; to the Foxes, three thousand dollars; to the Sioux, two thousand dollars; to the Yankton and Santee bands of Sioux, three thousand dollars; to the Omahas, two thousand five hundred dollars; and to the Ottoes and Missouris, two thousand five hundred dollars—to be paid annually for ten successive years. In addition to these annuities, the Government agreed to furnish some of the tribes with blacksmiths and agricultural implements to the amount of two hundred dollars, at the expense of the United States, and to set apart three thousand dollars annually for the education of the children of these tribes. It does not appear that any fort was erected in this territory prior to the erection of Fort Atkinson on the Neutral Ground, in 1840-1.

This treaty was made by William Clark, Superintendent of Indian affairs, and Col. Willoughby Morgan, of the United States First Infantry, and came into effect by proclamation, February 24, 1831.

10. *Treaty with the Winnebagoes.*—Made at Fort Armstrong, Rock Island, September 15, 1832, by Gen. Winfield Scott and Hon. John Reynolds, Governor of Illinois. In this treaty the Winnebagoes ceded to the United States all their land lying on the east side of the Mississippi, and in part consideration therefor the United States granted to the Winnebagoes, to be held as other Indian lands are held, that portion of Iowa known as the Neutral Ground. The exchange of

the two tracts of country was to take place on or before the 1st day of June, 1833. In addition to the Neutral Ground, it was stipulated that the United States should give the Winnebagoes, beginning in September, 1833, and continuing for twenty-seven successive years, ten thousand dollars in specie, and establish a school among them, with a farm and garden, and provide other facilities for the education of their children, not to exceed in cost three thousand dollars a year, and to continue the same for twenty-seven successive years. Six agriculturists, twelve yoke of oxen and plows and other farming tools were to be supplied by the Government.

11. *Treaty of 1832 with the Sacs and Foxes.*—Already mentioned as the Black Hawk purchase.

12. *Treaty of 1836*, with the Sacs and Foxes, ceding Keoknk's Reserve to the United States; for which the Government stipulated to pay thirty thousand dollars, and an annuity of ten thousand dollars for ten successive years, together with other sums and debts of the Indians to various parties.

13. *Treaty of 1837.*—On the 21st of October. 1837, a treaty was made at the city of Washington, between Carey A. Harris, Commissioner of Indian Affairs, and the confederate tribes of Sacs and Foxes, ratified February 21, 1838, wherein another slice of the soil of Iowa was obtained, described in the treaty as follows: "A tract of country containing 1,250,000 acres, lying west and adjoining the the tract conveyed by them to the United States in the treaty of September 21, 1832. It is understood that the points of termination for the present cession shall be the northern and southern points of said tract as fixed by the survey made under the authority of the United States, and that a line shall be drawn between them so as to intersect a line extended westwardly from the angle of said tract nearly opposite to Rock Island, as laid down in the above survey, so far as may be necessary to include the number of acres hereby ceded, which last mentioned line. it is estimated. will be about twenty-five miles." This piece of land was twenty-five miles wide in the middle, and ran off to a point at both ends, lying directly back of the Black Hawk Purchase, and of the same length.

14. *Treaty of Relinquishment.*—At the same date as the above treaty, in the city of Washington, Carey A. Harris, Commissioner, the Sacs and Foxes ceded to the United States all their right and interest in the country lying south of the boundary line between the Sacs and Foxes and Sioux, as described in the treaty of August 19, 1825, and between the Mississippi and Missouri Rivers, the United States paying for the same one hundred and sixty thousand dollars. The Indians also gave up all claims and interests under the treaties previously made with them, for the satisfaction of which no appropriations had been made.

15. *Treaty of 1842.*—The last treaty was made with the Sacs and Foxes October 11, 1842; ratified March 23, 1843. It was made at the Sac and Fox agency (Agency City), by John Chambers, Commissioner on behalf of the United States. In this treaty the Sac and Fox Indians "ceded to the United States all their lands west of the Mississippi to which they had any claim or title." By the terms of this treaty they were to be removed from the country at the expiration of three years, and all who remained after that were to move at their own expense. Part of them were removed to Kansas in the Fall of 1845, and the rest the Spring following.

SPANISH GRANTS.

While the territory now embraced in the State of Iowa was under Spanish rule as a part of its province of Louisiana, certain claims to and grants of land were made by the Spanish authorities, with which, in addition to the extinguishment of Indian titles, the United States had to deal. It is proper that these should be briefly reviewed.

Dubuque—on the 22d day of September, 1788, Julien Dubuque, a Frenchman, from Prairie du Chien, obtained from the Foxes a cession or lease of lands on the Mississippi River for mining purposes, on the site of the present city of Dubuque. Lead had been discovered here eight years before, in 1780, by the wife of Peosta Fox, a warrior, and Dubuque's claim embraced nearly all the lead bearing lands in that vicinity. He immediately took possession of his claim and commenced mining, at the same time making a settlement. The place became known as the "Spanish Miners," or, more commonly, "Dubuque's Lead Mines."

In 1796, Dubuque filed a petition with Baron de Carondelet, the Spanish Governor of Louisiana, asking that the tract ceded to him by the Indians might be granted to him by patent from the Spanish Government. In this petition Dubuque rather indefinitely set forth the boundaries of his claim as "about seven leagues along the Missippi River, and three leagues in width from the river," intending to include, as is supposed, the river front between the Little Maquoketa and the Tete des Mertz Rivers, embracing more than twenty thousand acres. Carondelet granted the prayer of the petition, and the grant was subsequently confirmed by the Board of Land Commissioners of Louisiana.

In October 1804, Dubuque transferred the larger part of his claim to Auguste Choteau, of St. Louis, and on the 17th of May, 1805, he and Choteau jointly filed their claims with the Board of Commissioners. On the 20th of September, 1806, the Board decided in their favor, pronouncing the claim to be a regular Spanish grant, made and completed prior to the 1st day of October, 1800, only one member, J. B. C. Lucas, dissenting.

Dubuque died march 24, 1810. The Indians, understanding that the claim of Dubuque under their former act of cession was only a permit to occupy the tract and work the mines during his life, and that at his death they reverted to them, took possession and continued mining operations, and were sustained by the military authority of the United States, notwithstanding the decision of the Commissioners. When the Black Hawk purchase was consummated the Dubuque claim thus held by the Indians was absorbed by the United States, as the Sacs and Foxes made no reservation of it in the treaty of 1832.

The heirs of Choteau, however, were not disposed to relinquish their claim without a struggle. Late in 1832, they employed an agent to look after their interests, and authorized him to lease the right to dig lead on the lands. The miners who commenced work under this agent were compelled by the military to abandon their operations, and one of the claimants went to Galena to institute legal proceedings, but found no court of competent jurisdiction, although he did bring an action for the recovery of a quantity of lead dug at Dubuque, for the purpose of testing the title. Being unable to identify the lead, however, he was non-suited.

By act of Congress, approved July 2, 1836, the town of Dubuque was surveyed and platted. After lots had been sold and occupied by the purchasers, Henry Choteau brought an action of ejectment against Patrick Malony, who held land in Dubuque under a patent from the United States, for the recovery of seven undivided eighth parts of the Dubuque claim, as purchased by Auguste Choteau in 1804. The case was tried in the District Court of the United States for the District of Iowa, and was decided adversely to the plaintiff. The case was carried to the Supreme Court of the United States on a writ of error, when it was heard at the December term, 1853, and the decision of the lower court was affirmed, the court holding that the permit from Carondolet was merely a lease, or permit to work the mines; that Dubuque asked, and the Governor of Louisiana granted, nothing more than the "peaceable possession " of certain lands obtained from the Indians; that Carondolet had no legal authority to make such a grant as claimed, and that, even if he had, this was but an "inchoate and imperfect title."

Girard.—In 1795, the Lieutenant Governor of Upper Louisiana granted to Basil Girard five thousand eight hundred and sixty acres of land, in what is now Clayton County, known as the "Girard Tract." He occupied the land during the time that Iowa passed from Spain to France, and from France to the United States, in consideration of which the Federal Government granted a patent of the same to Girard in his own right. His heirs sold the whole tract to James H. Lockwood and Thomas P. Burnett, of Prairie du Chien, for three hundred dollars.

Honori.—March 30, 1799, Zenon Trudeau, acting Lieutenant Governor of Upper Louisiana, granted to Louis Honori a tract of land on the site of the present town of Montrose, as follows: " It is permitted to Mr. Louis (Fresson) Honori, or Louis Honore Fesson, to establish himself at the head of the rapids of the River Des Moines, and his establishment once formed, notice of it shall be given to the Governor General, in order to obtain for him a commission of a space sufficient to give value to such establishment, and at the same time to render it useful to the commerce of the peltries of this country, to watch the Indians and keep them in the fidelity which they owe to His Majesty."

Honori took immediate possession of his claim, which he retained until 1805. While trading with the natives he became indebted to Joseph Robedoux, who obtained an execution on which the property was sold May 13, 1803, and was purchased by the creditor. In these proceedings the property was described as being " about six leagues above the River Des Moines." Robedoux died soon after he purchased the property. Auguste Choteau, his executor, disposed of the Honori tract to Thomas F. Reddeck, in April, 1805, up to which time Honori continued to occupy it. The grant, as made by the Spanish Government, was a league square, but only one mile square was confirmed by the United States. After the half-breeds sold their lands, in which the Honori grant was included, various claimants resorted to litigation in attempts to invalidate the title of the Reddeck heirs, but it was finally confirmed by a decision of the Supreme Court of the United States in 1839, and is the oldest legal title to any land in the State of Iowa.

THE HALF-BREED TRACT.

Before any permanent settlement had been made in the Territory of Iowa, white adventurers, trappers and traders, many of whom were scattered along the Mississippi and its tributaries, as agents and employes of the American Fur Company, intermarried with the females of the Sac and Fox Indians, producing a race of half-breeds, whose number was never definitely ascertained. There were some respectable and excellent people among them, children of men of some refinement and education. For instance: Dr. Muir, a gentlemen educated at Edinburgh, Scotland, a surgeon in the United States Army, stationed at a military post located on the present site of Warsaw, married an Indian woman, and reared his family of three daughters in the city of Keokuk. Other examples might be cited, but they are probably exceptions to the general rule, and the race is now nearly or quite extinct in Iowa.

A treaty was made at Washington, August 4, 1824, between the Sacs and Foxes and the United States, by which that portion of Lee County was reserved to the half-breeds of those tribes, and which was afterward known as "The Half-Breed Tract." This reservation is the triangular piece of land, containing about 119,-000 acres, lying between the Mississippi and Des Moines Rivers. It is bounded on the north by the prolongation of the northern line of Missouri. This line was intended to be a straight one, running due east, which would have caused it to strike the Mississippi River at or below Montrose; but the surveyor who run it took no notice of the change in the variation of the needle as he proceeded eastward, and, in consequence, the line he run was bent, deviating more and more to the northward of a direct line as he approached the Mississippi, so that it struck that river at the lower edge of the town of Fort Madison. "This erroneous line," says Judge Mason, "has been acquiesced in as well in fixing the northern limit of the Half-Breed Tract as in determining the northern boundary line of the State of Missouri." The line thus run included in the reservation a portion of the lower part of the city of Fort Madison, and all of the present townships of Van Buren, Charleston, Jefferson, Des Moines, Montrose and Jackson.

Under the treaty of 1824, the half-breeds had the right to occupy the soil but could not convey it, the reversion being reserved to the United States. But on the 30th day of January, 1834, by act of Congress, this reversionary right was relinquished, and the half-breeds acquired the lands in fee simple. This was no sooner done, than a horde of speculators rushed in to buy land of the half-breed owners, and, in many instances, a gun, a blanket, a pony or a few quarts of whisky was sufficient for the purchase of large estates. There was a deal of sharp practice on both sides; Indians would often claim ownership of land by virtue of being half-breeds and had no difficulty in proving their mixed blood by the Indians, and they would then cheat the speculators by selling land to which they had no rightful title. On the other hand, speculators often claimed land in which they had no ownership. It was diamond cut diamond, until at last things became badly mixed. There was no authorized surveys, and no boundry lines to claims, and, as a natural result, numerous conflicts and quarrels ensued.

To settle these difficulties, to decide the validity of claims or sell them for the benefit of the real owners, by act of the Legislature of Wisconsin Territory, approved January 16, 1838, Edward Johnstone, Thomas S. Wilson and David Brigham were appointed Commissioners, and clothed with power to effect these objects. The act provided that these Commissioners should be paid six dollars a day each. The commission entered upon its duties and continued until the next session of the Legislature, when the act creating it was repealed, invalidating all that had been done and depriving the Commissioners of their pay. The repealing act, however, authorized the Commissioners to commence action against the owners of the Half-Breed Tract, to receive pay for their services, in the District Court of Lee County. Two judgments were obtained, and on execution the whole of the tract was sold to Hugh T. Reid, the Sheriff executing the deed. Mr. Reid sold portions of it to various parties, but his own title was questioned and he became involved in litigation. Decisions in favor of Reid and those holding under him were made by both District and Supreme Courts, but in December, 1850 these decisions were finally reversed by the Supreme Court of the United States in the case of Joseph Webster, plantiff in error, vs. Hugh T. Reid, and the judgment titles failed. About nine years before the "judgment titles" were finally abrogated as a above, another class of titles were brought into competition with them, and in the conflict between the two, the final decision was obtained. These were the titles based on the "decree of partition" issued by the United States District Court for the Territory of Iowa, on the 8th of May, 1841, and certified to by the Clerk on the 2d day of June of that year. Edward Johnstone and Hugh T. Reid, then law partners at Fort Madison, filed the petition for the decree in behalf of the St. Louis claimants of half-breed lands. Francis S. Key, author of the Star Spangled Banner, who was then attorney for the new York Land Company, which held heavy interest in these lands, took a leading part in the measure, and drew up the document in which it was presented to the court. Judge Charles Mason, of Burlington, presided. The plan of partition divided the tract into one hundred and one shares, and arranged that each claimant should draw his proportion by lot, and should abide the result, whatever it might be. The arrangement was entered into, the lots drawn, and the plat of the same filed in the Recorder's office, October 6, 1841. Upon this basis the titles to land in the Half-Breed Tract are now held.

EARLY SETTLEMENTS.

The first permanent settlement by the whites within the limits of Iowa was made by Julien Dubuque, in 1788, when with a small party of miners, he settled on the site of the city that now bears his name, where he lived until his death, in 1810. Louis Honori settled on the site of the present town of Montrose, probably in 1799, and resided there until 1805, when his property passed into other hands. Of the Girard settlement, opposite Prairie du Chien, little is known except that it was occupied by some parties prior to the commencement of the present century and contained three cabins in 1805. Indian traders, although not strictly to be considered settlers had established themselves at various points at an early date. A Mr. Johnson, Agent of the American Fur Company, had a trading post below Burlington, where he carried on traffic with the Indians some time before the United States possessed the country. In 1820, Le Moliese, a French trader, had a station at what is now Sandusky, six miles above Keokuk, in Lee County. In 1829, Dr. Isaac Galland made a settlement on the Lower Rapids, at what is now Nashville.

The first settlement in Lee County was made in 1820, by Dr. Samuel C. Muir, a surgeon in the United States army, who had been stationed at Fort Edwards, now Warsaw, Ill., and who built a cabin where the city of Keokuk now stands.

Messrs. Reynolds & Culver, who had leased Dr. Muir's claim at Keokuk, subsequently employed as their agent Mr. Moses Stillwell, who arrived with his family in 1828, and took possession of Muir's cabin. His brothers-in-law, Amos and Valencourt Van Ansdal, came with him and settled near.

His daughter, Margaret Stillwell (afterward Mrs. Ford) was born in 1831, at the foot of the rapids, called by the Indians Puch-a-she-tuck, where Keokuk now stands. She was probably the first white American child born in Iowa.

In 1831, Mr. Johnson, agent of the American Fur Company, who had a station at the foot of the rapids, removed to another location, and, Dr. Muir having returned from Galena, he and Isaac R. Campbell took the place and buildings vacated by the Company, and carried on trade with the Indians and half-breeds. Campbell, who had first visited and traveled through the southern part of Iowa, in 1821, was an enterprising settler, and besides trading with the natives, carried on a farm and kept a tavern.

Dr. Muir died of cholera in 1832.

3

In 1830, James L. and Lucius H. Langworthy, brothers and natives of Vermont, visited the Territory for the purpose of working the lead mines at Dubuque. They had been engaged in lead
mining at Galena, Illinois, the former as early as 1824. The lead
mines in the Dubuque region were an object of great interest to
the miners about Galena, for they were known to be rich in lead
ore. To explore these mines and to obtain permission to work
them was therefore eminently desirable.

In 1829, James L. Langworthy resolved to visit the Dubuque,
mines. Crossing the Mississippi at a point now known as Dunleith
in a canoe, and swimming his horse by his side, he landed on the
spot now known as Jones Street Levee. Before him spread out a
beautiful prairie, on which the city of Dubuque now stands. Two
miles south, at the mouth of Catfish Creek, was a village of Sacs
and Foxes. Thither Mr. Langworthy proceeded, and was well received by the natives. He endeavored to obtain permission from
them to mine in their hills, but this they refused. He, however,
succeeded in gaining the confidence of the chief to such an extent
as to be allowed to travel in the interior for three weeks and explore the country. He employed two young Indians as guides,
and traversed in different directions the whole region lying between the Maquoketa and Turkey Rivers. He returned to the
village, secured the good will of the Indians, and, returning to
Galena, formed plans for future operations, to be executed as soon
circumstances would permit.

In 1830, with his brother, Lucius H., and others, having obtained the consent of the Indians, Mr. Langworthy crossed the
Mississippi and commenced mining in the vicinity around Dubuque.

At this time, the lands were not in the actual possession of the
United States. Although they had been purchased from France,
the Indian title had not been extinguished, and these adventurous
persons were beyond the limits of any State or Territorial government. The first settlers were therefore obliged to be their own
law-makers, and to agree to such regulations as the exigencies of
the case demanded. The first act resembling civil legislation
within the limits of the present State of Iowa was done by the
miners at this point, in June, 1830. They met on the bank of the
river, by the side of an old cottonwood drift log, at what is now
the Jones Street Levee, Dubuque, and elected a committee, consisting of J. L. Langworthy, H. F. Lander, James McPhetres,
Samuel Scales, and E. M. Wren. This may be called the first
Legislature in Iowa, the members of which gathered around that
old cottonwood log, and agreed to and reported the following,
written by Mr. Langworth, on a half-sheet of coarse, unruled
paper, the old log being the writing desk:

We, a Committee having been chosen to draft certain rules and regulations
(laws) by which we as miners, will be governed, and having duly considered

the subject, do unanimously agree that we will be governed by the regulations on the east side of the Mississippi River,* with the following exceptions, to-wit:

ARTICLE I. That each and every man shall hold 200 yards square of ground by working said ground one day in six.

ARTICLE II. We further agree that there shall be chosen, by the majority of the miners present, a person who shall hold this article, and who shall grant letters of arbitration on application having been made, and that said letters of arbitration shall be obligatory on the parties so applying.

The report was accepted by the miners present, who elected Dr. Jarote, in accordance with Article 2. Here, then, we have, in 1830, a primitive Legislature elected by the people, the law drafted by it being submitted to the people for approval, and under it Dr. Jarote was elected first Governor within the limits of the present State of Iowa. And it is to be said that the laws thus enacted were as promptly obeyed, and the acts of the executive officer thus elected as duly respected, as any have been since.

The miners who had thus erected an independent government of their own on the west side of the Mississippi River, continued to work successfully for a long time, and the new settlement attracted considerable attention. But the west side of the Mississippi belonged to the Sac and Fox Indians, and the Government in order to preserve peace on the frontier, as well as to protect the Indians in their rights under the treaty, ordered the settlers not only to stop mining, but to remove from the Indian territory. They were simply intruders. The execution of this order was entrusted to Col. Zachary Taylor, then in command of the military post at Prairie du Chien, who, early in July, sent an officer to the miners with orders to forbid settlement, and to command the miners to remove within ten days to the east side of the Mississippi, or they would be driven off by armed force. The miners, however, were reluctant about leaving the rich "leads" they had already discovered and opened, and were not disposed to obey the order to remove with any considerable degree of alacrity. In due time, Col. Taylor dispatched a detachment of troops to enforce his order. The miners, anticipating their arrival, had, excepting three, recrossed the river, and from the east bank saw the troops land on the western shore. The three who had lingered a little too long were, however, permitted to make their escape unmolested. From this time, a military force was stationed at Dubuque to prevent the settlers from returning, until June, 1832. The Indians returned, and were encouraged to operate the rich mines opened by the late white occupants.

In June, 1832, the troops were ordered to the east side to assist in the annihilation of the very Indians whose rights they had been protecting on the west side. Immediately after the close of the Black Hawk war, and the negotiations of the treaty in September, 1832, by which the Sacs and Foxes ceded to the United States the

*Established by the Superintendent of U. S. Lead Mines at Fever River.

tract known as the " Black Hawk Purchase," the settlers, supposing that now they had a right to re-enter the territory, returned
and took possession of their claims, built cabins, erected furnaces
and prepared large quantities of lead for market. Dubuque was
becoming a noted place on the river, but the prospects of the hardy
and enterprising settlers and miners were again ruthlessly inter-
fered with by the Government, on the ground that the treaty with
the Indians would not go into force until June 1, 1833, although
they had withdrawn from the vicinity of the settlement. Col Taylor was again ordered by the War Department to remove the miners, and in January, 1833, troops were again sent from Prairie du
Chien to Dubuque for that purpose. This was a serious and perhaps unnecessary hardship imposed upon the settlers. They were
compelled to abandon their cabins and homes in midwinter. It
must be now said, simply that " red tape " should be respected.
The purchase had been made, the treaty ratified, or was sure to be;
the Indians had retired, and, after the lapse of nearly fifty years,
no very satisfactory reason for this rigorous action of the Government can be given.

But the orders had been given, and there was no alternative but
to obey. Many of the settlers recrossed the river, and did not return; a few, however, removed to an island near the east bank of
the river, built rude cabins of poles, in which to store their lead
until spring, when they could float the fruits of their labor to St.
Louis for sale, and where they could remain until the treaty went
into force, when they could return. Among these were James L.
Langworthy, and his brother Lucius, who had on hand about three
hundred thousand pounds of lead.

Lieut. Covington, who had been placed in command at Dubuque
by Col. Taylor, ordered some of the cabins of the settlers to be torn
down, and wagons and other property to be destroyed. This wan-
ton and inexcusable action on the part of a subordinate clothed with
a little brief authority was sternly rebuked by Col. Taylor, and Covington was superseded by Lieut. Geo. Wilson, who pursued a just
and friendly course with the pioneers, who were only waiting for
the time when they could repossess their claims.

June 1, 1833, the treaty formally went into effect, the troops
were withdrawn and the Langworthy brothers and a few others at
once returned and resumed possession of their home claims and
mineral prospects, and from this time the first permanent settlement of this portion of Iowa must date. Mr. John P. Sheldon
was appointed Superintendent of the mines by the Government,
and a system of permits to miners and licenses to smelters was
adopted, similar to that which had been in operation at Galena,
since 1825, under Lieut. Martin Thomas, and Capt. Thomas C. Le-
gate. Substantially the primitive law enacted by the miners assembled around that old cottonwood drift log in 1830 was adopted and
enforced by the United States Government, except that miners were

required to sell their mineral to licensed smelters and the smelter was required to give bonds for the payment of six per cent. of all lead manufactured to the Government. This was the same rule adopted in the United States mines on Fever River in Illinois, except that, until 1830, the Illinois miners were compelled to pay ten per cent. tax. This tax upon the miners created much dissatisfaction among the miners on the west side as it had on the east side of the Mississippi. They thought they had suffered hardships and privationsenough in opening the way for civilization, without being subjected to the imposition of an odious Government tax upon their means of subsistence, when the Federal Government could better afford to aid than to extort from them. The measure soon became unpopular. It was difficult to collect the taxes, and the whole system was abolished in about ten years.

During 1833, after the Indian title was fully extinguished, about five hundred people arrived at the mining district, about one hundred and fifty of them from Galena.

In the same year Mr. Langworthy assisted in building the first school house in Iowa, and thus was formed the nucleus of the now populous and thriving city of Dubuque. Mr. Langworthy lived to see the naked prairie on which he first landed become the site of a city of fifteen thousand inhabitants, the small school house which he aided in constructing replaced by three substantial edifices, wherein two thousand children were being trained, churches erected in every part of the city, and railroads connecting the wilderness which he first explored with all the eastern world. He died suddenly on the 13th of March, 1865, while on a trip over the Dubuque & Southwestern Railroad, at Monticello, and the evening train brought news of his death and his remains.

Lucius H. Langworthy, his brother, was one of the most worthy, gifted and influential of the old settlers of this section of Iowa. He died, greatly lamented by many friends, in June, 1865.

The name Dubuque was given to the settlement by miners at a meeting held in 1834.

In 1832 Captain James White made a claim on the present site of Montrose. In 1834 a military post was established at this point and a garrison of cavaly was stationed here, under the command of Col. Stephen W. Kearney. The soldiers were removed from this post to Fort Leavenworth, Kansas, in 1837.

During the same year, 1832, soon after the close of the Black Hawk War, Zachariah Hawkins, Benjamin Jennings, Aaron White, Augustine Horton, Samuel Gooch, Daniel Thompson and Peter Williams made claims at Fort Madison. In 1833, these claims were purchased by John and Nathaniel Knapp, upon which, in 1835, they laid out the town. The next summer, lots were sold. The town was subsequently re-surveyed and platted by the United States Government.

At the close of the Black Hawk War, parties who had been impatiently looking across upon " Flint Hills," now Burlington, came over from Illinois and made claims. The first was Samuel S. White, in the fall of 1832, who erected a cabin on the site of the city of Burlington. About the same time, David Tothero made a claim on the prairie about three miles back from the river, at a place since known as the farm of Judge Morgan. In the winter of that year, they were driven off by the military from Rock Island, as intruders upon the rights of the Indians, and White's cabin was burnt by the soldiers. He retired to Illinois, where he spent the winter, and in the summer, as soon as the Indian title was extinguished, returned and rebuilt his cabin. White was joined by his brother-in-law, Doolittle, and they laid out the original town of Burlington, in 1834.

All along the river borders of the Black Hawk Purchase settlers were flocking into Iowa. Immediately after the treaty with the Sacs and Foxes, in September, 1832, Col. George Davenport made the first claim on the spot where the thriving city of Davenport now stands. As early as 1827, Col. Davenport had established a flatboat ferry, which ran between the island and the main shore of Iowa, by which he carried on a trade with the Indians west of the Mississippi. In 1833, Capt. Benjamin W. Clark moved across from Illinois, and laid the foundation of the town of Buffalo, in Scott county, which was the first actual settlement within the limits of that county. Among other early settlers in this part of the Territory were Adrian H. Davenport, Col. John Sullivan, Mulligan and Franklin Easly, Capt. John Coleman, J. M. Camp, William White, H. W. Higgins, Cornelius Harrold, Richard Harrison, E. H. Shepherd and Dr. E. S. Barrows.

The first settlers of Davenport were Antoine LeClaire, Col. George Davenport, Major Thomas Smith, Major William Gordon, Philip Hambaugh, Alexander W. McGregor, Leyi S. Colton, Capt. James May and others. Of Antoine LeClaire, as the representative of the two races of men who, at this time occupied Iowa, Hon. C. C. Nourse, in his admirable Centennial Address, says: " Antoine LeClaire was born in St. Joseph, Michigan, in 1797. His father was French, his mother a granddaughter of a Pottawattamie chief. In 1818, he acted as official interpreter to Col. Davenport, at Fort Armstrong (now Rock Island). He was well acquainted with a dozen Indian dialects, and was a man of strict integrity and great energy. In 1820 he married the granddaughter of a Sac chief. The Sac and Fox Indians reserved for him and his wife two sections of land in the treaty of 1833, one at the town of LeClaire and one at Davenport. The Pottawattamies, in the treaty at Prairie du Chien, also reserved for him two sections of land, at the present site of Moline, Ill. He received the appointment of Postmaster and Justice of the Peace in the Black Hawk Purchase, at an early day. In 1833, he bought for $100 a claim on the land upon which the original town of Davenport was surveyed and platted in 1836. In 1836, LeClaire built the hotel, known since, with its valuable addition, as the LeClaire House. He died September 25, 1861."

In Clayton county, the first settlement was made in the Spring of 1832, on Turkey River, by Robert Hatfield and William W. Wayman. No further settlements were made in this part of the State till the beginning of 1836.

In that portion now known as Muscatine county, settlements were made in 1834, by Benjamin Nye, John Vanater and G. W. Kasey, who were the first settlers. E. E. Fay, William St. John, N. Fullington H. Reece, Jona. Pettibone, R. P. Lowe, Stephen Whicher, Abijah Whiting, J. E. Fletcher, W. D. Abernethy and Alexis Smith were early settlers of Muscatine.

During the summer of 1835, William Bennett and his family, from Galena, built the first cabin within the present limits of Delaware county, in some timber since known as Eads' Grove.

The first postoffice in Iowa was established at Dubuque in 1833. Milo H. Prentice was appointed postmaster.

The first Justice of the Peace was Antoine LeClaire, appointed in 1833, as "a very suitable person to adjust the difficulties between the white settlers and the Indians still remaining there."

The first Methodist Society in the Territory was formed at Dubuque on the 18th of May, 1834, and the first class meeting was held June 1st of that year.

The first church bell brought into Iowa was in March, 1834.

The first mass of the Roman Catholic Church in the Territory was celebrated at Dubuque, in the house of Patrick Quigley, in the fall of 1833.

The first school house in the Territory was erected by the Dubuque miners in 1833.

The first Sabbath school was organized at Dubuque early in the Summer of 1834.

The first woman who came to this part of the Territory with a view to permanent residence, was Mrs. Noble F. Dean, in the Fall of 1832.

The first family that lived in this part of Iowa was that of Hosea T. Camp, in 1832.

The first meeting house was built by the Methodist Episcopal Church, at Dubuque, in 1834.

The first newspaper in Iowa was the Dubuque *Visitor*, issued May 11th, 1836. John King, afterward Judge King, was editor, and William C. Jones, printer.

The pioneers of Iowa, as a class, were brave, hardy, intelligent and enterprising people.

As early as 1824, a French trader named Hart had established a trading post, and built a cabin on the bluffs above the large spring now known as "Mynster Spring," within the limits of the pres-

ent city of Council Bluffs, and had probably been there some time,
as the post was known to the employes of the American Fur
Company as *Lacote de Hart*, or "Hart's Bluff." In 1827, an
agent of the American Fur Company, Francis Guittar, with others,
encamped in the timber at the foot of the bluffs, about on the
present location of Broadway, and afterward settled there. In
1839, a block house was built on the bluff in the east part of the
city. The Pottawattamie Indians occupied this part of the State
until 1846-7, when they relinquished the territory and removed to
Kansas. Billy Caldwell was then principal chief. There were no
white settlers in that part of the State, except Indian traders,
until the arrival of the Mormons under the lead of Brigham
Young. These people, on their way westward, halted for the
Winter of 1846-7 on the west bank of the Missouri River, about
five mile above Omaha, at a now place called Florence. Some of
them had reached the eastern bank of the river the Spring before,
in season to plant a crop. In the Spring of 1847, Young and a
portion of the colony pursued their journey to Salt Lake, but a
large portion of them returned to the Iowa side and settled mainly
within the limits of Pottawattamie County. The principal settlement of this strange community was at a place called "Miller's
Hollow," on Indian Creek, and afterward named Kanesville, in
honor of Col. Kane, of Pennsylvania, who visited them soon afterward. The Mormon settlement extended over the county and into
neighboring counties, wherever timber and water furnished
desirable locations. Orson Hyde, priest, lawyer and editor, was
installed as President of the Quorum of Twelve, and all that part
of the State remained under Mormon control for several years.
In 1846, they raised a battalion, numbering some five hundred men,
for the Mexican war. In 1848, Hyde started a paper called the
Frontier Guardian, at Kanesville. In 1849, after many of the
faithful had left to join Brigham Young at Salt Lake, the Mormons in this section of Iowa numbered 6,552, and in 1850, 7,828,
but they were not all within the limits of Pottawattamie County.
This county was organized in 1848, all the first officials being Mormons. In 1852, the order was promulgated that all the true be-
lievers should gather together at Salt Lake. Gentiles flocked in,
and in a few years nearly all the first settlers were gone.

May 9, 1843, Captain James Allen, with a small detachment of
troops on board the steamer Ione, arrived at the present site of the
capital of the State, Des Moines. The Ione was the first steamer
to ascend the Des Moines River to this point. The troops and
stores were landed at what is now the foot of Court avenue, Des
Moines, and Capt. Allen returned in the steamer to Fort Sanford
to arrange for bringing up more soldiers and supplies. In due
time they, too, arrived, and a fort was built near the mouth of
Raccoon Fork, at its confluence with the Des Moines, and named
Fort Des Moines. Soon after the arrival of the troops, a trading

post was established on the east side of the river, by two noted Indian traders named Ewing, from Ohio.

Among the first settlers in this part of Iowa were Benjamin Bryant, J. B. Scott, James Drake (gunsmith), John Sturtevant, Robert Kinzie, Alexander Turner, Peter Newcomer, and others.

The Western States have been settled by many of the best and most enterprising men of the older States, and a large immigration of the best blood of the Old World, who, removing to an arena of larger opportunities, in a more fertile soil and congenial climate, have developed a spirit and an energy peculiarly Western. In no country on the globe have enterprises of all kinds been pushed forward with such rapidity, or has there been such independence and freedom of competition. Among those who have pioneered the civilization of the West, and been the founders of great States, none have ranked higher in the scale of intelligence and moral worth than the pioneers of Iowa, who came to the territory when it was an Indian country, and through hardship, privation and suffering, laid the foundations of the populous and prosperous commonwealth which to-day dispenses its blessings to a million and a quarter of people. From her first settlement and from the first organization as a territory to the present day, Iowa has had able men to manage her affairs, wise statesmen to shape her destiny and frame her laws, and intelligent and impartial jurists to administer justice to her citizens; her bar, pulpit and press have been able and widely influential; and in all the professions, arts, enterprises and industries which go to make up a great and prosperous commonwealth, she has taken and holds a front rank among her sister States of the West.

TERRITORIAL HISTORY.

By act of Congress, approved October 31, 1803, the President of the United States was authorized to take possession of the territory included in the Louisiana purchase, and provided for a temporary government. By another act of the same session, approved March 26, 1804, the newly acquired country was divided: October 1st, 1804, into the Territory of Orleans, south of the thirty-third parallel of north latitude, and the district of Louisiana, which latter was placed under the authority of the officers of Indian Territory.

In 1802, the district of Louisana was organized as a Territory, with a government of its own. In 1807, Iowa was included in the Territory of Illinois, and in 1812 in the Territory of Missouri. When Missouri was admitted as a State, March 2, 1821, "Iowa," says Hon. C. C. Nourse, "was left a political orphan," until by act of Congress, approved June 28, 1834, the Black Hawk purchase having been made, all the territory west of the Mississippi and north of the northern boundary of Missouri, was made a part of

Michigan Territory. Up to this time there had been no county or other organization in what is now the State of Iowa, although one or two Justices of the Peace had been appointed and a post-office was established at Dubuque in 1833. In September, 1834, however, the Territorial Legislature of Michigan created two counties on the west side of the Mississippi River, viz: Dubuque and Des Moines, separated by a line drawn westward from the foot of Rock Island. These counties were partially organized. John King was appointed Chief Justice of Dubuque County, and Isaac Leffler, of Burlington, of Des Moines County. Two Associate Justices in each county, were appointed by the Governor.

On the first Monday in October, 1835, Gen. Geo. W. Jones, now a citizen of Dubuque, was elected a Delegate to Congress from this part of Michigan Territory. On the 20th of April, 1836, through the efforts of Gen. Jones, Congress passed a bill creating the Territory of Wisconsin, which went into operation, July 4, 1836, and Iowa was then included in.

THE TERRITORY OF WISCONSIN,

of which Gen Henry Dodge was appointed Governor; John S. Horner, Secretary of the Territory; Charles Dunn, Chief Justice; David Irwin and Wm. C. Frazer, Associate Justices.

September 9, 1836, Gov. Dodge ordered the census of the new territory to be taken. This census resulted in showing a population of 10,531 in the counties of Dubuque and Des Moines. Under the apportionment, these two counties were entitled to six members of the Council and thirteen of the House of Representatives. The Governor issued his proclamation for an election to be held on the first Monday of October, 1836, on which day the following members of the First Territorial Legislature of Wisconsin were elected from the two counties in the Black Hawk purchase:

Dubuque County.– *Council:* John Fally, Thomas McKnight, Thomas McCarney. *House:* Loring Wheeler, Hardin Nowlan, Peter Hill Engle, Patrick Cuigley, Hosea T. Camp.

Des Moines County.—*Council:* Jeremiah Smith, Jr., Joseph R. Teas, Arthur B. Inghram. *House:* Isaac Leffler, Thomas Blair, Warren L. Jenkins, John Box, George W. Teas, Eli Reynolds, David R. Chance.

The first Legislature assembled at Belmont, in the present State of Wisconsin, on the 25th day of October, 1836, and was organized by electing Henry T. Baird President of the Council, and Peter Hill Engle, of Dubuque, Speaker of the House. It adjourned December 9, 1836.

The second Legislature assembled at Burlington, November, 10, 1837. Adjourned January 20, 1838. The third session was at Burlington; commenced June 1st, and adjourned June 12, 1838.

During the first session of the Wisconsin Territorial Legislature in 1836, the County of Des Moines was divided into Des Moines

Lee, Van Buren, Henry, Muscatine and Cook (the latter being subsequently changed to Scott) and defined their boundaries. During the second session, out of the territory embraced in Dubuque County, were created the counties of Dubuque, Clayton, Fayette, Delaware, Buchanan, Jackson, Jones, Linn, Clinton and Cedar, and their boundaries defined, but the most of them were not organized until several years afterward, under the authority of the Territorial Legislature of Iowa.

The question of a separate territorial organization for Iowa, which was then a part of Wisconsin Territory, began to be agitated early in the autumn of 1837. The wishes of the people found expression in a convention held at Burlington on the 1st of November, which memorialized Congress to organize a Territory west of the Mississippi, and to settle the boundary line between Wisconsin Territory and Missouri. The Territorial Legislature of Wisconsin, then in session at Burlington, joined in the petition. Gen. Geo. W. Jones, of Dubuque, then residing at Sinsinawa Mound, in what is now Wisconsin, was Delegate to Congress from Wisconsin Territory, and labored so earnestly and successfully, that "An act to divide the Territory of Wisconsin, and to establish the Territorial Government of Iowa," was approved June 12, 1838, to take effect, and be in force on and after July 3, 1838. The new Territory embraced "all that part of the present Territory of Wisconsin which lies west of the Mississippi River, and west of a line drawn due north from the head water or sources of the Mississippi to the territorial line." The organic act provided for a Governor, whose term of office should be three years, and for a Secretary, Chief Justice, two Associate Justices, and Attorney and Marshal, who should serve four years, to be appointed by the President, by and with the advice and consent of the Senate. The act also provided for the election, by the white male inhabitants, citizens of the United States, over twenty-one years of age, of a House of Representatives, consisting of twenty-six members, and a Council, to consist of thirteen members. It also appropriated $5,000 for a public library, and $20,000 for the erection of public buildings.

President Van Buren appointed Ex-Governor Robert Lucas, of Ohio, to be the first Governor of the new Territory. William B. Conway, of Pittsburgh, was appointed Secretary of the Territory; Charles Mason, of Burlington, Chief Justice, and Thomas S. Wilson, of Dubuque, and Joseph Williams, of Pennsylvania, Associate Judges of the Supreme and District Courts; Mr. Van Allen, of New York, Attorney; Francis Gehon, of Dubuque, Marshal; Augustus C. Dodge, Register of the Land Office at Burlington, and Thomas McKnight, Receiver of the Land Office at Dubuque. Mr. Van Allen, the District Attorney, died at Rockingham, soon after his appointment, and Col. Charles Weston was appointed to fill his vacancy. Mr. Conway, the Secretary, also died at Burlington, during the second session of the Legislature, and James Clarke, editor of the *Gazette*, was appointed to succeed him.

Immediately after his arrival, Governor Lucas issued a proclamation for the election of members of the first Territorial Legislature, to be held on the 10th of September, dividing the Territory into election districts for that purpose, and appointing the 12th day of November for meeting of the Legislature to be elected, at Burlington.

The first Territorial Legislature was elected in September and assembled at Burlington on the 12th of November, and consisted of the following members:

Council.—Jesse B. Brown, J. Keith, E. A. M. Swazy, Arthur Ingram, Robert Ralston, George Hepner, Jesse J. Payne, D. B. Hughes, James M. Clark, Charles Whittlesey, Jonathan W. Parker, Warner Lewis, Stephen Hempstead.

House.—William Patterson, Hawkins Taylor, Calvin J. Price, James Brierly, James Hall, Gideon S. Bailey, Samuel Parker, James W. Grimes, George Temple, Van B. Delashmutt, Thomas Blair, George H. Beeler,* William G. Coop, William H. Wallace, Asbury B. Porter, John Frierson, William L. Toole, Levi Thornton, S. C. Hastings, Robert G. Roberts, Laurel Summers,† Jabez A. Burchard, Jr., Chauncey Swan, Andrew Bankson, Thomas Cox and Hardin Nowlin.

Notwithstanding a large majority of the members of both branches of the Legislature were Democrats, yet Gen. Jesse B. Browne (Whig), of Lee County, was elected President of the Council, and Hon. William H. Wallace (Whig), of Henry County, Speaker of the House of Representatives—the former unanimously and the latter with but little opposition. At that time, national politics were little heeded by the people of the new Territory, but in 1840, during the Presidential campaign, party lines were strongly drawn.

At the election in September, 1838, for members of the Legislature, a Congressional Delegate was also elected. There were four candidates, viz: William W. Chapman and David Rohrer, of Des Moines County; B. F. Wallace, of Henry County, and P. H. Engle, of Dubuque County. Chapman was elected, receiving a majority of thirty-six over Engle.

The first session of the Iowa Territorial Legislature was a stormy and exciting one. By the organic law, the Governor was clothed with almost unlimited veto power. Governor Lucas seemed disposed to make free use of it, and the independent Hawkeyes could not quietly submit to arbitrary and absolute rule, and the result was an unpleasant controversy between the Executive and Legislative departments. Congress, however, by act approved March 3,

---

*Cyrus S. Jacobs, who was elected for Des Moines County, was killed in an unfortunate encounter at Burlington before the meeting of the Legislature, and Mr. Beeler was elected to fill the vacancy.

†Samuel R. Murray was returned as elected from Clinton County, but his seat was successfully contested by Burchard.

1839, amended the organic law by restricting the veto power of the Governor to the two-thirds rule, and took from him the power to appoint Sheriffs and Magistrates.

Among the first important matters demanding attention was the location of the seat of government and provision for the erection of public buildings, for which Congress had appropriated $20,000. Governor Lucas, in his message, had recommended the appointment of Commissioners, with a view to making a central location. The extent of the future State of Iowa was not known or thought of. Only on a strip of land fifty miles wide, bordering on the Mississippi River, was the Indian title extinguished, and a central location meant some central point in the Black Hawk Purchase. The friends of a central location supported the Governor's suggestion. The southern members were divided between Burlington and Mount Pleasant, but finally united on the latter as the proper location for the seat of government. The central and southern parties were very nearly equal, and, in consequence, much excitement prevailed. The central party at last triumphed, and on the 21st day of January, 1839, an act was passed, appointing Chauncey Swan, of Dubuque County; John Ronalds, of Louisa County, and Robert Ralston, of Des Moines County, Commissioners, to select a site for a permanent seat of Government within the limits of Johnson County.

Johnson County had been created by act of the Territorial Legislature of Wisconsin, approved December 21, 1837, and organized by act passed at the special session at Burlington in June, 1838, the organization to date from July 4th, following. Napoleon, on the Iowa River, a few miles below the future Iowa City, was designated as the county seat, temporarily.

Then there existed good reason for locating the capital in the county. The Territory of Iowa was bounded on the north by the British Possessions; east, by the Mississippi River to its source; thence by a line drawn due north to the northern boundary of the United States; south, by the State of Missouri, and west, by the Missouri and White Earth Rivers. But this immense territory was in undisputed possession of the Indians, except a strip on the Mississippi, known as the Black Hawk Purchase. Johnson County was, from north to south, in the geographical center of this purchase, and as near the east and west geographical center of the future State of Iowa as could then be made, as the boundary line between the lands of the United States and the Indians, established by the treaty of October 21, 1837, was immediately west of the county limits.

The Commissioners, after selecting the site, were directed to lay out 640 acres into a town, to be called Iowa City, and to proceed to sell lots and erect public buildings thereon, Congress having granted a section of land to be selected by the Territory for this purpose. The Commissioners met at Napoleon, Johnson County,

May 1, 1839, selected for a site Section 10, in Township 79 North
of Range 6, West of the Fifth Principal Meridian, and immediately surveyed it and laid off the town. The first sale of lots took
place August 16, 1839. The site selected for the public buildings
was a little west of the geographical center of the section, where
a square of ten acres on the elevated grounds overlooking the river
was reserved for the purpose. The capitol is located in the center
of this square. The second Territorial Legislature, which assembled in November, 1839, passed an act requiring the Commissioners to adopt such plan for the building that the aggregate cost
when complete, shovld not exceed $51,000, and if they had already
adopted a plan involving a greater expenditure, they were directed
to abandon it. Plans for the building were designed and drawn
by Mr. John F. Rague, of Springfield, Ill., and on the 4th day of
July, 1840, the corner stone of the edifice was laid with appropriate ceremonies. Samuel C. Trowbridge was Marshal of the
day, and Gov. Lucas delivered the address on that occasion.

When the Legislature assembled at Burlington in special session
July 13, 1840, Gov. Lucas announced that on the 4th of that
month he had visited Iowa City, and found the basement of the
capitol nearly completed. A bill authorizing a loan of $20,000
for the building was passed, January 15, 1841, the unsold lots of
Iowa City being the security offered, but only $5,500 was obtained
under the act.

THE BOUNDARY QUESTION.

The boundary line between the Territory of Iowa and the State
of Missouri was a difficult question to settle in 1838, in consequence of claims arising from taxes and titles, and at one time
civil war was imminent. In defining the boundaries of the counties bordering on Missouri, the Iowa authorities had fixed a line
that has since been established as the boundary between Iowa and
Missouri. The Constitution of Missouri defines her northern
boundary to be the parallel of the latitude which passes through
the rapids of the Des Moines River. The lower rapids of the
Mississippi immediately above the mouth of the Des Moines River
had always been known as the Des Moines Rapids, or "the rapids
of the Des Moines River." The Missourians (evidently not well
versed in history or geography) insisted on running the northern
boundary line from the rapids in the Des Moines River, just below
Keosauqua, thus taking from Iowa a strip of territory eight or ten
miles wide. Assuming this as her northern boundary line, Missouri attempted to exercise jurisdiction over the disputed territory
by assessing taxes, and sending her Sheriffs to collect them by distraining the personal property of the settlers. The Iowans, however, were not disposed to submit, and the Missouri officials were
arrested by the Sheriffs of Davis and Van Buren Counties and

confined in jail. Gov. Boggs, of Missouri, called out his militia to enforce the claim and sustain the officers of Missouri. Gov. Lucas called out the militia of Iowa, and both parties made active preparations for war. In Iowa, about 1,200 men were enlisted, and 500 were actually armed and encamped in Van Buren County, ready to defend the integrity of the Territory. Subsequently, Gen. A. C. Dodge, of Burlington, Gen. Churchman, of Dubuque, and Dr. Clark, of Fort Madison, were sent to Missouri as envoys plenipotentiary, to effect, if possible, a peaceable adjustment of the difficulty. Upon their arrival, they found that the County Commissioners of Clarke County, Missouri, had rescinded their order for the collection of the taxes, and that Gov. Boggs had despatched messengers to the Governor of Iowa proposing to submit an agreed case to the Supreme Court of the United States for the final settlement of the boundary question. This proposition was declined, but afterward Congress authorized a suit to settle the controversy, which was instituted, and which resulted in a judgment for Iowa. Under this decision, William G. Miner, of Missouri, and Henry B. Hendershott were appointed Commissioners to survey and establish the boundary. Mr. Nourse remarks that "the expenses of the war on the part of Iowa were never paid, either by the United States or the Territorial Government. The patriots who furnished supplies to the troops had to bear the cost and charges of the struggle."

The first legislative assembly laid the broad foundation of civil equality, on which has been constructed one of the most liberal governments in the Union. Its first act was to recognize the equality of woman with man before the law, by providing that "no action commenced by a single woman, who intermarries during the pendency thereof, shall abate on account of such marriage." This principle has been adopted by all subsequent legislation in Iowa, and to-day woman has full and equal civil rights with man, except only the right of the ballot.

Religious toleration was also secured to all, personal liberty strictly guarded, the rights and privileges of citizenship extended to all white persons, and the purity of elections secured by heavy penalties against bribery and corruption. The judiciary power was vested in a Supreme Court, District Court, Probate Court, and Justices of the Peace. Real estate was made divisible by will, and intestate property divided equitably among heirs. Murder was made punishable by death, and proportionate penalties fixed for lesser crimes. A system of free schools, open for every class of white citizens, was established. Provision was made for a system of roads and highways. Thus, under the territorial organization, the country began to emerge from a savage wilderness, and take on the forms of civil government.

By act of Congress of June 12, 1838, the lands which had been purchased of the Indians were brought into market, and land

offices opened in Dubuque and Burlington. Congress provided for
military roads and bridges, which greatly aided the settlers, who
were now coming in by thousands, to make their homes on the
fertile prairies of Iowa—" the Beautiful Land." The fame of the
country had spread far and wide; even before the Indian title was
extinguished, many were crowding the borders, impatient to cross
over and stake out their claims on the choicest spots they could
find in the new Territory. As soon as the country was open for
settlement, the borders, the Black Hawk Purchase, all along the
Mississippi, and up the principal rivers and streams, and out over
the broad rolling prairies, began to be thronged with eager land
hunters and immigrants, seeking homes in Iowa. It was a sight
to delight the eyes of all comers from every land—its noble streams,
beautiful and picturesque hills and valleys, broad and fertile
prairies extending as far as the eye could reach, with a soil surpassing in richness anything which they had ever seen. It is not to
be wondered at that immigration into Iowa was rapid, and that
within less than a decade from the organization of the Territory it
contained a hundred and fifty thousand people.

As rapidly as the Indian titles were extinguished and the original owners removed, the resistless tide of emigration flowed
westward. The following extract from Judge Nourse's Centennial
Address shows how the immigrants gathered on the Indian
boundary, ready for the removal of the barrier:

In obedience to our progressive and aggressive spirit, the Government of the
United States made another treaty with the Sac and Fox Indians, on the 11th
day of August, 1842; for the remaining portion of their land in Iowa. The treaty
provided that the Indians should retain possession of all the lands thus ceded
until May 1, 1843, and should occupy that portion of the ceded territory west of
a line running north and south through Redrock, until October 11, 1845. These
tribes, at this time, had their principal village at Ot-tum-wa-no, now called Ottumwa. As soon as it became known that the treaty had been concluded, there
was a rush of immigration to Iowa, and a great number of temporary settlements were made near the Indian boundary, waiting for the 1st day of May.
As the day approached, hundreds of families encamped along the line, and their
tents and wagons gave the scene the appearance of a military expedition. The
country beyond had been thoroughly explored, but the United States military
authorities had prevented any settlement or even the making out of claims by
any monuments whatever.

To aid them in making out their claims when the hour should arrive, the settlers had placed piles of dry wood on the rising ground, at convenient distances,
and a short time before twelve o'clock on the night of the 30th of April, these
were lighted, and when the midnight hour arrived it was announced by the discharge of firearms. The night was dark, but this army of occupation pressed
forward, torch in hand, with axe and hatchet, blazing lines with all manner of
curves and angles. When daylight came and revealed the confusion of these
wonderful surveys, numerous disputes arose, settled generally by compromise,
but sometimes by violence. Between midnight of the 30th of April and sundown
of the 1st of May, over one thousand families had settled on their new purchase.

While this scene was transpiring, the retreating Indians were enacting one
more impressive and melancholy. The winter of 1842-43 was one of unusual
severity, and the Indian prophet, who had disapproved of the treaty, attributed
the severity of the winter to the anger of the Great Spirit, because they had sold
their country. Many religious rites were performed to atone for the crime.

When the time for leaving Ot-tum-wa-no arrived, a solemn silence pervaded the Indian camp, and the faces of their stoutest men were bathed in tears; and when their cavalcade was put in motion, toward the setting sun, there was a spontaneous outburst of frantic grief from the entire procession.

The Indians remained the appointed time beyond the line running north and south through Redrock. The Government established a trading post and military encampment at the Raccoon Fork of the Des Moines River, then and for many years known as Fort Des Moines. Here the red man lingered until the 11th of October, 1845, when the same scene that we have before described was re-enacted, and the wave of immigration swept over the remainder of the "New Purchase." The lands thus occupied and claimed by the settlers still belonged in fee to the General Government. The surveys were not completed until some time after the Indian title was extinguished. After their survey, the lands were publicly proclaimed or advertised for sale at public auction. Under the laws of the United States, a pre-emption or exclusive right to purchase public lands could not be acquired until after the lands had thus been publicly offered and not sold for want of bidders. Then, and not until then, an occupant making improvements in good faith might acquire a right over others to enter the land at the minimum price of $1.25 per acre. The "claim laws" were unknown to the United States statutes. They originated in the "eternal fitness of things," and were enforced, probably, as belonging to that class of natural rights not enumerated in the constitution, and not impaired or disparaged by its enumeration.

The settlers organized in every settlement prior to the public land sales, appointed officers, and adopted their own rules and regulations. Each man's claim was duly ascertained and recorded by the Secretary. It was the duty of all to attend the sales. The Secretary bid off the lands of each settler at $1.25 per acre. The others were there to see, first, that he did his duty and bid in the land, and, secondly, to see that no one else bid. This, of course, sometimes led to trouble, but it saved the excitement of competition, and gave a formality and degree of order and regularity to the proceedings they would not otherwise have attained. As far as practicable, the Territorial Legislature recognized the validity of these "claims" upon the public lands, and in 1839 passed an act legalizing their sale and making their transfer a valid consideration to support a promise to pay for the same. (Acts of 1843, p. 456). The Supreme Territorial Court held this law to be valid. (See Hill v. Smith, 1st Morris Rep. 70). The opinion not only contains a decision of the question involved, but also contains much valuable erudition upon that "spirit of Anglo-Saxon liberty" which the Iowa settlers unquestionably inherited in a direct line of descent from the said "Anglo-Saxons." But the early settler was not always able to pay even this dollar and twenty-five cents per acre for his land.

Many of the settlers had nothing to begin with, save their hands, health and courage and their family jewels, " the pledges of love," and the " consumers of bread." It was not so easy to accumulate money in the early days of the State, and the " beautiful prairies," the " noble streams," and all that sort of poetic imagery, did not prevent the early settlers from becoming discouraged.

An old settler, in speaking of the privations and trials of those early days, says:

Well do the "old settlers" of Iowa remember the days from the first settlement to 1840. Those were days of sadness and distress. The endearments of home in another land had been broken up; and all that was hallowed on earth, the home of childhood, and the scenes of youth, were severed; and we sat down by the gentle waters of our noble river, and often "hung our harps on the willows."

Another, from another part of the state testifies:

There was no such thing as getting money for any kind of labor. I laid brick at $3.00 per thousand, and took my pay in anything I could eat or wear. I

4

built the first Methodist Church at Keokuk, 42x60 feet, of brick. for $600, and took my pay in a subscription paper, part of which I never collected, and upon which I only received $50.00 in money. Wheat was hauled 100 miles from the interior, and sold for 37½ cents per bushel.

Another old settler, speaking of a later period, 1843, says:

Land and everything had gone down in value to almost nominal prices. Corn and oats could be bought for six or ten cents a bushel; pork, $1.00 per hundred and the best horse a man could raise sold for $50.00. Nearly all were in debt and the Sheriff and Constable, with legal processes, were common visitors at almost every man's door. These were indeed "the times that tried men's souls."

"A few," says Mr. Nourse, " who were not equal to the trial, returned to their old homes, but such as had courage and faith to be the worthy founders of a great State remained, to more than realize the fruition of their hopes, and the reward of their self-denial."

On Monday, December 6, 1841, the fourth Legislative Assembly met, at the new capital, Iowa City, but the capitol building could not be used, and the Legislature occupied a temporary frame house, that had been erected for that purpose, during the session of 1841-2. At this session, the Superintendent of Public Buildings (who, with the Territorial Agent, had superseded the Commissioners first appointed), estimated the expense of completing the building at $33,330, and that rooms for the use of the Legislature could be completed for $15,600.

During 1842, the Superintendent commenced obtaining stone from a new quarry, about ten miles northeast of the city. This is now known as the "Old Captain Quarry," and contains, it is thought, an immense quantity of excellent building stone. Here all the stone for completing the building was obtained, and it was so far completed that on the 5th day of December, 1842, the Legislature assembled in the new capitol. At this session, the Superintendent estimated that it would cost $39,143 to finish the building. This was nearly $6,000 higher than the estimate of the previous year, notwithstanding a large sum had been expended in the meantime. This rather discouraging discrepancy was accounted for by the fact that the officers in charge of the work were constantly short of funds. Except the Congressional appropriation of $20,000 and the loan of $5,500, obtained from the Miners' Bank, of Dubuque, all the funds for the prosecution of the work were derived from the sale of the city lots (which did not sell very rapidly), from certificates of indebtedness, and from scrip, based upon unsold lots, which was to be received in payment for such lots when they were sold. At one time the Superintendent made a requisition for bills of iron and glass, which could not be obtained nearer than St. Louis. To meet this, the Agent sold some lots for a draft, payable at Pittsburgh, Pa., for which he was compelled to pay twenty-five per cent. exchange. This draft, amounting to $507, that officer reported to be more than one-half the cash actually handled by him during the entire season, when the disbursement amounted to very nearly $24,000.

With such uncertainty, it could not be expected that estimates could be very accurate. With all these disadvantages, however, the work appears to have been prudently prosecuted, and as rapidly as circumstances would permit.

Iowa remained a Territory from 1838 to 1846, during which the office of Governor was held by Robert Lucas, John Chambers and James Clarke.

STATE ORGANIZATION.

By an act of the Territorial Legislature of Iowa, approved February 12, 1844, the question of the formation of a State Constitution and providing for the election of Delegates to a convention to be convened for that purpose was submitted to the people, to be voted upon at their township elections in April following. The vote was largely in favor of the measure, and the Delegates elected assembled in convention at Iowa City, on the 7th of October, 1844. On the first day of November following, the convention completed its work and adopted the first State Constitution.

The President of the convention, Hon. Shepherd Leffler, was instructed to transmit a certified copy of this Constitution to the Delegate in Congress, to be by him submitted to that body at the earliest practicable day. It was also provided that it should be submitted, together with any conditions or changes that might be made by Congress, to the people of the Territory, for their approval or rejection, at the township election in April, 1845.

The boundaries of the State, as defined by this Constitution, were as follows:

Beginning in the middle of the channel of the Mississippi River, opposite mouth of the Des Moines River, thence up the said river Des Moines, in the middle of the main channel thereof, to a point where it is intersected by the Old Indian Boundary line, or line run by John C. Sullivan, in the year 1816; thence westwardly along said line to the "old" northwest corner of Missouri; thence due west to the middle of the main channel of the Missouri River; thence up in the middle of the main channel of the river last mentioned to the mouth of the Sioux or Calumet River; thence in a direct line to the middle of the main channel of the St. Peters River, where the Watonwan River—according to Nicollet's map—enters the same; thence down the middle of the main channel of said river to the middle of the main channel of the Mississippi River; thence down the middle of the main channel of said river to the place of beginning.

These boundaries were rejected by Congress, but by act approved March 3, 1845, a State called Iowa was admitted into the Union, provided the people accepted the act, bounded as follows:

Beginning at the mouth of the Des Moines River, at the middle of the Mississippi, thence by the middle of the channel of that river to a parallel of latitude passing through the mouth of the Mankato or Blue Earth River; thence west, along said parallel of latitude, to a point where it is intersected by a meridian line seventeen degrees and thirty minutes west of the meridian of Washington City; thence due south, to the northern boundary line of the State of Missouri; thence eastwardly, following that boundary to the point at which the same intersects the Des Moines River; thence by the middle of the channel of that river to the place of beginning.

These boundaries, had they been accepted, would have placed the northern boundary of the State about thirty miles north of its present location, and would have deprived it of the Missouri slope and the boundary of that river. The western boundary would have been near the west line of what is now Kossuth County. But it was not so to be. In consequence of this radical and unwelcome change in the boundaries, the people refused to accept the act of Congress and rejected the Constitution at the election, held August 4, 1845, by a vote of 7,656 to 7,235.

A second Constitutional Convention assembled at Iowa City on the 4th day of May, 1846, and on the 18th of the same month another Constitution for the new State with the present boundaries, was adopted and submitted to the people for ratification on the 3d day of August following, when it was accepted; 9,492 votes were cast "for the Constitution," and 9,036 "against the Constitution." The Constitution was approved by Congress, and by act of Congress approved December 28, 1846, Iowa was admitted as a sovereign State in the American Union.

Prior to this action of Congress, however, the people of the new State held an election under the new Constitution on the 26th day of October, and elected Ŏreset Briggs, Governor; Elisha Cutler, Jr., Secretary of State; Joseph T. Fales, Auditor; Morgan Reno, Treasurer; and members of the Senate and House of Representatives.

At this time there were twenty-seven organized counties in the State, with a population of nearly 100,000, and the frontier settlements were rapidly pushing toward the Missouri River. The Mormons had already reached there.

The first General Assembly of the State of Iowa was composed of nineteen Senators and forty Representatives. It assembled at Iowa City, November 30, 1846, about a month *before* the State was admitted into the Union.

At the first session of the State Legislature, the Treasurer of State reported that the capitol building was in a very exposed condition, liable to injury from storms, and expressed the hope that some provision would be made to complete it, at least sufficiently to protect it from the weather. The General Assembly responded by appropriating $2,500 for the completion of the public buildings. At the first session also arose the question of the re-location of the capital. The western boundary of the State, as now determined, left Iowa City too far toward the eastern and southern boundary of the State; this was conceded. Congress had appropriated five sections of land for the erection of public buildings, and toward the close of the session a bill was introduced providing for the re-location of the seat of government, involving to some extent the location of the State University, which had already been discussed. This bill gave rise to a deal of discussion and parliamentary maneuvering, almost purely sectional in its character. It provided for the appointment of three Commissioners, who were authorized to make a location as near the geographical center of the State as a healthy and eligible site could be obtained; to select the five sections of land donated by Congress; to survey and plat into town lots not exceeding one section of the land so selected; to sell lots at public sale, not to exceed two in each block. Having done this, they were then required to suspend further operations, and make a report of their proceedings to the Governor. The bill passed both Houses by decisive votes, received the signature of the Governor, and became a law, Soon after, by "An act to locate and establish a State University," approved February 25, 1847, the unfinished public buildings at Iowa City, together with the ten acres of land on which they were situated, were granted for the use of the University, reserving their use, however, by the general Assembly and the State officers, until other provisions were made by law.

The Commissioners forthwith entered upon their duties, and selected four sections and two half sections in Jasper County. Two of these sections are in what is now Des Moines Township, and the others in Fairview Township, in the southern part of that county. These lands are situated between Prairie City and Monroe, on the Keokuk & Des Moines Railroad, which runs diagonally through them. Here a town was platted, called Monroe City, and a sale of lots took place. Four hundred and fifteen lots were sold, at prices that were not considered remarkably remunerative. The cash payments (one-fourth) amounted to $1,797.43, while the expenses of the sale and the claims of the Commissioners for services amounted to $2,206.57. The Commissioners made a report of their proceedings to the Governor, as required by law, but the location was generally condemned.

When the report of the Commissioners, showing this brilliant financial operation, had been read in the House of Representatives, at the next session, and while it was under consideration, an indignant member, afterward known as the eccentric Judge McFarland, moved to refer the report to a select Committee of Five, with instructions to report "how much of said city of Monroe was under water and how much was burned." The report was referred, without the instructions, however, but Monroe City never became the seat of government. By an act approved January 15, 1849, the law by which the location had been made was repealed and the new town was vacated, the money paid by purchasers of lots being refunded to them. This, of course, retained the seat of government at Iowa City, and precluded, for the time, the occupation of the building and grounds by the University.

At the same session, $3,000 more were appropriated for completing the State building at Iowa City. In 1852, the further sum of $5,000, and in 1854 $4,000 more were appropriated for the same purpose, making the whole cost $123,000, paid partly by the General Government and partly by the State, but principally from the proceeds of the sale of lots in Iowa City.

But the question of the permanent location of the seat of government was not settled, and in 1851 bills were introduced for the removal of the capital to Pella and to Fort Des Moines. The latter appeared to have the support of the majority, but was finally lost in the House on the question of ordering it to its third reading.

At the next session, in 1853, a bill was introduced in the Senate for the removal of the seat of Government to Fort Des Moines, and, on final vote, was just barely defeated. At the next session, however, the effort was more successful, and on the 15th day of January, 1855, a bill re-locating the capital within two miles of the Raccoon Fork of the Des Moines, and for the appointment of Commissioners, was approved by Gov. Grimes. The site was selected in 1856, in accordance with the provisions of this act, the land being donated to the State by citizens and property-holders of Des Moines. An association of citizens erected a building for a temporary capitol, and leased it to the State at a nominal rent.

The third Constitutional Convention to revise the Constitution of the State assembled at Iowa City, January 19, 1857. The new Constitution framed by this convention was submitted to the people at an election held August 3, 1857, when it was approved and adopted by a vote of 40,311 "for" to 38,681 "against," and on the 3d day of September following was declared by a proclamation of the Governor to be the Supreme law of the State of Iowa.

Advised of the completion of the temporary State House of Des Moines, on the 19th of October following, Governor Grimes issued another proclamation, declaring the city of Des Moines to be the capital of the State of Iowa.

The removal of the archives and offices was commenced at once and continued through the fall. It was an undertaking of no small magnitude; there was not a mile of railroad to facilitate the work, and the season was unusually disagreeable. Rain, snow and other accompaniments increased the difficulties, and it was not until December that the last of the effects—the safe of the State Treasurer, loaded on two large "bob-sleds"—drawn by ten yoke of oxen was deposited in the new capitol. It is not imprudent now to remark that, during this passage over hills and prairies, across rivers, through bottom lands and timber, the safes belonging to the several departments contained large sums of money, mostly individual funds, however. Thus, Iowa City ceased to be the capital of the State, after four Territorial Legislatures, six State Legislatures and three Constitutional Conventions had held their sessions there. By the exchange, the old capitol at Iowa City, became the seat of the University, and except the rooms occupied by the United States District Court, passed under the immediate and direct control of the Trustees of that institution.

Des Moines was now the permament seat of government, made so by the fundamental law of the State, and on the 11th day of January, 1858, the seventh General Assembly convened at the new capital. The buildings used for governmental purposes was purchased in 1864. It soon became inadequate for the purposes for which it was designed, and it became apparent that a new, large and permanent State House must be erected. In 1870, the General Assembly made an appropriation and provided, for the appointment of a Board of Commissioners to commence the work. The board consisted of Gov. Samuel Merrill, ex-officio, President; Grenville M. Dodge, Council Bluffs; James F. Wilson, Fairfield; James Dawson, Washington; Simon G. Stein, Muscatine; James O. Crosby, Gainsville; Charles Dudley, Agency City; John N. Dewey, Des Moines; William L. Joy, Sioux City; Alexander R. Fulton, Des Moines, Secretary,

The act of 1870 provided that the building should be constructed of the best material and should be fire proof, to be heated and ventilated in the most approved manner; should contain suitable legislative halls, rooms for State officers, the judiciary, library, committees, archieves and the collections of the State Agricultural Society, and for all purposes of State Government, and should be erected on grounds held by the State for that purpose. The sum first appropriated was $150,000; and the law provided that no contract should be made, either for constructing or furnishing the building, which should bind the State for larger sums than those at the time appropriated. A design was drawn and plans and specifications furnished by Cochrane & Piquenard, architects, which were accepted by the board, and on the 23d of November, 1871, the corner stone was laid with appropriate ceremonies. The estimated cost and present value of the capitol is fixed at $2,000,000,

From 1858 to 1860, the Sioux became troublesome in the northwestern part of the State. These warlike Indians made frequent plundering raids upon the settlers, and murdered several families. In 1861, several companies of militia were ordered to that portion of the State to hunt down and punish the murderous thieves. No battles were fought, however, for the Indians fled when they ascertained that systematic and adequate measures had been adopted to protect the settlers.

"The year 1856 marked a new era in the history of Iowa. In 1854, the Chicago & Rock Island Railroad had been completed to the east bank of the Mississippi River, opposite Davenport. In 1854, the corner stone of a railroad bridge, that was to be the first to span the 'Father of Waters,' was laid with appropriate ceremonies at this point. St. Louis had resolved that the enterprise was unconstitutional, and by writs of injunction made an unsuccessful effort to prevent its completion. Twenty years later in her history, St. Louis repented her folly, and made atonement for her sin by imitating our example. On the first day of January, 1856, this railroad was completed to Iowa City. In the meantime, two other railroads had reached the east bank of the Mississippi—one opposite Burlington, and one opposite Dubuque—and these were being extended into the interior of the State. Indeed, four lines of railroad had been projected across the State from the Mississippi to the Missouri, having eastern connections. On the 15th of May, 1856, the Congress of the United States passed an act granting to the State, to aid in the construction of railroads, the public lands in alternate sections, six miles on either side of the proposed line. An extra session of the General Assembly was called in July of this year, that disposed of the grant to the several companies that proposed to complete these enterprises. The population of our State at this time had increased to 500,000. Public attention had been called to the necessity of a railroad across the continent. The position of Iowa, in the very heart and center of the Republic, on the route of this great highway across the continent, began to attract attention. Cities and towns sprang up through the State as if by magic. Capital began to pour into the State, and had it been employed in developing our vast coal measures and establishing manufactories among us, or if it had been expended in improving our lands, and building houses and barns, it would have been well. But all were in haste to get rich, and the spirit of speculation ruled the hour.

"In the meantime every effort was made to help the speedy completion of the railroads. Nearly every county and city on the Mississippi, and many in the interior, voted large corporate subscriptions to the stock of the railroad companies, and issued their negotiable bonds for the amount." Thus enormous county and city debts were incurred, the payment of which these municipalities tried to avoid upon the plea that they had exceeded the constitutional limitation of their powers. The Supreme Court of the United States held these bonds to be valid; and the courts by mandamus compelled the city and county authorities to levy taxes to pay the judgments. These debts are not all paid even yet, but the worst is over and ultimately the burden will be entirely removed.

The first railroad across the State was completed to Council Bluffs in January, 1871. The others were completed soon after. In 1854 there was not a mile of railroad in the State. In 1874, twenty years after, there were 3,765 miles in successful operation."

GROWTH AND PROGRESS.

When Wisconsin Territory was organized, in 1836, the entire population of that portion of the Territory now embraced in the State of Iowa was 10,531. The Territory then embraced two counties; Dubuque and Des Moines, erected by the Territory of Michigan, in 1834. From 1836 to 1838, the Territorial Legislature of Wisconsin increased the number of counties to sixteen, and the population had increased to 22,859. Since then the counties have increased to ninety-nine. and the population, in 1875, was 1,366,-000. The following table will show the population at different periods, since the erection of Iowa Territory:

Year.	Population.	Year.	Population.
1838	22,589	1859	638,775
1840	43,115	1860	674,913
1844	75,152	1863	701,732
1846	97,588	1865	754,699
1847	116,651	1867	902,040
1849	152,988	1869	1,040,819
1850	191,982	1870	1,191,727
1851	204,774	1873	1,251,333
1852	230,713	1875	1,366,000
1854	326,013	1880	1,624,463
1856	519,055		

The most populous county in the State is Dubuque. Not only in population, but in everything contributing to the growth and greatness of a State has Iowa made rapid progress. In a little more than thirty years, its wild but beautiful prairies have advanced from the home of the savage to a highly civilized commonwealth, embracing all the elements of progress which characterize the older States.

Thriving cities and towns dot its fair surface; an iron net-work of thousands of miles of railroads is woven over its broad acres; ten thousand school houses. in which more than five hundred thousand children are being taught the rudiments of education, testify to the culture and liberality of the people; high schools, colleges and universities are generously endowed by the State; manufactories spring up on all her water courses, and in most of her cities and towns.

Whether measured from the date of her first settlement. her organization as a Territory. or admission as a State, Iowa has thus far shown a growth unsurpassed, in a similar period, by any commonwealth on the face of the earth; and, with her vast extent of fertile soil, with her inexhaustible treasures of mineral wealth, with a healthful, invigorating climate; an intelligent, liberty-loving people; with equal, just and liberal laws, and her free schools, the future of Iowa may be expected to surpass the most hopeful anticipations of her present citizens.

Looking upon Iowa as she is to-day—populous, prosperous and happy—it is hard to realize the wonderful changes that have occurred since the first white settlements were made within her borders. When the number of States was only twenty-six, and their total population about twenty millions, our republican form of government was hardly more than an experiment, just fairly put upon trial. The development of our agricultural resources and inexhaustible mineral wealth had hardly commenced. Westward the "Star of Empire" had scarcely started on its way. West of the great Mississippi was a mighty empire, but almost unknown, and marked on the maps of the period as "The Great American Desert."

Now, thirty-eight stars glitter on our national escutcheon, and forty-five millions of people, who know their rights and dare maintain them, tread American soil, and the grand sisterhood of States extends from the Gulf of Mexico to the Canadian border, and from the rocky coast of the Atlantic to the golden shores of the Pacific.

THE AGRICULTURAL COLLEGE AND FARM.

Ames, Story County.

The Iowa State Agricultural College and Farm were established by an act of the General Assembly, approved March 22d, 1858. A Board of Trustees was appointed, consisting of Governor R. P. Lowe, John D. Wright, William Duane Wilson, M. W. Robinson, Timothy Day, Richard Gaines, John Pattee, G. W. F. Sherwin, Suel Foster, S. W. Henderson, Clement Coffin and E. G. Day; the Governors of the State and President of the College being ex-officio members. Subsequently the number of Trustees was reduced to five. The Board met in June, 1859, and received propositions for the location of the College and Farm from Hardin, Polk, Story and Boone, Marshall, Jefferson and Tama Counties. In July, the proposition of Story County and some of its citizens and by the citizens of Boone County was accepted, and the farm and the site for the buildings were located. In 1860-61, the farm-house and barn were erected. In 1862, Congress granted to the State 240,-000 acres of land for the endowment of schools of agriculture and the mechanical arts, and 195,000 acres were located by Peter Melendy, Commissioner, in 1862-63. In 1864, the General Assembly appropriated $20,000 for the erection of the college building.

In June of that year, the Building Committee proceeded to let the contract. The $20,000 appropriated by the General Assembly were expended in putting in the foundations and making the brick for the structure. An additional appropriation of $91,000 was made in 1866, and the building was completed in 1868.

Tuition in this college is made by law forever free to pupils from the State over sixteen years of age, who have been resident of the State six months previous to their admission. Each county in the State has a prior right of tuition for three scholars from each county; the remainder, equal to the capacity of the college, are by the trustees distributed among the counties in proportion to the population, and subject to the above rule. All sale of ardent spirits, wine or beer, are prohibited by law within a distance of three miles from the college, except for sacramental, mechanical or medical purposes.

The course of instruction in the Agricultural College embraces the following branches: Natural Philosophy, Chemistry, Botany, Horticulture, Fruit Growing, Forestry, Animal and Vegetable Anatomy, Geology, Mineralogy, Meteorology, Entomology, Zoology, the Veterinary Art, Plane Mensuration, Leveling, Surveying, Bookkeeping, and such Mechanical Arts as are directly connected with agriculture; also such other studies as the Trustees may, from time to time, prescribe, not inconsistent with the purposes of the institution. The funds arising from the lease and sale of lands, and interest on investments are sufficient for the support of the institution.

The Board of Trustees, in 1881, was composed of Charles W. Tenney, Plymouth; George H. Wright, Sioux City; Henry G. Little, Grinnell; William McClintock, West Union; John N. Dixon, Oskaloosa. A. S. Welch, President of the Faculty; W. D. Lucas, Treasurer; E. W. Stanton, Secretary.

The Trustees are elected by the General Assembly, in Joint Convention, for four years, three being elected at one session and two the next.

THE STATE UNIVERSITY.

Iowa City, Johnson County.

In the famous Ordinance of 1787, enacted by Congress before the Territory of the United States extended beyond the Mississippi River, it was declared that in all the territory northwest of the Ohio River; "Schools and the means of education shall forever be encouraged." By act of Congress, approved July 20, 1840, the Secretary of the Treasury was authorized "to set apart and reserve from sale, out of any of the public lands within the Territory of Iowa, to which the Indian title has been or may be extinguished, and not otherwise appropriated, a quantity of land, not exceeding the entire townships, for the use and support of a university within said Territory when it becomes a State, and for no other use or purpose whatever; to be located in tracts of not less than an entire section, corresponding with any of the large divisions into which the public land are authorized to be surveyed."

William W. Dodge, of Scott County, was appointed by the Secretary of the Treasury to make the selections. He selected Section 5, in Township 78, north of Range 3, east of the Fifth Principal Meridian, and then removed from the Territory. No more land were selected until 1846, when, at the request of the Assembly, John M. Whitaker, of Van Buren County, was appointed, who selected the remainder of the grant except about 122 acres.

In the first Constitution, under which Iowa was admitted to the Union, the people directed the disposition of the proceeds of this munificent grant in accordance with its terms, and instructed the

General Assembly to provide, as soon as may be, effectual means
for the improvement and permanent security of the funds of the
university derived from the lands.

The first General Assembly, by act approved February 25, 1847,
established the "State University of Iowa" at Iowa City, then
the Capital of the State, "with such other branches as public convenience may hereafter require." The "public buildings at
Iowa City, together with the ten acres of land in which they are
situated, were granted for the use of said university *provided*,
however, that the sessions of the Legislature and State offices
should be held in the capitol until otherwise provided by law. The
control and management of the University were committed to a
Board of fifteen Trustees, to be appointed by the Legislature, five
of whom were to be chosen bienially. The Superintendent of
Public Instruction was made President of this Board. Provisions
were made for the disposal of the two townships of land, and for
the investment of the funds arising therefrom. The act further
provides that the University shall never be under the exclusive
control of any religious denomination whatever, and as soon as
the revenue for the grant and donations amounts to $2,000 a year,
the University should commence and continue the instruction,
free of charge, of fifty students annually. The General Assembly
retained full supervision over the University, its officers and the
grants and donations made and to be made to it by the State.

The organization of the University at Iowa City was impracticable, however. so long as the seat of government was retained there.

In January, 1849, two branches of the University and three
Normal Schools were established. The branches were located—
one at Fairfield, and the other at Dubuque, and were placed upon
an equal footing, in respect to funds and all other matters, with
the University established at Iowa City. "This act," says Col.
Benton, "created *three* State Universities, with equal rights and
powers, instead of a 'University with such branches as public convenience *may hereafter demand*,' as provided by the Constitution."

The Board of Directors of the Fairfield Branch consisted of
Barnet Ristine, Christian W. Slagle, Daniel Rider, Horace Gaylord, Bernhart Henn and Samuel S. Bayard. At the first meeting
of the Board Mr. Henn was elected President, Mr. Slagle Secretary,
and Mr. Gaylord Treasurer. Twenty acres of land were purchased,
and a building erected thereon, costing $2,500. This building was
nearly destroyed by a hurricane, in 1850, but was rebuilt more
substantially, all by contributions of the citizens of Fairfield. This
branch never received any aid from the State or from the University Fund, and by act approved January 24, 1853, at the request of
the Board, the General Assembly terminated its relation to the State.

The branch at Dubuque was placed under the control of the Superintendent of Public Instruction. The Trustees never organized, and its existence was only nominal.

The Normal Schools were located at Andrew, Oskaloosa and Mount Pleasant, respectively. Each was to be governed by a board of seven Trustees, to be appointed by the Trustees of the University. Each was to receive $500 annually from the income of the University fund, upon condition that they should educate eight common school teachers, free of charge for tuition, and that the citizens should contribute an equal sum for the erection of the requisite buildings. The several Boards of Trustees were appointed. At Andrew, the school was organized November 21, 1849. A building was commenced and over $1,000 expended on it, but it was never completed. At Oskaloosa, the Trustees organized in April, 1852. This school was opened in the Court House, September 13, 1852. A two-story brick building was completed in 1853, costing $2,473. The school at Mount Pleasant was never organized. Neither of these schools received any aid from the University Fund, but in 1857 the Legislature appropriated $1,000 each for those at Oskaloosa and Andrew, and repealed the law authorizing the payment of money to them from the University Fund. From that time they made no further effort to continue in operation.

At a special meeting of the Board of Trustees, held February 21, 1850, the "College of Physicians and Surgeons of the Upper Mississippi," established at Davenport, was recognized as the "College of Physicians and Surgeons of the State University of Iowa," expressly stipulating, however, that such recognition should not render the University liable for any pecuniary aid, nor was the Board to have any control over the property or management of the Medical Association. Soon after, this College was removed to Keokuk, its second session being opened there in November, 1850. In 1851, the General Assembly confirmed the action of the Board, and by act approved January 22, 1855, placed the Medical College under the supervision of the Board of Trustees of the University, and it continued in operation until this arrangement was terminated by the new Constitution, September 3, 1857.

From 1847 to 1855, the Board of Trustees was kept full by regular elections by the Legislature, and the Trustees held frequent meetings, but there was no effectual organization of the University. In March, 1855, it was partially opened for a term of sixteen weeks. July 16, 1855, Amos Dean, of Albany, N. Y., was elected President, but he never entered fully upon its duties. The University was again opened in September, 1855, and continued in operation until June, 1856, under Professors Johnson, Welton, Van Valkenburg and Guffin.

In the Spring of 1856, the capital of the State was located at Des Moines; but there were no buildings there, and the capitol at Iowa City was not vacated by the State until December, 1857.

In June, 1856, the faculty was re-organized, with some changes, and the University was again opened on the third Wednesday of

September, 1856. There were one hundred and twenty-four students—eighty-three males and forty-one females in attendance during the year 1856-7, and the first regular catalogue was published.

Article IX, Section 11, of the new State Constitution, which went into force September 3, 1857, provided as follows:

The State University shall be established at one place, without branches at any other place; and the University fund shall be applied to that institution, and no other.

Article XI, Section 8, provided that

The seat of Government is hereby permanently established, as now fixed by law, at the city of Des Moines, in the county of Polk; and the State University at Iowa City, in the county of Johnson.

The new Constitution created the Board of Education, consisting of the Lieutenant Governor, who was ex officio President, and one member to be elected from each judicial district in the State. This Board was endowed with "full power and authority to legislate and make all needful rules and regulations in relation to common schools and other educational institutions," subject to alteration, amendment or repeal by the General Assembly, which was vested with authority to abolish or re-organize the Board at any time after 1863.

In December, 1857, the old capitol building, now known as Central Hall of the University, except the rooms occupied by the United States District Court, and the property, with that exception, passed under the control of the Trustees, and became the seat of the University. The old building had had hard usage, and its arrangement was illy adapted for University purposes. Extensive repairs and changes were necessary, but the Board was without funds for these purposes.

The last meeting of the Board, under the old law, was held in January, 1858. At this meeting, a resolution was introduced, and seriously considered, to exclude females from the University; but it finally failed.

March 12, 1858, the first Legislature under the new Constitution enacted a new law in relation to the University, but it was not materially different from the former. March 11, 1858, the Legislature appropriated $3,000 for the repair and modification of the old capitol building, and $10,000 for the erection of a boarding house, now known as South Hall.

The Board of Trustees created by the new law met and duly organized April 27, 1858, and determined to close the University until the income from its fund should be adequate to meet the current expenses, and the buildings should be ready for occupation. Until this term, the building known as the "Mechanics' Academy" had been used for the school. The Faculty, except the Chancellor (Dean), was dismissed, and all further instruction suspended, from the close of the term then in progress until September, 1859. At this meeting, a resolution was adopted excluding females from the University after the close of the existing term; but this was afterward, in August, modified, so as to admit them to the Normal Department.

An "Act for the Government and Regulation of the State University of Iowa," approved December 25, 1858, was mainly a re-enactment of the law of March 12, 1858, except that changes were made in the Board of Trustees, and manner of their appointment. This law provided that both sexes were to be admitted on equal terms to all departments of the institution, leaving the Board no discretion in the matter.

At the annual meeting, June 28, 1860, a full Faculty was appointed, and the University re-opened, under this new organization, September 19, 1860 (third Wednesday); and at this date the actual existence of the University may be said to commence.

August, 19, 1862, Dr. Totten having resigned, Prof. Oliver M. Spencer was elected President and the honorary degree of Doctor of Laws was conferred upon Judge Samuel F. Miller. of Keokuk.

At the commencement, in June, 1863, was the first class of graduates in the Collegiate Department.

The Board of Education was abolished March 19, 1864, and the office of Superintendent of Public Instruction was restored ; the General Assembly resumed control of the subject of education, and on March 21, an act was approved for the goverment of the University. It was substantially the same as the former law, but provided that the Governor should be ex-officio President of the Board of Trustees. Until 1858, the Superintendent of Public Instruction had been ex-officio President. During the period of the Board of Education, the University Trustees were elected by it, and elected their own President.

The North Hall was completed late in 1866.

The Law Department was established in June, 1868, and, in September following an arrangement was perfected with the Iowa Law School, at Des Moines, which had been in successful operation for three years, by which that institution was transferred to Iowa City and merged in the Law Department of the University.

At a special meeting of the Board, on the 17th of September, 1868, a committee was appointed to consider the expediency of establishing a Medical Department. This Committee reported at once in favor of the proposition, the Faculty to consist of the President of the University and seven Professors, and recommended that, if practicable, the new department should be opened at the commencement of the University year, in 1869-70.

By an act of the General Assembly, approved April 11, 1870, the "Board of Regents" was instituted as the governing power of the University, and since that time it has been the fundamental law of the institution. The Board of Regents held its first meeting June 28, 1870.

The South Hall having been fitted up for the purpose, the first
term of the Medical Department was opened October 24, 1870, and
continued until March, 1871.

In June, 1874, the "Chair of Military Instruction" was established, and the President of the United States was requested to
detail an officer to perform its duties. At the annual meeting, in
1876, a Department of Homœopathy was established. In March,
1877, a resolution was adopted, affiliating the High Schools of the
State with the University.

In 1872, the *ex-officio* membership of the Superintendent of
Public Instruction was abolished; but it was restored in 1876.

The Board of Regents, in 1881, was composed as follows:
John H. Gear, Governor, *ex-officio*, President; Carl W. vonCoelln,
Superintendent of Public Instruction, *ex-officio;* J. L. Pickard,
President of the University, *ex-officio;* C. W. Slagle, Fairfield,
First District; D. N. Richardson, Davenport, Second District; H.
C. Bulis, Decorah, Third District; A. T. Reeve, Hampton, Fourth
District; J. N. W. Rumple, Marengo, Fifth District; W. O.
Crosby, Centerville, Sixth District; T. S. Parr, Indianola, Seventh
District; Horace Everett, Council Bluffs, Eighth District; J. F.
Duncombe, Fort Dodge, Ninth District. John N. Coldren, Iowa
City, Treasurer; W. J. Haddock, Iowa City, Secretary.

The Regents are elected by the General Assembly, in Joint
Convention, for six years, one-third being elected at each regular
session, one member to be chosen from each Congressional
District.

The present educational corps of the University consists of the
President, nine Professors in the Collegiate Department, one Professor and six Instructors in Military Science; Chancellor, three
Professors and four Lecturers in the Law Department; eight
Professor Demonstrators of Anatomy; Prosector of Surgery and
two Lecturers in the Medical Department, and two Professors in
the Homœopathic Medical Department.

STATE HISTORICAL SOCIETY.

By act of the General Assembly, approved January 28, 1857, a
State Historical Society was provided for in connection with the
University. At the commencement, an appropriation of $250 was
made, to be expended in collecting, embodying, and preserving in
an authentic form, a library of books, pamphlets, charts, maps,
manuscripts, papers, paintings, statuary, and other materials illus-
trative of the history of Iowa; and with the further object to
rescue from oblivion the memory of the early pioneers; to obtain
and preserve various accounts of their exploits, perils and hardy
adventures; to secure facts and statements relative to the history
and genius, and progress and decay of the Indian tribes of Iowa,
to exhibit faithfully the antiquities and past and present resources

of the State; to aid in the publication of such collections of the Society as shall, from time to time be deemed of value and interest; to aid in binding its books, pamphlets, manuscripts and papers, and in defraying other necessary incidental expenses of the Society.

There was appropriated by law to this institution, till the General Assembly shall otherwise direct, the sum of $500 per annum. The Society is under the management of a Board of Curators, consisting of eighteen persons, nine of whom are appointed by the Governor, and nine elected by the members of the Society. The Curators receive no compensation for their services. The annual meeting is provided for by law, to be held at Iowa City on Monday preceding the last Wednesday in June of each year.

The State Historical Society has published a series of very valuable collections, including history, biography, sketches, reminiscences, etc., with quite a large number of finely engraved portraits of prominent and early settlers, under the title of "Annals of Iowa."

THE PENITENTIARY.

Located at Fort Madison, Lee County.

The first act of the Territorial Legislature, relating to a Penitentiary in Iowa, was approved January 25, 1839, the fifth section of which authorized the Governor to draw the sum of $20,000 appropriated by an act of Congress approved July 7, 1838, for public buildings in the Territory of Iowa. It provided for a Board of Directors of three persons elected by the Legislature, who should direct the building of the Penitentiary, which should be located within one mile of the public square, in the town of Fort Madison, Lee County, provided Fort Madison should deed to the Directors a tract of land suitable for a site, and assign them, by contract, a spring or stream of water for the use of the Penitentiary. To the Directors was also given the power of appointing the Warden; the latter to appoint his own assistants.

The first Directors appointed were John S. David and John Claypole. They made their first report to the Legislative Council November 9, 1839. The citizens of the town of Fort Madison had executed a deed conveying ten acres of land for the building site. Amos Ladd was appointed Superintendent of the building June 5, 1839. The building was designed of sufficient capacity to contain one hundred and thirty-eight convicts, and estimated to cost $55,933.90. It was begun on the 9th of July, 1839; the main building and Warden's house were completed in the Fall of 1841. Other additions were made from time to time till the building and arrangements were all complete according to the plan of the Directors. It has answered the purpose of the State as a

Penitentiary for more than thirty years, and during that period many items of practical experience in prison management have been gained.

ADDITIONAL PENITENTIARY.

Located at Anamosa, Jones County.

By an Act of the Fourteenth General Assembly, approved April 23, 1872, William Ure, Foster L. Downing and Martin Heisey were constituted Commissioners to locate and provide for the erection and control of an additional Penitentiary for the State of Iowa. These Commissioners met on the 4th of the following June, at Anamosa, Jones County, and selected a site donated by the citizens, within the limits of the city. L. W. Foster & Co., architects, of Des Moines, furnished the plan, drawings and specifications, and work was commenced on the building on the 28th day of September, 1872. May 13, 1873, twenty convicts were transferred to Anamosa from the Fort Madison Penitentiary. The entire enclosure includes fifteen acres, with a frontage of 663 feet.

IOWA HOSPITAL FOR THE INSANE.

Mount Pleasant, Henry County.

By an act of the General Assembly of Iowa, approved January 24, 1855, $4,425 were appropriated for the purchase of a site, and $50,000 for building an Insane Hospital, and the Governor (Grimes), Edward Johnston, of Lee County, and Charles S. Blake, of Henry County, were appointed to locate the institution and Superintend the erection of the building. These Commissioners located the institution at Mt. Pleasant, Henry County. A plan for a building designed to accommodate 300 patients was accepted, and in October work was commenced. Up to February 25, 1858, and including an appropriation made on that date, the Legislature had appropriated $258,555.67 to this institution, but the building was not finished ready for occupancy by patients until March 1, 1861. April 18, 1876, a portion of the hospital building was destroyed by fire.

Trustees, 1881:—Timothy Whiting, Mt. Pleasant; J. H. Kulp, Davenport; Denison A. Hurst, Oskaloosa; John Conaway, Brooklyn; L. E. Fellows, Lansing. Mark Ranney, M. D., Mt. Pleasant, is the Medical Superintendent; C. V. Arnold, Mt. Pleasant, Treasurer.

HOSPITAL FOR THE INSANE

Independence, Buchanan County.

In the winter of 1867–8 a bill providing for an additional Hospital for the insane was passed by the Legislature, and an appropriation of $125,000 was made for that purpose. Maturin L.

Fisher, of Clayton County; E, G. Morgan, of Webster County, and Albert Clark, of Buchanan County, were appointed Commissioners to locate and supervise the erection of the building.

The Commissioners met and commenced their labors on the 8th day of June, 1868, at Independence. The act under which they were appointed required them to select the most eligible and desirable location, of not less than 320 acres, within two miles of the City of Independence, that might be offered by the citizens free of charge to the State. Several such tracts were offered, but the Commissioners finally selected the south half of southwest quarter of Section 5; the north half of northeast quarter of Section 7; the north half of northwest quarter of Section 8, and the north half of northeast quarter of Section 8, all in Township 88 north, Range 9 west of the Fifth Principal Meridian. This location is on the west side of the Wapsipinicon River, and about a mile from its banks, and about the same distance from Independence.

The contract for erecting the building was awarded for $88,114. The contract was signed November 7, 1868, and work was at once commenced. The main buildings were constructed of dressed limestone, from the quarries at Anamosa and Farley. The basements are of the local granite worked from the immense boulders found in large quantities in this portion of the State.

In 1872, the building was so far completed that the Commissioners called the first meeting of the Trustees, on the 10th day of July of that year. The building was ready for occupancy April 21, 1873.

In 1877, the south wing was built, but was not completed ready for occupancy until the Spring or Summer of 1878.

Trustees, 1881:—Erastus G. Morgan, Fort Dodge, President; Jed. Lake, Independence; Mrs. Jennie C. McKinney, Decorah; Lewis H. Smith, Algona; David Hammer, McGregor; A. Reynolds, M. D., Independence, Medical Superintendent; W. G. Donnan, Independence, Treasurer.

IOWA COLLEGE FOR THE BLIND.

Vinton, Benton County.

In August, 1852, Prof. Samuel Bacon, himself blind, established an Institution for the Instruction of the blind of Iowa, at Keokuk.

By act of the General Assembly, entitled, "An act to establish an Asylum for the Blind," approved January 18, 1853, the institution was adopted by the State, removed to Iowa City, February 3d, and opened for the reception of pupils April 4, 1853, free to all the blind in the State.

The Board of Trustees appointed Prof. Samuel Bacon. Principal; T. J. McGittigen, Teacher of Music, and Mrs. Sarah K. Bacon, Matron. Twenty-three pupils were admitted during the first term.

In his first report, made in 1854, Prof. Bacon suggested that the name should be changed from "Asylum for the Blind," to that of "Institution for the Instruction of the Blind." This was done in 1855, when the General Assembly made an annual appropriation for the College of $55 per quarter for each pupil. This was subsequently changed to $3.000 per annum, and a charge of $25 as an admission fee for each pupil, which sum, with the amounts realized from the sale of articles manufactured by the blind pupils, proved sufficient for the expenses of the institution during Mr. Bacon's administration.

On the 8th of May, 1858. the Trustees met at Vinton, and made arrangements for securing the donation of $5,000 made by the citizens of that town.

In June of that year a quarter section of land was donated for the College, by John W. O. Webb and others, and the Trustees adopted a plan for the erection of a suitable building. In 1860, the plan was modified, and the contract for enclosing let for $10,420.

In August, 1862, the building was so far completed that the goods and furniture of the institution were removed from Iowa City to Vinton, and early in October the School was opened there with twenty-four pupils.

Trustees, 1881:—Clinton O. Harrington, Vinton; S. H. Watson, Vinton, Treasurer; J. F. White, Sidney; M. H. Westerbrook, Lyons; W. H. Leavitt, Waterloo; Jacob Springer. Watkins; Rev. Robert Carothers, Principal of the Institution, and Secretary of the Board.

INSTITUTION FOR THE DEAF AND DUMB.

Council Bluffs, Pottawattamie County.

The Iowa Institution for the Deaf and Dumb was established at Iowa City by an act of the General Assembly, approved January 24, 1855. The number of deaf mutes then in the State was 301; the number attending the Institution, 50.

A strong effort was made, in 1866, to remove this important institution to Des Moines, but it was located permanently at Council Bluffs, and a building rented for its use. In 1868, Commissioners were appointed to locate a site for, and to superintend the erection of a new building, for which the Legislature appropriated $125,-000 to commence the work of construction. The Commissioners selected ninety acres of land about two miles south of the city of Council Bluffs. The main building and one wing were completed October 1, 1870, and immediately occupied by the Institution. February 25, 1877, the main building and east wing were destroyed by fire; and August 6th, following, the roof of the new west wing was blown off and the walls partially demolished by a tornado. At the time of the fire, about one hundred and fifty pupils were in attendance. After the fire, half the classes were dismissed and the number of scholars reduced to about seventy, and in a week or two the school was in running order.

Trustees, 1881 :—B. F. Clayton, Macedonia, President; J. H. Stubenrauch, Pella, Treasurer; Louis Weinstein, Burlington. Rev. A. Rogers, Superintendent.

SOLDIERS' ORPHANS' HOMES.

Davenport, Cedar Falls, Glenwood.

The movement which culminated in the establishment of this beneficient institution was originated by Mrs. Annie Wittenmeyer, during the civil war of 1861-65. This noble and patriotic lady called a convention at Muscatine, on the 7th of October, 1863, for the purpose of devising measures for the support and education of the orphan children of the brave sons of Iowa, who had fallen in defense of national honor and integrity. So great was the public interest in the movement that there was a large representation from all parts of the State on the day named, and an association was organized called the Iowa State Orphan Asylum.

The first meeting of the Trustees was held February 14, 1864, in the Representative Hall, at Des Moines. Committees from both branches of the General Assembly were present and were invited to participate in their deliberations. Arrangements were made for raising funds.

At the next meeting, in Davenport, in March, 1864, the Trustees decided to commence operations at once, and a committee was appointed to lease a suitable building, solicit donations, and procure suitable furniture. This committee secured a large brick building in Lawrence, Van Buren County, and engaged Mr. Fuller, of Mt. Pleasant, as Steward.

At the annual meeting, in Des Moines, in June, 1864, Mrs. C. B. Baldwin, Mrs. G. G. Wright, Mrs. Dr. Horton, Miss Mary E. Shelton and Mr. George Sherman, were appointed a committee to furnish the building and take all necessary steps for opening the "Home," and notice was given that at the next meeting of the Association, a motion would be made to change the name of the Institution to Iowa Orphans' Home.

The work of preparation was conducted so vigorously that on the 13th day of July following, the Executive Committee announced that they were ready to receive the children. In three weeks twenty-one were admitted, and the number constantly increased, so that, in a little more than six months from the time of opening, there were seventy children admitted, and twenty more applications, which the Committee had not acted upon—all Orphans of Soldiers.

The "Home" was sustained by the voluntary contributions of. the people, until 1866, when it was assumed by the State. In that year, the General Assembly provided for the location of several such "Homes" in the different counties, and which were established at Davenport, Scott County; Cedar Falls, Black Hawk County, and at Glenwood, Mills County.

The Board of Trustees, elected by the General Assembly, had the oversight and management of the Soldiers' Orphans' Homes of the State, and consisted of one person from each county in which such Home was located, and one for the State at large, who held their offices two years, or until their successors were elected and qualified. An appropriation of $10 per month for each orphan actually supported was made by the General Assembly.

The Home in Cedar Falls was organized in 1865, and an old hotel building was fitted up for it. January, 1866, there were ninety-six inmates.

October 12, 1869, the Home was removed to a large brick building, about two miles west of Cedar Falls, and was very prosperous for several years, but in 1876, the General Assembly established a State Normal School at Cedar Falls, and appropriated the buildings and grounds for that purpose.

By "An act to provide for the organization and support of an asylum at Glenwood, in Mills County, for feeble minded children," approved March 17, 1876, the buildings and grounds used by the Soldiers' Orphans' Home at that place were appropriated for this purpose. By another act, approved March 15, 1876, the soldiers' orphans, then at the Homes at Glenwood and Cedar Falls, were to be removed to the Home at Davenport within ninety days thereafter, and the Board of Trustees of the Home were authorized to receive other indigent children into that institution, and provide for their education in industrial pursuits.

Trustees 1881.—C. M. Holton, Iowa City; Seth P. Bryant, Davenport; C. C. Horton, Muscatine. S. W. Pierce, Davenport, Superintendent.

STATE NORMAL SCHOOL.

Cedar Falls, Black Hawk County.

Chapter 129 of the laws of the Sixteenth General Assembly, in 1876, established a State Normal School at Cedar Falls, Black Hawk County, and required the Trustees of the Soldiers' Orphans' Home to turn over the property in their charge to the Directors of the new institution.

The Board of Directors met at Cedar Falls June 7, 1876, and duly organized. The Board of Trustees of the Soldiers' Orphans'

Home met at the same time for the purpose of turning over to the Directors the property of that institution, which was satisfactorily done and properly receipted for as required by law.

On the 12th of July, 1876, the Board again met, when executive and teachers' committees were appointed and their duties assigned. A Steward and a Matron were elected, and their respective duties defined.

The buildings and grounds were repaired and fitted up as well as the appropriation would admit, and the first term of school opened September 6, 1876, commencing with twenty-seven and closing with eighty-seven students.

Directors, 1881:—C. C. Cory, Pella; E. H. Thayer, Clinton; G. S. Robinson, Storm Lake; N. W. Boyes, Dubuque; L. D. Lewelling, Mitchellville; J. J. Tollerton, Cedar Falls; E. Townsend, Cedar Falls, Treasurer.

ASYLUM FOR FEEBLE MINDED CHILDREN.

Glenwood, Mills County.

Chapter 152 of the laws of the Sixteenth General Assembly, approved March 17, 1876, provided for the establishment of an asylum for feeble minded children at Glenwood, Mills County, and the buildings and the grounds of the Soldiers' Orphans' Home at that place were to be used for that purpose. The asylum was placed under the management of three Trustees, one at least of whom should be a resident of Mills County. Children between the ages of 7 and 18 years are admitted. Ten dollars per month for each child actually supported by the State was appropriated by the act, and $2,000 for salaries of officers and teachers for two years.

Hon. J. W. Cattell, of Polk County; A. J. Russell, of Mills County, and W. S. Robertson, were appointed Trustees, who held their first meeting at Glenwood, April 26, 1876. The Trustees found the house and farm which had been turned over to them in a shamefully dilapidated condition. The fences were broken down and the lumber destroyed or carried away; the windows broken, doors off their hinges, floors broken and filthy in the extreme, cellars reeking with offensive odors from decayed vegetables, a ld every conceivable variety of filth and garbage; drains obstructed, cisterns broken, pump demoralized, wind-mill broken, roof leaky, and the whole property in the worst possible condition. It was the first work of the Trustees to make the house tenable.

The Institution was opened September 1, 1876; the first pupil admitted September 4, and the school was organized September 10.

Trustees, 1881:—Fred. O'Donnell, Dubuque; S. B. Thrall, Ottumwa; E. R. S. Woodrow, Glenwood; O. W. Archibald, M. D., Medical Superintendent.

THE REFORM SCHOOL.

Eldora, Hardin County.

By "An act to establish and organize a State Reform School for Juvenile Offenders," approved March 31, 1868, the General Assembly established a State Reform School at Salem, Lee (Henry) County; provided for a Board of Trustees, to consist of one person from each Congressional District. For the purpose of immediately opening the school, the Trustees were directed to accept the proposition of the Trustees of White's Iowa Manual Labor Institute, at Salem, and lease, for not more than ten years, the lands, buildings, etc., of the Institute, and at once proceed to prepare for and open a reform school as a temporary establishment.

The contract for fitting up the buildings was let September 21, 1868, and on the 7th of October following, the first inmate was received from Jasper County. The law provided for the admission of children of both sexes under 18 years of age. In 1876, this was amended, so that they are now received at ages over 7 and under 16 years.

April 19, 1872, the Trustees were directed to make a permanent location for the school, and $45,000 was appropriated for the erection of the necessary buildings. The Trustees were further directed, as soon as practicable, to organize a school for girls in the buildings where the boys were then kept.

The Trustees located the school at Eldora, Hardin County, and in the code of 1873, it is permanently located there by law.

The institution is managed by five Trustees, who are paid mileage, but no compensation for their services.

The object is the reformation of children of both sexes, under the age of 16 and over 7 years of age; and the law requires that the Trustees shall require the boys and girls under their charge to be instructed in piety and morality, and in such branches of useful knowledge as are adapted to their age and capacity, and in some regular course of labor, either mechanical, manufacturing or agricultural, as is best suited to their age, strength, disposition and capacity, and as may seem best adapted to secure the reformation and future benefit of the boys and girls.

A boy or girl committed to the State Reform School is there kept, disciplined, instructed, employed and governed, under the direction of the Trustees, until he or she arrives at the age of majority, or is bound out, reformed or legally discharged. The binding out or discharge of a boy or girl as reformed, or having arrived at the age of majority, *is a complete release* from all penalties incurred by conviction of the crime for which he or she is committed.

Trustees, 1881:— J. A. Parvin, Muscatine, President; W. J. Moir, Eldorado, Treasurer; W. G. Stewart, Dubuque; J. T. Moor-

head, Ely; T. E. Corkhill, Mount Pleasant; B. J. Miles, Eldora,
Superintendent. L. D. Lewelling is Superintendent of the Girl's
Department, at Mitchellville, Polk County.

FISH HATCHING ESTABLISHMENT.

Near Anamosa, Jones County.

The Fifteenth General Assembly, in 1874, passed "An act to
provide for the appointment of a Board of Fish Commissioners for
the construction of Fishways for the protection and propagation
of Fish," also, "an act to provide for furnishing the rivers and
lakes with fish and fish spawn." This act appropriated $3,000 for
the purpose. In accordance with the provisions of the first act
above mentioned, on the 9th of April, 1874, S. B. Evans of Ottumwa, Wapello County; B. F. Shaw of Jones County, and Charles
A. Haines, of Black Hawk County, were appointed to be Fish Commissioners by the Governor. These Commissioners met at Des
Moines, May 10, 1874, and organized by the election of Mr. Evans,
President; Mr. Shaw, Secretary and Superintendent, and Mr.
Haines, Treasurer.

The State was partitioned into three districts or divisions to enable the Commissioners to better superintend the construction of
fishways as required by law. At this meeting, the Superintendent was authorized to build a State Hatching House; to procure the
spawn of valuable fish adapted to the waters of Iowa; hatch and
prepare the young fish for distribution, and assist in putting them
into the waters of the State.

In compliance with these instructions, Mr. Shaw at once commenced work, and in the summer of 1874, erected a "State Hatching House" near Anamosa, 20x40 feet, two stories; the second story
being designed for a tenement; the first story being the "hatching
room." The hatching troughs are supplied with water from a
magnificent spring, four feet deep and about ten feet in diameter,
affording an abundant and unfailing supply of pure running water.
During the first year, from May 10, 1874, to May 10, 1875, the Commissioners distributed within the State 100,000 Shad, 300,000
California Salmon, 10,000 Bass, 80,000 Penobscot (Maine) Salmon,
5,000 land-locked Salmon, 20,000 of other species.

By act approved March 10, 1876, the law was amended so that
there should be one instead of three Fish Commissioners, and B. F.
Shaw was appointed, and the Commissioner was authorized to purchase twenty acres of land, on which the State Hatching House
was located near Anamosa.

In the fall of 1876, Commissioner Shaw gathered from the
sloughs of the Mississippi, where they would have been destroyed,
over a million and a half of small fish, which were distributed in
the various rivers of the State and turned into the Mississippi.

In 1875-6, 533,000 California Salmon, and in 1877, 303,500 Lake Trout were distributed in various rivers and lakes in the State. The experiment of stocking the small streams with brook trout is being tried, and 81,000 of the speckled beauties were distributed in 1877. In 1876, 100,000 young eels were distributed. These came from New York, and they are increasing rapidly.

A. A. Mosier, of Spirit Lake, was appointed Assistant Fish Commissioner, by the Governor, under Chapter 156, Laws of 1880.

THE PUBLIC LANDS.

The grants of public lands made in the State of Iowa, for various purposes, are as follows:

1. The 500,000 Acre Grant.
2. The 16th Section Grant.
3. The Mortgage School Lands.
4. The University Grant
5. The Saline Grant.
6. The Des Moines River Grant.
7. The Des Moines River School Lands.
8. The Swamp Land Grant.
9. The Railroad Grant.
10. The Agricultural College Grant.

I. THE FIVE HUNDRED THOUSAND ACRE GRANT.

When the State was admitted into the Union, she became entitled to 500,000 acres of land by virtue of an act of Congress, approved September 4, 1841, which granted to each State therein specified 500,000 acres of public land for internal improvements; to each State admitted subsequently to the passage of the act, an amount of land which, with the amount that might have been granted to her as a Territory, would amount to 500,000 acres. All these lands were required to be selected within the limits of the State to which they were granted.

The Constitution of Iowa declares that the proceeds of this grant, together with all lands then granted or to be granted by Congress for the benefit of schools, shall constitute a perpetual fund for the support of schools throughout the State. By an act approved January 15, 1849, the Legislature established a Board of School Fund Commissioners, and to that Board was confided the selection, care and sale of these lands for the benefit of the School Fund. Until 1855, these Commissioners were subordinate to the Superintendent of Public Instruction, but on the 15th of January of that year, they were clothed with exclusive authority in the management and sale of school lands. The office of School Fund Commissioner was abolished March 23, 1858, and that officer in each county was required to transfer all papers to and make full settlement with the County Judge. By this act, County Judges and Township Trustees were made the agents of the State to control and sell the sixteenth sections; but no further provision was made for the sale of the 500,000 acre grant until April 3d, 1860, when the entire management of the school lands was committed to the Boards of Supervisors of the several counties.

II. THE SIXTEENTH SECTIONS.

By the provisions of the act of Congress admitting Iowa to the Union, there was granted to the new State the sixteenth section in every township, or where that section had been sold, other lands of like amount for the use of schools. The Constitution of the State provides that the proceeds arising from the sale of these sections shall constitute a part of the permanent school fund. The control and sale of these lands were vested in the School Fund Commissioners of the several counties until March 23, 1858, when they were transferred to the County Judges and Township Trustees, and were finally placed under the supervision of the County Boards of Supervisors in January, 1861.

III. THE MORTGAGE SCHOOL LANDS.

These do not belong to any of the grants of land proper. They are lands that have been mortgaged to the school fund, and became school lands when bid off by the State by virtue of a law passed in 1862. Under the provisions of the law regulating the management and investment of the permanent school fund, persons desiring loans from that fund are required to secure the payment thereof with interest at ten per cent. per annum, by promissory notes endorsed by two good sureties and by mortgage on unincumbered real estate, which must be situated in the county where the loan is made, and which must be valued by three appraisers. Making these loans and taking the required securities was made the duty of the County Auditor, who was required to report to the Board of Supervisors at each meeting thereof, all notes, mortgages and abstracts of title connected with the school fund, for examination.

When default was made of payment of money so secured by mortgage, and no arrangement made for extension of time as the law provides, the Board of Supervisors were authorized to bring suit and prosecute it with diligence to secure said fund; and in action in favor of the county for the use of the school fund, an injunction may issue without bonds, and in any such action, when service is made by publication, default and judgment may be entered and enforced without bonds. In case of sale of land on execution founded on any such mortgage, the attorney of the board, or other person duly authorized, shall, on behalf of the State or county for the use of said fund, bid such sum as the interests of said fund may require, and if struck off to the State the land shall be held and disposed of as the other lands belonging to the fund.

These lands are known as the Mortgage School Lands, and reports of them, including description and amount, are required to be made to the State Land Office.

IV. UNIVERSITY LANDS.

By act of Congress, July 20, 1840, a quantity of land, not exceeding two entire townships, was reserved in the Territory of Iowa for the use and support of a university within said Territory when it should become a State. This land was to be located in tracts of not less than an entire section, and could be used for no other purpose than that designated in the grant. In an act supplemental to that for the admission of Iowa, March 3, 1845, the grant was renewed, and it was provided that the lands should be used "solely for the purpose of such university, in such manner as the Legislature may prescribe."

Under this grant there were set apart and approved by the Secretary of the Treasury, for the use of the State, the following lands.

	ACRES.
In the Iowa City Land District, Feb. 29, 1849............	20,150.49
In the Fairfield Land District, Oct. 17, 1849.............	9,685.20
In the Iowa City Land District, Jan. 28, 1850............	2,571.81
In the Fairfield Land District, Sept. 10, 1850............	3,198.20
In the Dubuque Land District, May 19, 1852.............	10,552.24
Total...	45,957.94

These lands were certified to the State November 19, 1859. The University lands are placed by law under the control and management of the Board of Trustees of the Iowa State University. Prior to 1865, there had been selected and located under 282 patents, 22,892 acres in sixteen counties, and 23,036 acres unpatented, making a total of 45,928 acres.

V. SALINE LANDS.

By act of Congress, approved March 3, 1845, the State of Iowa was granted the use of the salt springs within her limits, not exceeding twelve. By a subsequent act, approved May 27, 1852, Congress granted the springs to the State in fee simple, together with six sections of land contiguous to each, to be disposed of as the Legislature might direct. In 1861, the proceeds of these lands then to be sold were constituted a fund for founding and supporting a lunatic asylum, but no sales were made. In 1856, the proceeds of the saline lands were appropriated to the Insane Asylum, repealed in 1858. In 1860, the saline lands and funds were made a part of the permanent fund of the State University. These lands were located in Appanoose, Davis, Decatur, Lucas, Monroe, Van Buren and Wayne Counties.

VI. THE DES MOINES RIVER GRANT.

By act of Congress, approved August 8, 1846, a grant of land was made for the improvement of the navigation of Des Moines River, as follows:

Be it enacted by the Senate and House of Representatives of the United States of America in Congress assembled, That there be, and hereby is, granted to said Territory of Iowa, for the purpose of aiding said Territory to improve the navigation of the Des Moines River from its mouth to the Raccoon Fork (so called) in said Territory, one equal moiety, in alternate sections, of the public lands (remaining unsold and not otherwise disposed of, incumbered or appropriated), in a strip five miles in width on each side of said river, to be selected within said Territory by an agent or agents to be appointed by the Governor thereof, subject to the approval of the Secretary of the Treasury of the United States.

Sec. 2. *And be it further enacted,* That the lands hereby granted shall not be conveyed or disposed of by said Territory, nor by any State to be formed out of the same, except as said improvement shall progress; that is, the said Territory or State may sell so much of said lands as shall produce the sum of thirty thousand dollars, and then the sales shall cease until the Governor of said Territory or State shall certify the fact to the President of the United States that one-half of said sum has been expended upon said improvements, when the said Territory or State may sell and convey a quantity of the residue of said lands sufficient to replace the amount expended, and thus the sales shall progress as the proceeds thereof shall be expended, and the fact of such expenditure shall be certified as aforesaid.

Sec. 3. *And be it further enacted,* That the said River Des Moines shall be and forever remain a public highway for the use of the Government of the United States, free from any toll or other charge whatever, for any property of the United States or persons in their service passing through or along the same; *Provided always,* That it shall not be competent for the said Territory or future State of Iowa to dispose of said lands, or any of them, at a price lower than, for the time being, shall be the minimum price of other public lands.

Sec. 4. *And be it further enacted,* That whenever the Territory of Iowa shall be admitted into the Union as a State, the lands hereby granted for the above purpose shall be and become the property of said State for the purpose contemplated in this act, and for no other: *Provided,* the Legislature of the State of Iowa shall accept the said grant for the said purpose." Approved August 8, 1846.

By joint resolution of the General Assembly of Iowa, approved January 9, 1847, the grant was accepted for the purpose specified. By another act, approved February 24, 1847, entitled "An act creating the Board of Public Works, and providing for the improvement of the Des Moines River," the Legislature provided for a Board consisting of a President, Secretary and Treasurer, to be elected by the people. This Board was elected August 2, 1847, and was organized on the 22d of September following. The same act defined the nature of the improvement to be made, and provided that the work should be paid for from the funds to be derived from the sale of lands to be sold by the Board.

Agents appointed by the Governor selected the sections designated by "odd numbers" throughout the whole extent of the grant, and this selection was approved by the Secretary of the Treasury. But there was a conflict of opinion as to the extent of the grant. It was held by some that it extended from the mouth of the Des Moines River only to the Raccoon Forks; others held, as the agents to make selection evidently did, that it extended from the mouth to the headwaters of the river. Richard M. Young, Commissioner of the General Land Office, on the 23d of February, 1848, construed the grant to mean that "the State is entitled to the alternate sections within five miles of the Des Moines River, throughout the whole extent of that river within the limits of Iowa." Under this construction, the alternate sections above the Raccoon Forks would, of course, belong to the State; but on the 19th of June, 1848, some of these lands were, by proclamation, thrown into market. On the 18th of September, the Board of Public Works filed a remonstrance with the Commissioner of the General Land Office. The Board also sent in a protest to the State Land Office, at which the sale was ordered to take place. On the 8th of January, 1849, the Senators and Representatives in Congress from Iowa also protested against the sale, in a communication to Hon. Robert J. Walker, Secretary of the Treasury, to which the Secretary replied, concurring in the opinion that the grant extended the whole length of the Des Moines River in Iowa.

On the 1st of June, 1849, the Commissioner of the General Land Office directed the Register and Receiver of the Land Office at Iowa City "to withhold from sale all lands situated in the odd numbered sections within five miles on each side of the Des Moines River, above the Raccoon Forks." March 13, 1850, the Commissioner of the General Land Office submitted to the Secretary of the Interior a list "showing the tracts falling within the limits of the Des Moines River grant, above the Raccoon Forks, etc., under the decision of the Secretary of the Treasury, of March 2, 1849," and on the 6th of April following, Mr. Ewing, then Secretary of the Interior, reversed the decision of Secretary Walker, but ordered the lands to be withheld from sale until Congress could have an opportunity to pass an explanatory act. The Iowa authorities appealed from this decision to the President (Taylor), who referred the matter to the Attorney General (Mr. Johnson). On the 19th of July, Mr. Johnson submitted as his opinion, that by the terms of the grant itself, it extended to the very source of the Des Moines, but before his opinion was published President Taylor died. When Mr. Tyler's cabinet was formed, the question was submitted to the new Attorney General (Mr. Crittenden), who, on the 30th of June, 1851, reported that in his opinion the grant did not extend above the Raccoon Forks. Mr. Stewart, Secretary of the Interior, concurred with Mr. Crittenden at first, but subsequently conse..ted to lay the whole subject before the President and Cabinet, who decided in favor of the State.

October 29, 1851, Mr. Stewart directed the Commissioner of the General Land Office to "submit for his approval such lists as had been prepared, and to proceed to report for like approval lists of the alternate sections claimed by the State of Iowa above the Raccoon Forks, as far as the surveys have progressed, or may hereafter be completed and returned." And on the following day, three lists of these lands were prepared in the General Land Office.

The lands approved and certified to the State of Iowa under this grant, and all lying above the Raccoon Forks, are as follows:

By Secretary Stewart, Oct. 30, 1851............... 81,707.93 acres.
　　　　　　March 10, 1852..............143,908.37　　"
By Secretary McLellan, Dec. 17, 1853.............. 33,142.43　　"
　　　　　　Dec. 30, 1853.............. 12,813.51　　"

　　　Total......................................271,572.24 acres.

The Commissioners and Register of the Des Moines River Improvement, in their report to the Governor, November 30, 1852, estimate the total amount of lands then available for the work, including those in possession of the State and those to be surveyed and approved, at nearly a million acres. The indebtedness then standing against the fund was about $108,000, and the Commissioners estimated the work to be done would cost about $1,200,000,

January 19. 1853, the Legislature authorized the Commissioners to sell "any or all the lands which have or may hereafter be granted, for not less than $1,300,000."

On the 24th of January, 1853, the General Assembly provided for the election of a Commissioner by the people, and appointed two Assistant Commissioners, with authority to make a contract, selling the lands of the Improvement for $1,300,000. This new Board made a contract, June 9, 1855, with the Des Moines Navigation & Railroad Company, agreeing to sell *all* the lands donated to the State by Act of Congress of August 8, 1846, which the State had not sold prior to December 23, 1853, for $1,300,000, to be expended on the improvement of the river, and in paying the indebtedness then due. This contract was duly reported to the Governor and General Assembly.

By an act approved January 25, 1855, the Commissioner and Register of the Des Moines River Improvement were authorized to negotiate with the Des Moines Navigation & Railroad Company for the purchase of lands in Webster County, which had been sold by the School Fund Commissioner as school lands, but which had been certified to the State as Des Moines River lands, and had, therefore, become the property of the Company, under the provisions of its contract with the State.

March 21, 1856, the old question of the extent of the grant was again raised, and the Commissioner of the General Land Office decided that it was limited to the Raccoon Fork. Appeal was made to the Secretary of the Interior, and by him the matter was referred to the Attorney General, who decided that the grant ex-

tended to the northern boundary of the State; the State relinquished its claim to the lands lying along the river in Minnesota,
and the vexed question was supposed to be finally settled.

The land which had been certified, as well as those extending to
the northern boundary within the limits of the grant, were reserved
from pre-emption and sale by the General Land Commissioner, to
satisfy the grant of August 8, 1846, and they were treated as having passed to the State, which from time to time sold portions of
them prior to their final transfer to the Des Moines Navigation &
Railroad Company, applying the proceeds thereof to the improvement of the river in compliance with the terms of the grant.
Prior to the final sale to the Company, June 9, 1854, the State had
sold about 327,000 acres, of which amount 58,830 acres were located above the Raccoon Fork. The last certificate of the General
Land Office bears date December 30, 1853.

After June 9th, 1854, the Des Moines Navigation & Railroad
Company carried on the work under its contract with the State.
As the improvement progressed, the State, from time to time, by
its authorized officers, issued to the Company, in payment for said
work, certificates for lands. But the General Land Office ceased
to certify lands under the grant of 1846. The State had made no
other provision for paying for the improvements, and disagree-
ments and misunderstanding arose between the State authorities
and the Company.

March 22, 1858, a joint resolution was passed by the Legislature
submitting a proposition for final settlement to the Company,
which was accepted. The Company paid to the State $20,000 in
cash, and released and conveyed the dredge boat and materials
named in the resolution; and the State, on the 3d day of May,
1858, executed to the Des Moines Navigation & Railroad Company
fourteen deeds or patents to the lands, amounting to 256,703.64
acres. These deeds were intended to convey all the lands of this
grant certified to the State by the General Government not previously sold; but, as if for the purpose of covering any tract or
parcel that might have been omitted, the State made another deed
of conveyance on the 18th day of May, 1858. These fifteen deeds,
it is claimed, by the Company, convey 266,108 acres, of which
about 53,367 are below the Raccoon Fork, and the balance, 212,741
acres, are above that point.

Besides the lands deeded to the Company, the State had deeded
to individual purchasers 58,830 acres above the Raccoon Fork,
making an aggregate of 271,571 acres deeded above the Fork, all
of which had been certified to the State by the Federal Government.

By act approved March 28, 1858, the Legislature donated the remainder of the grant to the Keokuk, Fort Des Moines & Minnesota Railroad Company, upon condition that said Company assumed
all liabilities resulting from the Des Moines River improvement
operations, reserving 50,000 acres of the land in security for the

payment thereof, and for the completion of the locks and dams at Bentonsport, Croton, Keosauqua and Plymouth. For every three thousand dollars' worth of work done on the locks and dams, and for every three thousand dollars paid by the Company of the liabilities above mentioned, the Register of the State Land Office was instructed to certify to the Company 1,000 acres of the 50,000 acres reserved for these purposes. Up to 1865, there had been presented by the Company, under the provisions of the act of 1858, and allowed, claims amounting to $109,579.37, about seventy-five per cent. of which had been settled.

After the passage of the Act above noticed, the question of the extent of the original grant was again mooted, and at the December Term of the Supreme Court of the United States, in 1859-60, a decision was rendered declaring that the grant did *not* extend above Raccoon Fork, and that all certificates of land *above* the Fork had been issued without authority of law and were, therefore, void (see 23 How., 66).

The State of Iowa had disposed of a large amount of land without authority, according to this decision, and appeal was made to Congress for relief, which was granted on the 3d day of March, 1861, in a joint resolution relinquishing to the State all the title which the United States then still retained in the tracts of land along the Des Moines River above Raccoon Fork, that had been improperly certified to the State by the Department of the Interior, and which is now held by *bona fide* purchasers under the State of Iowa.

In confirmation of this relinquishment, by act approved July 12. 1862, Congress enacted:

That the grant of lands to the then Territory of Iowa for the improvement of the Des Moines River, made by the act of August 8, 1846, is hereby extended so as include the alternate sections (designated by odd numbers) lying within five miles of said river, between the Raccoon Fork and the northern boundary of said State; such lands are to be held and applied in accordance with the provisions of the original grant, except that the consent of Congress is hereby given to the application of a portion thereof to aid in the construction of the Keokuk, Fort Des Moines & Minnesota Railroad, in accordance with the provisions of the act of the General Assembly of the State of Iowa approved March 22, 1858. And if any of the said lands shall have been sold or otherwise disposed of by the United States before the passage of this act, except those released by the United States to the grantees of the State of Iowa, under joint resolution of March 3, 1861, the Secretary of the Interior is hereby directed to set apart an equal amount of lands within said State to be certified in lieu thereof: *Provided*, that if the State shall have sold and conveyed any portion of the lands lying within the limits of the grant the title of which has proved invalid, any lands which shall be certified to said State in lieu thereof by virtue of the provisions of this act, shall inure to and be held as a trust fund for the benefit of the person, or persons, respectively, whose titles shall have failed as aforesaid.

The grant of lands by the above act of Congress was accepted by a joint resolution of the General Assembly, Sept. 11, 1862, in extra session. On the same day, the Governor was authorized to appoint one or more Commissioners to select the lands in accordance with the

grant. These Commissioners were instructed to report their selections to the Registrar of the State Land Office. The lands so selected were to be held for the purposes of the grant, and were not
to be disposed of until further legislation should be had. D. W.
Kilburne, of Lee County, was appointed Commissioner, and, on the
25th day of April, 1864, the General Land Officer authorized the
selection of 300,000 acres from the vacant public lands as a part of
the grant of July 12, 1862, and the selections were made in the
Fort Dodge and Sioux City Land Districts.

Many difficulties, controversies and conflicts, in relation to claims
and titles, grew out of this grant, and these difficulties were en-
hanced by the uncertainty of its limits until the act of Congress of
July, 1862. But the General Assembly sought, by wise and appropriate legislation, to protect the integrity of titles derived from
the State. Especially was it the determination to protect the actual
settlers, who had paid their money and made improvements prior
to the final settlement of the limits of the grant by Congress.

VII.—THE DES MOINES RIVER SCHOOL LANDS.

These lands constituted a part of the 500,000 acre grant made
by Congress in 1841; including 28,378.46 acres in Webster County,
selected by the Agent of the State under that grant, and approved
by the Commissioner of the General Land Office February 20, 1851.
They were ordered into the market June 6, 1853, by the Superintendent of Public Instruction, who authorized John Tolman,
School Fund Commissioner for Webster County, to sell them as
school lands. Subsequently, when the act of 1846 was construed
to extend the Des Moines River grant above Raccoon Fork, it was
held that the odd numbered sections of these lands within five
miles of the river were appropriated by that act, and on the 30th
day of December, 1853, 12,813.51 acres were set apart and approved to the State by the Secretary of the Interior, as a part of
the Des Moines River grant. January 6, 1854, the Commissioner
of the General Land Office transmitted to the Superintendent of
Public Instruction a certified copy of the lists of these lands, indorsed by the Secretary of the Interior. Prior to this action of
the Department, however, Mr. Tolman had sold to individual purchasers 3,194.28 acres as school lands, and their titles were, of
course, killed. For their relief, an act, approved April 2, 1860,
provided that, upon application and proper showing, these purchasers should be entitled to draw from the State Treasury the amount
they had paid, with 10 per cent. interest, on the contract to purchase made with Mr. Tolman. Under this act, five applications
were made prior to 1864, and the applicants received, in the aggregate, $949.53.

By an act approved April 7, 1862, the Governor was forbidden
to issue to the Dubuque & Sioux City Railroad Company any certificate of the completion of any part of said road, or any convey-

ance of lands, until the company should execute and file, in the State Land office, a release of its claim—first to certain swamp lands; second, to the Des Moines River Lands sold by Tolman; third, to certain other river lands. That act provided that "the said company shall transfer their interests in those tracts of land in Webster and Hamilton Counties heretofore sold by John Tolman, School Fund Commissioner, to the Register of the State Land Office in trust, to enable said Register to carry out and perform said contracts in all cases when he is called upon by the parties interested to do so, before the 1st day of January, A. D., 1864.

The company filed its release to the Tolman lands, in the Land Office, February 27, 1864, at the same time entered its protest that it had no claim upon them, never had pretended to have, and had never sought to claim them. The Register of the State Land Office, under the advice of the Attorney General, decided that patents would be issued to the Tolman purchasers in all cases where contracts had been made prior to December 23, 1853, and remaining uncancelled under the act of 1860. But before any were issued, on the 27th of August, 1864, the Des Moines Navigation & Railroad Company commenced a suit in Chancery, in the District Court of Polk County, to enjoin the issue of such patents. On the 30th of August, an *ex parte* injunction was issued. In January, 1868, Mr. J. A. Harvey, Register of the Land Office, filed in the court an elaborate answer to plaintiffs' petition, denying that the company had any right to or title in the lands. Mr. Harvey's successor, Mr. C. C. Carpenter, filed a still more exhaustive answer February 10, 1868. August 3, 1868, the District Court dissolved the injunction. The company appealed to the Supreme Court, where the decision of the lower court was affirmed in December, 1869.

VIII.   SWAMP LAND GRANT.

An act of Congress, approved March 28, 1850, to enable Arkansas and other States to reclaim swampy lands within their limits, granted all the swamp and overflowed lands remaining unsold within their respective limits to the several States. Although the total amount claimed by Iowa under this act does not exceed 4,000,000 acres, it has, like the Des Moines River and some of the land grants, cost the State considerable trouble and expense, and required a deal of legislation. The State expended large sums of money in making the selections, securing proofs, etc., but the General Government appeared to be laboring under the impression that Iowa was not acting in good faith; that she had selected a large amount of lands under the swamp land grant, transferred her interest to counties, and counties to private speculators, and the General Land Office permitted contests as to the character of the lands already selected by the Agents of the State as "swamp lands."

Congress, by joint resolution Dec. 18, 1856, and by act March 3,
1857, saved the State from the fatal result of this ruinous policy.
Many of these lands were selected in 1854 and 1855, immediately
after several remarkably wet seasons, and it was but natural that
some portions of the selections would not appear swampy after a
few dry seasons. Some time after these first selections were made
persons desired to enter parcels of the so-called swamp lands and
offering to prove them to be dry. In such cases the General Land
Office ordered hearing before the local land officers, and if they
decided the land to be dry, it was permitted to be entered and the
claim of the State rejected. Speculators took advantage of this.
Affidavits were bought of irresponsible and reckless men, who,
for a few dollars, would confidently testify to the character of lands
they never saw. These applications multiplied until they covered
3,000,000 acres. It was necessary that Congress should confirm
all these selections to the State, that this gigantic scheme of fraud
and plunder might be stopped. The act of Congress of March 3,
1857, was designed to accomplish this purpose. But the Commissioner of the General Land Office held that it was only a qualified
confirmation, and under this construction sought to sustain the
action of the Department in rejecting the claim of the State, and
certifying them under act of May 15, 1856, under which the railroad companies claimed all swamp land in odd numbered sections
within the limits of their respective roads. This action led to
serious complications. When the railroad grant was made, it was
not intended, nor was it understood that it included any of the
swamp lands. These were already disposed of by previous grant.
Nor did the companies expect to receive any of them, but under
the decision of the Department adverse to the State the way was
opened, and they were not slow to enter their claims. March 4,
1862, the Attorney General of the State submitted to the General
Assembly an opinion that the railroad companies were not entitled
even to contest the right of the State to these lands, under the
swamp land grant. A letter from the Acting Commissioner of
the General Land Office expressed the same opinion, and the General Assembly by joint resolution, approved April 7, 1862, expressly
repudiated the acts of the railroad companies, and disclaimed any
intention to claim these lands under any other than the act of
Congress of September 28. 1850. A great deal of legislation has
been found necessary in relation to these swamp lands.

IX. THE RAILROAD GRANT.

One of the most important grants of public lands to Iowa for
purposes of internal improvement was that known as the "Railroad
Grant," by act of Congress, approved May 15, 1856.. This act
granted to the State of Iowa, for the purpose of aiding in the construction of railroads from Burlington, on the Mississippi River,
to a point on the Missouri River, near the mouth of Platte River;

from the city of Davenport, via Iowa City and Fort Des Moines to Council Bluffs; from Lyons City northwesterly to a point of intersection with the main line of the Iowa Central Air Line Railroad, near Maquoketa; thence on said main line, running as near as practicable to the Forty-second Parallel; across the said State of Iowa to the Missouri River; from the city of Dubuque to a point on the Missouri River near Sioux City, with a branch from the mouth of the Tete des Morts, to the nearest point on said road, to be completed as soon as the main road is completed to that point, every alternate section of land, designated by odd numbers, for six sections in width, on each side of said roads. It was also provided that if it should appear, when the lines of those roads were definitely fixed, that the United States had sold, or right of pre-emption had attached to any portion of said land, the State was authorized to select a quantity equal thereto, in alternate sections, or parts of sections, within fifteen miles of the lines so located. The lands remaining to the United States within six miles on each side of said roads were not to be sold for less than the double minimum price of the public lands when sold, nor were any of said lands to become subject to private entry until they had been first offered at public sale at the increased price.

Section 4 of the act provided that the lands granted to said State shall be disposed of by said State only in the manner following, that is to say: "That a quantity of land not exceeding one hundred and twenty sections for each of said roads, and included within a continuous length of twenty miles of each of said roads, may be sold; and when the Governor of said State shall certify to the Secretary of the Interior that any twenty continuous miles of any of said roads is completed, then another quantity of land hereby granted, not to exceed one hundred and twenty sections for each of said roads having twenty continuous miles completed as aforesaid, and included within a continuous length of twenty miles of each of such roads, may be sold; and so from time to time until said roads are completed, and if any of said roads are not completed within ten years, no further sale shall be made, and the lands unsold shall revert to the United States."

At a special session of the General Assembly of Iowa, by act approved July 14, 1856, the grant was accepted and the lands were granted by the State to the several railroad companies named, provided that the lines of their respective roads should be definitely fixed and located before April 1, 1857; and provided further, that if ·either of said companies should fail to have seventy-five miles of road completed and equipped by the 1st day of December, 1859, and its entire road completed by December 1, 1865, it should be competent for the State of Iowa to resume all rights to lands remaining undisposed of by the company so failing.

The railroad companies, with the single exception of the Iowa Central Air Line, accepted the several grants in accordance with the provisions of the above act, located their respective roads and and selected their lands. The grant to the Iowa Central was again granted to the Cedar Rapids and Missouri River Railroad Company, which accepted it.

By act, approved April 7, 1862, the Dubuque & Cioux City Railroad Company was required to execute a release to the State of certain swamp and school lands, included within the limits of its grant, in compensation for an extension of the time fixed for the completion of its road.

A careful examination of the act of Congress does not reveal any special reference to railroad *companies*. The lands were granted to the *State*, and the act evidently contemplated the sale of them *by the* State, and the appropriation of the proceeds to aid in the construction of certain lines of railroad within its limits. Section 4 of the act clearly defines the authority of the State in disposing of the lands.

Lists of all the lands embraced by the grant were made, and certified to the State by the proper authorities. Under an act of Congress approved August 3, 1864, entitled, "*An act to rest in the several States and Territories the title in fee of the lands which have been or may be certified to them,*" these certified lists, the originals of which are filed in the General Land Office, conveyed to the State " the fee simple title to all the lands embraced in such lists that are of the character contemplated " by the terms of the act making the grant, and " intended to be granted thereby; but where lands embraced in such lists are not of the character embraced by such act of Congress, and were not intended to be granted thereby, said lists, so far as these lands are concerned, shall be perfectly null and void; and no right, title, claim or interest shall be conveyed thereby." Those certified lists made under the act of May 15, 1856, were forty-three in number, viz: For the Burlington & Missouri River Railroad, nine: for the Mississippi & Missouri Railroad, eleven; for the Iowa Central Air line, thirteen; and for the Dubuque & Sioux City Railroad, ten. The lands thus approved to the State were as follows:

Burlington & Missouri River R R	287,095.34 acres.
Mississippi & Missouri River R R	774,674.36 "
Cedar Rapids & Missouri River R R	775,454.19 "
Dubuque & Sioux City R R	1,226,558.32 "

A portion of these had been selected as swamp lands by the State, under the act of September 28, 1850, and these, by the terms of the act of August 3, 1854, could not be turned over to the railroads unless the claim of the State to them as swamp was first rejected. It was not possible to determine from the records of the State Land Office the extent of the conflicting claims arising under the two grants, as copies of the swamp land selections in some of the counties were not filed of record. The Commissioner of the General Land Office, however, prepared lists of the lands claimed by the State as swamp under act of September 28, 1850, and also claimed by the railroad companies under act of May 15, 1856, amounting to 553,293.33 acres, the claim to which as swamp had been rejected by the Department. These were consequently certified the State as railroad lands. There was no mode other than the act of July, 1856, prescribed for transferring the title to these lands from the State to the companies. The courts had decided that, for the purposes of the grant, the lands belonged to the State, and to her the companies should look for their titles. It was generally accepted that the act of the Legislature of July, 1856, was all that was necessary to complete the transfer of title. It was assumed that all the rights and powers conferred upon the State by the act of Congress of May 14, 1856, were by the act of the General Assembly transferred to the companies: in other words, that it was designed to put the companies in the place of the State as the grantees from Congress—and, therefore, that which perfected the title thereto to the State perfected the title to the companies by virtue of the act of July, 1856. One of the companies, however, the Burlington & Missouri River Railroad Company. was not entirely satisfied with this construction. Its managers thought that some further and specific action of the State authorities in addition to the act of the Legislature was necessary to complete their title. This induced Gov. Lowe to attach to the certified lists his official certificate, under the broad seal of the State. On the 9th of November, 1859, the Governor thus certified to them (commencing at the Missouri River) 187,297.44 acres, and December 27th, 43,775.70 acres, an aggregate of 231,073.14 acres. These were the only lands under the grant that were certified by the State authorities with any design of perfecting the title already vested in the company by the act of July, 1856. The lists which were afterward furnished to the company were simply certified by the Governor as being correct copies of the lists received by the State from the United States General Land Office. These subsequent lists embraced lands that had been claimed by the State under the Swamp Land Grant.

It was urged against the claim of the Companies that the effect of the act of the Legislature was simply to substitute them for the State as parties to the grant. 1st. That the lands were granted to the State to be held in trust for the accomplishment of a specific purpose, and therefore the State could not part with the title until that purpose should have been accomplished. 2d. That it was not the intention of the act of July 14, 1856, to deprive the State of the control of the lands, but on the contrary that she should retain supervision of them and the right to withdraw all rights and powers and resume the title conditionally conferred by that act upon the companies in the event of their failure to complete their part of the contract. 3d. That the certified lists from the General Land Office vested the title in the State only by virtue of the act of Congress approved August 3, 1854. The State Land Office held that the proper construction of the act of July 14, 1856, when accepted by the companies, was that it became a *conditional contract* that might ripen into a positive sale of the lands as from time to time the work should progress, and as the State thereby became authorized by the express terms of the grant to sell them.

This appears to have been the correct construction of the act, but by a subsequent act of Congress, approved June 2, 1864, amending the act of 1856, the terms of the grant were changed, and numerous controversies arose between the companies and the State.

The ostensible purpose of this additional act was to allow the Davenport & Council Bluffs Railroad "to modify or change the location of the uncompleted portion of its line," to run through the town of Newton, Jasper County, or as nearly as practicable to that point. The original grant had been made to the State to aid in the construction of railroads within its limits, and not to the companies, but Congress, in 1864, appears to have been utterly ignorant of what had been done under the act of 1856, or, if not, to have utterly disregarded it. The State had accepted the original grant. The Secretary of the Interior had already certified to the State all the lands intended to be included in the grant within fifteen miles of the lines of the several railroads. It will be remembered that Section 4. of the act of May 15, 1856, specifies the manner of sale of these lands from time to time as work on the railroads should progress, and also provided that "if any of said roads are not completed within ten years, no *further* sale shall be made, and the lands *unsold shall revert to the United States.*" Having vested the title to these lands in trust, in the State of Iowa, it is plain that until the expiration of the ten years there could be no reversion, and the State, not the United States, must control them until the grant should expire by limitation. The United States authorities could not rightfully require the Secretary of the Interior to certify directly to the companies any portion of the lands already certified to the State. And yet Congress, by its act of June 2, 1864, provided that whenever the Davenport & Council Bluffs Railroad Company should file in the General Land Office, at Washington, a map definitely showing such new location, the Secretary of the Interior should cause to be certified and conveyed to said Company, from time to time, as the road progressed, out of any of the lands belonging to the United States, not sold, reserved, or otherwise disposed of, or to which a pre-emption claim or right of homestead had not attached, and on which a *bona fide* settlement and improvement had not been made under color of title derived from the United States, or from the State of Iowa, within six miles of such newly located line, an amount of land per mile equal to that originally authorized to be granted to aid in the construction of said road by the act to which this was an amendment.

The term "out of any lands *belonging to the United States*, not sold, reserved or otherwise disposed of, etc.," would seem to indicate that Congress did intend to grant lands already granted, but when it declared that the Company should have an amount per mile *equal* to that originally *authorized to be granted*, it is plain that the framers of the bill were ignorant of the real terms of the original grant, or that they designed that the United States should *resume* the title it had already parted with two years before the lands could revert to the United States under the original act, which was not repealed.

A similar change was made in relation to the Cedar Rapids & Missouri Railroad, and dictated the conveyance of lands in a similar manner.

Like provision was made for the Dubuque & Sioux City Railroad, and the Company was permitted to change the location of its line between Fort Dodge and Sioux City, so as to secure the best route between those points; but this change of location was not to impair the right to the land granted in the original act, nor did it change the location of those lands.

By the same act, the Mississippi & Missouri Railroad Company was authorized to transfer and assign all or any part of the grant to any other company or person, "if, in the opinion of said Company, the construction of said railroad across the State of Iowa would be thereby sooner and more satisfactorily completed; but such assignee should not in any case be released from the liabilities and conditions accompanying this grant, nor acquire perfect title in any other manner than the same would have been acquired by the original grantee."

Still further, the Burlington & Missouri River Railroad was not forgotten, and was, by the same act, empowered to receive an amount of land per mile equal to that mentioned in the original act, and if that could not be found within the limits of six miles from the line of said road, then such selection might be made along such line within twenty miles thereof out of any public lands belonging to the United States, not sold, reserved or otherwise disposed of, or to which a pre-emption claim or right of homestead had not attached.

Those acts of Congress, which evidently originated in the "lobby," occasioned much controversy and trouble. The Department of the Interior, however, recognizing the fact that when the Secretary had certified the lands to the State, under the act of 1856, that act divested the United States of title, under the vesting act of August, 1854, refused to review its action, and also refused to order any and all investigations for establishing adverse claims (except in pre-emption cases), on the ground that the

United States had parted with the title, and. therefore, could exercise no control over the land.

May 12, 1864, before the passage of the amendatory act above described. Congress granted to the State of Iowa, to aid in the construction of a railroad from McGregor to Sioux City, and for the benefit of the McGregor Western Railroad Company, every alternate section of land, designated by odd numbers, for ten sections in width on each side of the proposed road, reserving the right to substitute other lands, whenever it was found that the grant infringed upon pre-empted lands, or on lands that had been reserved or disposed of for any other purpose. In such cases, the Secretary of the Interior was instructed to select, in lieu, lands belonging to the United States lying nearest to the limits specified.

X.   AGRICULTURAL COLLEGE AND FARM LAND.

An Agricultural College and Model Farm was established by act of the General Assembly, approved March 22, 1858. By the eleventh section of the act, the proceeds of the five-section grant made for the purpose of aiding in the erection of public buildings was appropriated, subject to the approval of Congress, together with all lands that Congress might thereafter grant to the State for the purpose for the benifit of the institution. On the 23d of March, by joint resolution, the Legislature asked the consent of Congress to the proposed transfer. By act approved July 11, 1862, Congress removed the restrictions imposed in the "five-section grant," and authorized the General Assembly to make such disposition of the lands as should be deemed best for the interests of the State. By these several acts, the five sections of land in Jasper County certified to the State to aid in the erection of public buildings under the act of March 3, 1845, entitled: " An act supplemental to the act for the admission of the States of Iowa and Florida into the Union," were fully appropriated for the benefit of the Iowa Agricultural College and Farm. The institution is located in Story County. Seven hundred and twenty-one acres in that and two hundred in Boone County were donated to it by individuals interested in the success of the enterprise.

By act of Congress approved July 2, 1822, an appropriation was made to each State and Territory of 30.000 acres for each Senator and Representative in Congress, to which, by the apportionment under the census of 1850, they were respectively entitled. This grant was made for the purpose of endowing colleges of agriculture and mechanic arts.

Iowa accepted this grant by an act passed at an extra session of its Legislature, approved September 11, 1862, entitled " An act to accept of the grant, and carry into execution the trust conferred upon the State of Iowa by an act of Congress entitled 'An act granting public lands to the several States and Territories which may provide colleges for the benefit of agriculture and the mechanic arts,' approved July 2, 1862." This act made it the duty of the Governor to appoint an agent to select and locate the lands, and provided that none should be selected that were claimed by any county as swamp lands. The agent was required to make report of his doings to the Governor, who was instructed to submit the list of selections to the Board of Trustees of the Agricultural College for their approval. One thousand dollars were appropriated to carry the law into effect. The State, having two Senators and six Representatives in Congress, was entitled to 240,000 acres of land under this grant, for the purpose of establishing and maintaining an Agricultural College. Peter Melendy, Esq., of Black Hawk County, was appointed to make the selections, and during August, September and December, 1863, located them in the Fort Dodge, Des Moines and Sioux City Land Districts. December 8, 1864, these selections were certified by the Commissioner of the General Land Office, and were approved to the State by the Secretary of the Interior December 13, 1864. The title to these lands was vested in the State in fee simple, and conflicted with no other claims under other grants.

The agricultural lands were approved to the State as 240,000.96 acres; but 35,691.66 acres were located within railroad limits, which were computed at the rate of two acres for one, the actual amount of land approved to the State under this grant was only 204,309.30 acres, located as follows:

In Des Moines Land District	6,804.96 acres.
. In Sioux City Land District	59,025.37 "
In Fort Dodge Land District	138,478.97 "

By act of the General Assembly, approved March 29, 1864, entitled, "An act authorizing the Trustees of the Iowa State Agricultural College and Farm, to sell all lands acquired, granted, donated or appropriated for the benefit of said College, and to make an investment of the proceeds thereof," all these lands were granted to the Agricultural College and Farm, and the Trustees were authorized to take possession and sell or lease them. They were then under the control of the Trustees, lands as follows:

Under the act of July 2, 1852	304,309.30 acres.
Of the five-section grant	3,200.00 "
Lands donated in Story County	721.00 "
Lands donated in Boone County	200.00 "
Total	208,430.30 acres.

The Trustees opened an office at Fort Dodge, and appointed Hon. G. W. Bassett their agent for the sale of these lands.

THE PUBLIC SCHOOLS.

The germ of the free public school system of Iowa, which now ranks second to none in the United States, was planted by the first settlers. They had migrated to the "Beautiful Land" from other

L. & C.

and older States, where the common school system had been tested by many years' experience, bringing with them some knowledge of its advantages, which they determined should be enjoyed by the children of the land of their adoption. The system thus planted was expanded and improved in the broad fields of the West, until now it is justly considered one of the most complete, comprehensive and liberal in the country.

Nor is this to be wondered at when it is remembered humble log school houses were built almost as soon as the log cabin of the earliest settlers were occupied by their brave builders. In the lead mining regions of the State, the first to be occupied by the white race, the hardy pioneers provided the means for the education of their children even before they had comfortable dwellings for their families. School teachers were among the first immigrants to Iowa. Wherever a little settlement was made, the school house was the first united public act of the settlers; and the rude, primitive structures of the early time only disappeared when the communities had increased in population and wealth, and were able to replace them with more commodious and comfortable buildings. Perhaps in no single instance has the magnificent progress of the State of Iowa been more marked and rapid than in her common school system and in her school houses, which, long since, superseded the log cabins of the first settlers. To-day, the school houses which everywhere dot the broad and fertile prairies of Iowa are unsurpassed by those of any other State in the great Union. More especially is this true in all her cities and villages, where liberal and lavish appropriations have been voted, by a generous people, for the erection of large, commodious and elegant buildings, furnished with all the modern improvements, and costing from $10,000 to $60,000 each. The people of the State have expended more than $10,000,000 for the erection of public school buildings.

The first house erected in Iowa was a log cabin at Dubuque, built by James L. Langworthy and a few other miners, in the Autumn of 1833.

Mrs. Caroline Dexter commenced teaching in Dubuque in March, 1836. She was the first female teacher there, and probably the first in Iowa. The first tax for the support of schools at Dubuque was levied in 1840.

Among the first buildings erected at Burlington was a commodious log school house in 1834, in which Mr. Johnson Pierson taught the first school in the Winter of 1834-5.

The first school in Muscatine County was taught by George Bumgardner, in the Spring of 1837, and in 1839, a log school house was erected in Muscatine, which served for a long time for school house, church and public hall. The first school in Davenport was taught in 1838. In Fairfield Miss Clarissa Sawyer, James F. Chambers and Mrs. Reed taught school in 1839.

When the site of Iowa City was selected as the capital of the Territory of Iowa, in May, 1839, it was a perfect wilderness. The first sale of lots took place August 18, 1839, and before January 1, 1840, about twenty families had settled within the limits of the town: and during the same year, Mr. Jesse Berry opened a school in a small frame building he had erected, on what is now College street.

The first settlement in Monroe County was made in 1843, by Mr. John R. Gray, about two miles from the present site of Eddyville; and in the Summer of 1844, a log school house was built, and the first school was opened. About a year after the first cabin was built at Oskaloosa, a log school house was built.

At Fort Des Moines, now the Capital of the State, the first school was taught in the Winter of 1846–7.

The first school in Pottawattamie County was opened at Council Point, prior to 1849.

The first school in Decorah was taught in 1853. In Osceola, the first school was opened by Mr. D. W. Scoville. The first school at Fort Dodge was taught in 1855, by Cyrus C. Carpenter, since Governor of the State. In Crawford County, the first school house was built in Mason's Grove, in 1856, and Morris McHenry first occupied it as teacher.

During the first twenty years of the history of Iowa, the log school houses prevailed, and in 1861, there were 893 of these primitive structures in use for school purposes in the State. Since that time they have been gradually disappearing. In 1865, there were 796; in 1870, 336; and in 1875, 121.

Iowa Territory was created July 3, 1838. January 1, 1839, the Territorial Legislature passed an act providing that "there shall be established a common school, or schools, in each of the counties in this Territory, which shall be open and free for every class of white citizens between the ages of five and twenty-one years." The second section of the act provided that "the County Board shall, from time to time, form such districts in their respective counties whenever a petition may be presented for the purpose by a majority of the voters resident within such contemplated district." These districts were governed by boards of trustees, usually of three persons; each district was required to maintain school at least three months in every year; and later, laws were enacted providing for county school taxes for the payment of teachers, and that whatever additional sum might be required should be assessed upon the parents sending, in proportion to the length of time sent.

When Iowa Territory became a State, in 1846, with a population of 100,000, and with 20,000 pupils within its limits, about four hundred school districts had been organized. In 1850, there were 1,200, and in 1857, the number had increased to 3,265.

In March, 1858, the Seventh General Assembly enacted that "each civil township is declared a school district," and provided that these should be divided into sub-districts. This law went into force March 20, 1858, and reduced the number of school districts from about 3,500 to less than 900.

This change of school organization resulted in a very material reduction of the expenditures for the compensation of District Secretaries and Treasurers. An effort was made for several years, from 1867 to 1872, to abolish the sub-district system. The Legislature of 1870, provided for the formation of independent districts from the sub-districts of district townships. The system of graded schools was inaugurated in 1849; and new schools, in which more than one teacher is employed, are universally graded.

The first official mention of Teachers' Institutes in the educational records of Iowa, occurs in the annual report of Hon. Thomas H. Benton, Jr., made December 2, 1850.

In March, 1858, an act was passed authorizing the holding of Teachers' Institutes for periods not less than six working days, whenever not less than thirty teachers should desire. The Superintendent was authorized to expend not exceeding $100 for any one Institute, to be paid out by the County Superintendent as the Institute might direct for teachers and lecturers, and one thousand dollars was appropriated to defray the expenses of these Institutes.

The Board of Education at its first session, commencing December 6, 1858, enacted a code of school laws which retained the existing provisions for Teachers' Institutes. In March, 1860, the General Assembly amended the act of the Board by appropriating "a sum not exceeding fifty dollars annually for one such Institute, held as provided by law in each county."

By act approved March 19, 1874, Normal Institutes were established in each county, to be held annually by the County Superintendent, and in 1876 the Sixteenth General Assembly established the first permanent State Normal School at Cedar Falls, Black Hawk County, appropriating the building and property of the Soldiers' Orphans' Home at that place for that purpose.

The public school system of Iowa is admirably organized, and if the various officers who are entrusted with the educational interests of the commonwealth are faithful and competent, should and will constantly improve.

"The public schools are supported by funds arising from several sources. The sixteenth section of every Congressional Township was set apart by the General Government for school purposes, being one-thirty-sixth part of all the lands of the State. The minimum price of these lands was fixed at one dollar and twenty-five cents per acre. Congress also made an additional donation to the State of five hundred thousand acres, and an appropriation of five per cent. on all the sales of public lands to the school fund. The State gives to this fund the proceeds of the sales of all lands which escheat to it; the proceeds of all fines for the violation of the liquor and criminal laws. The money derived from these sources constitutes the permanent school fund of the State, which cannot be diverted to any other purpose. The penalties collected by the courts for fines and forfeits go to the school fund in the counties where collected. The proceeds of the sale of lands and the five per cent. fund go into the State Treasury, and the State distributes these proceeds to the several counties according to their request, and the counties loan the money to individuals for long terms at eight per cent. interest, on security of land valued at three times the amount of the loan, exclusive of all buildings and improvements thereon. The interest on these loans is paid into the State Treasury, and becomes the available school fund of the State. The counties are responsible to the State for all money so loaned, and the State is likewise responsible to the school fund for all moneys transferred to the counties. The interest on these loans is apportioned by the State Auditor semi-annually to the several counties of the State, in proportion to the number of persons between the ages of five and twenty-one years. The counties also levy an annual tax for school purposes, which is apportioned to the several district townships in the same way. A district tax is also levied for the same purpose. The money arising from these several sources constitutes the support of the public schools, and is sufficient to enable every sub-district in the State to afford from six to nine months' school each year."

The taxes levied for the support of schools are self-imposed. Under the admirable school laws of the State, no taxes can be legally assessed or collected for the erection of school houses until they have been ordered by the election of the district at a school meeting legally called. The school houses of Iowa are the pride of the State and an honor to the people. If they have been sometimes built at a prodigal expense, the tax payers have no one to blame but themselves. The teachers' and contingent funds are determined by the Directors, under certain legal restrictions. These boards are elected annually, except in the independent districts, in which the board may be entirely changed every three years. The only exception to this mode of levying taxes for support of schools is the county school tax, which is determined by the County Board of Supervisors. The tax is from one to three mills on the dollar; usually, however, but one.

In his admirable message to the General Assembly, just previous to retiring from the Gubernatorial chair, Gov. Gear has the following to say concerning the public schools of Iowa:

"The number of school children reported is 594,750. Of this number 384,192 are, by approximation, between the ages of six and sixteen years. The number of all ages enrolled in the schools is 431,513, which shows that much the greater proportion of children of school age avail themselves of the benefits of our educational system. The average attendance is 254,088. The schools of the State have been in session, on an average, 148 days.

"There is, doubtless, quite a percentage of children who attend schools other than those of a public character. Yet the figures I have quoted show clearly that very many children, through the negligence or unwillingness of parents, do not attend school at all, but are in a fair way to grow up in ignorance. I, therefore, earnestly suggest that you consider the expediency of enacting a compulsory educational law, which should require attendance upon schools of some kind, either public or private. To me it does seem as if the State shall not have done her full duty by the children, until she shall have completed her educational system by some such enactment.

"The interest in the normal institutes is maintained, and, beyond doubt, they render great aid in training the teachers who attend them.

"The receipts for all school purposes throughout the State were $5,006,023.60, and the expenditures $5,129,279.49; but of these receipts and expenditures about $400,000 was of money borrowed to refund outstanding bonds at lower rates of interest.

"The amount on hand aggregated, at the end of the fiscal year, $2,653,356.55. This sum is, in my judgment, much larger than the necessities of the schools require, and it would be well to impose some check to prevent an excessive or unnecessary levy of taxes for school purposes."

The significance of such facts as these is unmistakable. Such lavish expenditures can only be accounted for by the liberality and public spirit of the people, all of whom manifest their love of popular education and their faith in the public schools by the annual dedication to their support of more than one per cent. of their entire taxable property; this too, uninterruptedly through a series of years, commencing in the midst of a war which taxed their energies and resources to the extreme, and continuing through years of general depression in business—years of moderate yield of produce, of discouragingly low prices, and even amid the scanty surroundings and privations of pioneer life. Few human enterprises have a grander significance or give evidence of a more noble purpose than the generous contributions from the scanty resources of the pioneer for the purposes of public education.

POLITICAL RECORD.

TERRITORIAL OFFICERS.

Governors—Robert Lucas, 1838–41; John Chambers, 1841–45; James Clarke, 1845.

Secretaries—William B. Conway, 1838, died 1839; James Clarke, 1839; O. H. W. Stull, 1841; Samuel J. Burr, 1843; Jesse Williams, 1845.

Auditors—Jesse Williams, 1840; Wm. L. Gilbert, 1843; Robert M. Secrest, 1845.

Treasurers—Thornton Bayliss, 1839; Morgan Reno, 1840.
Judges—Charles Mason, Chief Justice, 1838; Joseph Williams, 1838, Thomas S. Wilson, 1838.
Presidents of Council—Jesse B. Browne, 1838-9 ; Stephen Hempstead, 1839-40; M. Bainridge, 1840-1; Jonathan W. Parker, 1841-2; John D. Elbert, 1842-3; Thomas Cox, 1843-4; S. Clinton Hastings, 1845; Stephen Hempstead, 1845-6.
Speakers of the House—William H. Wallace, 1838-9; Edward Johnston, 1839-40; Thomas Cox, 1840-1; Warner Lewis, 1841-2; James M. Morgan, 1842-3; James P. Carleton, 1843-4; James M. Morgan, 1845; George W. McCleary, 1845-6.
First Constitutional Convention, 1844—Shepherd Leffler, President; Geo. S. Hampton, Secretary.
Second Constitutional Convention, 1846—Enos Lowe, President; William Thompson, Secretary.

OFFICERS OF THE STATE GOVERNMENT.

Governors—Ansel Briggs, 1846 to 1850; Stephen Hempstead, 1850 to 1854; James W. Grimes, 1854 to 1858; Ralph P. Lowe, 1858 to 1860; Samuel J. Kirkwood, 1860 to 1864; William M. Stone, 1864 to 1868; Samuel Morrill, 1868 to 1872; Cyrus C. Carpenter, 1872 to 1876; Samuel J. Kirkwood, 1876 to 1877; Joshua G. Newbold, Acting, 1877 to 1878; John H. Gear, 1878 to 1882; Buren R. Sherman, 1882 to ——.
Lieutenant Governors—Office created by the new Constitution September 3, 1857—Oran Faville, 1858-9; Nicholas J. Rusch, 1860-1; John R. Needham, 1862-3; Enoch W. Eastman, 1864-5; Benjamin F. Gue, 1866-7; John Scott, 1868-9; M. M. Walden, 1870-1; H. C. Bulis, 1872-3; Joseph Dysart, 1874-5; Joshua G. Newbold, 1876-7; Frank T. Campbell, 1878-82; O. H. Manning, 1882 to ——.
Secretaries of State—Elisha Cutler, Jr., Dec. 5, 1846, to Dec. 4, 1848; Josiah H. Bonney, Dec. 4,1848, to Dec. 2,1850; George W. McCleary, Dec. 2, 1850,to Dec. 1,1856; Elijah Sells, Dec. 1, 1856, to Jan. 5, 1863; James Wright, Jan. 5, 1863, to Jan. 7, 1867; Ed. Wright, Jan. 7, 1867, to Jan. 6, 1873; Josiah T. Young, Jan. 6, 1873, to 1879; J. A. T. Hull, 1879 to ——.
Auditors of State—Joseph T. Fales, Dec. 5, 1846, to Dec. 2,1850; William Pattee, Dec. 2,1850,to Dec. 4,1854; Andrew J. Stevens, Dec. 4, 1854, resigned in 1855; John Pattee, Sept. 22, 1855, to Jan. 3, 1859; Jonathan W. Cattell, 1859,to 1865; John A. Elliot, 1865 to 1871; John Russell, 1871 to 1875; Buren R. Sherman, 1875 to 1881; W. V. Lucas, 1881 to ——.
Treasurers of State—Morgan Reno, Dec. 18, 1846, to Dec. 2, 1850; Israel Kister, Dec. 2, 1850, to Dec. 4, 1852, Martin L. Morris, Dec. 4, 1852, to Jan. 2, 1859; John W. Jones, 1859 to 1863; William H. Holmes, 1863 to 1867; Samuel E. Rankin, 1867 to

1873; William Christy, 1873 to 1877; George W. Bemis, 1877 to 1881; Edwin G. Conger, 1881 to ——.

Superintendents of Public Instruction—Office created in 1847— James Harlan, June 5, 1845 (Supreme Court decided election void); Thomas H. Benton, Jr., May 23, 1844, to June 7, 1854; James D. Eads, 1854-7; Joseph C. Stone, March to June, 1857; Maturin L. Fisher, 1857 to Dec. 1858, when the office was abolished and the duties of the office devolved upon the Secretary of the Board of Education.

Secretaries of the Board of Education—Thomas H. Benton, Jr., 1859–1863; Oran Faville, Jan. 1, 1864. Board abolished March 23, 1864.

Superintendents of Public Instruction—Office re-created March 23, 1864—Oran Faville, March 28, 1864, resigned March 1, 1867; D. Franklin Wells, March 4, 1867, to Jan., 1870; A. S. Kissell, 1870 to 1872; Alonzo Abernethy, 1872 to 1877; Carl W. von Coelln, 1877 to 1882; J. W. Akers, 1882 to ——.

State Binders—Office created February 21, 1855—William M. Coles, May 1, 1855, to May 1, 1859; Frank M. Mills, 1859 to 1867; James S. Carter, 1867 to 1870; J. J. Smart, 1870 to 1874; H. A. Perkins, 1874 to 1878; Matt Parrott, 1878 to ——.

Registers of the State Land Office—Anson Hart, May 5, 1855, to May 13, 1857; Theodore S. Parvin, May 13, 1857, to Jan. 3, 1859; Amos B. Miller, Jan. 3, 1859, to October, 1862; Edwin Mitchell, Oct. 31, 1862, to Jan. 5, 1863; Josiah A. Harvey, Jan. 5, 1863, to Jan. 7, 1867; Cyrus C. Carpenter, Jan. 7, 1867, to January, 1871; Aaron Brown, January, 1871, to January, 1875; David Secor, January, 1875, to 1879; J. K. Powers, 1879 to ——.

State Printers—Office created Jan. 3, 1840—Garrett D. Palmer and George Paul, 1849; William H. Merritt, 1851 to 1853; William A. Hornish, 1853 (resigned May 16, 1853); Mahoney & Dorr, 1853 to 1855; Peter Moriarty, 1855 to 1857; John Teesdale, 1857 to 1861; Francis W. Palmer, 1861 to 1869; Frank M. Mills, 1869 to 1870; G. W. Edwards, 1870 to 1872; R. P. Clarkson, 1872 to 1878; Frank M. Mills, 1878 to ——.

Adjutants General—Daniel S. Lee, 1851–5; Geo. W. McCleary, 1855–7; Elijah Sells, 1857; Jesse Bowen, 1857–61; Nathaniel Baker, 1861 to 1877; John H. Looby, 1877 to 1879; W. L. Alexander, 1879 to ——.

Attorneys General—David C. Cloud, 1853–56; Samuel A. Rice, 1856-60; Charles C. Nourse, 1861–4; Isaac L. Allen, 1865 (resigned January, 1866); Frederick E. Bissell, 1866 (died June 12, 1867); Henry O'Connor, 1867–72; Marsena E. Cutts, 1872–6; John F. McJunkin, 1877 to 1881; Smith McPherson, 1881 to ——.

Presidents of the Senate—Thomas Baker, 1846–7; Thomas Hughes, 1848; John J. Selman, 1848–9; Enos Lowe, 1850–1; William E. Leffingwell, 1852–3; Maturin L. Fisher, 1854–5; William

W. Hamilton, 1856-7. Under the New Constitution, the Lieutenant Governor is President of the Senate.
Speakers of the House—Jesse B. Brown, 1847-8; Smiley H. Bonhan, 1849-50; George Temple, 1851 2; James Grant, 1853-4; Reuben Noble, 1855-6; Samuel McFarland, 1856-7; Stephen B. Sheledy, 1858-9; John Edwards, 1860-1; Rush Clark, 1862-3; Jacob Butler, 1864-5; Ed. Wright, 1866-7; John Russell, 1868-9; Aylett R. Cotton, 1870-1; James Wilson, 1872 3; John H. Gear, 1874-7; John Y. Stone, 1878-9; Lore Alford, 1880-1; G. R. Struble, 1882 to ——.
New Constitutional Convention, 1859—Francis Springer. President; Thos. J. Saunders, Secretary.

STATE OFFICERS, 1882.

Buren R. Sherman, Governor; O. H. Manning, Lieutenant Governor; John A. T. Hull, Secretary of State; William V. Lucas, Auditor of State; Edwin H. Conger, Treasurer of State; James K. Powers, Register of State Land Office; W. L. Alexander, Adjutant General: Smith McPherson, Attorney General; Edward J. Holmes, Clerk of the Supreme Court; Jno. S. Runnells, Reporter Supreme Court; J. W. Akers, Superintendent of Public Instruction; Frank M. Mills, State Printer; Matt. Parrott, State Binder; Prof. Nathan R. Leonard, Superintendent of Weights and Measures; Mrs. S. B. Maxwell, State Librarian.

THE JUDICIARY.

SUPREME COURT OF IOWA, 1882.

Chief Justice, Austin Adams, Dubuque; Associate Judges, William H. Seevers, Oskaloosa; James G. Day, Sidney; James H. Rothrock, Tipton; Joseph M. Beck, Fort Madison.

DISTRICT COURTS, 1882.

First Judicial District, Abraham H. Stutsman, Burlington; Second Judicial District, Edward L. Burton, Ottumwa; Third Judicial District, R. C. Henry, Mount Ayr; Fourth Judicial District, Charles H. Lewis, Cherokee; Fifth Judicial District, William H. McHenry, Des Moines; Sixth Judicial District, John C. Cook, Newton; Seventh Judicial District, Walter I. Hayes, Clinton; Eighth Judicial District, John Shane, Vinton; Ninth Judicial District, Sylvester Bagg, Waterloo; Tenth Judicial District, Ezekiel E. Cooley, Decorah; Eleventh Judicial District, James W. McKenzie, Hampton; Twelfth Judicial District, Geo. W. Ruddick, Waverly; Thirteenth Judicial District, Joseph R. Reed, Council Bluffs; Fourteenth Judicial District, Ed. R. Duffie, Sac City.

CIRCUIT COURTS, 1882.

First Judicial Circuit, First District, William J. Jeffries, Mt. Pleasant; Second Judicial Circuit, First District, Charles Phelps,

Burlington; Second Judicial Circuit, H. C. Traverse, Bloomfield;
Third Judicial Circuit, D. D. Gregory. Afton; Fourth Judicial
Circuit, J. R. Zuver, Sioux City; First Judicial Circuit, Fifth
District, Josiah Given, Des Moines; Second Judicial Circuit,
Fifth District, Stephen A. Callvert, Adel; Sixth Judicial Circuit,
W. R. Lewis, Montezuma; First Judicial Circuit, Seventh District,
Charles W. Chase, Clinton; Second Judicial Circuit, Seventh Dis-
trict, DeWitt C. Richman, Muscatine; Eighth Judicial Circuit,
Christian Hedges, Marengo; Ninth Judicial Circuit, Benjamin W.
Lacy. Dubuque; Tenth Judicial Circuit, Charles T. Granger, Wau-
kon; Eleventh Judicial Circuit, D. D. Miracle, Webster City;
Twelfth Judicial Circuit, Robert G. Reineger, Charles City; Thir-
teenth Judicial Circuit, C. F. Loofbourrow, Atlantic; Fourteenth
Judicial Circuit, John N. Weaver, Algona.

CONGRESSIONAL REPRESENTATION.

UNITED STATES SENATORS.

(The first General Assembly failed to elect Senators.)
George W. Jones, Dubuque, Dec. 7, 1848-1858; Augustus C.
Dodge, Burlington, Dec. 7, 1848-1855; James Harlan, Mt. Pleas-
ant, Jan. 6, 1855-1865; James W. Grimes, Burlington, Jan. 26,
1858-died 1870; Samuel J. Kirkwood, Iowa City, elected Jan. 13,
1866, to fill vacancy caused by resignation of James Harlan; James
Harlan, Mt. Pleasant, March 4, 1866-1872; James B. Howell,
Keokuk, elected Jan. 20, 1870, to fill vacancy caused by the death of
J. W. Grimes –term expired March 3d; George G. Wright, Des
Moines, March 4, 1871-1877; William B. Allison, Dubuque,
March 4, 1872; Samuel J. Kirkwood, March 4, 1877; James W.
McDill, appointed to fill vacancy caused by the resignation of S.
J. Kirkwood, in 1881, and elected Jan. 1882, to fill the unexpired
term; James F. Wilson, elected Jan. 1882, for the full term, be-
ginning March 4, 1883.

MEMBERS OF HOUSE OF REPRESENTATIVES.

Twenty-ninth Congress—1846 to 1847.—S. Clinton Hastings;
Shepherd Leffler.
Thirtieth Congress—1847 to 1849.—First District, William
Thompson; Second District, Shepherd Leffler.
Thirty-first Congress—1849 to 1851.—First District, First Ses-
sion, Wm. Thompson; unseated by the House of Representatives
on a contest, and election remanded to the people. First District,
Second Session, Daniel F. Miller. Second District, Shepherd
Leffler.
Thirty-second Congress—1851 to 1853.—First District, Bern-
hart Henn. Second District, Lincoln Clark.
Thirty-third Congress—1853 to 1855.—First District, Bernhart
Henn. Second District, John P. Cook.

Thirty-fourth Congress—1855 to 1857.—First District, Augustus Hall. Second District, James Thorington.

Thirty-fifth Congress—1857 to 1859.—First District, Samuel R. Curtis. Second District, Timothy Davis.

Thirty-sixth Congress—1859 to 1861.—First District, Samuel R. Curtis. Second District, William Vandever.

Thirty-seventh Congress—1861 to 1863.—First District, First Session, Samuel R. Curtis.* First District, Second and Third Sessions, James F. Wilson. Second District, William Vandever.

Thirty-eighth Congress—1863 to 1865.—First District, James F. Wilson. Second District, Hiram Price; Third District, William B. Allison; Fourth District, Josiah B. Grinnell; Fifth District, John A. Kasson; Sixth District, Asahel W. Hubbard.

Thirty-ninth Congress—1865 to 1867.—First District, James F. Wilson; Second District, Hiram Price; Third District, William B. Allison; Fourth District, Josiah B. Grinnell, Fifth District, John A. Kasson; Sixth District, Asahel W. Hubbard.

Fortieth Congress—1867 to 1869.—First District, James F. Wilson; Second District, Hiram Price; Third District, William B. Allison; Fourth District, William Loughridge; Fifth District, Grenville M. Dodge; Sixth District, Asahel W. Hubbard.

Forty-first Congress—1869 to 1871.—First District, George W. McCrary; Second District, William Smyth; Third District, William B. Allison; Fourth District, William Loughridge; Fifth District, Frank W. Palmer; Sixth District, Charles Pomeroy.

Forty-second Congress—1871 to 1873.—First District, George W. McCrary; Second District, Aylett R. Cotton; Third District, W. G. Donnan; Fourth District, Madison M. Waldon; Fifth District, Frank W. Palmer; Sixth District, Jackson Orr.

Forty-third Congress—1873 to 1875.—First District, George W. McCrary; Second District, Aylett R. Cotton; Third District, William G. Donnan; Fourth District, Henry O. Pratt; Fifth District, James Wilson; Sixth District, William Loughridge; Seventh District, John A. Kasson; Eighth District, James W. McDill; Ninth District, Jackson Orr.

Forty-fourth Congress—1875 to 1877.—First District, George W. McCrary; Second District, John Q. Tufts; Third District, L. L. Ainsworth; Fourth District, Henry O. Pratt; Fifth District, James Wilson; Sixth District, Ezekiel S. Sampson; Seventh District, John A. Kasson; Eighth District, James W. McDill; Ninth District, Addison Oliver.

Forty-fifth Congress—1877 to 1879.—First District, J. C. Stone; Second District, Hiram Price; Third District, T. W. Burdick; Fourth District, H. C. Deering; Fifth District, Rush Clark; Sixth District, E. S. Sampson; Seventh District, H. J. B. Cummings; Eighth District, W. F. Sapp; Ninth District, A. Oliver.

*Vacated seat by acceptance of commission as Brigadier General, and J. F. Wilson chosen his successor.

Forty-sixth Congress.—1879 to 1881.—First District, Moses A.
McCoid; Second District, Hiram Price; Third District, Thomas
Updegraff; Fourth District, Nathaniel C. Deering; Fifth District,
W. G. Thompson; Sixth District, James B. Weaver; Seventh Dis-
trict, Edward H. Gillette; Eighth District, William F. Sapp;
Ninth District, Cyrus C. Carpenter.

Forty-Seventh Congress—1881 to 1883.—First District, Moses
A. McCoid; Second District, Sewall S. Farwell; Third District,
Thomas Updegraff; Fourth District, Nathaniel C. Deering; Fifth
District, W. G. Thompson; Sixth District, Madison E. Cutts;
Seventh District, John A. Kasson; Eighth District, William P.
Hepburn; Ninth District, Cyrus C. Carpenter.

WAR RECORD.

The State of Iowa may well be proud of her record during the
War of the Rebellion, from 1861 to 1865. The following brief
but comprehensive sketch of the history she made during that trying period, is largely from the pen of Col. A. P. Wood, of Dubuque, the author of "The History of Iowa and the War," one of
the best works of the kind yet written.

"Whether in the promptitude of her responses to the calls made
on her by the General Government, in the courage and constancy
of her soldiery in the field, or in the wisdom and efficiency with
which her civil administration was conducted during the trying
period covered by the War of the Rebellion, Iowa proved herself
the peer of any loyal State. The proclamation of her Governor,
responsive to that of the President, calling for volunteers to compose her First Regiment, was issued on the fourth day after the
fall of Sumter. At the end of only a single week, men enough
were reported to be in quarters (mostly in the vicinity of their
own homes) to fill the regiment. These, however, were hardly
more than a tithe of the number who had been offered by company commanders for acceptance under the President's call. So
urgent were these offers that the Governor requested (on the 24th
of April) permission to organize an additional regiment. While
awaiting an answer to this request, he conditionally accepted a
sufficient number of companies to compose two additional regiments. In a short time, he was notified that both of these would
be accepted. Soon after the completion of the Second and Third
Regiments (which was near the close of May), the Adjutant General of the State reported that upwards of one hundred and seventy
companies had been tendered to the Governor to serve against the
enemies of the Union.

"Much difficulty and considerable delay occurred in fitting these
regiments for the field. For the First Infantry a complete outfit
(not uniform) of clothing was extemporized—principally by the
volunteered labor of loyal women in the different towns—from

material of various colors and qualities, obtained within the limits of the State. The same was done in part for the Second Infantry. Meantime, an extra session of the General Assembly had been called by the Governor, to convene on the 15th of May. With but little delay, that body authorized a loan of $800,000, to meet the extraordinary expenses incurred, and to be incurred, by the Executive Department, in consequence of the new emergency. A wealthy merchant of the State (Ex-Governor Merrill, then a resident of McGregor) immediately took from the Governor a contract to supply a complete outfit of clothing for the three regiments organized, agreeing to receive, should the Governor so elect, his pay therefor in State bonds at par. This contract he executed to the letter, and a portion of the clothing (which was manufactured in Boston, to his order) was delivered at Keokuk, the place at which the troops had rendezvoused, in exactly one month from the day on which the contract had been entered into. The remainder arrived only a few days later. This clothing was delivered to the regiment, but was subsequently condemned by the Government, for the reason that its color was gray, and blue had been adopted as the color to be worn by the national troops."

Other States also clothed their troops, sent forward under the first call of President Lincoln, with gray uniforms, but it was soon found that the Confederate forces were also clothed in gray, and that color was at once abandoned by the Union troops. If both armies were clothed alike, annoying if not fatal mistakes were liable to be made.

But while engaged in these efforts to discharge her whole duty, in common with all the other Union-loving States in the great emergency, Iowa was compelled to make immediate and ample provision for the protection of her own borders, from threatened invasion on the south by the Secessionists of Missouri, and from incursions from the west and northwest by bands of hostile Indians, who were freed from the usual restraint imposed upon them by the presence of regular troops stationed at the frontier posts. These troops were withdrawn to meet the greater and more pressing danger threatening the life of the nation at its very heart.

To provide for the adequate defense of her borders from the ravages of both rebels in arms against the Government, and of the more irresistible foes from the Western plains, the Governor of the State was authorized to raise and equip two regiments of infantry, a squadron of cavalry (not less than five companies) and a battalion of artillery (not less than three companies). Only cavalry were enlisted for home defense, however, "but," says Col. Wood, "in times of special danger, or when calls were made by the Unionists of Northern Missouri for assistance against their disloyal enemies, large numbers of militia on foot often turned out, and remained in the field until the necessity for their services had passed.

" The first order for the Iowa volunteers to move to the field
was received on the 13th of June. It was issued by Gen. Lyon,
then commanding the United States forces in Missouri. The
First and Second Infantry immediately embarked in steamboats,
and moved to Hannibal. Some two weeks later, the Third Infantry was ordered to the same point. These three, together with
many other of the earlier organized Iowa regiments, rendered their
first field service in Missouri. The First Infantry formed a part
of the little army with which Gen. Lyon moved on Springfield,
and fought the bloody battle of Wilson's Creek. It received un-
qualified praise for its gallant bearing on the field. In the following month (September), the Third Iowa, with but very slight support, fought with honor the sanguinary engagement of Blue
Mills Landing; and in November, the Seventh Iowa, as a part of
a force commanded by Gen. Grant, greatly distinguished itself in
the battle of Belmont, where it poured out its blood like water—
losing more than half of the men it took into action.

" The initial operations in which the battles referred to took
place, were followed by the more important movements led by
Gen. Grant, Gen. Curtis, of this State, and other commanders,
which resulted in defeating the armies defending the chief
strategic lines held by the Confederates in Kentucky, Tennessee,
Missouri and Arkansas, and compelling their withdrawal from
much of the territory previously controlled by them in those
States. In these and other movements, down to the grand culminating campaign by which Vicksburg was captured and the Confederacy permanently severed on the line of the Mississippi River,
Iowa troops took part in steadily increasing numbers. In the investment and siege of Vicksburg, the State was represented by
thirty regiment and two batteries, in addition to which, eight
regiments and one battery were employed on the outposts of the
besieging army. The brilliancy of their exploits on the many
fields where they served, won for them the highest meed of praise,
both in military and civil circles. Multipled were the terms in
which expression was given to this sentiment, but these words of
one of the journals of a neighboring State, 'The Iowa troops have
been heroes among heroes,' embody the spirit of all.

"In the veteran re-enlistments that distinguished the closing
months of 1863, above all other periods in the history of re-enlistments for the national armies, the Iowa three years' men (who
were relatively more numerous than those of any other State)
were prompt to set the example of volunteering for another term
of equal length, thereby adding many thousands to the great
army of those who gave this renewed and practical assurance that
the cause of the Union should not be left without defenders.

"In all the important movements of 1864-65, by which the
Confederacy was penetrated in every quarter, and its military power
finally overthrown, the Iowa troops took part. Their drum-beat

was heard on the banks of every great river of the South, from the Potomac to the Rio Grande, and everywhere they rendered the same faithful and devoted service, maintaining on all occasions their wonted reputation for valor in the field and endurance on the march.

"Two Iowa three-year cavalry regiments were employed during the whole term of service in the operations that were in progress from 1863 to 1866 against the hostile Indians of the western plains. A portion of these men were among the last of the volunteer troops to be mustered out of service. The State also supplied a considerable number of men to the navy, who took part in most of the naval operations prosecuted against the Confederate power on the Atlantic and Gulf coasts, and the rivers of the West.

"The people of Iowa were early and constant workers in the sanitary field, and by their liberal gifts and personal efforts for the benefit of the soldiery, placed their State in front rank of those who became distinguished for their exhibition of patriotic benevolence during the period covered by the war. Agents appointed by the Governor were stationed at points convenient for rendering assistance to the sick and needy soldiers of the State, while others were employed in visiting, from time to time, hospitals, camps and armies in the field, and doing whatever the circumstances rendered possible for the health and comfort of such of the Iowa soldiers as might be found there.

"Some of the benevolent people of the State early conceived the idea of establishing a Home for such of the children of deceased soldiers as might be left in destitute circumstances. This idea first took form in 1863, and in the following year a Home was opened at Farmington, Van Buren County, in a building leased for that purpose, and which soon became filled to its utmost capacity. The institution received liberal donations from the general public, and also from the soldiers in the field. In 1865 it became necessary to provide increased accommodations for the large number of children who were seeking the benefits of its care. This was done by establishing a branch at Cedar Falls, in Black Hawk County, and by securing, during the same year, for the use of the parent Home, Camp Kinsman, near the city of Davenport. This property was soon afterward donated to the institution by act of Congress.

"In 1866, in pursuance of a law enacted for that purpose, the Soldiers' Orphans' Home (which then contained about four hundred and fifty inmates) became a State institution, and thereafter the sums necessary for its support were appropriated from the State treasury. A second branch was established at Glenwood, Mills County. Convenient tracts were secured, and valuable improvements made at the different points. Schools were also established, and employments provided for such of the children as were of suitable age. In all ways the provision made for these wards of the State has been such as to challenge the approval of every benevolent mind. The number of children who have been inmates of the Home from its foundation to the present time is considerably more than two thousand.

"At the beginning of the war, the population of Iowa included about one hundred and fifty thousand men, presumably liable to render military service. The State raised, for general service, thirty-nine regiments of infantry; nine regiments of cavalry, and four companies of artillery, composed of three years' men; one regiment of Infantry, composed of three months' men; and four regiments and one battallion of infantry composed of one hundred days' men. The original enlistments in these various organizations, including seventeen hundred and twenty-seven men raised by draft, numbered a little more than sixty-nine thousand. The re-enlistments, including upward of seven thousand veterans, numbered very nearly eight thousand. The enlistments in the regular army and navy, and organizations of other States, will, if added, raise the total to upward of eighty thousand. The number of men who, under special enlistments, and as militia, took part at different times in the operations on the exposed borders of the State, was probably as many as five thousand.

"Iowa paid no bounty on account of the men she placed in the field. In some instances, toward the close of the war, bounty to a comparatively small amount was paid by cities and towns. On only one occasion—that of the call of July 18, 1864—was a draft made in Iowa. This did not occur on account of her proper liability, as established by previous rulings of the War Department, to supply men under that call, but grew out of the great necessity that there existed for raising men. The Government insisted on temporarily setting aside, in part, the former rule of settlements, and enforcing a draft in all cases where sub-districts in any of the States should be found deficient in their supply of men. In no instance was Iowa, as a whole, found to be indebted to the General Government for men, on a settlement of her quota accounts."

It is to be said to the honor and credit of Iowa, that while many of the loyal States, older and larger in population and wealth, incurred heavy State debts for the purpose of fulfilling their obligations to the General Government, Iowa, while she was foremost in duty, while she promptly discharged all her obligations to her sister States and the Union, found herself at the close of the war without any material addition to her pecuniary liabilities incurred before the war commenced. Upon final settlement after the restoration of peace, her claims upon the Federal Government were found to be fully equal to the amount of her bonds issued and sold during the war to provide the means for raising and equipping her troops sent into the field, and to meet the inevitable demands upon her treasury in consequence of the war.

STATEMENT showing the number of men furnished and casualties in Iowa regiments during the War of the Rebellion.

Regiments.	No. of Men.	Total Casualties.	Killed or died of wounds.	Died of Disease.
1st Battery	149	124	10	51
2d Battery	123	62	2	29
3d Battery	142	79	4	33
4th Battery	152	17	..	5
1st Cavalry	1478	543	54	187
2d Cavalry	1394	602	65	191
3d Cavalry	1360	770	77	224
4th Cavalry	1227	590	48	186
5th Cavalry	1245	452	43	127
6th Cavalry	1125	193	21	59
7th Cavalry	562	402	40	92
8th Cavalry	1234	274	33	91
9th Cavalry	1178	258	15	162
Sioux City Cavalry	93	7	..	...
Co. A, 11th Penn. Cavalry	87	5	1	4
1st Infantry	959	165	17	7
2d Infantry	1247	758	72	107
3d Infantry	1074	749	80	99
2d and 3d Inf. Consolidated	....	23	18	9
4th Infantry	1184	973	108	237
5th Infantry	1037	699	88	90
6th Infantry	1013	855	132	124
7th Infantry	1138	885	129	135
8th Infantry	1027	761	93	137
9th Infantry	1090	973	133	208
10th Infantry	1027	739	91	134
11th Infantry	1022	610	79	148
12th Infantry	981	768	62	243
13th Infantry	989	852	99	182
14th Infantry	840	526	50	122
14th Inf. Res. Batt	....	11	..	...
15th Infantry	1196	1029	130	194
16th Infantry	918	819	89	217
17th Infantry	950	614	61	97
18th Infantry	875	449	33	109
19th Infantry	985	562	86	91
20th Infantry	925	359	13	130
21st Infantry	980	531	66	157
22d Infantry	1108	634	105	126
23d Infantry	961	570	69	196
24th Infantry	959	761	111	197
25th Infantry	995	564	61	199
26th Infantry	919	562	69	204
27th Infantry	940	530	21	162
28th Infantry	956	696	76	180
29th Infantry	1005	511	36	248
30th Infantry	978	646	63	233
31st Infantry	977	540	27	261
32d Infantry	925	589	89	203
33d Infantry	985	580	62	196
34th Infantry	953	561	6	228

Statement of Number of Men, Casualties, etc.—continued.

Regiments.	No. of Men.	Total Casualties.	Killed or Died of Wounds	Died of Disease
34th Consolidated......................	....	72	5	13
35th Infantry............................	984	510	42	182
36th Infantry............................	986	619	59	226
37th Infantry............................	914	503	3	141
38th Infantry............................	910	431	1	310
39th Infantry............................	933	406	54	119
40th Infantry............................	900	361	15	179
41st Infantry............................	294	17	..	2
44th Infantry............................	867	15	..	14
45th Infantry............................	912	22	1	17
46th Infantry............................	892	28	1	23
47th Infantry............................	884	47	..	45
48th Infantry............................	346	4	..	4
1st African Infantry.....................	903	383	5	331
Totals..................	56,364	30,394	3,139	8,695

ABSTRACT OF IOWA STATE LAWS.

BILLS OF EXCHANGE AND PROMISSORY NOTES.

Upon negotiable bills, and notes payable in this State, grace shall be allowed according to the law merchant. All the above mentioned paper falling due on Sunday,'New Year's Day, the Fourth of July, Christmas, or any day appointed or recommended by the President of the United States or the Governor of the State, as a day of fast or thanksgiving, shall be deemed as due on the day previous. No defense can be made against a negotiable instrument (assigned before due) in the hands of the assignee without notice, except fraud was used in obtaining the same. To hold an indorser, due diligence must be used by suit against the maker or his representative. Notes payable to persons named or to order, in order to absolutely transfer title, must be indorsed by the payee. Notes payable to bearer may be transferred by delivery, and when so payable, every indorser thereon is held as a guarantor of payment, unless otherwise expressed.

In computing interest or discount on negotiable instruments, a month shall be considered a calendar month or twelfth of a year, and for less than a month, a day shall be considered a thirtieth part of a month. Notes only bear interest when so expressed; but after due, they draw the legal interest, even if not stated.

INTEREST.

The legal rate of interest is six per cent. Parties may agree, in writing, on a rate not exceeding ten per cent. If a rate of interest greater than ten per cent. is contracted for, it works a forfeiture of ten per cent. to the school fund, and only the principal sum can be recovered.

DESCENT.

The personal property of the deceased (except (1) that necessary for payment of debts and expenses of administration; (2) property set apart, to widow, as exempt from execution; (3) allowance by court, if necessary, of twelve month's support to widow, and to children under fifteen years of age), including life insurance, descends as does real estate.

One-third in value (absolutely) of all estates in real property, possessed by husband at any time during marriage, which have not been sold on execution or other judicial sale, and to which the wife has made no relinquishment of her right, shall be set apart as her property, in fee simple, if she survive him.

The same share shall be set apart to the surviving husband of a deceased wife.

The widow's share cannot be affected by any will of her husband's, unless she consents, in writing thereto, within six months after notice to her of provisions of the will.

The provisions of the statutes of descent apply alike to surviving husband or surviving wife.

Subject to the above, the remaining estate of which the decedent died seized, shall in absence of other arrangements by will, descend;

First. To his or her children and their descendants in equal parts; the descendants of the deceased child or grandchild taking the share of their deceased parents in equal shares among them.

Second. Where there is no child, nor descendant of such child, and no widow or surviving husband, then to the parents of the deceased in equal parts; the surviving parent, if either be dead, taking the whole; and if there is no parent living, then to the brothers and sisters of the intestate and their descendants,

Third. When there is a widow or surviving husband, and no child or children, or descendants of the same, then one-half of the estate shall descend to such widow or surviving husband, absolutely; and the other half of the estate shall descend as in other cases where there is no widow or surviving husband, or child or children or descendants of the same.

Fourth. If there is no child, parent, brother or sister, or descendants of either of them, then to wife of intestate, or to her heirs, if dead, according to like rules.

Fifth. If any intestate leaves no child, parent, brother or sister or descendant of either of them, and no widow or surviving husband, and no child, parent, brother or sister (or descendant of either of them) of such widow or surviving husband, it shall escheat to the State.

WILLS AND ESTATES OF DECEASED PERSONS.

No exact form of words are necessary in order to make a will good at law. Every male person of the age of twenty-one years, and every female of the age of eighteen years, of sound mind and memory, can make a valid will; it must be in writing, signed by the testator, or by some one in his or her presence, and by his or her express direction, and attested by two or more competent witnesses. Care should be taken that the witnesses are not interested in the will. Inventory to be made by the executor or administrator within fifteen days from date of letters testamentary or of administration. Executors' and administrators' compensation on amount of personal estate distributed, and for proceeds of sale of real estate, five per cent. for first one thousand dollars, two and one-half per cent. on overplus up to five thousand dollars, and one per cent. on overplus above five thousand dollars, with such additional allowance as shall be reasonable for extra services.

Within *ten days* aftes the receipt of letters of administration, the executor or administrator shall give such *notice of appointment* as the court or clerk shall direct.

Claims (other than preferred) must be filed *within one year thereafter*, are forever barred, *unless the claim is pending* in the District or Supreme Court, or *unless peculiar circumstances* entitle the claimant to equitable relief.

Claims are *classed* and *payable* in the following order:

1. Expenses of administration.
2. Expenses of last sickness and funeral.
3. Allowance to widow and children, if made by the court.
4. Debts preferred under laws of the United States.
5. Public rates and taxes.
6. Claim filed within six months after the *first publication* of the notice given by the executors of their appointment.
7. All other debts.
8. Legacies.

The *award*, or property which must be *set apart to the widow in her own right*, by the executor, includes all personal property which, in the hands of the deceased, as head of a family, would have been *exempt from execution*.

TAXES.

The owners of personal property, on the first day of January of each year, and the owners of real property on the first day of November of each year, *are liable* for the taxes thereon.

The following property is exempt from taxation, viz.:

1. The property of the United States and of this State, including university, agricultural college and school lands and all property leased to the State; property of a county, township, city, incorporated town or school district when devoted entirely to the public use and not held for pecuniary profit; public grounds, including all places for the burial of the dead; fire engines and all implements for extinguishing fires, with the grounds used exclusively for their buildings and for the meetings of the fire companies; all public libraries, grounds and buildings of literary, scientific, benevolent, agricultural and religious institutions, and societies devoted solely to the appropriate objects of these institutions, not exceeding 640 acres in extent, and not leased or otherwise used with a view of pecuniary profit; and all property leased to agricultural, charitable institutions and benevolent societies, and so devoted during the term of such lease; *provided*, that all deeds, by which such

property is held, shall be duly filed for record before the property therein described shall be omitted from the assessment.

2. The books, papers and apparatus belonging to the above institutions; used solely for the purposes above contemplated, and the like property of students in any such institution, used for their education.

3. Money and credits belonging exclusively to such institutions and devoted solely to sustaining them, but not exceeding in amount or income the sum prescribed by their charter.

4. Animals not hereafter specified, the wool shorn from sheep, belonging to the person giving the list, his farm produce harvested within one year previous to the listing; private libraries not exceeding three hundred dollars in value; family pictures, kitchen furniture, beds and bedding requisite for each family; all wearing apparel in actual use, and all food provided for the family; but no person from whom a compensation for board or lodging is received or expected, is to be considered a member of the family within the intent of this clause.

5. The polls or estates or both of persons who, by reason of age or infirmity, may, in the opinion of the Assessor, be unable to contribute to the public revenue; such opinion and the fact upon which it is based being in all cases reported to the Board of Equalization by the Assessor or any other person, and subject to reversal by them.

6. The farming utensils of any person who makes his livelihood by farming, and the tools of any mechanic, not in either case to exceed three hundred dollars in value.

7. Government lands entered or located, or lands purchased from this State, should not be taxed for the year in which the entry, location or purchase is made.

There is also a suitable exemption, in amount, for planting fruit trees or forest trees or hedges.

Where buildings are destroyed by fire, tornado, or other unavoidable casualty, after being assessed for the year, the Board of Supervisors may rebate taxes for that year on the property destroyed, *if same has not been sold for taxes, and if said taxes have not been delinquent for thirty days* at the time of destruction of property, and the rebate shall be allowed for such loss only as is not covered by insurance.

All other property is subject to taxation. Every inhabitant of full age and sound mind shall assist the Assessor in listing all taxable property of which he is the owner, or which he controls or manages, either as agent, guardian, father, husband, trustee, executor, accounting officer, partner, mortgagor or lessor, mortgagee or lessee.

Road beds of railway corporations shall not be assessed to owners of adjacent property, but shall be considered the property of the companies for purposes of taxation; nor shall real estate used as a public highway be assessed and taxed as part of adjacent lands whence the same was taken for such public purpose.

The property of railway, telegraph and express companies shall be listed and assessed for taxation as the property of an individual would be listed and assessed for taxation. Collection of taxes made as in the case of an individual.

The Township Board of Equalization shall meet first Monday in April of each year. Appeal lies to the Circuit Court.

The County Board of Equalization (the Board of Supervisors) meet at their regular session in June of each year. Appeal lies to the Circuit Court.

Taxes become delinquent February 1st of each year, payable without interest or penalty, at any time before March 1st of each year.

Tax sale is held on first Monday in October of each year.

Redemption may be made at any time within three years after date of sale, by paying to the County Auditor the *amount* of sale, and *twenty per centum* of such amount immediately added as *penalty with ten per cent. interest per annum* on the whole amount thus made from the day of sale, and also subsequent taxes, interest and costs paid by purchaser after March 1st of each year, and a similar *penalty* of twenty per centum added as before, with ten per cent. *interest* as before.

If *notice* has been given, by purchaser, of the date at which the redemption is limited, the cost of same is added to the redemption money. Ninety days notice is required, by the statute, to be published by the purchaser or holder of certificate, to terminate the right of redemption.

JURISDICTION OF COURTS.

DISTRICT COURTS

have jurisdiction, general and original, both civil and criminal, except in such cases where Circuit Courts have exclusive jurisdiction. District Courts have *exclusive supervision* over courts of Justices of the Peace and Magistrates, in criminal matters, on appeal and writs of error.

CIRCUIT COURTS

have jurisdiction, general and original, with the District Courts, in all civil actions and special proceedings, and *exclusive jurisdiction* in all appeals and writs of error from inferior courts, in civil matters. And *exclusive jurisdiction* in matters of estates and general probate business.

JUSTICES OF THE PEACE

have jurisdiction in civil matters where $100 or less is involved. By consent of parties, the jurisdiction may be extended to an

8

amount not exceeding $300. They have jurisdiction to try and determine all public offense less than felony. committed within their respective counties, in which *the fine,* by law, does not exceed *$100* or *the imprisonment thirty days.*

LIMITATION OF ACTIONS.

Action for injuries to the person or reputation; for a statute penalty, and to enforce a mechanics' lien, must be brought in two (2) years.

Those against a public officer within three (3) years.

Those founded on unwritten contracts: for injuries to property; for relief on the ground of fraud; and all other actions not otherwise provided for, within five (5) years.

Those founded on written contracts: on judgments of any court (except those provided for in next section), and for the recovery of real property, within ten (10) years.

Those founded on judgment of any court of record in the United States, within twenty (20) years.

All above limits, except those for penalties and forfeitures, are extended in favor of minors and insane persons, until one year after the disability is removed—time during which defendant is a non-resident of the State shall not be included in computing any of the above periods.

Actions for the recovery of real property, sold for non-payment of taxes, must be brought within five years after the Treasurer's Deed is executed and recorded, except where a minor or convict or insane person is the owner, and they shall be allowed five years after disability is removed, in which to bring action.

JURORS.

All qualified electors of the State, of good moral character, sound judgment, and in full possession of the senses of hearing and seeing, are competent jurors in their respective counties.

United States officers, practicing attorneys, physicians and clergymen, acting professors or teachers in institutions of learning and persons disabled by bodily infirmity or over sixty-five years of age, are exempt from liability to act as jurors.

Any person may be excused from serving on a jury when his own interests or the public's will be materially injured by his attendance, or when the state of his health, or the death, or sickness of his family requires his absence.

CAPITAL PUNISHMENT

was restored by the Seventeenth General Assembly, making it optional with the jury to inflict it or not.

A MARRIED WOMAN

may convey or incumber real estate, or interest therein, belonging to her; may control the same or contract with reference thereto, as other persons may convey, incumber, control or contract.

She may own, acquire, hold, convey and devise property, as her husband may.

Her husband is not liable for civil injuries committed by her.

She may convey property to her husband, and he may convey to her.

She may constitute her husband her attorney in fact.

EXEMPTIONS FROM EXECUTION.

A resident of the State and head of a family may hold the following property exempt from execution: All wearing apparel of himself and family kept for actual use and suitable to the condition, and the trunks or other receptacles necessary to contain the same, one musket or rifle and shot-gun; all private libraries, family Bibles, portraits, pictures, musical instruments, and paintings not kept for the purpose of sale; a seat or pew occupied by the debtor or his family in any house of public worship; an interest in a public or private burying ground not exceeding one acre; two cows and a calf; one horse, unless a horse is exempt as hereinafter provided; fifty sheep and the wool therefrom, and the materials manufactured from said wool; six stands of bees; five hogs and all pigs under six months; the necessary food for exempted animals for six months; all flax raised from one acre of ground, and manufactures therefrom; one bedstead and necessary bedding for every two in the family; all cloth manufactured by the defendant not exceeding one hundred yards; household and kitchen furniture not exceeding $200 in value; all spinning wheels and looms; one sewing machine and other instruments of domestic labor kept for actual use; the necessary provisions and fuel for the use of the family for six months; the proper tools, instruments, or books of the debtor, if a farmer, mechanic, surveyor, clergyman, lawyer, physician, teacher or professor; the horse or the team, consisting of not more than two horses or mules, or two yokes of cattle, and the wagon or other vehicle, with the proper harness or tackle, by the use of which the debtor, if a physician, public officer, farmer, teamster or other laborer, habitually earns his living; and to the debtor, if a printer, there shall also be exempt a printing press and the types, furniture and material necessary for the use of such printing press, and a newspaper office to the value of twelve hundred dollars; the earnings of such debtor, or those of his family, at any time within ninety days next preceding the levy.

Persons unmarried and not the head of a family, and non-residents, have exempt their own ordinary wearing apparel and trunks to contain the same.

There is also exempt, to a head of a family, a homestead, not exceeding forty acres; or, if inside city limits, one-half acre with improvements, value not limited. The homestead is liable for all debts contracte1 prior to its acquisition as such, and is subject to mechanics' lien for work or material furnished for the same.

An article, otherwise exempt, is liable, on execution, for the purchase money thereof.

Where a debtor, if a head of a family, has started to leave the State, he shall have exempt only the ordinary wearing apparel of himself and family, and other property in addition, as he may select, in all not exceeding seventy-five dollars in value.

A policy of life insurance shall inure to the separate use of the husband or wife and children, entirely independent of his or her creditors.

ESTRAYS.

An unbroken animal shall not be taken up as an estray between May 1st and November 1st, of each year, unless the same be found within the lawful enclosure of a householder who alone can take up such animal, unless some other person gives him notice of the fact of such animal coming on his place; and if he fails, within five days thereafter, to take up such estray, any other householder of the township may take up such estray and proceed with it as if taken on his own premises, provided he shall prove to the Justice of the Peace such notice, and shall make affidavit where such estray was taken up.

Any swine, sheep, goat, horse, neat cattle or other animal distrained (for damage done to one's enclosure), when the owner is not known, shall be treated as an estray.

Within five days after taking up an estray, notice, containing a full description thereof, shall be posted up in three of the most public places in the township; and in ten days, the person taking up such estray shall go before a Justice of the Peace in the township and make oath as to where such estray was taken up, and that the marks or brands have not been altered, to his knowledge. The estray shall then be appraised, by order of the Justice, and the appraisment, description of the size, age, color, sex, marks and brands of the estray shall be entered by the Justice in a book kept for that purpose, and he shall, within ten days thereafter, send a certified copy thereof to the County Auditor.

When the appraised value of an estray does not exceed five dollars, the Justice need not proceed further than to enter the description of the estray on his book, and if no owner appears within six months, the property shall vest in the finder, if he has complied with the law and paid all costs.

Where appraised value of estray exceeds five and is less than ten dollars, if no owner appears in nine months, the finder has the property, if he has complied with the law and paid costs.

An estray, legally taken up, may be used or worked with care and moderation.

If any person unlawfully take up an estray, or take up an estray and fail to comply with the law regarding estrays, or use or work it contrary to above, or work it before having it appraised, or keep such estray out of the county more than five days at one time, before acquiring ownership, such offender shall forfeit to the county twenty dollars, and the owner may recover double damages with costs.

If the owner of any estate fail to claim and prove his title for one year after the taking up, and the finder shall have complied with the law, a complete title vests in the finder.

But if the owner appear within eighteen months from the taking up, prove his ownership and pay all costs and expenses, the finder shall pay him the appraised value of such estray. or may, at his option, deliver up the estray.

WOLF SCALPS.

A bounty of one dollar is paid for wolf scalps.

MARKS AND BRANDS.

Any person may adopt his own mark or brand for his domestic animals, and have a description thereof recorded by the Township Clerk.

No person shall adopt the recorded mark or brand of any other person residing in his township.

DAMAGES FROM TRESPASS.

When any person's lands are enclosed by a *lawful* fence, the owner of any domestic animal injuring said lands is liable for the damages, and the damages may be recovered by suit against the owner, or may be made by distraining the animals doing the damage; and if the party injured elects to recover by action against the owner, no appraisement need be made by the Trustees, as in case of distraint.

When trespassing animals are distrained, within twenty-four hours, Sunday not included, the party injured shall notify the owner of said animals, if known; and if the owner fails to satisfy the party within twenty-four hours thereafter, the party shall have the township Trustees assess the damage, and notice shall be posted up in three conspicuous places in the township, that the stock or part thereof, shall, *on the tenth day after posting the notice*, between the hours of 1 and 3 P. M., be sold to the highest bidder, to satisfy said damages, with costs.

Appeal lies, within twenty days, from the action of the Trustees, to the Circuit Court.

Where stock is retained, by police regulation, or by law, from running at large, any person injured in his improved or cultivated lands by any domestic animal, may, by action against the owner of such animal, or by distraining such animal, recover his damages, whether the lands whereon the injury was done were inclosed by a lawful fence or not.

FENCES.

A lawful fence is fifty-four inches high, made of rails, wire or boards, with posts not more than ten feet apart where rails are used, and eight feet where boards are used; substantially built and kept in good repair; or any other fence which, in the opinion of the Fence Viewers, shall be declared a lawful fence—provided the lower rail, wire or board be not more than twenty nor less than sixteen inches from the ground.

The respective owners of lands enclosed with fences shall maintain partition fences between their own and next adjoining enclosure so long as they improve them in equal shares, unless otherwise agreed between them.

If any party neglect to maintain such partition fence as he should maintain, the Fence Viewers (the township Trustees), upon complaint of aggrieved party, may, upon due notice to both parties, examine the fence, and, if found insufficient, notify the delinquent party, *in writing*, to repair or re-build the same within such time as they judge reasonable.

If the fence be not repaired or rebuilt accordingly, the complainant may do so, and the same being adjudged sufficient by the Fence Viewers, and the value thereof, with their fees, being ascertained and certified under their hands, the complainant may demand of the delinquent the sum so ascertained, and if the same be not paid in one month after demand, may recover it with one per cent a month interest, by action.

In case of disputes, the Fence Viewers may decide as to who shall erect or maintain partition fences, and in what time the same shall be done; and in case any party neglect to maintain or erect such part as may be assigned to him, the aggrieved party may erect and maintain the same, and recover double damages.

No person, not wishing his land inclosed, and not using it otherwise than in common, shall be compelled to maintain any partition fence; but when he uses or incloses his land otherwise than in common, he shall contribute to the partition fences.

Where parties have had their lands inclosed in common, and one of the owners desires to occupy his separate and apart from the other, and the other refuses to divide the line or build a sufficient fence on the line when divided, the Fence Fiewers may divide and assign, and upon neglect of the other to build as ordered by the Viewers, the one may build the other's part and recover as above.

And when one incloses land which has lain uninclosed, he must pay for one-half of each partition fence between himself and his neighbors.

Where one desires to lay not less than twenty feet of his lands, adjoining his neighbor, out to the public to be used in common, he must give his neighbor six months' notice thereof.

Where a fence has been built on the land of another through mistake, the owner may enter upon such premises and remove his fence and material within six months after the division line has been ascertained. Where the material to build such a fence has been taken from the land on which it was built, then, before it can be removed, the person claiming must first pay for such material to the owner of the land from which it was taken, nor shall such a fence be removed at a time when the removal will throw open or expose the crops of the other party; a reasonable time must be given beyond the six months to remove crops.

MECHANICS' LIENS.

Every mechanic, or other person who shall do any labor upon, or furnish any materials, machinery or fixtures for any building, erection or other improvement upon land, including those engaged in the construction or repair of any work of internal improvement, by virtue of any contract with the owner, his agent, trustee, contractor, or sub-contractor, shall have a lien, on complying with the forms of law, upon the building or other improvement for his labor done or materials furnished.

It would take too large a space to detail the manner in which a sub-contractor secures his lien. He should file, within thirty days after the last of the labor was performed, or the last of the material shall have been furnished, with the Clerk of the District Court a true account of the amount due him, after allowing all credits, setting fort the time when such material was furnished or labor performed, and when completed, and containing a correct description of the property sought to be charged with the lien, and the whole verified by affidavit.

A principal contractor must file such an affidavit within ninety days, as above.

Ordinarily, there are so many points to be examined in order to secure a mechanics' lien, that it is much better, unless one is accustomed to managing such liens, to consult at once with an attorney.

Remember that the proper time to file the claim is ninety days for a principal contractor, thirty days for a sub-contractor, as above; and that actions to enforce these liens must be commenced within two years, and the rest can much better better be done with an attorney.

ROADS AND BRIDGES.

Persons meeting each other on the public highways, shall give one-half of the same by turning to the right. All persons failing to observe this rule shall be liable to pay all damages resulting therefrom, together with a fine, not exceeding five dollars.

The prosecution must be instituted on the complaint of the person wronged.

Any person guilty of racing horses, or driving upon the public highway, in a manner likely to endanger the persons or the lives of others, shall, on conviction, be fined not exceeding one hundred dollars or imprisoned not exceeding thirty days.

It is a misdemeanor, without authority from the proper Road Supervisor, to break upon, plow or dig within the boundary lines of any public highway.

The money tax levied upon the property in each road district in each township (except the general Township Fund, set apart for purchasing tools, machinery and guide boards), whether collected by the Road Supervisor or County Treasurer, shall be expended for highway purposes in that district, and no part thereof shall be paid out or expended for the benefit of another district.

The Road Supervisor of each district, is bound to keep the roads and bridges therein, in as good condition as the funds at his disposal will permit; to put guide boards at cross roads and forks of highways in his district; and when notified in writing that any portion of the public highway, or any bridge is unsafe, must in a reasonable time repair the same, and for this purpose may call out any or all the able bodied men in the district, but not more than two days at one time, without their consent.

Also, when notified in writing, of the growth of any Canada thistles upon vacant or non-resident lands or lots, within his district, the owner, lessee or agent thereof being unknown, shall cause the same to be destroyed.

Bridges when erected or maintained by the public, are parts of the highway, and must not be less than sixteen feet wide.

A penalty is imposed upon any one who rides or drives faster than a walk across any such bridge.

The manner of establishing, vacating or altering roads, etc., is so well known to all township officers, that it is sufficient here to say that the first step is by petition, filed in the Auditor's office, addressed in substance as follows:

The Board of Supervisors of ——— County: The undersigned asks that a highway, commencing at ——— and running thence ——— and terminating at ———, be established, vacated or altered (as the case may be).

When the petition is filed, all necessary and succeeding steps will be shown and explained to the petitioners by the Auditor.

ADOPTION OF CHILDREN.

Any person competent to make a will can adopt as his own the minor child of another. The consent of both parents, if living and not divorced or separated. and if divorced or separated, or if unmarried, the consent of the parent lawfully having the custody of the child; or if either parent is dead, then the consent of the survivor, or if both parents be dead, or the child have been and remain abandoned by them, then the consent of the Mayor of the city where the child is living.or if not in the city, then of the Clerk of the Circuit Court of the county shall be given to such adoption by an instrument in writing, signed by the party or parties consenting, and stating the names of the parties, if known, the name of the child, if known, the name of the person adopting such child, and the residence of all, if known, and declaring the name by which the child is hereafter to be called and known, and stating, also, that such child is given to the person adopting, for the purpose of adoption as his own child.

The person adopting shall also sign said instrument, and all the parties shall acknowledge the same in the manner that deeds conveying lands shall be acknowledged.

The instrument shall be recorded in the office of the County Recorder.

SURVEYORS AND SURVEYS.

There is in every county elected a Surveyor known as County Surveyor, who has power to appoint deputies, for whose official acts he is responsible. It is the duty of the County Surveyor, either by himself or his Deputy, to make all surveys that he may be called upon to make within his county as soon as may be after application is made. The necessary chainmen and other assistance must be employed by the person requiring the same to be done, and.to be by him paid, unless otherwise agreed: but the chainmen must be disinterested persons and approved by the Surveyor and sworn by him to measure justly and impartially. Previous to any survey. he shall furnish himself with a copy of the field notes of the original survey of the same land, if there be any in the office of the County Auditor, and his survey shall be made in accordance therewith.

Their fees are three dollars per day. For certified copies of field notes. twenty-five cents.

SUPPORT OF POOR.

The father. mother and children of any poor person who has applied for aid, and who is unable to maintain himself by work, shall, jointly or severally, maintain such poor person in such manner as may be approved by the Township Trustees.

In the absence or inability of nearer relatives, the same liability shall extend to the grandparents, if of ability without personal labor, and to the male grandchildren who are of ability, by personal labor or otherwise.

The Township Trustees may, upon the failure of such relative to maintain a poor person, who has made application for relief, apply to the Circuit Court for an order to compel the same.

Upon ten days' notice, in writing, to the parties sought to be charged, a hearing may be had, and an order made for entire or partial support of the poor person.

Appeal may be taken from such judgment as from other judgments of the Circuit Court.

When any person, having any estate, abandons either children, wife or husband, leaving them chargeable, or likely to become chargeable, upon the public for support, upon proof of above fact, an order may be had from the Clerk of the Circuit Court, or Judge, authorizing the Trustees or the Sheriff to take into possession such estate.

The Court may direct such personal estate to be sold, to be applied, as well as the rents and profits of the real estate, if any, to the support of children, wife or husband.

If the party against whom the order is issued return and support the person abandoned, or give security for the same, the order shall be discharged, and the property taken returned.

The mode of relief for the poor, through the action of the Township Trustees, or the action of the Board of Supervisors, is so well known to every township officer, and the circumstances attending application for relief are so varied, that it need now only be said that it is the duty of each county to provide for its poor, no matter at what place they may be.

LANDLORD AND TENANT.

A tenant giving notice to quit demised premises at a time named, and afterward holding over, and a tenant or his assignee willfully holding over the premises after the term, and after notice to quit, shall pay double rent.

Any person in possession of real property, with the assent of the owner, is presumed to be a tenant at will until the contrary is shown.

Thirty days' notice, in writing, is necessary to be given by either party before he can terminate a tenancy at will; but when, in any case, a rent is reserved payable at intervals of less than thirty days, the length of notice need not be greater than such interval between the days of payment. In case of tenants occupying and cultivating farms, the notice must fix the termination of the tenancy to take place on the 1st day of March, except in cases of field tenants or croppers, whose leases shall be held to expire when the crop is harvested; provided, that in case of a crop of corn, it shall not be later than the 1st day of December, unless otherwise agreed upon. But when an express agreement is made, whether the same has been reduced to writing or not, the tenancy shall cease at the time agreed upon, without notice.

If such tenant cannot be found in the county, the notices above required may be given to any sub-tenant or other person in possession of the premises; or, if the premises be vacant, by affixing the notice to the principal door of the building or in some conspicuous position on the land, if there be no building.

The landlord shall have a lien for his rent upon all the crops grown on the premises, and upon any other personal property of the tenant used on the premises during the term, and not exempt from execution, for the period of one year after a year's rent or the rent of a shorter period claimed falls due; but such lien shall not continue more than six months after the expiration of the term.

The lien may be effected by the commencement of an action, within the period above described, for the rent alone;   d the landlord is entitled to a writ of attachment, upon filing an affidavit that the action is commenced to recover rent accrued within one year previous thereto upon the premises described in the affidavit.

WEIGHTS AND MEASURES.

Whenever any of the following articles shall be contracted for, or sold or delivered, and no special contract or agreement shall be made to the contrary, the weight per bushel shall be as follows, to-wit:

Apples, Peaches or Quinces........48	Sand.......................130
Cherries, Grapes, Currants or Goose-	Sorghum Seed....................30
berries..........................40	Broom Corn Seed................30
Strawberries, Raspberries or Black-	Buckwheat..... 52
berries...........................32	Salt.............................50
Osage Orange Seed................32	Barley.... 48
Millet Seed......................45	Corn Meal.......................48
Stone Coal......................80	Castor Beans....................46
Lime............................80	Timothy Seed....................45
Corn in the ear.... 70	Hemp Seed.......................44
Wheat...........................60	Dried Peaches...................33
Potatoes........ 60	Oats............................33
Beans...........................60	Dried Apples....................24
Clover Seed......................60	Bran............................20
Onions..................... 57	Blue Grass Seed.................14
Shelled Corn....................56	Hungarian Grass Seed...........45
Rye.............................56	Flax Seed.......................56
Sweet Potatoes...................46	

Penalty for giving less than above standard is treble damages and costs and five dollars addition thereto as a fine.

DEFINITION OF COMMERCIAL TERMS.

$——means dollars, being a contraction of U. S., which was formerly placed before any denomination of money, and meant, as it means now, United States Currency.

£——means *pounds*, English money.

@ stands for *at* or *to*; ℔ for *pounds*, and bbl. for *barrels*; ℔ for *per* or *by the*. Thus, Butter sells at 20@30c ℔ ℔, and Flour at $8@$12 ℔ bbl.

May 1. Wheat sells at $1.20@$1.25, "seller June." *Seller June* means that the person who sells the wheat has the privilege of delivering it at any time during the month of June.

Selling *short*, is contracting to deliver a certain amount of grain or stock, at a fixed price, within a certain length of time, when the seller has not the stock on hand. It is for the interest of the person selling "short" to depress the market as much as possible, in order that he may buy and fill his contract at a profit. Hence the "shorts" are termed "bears."

Buying *long*, is to contract to purchase a certain amount of grain or shares of stock at a fixed price, deliverable within a stipulated time, expecting to make a profit by the rise in prices. The "longs" are termed "bulls," as it is for their interest to "operate" so as to "toss" the prices upward as much as possible.

NOTES.

Form of note is legal, worded in the simplest way, so that the amount and time of payment are mentioned:

$100.   CHICAGO, Ill., Sept. 15, 1876.

Sixty days from date I promise to pay to E. F. Brown or order, one hundred dollars, for value received.   L. D. LOWRY.

A note to be payable in anything else than money needs only the facts substituted for money in the above form.

ORDERS.

Orders should be worded simply, thus:

Mr. F. H. COATS: CHICAGO, Sept. 15, 1876.

Please pay to H. Birdsall twenty-five dollars, and charge to
                                             F. D. SILVA.

RECEIPTS.

Receipts should always state when received and what for, thus:

$100.   CHICAGO, Sept. 15, 1876.

Received of J. W. Davis, one hundred dollars, for services rendered in grading his lot in Fort Madison, on account.
                                          THOMAS BRADY.

If receipt is in full, it should be so stated.

BILLS OF PURCHASE.

W. N. MASON,   SALEM, Illinois, Sept. 18, 1876.
                    Bought of A. A. GRAHAM.
4 Bushels of Seed Wheat at $1.50.......................$6 00
2 seamless Sacks   "   30...................... 60
                                                           ———
                    Received payment, $6 60
                                        A. A. GRAHAM.

CONFESSION OF JUDGMENT.

$——.   ——, Iowa, ——, 18—.
—— after date — promises to pay to the order of ——, ——
dollars, at ——, for value received, with interest at ten per cent.
per annum after —— until paid. Interest payable ——, and on
interest not paid when due, interest at same rate and conditions.

A failure to pay said interest, or any part thereof, within 20 days after due,
shall cause the whole note to become due and collectible at once.
If this note is sued, or judgment is confessed hereon, $—— shall b· allowed
as attorney fees.

No. —.   P. O. ——,   ——.

CONFESSION OF JUDGMENT.

— vs. —.   In —— Court of —— County, Iowa, ———, of
—— County, Iowa, do hereby confess that —— justly indebted
to ——, in the sum of —— dollars, and the further sum of
$—— as attorney fees, with interest thereon at ten per cent. from
——, and — hereby confess judgment against —— as defendant in favor of said ——, for said sum of $——, and $— as
attorney fees, hereby authorizing the Clerk of the —— Court of
said county to enter up judgment for said sum against —— with
costs, and interest at 10 per cent. from ——, the interest to be
paid ——.
    Said debt and judgment being for——,
    It is especially agreed, however, That if this judgment is paid
within twenty days after due, no attorney fees need be paid. And
—— hereby sell, convey and release all right of homestead we now
occupy in favor of said —— so far as this judgment is concerned,
and agree that it shall be liable on execution for this judgment.
    Dated ——, 18- ·.
                                        ——— ———,
                                        ——— ———.

THE STATE OF IOWA, {
    ——— County. }
    —— being duly sworn according to law, depose and say that
the foregoing statement and Confession of Judgment was read
over to ——, and that — understood the contents thereof, and

that the statements contained therein are true, and that the sums therein mentioned are justly to become due said ———— as afore-said.

Sworn to and subscribed before me and in may presence by the said ———— this —— day of ————, 18—.

———— ————, Notary Public.

ARTICLES OF AGREEMENT.

An agreement is where one party promises to another to do a certain thing in a certain time for a stipulated sum. Good business men always reduce an agreement to writing, which nearly always saves misunderstandings and trouble. No particular form is necessary, but the facts must be clearly and explicitly stated, and there must, to make it valid, be a reasonable consideration.

GENERAL FORM OF AGREEMENT.

THIS AGREEMENT, made the second day of June, 1878, between John Jones, of Keokuk. County of Lee, State of Iowa, of the first part, and Thomas Whiteside, of the same place, of the second part—

WITNESSETH, That the said John Jones, in consideration of the agreement of the party of the second part, hereinafter contained, contracts and agrees to and with the said Thomas Whiteside, that he will deliver in good and marketable condition, at the Village of Melrose, Iowa, during the month of November, of this year; One Hundred Tons of Prairie Hay, in the following lots,* and at the following specified terms; namely, twenty-five tons by the seventh of November, twenty-five tons additional by the four-teenth of the month, twenty-five tons more by the twenty-first, and the entire one hundred tons to be all delivered by the thirtieth of November.

And the said Thomas Whiteside, in consideration of the prompt fulfillment of this contract, on the part of the party of the first part, contracts to and agrees with the said John Jones, to pay for said hay five dollars per ton, for each ton as soon as delivered.

In case of failure of agreement by either of the parties hereto, it is hereby stipulated and agreed that the party so failing shall pay to the other One Hundred dollars, as fixed and settled damages.

In witness whereof, we have hereunto set our hands the day and year first above written.   JOHN JONES,

THOMAS WHITESIDE.

AGREEMENT WITH CLERK FOR SERVICES.

THIS AGREEMENT, made the first day of May, one thousand eight hundred and seventy-eight, between Reuben Stone, of Du-buque, County of Dubuque, State of Iowa, party of the first part, and George Barclay, of McGregor, County of Clayton, State of Iowa, party of the second part—

WITNESSETH, that said George Barclay agrees faithfully and diligently to work as clerk and salesman for the said Reuben Stone, for and during the space of one year from the date thereof, should both live such length of time, without absenting himself from his occupation; during which time he, the said Barclay, in the store of said Stone, of Dubuque, will carefully and honestly attend, doing and performing all duties as clerk and salesman aforesaid, in accordance and in all respects as directed and desired by the said Stone.

In consideration of which services, so to be rendered by the said Barclay, the said Stone agrees to pay to said Barclay the annual sum of one thousand dollars, payable in twelve equal monthly payments, each upon the last day of each month; provided that all dues for days of absence from business by said Barclay, shall be deducted from the sum otherwise by the agreement due and payable by the said Stone to the said Barclay.

Witness our hands.   REUBEN STONE.
                                              GEORGE BARCLAY.

BILLS OF SALE.

A bill of sale is a written agreement to another party, for a consideration to convey his right and interest in the personal property. *The purchaser must take actual possession of the property, or the bill of sale must be acknowledged and recorded.*

COMMON FORM OF BILL OF SALE.

KNOW ALL MEN by this instrument, that I, Louis Clay, of Burlington, Iowa, of the first part, for and in consideration of Five Hundred and Ten Dollars, to me paid by John Floyd, of the same place, of the second part, the receipt whereof is hereby acknowledged, have sold, and by this instrument do convey unto the said Floyd, party of the second part, his executors, administrators and assigns, my undivided half of ten acres of corn, now growing on the farm of Thomas Tyrell, in the town above mentioned; one pair of horses; sixteen sheep, and five cows, belonging to me and in my possession at the farm aforesaid; to have and to hold the same unto the party of the second part, his executors and assigns forever. And I do, for myself and legal representatives, agree with the said party of the second part, and his legal representatives, to warrant and defend the sale of the afore-mentioned property and chattels unto the said party of the second part, and his legal representatives, against all and every person whatsoever.

In witness whereof, I have hereunto affixed my hand, this tenth day of October, one thousand eight hundred and seventy-six.

                                              LOUIS CLAY.

NOTICE TO QUIT.

To JOHN WONTPAY:

You are hereby notified to quit the possession of the premises you now occupy to wit:

[*Insert Description.*]

on or before thirty days from the date of this notice.

Dated January 1, 1878.   Landlord.

[*Reverse for Notice to Landlord.*]

GENERAL FORM OF WILL FOR REAL AND PERSONAL PROPERTY.

1. Charles Mansfield, of the town of Bellevue, County of Jackson, State of Iowa, being aware of the uncertainty of life, and in failing health, but of sound mind and memory, do make and declare this to be my last will and testament, in manner following, to-wit:

First. I give, devise and bequeath unto my eldest son, Sidney H. Mansfield, the sum of Two Thousand Dollars of bank stock, now in the Third National Bank, of Cincinnati, Ohio, and the farm owned by myself, in the Township of Iowa, consisting of one hundred and sixty acres, with all the houses, tenements and improvements thereunto belonging; to have and to hold unto my said son, his heirs and assigns, forever.

Second. I give, devise and bequeath to each of my two daughters, Anna Louise Mansfield and Ida Clara Mansfield, each Two Thousand Dollars in bank stock in the Third National Bank of Cincinnati, Ohio; and also, each one quarter section of land, owned by myself, situated in the Township of Fairfield, and recorded in my name in the Recorder's office, in the county where such land is located. The north one hundred and sixty acres of said half section is devised to my eldest daughter, Anna Louise.

Third. I give, devise and bequeath to my son Frank Alfred Mansfield, five shares of railroad stock in the Baltimore & Ohio Railroad, and my one hundred and sixty acres of land, and saw-mill thereon, situated in Manistee, Michigan, with all the improvements and appurtenances thereunto belonging, which said real estate is recorded in my name, in the county where situated.

Fourth. I give to my wife, Victoria Elizabeth Mansfield, all my household furniture, goods, chattels and personal property, about my home, not hitherto disposed of, including Eight Thousand Dollars of bank stock in the Third National Bank of Cincinnati, Ohio, fifteen shares in the Baltimore & Ohio Railroad, and the free and unrestricted use, possession and benefit of the home farm so long as she may live, in lieu of dower, to which she is entitled by law—said farm being my present place of residence.

Fifth. I bequeath to my invalid father, Elijah H. Mansfield the income from rents of my store building at 145 Jackson street

Chicago, Illinois, during the term of his natural life. Said building and land therewith to revert to my said sons and daughters in equal proportion, upon the demise of my said father.

Sixth. It is also my will and desire that, at the death of my wife, Victoria Elizabeth Mansfield, or at any time when she may arrange to relinquish her life interest in the above mentioned homestead, the same may revert to my above named children, or to the lawful heirs of each.

And lastly. I nominate and appoint as the executors of this, my last will and testament, my wife, Victoria Elizabeth Mansfield and my eldest son, Sidney H. Mansfield.

I further direct that my debts and necessary funeral expenses shall be paid from moneys now on deposit in the Savings Bank of Bellevue, the residue of such moneys to revert to my wife, Victoria Elizabeth Mansfield, for her use forever.

In witness whereof, I Charles Mansfield, to this my last will and testament, have hereunto set my hand and seal, this fourth day of April, eighteen hundred and seventy-two.

CHARLES MANSFIELD.

Signed and declared by Charles Mansfield, as and for his last will and testament, in the presence of us, who, at his request, and in his presence, and in the presence of each other, have subscribed our names hereunto as witness thereof.

PETER A. SCHENCK, Dubuque, Iowa.
FRANK E. DENT, Bellevue, Iowa.

CODICIL.

Whereas I, Charles Mansfield, did, on the fourth day of April, one thousand eight hundred and seventy-two, make my last will and testament, I do now, by this writing, add this codicil to my said will, to be taken as a part thereof.

Whereas, by the dispensation of Providence, my daughter, Anna Louise, has deceased, November fifth, eighteen hundred and seventy-three, and whereas a son has been born to me, which son is now christened Richard Albert Mansfield. I give and bequeath unto him my gold watch, and all right, interest and title in lands and bank stock and chattels bequeathed to my deceased daughter, Anna Louise, in the body of this will.

In witness whereof, I hereunto placed my hand and seal, this tenth day of March, eighteen hundred and seventy-five.

CHARLES MANSFIELD.

Signed, sealed, published and declared to us by the testator, Charles Mansfield, as and for a codicil to be annexed to his last will and testament. And we, at his request, and in his presence, and in the presence of each other, have subscribed our names as witnesses thereto, at the date hereof.

FRANK E. DENT, Bellevue, Iowa.
JOHN C. SHAY, Bellevue, Iowa.

9

(Form No. 1.)

SATISFACTION OF MORTGAGE.

STATE OF IOWA, } ss.
 ....County,   }

I,......, of the County of...., State of Iowa, do hereby acknowledge that a certain Indenture of......., bearing date the ....day of...., A. D. 18.., made and executed by......and...... his wife, to said......on the following described Real Estate, in the County of...., and State of Iowa, to-wit: (here insert description) and filed for record in the office of the Recorder of the County of...., and State of Iowa, on the....day of......, A. D. 18.., at....o'clock .M.; and recorded in Book of ......Mortgage Records, on page...., is redeemed, paid off, satisfied and discharged in full.   ...... [SEAL.]

STATE OF IOWA, } ss.
 ....County,   }

Be it Remembered. That, on this.... day of ...., A. D. 18.., before me the undersigned, a ...... in and for said county, personally appeared ...., to me personally known to be the identical person who executed the above (satisfaction of mortgage) as grantor, and acknowledged .... signature thereto to be .... voluntary act and deed.

Witness my hand and ...... seal. the day and year last above written.   ....

ONE FORM OF REAL ESTATE MORTGAGE.

KNOW ALL MEN BY THESE PRESENTS: That ...., of .... County, and State of ...., in consideration of ...... dollars, in hand paid by ...... of .... County, and State of .....do hereby sell and convey unto the said ..... the following described premises, situated in the County of ...., and State of ...., to-wit: (here insert description) and .... do hereby covenant with the said ...... that .... lawfully seized of said premises, that they are free from incumbrance, that .... have good right and lawful authority to sell and convey the same; and ...: do hereby covenant to warrant and defend the same against the lawful claims of all persons whomsoever. To be void upon condition that the said ...... shall pay the full amount of principal and interest at the time therein specified, of .... certain promissory note for the sum of .... dollars.

One note for $...., due ....., 18.., with interest annually at ... per cent.
One note for $...., due ....., 18.., with interest annually at ... per cent.
One note for $...., due .... , 18.., with interest annually at ... per cent.

One note for $..., due ....., 18... with interest annually at ... per cent.

And the said Mortgagor agrees to pay all taxes that may be levied upon the above described premises. It is also agreed by the Mortgagor that if it becomes necessary to foreclose this mortgage, a reasonable amount shall be allowed as an attorney's fee for foreclosing. And the said ...... hereby relinquishes all her right of dower and homestead in and to the above described premises.

Signed the .... day of ...., A. D. 18...

....
....

[Acknowledge as in Form No. 1.]

SECOND FORM OF REAL ESTATE MORTGAGE.

THIS INDENTURE, made and executed .... by and between .... of the county of .... and State of...., part of the first part, and ...... of the county of .... and State of .... party of the second part, *Witnesseth*, that the said part of the first part, for and in consideration of the sum of .... dollars, paid by the said party of the second part, the receipt of which is hereby acknowledged, have granted and sold, and do by these presents, grant, bargain, sell, convey and confirm, unto the said party of the second part, ... heirs and assigns forever, the certain tract or parcel of real estate situated in the county of .... and State of ..... described as follows, to-wit:

(Here insert description.)

The said part of the first part represent to and covenant with the part of the second part, that he have good right to sell and convey said premises, that they are free from encumbrance and that he will warrant and defend them against the lawful claims of all persons whomsoever, and do expressly hereby release all rights of dower in and to said premises, and relinquish and convey all rights of homestead therein.

This Instrument is made, executed and delivered upon the following conditions, to-wit:

First. Said first part agree to pay said .... or order ....

Second. Said first part further agree as is stipulated in said note, that if he shall fail to pay any of said interest when due, it shall bear interest at the rate of ten per cent. per annum, from the time the same becomes due, and this mortgage shall stand as security for the same.

Third. Said first part further agree that he will pay all taxes and assessments levied upon said real estate before they become delinquent, and if not paid the holder of this mortgage may declare the whole sum of money herein secured due and collectible at once, or he may elect to pay such taxes or assessments, and be entitled to interest on the same at the rate of ten per cent. per annum, and this mortgage shall stand as security for the amount so paid.

Fourth. Said first part further agree that if he fail to pay any of said money, either principal or interest, within .... days after the same becomes due, or fail to conform or comply with any of the foregoing conditions or agreements, the whole sum herein secured shall become due and payable at once. and this mortgage may thereupon be foreclosed immediately for the whole of said money, interest and costs.

Fifth. Said first part further agree that in the event of the non-payment of either principal, interest or taxes when due, and upon the filing of a bill of foreclosure of this mortgage, an attorney's fee of .... dollars shall become due and payable, and shall be by the court taxed, and this mortgage shall stand as security therefor, and the same shall be included in the decree of foreclosure and shall be made by the Sheriff on general or special execution with the other money, interest and costs, and the contract embodied in this mortgage and the note described herein, shall in all respects be governed, constructed and adjudged by the laws of ......, where the same is made. The foregoing conditions being performed, this conveyance to be void, otherwise in full force and virtue.

. . . .
. . . .

[Acknowledge as in form No. 1.]

FORM OF LEASE.

THIS ARTICLE OF AGREEMENT, Made and entered into on this .... day of ...., A. D. 187., by and between ...., of the county of ......, and State of Iowa, of the first part, and ...... of the county of ......, and State of Iowa, of the second part, witnesseth, that the said party of the first part has this day leased unto the party of the second part the following described premises, to-wit:

Here insert Description.

for the term of .... from and after the .. day of ...., A. D. 187.., at the .... (rent) of .... dollars, to be paid as follows, to-wit:

Here insert Terms.

And it is further agreed that if any rent shall be due and unpaid, or if default be made in any of the covenants herein contained, it shall then be lawful for the said party of the first part to re-enter the said premises, or to destrain for such rent; or he may recover possession thereof, by action of forcible entry and de-

tainer, notwithstanding the provision of Section 3,612 of the
Code of 1873; or he may use any or all of said remedies.

And the said party of the second part agrees to pay to the party
of the first part the rent as above stated, except when said premises
are untenantable by reason of fire, or from any other cause than
the carelessness of the party of the second part, or persons ....
family, or in .... employ, or by superior force and inevitable necessity. An l the said party of the second part covenants that
.... will use the said premises as a ...., and for no other purpose
whatever; and that .... especially will not use said premises, or
permit the same to be used, for any unlawful business or purpose
whatever; that .... will not sell, assign, underlet or relinquish
said premises without the written consent of the lessor, under
penalty of a forfeiture of all .... rights under this lease, at the
election of the party of the first part; and that .... will use all
due care and diligence in guarding said property, with the buildings, gates, fences, trees, vines, shrubbery, etc., from damage by
fire, and the depredations of animals; that .... will keep buildings, gates, fences, etc.. in as good repair as they now are, or may
at any time be placed by the lessor, damages by superior force, inevitable necessity, or fire from any other cause than from the
carelessness of the lessee, or persons of .... family, or in ....
employ, excepted; and that at the expiration of this lease, or upon
a breach by said lessee of any of the said covenants herein contained, ... will, without further notice of any kind, quit and
surrender the possession and occupancy of said premises in as good
condition as reasonable use, natural wear and decay thereof will
permit, damages by fire as aforesaid, superior force, or inevitable
necessity, only excepted.

In witness whereof. the said parties have subscribed their names
on the date first above written.

In presence of .   .
....

FORM OF NOTE.

$....   .... .., 18..,
On or before the .. day of ...., 18.., for value received, I
promise to pay.......... .... or order, ... dollars, with interest from date until paid, at ten per cent. per annum, payable annually, at .... Unpaid interest shall bear interest at ten per
cent. per annum. On failure to pay interest within .... days
after due, the whole sum, principal and interest, shall become due
at once.

[..... ......

CHATTEL MORTGAGE.

KNOW ALL MEN BY THESE PRESENTS: That........ of ....
County, and State of .... in consideration of .... dollars, in hand

paid by ...., of .... County and State of .... do hereby sell and convey unto the said .... the following described personal property, now in the possession of .... in the County .... and State of ...., to-wit:

Here insert Description.

And .... do hereby warrant the title of said property, and that it is free from any incumbrance or lien. The only right or interest retained by grantor in and to said property being the right of redemption as herein provided. This conveyance to be void upon condition that the said grantor shall pay to said grantee, or his assigns, the full amount of principal and interest at the time therein specified, of .... certain promissory notes of even date herewith, for the sum of .... dollars,

One note for $...., due ......, 18.., with interest annually at .... per cent.
One note for $...., due ......, 18.., with interest annually at .... per cent.
One note for $...., due ......, 18.., with interest annually at .... per cent.
One note for $...., due ......, 18.., with interest annually at .... per cent.

The grantor to pay all taxes on said property, and if at any time any part or portion of said notes should be due and unpaid, said grantee may proceed by sale or foreclosure, to collect and pay himself the unpaid balance of said notes, whether due or not, the grantor to pay all necessary expenses of such foreclosure, including $.... Attorney's fees, and whatever remains after paying off said notes and expenses, to be paid over to said grantor.

Signed the .... day of ...., 18...

[Acknowledged as in form No. 1.]   ....

WARRANTY DEED.

KNOW ALL MEN BY THESE PRESENTS : That .... of .... County, and State of ...., in consideration of the sum of ...... Dollars, in hand paid by .... of .... County and State of ...., do hereby sell and convey unto the said .... and to .... heirs and assigns, the following described premises, situated in the County of ...., State of Iowa, to-wit:

Here insert Description.

And I do hereby covenant with the said .... that .. lawfully seized in fee simple, of said premises, that they are free from incumbrance; that .. ha good right and lawful authority to sell the same, and .. do hereby covenant to warrant and defend the said premises and appurtenances thereto belonging, against the lawful claims of all persons whomsoever; and the said .... hereby relinquishes all her right of dower and of homestead in and to the above described premises.

Signed the .... day of ...., A. D. 18...

IN PRESENCE OF

....

[Acknowledged as in Form No. 1.]

QUIT CLAIM DEED.

KNOW ALL MEN BY THESE PRESENTS: That ...... of ..... County, State of ...., in consideration of the sum of .... dollars to .... in hand paid by ...., of .... County, State of ...., the receipt whereof ... do hereby acknowledge, have bargained, sold and quit-claimed, and by these presents do bargain, sell and quit-claim unto the said .... and to .. heirs and assigns forever, all .. right, title, interest, estate, claim and demand, both at law and in equity, and as well in possession as in expectancy, of, in and to the following described premises, to wit: [here insert description] with all and singular the hereditaments and appurtenances thereto belonging.

Signed this ... day of ...., A. D., 18...

SIGNED IN PRESENCE OF ....

....

....

.... [Acknowledged as in form No. 1.]

BOND FOR DEED.

KNOW ALL MEN BY THESE PRESENTS: That .... of ...... County, and State of .... am held and firmly bound unto ...... of .... County, and State of ...., in the sum of ...... Dollars, to be paid to the said ......, his executors or assigns, for which payment well and truly to be made, I bind myself firmly by these presents. Signed the .... day of ...... A. D. 18...

The condition of this obligation is such, that if said obligee shall pay to said obligor, or his assigns, the full amount of principal and interest at the time therein specified, of .. certain promissory note, of even date herewith, for the sum of .... Dollars,

One note for $...., due ......, 18.., with interest annually at .. per cent.

One note for $...., due ......, 18... with interest annually at .. per cent.

One note for $...., due ......, 18.., with interest annually at .. per cent.

and pay all taxes accruing upon the lands herein described, then said obligor shall convey to the said obligee, or his assigns, that certain tract or parcel of real estate, situated in the County of .... and State of Iowa, described as follows, to wit: [here insert description] by a Warranty Deed, with the usual covenants, duly executed and acknowledged.

If said obligee should fail to make the payments as above stipulated, or any part thereof, as the same becomes due, said obligor may at his option, by notice to the obligee terminate his liability under the bond and resume the possession and absolute control of said premises, time being the essence of this agreement.

On the fulfillment of the above conditions this obligation to become void, otherwise to remain in full force and virtue; unless terminated by the obligor as above stipulated.

[Acknowledged as in form No. 1]

CHARITABLE, SCIENTIFIC AND RELIGIOUS ASSOCIATIONS.

Any three or more persons of full age, citizens of the United States, a majority of whom shall be citizens of this State, who desire to associate themselves for benevolent, charitable, scientific, religious or missionary purposes, may make, sign and acknowledge before any officer authorized to take acknowledgements of deeds in this State, and have recorded in the office of the Recorder of the county in which the business of such society is to be conducted, a certificate in writing, in which shall be stated the name or title by which such society shall be known, the particular business and objects of such society, the number of Trustees, Directors or Managers to conduct the same, and the names of the Trustees, Directors or Managers of such society for the first year of its existence.

Upon filing for record the certificate, as aforesaid, the persons who shall have signed and acknowledged such certificate, and their associates and successors, shall, by virtue hereof, be a body politic and corporate by the name stated in such certificate, and that they and their successors shall and may have succession, and shall be persons capable of suing and being sued, and may have and use a common seal, which they may alter or change at pleasure; and they and their successors, by their corporate name, shall be capable of taking, receiving, purchasing and holding real and personal estate and of making by-laws for the management of its affairs, not inconsistent with law.

The society so incorporated may, annually or oftener, elect from its members its Trustees, Directors or Managers at such time and place, and in such manner as may be specified in its by-laws, who shall have the control and management of the affairs and funds of the society, a majority of whom shall be a quorum for the transaction of business, and whenever any vacancy shall happen among such Trustees, Directors or Managers, by death, resignation or neglect to serve, such vacancy shall be filled in such manner as shall be provided by the by-laws of such society. When the body corporate consists of the Trustees, Directors or Managers of any benevolent, charitable, literary, scientific, religious or missionary institution, which is or may be established in the State, and which is or may be under the patronage, control, direction or supervision of any synod, conference, association or other ecclesiastical body in such State, established agreeably to the laws thereof, such ecclesiastical body may nominate and appoint such Trustees, Directors or

Managers, according to usages of the appointing body, and may fill any vacancy which may occur among such Trustees, Directors or Managers; and when any such institution may be under the patronage, control, direction or supervision of two or more of such synods, conferences, associations or other ecclesiastical bodies, such bodies may severally nominate and appoint such proportion of such Trustees, Directors or Managers as shall be agreed upon by those bodies immediately concerned. And any vacancy occurring among such appointees last named, sh ll be filled by the synod, conference, association or body having appointed the last incumbent.

In case any election of Trustees, Directors or Managers shall not be made on the day designated by the by-laws, said society for that cause shall not be dissolved, but such election may take place on any other day selected by such by-laws.

Any corporation formed under this chapter shall be capable of taking, holding or receiving property by virtue of any devise or bequest contained in any last will or testament of any person whatsoever; but no person leaving a wife, child or parent, shall devise or bequeath to such institution or corporation more than one-fourth of his estate after the payment of his debts, and such devise or bequest shall be valid only to the extent of such one-fourth.

Any corporation in this State of an academical character, the membership of which shall consist of lay members and pastors of churches, delegates to any synod, conference or council holding its annual meetings alternately in this and one or more adjoining States, may hold its annual meeting for the election of officers and the transaction of business in any adjoining State to this, at such place therein as the said synod, conference or council shall hold its annual meetings; and the elections so held and business so transacted shall be as legal and binding as if held and transacted at the place of business of the corporation in this State.

The provisions of this chapter shall not extend or apply to any association or individual who shall, in the certificate filed with the Recorder, use or specify a name or style the same as that of any previously existing incorporated society in the county.

The Trustees, Directors or stockholders of any existing benevolent, charitable, scientific, missionary or religious corporation may, by conforming to the requirements of Section 1,095 of this chapter, re-incorporate themselves or continue their existing corporate powers, and all the property and effects of such existing corporation shall vest in and belong to the corporation so re-incorporated or continued.

INTOXICATING LIQUORS.

No intoxicating liquors (alcohol, spirituous and vinous liquors), except wine manufactured from grapes, currants or other fruit grown in the State, shall be manufactured or sold, except for mechanical, medicinal, culinary or sacramental purposes; and even such sale is limited as follows:

Any citizen of the State, except hotel keepers, keepers of saloons, eating houses, grocery keepers and confectioners, is permitted to buy and sell, within the county of his residence, such liquors for such mechanical, etc., purposes only, provided he shall obtain the consent of the Board of Supervisors. In order to get that consent he must get a certificate from a majority of the electors of the town or township or ward in which he desires to sell, that he is of good moral character, and a proper person to sell such liquors.

If the Board of Supervisors grant him permission to sell such liquors, he must give bonds, and shall not sell such liquors at a greater profit than thirty-three per cent. on the cost of the same. Any person having a permit to sell, shall make, on the last Saturday of every month, a return in writing to the Auditor of the county, showing the kind and quantity of the liquors purchased by him since the date of his last report, the price paid and the amount of freights paid on the same; also the kind and quantity of liquors sold by him since the date of his last report, to whom sold, for what purpose and at what price, also the kind and quantity of liquors on hand; which report shall be sworn to by the person having the permit, and shall be kept by the Auditor, subject at all times to the inspection of the public.

No person shall sell or give away any intoxicating liquors, including wine or beer, to any minor, for any purpose whatever, except upon written order of parent, guardian or family physician; or sell the same to an intoxicated person or a person in the habit of becoming intoxicated.

Any person who shall mix any intoxicating liquor with any beer, wine or cider, by him sold, and shall sell or keep for sale, as a beverage, such mixture, shall be punished as for sale of intoxicating liquor.

But nothing in the chapter containing the laws governing the sale, or prohibiting the sale of intoxicating liquors, shall be construed to forbid the sale by the importer thereof of foreign intoxicating liquor, imported under the authority of the laws of the United States, regarding the importation of such liquors, and in accordance with such laws; provided that such liquor, at the time of the sale by the importer, remains in the original casks or packages in which it was by him imported, and in quantities not less than the quantities in which the laws of the United States require such liquors to be imported, and is sold by him in such original casks or packages, and in said quantities only.

All payment or compensation for intoxicating liquor sold in violation of the laws of this State, whether such payments or compensation be in money, goods, lands, labor, or anything else whatsoever, shall be held to have been received in violation of law and equity and good conscience, and to have been received upon a valid promise and agreement of the receiver, in consideration of the receipt thereof, to pay on demand to the person furnishing such consideration, the amount of the money on the just value of the goods or other things.

All sales, transfers, conveyances, mortgages, liens, attachments, pledges and securities of every kind, which, either in whole or in part, shall have been made on account of intoxicating liquors sold contrary to law, shall be utterly null and void.

Negotiable paper in the hands of holders thereof, in good faith, for valuable consideration, without notice of any illegality in its inception or transfer, however, shall not be affected by the above provisions. Neither shall the holder of land or other property who may have taken the same in good faith, without notice of any defect in the title of the person from whom the same was taken, growing out of a violation of the liquor law, be affected by the above provision.

Every wife, child, parent, guardian, employer, or other person, who shall be injured in person or property or means of support, by an intoxicated person, or in consequence of the intoxication, has a right of action against any person who shall, by selling intoxicating liquors, cause the intoxication of such person, for all damages actually sustained as well as exemplary damages.

For any damages recovered, the person and real property (except homestead, as now provided) of the person against whom the damages are recovered, as well as the premises or property, personal or real, occupied and used by him, with consent and knowledge of owner, either for manufacturing or selling intoxicating liquors contrary to law, shall be liable.

The only other exemption, besides the homestead, from this sweeping liability, is that the defendant may have enough for the support of his family for six months, to be determined by the Township Trustee.

No ale, wine, beer or other malt or vinous liquors shall be sold within two miles of the corporate limits of any municipal corporation, except at wholesale, for the purpose of shipment to places outside of such corporation and such two mile limits. The power of the corporation to prohibit or license sale of liquors not prohibited by law is extended over the two miles.

No ale, wine beer or other malt or vinous liquors shall be sold on the day on which any election is held under the laws of this State, within two miles of the place where said election is held; except only that any person holding a permit may sell upon the prescription of a practicing physician.

SUGGESTIONS TO THOSE PURCHASING BOOKS BY SUBSCRIPTION.

The business of *publishing books by subscription*, having so often been brought into disrepute by agents making representations and declarations *not authorized by the publisher*, in order to prevent that as much as possible, and that there may be more general knowledge of the relation such agents bear to their principal, and the law governing such cases, the following statement is made:

A subscription is in the *nature of a contract* of mutual promises, by which the subscriber agrees to *pay a certain sum* for the work described; the *consideration is concurrent* that the publisher shall *publish the book named*, and deliver the same, for which the subscriber is to pay the price named. *The nature and character of the work is described by the prospectus and sample shown.* These should be *carefully examined before subscribing*, as they are the basis and consideration of the promise to pay, and not the too *often exaggerated statements of the agent*, who is *merely employed* to *solicit subscriptions*, for which he is usually *paid a commission* for each subscriber, and has *no authority to change or alter* the conditions upon which the subscriptions are authorized to be made by the publisher. Should the *agent assume* to agree to make the subscription conditional or *modify or change the agreement of the publisher*, as set out by the prospectus and sample, in order to *bind the principal*, the *subscriber* should see that such condition or changes are stated *over or in connection with his signature*, so that the publisher may have notice of the same.

All persons making contracts in reference to matters of this kind, or any other business, should remember *that the law as written is*, that they can *not be altered, varied or rescinded verbally*, but if done at all, must be done in writing. It is therefore important that all persons contemplating subscribing should distinctly understand that all talk before or after the subscription is made, is not admissible as evidence, and is no part of the contract.

Persons employed to solicit subscriptions are known to the trade as canvassers. They are agents appointed to do a particular business in a prescribed mode, and have no authority to do it in any other way to the prejudice of their principal, nor can they bind their principal in any other matter. They can not collect money or agree that payment may be made in anything else but money. They cannot extend the time of payment beyond the time of delivery, nor bind their principal for the payment of expenses incurred in their business.

It would save a great deal of trouble, and often serious loss, if persons, before signing their names to any subscription book, or any written instrument, would examine carefully what it is; if they can not read themselves, call on some one disinterested who can.

PRACTICAL RULES FOR EVERY DAY USE.

How to find the gain or loss per cent. when the cost and selling price are given.

RULE.—Find the difference between the cost and selling price, which will be the gain or loss.

Annex two ciphers to the gain or loss, and divide it by the cost price; the result will be the gain or loss per cent.

How to change gold into currency.

RULE.—Multiply the given sum of gold by the price of gold.

How to change currency into gold.

RULE.—Divide the amount in currency by the price of gold.

How to find each partner's share of the gain or loss in a copartnership business.

RULE.—Divide the whole gain or loss by the entire stock the quotient will be the gain or loss per cent.

Multiply each partner's stock by this per cent., the result will be each one's share of the gain or loss.

How to find gross and net weight and price of hogs.

A short and simple method for finding the net weight, or price of hogs, when the gross weight or price is given, and vice versa.

NOTE.—It is generally assumed that the gross weight of Hogs diminished by 1-5 or 2) per cent. of itself gives the net weight, and the net weight increased by ⅕ or 25 per cent. of itself equals the gross weight.

To find the net weight or gross price.

Multiply the given number by .08 (tenths).

To find the gross weight or net price.

Divide the given number by .08 (tenths).

How to find the capacity of a granary, bin or wagon-bed.

RULE.—Multiply by short method) the number of cubic feet by 6,308, and point off ONE decimal place—the result will be the correct answer in bushels and tenths of a bushel.

For only an approximate answer, multiply the cubic feet by 8, and point off one decimal place.

How to find the contents of a corn-crib.

RULE.—Multiply the number of cubic feet by 54, short method, or by 4½ ordinary method, and point off ONE decimal place—the result will be the answer in bushels.

NOTE.—In estimating corn in the ear, the quality and the time it has been cribbed must be taken into consideration, since corn will shrink considerably during winter and spring. This rule generally holds good for corn measured at the time it is cribbed, provided it is sound and clean.

How to find the contents of a cistern or tank.

RULE.—Multiply the square of the mean diameter by the depth (all in feet) and this product by 5,681 (short method), and point off

ONE decimal place—the result will be the contents in barrels of
31½ gallons.

How to find the contents of a barrel or cask.

RULE.—Under the square of the mean diameter, write the length
(all in inches) in REVERSED order, so that its UNITS will fall under
the TENS; multiply by short method, and this product again by
430; point off one decimal place, and the result will be the answer
in wine gallons.

How to measure boards.

RULE.—Multiply the length (in feet) by the width (in inches)
and divide the product by 12—the result will be the contents in
square feet.

How to measure scantlings, joists, planks, sills, etc.

RULE.—Multiply the width, the thickness, and the length together (the width and thickness in inches, and the length in feet),
and divide the product by 12—the result will be square feet.

How to find the number of acres in a body of land.

RULE.- Multiply the length by the width (in rods), and divide
the product by 160 (carrying the division to 2 decimal places if
there is a remainder); the result will be the answer in acres and
hundredths.

When the opposite sides of a piece of land are of unequal length,
add them together and take one-half for the mean length or width.

How to find the number of square yards in a floor or wall.

RULE.—Multiply the length by the width or height (in feet),
and divide the product by 9, the result will be square yards.

How to find the number of bricks required in a building.

RULE.—Multiply the number of cubic feet by 22½.

The number of cubic feet is found by multiplying the length,
height and thickness (in feet) together.

Bricks are usually made 8 inches long, 4 inches wide, and two
inches thick; hence, it requires 27 bricks to make a cubic foot
without mortar, but it is generally assumed that the mortar fills
1-6 of the space.

How to find the number of shingles required in a roof.

RULE.—Multiply the number of square feet in the roof by 8, if
the shingles are exposed 4½ inches, or by 7 1-5 if exposed 5 inches.

To find the number of square feet, multiply the length of the
roof by twice the length of the rafters.

To find the length of the rafters, at ONE-FOURTH pitch, multiply
the width of the building by .56 (hundredths); at ONE-THIRD pitch
by .6 (tenths); at TWO-FIFTHS pitch, by .64 (hundredths); at ONE-
HALF pitch, by .71 (hundredths). This gives the length of the
rafters from the apex to the end of the wall, and whatever they
are to project must be taken into consideration.

NOTE.—By ¼ or ⅓ pitch is meant that the apex or comb of the roof is to be ¼ or ⅓
the width of the building **higher** than the walls or base of the rafters.

How to reckon the cost of hay.

RULE.—Multiply the number of pounds by half the price per ton, and remove the decimal point three places to the left.

How to measure grain.

RULE.—Level the grain, ascertain the space it occupies in cubic feet; multiply the number of cubic feet by 8, and point off one place to the left.

NOTE.—Exactness requires the addition to every three hundred bushels of one extra bushel.

The foregoing rule may be used for finding the number of gallons, by multiplying the number of bushels by 8.

If the corn in the box is in the ear, divide the answer by 2, to find the number of bushels of shelled corn, because it requires 2 bushels of ear corn to make 1 of shelled corn.

Rapid rules for measuring land without instruments.

In measuring land, the first thing to ascertain is the contents of any given plot in square yards; then, given the number of yards, find out the number of rods and acres.

The most ancient and simplest measure of distance is a step. Now, an ordinary-sized man can train himself to cover one yard at a stride, on the average, with sufficient accuracy for ordinary purposes.

To make use of this means of measuring distances, it is essential to walk in a straight line; to do this, fix the eye on two objects in a line straight ahead, one comparatively near, the other remote. and, in walking, keep these objects constantly in line.

Farmers and others by adopting the following simple and ingenious contrivance, may always carry with them the scale to construct a correct yard measure.

Take a foot rule, and commencing at the base of the little finger of the left hand, mark the quarters of the foot on the outer borders of the left arm, pricking in the marks with indelible ink.

To find how many rods in length will make an acre, the width being given.

RULE.—Divide 160 by the width, and the quotient will be the answer.

How to find the number of acres in any plot of land, the number of rods being given.

RULE.—Divide the number of rods by 8, multiply the quotient by 5, and remove the decimal point two places to the left.

The diameter being given, to find the circumference.

RULE.—Multiply the diameter by 3 1-7.

To find the diameter, when the circumference is given.

RULE.—Divide the circumference by 3 1-7.

To find how many solid feet a round stick of timber of the same thickness throughout will contain when squared

RULE.—Square half the diameter in inches, multiply by 2, multiply by the length in feet, and divide the product by 144.

General rule for measuring timber, to find the solid contents in feet.
RULE.—Multiply the depth in inches by the breadth in inches, and then multiply by the length in feet, and divide by 144.

To find the number of feet of timber in trees with the bark on.
RULE.—Multiply the square of one-fifth of the circumference in inches, by twice the length, in feet, and divide by 144. Deduct 1-10 to 1-15 according to the thickness of the bark.

Howard's new rule for computing interest.
RULE.—The reciprocal of the rate is the time for which the interest on any sum of money will be shown by simply removing the decimal point two places to the left; for ten times that time, remove the point one place to the left; for 1-10 of the same time, remove the point three places to the left.
Increase or diminish the results to suit the time given.

NOTE —The reciprocal of the rate is found by **inverting** the rate; thus 3 per cent. per month, inverted, becomes ⅓ of a month, or 10 days
When the rate is expressed by one figure, always write it thus: 3-1, three ones.

Rule for converting English into American currency.
Multiply the pounds, with the shillings and pence stated in decimals, by 400 plus the premium in fourths, and divide the product by 90.

U. S. GOVERNMENT LAND MEASURE.

A township—36 sections each a mile square.
A section—640 acres.
A quarter section, half a mile square—160 acres.
An eighth section, half a mile long, north and south, and a quarter of a mile wide—80 acres.
A sixteenth section, a quarter of a mile square—40 acres.
The sections are all numbered 1 to 36, commencing at the northeast corner.
The sections are divided into quarters, which are named by the cardinal points. The quarters are divided in the same way. The description of a forty-acre lot would read: The south half of the west half of the south-west quarter of section 1 in township 24, north of range 7 west, or as the case might be; and sometimes will fall short and sometimes overrun the number of acres it is supposed to contain.
The nautical mile is 795 4-5 feet longer than the common mile.

SURVEYORS' MEASURE.

7 92-100 inches.................................make 1 link.
25 links... " 1 rod.
4 rods.. " 1 chain.
80 chains....................................... " 1 mile.
NOTE.—A chain is 100 links, equal to 4 rods or 66 feet,

Shoemakers formerly used a subdivision of the inch called a barleycorn; three of which made an inch.

Horses are measured directly over the fore feet, and the standard of measure is four inches—called a hand.

In Biblical and other old measurements, the term span is sometimes used, which is a length of nine inches.

The sacred cubit of the Jews was 24.024 inches in length.

The common cubit of the Jews was 21.704 inches in length.

A pace is equal to a yard or 36 inches.

A fathom is equal to 6 feet.

A league is three miles, but its length is variable, for it is, strictly speaking, a nautical term, and should be three geographical miles, equal to 3.45 statute miles, but when used on land, three statute miles are said to be a league.

In cloth measure an aune is equal to 1¼ yards, or 45 inches.

An Amsterdam ell is equal to 26.796 inches.

A Trieste ell is equal to 25.284 inches.

A Brabant ell is equal to 27.116 inches.

MISCELLANEOUS TABLE.

12 units, or things, 1 Dozen.	196 pounds, 1 Barrel of Flour.
12 dozen, 1 Gross.	200 pounds, 1 Barrel of Pork.
20 things, 1 Score.	56 pounds, 1 Firkin of Butter.
24 sheets of paper, 1 Quire.	20 quires paper, 1 Ream.
4 ft. wide, 4 ft. high, and 8 feet long, 1 Cord Wood.	

HOW TO KEEP ACCOUNTS.

Every farmer and mechanic, whether he does much or little business, should keep a record of his transactions in a clear and systematic manner. For the benefit of those who have not had the opportunity of acquiring a primary knowledge of the principles of book-keeping, we here present a simple form of keeping accounts which is easily comprehended, and well adapted to record the business transactions of farmers, mechanics and laborers.

1882.		A. H. JACKSON.	Dr.	Cr.
Jan.	10	To 7 bushels Wheat....................at $1.25	$8 75	
"	17	By shoeing span of horses......................		$2 50
Feb.	4	To 14 bushels Oats.....................at $ .45	6 30	
"	4	To 5 ℔ Butter ....at 25	1 25	
March	8	By new Harrow		18 00
"	8	By sharpening 2 Plows...		40
"	13	By new Double-Tree...........................		2 25
"	17	To Cow and Calf..............................	48 00	
April	9	To half ton of Hay...........................	6 25	
"	9	By Cash......................................		25 00
May	6	By repairing Corn-Planter.....................		4 75
"	24	To one Sow with Pigs.........................	17 50	
July	4	By Cash, to balance account		35 15
			$88 05	$88 05

1

1882.		CASSA MASON.	Dr.		Cr.	
March	21	By 3 days' labor ....at $1.25			$3	75
"	21	To 2 Shoats ....at 3.00	$6	00		
"	23	To 18 Bushels Corn....................at .45	8	10		
May	1	By 1 month's Labor..........................			25	
"	1	To Cash...............................	10	00		00
June	19	By 8 day's Mowing....................at $1.50			12	
"	26	To 50 ℔ Flour.............................	2	75		
July	10	To 27 ℔ Meat ....at $ .10	2	70		00
"	29	By 9 Days Harvesting.................at 2.00			18	00
Aug.	12	By 6 days' Labor....................at 1.50			9	00
Sept.	1	To Cash	20	00		
		To Cash to balance account..................	18	20		
			$67	75	$67	75

INTEREST TABLE.

A SIMPLE RULE FOR ACCURATELY COMPUTING INTEREST AT ANY GIVEN
PER CENT FOR ANY LENGTH OF TIME.

Multiply the *principal* (amount of money at interest) by the *time reduced to
days*; then divide this *product* by the *quotient* obtained by dividing 360 (the number of days in the interest year) by the *per cent.* of interest, and *the quotient thus
obtained* will be the required interest.

ILLUSTRATION.

Require the interest of $462.50 for one month and
eighteen days at 6 per cent. An interest month is 30
days; one month and eighteen days equal 48 days.
$462.50 multiplied by .48 gives $222.0000; 360 divided
by 6 (the per cent. of interest) gives 60, and $222.0000
divided by 60 will give you the exact interest, which
is $3.70. If the rate of interest in the above example
were 12 per cent., we would divide the $222.0000 by 30
(because 360 divided by twelve gives 30); if 4 per cent.
we would divide by 90; if 8 per cent., by 45; and in
like manner for any other per cent.

Solution.
$462.50
.48
———
370000
6)360 ⎞ 185000
——— ⎟ ———
60 ⎠ $222.0000($3.70
180
—
420
430
—
0

NAMES OF THE STATES OF THE UNION, AND THEIR SIGNIFICATIONS.

Virginia— The oldest of the States, was so called in honor of
Queen Elizabeth, the " Virgin Queen," in whose reign Sir Walter
Raleigh made his first attempt to colonize that region.

Florida—Ponce de Leon landed on the coast of Florida on Easter
Sunday, and called the country in commemoration of the day, which
was the Pasqua Florida of the Spaniards, or "Feast of Flowers."

Louisiana was called after Louis the Fourteenth, who at one
time owned that section of the country.

Alabama was so named by the Indians, and signifies " Here we
Rest."

Mississippi is likewise an Indian name, meaning "Long
River."

Arkansas, from Kansas, the Indian word for " Smoky Water." Its prefix was really *arc*, the French word for " bow."

The *Carolinas* were originally one tract, and were called "Carolina," after Charles the Ninth of France.

Georgia owes its name to George the Second of England, who first established a colony there in 1732.

Tennessee is the Indian name for the "River of the Bend," *i. e.*, the Mississippi which forms its western boundary.

Kentucky is the Indian name for " at the head of the river."

Ohio means " beautiful;" *Iowa*, "the beautiful land;" *Minnesota*, " cloudy water," and *Wisconsin*, " wild-rushing channel."

Illinois is derived from the Indian word *illini*, men, and the French suffix *ois*, together signifying " tribe of men."

Michigan was called by the name given the lake, *fish-weir*, which was so styled from its fancied resemblance to a fish trap.

Missouri is from the Indian word " muddy," which more properly applies to the river that flows through it.

Oregon owes its Indian name to its principal river.

Cortez named *California*.

Massachusetts is the Indian name for " The country around the great hills."

Connecticut, from the Indian Quon-ch-ta-Cut, signifying "Long River."

Maryland, after Henrietta Maria, Queen of Charles the First, of England.

New York was named by the Duke of York.

Pennsylvania, means " Penn's Woods," and was so called after Wm. Penn, its owner.

Delaware, after Lord De La Ware.

New Jersey, so called in honor of Sir George Carteret, who was Governor of the Island of Jersey, in the British Channel.

Maine was called after the province of Maine in France, in compliment of Queen Henrietta of England, who owned that province.

Vermont, from the French word *Vert Mont*, signifying Green Mountain.

New Hampshire, from Hampshire County in England. It was formerly called Laconia.

The little State of *Rhode Island* owes its name to the Island of Rhodes in the Mediterranean, which domain it is said to greatly resemble.

Texas is the American word for the Mexican name by which all that section of the country was called before it was ceded to the United States.

POPULATION OF THE SEVERAL COUNTIES OF IOWA, 1880 CENSUS.

COUNTIES.	Organized.	COUNTY SEAT.	Population in 1880.
Adair	1854	Greenfield	11,199
Adams	1853	Corning	11,888
Allamakee	1849	Waukon	19,791
Appanoose	1846	Centerville	16,936
Audubon	1855	Audubon	7,448
Benton	1846	Vinton	24,888
Blackhawk	1853	Waterloo	23,913
Boone	1849	Boonsboro	20,838
Bremer	1853	Waverly	14,081
Buchanan	1847	Independence	18,547
Buena Vista	1858	Storm Lake	7,537
Butler	1854	Butler Center	14,293
Calhoun	1855	Rockwell City	5,595
Carroll	1856	Carroll	12,351
Cass	1853	Atlantic	16,943
Cedar	1836	Tipton	18,937
Cerro Gordo	1855	Mason City	11,461
Cherokee	1856	Cherokee	8,240
Chickasaw	1853	New Hampton	14,534
Clarke	1851	Osceola	11,512
Clay	1858	Spencer	4,248
Clayton	1838	Elkader	28,829
Clinton	1840	Clinton	36,764
Crawford	1855	Denison	12,413
Dallas	1847	Adel	18,746
Davis	1844	Bloomfield	16,468
Decatur	1850	Leon	15,336
Delaware	1840	Delhi	17,952
Des Moines	1834	Burlington	33,099
Dickinson	1857	Spirit Lake	1,901
Dubuque	1834	Dubuque	42,997
Emmet	1859	Swan Lake	1,550
Fayette	1850	West Union	22,258
Floyd	1854	Charles City	14,677
Franklin	1855	Hampton	10,248
Fremont	1849	Sidney	17,653
Greene	1854	Jefferson	12,725
Grundy	1856	Grundy Center	12,639
Guthrie	1851	Guthrie Center	14,863
Hamilton	1857	Webster City	11,252
Hancock	1858	Concord	3,453
Hardin	1853	Eldora	17,808
Harrison	1853	Logan	16,649
Henry	1836	Mt. Pleasant	20,826
Howard	1855	Cresco	10,837
Humboldt	1857	Dakota	5,341
Ida	1858	Ida Grove	4,382
Iowa	1845	Marengo	19,221
Jackson	1838	Maquoketa	23,771
Jasper	1846	Newton	25,962
Jefferson	1838	Fairfield	17,478

POPULATION OF THE SEVERAL COUNTIES OF IOWA, 1880 CENSUS.

COUNTIES.	Organized.	COUNTY SEATS.	Population in 1880.
Johnson............	1848	Iowa City......................	25,249
Jones..............	1839	Anamosa......................	21,052
Keokuk............	1844	Sigourney.....................	21,259
Kossuth........	1855	Algona........................	6,179
Lee...............	1837	Ft. Madison....................	34,859
Linn..............	1839	Marion........................	37,235
Louisa.............	1839	Wapello.......................	13,146
Lucas..............	1849	Chariton......................	14,530
Lyon....	1872	Rock Rapids...................	1,968
Madison............	1850	Winterset.....................	17,225
Mahaska...,..... ...	1844	Oskaloosa.....................	25,201
Marion....	1845	Knoxville.....................	25,111
Marshall...........	1850	Marshalltown..................	23,752
Mills..............	1851	Glenwood..... ,..............	14,135
Mitchell....	1854	Osage.........................	14,361
Monona............	1854	Onawa........................	9,055
Monroe............	1851	Albia.........................	13,719
Montgomery....	1858	Red Oak......................	15,895
Muscatine..........	1838	Muscatine.....................	23,168
O'Brien............	1860	Primghar......................	4,155
Osceola............	1872	Sibley........................	2,219
Page..............	1851	Clarinda......................	19,667
Palo Alto..........	1857	Emmetsburg...................	4,131
Plymouth..........	1858	Le Mars......................	3,567
Pocahontas.........	1859	Pocahontas Center.............	3,713
Polk..............	1846	Des Moines....................	41,395
Pottawattamie......	1848	Council Bluffs.................	39,846
Poweshiek.........	1848	Montezuma....................	18,936
Ringgold...........	1855	Mt. Ayr......................	12,085
Sac....	1858	Sac City......................	8,774
Scott.............	1838	Davenport.....................	42,270
Shelby.............	1853	Harlan........................	12,696
Sioux.............	1860	Orange City...................	5,436
Story.............	1853	Nevada.......................	16,906
Tama..............	1854	Toledo........................	21,585
Taylor............	1851	Bedford.......................	15,635
Union.............	1853	Afton.........................	14,900
Van Buren..........	1837	Keosauqua....................	17,042
Wapello.....	1844	Ottumwa......................	25,282
Warren............	1839	Indianola.....................	19,578
Washington.........	1849	Washington....................	20,375
Wayne.............	1851	Corydon......................	16,127
Webster...........	1853	Fort Dodge....................	15,950
Winnebago.........	1857	Forest City...................	4,917
Winneshiek.........	1851	Decorah.......................	23,937
Woodbury..........	1853	Sioux City....................	14,997
Worth.............	1857	Northwood....................	7,953
Wright............	1855	Clarion.......................	5,062
Total..........		....	1,624,463

The total footings for the State of Iowa, according to the census, are, males, 848,235; females, 776.228; native, 1,363,015; foreign, 261.418; white, 1,614,510; colored (including 47 Chinese and 464 Indians and half-breeds), 9,953, total, 1,624,463.

POPULATION OF THE UNITED STATES.

The revised and corrected returns of the census bureau show the population of the several States and Territories of the country to be as follows:

Alabama	1,262,505	Montana	39,159
Arizona	40,440	Nebraska	452,402
Arkansas	802,525	Nevada	62,266
California	864,694	New Hampshire	336,991
Colorado	194,327	New Jersey	1,131,116
Connecticut	622,700	New Mexico	116,565
Dakota	135,177	New York	5,082,871
Delaware	146,608	North Carolina	1,399,750
District of Columbia	177,624	Ohio	3.198,062
Florida	269,493	Oregon	174,768
Georgia	1,542,180	Pennsylvania	4,282,891
Idaho	32,610	Rhode Island	276,531
Illinois	3,077,871	South Carolina	995,577
Indiana	1,978,301	Tennessee	1,542,359
Iowa	1,624,615	Texas	1,591,749
Kansas	996,086	Utah	143,963
Kentucky	1,648,690	Vermont	332.286
Louisiana	939,946	Virginia	1,512,565
Maine	648,936	Washington	75,116
Maryland	934,942	West Virginia	618,457
Massachusetts	1,783,085	Wisconsin	1,315,497
Michigan	1,636,937	Wyoming	20,789
Minnesota	780,773		
Mississippi	1,131,597	Grand total	50,155,783
Missouri	2,168,380		

" The science of Geology illustrates many astonishing facts."
Viewed in the light of authentic tests, the region of country over
which this work extends, presents ample study for the Geologist
and Antiquarian, for nowhere in the broad expanse of country
traversed by the writer—excepting, perhaps, some sections of the
country of mines—is there such a fine field for the labor of the
geologist.   As we stood upon the high bluffs viewing the beautiful valleys below, or rowed over any of these streams—commercial
arteries of this great country—and tried to peer up the steep sides
of the overhanging bluffs, we often imagined ourself living away
amid the dim cycles of the past; again we lived in the present,
wondering what unseen agencies and gigantic forces had been employed to transform what was evidently once a vast and almost
boundless sea, into one of the finest sections of land—food producing land—between the two great oceans. Again, as the author
examined with hammer and chisel, testing the chips by heat and
cold, acid and alkali, subjecting the fused residuum to the diaphragm
of the microscope, or the wonderful spectra of the spectroscope,
he was often amazed at the broad expanse of time that must have
elapsed to make this wonderful strata from that ungainly, shapeless
mass, which, as Sacred History teaches, was this earth's original form.
Furthermore, it seems almost incredible that little by little as these
sands accumulate, that there could have elapsed sufficient time for
these marine aggregations and changes.   This, however, is merely
prefaratory, and we must hasten on to the subject matter, accorded
to this limited space, for to do the subject anything like justice, a
book much larger than this entire history would be required.   The
reader will know by this why we have not gone more into detail
in our discussion of this interesting and valuable portion of the
work.

To the geologist, among the first things to attract the attention
in this section is the "Walled Lakes" of Northern Iowa, one of
them in Wright County—where we first made a survey—is about
three-eighths of a mile wide, with a wall or embankment from 2 to
10 feet high surrounding it, formerly supposed to be the work of
ancient races, a theory, however, now discountenanced, for practical tests and observation go to prove that they are the results of
natural causes, namely the periodical action of alternate heat and
cold, aided to a limited extent by the action of the waves.   These
little lakes are very shallow, and during the ordinary winter freeze
nearly solid, so that little or no water remains at the bottom. but

a little will generally be found in the middle. As a consequence all loose substances at the bottom adhere to the ice below, and the expansive power of water when freezing—which must be immense in such a large body as some of these lakes—acts equally in all directions from the center to the circumference, and annually whatever was on the bottom of the lake has by this means been carried to the shore. This process, imperceptible, perhaps, to the casual observer in a single season, has been going on from year to year, century after century, causing these embankments, formerly a great wonder to everyone, but perfectly simple to any and all, if the various strata of the walls be carefully examined and compared with each other.

The entire State contains very few what may be classed as large elevations, the highest point being but a trifle over twelve hundred feet higher than its lowest point as shown by barometrical surveys; there are two such points, and are nearly three hundred miles apart; then if we think for a moment, it will be seen the entire State is traversed by gently flowing rivers- rapids nearly unknown —hence we have the entire State resting entirely within, comprising a part of a vast plain, with no mountain or hill range within its limits.

A further idea of the general uniformity which characterizes the State may be gleaned from the survey from point to point, and the following statement of the general slopes in feet per mile, in straight lines across:

From the NE corner to the SE corner 1 foot 1 inch per mile.
From the NE corner to Spirit Lake 5 feet 5 inches per mile.
From the NW corner to Spirit Lake 5 feet per mile.
From the NW corner to the SW corner 2 feet per mile.
From the SW corner to the highest ridge 4 feet 1 inch per mile.
From the dividing ridge to the SE corner 5 feet 7 inches per mile.
From the highest point in the State to the lowest 4 feet per mile.

This statement shows a great uniformity, and a good degree of propriety in estimating the whole State as part of a great plain, the lowest point showing but 144 feet above sea level. This point, nearly at the mouth of Des Moines River, presents a geological formation of great interest, but being so far removed from the territory within the scope of the work we will not discuss it in this connection. Taking the highest point—near Spirit Lake— and the lowest point—near the mouth of the Des Moines—gives but a slight elevation and depression, and a general average of the entire State of eight hundred feet above the level of the sea, though from the nearest point the State is over a thousand miles from the sea coast, a rather remarkable instance, and another proof of being a part of a vast plain. Of course, when we consider the slightly diversified surface of Western Iowa, the formation of small valleys out of the general level, which have been evolved by the action of streams, lakes, etc., during the dim cycles of the past, it may appear a trifle jejune, but will not alter the general and accepted theory aforesaid.   Especially is this true with reference to the northwestern portion, the seeming deviation being much more apparent in the northeastern portion of the State.

It will be well enough to mention that the Missouri River, though washing as many or more miles of Iowa's shore than the Mississippi, drains but about one-third of its surface, going to partially prove that this plain of which we speak, extends away out in Nebraska, where we have unmistakable evidences of the Missouri having once threaded its course, the other side being the eastern border of the State, giving us once a vast ocean about one and two-thirds broader than the State.

Thus much with reference to the surface indications.   We will now go lower and see what can be found beneath this beautiful and somewhat phenomenal exterior.

In our tests of the soil, we will make but three general divisions, which of themselves not only differ in their physical character, but are widely separated in their ultimate origin.   These will be classed as drift, bluff, and alluvial, and belong respectively to the deposits bearing the same names, the first of which occupies over two-thirds the surface of the entire State.

Every person who has paid the least atention to any of the analytical sciences, so-called, knows that when we speak of soil, in the general acceptation of the term, that we mean disintegrated or powdered rock.

The drift deposit of Iowa was derived, to a considerable extent, from the rocks of Minnesota; but the greater part of Iowa drift was derived from its own rocks, much of which has been transported but a short distance.   In general terms the *constant* component element of the drift soil is that portion which was transported from the north, while the *inconstant* elements are those portions which were derived from the adjacent or underlying strata.   For example, in Western Iowa, wherever that cretaceous formation known as the Nishnabotany sandstone exists, the soil contains more sand than elsewhere.   The same may be said of the soil of some parts of the State occupied by the lower coal measures, the sandstones and sandy shales of that formation furnishing the sand.

We find upon examination, however, that in the section of Iowa of which this work treats, the drift contains more sand and gravel than any other portion of the State.   There is no question in my mind but this was derived from the cretaceous rocks that now do, or formerly did exist, and also in part from the conglomerate and pudding stone beds of the Sioux quartzite.

The bluff soil, then, is that which rests upon, and constitutes part of the bluff deposit, and is found only in the western portion along the Missouri River.   Chemical analysis shows but one per cent., generally less, of alumina, at the same time it contains other constituent elements which render it little, if any, inferior for agricultural purposes; a very large portion of it is far out of reach of the highest floods, and must be very productive.

We now come to the alluvial. This is that portion called the flood plains of the river bottoms or valleys. That portion periodically flooded by the rivers, of course, is thereby rendered comparatively valueless for agricultural purposes for apparent reasons; but much of it, we might say by far the larger portion, is beyond the reach of floods, and is very rich in those elements which enter into plant life.

Speaking more properly of the geology of this particular section of Iowa, we find the rocks to range all along from the Azoic to the Merazoic inclusive. Taking the State as a whole, the surface is generally occupied by the evidences of the Palæozoic age. The following tabular statement gives each of these formations in the order in which they occur:

SYSTEMS.	GROUPS.	FORMATIONS.	THICKNESS IN FEET.
AGES.	PERIODS.	EPOCHS.	
Cretaceous.....	Post Tertiary......	Drift......................	10to200
		Inoceramous bed............	50
	Lower Cretaceous-	Woodbury Sandstone, Shales	130
		Nishnabotany Sandstone.....	100
		Upper Coal Measures........	200
	Coal Measures.-	Middle Coal Measures........	200
		Lower Coal Measures........	200
Carboniferous..		St. Louis Limestone.........	75
	Subcarboniferous.-	Keokuk Limestone...........	90
		Burlington Limestone........	196
		Kinderhook beds.............	175
Devonian......	Hamilton...........	Hamilton Limestone and Shales	200
Upper Silurian..	Niagara............	Niagara Limestone..........	350
	Cincinnati........	Maquoketa Shales...........	80
		Galena Limestone...........	250
	Trenton.	Trenton Limestone..........	200
Lower Silurian.		St. Peter's Sandstone........	80
		Lower Magnesian Limestone..	250
	Primordial.	Potsdam Sandstone..........	300
Azoic..........	Huronian...........	Sioux Quartzite.............	50

We now arrive at what is known as the Azoic system. In this section it is known and recognized by the specific name of Sioux quartzite, and is found exposed in natural ledges, only in a few spots away up in the extreme northwestern part of the State, upon the banks of the Big Sioux River, which position doubtless gave it its local name. This rock is intensely hard, disintegrates in sort of splinters; its color varying according to locality from nearly a yellow to a deep red. One thing connected with this rock is its process of metamorphism, which has been so complete all through the entire formation wherever found. Whether exposed to the surface or hidden hundreds of feet below the surface, the rock is found to be of almost uniform texture. As far as we have been able to examine, the dip is found to be from 4.75 to 5.20 degrees to the northward, but the trend of the outcrop is to the eastward and westward. In some rare cases the rock is profitably quarried, but generally speaking, it is very difficult to secure it in dry forms, except that into which it naturally cracks, and the tendency is into angular places. I have found the samples sent to be absolutely indestructible.

There are many other systems, of themselves very interesting to the scientific reader and investigator, but our limited space stands as an insurmountable barrier; hence we will have to pass the Lower Silurian system in the Primordial group of the eastern part of the State; it, however, is valueless for building purposes, and contains few if any, fossils. Then we have the Lower Magnesian Limestone, found but little here, containing a few crinoids and smaller fossils. Following this in point of interest, is the St. Peter's Sandstone, which exists in uniform thickness throughout the State where found, which is beneath the drift.

Of the Trenton Group of the Upper and Lower Silurian age, but little of interest to anyone can be said, save that it contains a great variety of fossils, and it makes very ornamental stone for cap and window sills. In this section of the State the drift contains more silex and gravel than elsewhere, as before stated, but in those sections where fossils are found, they are new to all I have read of science, open new fields of thought and investigation, and are found peculiar to the Hawkeye State.

Passing again the Galena Limestone of Dubuque, and other counties: This is always the upper formation of the Trenton Group. It seldom extends over twelve miles in width, though fully one hundred in length. In Dubuque County the greatest development of this limestone is exhibited. It is found to be merely a pure dolomite, with an occasional slight admixture of silicious matter. It is almost worthless for dressing; its principal value consisting of its formation being the source of lead ore, but the lead region of Iowa is confined to an area of say fifteen miles square. The one occurs in vertical fissures, which traverse the rock at regular intervals from east to west; some, however, is found in those which have a north and south course. Very small quantities of what is known as carbonate are found in it; its principal being what assayers call sulphuret of lead.

Probably one of the most important of all the geological formations of the State is the Coal-Measure group. This is divided into three formations, viz., the lower, middle and upper coal measures, each having a vertical thickness of about two hundred feet.

A line drawn upon the map of Iowa as follows, will represent the eastern and northern boundaries of the coal fields of the State: Commencing at the southeast corner of Van Buren County, carry

the line to the northeast corner of Jefferson County by a slight
easterly curve through the western portions of Lee and Henry
Counties. Produce this line until it reaches a point six or eight
miles northward from the one last named, and then carry it
northwestward, keeping it at about the same distance to the northward of Skunk River and its north branch that it had at first, until it reaches the southern boundary of Marshall County. a little
west of its center. Then carry it to a point three or four miles,
northeast of Eldora. Hardin County; thence westward to a
point a little north of Webster City. in Hamilton County; and
thence further westward to a point a little north of Fort Dodge.
in Webster County.

In consequence of the recedence to the southward of the borders
of the middle and upper coal measures, the lower coal measures
alone exist to the eastward and northward of Des Moines River.
They also occupy a large area westward and southward of that river,
but their southerly dip passes them below the middle coal measures
at no great distance from the river.

No other formation in the whole State possesses the economic
value of the lower coal measures. The clay that underlies almost
every bed of coal furnishes a large amount of material for potters'
use. The sandstone of these measures is usually soft and unfit,
but in some places, as near Red Rock, in Marion County, blocks of
large dimensions are obtained which make good building material,
samples of which can be seen in the State Arsenal at Des Moines.
On the whole, that portion of the State occupied by the lower coal
measures, is not well supplied with stone.

But few fossils have been found in any of the strata of the lower coal measures. but such animal remains as have been found are
without exception of marine origin.

Of fossil plants found in these measures all probably belong to
the class *acrogens*. Specimens of *calamites*, and several species of
ferns are found in all the coal measures, but the genus *lipeduden-
dron* seems not to have existed later than the epoch of the middle
coal measures.

This formation within the State of Iowa occupies a narrow belt of
territory in the southern central portion of the State, embracing a
superficial area of about fourteen hundred square miles. The counties more or less underlaid by this formation are Guthrie, Dallas, Polk,
Madison, Warren, Clarke, Lucas, Monroe, Wayne and Appanoose.

This formation is composed of alternating beds of clay, sandstone
and limestone, the clays or shales constituting the bulk of the formation, the limestone occurring in their bands. the lithological pe-
culiarities of which offer many contrasts to the limestones of the
upper and lower coal measures. The formation is also characterized by regular wave-like undulations, with a parallelism which indicates a widespread disturbance. though no dislocation of the strata
has been discovered.

Generally speaking, few species of fossils occur in these beds. Some of the shales and sandstone have afforded a few imperfectly preserved land plants—three or four species of ferns, belonging to the genera. Some of the carboniferous shales afford beautiful specimens of what appear to have been sea-weeds. Radiates are represented by corals. The mollusks are most numerously represented. *Trilobites* and *ostracoids* are the only remains known of articulates. Vertebrates are only known by the remains of *salachians*, or sharks, and ganoids.

The area occupied by this formation in Iowa is very great, comprising thirteen whole counties, in the southwestern part of the State. It adjoins by its northern and eastern boundaries the area occupied by the middle coal measures.

The prominent lithological features of this formation are its limestones, yet it contains a considerable proportion of shales and sandstones. Although it is known by the name of upper coal measures, it contains but a single bed of coal, and that only about twenty inches in maximum thickness.

The limestone exposed in this formation furnishes good material for building as in Madison and Fremont counties. The sandstones are quite worthless. No beds of clay for potters' use are found in the whole formation.

The fossils in this formation are much more numerous than in either the middle or lower coal measures. The vertebrates are represented by the fishes of the orders selachians and ganoids. The articulates are represented by the trilobites and ostracoids. Mollusks are represented by the classes *cephalopoda, gasteropoda, lamelli. branchiata, brachiapoda polyzoa.* Radiates are more numerous than in the lower and middle coal measures. Protogoans are represented in the greatest abundance, some layers of limestone being almost entirely composed of their small fusiform shells.

There being no rocks, in Iowa, of permian, triassic or jurassic age, the next strata in the geological series are of the cretaceous age. They are found in the western half of the State, and do not dip as do all the other formations upon which they rest, to the southward and westward, but have a general dip of their own to the north of westward, which, however, is very slight. Although the actual exposures of cretaceous rocks are few in Iowa, there is reason to believe that nearly all the western half of the State was originally occupied by them; but being very friable, they have been removed by denundation, which has taken place at two separate periods. The first period was during its elevation from the cretaceous sea, and during the long tertiary age that passed between the time of that elevation and the commencement of the glacial epoch. The second period was during the glacial epoch, when the ice produced their entire removal over considerable areas.

It is difficult to indicate the exact boundaries of these rocks: the following will approximate the outlines of the area:

From the northeast corner to the southwest corner of Kossuth County; thence to the southeast corner of Guthrie County; thence to the southeast corner of Cass County; thence to the middle of the south boundary of Montgomery County; thence to the middle of the north boundary of Pottawattamie County; thence to the middle of the south boundary of Woodbury County; thence to Sergeant's Bluffs; up the Missouri and Big Sioux Rivers to the northwest corner of the State; eastward along the State line to the place of beginning.

All the cretaceous rocks in Iowa are a part of the same deposits farther up the Missouri River, and in reality from their eastern boundary.

Nishnabotany Sandstone.—This rock has the most easterly and southerly extent of the cretaceous deposits of Iowa, reaching the southeastern part of Guthrie County and the southern part of Montgomery County. To the northward, it passes beneath the Woodbury sandstones and shales, the latter passing beneath inoceramus, or chalky, beds. This sandstone is, with few exceptions, almost valueless for economic purposes.

The only fossils found in this formation are a few fragments of angiospermous leaves.

Woodbury Sandstones and Shales.—These strata rest upon the Nishnabotany sandstone, and have not been observed outside of Woodbury County, hence their name. Their principal exposure is at Sergeant's Bluffs, seven miles below Sioux City.

This rock has no value except for purposes of common masonry.

Fossil remains are rare. Detached scales of a lepidoginoid species have been detected, but no other vertebrate remains. Of remains of vegetation, leaves of *salix* meekii and sassafras cretaceum have been occasionally found.

Inoceramus beds.—These beds rest upon the Woodbury sandstones and shales. They have not been observed in Iowa, except in the Bluffs which border the Big Sioux River in Woodbury and Plymouth Counties. They are composed almost entirely of calcareous material, the upper portion of which is extensively used for lime. No building material is to be obtained from these beds; and the only value they possess, except lime, are the marls, which at some time may be useful on the soil of the adjacent region.

The only vertebrate remains found in the Cretaceous rocks are the fishes. Those in the inoceramus beds of Iowa are two species of squoloid selachians, or cestratront, and three genera of teliosts. Molluscan remains are rare.

Extensive beds of peat exist in Northern Middle Iowa, which, it is estimated, contain the following areas:

Counties.	Acres.
Cerro Gordo	1,500
Worth	2 000
Winnebago	2,000
Hancock	1,500
Wright	500
Kossuth	700
Dickinson	80

Several other counties contain peat beds, but the character of the peat is inferior to that in the northern part of the State. The character of the peat named is equal to that of Ireland. The beds are of an average depth of four feet. It is estimated that each acre of these beds will furnish two hundred and fifty tons of dry fuel for each foot in depth. At present, owing to the sparseness of the population, this peat is not utilized; but, owing to its great distance from coal fields and absence of timber, the time is coming when their value will be realized, and the fact demonstrated that Nature has abundantly compensated the deficiency of other fuel.

GYPSUM.

The only deposits of the sulphates of the alkaline earths of any economic value in Iowa are those of gypsum at, and in the vicinity of Fort Dodge, in Webster County. All others are small and unimportant. The deposit occupies a nearly central position in Webster County, the Des Moines River running nearly centrally through it. along the valley sides of which the gypsum is seen in the form of ordinary rock cliff and ledges, and also occurring abundantly in similar positions along both sides of the valleys of the smaller streams and of the numerous ravines coming into the river valley.

The most northerly known limit of the deposit is at a point near the mouth of Lizard Creek, a tributary of the Des Moines River, and almost adjoining the town of Fort Dodge. The most southerly point at which it has been found exposed is about six miles, by way of the river, from this northerly point before mentioned. Our knowledge of the width of the area occupied by it is limited by the exposures seen in the valleys of the small streams and in the ravines which come into the valley within the distance mentioned. As one goes up these ravines and minor valleys, the gypsum becomes lost beneath the overlying drift. There can be no doubt that the different parts of this deposit, now disconnected by the valleys and ravines having been cut through it, were originally connected as a continuous deposit, and there seems to be as little reason to doubt that the gypsum still extends to considerable distance on each side of the valley of the river beneath the drift which covers the region to a depth of from twenty to sixty feet.

The country round about this region has the prairie surface ap-
proximating a general level which is so characteristic of the greater
part of the State, and which exists irrespective of the character or
geological age of the strata beneath, mainly because the drift is so
deep and uniformly distributed that it frequently almost alone
gives character to the surface. The valley sides of the Des
Moines River, in the vicinity of Fort Dodge, are somewhat abrupt,
having a depth there from the general level of the upland of about
one hundred and seventy feet, and consequently presents somewhat bold and interesting features in the landscape.

As one walks up and down the creeks and ravines which come
into the valley of the Des Moines River there, he sees the gypsum
exposed on either side of them, jutting out from beneath the drift
in the form of ledges and bold quarry fronts, having almost the
exact appearance of ordinary limestone exposures, so horizontal
and regular are its lines of stratification, and so similar in color is
it to some varieties of that rock. The principal quarries now
opened are on Two Mile Creek, a couple of miles below Fort
Dodge.

The reader will please bear in mind that the gypsum of this remarkable deposit does not occur in "heaps" or "nests" as it does
in most deposits of gypsum in the States farther eastward, but that
it exists here in the form of a regularly stratified, continuous formation, as uniform in texture, color and quality throughout the
whole region, and from top to bottom of the deposit as the granite
of the Quincy quarries is. Its color is a uniform gray, resulting
from alternating fine horizontal lines of nearly white, with similar
lines of darker shade. The gypsum of the white lines is almost
entirely pure, the darker lines containing the impurity. This is
at intervals barely sufficient in amount to cause the separation of
the mass upon those lines into beds or layers, thus facilitating the
quarrying of it into desired shapes. These bedding surfaces have
occasionally a clayey feeling to the touch, but there is nowhere
any intercalation of clay or other foreign substance in a separate
form. The deposit is known to reach a thickness of thirty feet at
the quarries referred to, but although it will probably be found to
exceed this thickness at some other points, at the natural exposures, it is seldom seen to be more that from ten to twenty feet
thick.

Since the drift is usually seen to rest directly upon the gypsum,
with nothing intervening, except at a few points where traces appear of an overlying bed of clayey material without doubt of the
same age as the gypsum, the latter probably lost something of its
thickness by mechanical erosion during the glacial epoch; and it
has, doubtless, also suffered some diminution of thickness since
then by solution in the waters which constantly percolate through
the drift from the surface. The drift of this region being somewhat clayey, particularly in its lower part, it has doubtless served

in some degree as a protection against the diminution of the
gypsum by solution in consequence of its partial imperviousness to
water. If the gypsum had been covered by a deposit of sand instead of the drift clays, it would have no doubt disappeared by being dissolved in the water that would have constantly reached it
from the surface. Water merely resting upon it would not dis-
solve it away to any extent, but it rapidly disappears under the action of running water. Where little rills of water at the time of
every rain run over the face of an unused quarry, from the surface
above it, deep grooves are thereby cut into it, giving it somewhat
the appearance of melting ice around a waterfall. The fact that
gypsum is now suffering a constant, but, of course, very slight,
diminution, is apparent in the fact the springs of the region contain more or less of it in solution in their waters.

Besides the clayed beds that that are sometimes seen to rest upon
the gypsum, there are occasionally others seen beneath them that
are also of the same age, and not of the age of the coal-measure
strata upon which they rest.

In neither the gypsum nor the associated clays has any trace of
any fossil remains been found, nor has any other indication of its
geological age been observed, except that which is afforded by its
stratigraphical relations; and the most that can be said with certainty is that it is nearer than the coal measures, and older than
the drift. The indications afforded by the stratigraphical relations
of the gypsum deposit of Fort Dodge are, however, of considerable
value.

As already shown, it rests in that region directly and uncon-
formably upon the lower coal measures; but going southward from
there, the whole series of coal-measure strata from the top of the
subcarboniferous group to the upper coal measures, inclusive, can
be traced without break or unconformability. The strata of the
latter also may be traced in the same manner up into the Permian
rocks of Kansas; and through this long series, there is no place or
horizon which suggests that the gypsum deposit might belong
there.

Again, no Tertiary deposits are known to exist within or near
the borders of Iowa to suggest that the gypsum might be of that
age; nor are any of the palaeozoic strata newer than the subcarboniferous unconformable upon each other as the other gypsum is
unconformable upon the strata beneath it. It therefore seems, in
a measure, conclusive, that the gypsum is of Mesozoic age, perhaps
older than the Cretaceous.

LITHOLOGICAL ORIGIN.

As little can be said with certainty concerning the lithological
origin of this deposit as can be said concerning its geological age,
for it seems to present itself in this relation, as in the former one

11

as an isolated fact. None of the associated strata show any traces
of a double decomposition of pre-existing materials, such as some
have supposed all deposits of gypsum to have resulted from. No
considerable quantity of oxide of iron nor any trace of native sulphur have been found in connection with it; nor has any salt been
found in the waters of the region. These substances are common
in association with other gypsum deposits, and are regarded by some
persons as indicative of the method of or resulting from their origin
as such. Throughout the whole region, the Fort Dodge gypsum
has the exact appearance of a sedimentary deposit. It is arranged
in layers like the regular layers of limestone, and the whole mass,
from top to bottom, is traced with fine horizontal laminæ of alternating white and gray gypsum, parallel with the bedding surface
of the layers, but the whole so intimately blended as to form a solid
mass. The darker lines contain almost all the impurity there is
in the gypsum, and that impurity is evidently sedimentary in its
character. From these facts, and also from the further one that
no trace of fossil remains has been detected in the gypsum, it seems
not unreasonable to entertain the opinion that the gypsum of Fort
Dodge originated as a chemical precipitation in comparatively still
waters, which were saturated with sulphate of lime and destitute
of life; its stratification and impurities being deposited at the same
time as clayey impurities which had been held suspended in the
same waters.

Much has already been said of the physical properties or character of this gypsum, but as it is so different in some respects from
that of other deposits, there are yet other matters worthy of mention in connection with those. According to the results of a complete and exhaustive analysis by Prof. Emery, the ordinary gray
gypsum contains only about eight per cent. of impurity; and it is
possible that the average impurity for the whole deposit will not
exceed that proportion, so uniform in quality is it from top to bottom, and from one end of the region to the other.

When it is remembered that plaster for agricultural purposes is
sometimes prepared from gypsum that contains as much as thirty
per cent. of impurity, it will be seen that ours is a very superior
article for such purposes. The impurities are also of such a character that they do not in anyway interfere with its value for use
in the arts. Although the gypsum rock has a gray color, it becomes quite white by grinding, and still whiter by the calcining
process necessary in the preparation of plaster of Paris. These
tests have all been practically made in the rooms of the Geological
Survey, and the quality of the plaster of Paris still further tested
by actual use and experiment. No hesitation, therefore, is felt in
stating that the Fort Dodge gypsum is of as good a quality as any
in the country, even for the finest uses.

In view of the bounteousness of the primitive fertility of our
Iowa soils, many persons forget that a time may come when Na-

ture will refuse to respond so generously to our demand as she does now, without an adequate return. Such are apt to say that this vast deposit of gypsum is valueless to our commonwealth, except to the small extent that it may be used in the arts. This is undoubtedly a short-sighted view of the subject, for the time is even now rapidly passing away when a man may purchase a new farm for less money than he can re-fertilize and restore the partially wasted primitive fertility of the one he now occupies. There are farms even now in a large part of the older settled portions of the State that would be greatly benefited by the proper application of plaster, and such eras will continue to increase until it will be difficult to estimate the value of the deposit of gypsum at Fort Dodge. It should be remembered, also, that the inhabitants of an extent of country adjoining our State more than three times as great as its own area, will find it more convenient to obtain their supplies from Fort Dodge than from any other source.

For want of direct railroad communication between this region and other parts of the State, the only use yet made of the gypsum by the inhabitants is for the purpose of ordinary building stone. It is so compact that it is found to be comparatively unaffected by the frost, and its ordinary situation in walls of houses is such that it is protected from the dissolving action of water, which can at most reach it only from occasional rains, and the effect of these is too slight to be perceived after the lapse of several years.

One of the citizens of Fort Dodge, Hon. John F. Duncombe, built a large, fine residence of it, in 1861, the walls of which appear as unaffected by the exposure and as beautiful as they were when first erected. It has been so long and successfully used for building stone by the inhabitants that they now prefer it to the limestone of good quality, which also exists in the immediate vicinity. This preference is due to the cheapness of the gypsum, as compared with the stone. The cheapness of the former is largely due to the facility with which it is quarried and wrought. Several other houses have been constructed of it in Fort Dodge, including the depot building of the Dubuque & Sioux City Railroad. The company have also constructed a large culvert of the same material to span a creek near the town, limestone only being used for the lower courses, which come in contact with the water. It is a fine arch, each stone of gypsum being nicely hewn, and it will doubtless prove a very durable one. Many of the sidewalks in the town are made of the slabs or flags or gypsum which occur in some of the quarries in the form of thin layers. They are more durable than their softness would lead one to suppose. They also possess an advantage over stone in not becoming slippery when worn.

The method adopted in quarrying and dressing the blocks of gypsum is peculiar, and quite unlike that adopted in similar treatment of ordinary stone. Taking a stout auger-bit of an ordi-

nary brace, such as is used by carpenters, and filing the cutting
parts of it into a peculiar form, the quarryman bores his holes
into the gypsum quarry for blasting, in the same manner and
with as great facility as a carpenter would bore hard wood. The
pieces being loosened by blasting, they are broken up with sledges
into convenient sizes, or hewn into the desired shape by means of
hatchets or ordinary chopping axes, or cut by means by means of
ordinary wood-saws. So little grit does the gypsum contain that
these tools, made for working wood, are found to be better adapted
for working the former substance than those tools are which are
universally used for working stone.

MINOR DEPOSITS OF SULPHATE OF LIME.

Besides the great gypsum deposit of Fort Dodge, sulphate of
lime in the various forms of fibrous gypsum, selenite, and small,
amorphous masses, has also been discovered in various formations
in different parts of the State, including the coal-measure shales
near Fort Dodge, where it exists in small quantities quite inde-
pendently of the great gypsum deposit there. The quantity of
gypsum in these minor deposits is always too small to be of any
practical value, and frequently minute. They usually occur in
shales and shaly clays associated with strata that contain more or less
sulphuret of iron (iron pyrites). Gypsum has thus been detected in
the coal measures, the St. Louis limestone, the cretaceous strata,
and also in the lead caves of Dubuque. In most of these cases it
is evidently the result of double decomposition of iron pyrites and
carbonate of lime, previously existing there; in which cases the
gypsum is of course not an original deposit as the great one at
Fort Dodge is supposed to be.

The existence of these comparatively minute quantities of gypsum in the shales of the coal measures and the subcarboniferous
limestone which are exposed within the region of and occupy a
stratigraphical position beneath the great gypsum deposits, suggest the possibility that the former may have originated as a pre-
cipitate from percolating waters, holding gypsum in solution
which they had derived from that deposit in passing over or
through it. Since, however, the same substance is found in similar small quantities and under similar conditions in regions where
they could have had no possible connection with that deposit, it is
believed that none of those mentioned have necessarily originated
from it, not even those that are found in close proximity to it.

The gypsum found in the lead caves is usually in the form of
efflorescent fibers, and is always in small quantity. In the lower
coal-measure shale near Fort Dodge, a small mass was found in the
form of an intercolated layer, which had a distinct fibrous structure, the fibers being perpendicular to the plane of the layer. The
same mass had also distinct, horizontal planes of cleavage at right
angles with the perpendicular fibers. Thus, being more or less

transparent, the mass combined the characters of both fibrous gypsum and selenite. No anhydrous sulphate of lime (*anhydrite*) has been found in connection with the great gypsum deposit, nor elsewhere in Iowa, so far as yet known.

SULPHATE OF STRONTIA.

(*Celestine.*)

The only locality at which this interesting mineral has yet been found in Iowa, or, so far as is known, in the great valley of the Mississippi, is at Fort Dodge. It occurs there in very small quantity in both the shales of the lower coal measures and in the clays that overlie the gypsum deposit, and which are regarded as of the same age with it. The first is just below the city, near Rees' coal bank, and occurs as a layer intercolated among the coal measure shales, amounting in quantity to only a few hundred pounds' weight. The mineral is fibrous and crystaline, the fibers being perpendicular to the plane of the layer. Breaking also with more or less distinct horizontal planes of cleavage, it resembles, in physical character, the layer of fibro-crystaline gypsum before mentioned. Its color is light blue, is transparent and shows crystaline facets upon both the upper and under surfaces of the layer; those of the upper surface being smallest and most numerous. It breaks up readily into small masses along the lines of the perpendicular fibers or columns. The layer is probably not more than a rod in extent in any direction and about three inches in maximum thickness. Apparent lines of stratification occur in it, corresponding with those of the shales which imbed it.

The other deposit was still smaller in amount, and occurred as a mass of crystals imbedded in the clays that overlie the gypsum at Cummins' quarry in the valley of Soldier Creek. Here the mineral is nearly without color, and were it not for the form of the separate crystals would closely resemble a mass of impure chloride. These crystals are so closely aggregated that they enclose but little impurity in the mass, but in nearly every case brought to my notice their fundamental forms are obscured. The mineral of itself is of no practical value, and its occurrence is only interesting as a mineralogical fact.

Epsomite, or native epsom salts, having been discovered near Burlington, we have thus recognized in Iowa all the sulphates of the alkaline earths of natural origin; all of them, except the sulphate of lime, being in very small quantity. Even if the sulphate of magnesia were produced in nature, in large quantities, it is so very soluble that it can accumulate only in such positions as afford it complete shelter from the rains or running water. The epsomite mentioned was found beneath the overhanging cliff of Burlington limestone, near Starr's mill.

It occurs in the form of efflorescent encrustations upon the surface of stones and in similar small fragile masses among the fine debris that has fallen down beneath the overhanging cliff. The projection of the cliff over the perpendicular face of the strata beneath amounts to near twenty feet at the point where epsomite was found. Consequently the rains never reach far beneath it from any quarter. The rock upon which the epsomite accumulates is an impure limestone, containing also some carbonate of magnesia, together with a small proportion of iron pyrites in a finely divided condition. It is doubtless by double decomposition of these that the epsomite results. By experiments with this native salt in the office of the Survey, a fine article of epsom salts was produced, but the quantity that might be annually obtained there would amount to only a few pounds, and of course is of no practical value whatever, on account of its cheapness in the market.

WOODBURY COUNTY,

Woodbury County is situated on the western border of the State, in the third tier from the north line. It is twenty-four miles north and south, by from thirty to thirty-six miles east and west, embracing a superficial area of about 832 square miles, or 432,480 acres. About 146,000 acres of this land is Missouri River bottom, of great fertility, and unsurpassed for agricultural and grazing purposes. This bottom is from six to ten miles in width and mostly above high water mark in the Missouri River. Although apparently nearly level, it is dry and susceptible of easy tillage. The soil is a deep loam, with a sufficient proportion of silicious material to render it retentive of moisture, while it seldom remains for any length of time so wet as to prevent the farmer from giving attention to his crops. Immediately adjacent to the valleys are the bluffs, forming a narrow belt, usually too much broken for cultivation, but a short distance back the land becomes gently rolling, and is well adapted to farming purposes. The Missouri, one of the great rivers of the continent, forms the western boundary of the county as far up as the mouth of the Big Sioux River. Thence, to the northwest corner, a distance of about five miles, the latter stream marks the western boundary. The principal streams flowing through the interior are Floyd, east and west forks of the Little Sioux, and Maple Rivers. Perry Creek is also a stream of considerable size. All these streams flow through rich and beautiful valleys, and receive many small affluents that completely drain the entire surface. The Little Sioux and Floyd Rivers furnish water power for machinery. There is a deficiency of native timber in this, as in other counties of this part of the State. There are some groves of valuable timber, however, bordering on the Missouri and along the Big and Little Sioux Rivers. The varieties common are cottonwood, hickory, oak, walnut, elm, and maple—the first named largely predominating along the Missouri River. It has been found that many kinds of timber may be easily propagated, and when planted on the prairies make a rapid growth.

The geological formation is such as to allow but few exposures of rock in the county, or indeed, in this portion of Iowa. The entire surface is covered by the peculiar formation known by the name of "bluff deposit," extending to the depth of many feet. The bed of the Missouri River at Sioux City is 340 feet above that of the Mississippi at Dubuque, in the same latitude. There are at Sioux City, and one or two other places, exposures of a sandstone formation of the cretaceous age, with a stratum of soft, chalky limestone overlying it. This is too soft for masonry, but is used for making quicklime. The sandstone is quarried for ordinary building purposes. The same formation appears on Big Sioux River about two miles above the mouth, and extends, with occasional exposures, to the northwest corner of the county. The surface of the "bluff deposit" is used for making brick. The clays in the cretaceous deposit furnish an excellent material for making pottery. Woodbury, however, must rely chiefly on its fertile prairies for its development into a prosperous and wealthy county.

On the 14th of May, 1804, Captains Lewis and Clarke, with forty-two men, under the direction of the War Department of the Government, started from their encampment at the mouth of Wood River, in what is now the State of Illinois, to explore the Missouri River and the unknown regions of the Northwest. After many strange adventures, and the accomplishment of a thousand miles of their journey, on the 18th of August they landed on the Nebraska side of the river, nearly opposite the southwest corner of the present County of Woodbury, where they held a council with a party of Ottoe and Missouri Indian Chiefs. On the morning of the 20th the Indians mounted their horses and left, having received some presents from the whites. On the 19th, in camp at the place where the council was held, Sergeant Charles Floyd, of the expedition, became very sick and remained so all night. The next morning, however, which was Monday, August 20, the party set out on their journey up the river. Having a "fine wind and fine weather," they made thirteen miles, and at two o'clock landed for dinner on the Iowa side of the river. Here Sergeant Floyd died. About one mile farther up the river, on the summit of a high bluff, his body was buried with the honors due to a brave soldier. His comrades marked the place with a cedar post, on which were inscribed his name and the date of his death. About one mile above, a small river flows into the Missouri, and here the party encamped until the next day. Captains Lewis and Clarke gave this stream the name of Floyd's River, to perpetuate the memory of the first man who had fallen in their expedition. The next day they set out early, passed the bluffs, now within the limits of Sioux City, which are mentioned in the journal of Patrick Gass, a member of the expedition, as "handsome, pale colored bluffs." Willow Creek and Big Sioux River, the latter just above where Sioux City now stands, are also mentioned. During a great freshet in the Spring of 1857, the turbulent Missouri washed away a portion of the bluff, so as to expose the remains of Sergeant Floyd. The citizens of Sioux City and vicinity collected the remains and re-interred them some distance back from the river on the same bluff.

The title of the Indians to the land in this portion of Iowa became extinct in 1847, and in the summer of 1848, forty-four years after the burial of Sergeant Floyd, a single pioneer, named William Thompson, settled at Floyd's Bluff—the first white man who became a permanent settler of the county. In the autumn of the same year his brother Charles and another man followed and spent the winter there, being, at that time the only white men in the county. Anticipating an immense immigration, he laid out a town here and named it in honor of himself—Thompsontown. Like other western towns, this for a while was supposed to be *the* point. To give it an air of business, and aid in its development, he erected here his cabin, and, on the organization of the county, in 1853, this was made the county seat. It was a sort of post for Indian traders for some years, but the city lots were too steep for cultivation, or for building, and, unfortunately, there was no place for a landing on the bank of the river, and the stakes are all that now remain to mark the progress of the town.

In may, 1849, Theophile Brughier, a native of Canada, but of French descent, settled at the mouth of the Big Sioux River, about two miles above where Sioux City now stands. Three years before he had visited the spot and made selection of the location. In 1835, at the age of twenty, Brughier left Canada and went to St. Louis, where he had an uncle who was a member of the American Fur Company. Under the advice of his uncle he engaged in the service of the company, but remained in their employ only a short time, when he joined the Yankton Sioux Indians and married a daughter of the somewhat distinguished chief, *Hu-yan-e-ka* (War Eagle). He became a prominent man in the tribe, and had acquired great influence among them. After remaining with the Indians, and sharing the fortunes of the tribe for some ten years, he concluded to change his manner of life, and notified the tribe of his intentions. Accordingly, with his faithful Indian wife and children, he left the post of the American Fur Company and came down the river and settled, as above stated, at the mouth of Big Sioux River. War Eagle, the Indian father-in-law of Brughier, died in his house in the fall of 1851, aged about sixty-five years. He was a noted warrior among the Sioux, but always a friend of the whites. He was first recognized as a Chief of the Yankton Sioux by Major Pilcher, the Indian agent. About the year 1830 he was for some time employed as a pilot on the Upper Mississippi. His remains, with those of his two daughters, one of them the deceased wife of Mr. Brughier, now repose on the summit of a lofty bluff on the Iowa side of the Big Sioux River, just above its mouth. Here are also the graves of several other Indians, as well as whites —eight or ten in all. From this romantic spot may be seen for many miles the broad winding Missouri, with its noble valley, the far off Blackbird Hills in Nebraska, with the intervening plains, islands and groves, and a portion of the rich bottom lands of Dakota, stretching as far as the eye can reach between the two rivers toward the northwest.

In the fall of 1849, Robert Perry, a man of somewhat eccentric character, but of fine education, removed from Washington, D. C., and settled on the small creek which meanders through Sioux City, where he remained two years, and then removed elsewhere. The creek now bears his name. The next year Paul Pacquette located at the crossing of Big Sioux River, about two miles above the mouth.

In the spring of 1852, Mr. Brughier sold a portion of his cultivated land, including what is now a part of Sioux City, to a Frenchman named Joseph Lionais, for one thousand dollars. About this time some difficulty occurred with the Indians at Fort Vermillion, and a small number of French descended the river and made a temporary settlement in the same vicinity. After this no further permanent improvement was made until the spring of 1854, when Doctor John K. Cook, who had a government contract for surveying, arrived with his party. Being impressed with the eligibility of the place for the location of a town, and the romantic beauty of its surroundings, he and his party immmediately located claims. Among those who selected and located claims at an early day in the vicinity of Sioux City, was the brave General Lyon, who fell at Wilson's Creek.

At the mouth of the Floyd River, Dr. Cook found encamped the red men of the forest, with Smutty Bear, their Chief, who ordered him to desist from his work under penalty of being driven from the place by his wariors, whom Smutty Bear would summon from the upper country. The belligerent Doctor boldly replied, through the interpreter, that he would go at once, if necessary, for a sufficient force to exterminate Smutty Bear and his band. Dr. Cook plainly told him that he had come there to make a survey, and he meant to complete his undertaking. The savages, impressed with the determination evinced by Dr. Cook, and intimidated by his well-timed threatenings, struck their tepees and departed, leaving him to complete his labors uninterrupted.

In the Winter of 1854-5, the town of Sioux City was laid out. Among the settlers at that time were the following: Hiram Nelson, Marshall Townsley, Franklin Wixon, G. W. Chamberlain, and Francis Chappel. About this time the Indians became troublesome, and began to steal horses, cattle and other property. Expeditions were fitted out against them, none of which, however, were attended with bloodshed. In the spring of 1855, Joseph Lionais sold his land for three thousand dollars, and on this an addition to Sioux City was laid out. It then contained two log cabins, but now comprises the principal business portion of the city. The first stage and mail arrived in Sioux City about the first week in September of this year, a postoffice having first been established. This event was hailed by the settlers as the beginning of the era of civilization. By Christmas Day there were seven log houses, two of them being hotels—the "Sioux City House," and the "Western Exchange." Two stores were opened, one of which was kept in a tent, and the other in a log cabin. Late in the season settlers came in rapidly, and many who could not obtain houses were obliged to camp out. In the Spring of 1856 the population had reached about 150. The land office had been opened here for pre-emptions, October 22, 1855, but the public lands were not offered for sale until May 4, 1857.

By an act of the Legislature the county seat had, 1853, been located at Floyd's Bluff. In the Spring of 1856 it was removed to Sioux City by a vote of the citizens of the county, the majority in favor of removal being fourteen. The county was organized in 1853.

The first steamboat freighted for Sioux City was the "Omaha," and arrived in June, 1856. Her freight consisted of ready framed houses and provisions. In July of this year a steam saw mill was erected. Mrs. S. H. Casady and Mrs. J. R. Myers were the first women who spent a Winter in Sioux City. Both came in the Summer of 1855. The first white child born in the place was a daughter of S. H. Casady and wife, in 1856.

Among transcriptions from the earliest records, we find the following:

SERGEANT'S BLUFFS, WOODBURY COUNTY, STATE OF IOWA:
To the organizing Sheriff of said County: We have fixed upon the southeast quarter of section 1, township 88, range 48, west of the Fifth Principal Meridian, as the point for the seat of justice for the aforesaid county of Woodbury, and set a stake on the avenue, coming east and west between lots 131 and 97, as laid down in Thompson's plat of Floyd's Bluffs, in said County, and recorded in the Recorder's Office of Pottawattamie County, Iowa, this 18th day of July, 1853.   THOMAS L. GRIFFEY,
                                        IRA PERYIER,
                                            Commissioners.

This appears to be a copy from the Pottawattamie County records. The next entry bears date of January 2, 1854, and mentions that Thomas L. Griffey is allowed for services as Locating Commissioner $18.50, the same being Order No. 1. It would seem that men were scarce; for Order No. 3 is also to Thomas L. Griffey for services as Locating Sheriff. July 16th, 1854. Ray Harvey is allowed $2 for hauling a box of books from Council Bluffs City. These were doubtless the first permanent records kept by the county. By a warrant—or bond, it is called in the record,—issued August 10, 1854, it appears that Leonard Bates had acted as Clerk of Elections, and that R. E. Knox acted as the first District Clerk, probably Clerk of Election.

August 12th, 1854, is the first entry bearing date of Sergeant's Bluffs, which appears to have been written there. This entry mentions that L. Bates is allowed $16.65 for services as Treasurer and Recorder, and is signed by M. Townsley, County Judge. On the same day, Lewis Cunningham is allowed $10.50 for services rendered as Assessor.

The officials mentioned appear to have been appointed to hold until the first election; for on August 16th of the year following,

John K. Cook gives his bond as County Judge; Samuel H. Casady as Treasurer; M. F. Moore, Prosecuting Attorney.

October 15th this entry appears: "John R. Myers was this day appointed District Clerk for this county, in place of Theophile Brughier, suspended by the District Judge at the last term of District Court." The proceedings, as appears by this record, are mixed as to dates, as if some were original entries and others were copied from an older book.

August 1, 1853, Thomas L. Griffey as Organizing Sheriff, appointed Orin B. Smith Prosecuting Attorney and Eli Lee, Coroner. On the 30th of the same month, Hiram Nelson gives his bonds as Treasurer and Recorder.

A petition is on record, asking Orin B. Smith, County Judge, to call an election on the first Monday of April, 1855, to decide whether the county seat shall not be removed from Sergeant's Bluffs to Sergeant's Bluffs City. The petition is signed by twenty-six persons. The first seat of justice was half way between Sioux City and the present station of Sergeant's Bluffs. It is called on the records indifferently, Sergeant's Bluffs, Thompsontown and Floyd's Bluffs.

The election removed the county capital to Sergeant's Bluffs City, now Sergeant's Bluffs Station, on the Sioux City & Pacific road, where it remained until March 3d. Here let the record under this date tell the story.

March term of County Court of Woodbury County:—Met at Sioux City, there being no place at the county seat for holding said court, first Monday of March.

Petition of S. P. Yeomans and George Weare and others—forty-nine others—praying for the removal of the county seat from its present location to Sioux City.

Remonstrance presented by F. E. Clark, J. D. M. Crockwell and others, against the removal of the county seat.

F. Chapel, Sheriff, sworn; that the notices of the presentation of the petition for the removal of the county seat were duly posted, according to law.

This is all that is disclosed by the records about the locating of the county seat at Sioux City. When it is remembered that the County Judge before whom the petition for removal came, was John K. Cook, the founder of Sioux City, no further record is needed to indicate what disposition was made of the petition for removal.

April 15th, 1859, Bernhard Henn, Jesse Williams, A. C. Dodge, and others, petition the County Judge, John K. Cook, to enter for them the west one-half of section 28, township 89, range 47, as a town-site in trust for the lot owners. This town-site in the petition is called East Sioux City, now part of Sioux City east addition, and now comprises the principal business and residence parts of the town.

The present officers of Woodbury County are: J. R. Zuver, Circuit Judge, Fourth Judicial District; C. H. Lewis, District Judge, Fourth Judicial District; S. M. Marsh, District Attorney;

Auditor, M. L. Sloan; Treasurer, John P. Allison; Clerk of Courts, J. H. Bolton; Recorder, Phil Carlin; Sheriff, D. McDonald; Coroner, Dr. W. O. Davis; Superintendent of Schools, N. E. Palmer; Surveyor, G. W. Oberholtzer; Attor.iey, G. W. Wakefield; Insane Commissioners, J. H. Bolton, Isaac Pendleton, Dr. J. M. Knott; Supervisors. P. C. Eberley, J. S. Horton, John Nairn, A. J. Weeks, D. T. Gilman.

SIOUX CITY.

While other cities may owe their location to some accident, the whim of an officer locating a military post, the ambition of a pioneer to have a townsite on his pre-emption, or the chance settlement of a trader, Sioux City's location was a matter of foresight and design by men worthy to be the founders of such a city.

When, in the summer of 1853, John K. Cook came into this part of Northwestern Iowa to survey the land for the Government, he had instructions from an association of capitalists and politicians to choose for them a site for a city, to be the metropolis of this part of the northwest. The principal men of the association were Gen. G. W. Jones and A. C. Dodge, Iowa's first Senators, Bernhard Henn, of Fairfield, also a Congressman; his partner in the banking business, Jesse Williams; Daniel Rider, also of Fairfield, and Wm. Montgomery, a Congressman from Pennsylvania, the author of the famous Montgomery Compromise: John K. Cook, who surveyed the land for the Government; and S. P. Yeomans, afterwards Register of the Government Land Office at Sioux City.

This land office was secured for the infant metropolis by the influence of the men who founded the city, and this and the business and settlement it brought, forced the town rapidly ahead of its many competitors.

Thompsontown, once the county seat, dwindled to a single farm house; Sergeant Bluffs, at first the most formidable rival, was soon outstripped, and the county seat that had been moved to that village from Thompsontown, was again moved to Sioux City.

Omadi, on the Nebraska side, once thought to be the coming town in this part of the northwest, has been swallowed up by the river, and the main channel is now where the main street was; of St. John, another Nebraska city of the future, only two or three farm houses remain on the town site, that covered one thousand acres; Dakota City and Covington, once formidable rivals of Sioux City, still exist, but only as villages. Sioux City has grown and prospered from the first. The securing of the Government Land Office was followed by the city securing the headquarters for the government expeditions against the hostile Sioux, and afterwards by its becoming the terminus of railroads created by land grant bills.

First its founders, and afterwards the leading men of the town, have been tireless in their efforts to advance the interests of the city. To this, even more than to its superior location, is the present prosperity of the city indebted.

The population of the city has more than doubled since 1870. According to the official figures of the federal census taken in June, 1880, the population was 7,367. But to-day we can easily calculate upon 10,000 being the correct figures, for not a single business-house is unoccupied, and although building boomed as never before last season, this winter sees many begging for houses to rent or quarters of some kind in which to locate. The demand for tenement houses is greater than the supply, and in many cases families are crowded into one room, not being able to secure more available quarters.

The population of the county, according to the census, excluding Sioux City, was 7,626, the whole county exceeding the town by 259. The county is divided into twenty-two townships, and the population of the whole county, including Sioux City, according to census figures, is given as follows:

Sioux City—First Ward...1,707
            Second Ward..2,074
            Third Ward...1,786
            Fourth Ward..1,800
Sioux City township 480
Arlington township 137
Concord township 340
Banner township... 64
Floyd township.. 194
Grange township 118
Grant Township.. 460
Kedron township... 316
Little Sioux township 876
Liberty township 721
Liston township 408
Lakeport township... 436
Union township 597
Moville township.. 117
Willow township... 242
Rock township... 250
Rutland township.. 197
Sloan township.. 312
Wolk Creek township... 418
Morgan township... 63
West Fork township 286
Woodbury township 594
                                                               _____
      Total...14,993

What has been said in regard to the city's population holds equally true of the county, outside of the city. Since the census enumeration many families have bought farms and settled in the county. In fact, the tide of immigration to Woodbury, which has never been greater than during the last year, did not set in until after June, and continued until cold weather set in. It is safe, therefore, to estimate the present population of the city and county at 19,000, at least.

SIOUX CITY'S RAILROAD INTERESTS.

The founders of Sioux City had not got fairly settled on their townsite before they began to agitate the question of securing railroads. The location of the town seemed made by nature for a railroad center, supposing that nature contemplated railroads when this section of the world was made. The great Missouri, coming down through its wide valley, flows in a general easterly course and here makes an abrupt bend to the south, the first great change in course above Kansas City. The Big Sioux comes down from the north, and at its head the Red River starts on its course north, the valleys of the two streams forming a natural route for a railroad from Sioux City to the British Possessions. The Niobrara coming from the west flows straight toward Sioux City until it joins the Missouri at the first great bend above the city. The Floyd coming from the northeast invited a road from the Minnesota lumber country, and afforded a route into the young metropolis for a road across the State, while the rock bluff that crops out above the town suggests a bridge site and lines beyond the Missouri. All these ideas were urged by the more progressive of the founders of the city, and, though visionary then to a commonplace mind, have been either made realities, or are in a fair way to become realities.

Sioux City was fortunate in having as a member of Congress, during the years in which land grants were being given to railroads, a citizen active, far-sighted and tireless, the late Judge Hubbard. It was this gentleman who secured the insertion of a clause in the original land grant bill of the Union Pacific providing for a branch of this road to Sioux City, who secured the change of the land grant from the bankrupt Dubuque & Missouri River road to the Iowa Falls & Sioux City, and finally, in 1864, by the help of the Minnesota Congressmen, procured the passage of a bill granting lands to the amount of 10 sections per mile to the Sioux City & St. Paul road. But in spite of the tempting offers of lands, and in the case of the Sioux City branch of the Union Pacific, of guaranteed government bonds as well, nothing was done toward building these roads until late in 1867.

Sioux City & Pacific.—John I. Blair, even then a veteran railroad man, in that year agreed to build the Sioux City branch of the Union Pacific if a modification of the line could be secured. What he wanted, and got, was permission to build from Missouri Valley north to Sioux City, a distance of 77 miles, and to build from Missouri Valley west, across the Missouri River to Fremont, a distance of 37 miles. The original bill did not contemplate any such line, but one crossing the River at Sioux City, and running southwest to a junction with the Union Pacific at Columbus. Mr. Blair having secured the change in the route asked; proceeded to build the road. Besides the land grant and government bonds, the wily railroader secured from Sioux City a tract of land amounting to about 14 acres near the business center of the town, and several thousand acres of swamp land from the county of Woodbury.

The road, under the name of the Sioux City & Pacific, was finished so as to allow the first passenger train to run from Missouri Valley to Sioux City on March 9, 1868. The citizens were wild with enthusiasm, and the newspapers flamed with head lines over this connection with the railroad world. The year following the completion of the Sioux City road, the Blair cut-off, between Missouri Valley, on the Northwestern, and Fremont, on the Union Pacific, was built. This gave a connection with the Union Pacific, of which great things were expected; but the bridging of the Missouri at Omaha sent most of the business that way, instead of across the river at Blair, where a transfer boat was used. From Blair a branch was started up the Elkhorn Valley, that has grown from year to year, until, at the close of 1881, it rested at Long Pine, 250 miles northwest of Blair. Surveys have been made for an extension from Long Pine west to the Wyoming line, and the line seems likely to become in reality, what it is in name, a Sioux City and Pacific road.

Illinois Central.—The general joy over securing the first railroad, took the very practical form of a move to secure other railroads. In the Spring of 1869, Mr. Blair and his associates began building from Sioux City east, and from Iowa Falls west, to secure the land grant of the Iowa Falls & Sioux City road. That year the west section was built to Cherokee, and from the east as far as Fort Dodge. Early in the summer of 1870 the road was finished. It was leased to the Illinois Central, a company that has since operated it. The rental paid is 35 per cent. of the gross earnings.

Chicago, St. Paul, Minneapolis and Omaha.—Fast following on this road came the Sioux City & St. Paul. As has been mentioned, Judge Hubbard, in 1864, when in Congress, procured a land grant for this project, but no work was done until 1872, when the franchises having passed to the St. Paul & Sioux City company, the road was built from the Minnesota State line to Le Mars. There connection was made with the Illinois Central, and the right to run trains over that company's track to Sioux City secured. The year following Sioux City voted the company $20,-000 in consideration of establishing repair shops in the town. Extensive shops were built, and these have since been enlarged until, during the past summer, over 200 men were employed there. In the Spring of 1881, the St. Paul & Sioux City road was consolidated with various Wisconsin roads and now forms a part of the Chicago, St. Paul, Minneapolis & Omaha railway.

The necessity of developing a system of roads in Nebraska diverging from this city, was early apparent to the public-spirited men who made the town the railroad center that it is. In this, as in most other railroad enterprises of the town, the late Judge Hubbard took a leading a part.

After much preliminary surveying and agitation, work was begun on a line from Covington to Ponca in the fall of 1876. The road, a narrow guage, was finished to Ponca early in 1877. Grading was done beyond that town into Cedar county, but the company became involved in litigation on account of the bonds issued by the Nebraska counties in aid of the road, and the line passed into the hands of a receiver.

At the time the Ponca line was building some little grading was done on a line which was projected between this city and Columbus on the Union Pacific road. This project rested with the resting of the Ponca line, and nothing more was done in the way of work on the Nebraska lines until the St. Paul & Sioux City acquired possession of the different interests in the Nebraska roads in the fall of 1879.

The winter following material was crossed for extensive work on the newly acquired road, and on the roads projected, and the next spring business began in earnest. The twenty-six miles of narrow gauge track between Covington, on the Nebraska shore opposite this city, and Ponca, was widened to standard gauge, and substantially rebuilt. Surveys have been made west of Ponca looking to an extension of this branch to Niobrara. This extension will be built in 1882, if a tax asked by the company be voted in Cedar County, which now seems probable.

In 1880 a track was built from Coburn Junction, on the Ponca line, to the south 52 miles, where the end of a track extending from Oakland to Omaha was met. This track had previously been bought by the St. Paul & Sioux City Company. This line gives a new connection between the lumber country of Minnesota and Wisconsin, and the Union Pacific road. In the winter of 1881-2 the 47 miles of track from Emerson Junction, on the Omaha line, was completed to Norfolk, the railroad center of Northern Nebraska. A bill recently introduced in Congress during the session of 1881-2, to revive the charter of the Sioux City branch of the Union Pacific, indicates that this line is to be extended from Norfolk west to some point on the Union Pacific.

The building of these numerous lines by the company in Nebraska will, at an early day, make necessary a bridge at this city. Soundings were made as early as 1869, and bed rock suitable for the foundation of bridge piers was found at depths ranging from 30 to 50 feet below low water mark. The range of bluffs that comes to the river edge in the west part of the city, forms a convenient approach on one side, which is all that any bridge site on the Missouri offers. The building of a bridge, which cannot be delayed for more than a year or two, will do much to fix the business of Northern Nebraska at this city. During 1881, the company has, in a measure, prepared for an increase in the Nebraska business by building nearly four miles of side track in the city, and by the purchase of depot grounds, at an expense of $20,000 near the business center of the town. A survey has been partially made between LeMars, where the company's track joins that of the Illinois Central, to this city, and there is good assurance that the company will build this track in 1882.

Right here it may be in order to speak of the company's land grant, some 20,000 acres of which, lying in this county and in Plymouth county, is in dispute, unfortunately, and so cannot be sold to settlers until the question between the State and the company is settled. The company has built 57½ miles of road in Iowa, which fact has been duly certified by the Governor to the General Government, and the land at the rate of ten sections per mile has been turned over to the State in trust for the railroad company. The State has, in turn, certified the land grant of 50 miles of road to the company. The lands for the other 7½ miles the State holds, claiming that the road was entitled to it only as sections of ten miles of road were completed, and the showing of the Railroad company was that the last section lacked 2½ miles of being ten miles long. The company holds that as the General Goverment has waived the ten-mile point, and certified the lands to the State for the use and benefit of the company the State should certify the lands for the 7½ miles of road built to the company. Meantime the State holds the lands in abeyance, and settlement is kept out. It would require only a part of the land thus held by the State to give the company the ten sections per mile for the 7½ miles built and unsubsidized. There is also a question between the St. Paul and the Milwaukee companies as to the ownership of about 185,000 acres of land in the vicinity of the crossing point of the two roads. This land is now being sold, and both companies join in giving title, and agree that the company that wins in the courts shall have the money for the disputed lands sold. If this dispute is settled in favor of the Milwaukee Company, it will take all the lands in dispute between the State and the St. Paul Company to make good the land grant of that Company.

Chicago, Milwaukee & St. Paul.—The first spike on the track leading from Sioux City to Yankton was driven in this city Aug. 12, 1872, and the track was finished to Yankton on the 28th of January following. This road is noticeable as the first built in this part of the west without a land grant. The construction company, Wicker & Meckling, of Chicago, obtained a tax from Sioux City, voted the Sioux City & Pembina road, and it was under this name that the road was built as far as the Big Sioux bridge. They also obtained $200,000 in bonds from Yankton County, and a lesser amount from stations along the route. This was the first

track in Dakota, south of the Northern Pacific, except a few miles
built across the line near where Watertown now is, but abandoned
after the land grant was secured. It had long been a favorite
plan of the public spirited men of this city to build a road north,
up the Big Sioux Valley, and the Sioux City & Pembina was organized in 1871 for this purpose. The leading spirit, as in most
other railroad projects in these parts, was Judge Hubbard. The
year following the organization, taxes were voted in aid of the road
by Sioux City township and by the townships in the west part of
Plymouth County, and some grading was done. But the financial
crisis of 1873 coming on, work was suspended. In 1875 the
owners of the track between Sioux City and Yankton began work
at Davis Junction on a road up the Big Sioux Valley, and
that year completed sixteen miles to Portlandville. In 1878 the
road was finished to Beloit, and in December, 1879, the track was
laid into Sioux Falls. It was in the spring of this year, 1879, that
John I. Blair reappeared on the railroad stage, after several years
absence, and bought what he supposed was a controlling interest
in the Yankton and Sioux Falls lines. At his suggestion the two
were consolidated into the Sioux City & Dakota Railway. In the
summer of 1880 the Chicago, Milwaukee & St. Paul Railway Company bought Mr. Wicker's interest in the Sioux City & Dakota
road, and after a tedious litigation Mr. Blair sold his interest to
the same company. The addition of a third road to Chicago by
this purchase was hailed with enthusiasm by our business men.
The connection, opening up as it does to the trade of the city, the
best part of Southeastern Dakota and Northern Iowa, has been a
great advantage, while as an eastern connection the new line has
done much to bring the freight rate down to a point that enabled
our wholesale dealers to compete with those of Omaha and St.
Paul. During the past year, 1881, the company has completed
its line up the Big Sioux Valley, from Sioux Falls to Flandrau,
where connection is made with the company's Southern Minnesota
division, and has partly graded a line from Yankton to Scotland,
which when ironed, will give our dealers a direct line to the lower
Jim River Valley. But the work that promised to be of most advantage to the city is the line surveyed southeast, ninety miles, to
a connection with the company's new main line, that during 1881
was nearly completed between Marion and Council Bluffs. This
line when built, as it is likely to be in 1882, will not only open up
a new section to the trade of our city, but will give a shorter track
between Sioux City and Chicago. Some steps have been taken toward securing shops of this company at this city, but nothing definite has as yet been assured.

Railroad Probabilities.—These are the railroad lines to which
Sioux City owes her importance as a commercial center. There
are besides several roads to get, which may be briefly mentioned:
The Iowa Railroad Land Company, the owners of the Maple Val-

ley branch of the Chicago & Northwestern, put a party of engineers in the field in December, 1881, to make a survey for a line between Sac City, the terminus of a spur of the branch mentioned, to Sioux City. There is good assurance that a part of this line, at least, will be built in 1882, and that the line will eventually be extended to a connection with the company's system of roads in Dakota. The Wabash, in the Summer of 1881, leased the Des Moines & Northwestern, a narrow gauge road running northwest from Des Moines. Late in the year the company secured an old roadbed and right of way from Rockwell City to Sac City, and there is the authority of the President of the Narrow Gauge Road for saying that it is to be extended either to Sioux City or Sioux Falls. The branch of the St. Paul Road that now extends down the Rock River to Doon, it is hoped, will be extended south to Sioux City, and an effort is being made to have the 20,000 acres of disputed land grant mentioned diverted to the aid of this extension. The St. Paul and the Sioux City & Pacific, together, have planned to extend from Fremont to Lincoln, and this Nebraska line, of the greatest usefulness to Sioux City, is likely to be built during 1882. Most important of all the expected lines, is the Central Pacific. During 1881, this company had a preliminary survey made between Corinne, near its eastern terminus, to the mouth of the Niobrara River. The short and natural route for a road coming down the Niobrara Valley, seeking a Chicago connection, is to cross the Missouri River at Sioux City. A letter written by Vice President Huntington of this road to one of our citizens says, that the Central Pacific will be extended from Corinne to some point on the Missouri River not yet determined on. As Sioux City presents a good bridge site, and is on the most direct route, there is a reasonable certainty that she will secure this prize. With the roads already built into this city, neither the Central Pacific, nor any other road, can afford to come within reaching distance of Sioux City and not send in a line.

BOATING BUSINESS.

The first steamboat came up the Missouri to Sioux City in the Spring of 1856. The river route was then the only one open for the bringing in of heavy freight; and the material for a number of residences and business houses, and several stocks of goods came in on this first boat. With the settlement of the country around the city, came a demand from the military posts and mining camps further up the river, for any surplus produce marketed in the city, and orders for goods began to be sent down to Sioux City. The up-river business of the city grew steadily, and new boats were added every year to the carrying trade. The opening of the rich mines in the Black Hills greatly increased this business, and there has been a steady increase in the amount of grain, pork and merchandise sent from the city to points further up the Missouri.

Sioux City is the headquarters of the Peck line of boats, which line comprises the steamers C. K. Peck, Nellie Peck, Terry, Peninah, Meade, and Far West. The Benton line, Coulson line and Kountz line of boats also find much profitable freight at this city. Costly experience has proved to the satisfaction of river men that the winter harbor here is the safest on the upper river, and numbers of the river steamers are put on the ways at this city for repair every winter.

Many of Sioux City's business men are interested in stock raising, mining, the fur trade, and other up-river enterprises, and their connection with the "up-country" forms a bond of union of great help to the trade of the city. Several hundred thousand bushels of corn and oats are sent every summer to points further up the Missouri, and more than half the immense out-put of the pork packing establishment finds a market in the same quarter, while the growth of the wholesale trade of our merchants in these parts has kept steady pace with the growth of this newest portion of the new Northwest.

During the winter of 1878, Congress made an appropriation for the improvement of the river, and the protection of the levee at Sioux City, and has, each subsequent winter, made further appropriations for carrying on the work. The first systematic attempt to prevent the encroachment of the river on our levee was made during the Summer of 1879, by Major Yonge, of the United States Engineer Corps. The work has been carried on every season since, with results, on the whole, satisfactory. The banks on either side now appear to be permanently fixed, and much valuable data has been obtained that will be of use when the improvement of the entire river below Sioux City is attempted, by government, as it evidently will be in the near future.

THE NEWSPAPERS.

. The press of Sioux City has been an important factor in the upbuilding of the city, and no other single agency has contributed more to make the city what it is. It has ever been said, that a town may be judged by the character of its newspapers. If this be true, Sioux City can make an excellent showing, as no city in the State of its size has as many or as good newspapers as are published here. To-day, it has one morning, two evening and three weekly journals, all well supported.

The pioneer newspaper of Sioux City, as well as of Woodbury County, was called the *Sioux City Eagle*, and the first number was issued July 4th, 1857, with S. W. Swiggett as editor and proprietor. It was independent in politics, and for those days, a sprightly, well conducted sheet. Its publication was continued for nearly three years, when it passed out of existence.

The next newspaper venture was made by F. M. Ziebach. The August previous, he, in conjunction with J. N. Cum-

mings, under the firm name of Cummings & Ziebach, began the
publication of the *Western Independent*—independent in politics—
at Sergeant's Bluffs, eight miles south of Sioux City. It was regularly published until the following July, when Mr. Ziebach purchased his partner's interest in the paper, and removed the material to Sioux City, which, even then, gave promise of being the
metropolis of the Northwest; and on July 22d, 1858, gave to Sioux
City its second weekly newspaper, the *Sioux City Register*. With
the change of name also came a change in politics, the Register
being the first to champion Democracy in Northwestern Iowa.

In 1859 William Freney purchased an interest in the paper, and
the year following it was consolidated with the *Eagle*. The *Register* was continued under the management of Ziebach & Freney until 1862, when Mr. Ziebach withdrew, leaving Mr. Freney to continue
it alone, which he did until 1871, when its publication was suspended.

Shortly after the consolidation of the *Register* and *Eagle*, in
1860, Pendleton & Swiggett started the *Sioux City Times*—Republican in politics. It survived only a few months.

Three years later, another attempt was made, by J. C. Stillman,
to establish a Republican paper, *The Sioux City Journal*, but it
ceased to exist before the publication of a dozen numbers. August
29th, 1864, it was resuscitated, under the editorial management of
J. V. Baugh, and its publication has been continued uninterruptedly ever since, though it has passed through many trying
ordeals, with several changes in its management.

In October of the same year, S. T. Davis, then Register of the
Land Office, succeeded Mr. Baugh as editor, but only remained in
charge until the close of the Presidential campaign in 1864, when
the paper passed into the hands of Mahlon Gore, a brilliant writer
and an accomplished journalist. In 1868, B. L. Northrup purchased an interest in the paper, but retired in a short time, leaving
Mr. Gore to continue it alone, which he did until May 1st, 1869,
when he disposed of it to George D. Perkins, who has been its
editor ever since.

The following January, H. A. Perkins bought an interest in the
paper, and the firm of Perkins Brothers was formed, and continued until July, 1875, when H. A. Perkins retired; but after an
absence of nearly two years, he returned; the firm name of Perkins Brothers was restored, and continues to the present time.

In 1870 a morning edition was issued from the office, and has
appeared regularly ever since. *The Daily Journal* has grown and
strengthened with its years, until to-day it ranks with the foremost papers of the State. It is a handsome, nine-column folio,
printed on a press of the latest pattern, and has a large and increasing circulation. The mechanical execution is in the highest
style of the art. Its editor, George D. Perkins, is a polished, con-
scientious and able writer, and a gentleman who has a high ideal
of journalism.

' *The Journal* building is a fine establishment, and the whole enterprise is an illustration of what may be accomplished by talent and energy, directed by sound financial ability and good management. Few papers have achieved a more decided and permanent success, than *The Sioux City Journal*, in the hands of its present proprietors, and, it may be added, none are more deserving of the grand success they have won, as they have built up an institution of which Sioux City may well feel proud.

In May, 1869, a stock company began the publication of the *Daily and Weekly Times*, a journal neutral in politics, with Charles Collins as the editor. In a short time Mr. Collins became sole proprietor, changing the publication from a morning to an evening paper. In 1872, the daily edition was discontinued, but the weekly was maintained until 1874, when it was purchased by Warner & Gore, made Democratic in politics, and the name changed to the *Sioux City Tribune*, under which name it has been continued until the present time, though many changes have occurred in its management. At the close of the Presidential campaign, in 1876, Mr. Warner retired, being succeeded by C. R. Smead, the style of the firm becoming Gore & Smead. August, 1877, Mr. Gore left the paper, because of ill health, Mr. Smead continuing its publication until December 6th of the same year, when Albert Watkins purchased an interest, and assumed editorial management. May 1st, 1879, Mr. Watkins bought his partner's interest, and continued the publication of the paper alone until July 1st, 1880, when he disposed of it to John C. Kelley, its present editor and proprietor. *The Tribune* is a six-column quarto, well printed, ably edited, and is on a solid financial footing, with a rapidly increasing business. It is an unfaltering advocate of Democracy, and the recognized organ of the party in the Northwest.

There is also issued from the Tribune office the *Anpao*, a monthly journal, in the Sioux dialect, in the interests of the Niobrara Mission. It is edited by Rev. Joseph W. Cook, and Rev. J. W. Cleveland, and published under the management of James R. Fraser.

The only German paper ever published here is the *Sioux City Weekly Courier*, which made its first appearance in 1870, under the management of Wetter & Danquard. After a short time, Mr. Wetter purchased his partner's interest and continued it alone for a few months, when he disposed of it to Dr. C. J. Krejci. Subsequently the paper passed into the hands of Chas. F. Schroeder, who, however, sold it to Herman Schorning. Mr. Schorning continued it until it became the property of its present publisher, Frederick Barth, in November, 1877. *The Courier* is Democratic in politics, under its present management, is well conducted, the only German paper in this section, and has a wide circulation.

The *Cosmopolite*, a sixteen-page monthly, was established by D. H. Talbot July 1st, 1879, and continued for two years. It was is-

sued mainly in the interest of private enterprises, but contained
much matter of general interest.

In August, 1881, Charles Collins commenced the *Sioux City Daily
Times*, an evening sheet, independent in politics. The *Times* is a
sprightly six-column folio, devoted to local news, and rapidly establishing itself on a firm footing. Its editor and proprietor, Mr.
Charles Collins, is a veteran journalist and a ready and forcible
writer.

Two weeks after the first issue of the *Daily Times*, another can-
didate for public favor made its appearance, the *Sioux City Daily
News*, published by Watkins & Jay. Like its contemporary, *The
Times*, it is a six-column folio, independent in politics, but with
Democratic tendencies.

The *Sioux City Grocer*, established in 1881, is a handsome
monthly, published by E. C. Palmer & Co., and issued in the interest of the grocery trade.

In August, 1877, Alex. Macready began the publication of the
Industrial Press, a weekly newspaper, advocating the Greenback
doctrine. It was continued about a year, when it ceased to exist.

The *Sioux City Gazette* was commenced by R. Goldie & Son.,
December 1st, 1877, but after a few issues suspended publication.

PORK PACKING.

Pork packing was begun, in a small way, in Sioux City, in the
winter of 1872-3. The building occupied was a small wooden affair
on Water street above Fifth. That season H. D. Booge & Co.
killed 5,000 hogs. The experiment was a success, and the following summer a large brick building was put up on the site of the
frame one, where the business first started. Additions to this
building were made from year to year, until its capacity was increased to 500 hogs per day, and there was no room for further extensions. In the spring of 1881, work was begun on the pork
house now occupied in the east part of the city. The site is all
that could be wished. The Floyd furnishes drainage, and the
nearness to railroads allows the cars of the different lines centering at the city to deliver hogs directly into the yards beside the
packing house, and to load the manufactured product directly from
the storage rooms into the cars. There is plenty of ground,
some fourteen acres of city lots having been bought. The new
building cost over $100,000, and more than a million and a half
of brick were used in its building. It is pronounced by competent
judges the most complete structure of the kind in the State. The
ice is run directly from the Floyd River into the great 6,000 ton
ice house. For summer packing this ice in skidded from the ice
house into the refrigerator that occupies an entire story of the
main building. A steam elevator connects the different floors.
In the fertilizer room, the parts that would otherwise go to waste,
are worked over into an odorless powder that is in demand for

enriching the worn-out fields of the east. Every part of the defunct porker is utilized, from the tough terminus of the snout, to the brush of bristles that beautifies the tip of the tail. The house has a capacity of 1,000 hogs per day, the capacity being measured by the hanging capacity. This has been found insufficient for the hogs offered, and the coming season an addition will be built that will increase the capacity about 50 per cent.

The firm conducting the business of Jas. E. Booge & Co., consists of Jas. E. Booge, of Sioux City, and John L. Merriam, A. H. Wilder and Wm. R. Merriam, of St. Paul. The first named gentleman has been connected with the business from the first, and the three others for several years. As appears from the report made to the Board of Trade, the pork house had, during the two months ending January 1st, 1882, killed 37,000 hogs, and paid for these $580,000. The labor bills during this time footed up $14,000 and the pay roll showed 188 men employed.

No other business in Sioux City does so much to advertise the name of the town. The hams made can be found on hotel tables from Chicago to San Francisco. The side meat goes mostly to the south, Memphis, New Orleans and Mobile being the principal points of sale. The lard goes to Chicago and the bacon finds a ready market all over the west, the heaviest demand coming from the mining camps and military posts of the Upper Missouri. The Sioux City Pork house has a practical monopoly of supplying hog products to the military posts in the northwest, having, during the past year, secured more than eighty per cent. of the contracts let. The position of the town as a railroad center, in the midst of one of the best corn growing sections of the Union, makes the steady supply of swine certain, and the exceptional advantages for the distribution of the product, allows prices to be paid that while renumerative to the hog grower, leaves a fair margin of profit to the packer.

THE CITY LIBRARY.

There is nothing perhaps that speaks higher for the culture and enterprise of the city, than its valuable Public Library and Reading Room. Both are well patronized and supported. About two thousand well selected volumes are on the shelves, and mostly all the popular magazines and leading newspapers of the country, religious and secular, are kept on file. The Library is a large and pleasant room, situated in the City Hall, on one of the leading business streets. Miss Helen Smith is at present, and has been for some years past, the Librarian.

FOUNDRY AND MACHINE SHOPS.

The Sioux City Foundry and Machine Shop, is the pioneer manufacturing establishment of the city. Started in 1871, in a small way, and doing work only of the simplest kind, it has grown

with the city, until now its buildings extend over several acres of
ground, and its manufactures embrace everything in the different
branches of the business, from the plain castings in iron and brass,
to the building of heavy machinery for steamboats, saw mills,
quartz mills, planing mills, etc. As the growth of the city and
the wants of the trade demanded, new buildings with the required
machinery, have been added, from time to time, until the works
are now undoubtedly the largest and most complete of the kind in
the West. The main building is of brick, two stories high, with
a frontage of 120 feet. There is also an extensive boiler shop, detached from the main building, 70 by 80 feet. The works give
employment to 40 men, and their trade extends throughout the
Northwest, even reaching to the Black Hills. The establishment
is in every way creditable to Sioux City, as well as to the country
tributary.

Plow Works.—The broad and liberal policy of the citizens of
Sioux City towards manufacturing enterprises of merit, is in striking contrast with the narrow, selfish course of many western cities.
At all times they have been ready and willing to extend a helping
hand to any enterprise that would add to the material wealth
and advance the interests of the city, and the many manufacturing
industries that have located here of late demonstrate, beyond question, that the policy which has been pursued is the only true one,
and one that will ultimately place Sioux City in the front rank of
the manufacturing towns of the State.

The Board of Trade, of which appropriate mention is made elsewhere, has performed an important part in attracting many desirable manufacturers hither, and among the first brought here,
through its influence, was the Sioux City Plow Company, an institution of which the city feels justly proud. In May, 1880, a stock
company of practical mechanics was organized under the above
name, and commenced the erection of a suitable building for the
manufacture of plows, and in the following September the first
plow was turned out. The next season, their goods were placed
upon the market and immediately sprang into public favor; and
though the works have a capacity of fifty finished plows per day,
so great has become the demand that the company has not been
able to fully meet the requirements of its trade, and an increase in
the building capacity of the works has become an imperative necessity. The Sioux City Plow is made with special reference to its
adaptability to the peculiar soil of this section, and possesses many
points of superiority over those of Eastern manufacture. The
works of the company, situated in the southeastern part of the
city, are substantial, two-story brick buildings, supplied with all
the necessary machinery for the turning out of first class work.

THE GAS WORKS.

Long before Sioux City had a population of five thousand souls
her streets were lighted with gas. Through the untiring energy

and public spirit of a few of her leading citizens, in February, 1872, the Sioux City Gas Light Company was incorporated with an authorized capital of $100,000. D. T. Hedges was President, George Weare, Treasurer, and John P. Allison, Secretary. A substantial brick building was soon erected, and on the evening of March 17th, 1873, the city was illuminated by gas, the event being duly celebrated. It was not expected by the projectors of the enterprise, that the works in a town like Sioux City then was, would be self-sustaining; but they had an abiding faith in its future. Time has demonstrated that their confidence was not misplaced. The hazardous venture of ten years ago, is now a paying investment. The city has always lent the company a helping hand, and encouraged and fostered it with its patronage, oftentimes when its finances would hardly justify the outlay. The works· are now operated by private parties, under a lease from the incorporators of the company. About three million feet of gas is made annually, of which the city is a large consumer, all the leading thoroughfares being lighted by gas.

SIOUX CITY BOARD OF TRADE.

During the autumn of 1872, the first Citizens' Association, for the general advancement of the business and manufacturing interests of the city was formed. The first meeting for the formation of this association was held November 21st, 1872, at the court room, which was at that time in the Hubbard block, on Fourth street. It was called by the Mayor, G. W. Kingsnorth. Hon. A. W. Hubbard introduced the following resolution, which was unanimously adopted:

"*Resolved*, That this meeting is in favor of organizing an association, the object of which shall be to induce manufactures to come to this place."

A provisional board was appointed; also committees to draft a constitution, by-laws, and for procuring members.

December 9th the committee reported a constitution, which was adopted; and that they had secured 221 names for membership. The name this association adopted was "The Sioux City Chamber of Commerce."

January 13th, 1873, the following officers were elected for the year: President, J. C. Flint; First Vice-President, A. W. Hubbard; Second Vice-President, S. T. Davis; Directors, J. H. Swan, M. C. Bogue, J. J. Saville, L. C. Sanborn, C. E. Hedges, A. Groninger, J. P. Dennis, E. W. Skinner, A. R. Wright, H. L. Warner. Board of Arbitration, J. C. C. Hoskins, W. L. Joy, L. Wynn, J. E. Booge, L. McCarty; Secretary, F. C. Thompson. Treasurer, J. M. Pinckney.

During the year the organization secured the location of Joseph Trudell's wagon shop; entertained the St. Paul Chamber of Commerce on its visit to Sioux City, September 10th; published a

twenty-four page pamphlet, containing statistics and description
of the city, and did a good deal of miscellaneous work toward securing railroads. Government improvement of river, etc.

In January, 1874, the following officers were elected for the
year: President, J. C. C. Hoskins; First Vice-President, J. H.
Swan; Second Vice-President, L. C. Sanborn; Directors, James E.
Booge, Thomas J. Stone, William R. Smith, Joseph Schulien, L.
McCarty, James M. Bacon, E. B. Crawford, George W. Kings-
north, E. E. Lewis, C. J. Kathrens. Committee on Arbitration,
W. S. Joy, H. L. Warner, D. T. Hedges, J. C. Flint, A. W.
Hubbard. F. C. Thompson was re-elected Secretary, and J. M.
Pinckney, Treasurer.

This organization—The Chamber of Commerce—was quite active during the year in working up the material interests of the
city; but a quorum of members did not respond to the call for the
annual meeting of 1875, and the officers previously elected held
over.

In October, 1877, the merchants of Sioux City met and formed
the Merchants Exchange, and the following officers were elected
for the year: President, J. M. Bacon; Vice President, L. C. Sanborn; Secretary, E. H. Bucknam; Treasurer, A. C. Davis; Directors, H. L. Warner, H. A. Jandt, E. W. Rice, F. L. Goewey,

During the year, the subject of cheap ferriage to Covington, the
adjusting of railroad freights and the commercial interests of Sioux
City in general, had the attention of the Exchange with marked
success. They raised by voluntary subscriptions $1,929.60 during
the year, and paid to secure cheap ferriage, $1,500.

In October, 1878, the following officers were elected for the
year: President, J. M. Bacon; Vice President, E. C. Tompkins;
Secretary, E. W. Bucknam; Directors, H. L. Warner, H. A. Jandt,
M. W. Murphy, S. Schulein, F. L. Goewey.

In October, 1879, the following officers were elected: President,
H. A. Jandt; Vice President, M. W. Murphy, Secretary, E. G.
Burkam, Jr.; Treasurer, A. C. Davis; Directors, J. M. Bacon,
William Tackaberry, F. L. Goewey, W. H. Livingston, G. H.
Howell.

During the year, the Exchange, in addition to other important
work, raised quite a boom for the Chicago, Milwaukee & St. Paul
Railroad towards the purchase of depot grounds.

The officers elected October, 1879, held over until July, 1881,
when the exchange was reorganized, the name changed to the
Sioux City Board of Trade, its scope extended so as to include as
eligible to membership all citizens of Sioux City and to embrace
in its work the securing of manufactories. The following officers
were elected for the balance of the year: President, H. A. Jandt;
Vice President, John Hornick; Treasurer, A. S. Garretson; Secretary, E. W. Skinner; Directors, F. H. Peavey, H. A. Perkins, W.
H. Beck, F. L. Goewey, E. C. Palmer, Geo. H. Howell, J. P. Dennis.

In November, 1881, the following officers were elected: President, F. H. Peavey; Vice President, John Hornick; Treasurer, A. S. Garretson; Secretary, E. W. Skinner; Directors, H. A. Jandt, F. L. Goewey, E. C. Palmer, W. H. Livingston, W. H. Beck, H. A. Perkins, R. S. Van Keuren.

During the first six months of the new organization, the Board of Trade has aided in securing for the city several important additions to its industrial and mercantile institutions, among which may be mentioned, a button factory, a chemical paint and color works, a branch of R. G. Dun & Co's Commercial agency, Cummings,Smith & Co.'s large wholesale boot and shoe house, a branch of the Consolidated Oil Tank Line Company; a United States Express Company's office, an iron pump factory, chemical works, increased telegraph facilities, and has in prospect a paper mill, a flax, twine and bagging mill, and several other industries.

The subject of railroad extensions, and increased rail facilities, and the improvement of the Missouri River by the Government, have also had consideration.

BUSINESS TRANSACTED.

The following extracts are taken from the *Journal's* last annual review of the city's business acchievements:

"During the year 1881, Sioux City merchants and dealers sold goods to the value of $6,427,626, giving employment to 412 persons, who received for salaries $197,425. These figures can be accepted as being as nearly correct as it is possible to give them, and if they err at all, it is in being too small, and that they are too small is clearly indicated by the amount of exchange sold by our three banks during the past year, as per figures furnished the Board of Trade, which was $10,256,127.02.

"It may also be stated that several dealers refused to state the amount of their business, and as no estimated figures are given, it must be evident to all that the total of $6,427,626 falls far short of naming the full volume of business. It would probably not be an exaggeration to place Sioux City's merchandise sales in 1881 at fully $8,000,000.

MANUFACTURING.

"This branch of industry is yet in its infancy in Sioux City, and yet, a very flattering showing is made, the value of manufactured articles in 1881 reaching a value of $1,189,050, in the production of which 555 persons found employment, and who received for wages $237,410. In these figures are not included the business of the St. Paul machine shops, which give employment to hundreds of men, and pay out many thousands of dollars for wages. Nor do they include the immense transactions at the new pork-house, which, during the two months it has been in operation, has killed 37,000 hogs, bought at a cost of $580,000,and which, during the time, has also paid out $36.000 for packing material, which includes cooperage. etc., and $14,000 for wages. This establishment has 188 men now on its pay-roll. Several new manufacturing enterprises have been started here this fall, others are projected with a certainty of their being put in operation, and another year Sioux City can make a much larger showing in this direction.

THE BUILDING RECORD.

"The opening of a late spring found Sioux City almost destitute of building material. The wrecking of the railroads by the spring floods delayed its arrival, so that it was nearly the middle of May before much progress was made in building. When this material did arrive, our contractors took hold of the work with a will.

"Our building record this year, in its sum total, very largely exceeds that of any previous year since the present writer has made his compilations. The amount expended is nearly $400,000 greater than in 1879, and $300,000 greater than in 1880. The number of buildings built is 308 greater than in 1879, and 265 greater than in 1880.

"In the erection of buildings for manufacturing purposes, the showing is still more gratifying, as the increase is over six fold. Our great pork-packing establishment, the butter and egg house, and the button factory, are valuable additions, not only in themselves, but from the fact that they give employment permanently to a great many men, and necessitate the building of many new homes, and very largely increase our population.

"Our tables again show, that Sioux City workingmen are building their own homes, and the vast majority of them are neat, warm and comfortable.

"The increased cost of building has not been as great as expected, and will not average over 15 per cent. above the amounts paid for similar work in the two previous years. This increase is not greater than the increase in the earnings, and profits of almost any business in the city, and ought not to deter anyone from building.

"We ought not to lose sight of the fact, that all of these new houses are full of people, and the smaller the house, the more people it seems to hold, and that our tables show the completion of nine large hotels and boarding-houses, all of which have all of the rooms that they can spare from transient guests let to permanent boarders. There can be no reason to doubt that the population of the school district of Sioux City, which takes in all of the town, is now fully 11,000 people."

CITY GOVERNMENT.

Mayor. W. R. Smith; Treasurer, G. R. Gilbert; City Solicitor, J. M. Cleland; Clerk. F. Barth; Marshal. J. R. Thompson; Deputy Marshal, John Colvin; Street Commissioner, James Scollard; Night Police, Thomas Budworth and Mike Ahern; Engineer, G.

W. Oberholtzer; Engineer of Steamer, H. A. Lyon; Chief of Fire
Department, Jas. P. Wall; Health Officer, Dr. J. W. Frazey;
Weighmaster, James Shanley; Librarian, Miss Helen Smith.

Councilmen.—First Ward, D. Dineen, R. G. Grady; Second
Ward, D. A. Magee, H. S. Harmon; Third Ward, N. Tiedeman,
R. S. Van Keuren; Fourth Ward, L. Humbert, E. C. Tompkins.

FIRE DEPARTMENT.

The fire department of the city is a volunteer organization,
composed of ninety members, fifty-five of whom are active, and
thirty-five exempt. The organization was first effected in 1874,
with E. R. Kirk, Chief of the Department. The fire apparatus
belonging to the city consists of one steamer, three hose carts,
2,500 feet of hose, and a hook and ladder truck, fully equipped.
The engine house is a substantial two-story brick building, located
in the central part of the city. The members of the company,
with the exception of the Chief and Engineer, render their services
gratuitously. James P. Wall is the present Chief, and the department is an able and efficient one.

THE TELEPHONE EXCHANGE.

The Sioux City Telephone Exchange was incorporated August
7th, 1880, and the construction of lines was soon after commenced.
December 10th, of the same year, the first telephone connection
was made, but only a few instruments were put in. The practic-
ability of this new and novel means of communication was soon
demonstrated, and the telephone rapidly grew in public favor, the
success of the Exchange being thereby assured. Lines were soon
extended all over the city, and communication established between
nearly every business house, as well as with many private residences. Over one hundred telephones are now in use in the city,
and new ones are constantly being put in. In December, 1881, a
line was extended to Sergeant's Bluffs, eight miles distant, and as
it is found to be entirely practicable, it is more than probable that
a few years will see Sioux City connected by telephone with all the
towns within a radius of twenty-five miles, thus bringing them all
into closer commercial relations with Sioux City as the head center.

THE POSTOFFICE.

The first postoffice was located in an unostentatious log building,
the private residence of the Postmaster, Dr. John K. Cook, who,
received his commission from President Pierce, by the first mail
that arrived in the place, July 20th, 1855. The arrival of the
first mail sack was an occasion of no small consequence to the
little sturdy band of settlers who had cast their fortunes in the
great unknown West, as the contents brought them tidings of
their Eastern friends, and seemed to link them once more with the
civilization from which they had been so long cut off. Though

the revenue derived, by the Postmaster from the office, was but a small sum, it is related that the Doctor discharged his onorous duties with such scrupulous care and fidelity, that he remained in his position, undisturbed by place-hunting politicians, until relieved at his own request. The mail service, thus early established. in 1855, though then only arriving weekly, via Council Bluffs, has continued uninterrupted. As the place grew in size and commercial importance, semi-weekly, then tri-weekly, and finally, in 1861, daily mails were established, and the postoffice was removed to more commodious quarters in the "corner grocery." Previous to the removal of the office, Dr. Cook was succeeded as Postmaster by Charles K. Smith, who retained the position until the close of James Buchanan's administration. On Lincoln's accession to the Presidency, A. R. Appleton, was appointed Postmaster, who, in turn, was succeeded by J. C. C. Hoskins, who was continued in office until March, 1878, when E. R. Kirk, the present incumbent, was appointed. Until the appointment of Mr. Kirk, the office was located according to the fancy of the official in charge, which not infrequently resulted in great inconvenience to the public.

The growth of the city to a place of several thousand inhabitants, with a dozen mails arriving and departing daily, rendered more commodious quarters necessary, and in 1879 the office was removed to its present central location, where a building had been specially erected for it. It is conveniently arranged, both for the benefit of the public and the rapid handling of the mails. The business of the office at present requires the services of five clerks, and is rapidly increasing.

However uninteresting statistics may be to the general reader, they are very significant to those who wish to trace the progress, determine the results, or estimate the future of a growing city, and as nothing affords a better index of the business of a place than the value of the business done at its postoffice, we append the following detailed exhibit of the Sioux City post office during the year 1881:

GENERAL ACCOUNT.

Receipts.

Stamps sold...$10,759.51
Envelopes sold.. 3,395.56
Postal cards sold... 1,662.57
Paper and Periodical Stamps sold............................   750.18
Postage due stamps sold.....................................   259.02
Box Rent.. 1,659.50

        Total...$18,446.34

Expenses.

General Expense Account...........................$3,069.49
Postmaster's Salary............................... 2,800.00
                                                 ----------- $5,869.49

        Net income...$12,576.85

MONEY ORDER BUSINESS.
Receipts.

4,524	Domestic orders issued	$57,570.75
	Fees on same	550.65
43	Canadian orders issued	1,307.05
	Fees on same	20.85
73	British orders issued	1,031.13
	Fees on same	30.45
50	German orders issued	813.19
	Fees on same	14.10
4,690	Total orders and fees on same	$ 61,338.17
2,610	Remittances received	294,989.29
	Balance on hand Jan. 1, 1881	2,082.98
		$358,410.44

Disbursements.

4,733	Domestic orders paid	$ 86,432.57
43	Canadian orders paid	1,620.58
39	British orders paid	824.76
61	German orders paid	2.104.05
4,876	Total money orders paid	$90,981.96
31	Domestic orders repaid	373.44
	Money order expense account	504.06
	Remitted to Omaha	364,650.00
	Balance on hand Jan. 1, 1882	1,900.98
		$358,410.44

MAILING DEPARTMENT.

Letters	603,148
Postal Cards	155,220
Transient printed matter	258,232
Merchandise packages	5,512
Total	1.022,112

REGISTRY DEPARTMENT.

Number of Letters received	6.808
Number of Letters dispatched, originating at Sioux City	2.211
Number of packages in transit	18,394
Total	27,413

SOCIETY ORGANIZATIONS.

Masonic.—Landmark Lodge No. 103, A. F. & A. M., was chartered June 2d, 1857. It is in a flourishing condition, and has a membership, at present, of about 140. Meetings are held the second Monday of each month.

Sioux City Chapter, R. A. M., No. 26, was organized April 9th, 1860, and has a membership of ninety-five. Meetings are held the third Tuesday of each month.

Columbia Commandery No. 18, K. T., holds stated conclaves on the first and third Fridays of each month. The present membership is forty-three.

I. O. O. F.—The Independent Order of Odd Fellows has a hall in Hedges' Block, corner of Fourth and Douglas streets.

14

Sioux City Lodge No. 164 was organized October 22d, 1868. Meetings are held regularly Monday night of each week. The membership is ninety-five.

Western Star Lodge No. 282 meets every Tuesday night. It was organized October 22d, 1874, and has a present membership of fifty-four.

Sioux City Encampment No. 44 meets regularly the second and fourth Thursdays of each month. It was organized October 20th, 1869, and has how fifty-five members.

Knights of Pythias.—Columbia Lodge No. 13 was organized July 10th, 1872, and has a membership of sixty-five. This society has no hall of its own, and meetings are held every Wednesday night in Odd Fellows' hall.

Endowment Section No. 302 also meets every Wednesday night.

Ancient Order of United Workmen: membership 100; meeting place Odd Fellows' hall. Officers: T. R. Galbraith, M. W.; Jas. Hutchins, F.; J. T. Orr, O.; Maris Peirce. S.; M. L. Sloan, F.; A. F. Nash, R.; H. A. Lyon, P. M. W., and delegate to State Lodge.

The Sioux City Medical Society was organized November 4th, 1872, and has for its object the mutual improvement of members. Meetings are held quarterly.

The Womans' Christian Temperance Union was organized in 1875, and has a membership of sixty-five. This is a most active organization, and has for its object the suppression of intemperance. The club has inviting and pleasant rooms in Hedges' Block, and meetings are held every Tuesday afternoon.

The Woman's Christian Association, was organized in 1875, by the christian ladies of the city. It has a large and increasing membership, and regular meetings are held quarterly.

The Muennerchor is a social and musical organization with forty-five members. Meetings are held the first Sunday in each month, in the society's hall on Fourth street.

Society of United Irishmen.—This society was organized September 1st, 1880, and has forty members. Meetings are held every Sunday afternoon.

Q. E. D. Club.—This is a gentleman's social club, organized November 20th, 1878. The membership is limited to twenty-one.

B. Neque D. Club.—A gentleman's social club, with rooms in Hedges' Block. It was organized September 1st, 1880, with a limited membership of twenty-five.

There are in addition several musical, literary and social organizations holding meetings.

THE ST. PAUL SHOPS.

The year following the completion of the Sioux City & St. Paul road, the city voted a tax of $20,000 to secure the location of the company's repair shops at this city, and work was immediately be-

gun on the extensive buildings now occupied by the company's
machine shops. These shops have been enlarged from time to
time, and, during the summer of 1881, had been increased to a capacity of 200 men, whose monthly pay-roll amounted to more than
$10,000. In these shops a specialty is made of repair work. All
the most improved machinery has been put in for this line. Besides the repair work, a great number of new freight cars have
been built. But the point in which the shops excel, is the re-
building of passenger cars, and the best trains now run by the
company are of cars that have been practically rebuilt in the shops
at Sioux City. The increased mileage of the road has, and will,
make necessary further enlargements of the shops, and this will
keep the St. Paul Railroad Machine Shops, what they have ever
been, one of the leading industrial establishments in the West.

SIOUX CITY WATER COMPANY.

The need of an adequate supply of water for the city for fire,
domestic and manufacturing purposes has long been apparent, and
various organizations have been started to give the city a water
supply; but it was not until the Spring of 1881 that anything tan-
gible was done. Then the Sioux City Water Company was organized, with David Magee as President. The plan of the company
was to secure a supply of water from an artesian well. Work on
this well was begun in October following, and by New Year's a
depth of 1.290 feet was reached, where the drill entered a rotten
sand-rock that promises, when it is curbed, to give a sufficient supply of water. The company, soon after the formation, secured a
fair franchise from the city for furnishing water for fire purposes.
Lots have been bought on Prospect Hill, a bluff rising 183 feet
above the level of the principal street, on which to build a reservoir, and the purpose of the company is to pump water from the
Missouri River, which flows at the foot of this bluff. to supply the
the reservoir in case the artesian well should fail to give a sufficient supply.

THE COURTS.

The first term of the Woodbury County Court was held at Sioux
City in March, 1855, John K. Cook acting as Judge. The first
term of District Court began September 3d, of that year, with
Samuel H. Riddle as Judge. In the early days of the city. court
was held in the now dilapidated brick building, yet standing on
lower Fourth street, near Virginia. Afterwards, the county built
the house now called the "old jail," on Virginia street, near
Seventh. This was used as a jail, and occasionally for court purposes, until the fall of 1876, when the commodious and imposing
edifice, which had been begun the previous spring. was completed.
Woodbury County points with pride to this Court House. No
other county in the State has one of more architectural beauty,

and few are larger and more convenient. The contractors were Sioux City men, C. E. & D. T. Hedges, and the building cost (complete) $100,000. The present Judiciary are: C. E. Lewis, of Cherokee, District Judge, and J. R. Zuver, of Sioux City, Circuit Judge. S. M. Marsh is District Attorney. A bill has been introduced in Congress, which, if it becomes a law, as now seems likely, will give Sioux City terms of the United States Court.

THE BUTTON FACTORY.

The Sioux City Button Manufacturing Company was incorporated October 15th, 1881, with a paid-up capital of $10,000. Its manufactory is located on the West Side, and is a substantial three-story brick building, well supplied with all necessary machinery. The works were set in operation in January, 1882, and the first finished buttons were turned out on the 26th of the same month. The factory, at present, is exclusively devoted to the manufacturing of buttons from horn, and when run to its full capacity, will afford employment for seventy operatives. The advantages enjoyed by the company in obtaining the raw material for its products, enable them to successfully compete with eastern manufacturers for trade in the East, while the freights that the latter have to pay, on the raw material and manufactured articles, will preclude the possibility of their entering western markets as competitors of this home manufactory. All grades of buttons will be made, and it is the intention of the company to handle their goods through jobbers only. The company is composed entirely of Sioux City men, and the machinery, excepting the lathes and presses, are nearly all of Sioux City make.

THE CHURCHES.

The moral and religious wants of the community are well supplied in this city. The church records run back as far as 1856. In 1857, Rev. Mr. Chessington, a Presbyterian missionary, organized a congregation of his denomination in the then frontier village, and the first church edifice built was by that society, the building being still standing on lower Fourth street, and now does duty as a grocery store. The churches now in this city are:

First Presbyterian,—Established in 1857; membership 193; church, corner Sixth and Nebraska streets.

Congregational,—Established 1857; membership, 184; church, on Douglas street, between Fifth and Sixth streets.

First Methodist Episcopal.—Established in 1857; membership, 175; church, corner of Sixth and Pierce streets.

St. Thomas Episcopal.—Established in 1859; membership, eighty-three; church, corner of Nebraska and Seventh streets.

First Baptist.—Established in 1860; membership, 155; church, corner Fifth and Nebraska streets.

St. Mary's (Catholic).—Established in 1856; membership, 130 families; church, corner Sixth and Pierce streets.

German Lutheran.—Established in 1877; membership thirty-three; church, on Jackson street, above Sixth street.

Swedish Evangelical Lutheran.—Established in 1875; membership, 160; church, corner of Virginia and Fifth streets.

Norwegian Lutheran.—Established in 1875; membership, seventy-three; church on Third street between Jones and Jennings streets.

Trefoldighedskirken.—Established in 1875; membership, forty-three; church on Sixth street, West Side.

Norwegian Methodist.—Established 1880; membership, sixty-two; church, on Court street, near Seventh street.

Swedish Baptist.—Established in 1881; membership, fifty-seven; church, on Wall street near Sixth street.

In connection with all these churches, flourishing Sunday Schools are maintained; the scholars in nearly every church outnumbering the membership. It shows a satisfactory growth in religious matters, that during 1881, three new churches, the Baptist, Swedish Baptist, and Norwegian Methodist, have been built or begun, and that a fourth, the First Methodist, took the preliminary steps for re-building and enlarging their place of worship.

WOODBURY COUNTY AGRICULTURAL SOCIETY.

The Woodbury County Agricultural Society was organized in 1870, and the present handsome fair grounds, located one and a half miles northwest of the city, were laid out soon after. Though the organization has met with many discouraging reverses, it has done much to advance the interests of farming, and created a laudable ambition to excel among the agriculturists of the county. Exhibitions have been held annually, with the exception of one or two seasons, when bad weather made it inexpedient to attempt it. Within the past two years unusual interest has been taken in the Society by the farming and stock-raising community, and the organization has been placed in a prosperous condition and on a solid financial footing. Men, identified with the pursuits, whose interests are represented by an association of this kind, have assumed the management, and made the Society in every way creditable to the county. The benefits arising from these annual exhibitions of the agricultural, mechanical, and manufacturing products of the country, are being recognized, and the hearty co-operation of all classes is accorded them. The grounds belonging to the Society have recently been improved by the planting of shade trees, and new buildings erected for the convenience of exhibitors. The officers of the association are: G. W. Kingsnorth President; Craig L. Wright, Vice-President; J. M. Cleland, Secretary; G. W. Wakefield, Treasurer; R. Hall, W. B. Tredway, R. A. Broadbent, J. M. Cleland, G. H. Wright, G. W. Wakefield,

G. W. Kingsnorth, C. L. Wright, W. P. Holman, B. P. Yeomans, Directors. The fair for 1882 is to be held September 12th, 13th and 14th.

MISCELLANEOUS MANUFACTORIES.

Among the manufacturing interests of the city, which can only be mentioned without giving any detailed account are: C. F. Hoyt's Vinegar Works, employing five men; John Beck's planing mill, fifteen men; A. J. Millard's wood working shop, four men; Barker & Petty, barrel and butter tub factory, fourteen men; R. Selzer's brewery, eleven men; Franz & Co's brewery, thirteen men; City flouring mills steam, ten men; the Floyd flouring mills, water power, eight men; the brick yards of J. Rochele, Thomas Green and C. B. Woodley, the two latter having steam power, and altogether employing ninety men during the season; John Griffin's candy factory, three men; and the wagon shops of Trudell Bros., Dineen Bros., and Reeve & Trudell, and Brown Bros., together employing forty-three men; and the cigar factories of Amsler & Radcliff, George Mauer, and A. M. Ashley, which furnish employment to twenty-four workmen. The following table, showing the business of these, and numerous smaller manufactories, during 1881, will give the reader some idea of the importance of these industries:

	No. Employes.	Wages paid.	Amount sales.
Iron and wood articles......................	106	$ 44,950	$ 167,400
Eatables.................................	79	37,780	457,350
Cigars.............	24	10,300	69,000
Beer....................................	24	21,000	110,000
Leather.................................	34	13,500	79,200
Clothing and other items..................	124	46,280	167,200
Brick....................................	90	18,000	43,400
Printing.................................	66	41,100	81,500
Marble..................................	8	4,500	14,000
Totals................................	555	$ 237,410	$1,189,050

This table does not include the output of the pork house, nor of the St. Paul shops. Owing, mostly, to the active exertions of the Board of Trade, several other manufacturing enterprises are either assured or in prospect. Among these are chemical works, for which part of the apparatus has arrived at this writing; a pump foundry, for which ground has been leased; clay pipe works, a large distillery, a flax mill, and numerous others yet too vague to take position as historical facts.

THE SCHOOLS OF SIOUX CITY.

Rapid and substantial as we have seen the growth of Sioux City to have been, in population and commercial importance, intellectual progress has been maintained in a degree fully equal to its material progress; and, to-day, it is the acknowledged educational center of the great Northwest. Fortunately, from the birth of the city to the present time, her school interests have been confided to earnest, active, representative men, with broad and liberal views of education, brought with them from their New England homes, where the advantages of common schools had been tested by experience, and under whose administration and fostering care a system of graded schools has been established which affords educational advantages unsurpassed by any city in the State. Her citizens have been liberal—even lavish—in the expenditure of money for the erection of elegant and commodious school buildings, and their equipments, with all the modern improvements calculated to facilitate the acquisition of a common school education.

The public schools of the city are embraced in what is known as the Independent School District of Sioux City, which was organized in July, 1869. The first Board of Directors was composed of six members, consisting of A. M. Hunt, President; William L. Joy, W. R. Smith, John Cleghorn, F. J. Lambert, and George Falkenhainer. John P. Allison was Treasurer and F. M. Ziebach, Secretary. The present Board of Directors consists of John P. Allison, President; William L. Joy, J. C. C. Hoskins, L. McCarty, C. R. Marks and A. Groninger, two of whom are elected every two years for a term of three years. During the first year after the organization of the district into an independent one, the first school house of any now in use was built. At present there are eleven school houses in use, of which three are rented, and the others belong to the district. Additional buildings are in contemplation to meet the growing wants of the district. The schools are all graded, as primary, secondary and intermediate, culminating in the High School, which latter, though few in its number of pupils, has attained a high degree of efficiency as a factor in the educational system of the city. The schools are under the management of A. Armstrong, Superintendent, with a corps of thirty-two able teachers. Instructors only of acknowledged ability and ripe experience are employed, who are emulous of attaining the the high standard of excellence for which Iowa, as a State, has become justly renowned. Of these, three are males, at an average salary of $90 per month, and twenty-nine females, at an average salary of $40 per month. The Superintendent, has general charge of all the schools, and receives a salary of $1,250 per annum. The last annual report of the County Superintendent gives the number of school age in the district, as 2,185, while the actual attendance upon school, as appears by the City Superintendent's report, is 1,329. School is in session ten months of the year, and the average cost per pupil is $1.27. The value of the school buildings is estimated at about $75,000. The grounds in most cases, are surrounded by substantial fences and adorned with shade and ornamental trees.

A CITY OF HOMES.

To give some idea, though necessarily an inadequate one, of the rapid growth and present prosperity of the city, the following figures are given, showing the number of new buildings and the cost of improvements made during the past three years:

	NO.	COST.
1879	103	$157,445
1880	146	257,085
1881	411	558,210

While many of these buildings were substantial business blocks, solid manufactories, and palatial residences, by far the greater number were the modest homes of mechanics, small tradesmen, and laborers. Sioux City is emphatically a city of homes. The possibility of securing a home of one's own, owing to the moderate price at which residence lots have been held, the prosperity of all classes, and the assistance given by loan and building associations, has been improved, and these have combined to make the city the Philadelphia of the West.

LAND INTERESTS.

As well as being a center of wealth and business for a large section of country, Sioux City is the center of a large land interest and business. The location of a government land office at this city, one of the first prizes secured by the founders of the infant metropolis, has naturally been followed by the centering of a large landed business at the city. The fertile acres in this part of Iowa were open to entry at $1.25 per acre for several years after being surveyed, and during the flush of times of 1856-7 hundreds of thousands of acres were entered by speculators in this part of the State. Then came the era of land grants to railroads, and these lands, as well as those of private speculators, were placed in the hands of Sioux City agents for sale. Among the resident proprietors of large landed estates may be mentioned T. J. Stone, Weare & Allison, D. T. Gilman, G. W. Wakefield, John Pierce and N. A. McFaul. The two latter, beside the lands which they own, are agents for non-resident and railroad lands, the former in selling the lands granted railroads in this part of Iowa, and the latter representing the Burlington and Missouri grant in Nebraska. The sales of these two firms alone amounted to several hundred thousand dollars during 1881.

It would be an error to suppose from the active demand for real estate that the country was becoming crowded. A careful study of the plats in the office of any Sioux City land dealer will show that not more than one-sixth part of the land in Woodbury County has yet passed into the hands of actual occupants. The county is capable of sustaining a population equal to that now scattered out over the entire northwest quarter of the State.

AS A DISTRIBUTING POINT.

Sioux City, situated as it is, on the convex side of the Missouri River, on its first great bend north of Kansas City, the waters of that great river flow toward it from an almost due westerly course for 150 miles, when they turn southward, while smaller streams flow toward it from the north and east. Its location thus seems to have been designed by nature as the natural spot for the great metropolis of the Upper Missouri, and the commerce of this rapidly growing empire flows as naturally toward this point as the waters have for ages. The natural advantages of this location for a commercial center, were seen and fully appreciated by the enterprising, intelligent men who selected it for a city, and they not not only laid it out on a grand scale for substantial business blocks and stately residences, but they worked to bring to the aid of its natural resources all the helps that the artificial arteries of commerce can command.

Its commanding geographical position, coupled with its eight lines of railroad and mighty river, has made it the distributing point for Dakota and Nebraska. All the supplies for the vast territory to the north and westward are necessarily handled by the railroads centering here, and the business thus brought to her very doors has contributed not a little to the upbuilding of the city, as it necessitated the erection of warehouses and the investment of capital in the wholesale and distributing business. The following table, prepared by the Secretary of the Board of Trade, will give some idea of the extent and character of this business during the year 1881:

	No. Employes.	Wages paid.	Gross sales.
General Merchandise........................	320	$ 148,225	$ 4,541,304
Grain..	18	15,500	549,322
Hides, Tallow and Furs......................	10	6,000	654,000
Wood and Coal..............................	16	5,000	188,000
Lumber..	23	12,400	375,000
Agricultural Implements, etc.................	25	30 0	170,000
Total..............	412	$ 197,425	$6,477,626

These figures can be accepted as being as nearly correct as it is possible to give them, and if the yerr at all it is in being too small, and that they are too small is clearly indicated by the amount of exchange sold by our three banks during the past year, as per figures furnished, which was $10,256,127.02.

Especially is this true of grain, as one firm, during the period covered by this table, purchased 600,000 bushels of wheat alone, and the shipments of corn and oats to the up-river military posts amounted to 15,000,000 pounds. The general merchandise sales of the city during the same year reached the gratifying total of 4,500,000 of dollars. Of this amount $1,456,000 was sold by the three wholesale dry goods houses, and about $100,000 in round numbers by the two wholesale grocery establishments. Of the other lines of trade engaged in the distribution business, of the magnitude of whose operations no definite figures can be given, may be mentioned:

The Standard Oil Company has put in tanks and a warehouse, whence illuminating and lubricating oil is distributed all over this part of the northwest.

The firms of F. H. Peavey & Co., H. G. Wyckoff, Booge Bros., and Knud Sunde send out coal, lime and plaster by the ton, carload or single barrel.

Two wholesale grocery houses, E. C. Palmer & Co. and Tackaberry, Van Keuren & Floyd, represent their line. One of the firms stated that its business in 1881 amounted to over $500,000, and the other refused to give figures.

The wholesale drug business is carried on by John Hornick and F. Hansen.

Liquors are sold in job lots by John Hornick, E. Ressegieu and Joseph Marks.

The cracker factory of Goodwin & Mosseau employs seven men, and has a trade extending throughout the Northwest.

In the wholesale saddlery hardware line there are J. M. McConnell & Co. and L. Humbert.

Dry goods and notions are wholesaled by Tootle, Livingston & Co. and by Jandt & Tompkins.

The jobbing of hardware is conducted by Peavey Bros. and Geowey & Co., the former firm selling only at wholesale.

Agricultural implements are sold in lots to dealers by Peavey Bros., W. L. Wilkins and Cottrell, Bruce & Co.

The shipping of grain is the specialty of F. H. Peavey & Co. and Davis & Wann, and is one of the lines of John H. Charles and Jas. E. Booge & Co.

The northwestern distributing point is at Sioux City for the Singer Sewing Machines, for which A. P. Provost is agent; the American Sewing Machines, represented by W. W. Griggs, and for Kimball's musical instruments, for which Arthur Hubbard is general agent.

During 1881, Smith & Farr, built an extensive butter and egg packing establishment, costing $20,000, which the growth of the trade in this produce imperatively demanded.

Oberne, Hosick & Co., of Chicago, have a branch house established here, which makes a specialty of hides and wool, and whose operations extend to the British Possessions.

Pinckney & Co., beside their retail book and stationery business, keep several men on the road selling their wares.

Cummings, Smith & Co. are exclusively engaged in the wholesale boot and shoe trade.

J. K. Prugh, in connection with his retail crockery and queen's-ware trade, devotes some attention to the wholesale line of his business.

Beside these, three banks, two of which are national banks, two express offices and the postoffice handle the currency used in the business of a wide extent of country. Numerous firms and individuals who do not figure before the public as being in the wholesale trade, are, by force of circumstances compelled to sell goods in job lots to out-of-town customers. Thus a number of our clothing merchants supply surrounding country stores, grocers send out shipments to dealers all the way between the city and Deadwood, and lumber dealers ship small lots and entire car lots to small dealers out of the city. By numberless channels the goods brought in bulk to this city are distributed, and the produce of the country collected and forwarded. Much of this business has not been cultivated, but has come to the city unasked. The need of more wholesale houses is the crying need of the city. The field is large, and the harvest is plenteous, but the laborers comparatively few.

INDIAN ANTIQUITIES.

When Lewis and Clark's expedition ascended the Missouri River, they found the Sioux in possession of the country on the north side of the river above the Big Sioux, and on both sides from the mouth of the Niobrara up to near where Ft. Buford now is. On the west side of the river, at the Blackbird Hills, was the Omaha village. This tribe, whose present village is about thirty miles southwest of Sioux City, had occupied the neighborhood of their present village from a time to which Indian tradition fixes no limit. Their peaceful ways had fixed the tribe not only in locality, but in numbers, and from the best accounts attainable they have never varied much in the the latter, from 1,200 souls. On account of this Chinese-like fixedness, this tribe has always been considered one of the most interesting by students. At this writing a cultured young lady of Boston, Miss A. C. Fletcher, is living with the tribe as a member, to study their religion and traditions. Though in the early treaties the government appears to recognize the title of the Omahas to the country about this city, it was the common hunting ground of this tribe and the Sioux.

The Sioux are, as a tribe. the opposite of the Omahas. While
the Omahas have remained stationary, the Sioux have grown.
From the time of Lewis and Clark's expedition to the time the first
lot was staked at Sioux City, the tribe had almost annihilated the
once formidable Rees and Mandans, reduced the Poncas to a petty
band, and extended their dominion to the south as far as the Platte,
north to the Saskatchawan.   Indian tradition says that the Sioux
are not an old tribe, but the descendants of a band of young braves
from different tribes that banded themselves together to form a
new tribe, and started from somewhere near the head of the south
Saskatchawan.   These Romans of the North subdued other tribes
and incorporated them with themselves, taking such wives as they
wanted from the conquered.   The name used by the tribe in speaking of themselves, Dacota—friends or allies—comes from this association of young men, rather than from the subsequent proceedings had.

The human bones disinterred in excavating for the foundations
of buildings in Sioux City, indicate that the Omahas, or some
other of the older tribes, occupied the country before the Sioux
came, for the Omahas bury their dead, while the Sioux expose the
bodies of their deceased friends on scaffolds.   Dr. Yeomans, one
of the first settlers of Sioux City, mentions in a letter recently
written to a resident, that. when he first saw the townsite, in the
fall of 1855, the trees on the east slope of Prospect Hill were ornamented with scaffolds, on which were the bones of Indians.   The
dead had been wrapped in their robes and blankets, and left there
to decay.

But before either the Omahas or the Sioux occupied the country
about Sioux City, it was the home of another and more civilized
people, of whom, unfortunately. but little can now be known.
Their principal city was on the Broken Kettle Creek, about seven
miles northwest of Sioux City.   There a circular elevation,
several acres in extent. rises to the height of from six to ten feet
above the level of the bottom land.   But few explorations of this
village mound have been made, and the most that is known of it
comes from observations taken of the side where the Broken Kettle Creek has cut into the mound. The soil of which the mound is
made appears to be different from that of either the neighboring
bluffs. or of the bottom land, from which it rises; nor is there any
depression near the mound to show from whence came the materials of which it is made.   In places, and at some little distance below the surface, are ashes and bones of some animals, as if the
mound had been built higher since it was first the site of a village.
Some human bones have been found, but scattered and broken, as
the animal bones were, and this gives rise to the horrid theory that
the villagers feasted on elk, man and buffalo flesh with equal enjoyment.   The few parts of skeletons found on the higher part of
this and neighboring mounds (for there are several mounds in the

same section) are supposed to be the result of Indian interments made long subsequent to the age when these mounds were the sites of populous towns. The peculiar feature of the mounds, and the one from which the creek takes its name, Broken Kettle, is the numerous remains of pottery found. These vessels, from the fragments found, (for no complete specimens have yet been discovered) appear to have been for all kinds of domestic use. They were made of clay found in the bluff not far off, and appear to have been moulded by hand, not turned on a wheel, before being baked. Some of them display considerable rude taste in ornamentation and design, and much patience in their making. A mound somewhat similar to those on the Broken Kettle, is reported to have been found on the Little Sioux, north of Correctionville, but with this exception the Broken Kettle mounds are unique, as is their pottery. It is to be regretted that these interesting remains have not been more fully explored, and it is to be hoped that at an early day some one actuated by a pure love of knowledge will investigate these relics of an earlier civilization.

THE INDIAN WAR.

In 1861, the beginning of the war of the Rebellion, fired the hearts of the pioneer patriots of Sioux City to such an extent that a company of cavalry was formed under the State law, with Capt. Tripp in command. This organization disbanded during the winter, and the following summer a company was enlisted under the name of the Sioux City Cavalry, under which name it was mustered into the government service, with A. J. Millard as Captain. During the Indian troubles following the massacres at New Ulm and Spirit Lake, this company did much to give confidence and courage to the frontier. It was the presence of this company that checked the stampede of settlers that came out of Dakota in the summer of 1862, and when Cordua and Roberts were killed by straggling Indians in Bacon's Hollow, three miles east of this city, the Sioux City Cavalry followed the trail of the murderers for several days, but without overtaking them. About the same time Sioux Falls was burned, and several murders committed by the Sioux in Union and Clay counties, in Dakota.

In the winter of 1862-3, General John Cook began the organization of a campaign against the Sioux, with Sioux City as a base of operations. The Sioux City Cavalry, as a company, went into the Seventh Iowa Cavalry, a part of which regiment, and all of the Sixth Iowa Cavalry, composed the force of which General Sully took command in the spring of 1863, when he relieved General Cook. After the campaign of that year, the expedition returned to spend the winter of 1863-4 at Sioux City, and the summer following went out on the campaign, which resulted in driving the hostile Sioux beyond the Missouri.

SLOAN.

This prosperous and enterprising little place is situated on the Sioux City & Pacific Railway, twenty-one miles below Sioux City, and four miles from the Missouri River. It possesses no corporate powers in itself, but is a part of Sloan Township, which was formerly a portion of Lakeport Township, but which, in January, 1876, was organized as a separate township, the first officers of which were: F. O. Hunting, President; G. R. Beall, J. R. Coe, Trustees, and Ed. Haakinson, Clerk. The present township officers are: W. J. Wray, President; F. O. Hunting, George W. Lee, Trustees, and W. G. Williamson, Clerk. The connection of township affairs with those of the village has been so close that it is scarcely possible to do justice to one without giving something of the other's history.

This place, although older than many other towns in Western Iowa, is still in its infancy, and though for several years it seemed to make but little progress, it is now rapidly building up, and bids fair to become an important point.

The date of the first permanent settlement in this section is not definitely known, but it is believed that Rufus Beall, now deceased, is entitled to that honor, as he first came here in 1856, and although he did not make his home in Sloan until 1865, he was a very large landholder in the vicinity as early as the first date given, and made several lengthy stays. George R. Beall, a nephew of Rufus Beall, is at present the oldest settler in the township, he having made it his place of residence as early as 1868. Another settler, who came the same year, was Andrew Fee.

Sloan proper was platted in 1870 by John I. Blair, at that time President of the Sioux City & Pacific Railway Company, and all deeds were made in his name. Blair received the land as a gift from one of the enterprising citizens of this place. Previous to the platting of the town, there was a store on the site which had been erected in 1868 by J. B. Johnston. There was also a post-office, which was known as Hamlin Postoffice; but the real place commenced, in a measure, its existence with the platting of the town. Among the settlers who came about or just before this time, were John Tully, now dead, R. C. Barnard, Fred. T. Evans, Ed. Haakinson, and others.

The population of the village is variously estimated at from 200 to 225, and it is probable that the latter figure is not too great. The nationalities represented are various, though the native American element is in the majority, many of the latter being from the State of New York. On the outskirts of the village is a strong Scandinavian representation. Taken in combination, the people of Sloan are as good citizens as could be wished for, and they would be welcomed with open arms to any locality.

A movement is on foot to secure incorporation, and the desired object will no doubt become an accomplished fact at an early day. The prevailing sentiment at present, however, seems to be that the population is hardly, as yet, up to the required standard, but as that drawback is fast being remedied, it will probably not prove an obstacle for any very extended period.

Sloan is well represented in the various lines of business necessary to a properly balanced village, and all show signs of prosperity.

The following are the various establishments: Three general merchandise stores, one grocery store and meat shop, a butcher shop, saloon, drug store, hardware store, blacksmith shop, blacksmith and wagon shop, hotel, restaurant, barber shop, livery and sale stable, furniture store, photograph gallery, lumber-yard, stock and grain dealer. In addition to these, the learned professions are represented by one clergyman, as elsewhere noticed, and one physician. The bar has no representative here. The postoffice is a money order office. The railroad shipments, which are rapidly increasing, will average two car-loads or more per day of stock and other products of the country.

CHURCHES, SCHOOLS AND SOCIETIES.

M. E. Church Society.—The first sermon preached in Sloan, subsequent to missionary work, was delivered by the Rev. Mr. Crane, of Dakota, a representative pioneer preacher, who held services with a congregation of seventeen, in a room over Beall & Evans' store. This was in October, 1870, and from that date, the Methodist Society of Sloan began its growth. Subsequent meetings were held in the school-house, Mr. Crane acting as supply preacher, and continuing in that capacity for several years. Mr. Crane was succeeded in his ministrations by various other itinerant clergymen, prominent among whom were Revs. Keister, Billings, Fawcett, Drake and Cuthbert. The society which started with two members, now has a membership of forty, and has a regular pastor, Rev. William Thomas, who has continued in that capacity since October, 1881. The Society is no longer in need of securing public buildings for the holding of its meetings, but has an excellent church edifice, with dimensions of 35x50 feet, which was dedicated in June, 1881, and which is a credit to the community.

Congregational Church Society.—The Congregational Church Society was organized in the Spring of 1879, by the Rev. A. M. Beeman, now of Spencer, who relinquished his charge in September, 1881, since which time the church, which has a membership of thirty-five, has depended upon supply preachers. The society has no building of its own, as yet, but a subscription has been started for the erection of one next season, upon the completion of which a resident pastor will be secured.

Sloan Lodge, I. O. G. T.—This is the only organization in the nature of a secret society in Sloan, and it, though the charter is still retained, does not hold regular meetings. It started with a small membership a year or so ago.

The organization of a Masonic Lodge in the village has been contemplated, but as yet nothing has been done in the way of work to that end.

Debating Societies.—Sloan has also a debating Society, but as yet it is small and in an embryo stage of life. The meetings are held in the school house.

Public Schools.—The public schools of the city consist of a primary and a higher school, the latter presided over by F. E. Chapin, and the former by Mrs. F. E. Chapin. The number of pupils in attendance is seventy. The school building was erected in 1881, and is a two-story, frame structure, with dimensions of 28x40 feet. Its interior arrangements consist of two large class-rooms, and a smaller recitation room. A smaller brick building had supplied the needs of the place for several years prior to the erection of the present school house. The School Board for this year consists of J. B. Crawford, President; F. O. Hunting and W. J. Wray. The school system of the place has been almost co-existent with itself, and reflects great credit on the community.

The people of Sloan are confident of a prosperous future, and deliberate observation by an unprejudiced observer would seem to confirm the belief. The country around is a grand one, and it would seem that nothing stands in the way of an ultimately large growth.

OTHER TOWNS IN WOODBURY COUNTY.

Smithland.—One of the early settlements in the county was Smithland, on the Little Sioux River, about thirty-five miles south-east of Sioux City. At this place in January, 1857, began, between the whites and Indians, the troubles immediately preceding the Spirit Lake massacre. The Indians made some threats against the whites, which caused the settlers to arrest and disarm some of Ink-pa-du-tah's band. The Indians stole other arms, and passing up the valley of Little Sioux River into Cherokee and Clay Counties, committed further depredations. When they arrived in Dickinson County, they committed the outrages which form so painful a chapter in the history of the State.

Correctionville—Lies in a bend of the Little Sioux River, near the line of Ida County. It was settled years ago, when Sioux City was little more than an Indian camping ground, and per force of circumstances still remains a village, though its situation and nat-ural resources would warrant it in becoming a town. A pioneer by the name of Shook came into what is now Kedron Township in Section 1, in 1853. R. Candreau, C. Bacon, and M. Kellogg came the next year. Shook sold out to Bacon, who was the first permanent settler.

Woodbury.—This village was formerly called Sergeant's Bluff City. The railroad station here is still called Sergeant's Bluff. It is situated on the Missouri bottom, six miles south of Sioux City. It was located in 1856, by Doctor J. D. M. Crockwell and Doctor Wright, of Independence, Iowa. In 1857-8 a newspaper was published here, of which mention has been made. In 1862 the manufacture of pottery was commenced at Woodbury, and the business has been lively and remunerative ever since.

Danbury, Salix, and Oto are other minor settlements in Woodbury County.

WOODBURY COUNTY BIOGRAPHIES.

SIOUX CITY.

D. D. Adams, of the firm of Devore & Adams, auctioneers and commission merchants—who established business at Sioux City in 1869—was born in 1848; served in the U. S. A. one and one-half years under Colonel La Grange, in Co. B., 1st W. C. He lost a brother at Helena, Ark., who was captain of the company. Previous to coming to this place, the subject of this sketch was engaged in business three years in Wis.

A. Akin, of the firm of Akin & Shulson, dealers in staple and fancy groceries, confectionery, etc., Chicago House, 4th St., Sioux City, Ia., was born in Otsego county, N. Y., March 8th, 1810. In 1827, he moved to Penn.; removed to Belvidere, Ill., in 1844; thence to Elgin, and from there to Chicago in 1852, where he served as justice of the peace and police magistrate for seven years, and also practiced law. He received a commission from President Lincoln to recruit. In 1864, he moved to Kansas, where he was for several years register in the U. S. land office, in Augusta and Wichita; was postmaster for several years, and prosecuting attorney for Morris county. He then moved back to Chicago, and remained two years, after which he came to Sioux City, in 1878, and located permanently.

Abel Anderson, dealer in groceries and provisions, corner of 4th and Jackson Sts., was born in Sweden in 1856; came to America in 1874, and settled in Sioux City. He is now one of the leading grocers of the city; his sales average $25,000 per year.

C. M. Anderson, photographer, was born in Sweden in 1849, came to America in 1852, and located in Chicago. In 1871, he moved to Rock Island, Ill. While there he took charge of a gal-

lery, and learned the art of photography. He came to Sioux City
in 1878; married Bertha Jorgenson, of Manitowoc, Wis. They
have two children--Emineretta and John E.

John Anderson, of the firm of Anderson & Olson, dealers in
boots, shoes, rubbers, etc., opposite High School building, was
born in Sweden in 1843; came to America in 1869, and settled in
Sioux City; married Anna Anderson. They have four children—
Mary, Albert, Carrie and Oscar.

L. B. Atwood, liveryman, established business in 1866; was
born in Livermore, Maine; came west and settled in Sioux
Falls, Dakota, in 1858; and the same year came to Sioux City,
which makes him one of the pioneers of this place. He has been
a member of the city council, and held other minor offices. He is
one of Sioux City's representative citizens.

F. W. Anthon, of the firm of Tiedeman & Anthon, dealers in
staple and fancy groceries, cigars, tobacco, etc., established business in 1875. He was born in Germany in 1836; came to America in 1857, and settled in Davenport, Ia.; removed to Sioux City
in 1870, and was for three years in charge of the Chicago Hotel.

Frank X. Babue, of the firm of Payette & Babue—shop opposite High School building—was born in Montreal, Canada in 1842;
came to the U. S. in 1854, and settled in N. Y. He moved to
Mass.; thence to Connecticut; thence to Vermont, and in 1875, he
came to Sioux City. He married Medrise Delier, of Canada.
They have five sons—Albert, Frank, Willie, Alphonso and Ed-
mund.

John Beck, proprietor of the Sioux City planing mills. This
mill was established Aug. 22nd, 1871. In this year the building
was enlarged, and machinery added, by Mr. B. and partner. In
1881, Mr. B. became sole proprietor. The amount of business
transacted by the establishment, is about $12,000 per annum. Mr.
Beck was born in Somerset county, Penn., in 1833; came west in
1857, and settled in Sioux City, and is therefore one of the oldest
settlers of Sioux City. He was engaged in contracting and building for eighteen years; has served as city alderman two years. He
married Nancy Culbertson, and has four children—Irene, Maggie, Eva and William E.

M. E. Bedford, of the firm of Bedford Brothers, dentists, began the practice of dentistry in Grand Rapids, Mich., in 1866; in
1872, located in Worthington, Minn., and engaged in the practice
in Sioux City in 1876, with his brother, L. N. Bedford, who, with
his assistant, R. F. Merrick, travels in Southern Minn., Northern
Iowa, Southeastern Dakota and Eastern Neb., in the practice of
dentistry in all its branches.

A. D. Bedford, M. D., was born in Pa., in 1848; graduated from Alleghany College in 1873; studied two terms at Tubingen, Germany, in 1874 and 1875. He was a teacher in the military school at Poughkeepsie, N. Y., during the year 1876; and in 1877, graduated from the Jefferson Medical College, Philadelphia. Came to Iowa, and practiced medicine in Waterloo two years, and came to Sioux City in 1879; was married in June, 1880, to R. McNeil, of Waterloo.

Geo. W. Beggs, M. D., is the son of the Rev. S. R. Beggs, the author of "Early Methodism in the West." He was born in Ill., in 1837, graduated from Evanston College in the literary department, and received the degree of A. M., and from the Rush Medical College, Chicago, in 1862, where he received the degree of D. D. During the late war, he was surgeon of the 105th Ill. regiment, and was with Gen. Sherman in his famous march to the sea. He came to Sioux City in 1866, and was married in 1865 to Lillian A. Sims. They have three daughters—Lizzie, Bertha and May.

A. L. Bennetts, proprietor of the New York Fruit Store—established business in 1879—was born in N. Y., in 1826; came west to Wis. in 1848, and, after traveling about, finally located at Fort Winnebago. He afterwards moved to Minnesota; from there to Saginaw, Mich.; thence to O.; then back to Mich.; from there to Chicago, and then to this city. He served in the late war two years under Gen. Burnside, in the 9th army corps. He has held various town offices. He married Grace Brigham, of Wis. They have three children.

Hon. J. H. Bolton, clerk of the circuit and district courts of Woodbury county, was born in Cleveland, O., in Jan., 1846; graduated at Harvard college in 1868. In 1869, he came to Sioux City, and engaged in the practice of law, which he continued until 1873, when he retired from business. He was elected to the 17th General Assembly, and in 1879, was elected to his present office. He married Sarah Thornton—now deceased—who was the daughter of James Thornton, the present consul to Aspinwall.

James E. Booge, of the firm of J. E. Booge & Co., pork packers, was born in Pittsford, Rutland county, Vt.; came to Sioux City in 1858, and has been engaged in his present business since 1869. This firm sell their hams for the north and west; mess pork to the north, and the government; their sides for the local trade and the south, and their lard to Chicago. Capital required in operating the business, about $500,000. During the year, 1881, they erected extensive buildings of brick and stone, five stories high, at a cost of $100,000. The works cover an area of five acres. They have every modern appliance, fertilizing works, etc., and employ in the busiest season, about 300 men, and run both winter and summer seasons, with a capacity, respectively, of 1,500 daily in winter, and

500 in summer.   J. E. Booge, Esq., who founded the establishment, is resident partner and entire manager.   The works have ample side-tracks connecting with every road in the city.

C. Borman, proprietor of Columbia House, on the corner of Fourth and Water streets, established business in 1870.   He has good stabling accommodations connected with the premises. Mr. B. was born in Germany in 1826.   He was in the German military service six years; came to America in 1854, and settled in Alleghany City, Pa.   He removed to Johnston, Pa.; thence to Omaha; thence to Sioux City, in 1868.   In 1879, he was township trustee for this town.   He married Federika Keller.   They have five children—Lena, Mina, Elizabeth, Charles and Oscar.

John Brennan, attorney-at-law; commercial collections, a specialty.

Napoleon Brouillette, dealer in groceries and provisions, was born in Montreal, Canada, Aug. 15th, 1852; came to the U. S. in 1869, and settled in Sioux City.   He entered the employ of H. D. Booge & Co., where he remained three years; was then employed in the store of Joe. Marks three years; then was with Geo. W. Felt, and after that, with J. B. Barringer two and one-half years. He married Jennie Irwin, of this place.   They have three children —Maud, Henry and William.

R. A. Broadbent, proprietor of livery stable, on Douglas street, between 4th and 5th streets; established business in 1869.   He was born in Ill., in 1844.   He moved to Fayette county, Iowa, and came to Sioux City in 1868.   He served in the late war two years in Co. F, 9th I. I., under Captain Guinn.

N. C. Brunk, proprietor of grocery store and restaurant, was born in Virginia in 1852; served as postmaster in Va. four years. In Oct., 1881, came west, and settled in Sioux City.   He was station agent for the B. & O. R. R., for some time.   He married Carrie Hite, of Middletown, Va..

E. H. Bucknam, of the firm of J. P. Dennis & Co., was born in Washington Co., Maine, in 1843; moved to Toledo, O., in 1866; thence to Chicago, where he remained until 1868, when he came to this place, and entered the above firm.

Phil. Carlin, County Recorder, is a native of Ill.; came to Iowa in 1860, and settled in Clinton Co.; removed to Woodbury Co., in 1871, and located at Union; was elected to his present office in 1880, and removed to Sioux City the same year.

H. B. Clingan, of the firm of H. B. & C. E. Clingan, physicians and surgeons, was born in O., in 1822; is a graduate of the Cleveland Medical College.   He practiced in O., from 1848 to 1855;

then moved to Benton Co., Iowa, and practiced there until 1877, when he came to Sioux City and opened his present office with his son C. E. Clingan.

Willis G. Clark, attorney at law and justice of the peace, was born in Penobscot Co., Maine, in 1853. He came to Minn., with his parents in 1857, and settled in Dakota Co. He is a graduate of Browns University. of Providence, R. I. He came to Sioux City in 1878, and was elected justice of the peace in 1880. Mr. C. has been actively engaged in local politics, and is a rising young attorney.

M. A. Comeau, carpenter and joiner,—shop opposite High School building—was born in the Province of Quebec, Canada; came to the U. S., and settled in Mass., in 1863. He removed to this place in 1879, and engaged in his present business. He married Mary Gelines, of Canada. They have four children—Malvinas, Edwin, Emma and Charles.

T. H. Conniff, Jr., attorney at law and justice of the peace, is a son of T. H. Conniff, of Houston, Minn., who has represented that state in the legislature, and was district attorney for several years. The subject of this sketch settled in Sioux City in 1869, is a graduate of the State University, and was admitted to the bar at Des Moines.

W. H. Corrigan, proprietor of sample room, No. 26 Pearl St., was born in Ozaukee Co., Wis., in 1850; come to this place in 1874, and entered the employ of the proprietor of the Washington House. He married Emma Shiable, of Sioux City. They have one child—Willie.

A. H. Crowell, of the firm of Crowell & Martin, commission merchants and wholesale dealers in foreign and domestic goods, green and dried fruits, confectionery, etc., corner of 3rd and Pearl streets, was born in Mass. in 1838; followed sailing eleven years; has visited almost every foreign clime, and is a man of wide experience. During the late war he was on a government transport. He located in Benton Harbor, Mich., where he engaged in the dry goods business. In April, 1880, he came to this place, where he embarked in his present business, under the firm name of Crowell & Co.; afterwards, Geo. N. Martin became a partner. The firm name was changed to its present name. This is the only exclusive commission house in the city.

Warren H. Cottrell was born in Rensselaer Co., N. Y., in 1852; removed to Waterloo, Ia.; graduated from the State University at Iowa City in the class of '79, and came to Sioux City, Nov. 15th, 1880. He is now a member of one of the leading agricultural implement firms of this place.

Jesse M. Cunningham, the leading hatter of the city, was born in N. Y. in 1858; came to Sioux City in 1869, and engaged in business with his father, until in April, 1881, he entered his present business.

C. W. Cutler, M. D., was born in Winneshiek Co., Ia., in 1858; moved with his parents in 1871 to Osage: graduated from Cedar Valley Seminary in 1877, and from Rush Medical College, Chicago, in 1880; practiced medicine in Osage one year, and in 1881, located in Sioux City. Although his arrival is of comparatively recent date, he is already in the enjoyment of a lucrative practice.

John Davelaar, of the firm of Davelaar Brothers, house, sign and ornamental painters—shop on Douglas street, between 3rd and 4th streets—established in 1879. He was born in Holland in 1838, came to America in 1848, and settled in Pittsburg, Pa.; moved to Wis., and in 1875, came to Sioux City, where he was engaged in the car shops several years. He served in the Union Army four and one-half years in the 1st Missouri L. A., was orderly sergeant, and has been county commissioner of Armstrong county, Dak. Bart Davelaar, of the above firm, was born in Holland in 1831; came to America in 1848, and settled in Pa.; removed to Wis., and in 1873 came to this place; was in the employ of Dineen Bros.

George Douglass, M. D., was born in Canada in 1843; graduated in 1868 from the Eclectic Medical College of Ohio: came to Iowa in 1870, and settled in Iowa county. He removed to Sioux City in 1872, where he is now in the practice of his profession. He held the office of county physician for several years, and in 1871, he married Sarah Tufts, daughter of John Tufts, of Grinnell, Iowa. They have one son—Bruce.

A. DePee, proprietor of the National House, corner of 3d and Nebraska streets, has lately remodeled and refurnished this hotel, and made it one of the best $1.00 per day houses in the city: has no bar connected with the house. He was born in Ind., in June, 1836, and removed in 1856 to Wis.; came to Iowa in April, 1869, and settled on a homestead in Woodbury county, where he farmed six and one-half years. He served in the U. S. A. one year, in Co. H, 46th W. V. I., under Captain Hoskins and Colonel Lovell.

Hon. S. T. Davis, attorney at law and dealer in real estate, was born in Pa. in 1828; was educated at Alleghany College, at Meadville, Pa.; came to Sioux City in 1856, and has been identified with many leading enterprises for the benefit of his adopted city. He was the founder of the Sioux City Journal, and with others organized the S. C. & St. P. R. R., and has taken an active interest in the construction of other roads leading into the city. He was appointed by President Lincoln register of the U. S. land office, which position he held eighteen months. He was elected to the state senate to fill a vacancy made by the resignation of Judge Oliver. Mr. D. was mayor of the city in 1871, and was prosecuting attorney for several years. He owns large landed property and business property in the city.

M. B. Davis, attorney at law, was born in Grafton county, N. H., in 1837; enlisted in the late war in 1861 in Co. I, 1st R. I. C.; served in that regiment two years, and then enlisted in Co. I, 1st N. H. C., and served from March, 1863, to August 1865; enlisted as a private, and came out a commissioned officer. He was taken prisoner at Paris, Va., and exchanged at the end of four weeks, and again taken prisoner at Winchester, Va., and escaped and reached the Union army at Harper's Ferry. He was again taken prisoner by Wade Hampton's troops, and taken to Richmond, and removed to Castle Thunder; thence to Salisbury, N. C., and was paroled in the spring of 1865 at Wilmington, N. C. He was engaged as a cavalry scout most of the time during his service. He came to Fort Madison, Ia., in 1866, where he practiced law until 1875, when he came to this city and opened an office.

M. C. Davis, one of the proprietors of city mill and elevator, was born in Pittsford, Rutland county, Vt., in 1835. He has been engaged in the milling business since 1855; came to Sioux City in 1869 and erected the elevator in 1870. The elevator has a capacity of 70,000 bushels; the mill was built in 1871, has a capacity of 125 barrels of flour per day, and employs 15 men.

George Devore, auctioneer, was born in Bedford county, Pa., in 1834; came to Sioux City in 1869, prior to which he was in business in Ill. He was justice of the peace twelve years, and has held other town offices; he has followed his present business since 1865.

Deming & Hatch, dentists, are former residents of Vt. They came to this city in Nov., 1880, and opened their present office Their practice is extensive and remunerative.

J. P. Dennis, of the firm of Dennis & Co., was born in Somerset county, Maine, in 1832, removed to N. Y. in 1851; thence to Dubuque, Ia., in 1853, and to this city in 1867. He served his country in the late war from 1862 until 1863 in Co. G, 40th I. I.

Thomas Dorman, baker and confectioner—No. 56, Pearl St.—was born in England in 1841; came to America in 1863, and settled in Chicago; removed to Omaha, Neb., 1867. During the late war he served two years under Gen. Myers. He married Amelia Gibbons, and has two children—Anne and Arthur.

Christ. Doss, proprietor of the Milwaukee House—located near depot—was born in Mecklingburg, Germany, in 1830; came to America in 1854, and settled in O., where he learned carpentry. Thence he removed to Dubuque, Ia.; came to this city in 1857, and was one of its pioneers. He married Mary Sohl, of Germany. They have five children—one son and four daughters.

L. H. Drumm, proprietor of the Washington meat market, which is one of the finest markets in the west, with all of the appurtenances that would do credit to an eastern city—was born in Bavaria in 1839; came to America in 1861 and settled in Cincinnati, O.; removed to Lyons, Ia.; thence to New Frankfort, Mo., and from there came to Sioux City. He married Helena Bitteghaffer, and has two children—Nellie H. and Eddie L.

J. W. Denton, of the late firm of Flinn & Denton, of the Central meat market, was born in Keokuk, Ia., in 1856; moved to Neb. in 1859, and in 1872 to Council Bluffs; came to this city in 1879.

D. Elliott, dealer in crockery, glass, wood and willow ware, house, hotel and steamboat furnishing goods, established this business in 1870; his establishment was destroyed by fire Dec. 5th, 1875; reopened Dec. 7th, of the same year. The building has two stories and basement, all of which he occupies, carrying one of the largest stocks of goods of this description west of Chicago. He was born in Pa.; has been in Ia. twenty years; was formerly in business in Iowa City. H. E. Sawyers, head salesman, for the above firm, has been connected with this house for more than twelve years. He was born in Davis county, Ia., in 1856; came to this city with his parents in 1857, where he has made his home ever since.

Rev. Fr. Eisenbe'ss, pastor of the First German Lutheran church, was born in Germany in 1851; came to America in 1870, and located at Fort Wayne, Ind., where he founded Concordia College. He then attended St. Louis college three years. He removed to Dixon county, Neb., by special call of the newly formed congregation, to do missionary work for this denomination; came to this city in 1878, and founded a church with fourteen members, which was incorporated in Jan., 1879. He married D. Steinmeyer, of St. Louis, and has two children—Dorothy and Ludmilla.

J. D. Farr, of the firm of Smith & Farr, wholesale dealers in butter and eggs, was born in Lewis county, N. Y., in 1843; came west in 1876; started in business with a small capital, and now does a business of one-half a million per annum.

S. S. Fessenden is the proprietor of the China Hall. This business was established in 1863; purchased 1871 by J. H. Fessenden, and by its present owner in 1877. Mrs. F. is a native of Cincinnati, O. J. H. Fessenden is a native of Concord, N. H., and is at present extensively engaged in mining in Col.

M. L. Flinn, of the firm of Flinn & Lessenich, proprietors of the Central meat market, (business was established in 1881), was born in Woodstock, Ill., in 1852; moved to Chicago, where he lived eight years, and came to this city in 1868. He was chief clerk in the

St. P. R. R. shops for nine years, and worked three years on the S. C. & P. R. R. He married Mary M. Wilkins, and has three children—Grace M., Frank M. and an infant.

Wm. S. Follis, dealer in real estate and insurance agent, does a general fire and marine insurance business.

P. Follis, proprietor of the Sioux City House, was born in Ireland in 1817; came to America in 1843, and settled in Fall River, Mass. He removed to Dubuque, Ia., Sept. 15th, 1845, and from there to this city in 1868. He has served as school director and in other town official capacities. He married Margaret Conway. They have four children—William S., Mary, Michael E. and Ellen.

J. W. Frazey, of the firm of Frazey & Bedford, physicians, was born in Pa., in 1833; studied medicine at Cleveland, O., and also at Ann Harbor, Mich., and graduated from Chicago Medical College; has been in the practice of his profession since 1853; was married to Rebecca Shertzer in 1853, and has one child—Ada, now the wife of Dr. C. E. Clingan.

J. Franz & Co., brewers. The business of this firm is conducted by Mrs. M. Franz and Mrs. Kate Hensler, the widows of the former proprietors, both of whom died in the spring of 1881. The brewery was built in 1868, is 150x40 ft., has a capacity of 10,000 brls. per year, and has bottling works connected with it, whose capacity is about 250,000 bottles per year. The foreman, John Arensdorf, is a practical brewer, having learned the business at Sedan France, and is in every respect well fitted for the position which he now holds. The financial affairs are under the charge of C. F. Hoyt and J. R. White. The firm employ about fifteen men about the establishment.

P. F. Gerard, proprietor of the sample room, newly fitted up and opened—Pearl st., between 3rd and 4th sts.—was born in O. in 1845; came to Iowa in 1855, and settled ten miles west of Marengo; removed to this city in 1870. He served in the late war about one year in Co. B, 9th Ill. C.

G. M. Gilbert, merchant tailor, was born in Brattleboro, Vt., in 1844, where he lived until 1862, when he enlisted in Co. B. 16th V. V. His term of enlistment expired a few days before the battle of Gettysburg, but his regiment took an active part in the engagement, and but few returned. He came to Ill. in 1864, and removed to this city in 1870. Mr. Gilbert established his business in Sioux City in 1873, and as the fruits of his proficiency and ability to please the purchasing public, has acquired a very extensive patronage of the most desirable kind, embracing, in addition to the Iowa trade, portions of Dakota, Nebraska, Minnesota and Missouri.

S. O. Gibbs, proprietor of American House—Jennings St., between 3rd and 4th Sts.—has newly refitted and refurnished his

hotel with a view to accommodating the traveling public, farmers
and boarders at reasonable rates. He was born in N. Y. in 1825;
removed to Wis., in 1869. The same year he came to this city,
where he worked at carpentering, and next opened a meat market.
He served in the U. S. A., at Leavenworth, Kan., was treasurer of
Concord township four years. In 1880 he visited Salt Lake City,
Utah.

P. P. Gibbs, proprietor of the St. Elmo Hotel, between 5th and
6th streets, was born in Pittsfield, Vt., in 1821; moved thence to
Brandon, where he served eighteen years as a magistrate, and held
many municipal and other offices of public trust. He was married in 1873 to Adeliza Sargent, of Pittsford, Vt., and has one
child—Irving. In June, 1881, Mr. Gibbs located in Sioux City,
and assumed the proprietorship of the hotel above mentioned,
which he has ever since continued to conduct to the satisfaction
of an increasing public patronage.

G. W. Goodwin is of the firm of Goodwin & Mousseau, proprietors of the steam bakery. They are manufactures of crackers, and
jobbers in confectionery—capacity, 60 bbls. per day—and the in-
ventors of the cracker factory machine-made bread, which they
find a ready sale for throughout this western country. He was
born in Pa., in 1833; removed to Ill., in 1853, and settled at Dixon; then removed to Vinton, Ia., where he was engaged in the
bakery business, under the name of Goodwin Bros. He served in
the U. S. A. three years in Battery F, 1st Ill. L. A., under Maj. T.
Cheney. He was a corporal while in the service; came to this city
in 1877, and is one of its substantial business men.

John H. Griffin, proprietor of candy factory—Fourth street—
established business in 1879. He was born in Chicago, Ill., in
1857; came to this city in 1873, and was engaged as a compositor
in The Journal office five years.

B. A. Guyton, M. D., is a graduate from the University of
Maryland in the class of '69. He settled in Sioux City in 1870,
and engaged in the practice of his profession.

John Hauer, dealer in hardware—lower Fourth street—established business in 1881. He came to Sioux City in 1861; was employed as clerk in the Groninger hardware store. He enlisted in
this city in the 14th I., under Col. Pattee, and served in the U. S.
A. all through the rebellion; was commissary sergeant most of
the time, also clerk in the commissary department. He married
Julia Reinke, and has five children—Lena, Tillie, Willie, Otto and
Emma.

F. S. Hansen, blacksmith, established business in 1878; was
born in Germany in 1849, and came to America in 1869, and settled in Sioux City. He removed to Missouri Valley; thence among

the Indians at Fort Berthold: thence to Plymouth county, Ia., and back to this city. He married Minnie F. Krouse, of this place, and has one child—George.

Capt. James Hayden. proprietor of the Central House—cor. of 3rd and Jackson sts.—has newly opened and furnished the house. He was born in Dublin in 1835; followed sailing from 1846 to 1875; and was the owner of several vessels during that time. He served in the navy during the late war, and was quartermaster a part of the time.

J. M. Heberling, express agent, was born in Pa. in 1846; came to Jackson county, Ia., in 1856, and moved to Cedar Rapids in 1878, where he was messenger of the C., N. W. R. R. between Cedar Rapids and Council Bluffs. He came to this city in Aug., 1881. He married Lizzie Todd, of Milwaukee, Wis.

L. A. Heckman, dealer in groceries, confectionery, etc.—4th st. —was born in Cleveland, O, in 1857; came to this city in 1877, and was in the employ of D. H. Talbot, in the Land Title office until 1879, when he engaged in his present business.

H. Hilgers. dealer in staple and fancy groceries, provisions, flour, etc.—7th st., west side—was born in Germany in 1832, came to America in 1852, and settled in Galena. Ill.; removed to this city and engaged in farming for thirteen years, when his health failing him for that pursuit, he engaged in his present business. He has served as school director.

F. C. Hills, of the firm of Hills & McKercher, successors to Groninger, dealers in hardware, stoves, tinware, wagon stock, barbed wire, etc., sole agents for Adams & Westlake's non-explosive coal oil stoves, also agents for rubber paint, galvanized iron cornice work a specialty—numbers 33 and 35. Pearl st.—was born in England in 1843, came to America in 1849, and settled in Oneida county, N. Y.; removed to Iowa in 1868, in the interest of the S. C. P. R. R. Co., and located in this city in March of that year. He was general traffic manager for the above road, and the first railroad agent in Sioux City. He served as 2nd sergeant in the late war in Co. E, 117th N. Y. I., under Col. Wm. R. Pease. Mr. McKercher, of the above firm, was born in Flint. Mich., and was for some times traveling salesman for a Chicago house. He came to this city in the winter of 1872–3.

John Hittle. retail grocer—cor. 4th and Douglas sts—established business in 1873. He was born in Ohio in 1835: moved to Ind., and in 1855 removed to Des Moines, Ia. He came to Sioux City in 1856, and in the fall of that year went to Sioux Falls, where he built a cabin for a Dubuque town company, returning to this place before winter. He was a fur trader for some years, and then entered the employ of H. D. Booge & Co., where he remained for fifteen years.

John Hopkins, proprietor of sample room—Pearl street, between 5th and 6th—was born in 1862; came to Sioux City in 1867; was in the employ of E. J. Ressegieu for some time. He married Jennie Pickett.

C. W. Hopkins, carriage and sign painter and grainer—cor. Douglas and 5th sts.—was born in Pa., in 1830; moved to Wis., in 1840, and in 1850 removed to Cal.; thence to Australia; thence to London, Eng.; thence to Canada; thence to Wis.; thence to Missouri Valley Junction, Ia., where he had charge of the R. R. paint shop five years, moving thence to this city.

C. F. Hoyt, proprietor of Sioux City Vinegar works, was born in Ill., in 1842; removed to Idaho in 1864, and engaged in mining for two years; located in this city in 1869 and went into the farm machinery business; established his present business in 1875.

B. S. Holmes, dealer in boots and shoes, clothing and gent's furnishing goods, was born in Norway in 1853; came to America in 1870, and settled in Chicago; came to this city in 1872 and engaged in the mercantile business; engaged in the boot and shoe business in 1880, and the 1st of Sept., 1881, he engaged in his present business.

J. C. C. Hoskins was born in N. H. in 1820; graduated at Dartmouth college in the class of '41; was engaged in teaching shool five years, and afterward followed his profession, that of civil engineering. He was employed by the Cochituate Water works, and afterward by the B. & O. R. R. Co., until the spring of 1857, when he came to this city. In 1863, he was appointed postmaster of Sioux City, and served in that capacity until June 30th, 1878. He was city engineer from 1858 to 1871; has been mayor of the city, and was justice of the peace twelve years; has served on the school board several terms. He was the first engineer for the S. C. & St. P. R. R., and made preliminary surveys, etc. Mr. Hoskins was a director of the Sioux City Savings bank, which was subsequently changed to the Sioux National bank, of which he continues to be a director.

Hon. E. H. Hubbard, attorney at law, was born in Rush county, Ind., in 1849; graduated from Yale College in the class of 1872, and was admitted to the bar in Sioux City, in 1874. He has represented Woodbury county in the state legislature.

W. B. Humphrey, proprietor of the Central book store, dealer in books, pictures, frames, paintings, wall paper, notions, periodicals, etc., No. 66, 4th street; came into possession of this business Nov. 22d, 1881. He was born in Maine in 1855; removed to Minneapolis, Minn., in 1870; thence to Sibley, where he was engaged in buying grain. From Sibley he came to this city. He was in the employ of the S. C. & St. P. R. R. company ten years, part of that time as station agent.

C. P. Ibs, proprietor of Eastern meat market, established business in 1871; owns the buildings that he occupies, and in 1874 fitted up his place of business with all the late improvements at a cost of $1,500. He was born in Germany in 1843; came to America in 1870, and located in this city. He learned his trade in Germany, where he was employed for a number of years in a market.

S. B. Jackson, ex-sheriff of Woodbury county, was born in Pa. in 1845; removed to Linn county, Ia., in 1864; thence to this city and engaged in the real estate business. He was elected mayor in 1877, and served three terms; was elected sheriff in 1879; his term expiring with the beginning of the present year; Mr. Jackson served two years in the late war in Co. B, 17th Pa. I.

Hon. Wm. L. Joy, president of the Sioux national bank of Sioux City, and member of the law firm of Joy & Wright, was born in Townshend, Windham county, Vt.: came to this city in 1855, and engaged in the practice of his profession with N. E. Hudson; he entered the present partnership in 1868. Mr. Joy was elected to the State legislature in 1864, and again in 1866.

James Junk, wholesale dealer in liquors and cigars, was born in N. Y. city; removed to Iowa City, Ia., in 1861, and enlisted in Co. A, 41st Ia. I., was transferred to the 7th Ia. C., and served in the U. S. A. until 1866, under Gen. Sully, on the frontier. He established his present business in 1868.

M. J. Kearney, dealer in groceries, provisions, etc.—established business in 1877. He was born in Ireland in 1856; came to America in Oct., 1875, and settled in New Haven, Conn.; removed to this city in 1876, where he has resided ever since, except one year spent in the Black Hills. He married Mary A. Toohey, of Sioux City, and had one child—Alice, now deceased.

E. R. Kirk, postmaster, was born in Ottawa county, O., in 1834; came to Sioux City in 1856, and in the following year engaged in the mercantile business, which business he continued until 1873; then held the office of deputy county treasurer; was appointed deputy collector of internal revenue in 1876, and was appointed postmaster in 1878. Mr. Kirk was married in 1859 to Mary P. Sawyers, and has five children—W. A., E. L., Charles, Frank and Mamie. W. A. Kirk, is deputy P. M., and E. L. Kirk is delivery clerk.

Frank Klepsch, proprietor of the Iowa House, (formerly owner of the Milwaukee House), has newly furnished and opened this hotel, and solicits patronage. He was born in Germany in 1838; came to America in 1867, and located at La Crosse, Wis.; removed to this city in 1869.

B. Kuhlman, proprietor of the Madison Hotel—between Pearl and Water sts.—was born in Germany in 1829; came to America in

1859, settled in Chicago, and engaged in the grocery business. In 1876 he removed to this city, and took charge of the Merchants' Hotel. He married Barbara Masath, of Germany. Mr. K. was in the military service in his native country during three years.

Samuel Krummann, proprietor of a fine dairy farm, (situated on Horse Shoe Lake, one and one-half miles from this city, and contains 45 acres) has in his dairy 36 milch cows, and owns a stock farm of 240 acres, situated four miles northeast of this city, on which he has 37 head of fine stock cattle, and nine head of horses. Mr. K. was born in Switzerland in 1830; came to America in 1852, and settled in Iowa in 1856. He was married in 1858 to C. Hacker, of Germany, and has five children—John, Samuel, Louis, Harry and Annie.

J. P. Langdon handles goods on commission and buys and sells second-hand goods; clothing a specialty. He was born in Green county, Mo., in 1847; removed to Kansas City in 1871, and engaged in the wall paper business; came to this city in 1876, and was engaged in painting until 1880, when he established his present business. He married Emily Jane Pierce, of Canada.

Alex. Larson, dealer in dry goods, notions and fancy goods, established business in 1881. He was born in Sweden, in 1847; came to America in 1869, and settled in Henry county, Ill.; removed to Mount Pleasant, Ia., in 1871; thence came to this city, and engaged in his present business. He was married to Huld Appelgren, of Sweden, and has two children—Gustave G., and Fredrick E. Mr. L. is now a naturalized citizen of the U. S.

Arthur G. Lascelles was born near Chester, Chester county, Eng., July 31st. 1855; came to America in 1880, and settled in Sioux City. He intends soon to erect a brick livery barn on the corner of 6th and Douglas sts.—50x150 ft. in dimensions.

Charles Lambert, dealer in harness, saddles, whips, etc.—corner of 4th and Nebraska sts.—was born in this city in 1858. He learned his trade with L. Humbert of this city, and engaged in his present business in 1879.

A. C. Larson, proprietor of the Oriental Steam laundry—cor. of Pearl and 3rd sts.,—was born in Denmark in 1857; came to America in 1870, and settled in Iowa; came to this city in 1880. He married Lydia Oleson.

William Lerch, proprietor of billiard hall, was born in Germany in 1841; came to America in 1864. He has built several of the business blocks in this city, and engaged in his present business in 1870.

John Lessenich, proprietor of the Chicago House, erected in 1881 at a cost of $12,000, and newly furnished throughout—cor. 4th and Jones sts.—was born in Prussia in 1826; came to America in

1854; removed to Chicago; from there to Sioux City in 1867, and built a hotel which burned in Feb., 1881. He has served as alderman, and also as township trustee.

P. L. Lindholm, dealer in furniture, established business in 1881. He was born in Sweden, in 1842; came to America in 1857, and settled in Boone, Ia.; removed to this city; thence to Yankton, Dak., and back to Sioux City in April, 1881. He married Ellen Ericson, of Sweden. They have five children—Annie, Albert, Emil, Henry and Frank.

E. W. Loft, of the firm of Corry & Loft, architects, was born in Dubuque, Ia., in 1855, and came to Sioux City in 1881.

G. W. Lower, former proprietor of Depot Hotel, was born in Onandaigua county, N. Y., in 1826; removed to Walworth county, Wis., in 1845; thence to Cedar Rapids, Ia., and to this city in 1868.

Wm. Lubert, tailor, established business in 1850. He was born in Mecklingburg, Schmern, Germany, in 1815; came to America in 1851, and settled in Cleveland, O. He removed to Bellefontaine; thence to Ill.; thence to this city. He married Henrietta Coner, and has four children—Gustavus, Jennie, Amelia and Carrie.

B. Luce, proprietor of a fine stock farm (situated eight miles northeast of Sioux City, in Woodbury county, and contains 240 acres), was born in Franklin county, Me., in 1838; came to this city in 1856, and engaged in blacksmithing until moving on to his farm. He married Louisa Meguier in 1855, and has six children —Harry, Fred, George, Jennie, Willie and Bartlett Louis.

Walter W. Lynch is of the firm of W. W. Lynch & Co.. upholsterers and repairers of all kinds of furniture, manufacturers of the self-adjusting spring bed, and agents for the American bird call, for which articles agents are wanted. The firm are also agents for a number of periodicals. Mr. Lynch was born in N. Y. in 1850; came west and engaged in railroading until he came to this city in 1881. He married Mary A. Montgomery.

H. A. Lyon, dealer in breech and muzzle loading guns, and all kinds of sporting goods and hunter's supplies. His machine shop is equipped with all kinds of machinery for repairing guns, and machinery of any kind. He also makes a specialty of safe work, such as opening safes whose locks have become unmanageable. In all, he has one of the finest gun establishmenes in the northwest. Mr. L. was born in Mass. in 1832; removed to Janesville, Wis.. in 1854, and came to Sioux City in 1868; is now engineer for the fire steamer here.

A. Macready, was born in Scotland in 1821; was raised and educated in Glasgow, where he graduated in 1842; came to America in 1846, and located at Patterson, N. J., where he took the management of two spinning mills. Afterwards he was connected with the banking house of John Thompson, now Thompson Bros. He was then sent to Kentucky as agent of the Breckenridge coal and coal oil companies, which made the first coal oil ever made. Mr. M. sold the first two barrels of oil ever sold in America, in the autumn of 1855. In 1856, he came to this city, where he brought a stock of goods, which he disposed of at Sergeant's Bluffs, where he built the first business house erected in Woodbury county, outside of Sioux City. He was appointed by President Lincoln agent of the Omaha Agency; was the first postmaster of Dakota City, and was appointed receiver in the land office at that place. He opened the first stage route from Fort Randall to Fort Dodge. In 1871, he retired from business.

D. A. Magee, of the firm of Hattenbach & Magee, grocers and wholesale dealers in cigars and tobacco, was born in Pa., in 1849; removed in 1855 to Davenport, Ia., and from there to Omaha in 1856, and engaged in milling. He came to this city in 1869, and took charge of the city mill and elevator until 1877, when he engaged in his present business. He is now serving his third term in the city council and is president of the Sioux City water works. He married Adelia Hattenbach in 1876, and has one child—Oliver G.

John Malmquist, of the firm of M. C. Carlstrom, & Co., dealers in foreign and American marble—Douglas st..opposite Journal office—was born in Sweden 1836; came to America in 1871, and settled in Vt.; removed to Mich.; thence to Chicago, where he remained four years, and came to this city in 1880. He married Julia Brown. They have three children—Harry, Edwin and Nathaniel.

Geo. Maurer, manufacturer of cigars and dealer in pipes and all smoking materials—4th. st.—was born in Austria in 1838; come to America in 1865, and settled in Cincinnati, O.; in the spring of 1869 he came to this city, where in 1873 he established the above business. While in Austria he served in the military five years and three months. He married Philomena Brunner, and has six children—Theresa, George, Anna, Flora, Minna and———.

Constant R. Marks, of the firm of Marks & Blood, attorneys at law, was born in Durham, Green county, N. Y., in 1841; graduated from the Albany law school, and in 1868 came to this city and opened his present office; in 1879 he was elected to the twelfth general assembly, and is at present a member of the school board. He served three months in the late war in Co. K, 8th Mass. V.

T. S. & J. P. Martin, dealers in dry goods and notions, came to this city from Galena, Ill., in 1867, and in April, 1879, established the above business, and have one of the best stores of the kind in the city. T. S. Martin was in the wholesale grocery business in the Black Hills from 1877 to 1879.

F. P. Mattocks, of the firm of Mattocks & Pape, proprietors of the London meat market, and wholesale dealers in fish, was born in Pa., in 1852; came west with parents and settled in northeastern Ia. in 1858. He came to this city in 1869 and engaged in farming; has served as constable in Concord township one term. He married Lillian Gibbs, and has two children—Samuel O. and Walter F.

L. McCarty, dealer in groceries, provisions, produce and live stock—corner 6th and Pearl sts—established business in 1867. He was born in Ireland in 1838; came to America in 1857, and settled in Dubuque, Ia.; removed to Manchester, where he remained four years, and came to this city in 1867. In The Sioux City Register, of 1868, Mr. M's. advertisement appears, there then being only one other similar advertisement in that paper, from this place. He has served as city treasurer, and was director of the Sioux City Savings bank—now National bank—and has served ten years as a member of the board of education. He married Eliza Clinton, of Manchester, in 1863. They have ten children—Thomas, Mary, Kate, Emma, Lizzie, Alice, Grace, Lawrence, Loretta and Helen.

Daniel McDonald, sheriff of Woodbury county, was born in Livingston county, N. Y., in 1844; removed to Wis. with his parents in 1849, and lived there until August 15th, 1862, when he enlisted in Co. B, 28th Wis. V.; served until 1865, and participated in a number of noted battles, among them being Helena, Little Rock, Pine Bluff and Spanish Fort battles. He came to this city in 1867, and engaged in the livery business; was deputy sheriff eight years, under John M. McDonald, and was elected to his present office in Oct., 1881.

G. R. McDougall, dealer in musical instruments, sewing machines, sheet music, music books, and all musical supplies, No. 71 Douglas street, established business in 1872. He was born in Ft. Edwards, N. Y., in 1824; removed to this city in 1856, and is one of the pioneers. He engaged in building, and the first year of his residence, he with others erected about thirty buildings. He next engaged in the furniture business. He has served as treasurer of this place, and was the first city marshal of Sioux City; has been an alderman and school treasurer several terms. He married Mary Macready, of this city, and has one child—Jennie Bell.

H. J. Merrill, proprietor of the Blue Front livery barn, (keeps first class turnouts), was born in Otsego county, N. Y., in 1838; removed to DeKalb county, Ill., in 1861, and thence to Sioux City. He served in the U. S. A. as sergeant of his brigade in Co. C, 105th Ill., under Captain Warner.

Captain A. J. Millard, undertaker, corner 9th and Douglas streets, was born in Saratoga Springs, N. Y.; came west in 1856, and in November of that year located in Sioux City, where he engaged in building operations under the firm name of McDougall & Millard, and continued in the business twenty-two years. In 1861 he raised a company of one hundred men, by a special order of the war department. The company was called the Sioux City cavalry, and was engaged against the Indians. He served with that company three years, six months of the time in an official capacity, by appointment of Gen. Sully. In 1863, he accompanied Gen. S. on an expedition as body-guard.

E. Morley, book-keeper in Sanborn & Follett's lumber office, was born in Chenango county, N. Y., in 1835; was engaged in various pursuits until 1867, when he came to this city and engaged as book-keeper.

S. Mosher, M. D., was born in N. Y. in 1835; removed to Chicago, and was engaged there in the practice of his profession. He came to this city in 1871; his wife is also a practicing physician. They treat all diseases, acute and chronic. Mrs. M. treats all diseases peculiar to ladies and children. Dr. M. gained quite a notoriety at one time by being held a prisoner by the bank robbers, Frank and Jesse James, who were escaping from Minn. Meeting the Dr., who was on his way into the country, east of this city, to make a professional visit, and thinking he was a detective, they held him prisoner for several hours, and then taking his horse, released him.

F. Munchrath, dealer in fancy goods, toys, books, stationery, etc., was born in Prussia in 1832; came to America in 1852, and located in Chicago, Ill.; removed to Sioux City in 1858, and built the first brick building in the city. He engaged in his present business in 1873. He married Gertrude Krudwig, and has seven children living.

Geo. W. Oberholtzer, civil engineer and county surveyor, was born in Chester county, Pa., in 1847; graduated at the Pennsylvania Polytechnic college in 1871; came to this city in 1872. The following year he was elected to his present office, and has been re-elected each successive year. He has been township trustee one term, and has, in his line of business, been connected with the railroads of this city.

Andrew G. Oleson, of the firm of Anderson & Oleson, dealers in boots, shoe, rubbers, etc—opposite High School building—was born in Sweden in 1834; came to America in 1873, and located in Mass.; removed to this city, and was engaged in the boot and shoe store of F. P. Dean.

Henry Page, carpenter and contractor, was born in Lancaster county, Pa., in 1820; removed to northern Ill. in 1855, and came to this city in 1870, where he was for a time engaged in building for Sharp & Beck.

J. N. Palmer, book keeper at City Mill and elevator, was born in Pittsford, Rutland county, Vt., in 1833. He was in the mercantile business, until he came to this city in 1873, and engaged in his present occupation.

Rev. Ira N. Pardee was born in Kingston, N. Y., in 1840; received his education at Armenia Seminary. He united with the church in 1857; his first pastoral charge was at Great Barrington, Mass., where he remained the full term; in 1861 he was transferred to the Wyoming conference, and was two years on the Ararat circuit; in 1862 he was removed to the Tallmanville, Pa., circuit, and in 1864, to the Newton, Pa., circuit. He was placed in charge of the Plymouth church in Wyoming Valley. In 1869 he was appointed to Great Bend station; to the Oneonta district in N. Y., in 1872, and in 1875 he was transferred to the Neb. conference and stationed in Omaha. In 1877 he was again transferred to the Northwestern Iowa conference, and stationed at Fort Dodge. He came to this city in 1880. For seven years he was prominent in Sunday School work in New York, and for the past two years he has managed the conference, held annually at Clear Lake, Ia.

J. K. Prugh, dealer in queensware, glassware, brackets, chandeliers, etc.—No. 57 Pearl st.—established business in April, 1881. Before coming to this place, he was engaged in the same line of business at Ottumwa, Ia. He has been in this business eighteen years.

A. P. Provost, manager of the Singer Sewing Machine Company, is a native of N. J.; removed to Ill., in 1860, and engaged in manufacturing carriages. He enlisted in the late war in the 73rd Ill., V. in 1864, and was discharged in June, 1865. He returned to his former occupation, which he continued until he took charge of this company's business at Council Bluffs; settled in this city in Feb., 1880.

James Puck, proprietor of the Davenport House, which was erected in 1881 at a cost of $5,000. This house is a brick structure, and newly furnished; has a barn in connection—4th. st., between Virginia and Court sts. Mr. Puck was born in Germany in 1835; came to America in 1853, and settled in Davenport, Ia. In 1869 he came to Sioux City and engaged in farming; then became one of the proprietors of the Chicago House, where he remained three years.

S. J. Quincy & W. D. Buckley, attorneys at law, were born in Otsego county, N. Y.; located in Sioux City in 1881. S. J. Quincy was admitted to the bar in N. Y., in 1879, and W. D. Buckley in Des Moines, Ia., the same year. They do a general law business.

A. J. Rederich, dentist, was born in N. Y. City in 1842; removed to Ill.. in 1853, and came to this city in 1870; graduated from a dental surgery college in Philadelphia in 1869, and opened his present office in 1870. He was married in Galena, Ill., to Alice Collins. They have three children—Mary, John, and Elmore.

Wm. T. Reeve, manufacturer of buggies, wagons, etc., also repairer and horseshoer, established business in 1872. He was born in Stockholm, St. Lawrence county, N. Y.. in 1847; removed to Wis.. in 1858; thence to Minn., in 1871, and came to this city the following year. He served in the U. S. A., two years in the 193rd N. Y. regiment, under Col. Van Patten. He was fife-major. In 1871 he married Laura J. Damron, of Minn. They have one child—Zenia M.

E. J. Ressegieu, wholesale dealer in liquors, 2d street, established business in 1873. He was born in N. Y. in 1849; removed to this city in 1867. He has just completed an addition to his place of business, 18 by 36 feet, which gives him a building 34 by 36 feet.

John Reinhart, tailor and proprietor of cleaning establishment, 3d street, between Pearl and Water streets, was born in Germany in 1839; came to America in 1856, and settled in Cincinnati, O.; removed to Sioux City in 1870. He served in the war of the rebellion three years in the 28th O. I. as sergeant, also served in the regular army three years as corporal.

Wm. Ring, barber, Pearl street under Dorman's bakery, was born in Germany in 1831: came to America in 1851: removed to St. Joe, Mo.; thence to Council Bluffs, and to Sioux City in 1867.

L. M. Rogers, dealer in flour and feed, lower 4th street, was born in Ill. in 1833; removed to Hardin county, Ia., where he was engaged in teaching school; thence to Cerro Gordo county; thence to Winnebago county. In 1858 he started for Pike's Peak, and that same year came to Sioux City. He was engaged in the revenue service here from 1868 to 1874. He has been deputy marshal of Woodbury county, and acted as special deputy U. S. marshal under Clark and Melendy. He served in the U. S. A. three years and four months under Capt. Millard, of this city; they were an independent company, but were afterwards attached to the 7th Iowa cavalry.

C. C. Rounsevell, dealer in second-hand goods, was born in 1853; came to Sac county, Ia., in the spring of 1869: removed to Osceola county in 1874; thence to this city in 1881. He married Adrienne Cook, of St. Gilman, Ia.

Hon. William Remsen Smith, Mayor of Sioux City, was born at Barnegat, Ocean county, New Jersey, December 30th, 1828. At sixteen, he went to New York City, whence he removed to Macon, Mich. Returning to New York City, he studied medicine, after which he again located at Macon, where he practiced three years in partnership with Dr. Joseph Howell. In 1856 Dr. Smith removed to Sioux City. Here he practiced medicine for eleven years. In the spring of 1861, he was a first lieutenant of the Sioux City cavalry. About this time he was appointed government surgeon, holding that position until 1863. In March, 1863, he was elected Mayor of Sioux City. For several years after the rebellion closed, he acted as examining surgeon for the pension bureau. He was appointed receiver of the U. S. land office in 1865, and was one of the incorporators of the First National Bank of Sioux City, and of the Sioux City & St. P. and S. C. and Pembina railroads. Dr. Smith has held a number of minor responsible public positions. He was one of the honorary commissioners of Iowa to the Paris exposition of 1878, traveled extensively through Europe, and while in England was made a member of the famous Cobden Club. He is now a correspondent of the leading agricultural journals of England. He was elected to his present office in 1881. In July, 1859, he was married to Rebecca Osborne, of Macon, Mich.

L. C. Sanborn, of the firm of Sanborn & Follett, proprietors of lumber yard and sawmill, (also own one-half interest in city mill and elevator), established business in 1856. The machinery for the saw mill was shipped on the first boat that landed at Sioux City. At that time there was but one store in this city. Mr. Sanborn was born in Chester, N. H., April 28th, 1827. In Jan., 1856, he came west, and in Feb. of the same year he located at this place. He voted for the first city mayor, and was a member of the city council many years; also has served as a member of the school board several terms.

Wm. Schudell, gunsmith, was born in Switzerland in 1851; came to America in 1872, and settled in N. Y., removed to this city in 1874. He married Phoebe Hofiler, of Germany. They had one child—William, now deceased.

Rudolph Selzer, brewer, was born in Germany in 1828; came to America in 1853, and settled in Omaha, Neb., where he built a brewery; removed to this city in 1860, and built the first brewery in Woodbury county. He was married in 1853 to Theresa Wasser, and has five children— Charles, Emma, Otto, Lewis and Fritz. Charles is foreman of the works, and Lewis is book-keeper and clerk.

Daniel Shannon, proprietor of Shannon's meat market, established business in 1879. He was born in Philadelphia, Pa., in 1846; removed to Ogle county, Ill., in 1858; thence to Nebraska City in 1873; thence to Chicago, Ill., in 1874; and came to this city in 1875. He has served as town clerk one term. He married Helen V. Utley, of Syracuse, Neb.

Frank L. Sharp, proprietor of Criterion sample room and billiard hall—corner 3d and Douglas sts.—was born in Ind. in 1853; removed to Sioux City in 1856.

Andrew Shulson was born in Norway in 1855; came to America in 1867, and settled in Canton, Dak., and engaged in farming, until he moved to Sioux City, where he entered the employ of the firm of E. C. Palmer & Co., and remained until 1881. He married Laura Lawson, of Canton, Dak.

E. W. Skinner, land, loan, and insurance agent, was born in Pa.; removed to Wis. in 1847, and located at Milwaukee; thence to Madison, and engaged in the manufacture of farm machinery and agricultural implements; also published the Wisconsin Farmer for several years. He came to Sioux City in 1872, and is secretary of the board of trade.

Mr. C. D. Shreeve, dealer in groceries, confectionery, dry goods, notions, etc.—corner of 4th and Iowa sts. Mr. C. D. Shreeve was born in La Porte county, Ind., in 1844; removed to Des Moines, Ia., in 1867; thence to Sioux City in 1881, and is superintendent of the city gas works. He served in the late war three years in the 4th Ind. cavalry. In Aug., 1881, he married Marie C. Raybuck, of Washington county, Penn. He has two children by a former marriage - Carl C. and Ora A.

M. L. Sloan, county auditor of Woodbury county, was born in Harrison county, O., in 1848; removed to Ia. in 1866, and to Sioux City in 1870, and was employed in the auditor's office as clerk. In 1877 was elected to his present office. He was married in 1875 to Ida M. Hill, and has two children—Isabella P. and Alice M.

F. M. Smith, of the firm of Smith & Farr, butter dealers, was born in Otsego county, N. Y., in 1835; removed to Sioux City in 1876, and engaged in his present business.

Thomas J. Stone, founder and cashier of the First National bank of Sioux City, was born in Niagara county, N. Y., in 1825; lived for several years on a farm near Mt. Vernon, O., and removed to Marion, Ia., in 1851. He came to this city in 1855, and engaged in banking and land business. He founded the First National bank in 1871, and is the largest stockholder in the bank; was elected county treasurer in 1871, and held the office until 1878. Mr. Stone's son, E. II., is a graduate of Yale College, and at present assistant cashier in the bank. He also has a daughter, Alice E.

Wm. Storey, proprietor of the North Star meat market, was born in England in 1848; came to America in 1866, and settled in Sioux City, where, for some time he was in the employ of J. Tucker and N. L. Witcher. He married Eveline Fenton. They have four children—Jane E., Emma M., Eveline M., and James E.

James Storey, proprietor of meat market, on Pearl street, was born in England in 1840; came to America in 1869, and settled in Sioux City. He is largely engaged in buying stock.

G. N. Swan, secretary and treasurer of Sioux City plow works, was born in Sweden in 1856; came to America in 1870, and settled in Lucas county, Ia.; removed to this city in 1880, and became a partner in his present business in the spring of 1881. The plow works were incorporated in May, 1880, with authorized capital of $100,000. A noteworthy feature of this establishment is the fact that the stockholders are all skilled mechanics, and all work in the different departments of the establishment. The buildings are of brick and situated within a few feet of the main track of the I. C. R. R., and have switching conveniences to the S. C. & P., and the C., St. P., M. & O. R. R's. They are now making a full line of walking plows, and will commence soon to include every variety of plows used in the west, also cultivators, harrows, and other agricultural implements.

Capt. J. H. Swan, attorney at law, was born in Canada in 1833; moved to Ohio at an early age, with his parents; thence to St. Paul, Minn., in 1851; spent some time among the Sioux Indians in western Minn.; removed to Le Sueur in 1854, and engaged in the study of the law; was admitted to the bar in 1857, and practiced until the beginning of the war of the rebellion, when he enlisted in Co. I, 3rd Minn. Vol., as first lieutenant. He was promoted to captain and served until 1865, and then went to Little Rock, Ark.; thence back to Le Sueur, where he remained until 1871, when he removed to Sioux City, and has been engaged as attorney for the C., M., St. P. & O. R. R. His son, C. M., is in partnership with him. They do a general law business.

William Z. Swarts, proprietor of the Red Front auction store, was born in Carlisle, Cumberland county, Pa., in 1840; removed to Wooster, O., in 1844. He enlisted in Co. I, 16th O. regiment, and remained in the army until Jan. 28th, 1866, when he was mustered out; served in the official capacity of orderly sergeant. He moved to Iowa City, Ia., in 1866; thence to Chicago in 1871, where he was engaged in auctioneering; thence to Sioux City in 1873.

C. R. Tappan, of the firm of Tappan Bros., dealers in carriage and buggy horses, (Teams matched and horses bought and sold. They make a speciality of breaking vicious and wicked horses. Any horse that they can not manage they agree to send back to the owner and pay charges both ways. They also stand in readiness to drive races, and train horses for the track.) C. R. Tappan was born in N. Y. in 1855; removed to Neb., in April, 1879; thence to Sioux City in Oct., 1881. B. M. Tappan was born in Onandaigua county, N. Y., in 1857; in Sept., 1881, he came to this city, and engaged in his present business.   They are thorough horsemen, and have had long experience in handling horses.

F. C. Thompson, dealer in real estate, and insurance agent, was born in Whitby, Upper Canada; removed with his parents to Erie county, N. Y.; thence to Ottumwa, Ia., in 1867, and engaged in the real estate and insurance business with C. C. Blake; thence to Sioux City in 1869.

N. Tiedeman, of the firm of Tiedeman & Anthon, dealers in staple and fancy groceries, cigars, tobacco, etc., was born in Prussia in 1842; came to America in the spring of 1866, located in Davenport, Ia., and engaged in farming; removed to Sioux City the same year; is now an alderman of the city.

Hugh Toohey, of the firm of Dussing & Toohey, proprietors of restaurant, corner of 6th and Pearl streets, established business in 1881.   He was born in Canada in 1859; came to Sioux City in 1870, and was engaged for a time as clerk in St. Elmo hotel; was also employed at the Hubbard house.

Joseph Trudell, manufacturer of carriages, buggies, etc., corner Pearl and 2d streets, is the patentee of the famous Trudell bolster plate, which is acknowledged to be the best thing of the kind ever invented.   He was born in Montreal, Canada, in 1820; removed to St. Lawrence county, N. Y., in 1828; thence back to Canada, where he married Sophia Maynard.   He next removed to Elgin, Ill.; thence to Dubuque, Ia., where he lived twenty-five years; thence in 1873 to Sioux City.   He has five sons and one daughter.

John Tucker, proprietor of the Globe meat market, Peirce street, Hubbard house block, established business in 1867.   In 1881 he refitted his place of business at a cost of $2,000, and has now all the modern improvements, his establishment being a credit to the city.   He was born in England in 1838; came to America in 1858, and settled in Va.   He removed to Sioux City in 1867.

Geo. W. Wakefield, attorney at law, was born in DeWitt county, Ill., in 1839.   He enlisted in Co. F. 41st Ill. Vol., and served three years; was wounded at Jackson, Miss., and returned to Ill.   He was admitted to the bar in De Witt county in 1867; came to Sioux City in 1868, and was elected county auditor in 1869, serving three years, after which he resumed the practice of the law.

Rev. D. R. Watson was born in Scotland in 1841; came to America in 1852; received his early education at White Star seminary, N. Y.   He graduated in the nine years' course at Madison University in 1868, and at Rochester Theological Seminary in 1871, with the title of A. M.   His first pastoral charge was at Lowville, N. Y.   He next went to Brandon, Vt., where he spent five years, and then to Wyoming Ter., where he remained five months.   He came to Sioux City in 1881.   In 1876 he married Carlie E. Copeley, and has two children—John R. and Robinson D.

W. L. Wilkins, dealer in agricultural implements, came to Sioux City in 1870, and soon afterwards engaged in business, under the firm name of Davis & Wilkins; next as Wilkins Bros.; subsequently W. L. Wilkins became sole proprietor. He has one of the leading establishments of the kind in the city. He handles all first class machinery, such as McCormick's, N. C. Thompson's and J. I. Case's various machinery. Harrison and Whitewater wagons, Racine wagon and carriage company's goods, windmills, barbed wire, and is also a dealer in grain.

A. C. Woodcock, dealer in groceries, produce, flour, etc., No. 116, 4th street, was born in Westmoreland county, Pa.; removed to West Va.; thence to O.; thence to Keokuk, Ia., where he wa employed in iron moulding; thence to this city. He served in the U. S. A. from Aug. 11th, 1862, to July, 1865, in Co. D, W. Va. Cav., under Gen. Custer, in the third division of Sheridan's corps; was first lieutenant, and acted as brigade commissary. He was at the final surrender at Appomattox. The night before the surrender, their division captured thirty-six pieces of artillery at Appomattox depot. His company was the last company fired upon in the war of the rebellion. He married Emma Van Kuren, of Medina. N. Y.

SLOAN.

R. C. Barnard, station agent and telegraph operator, was born in the District of Columbia in 1829; removed to Neb. in 1857. He platted the townsite of Grand Island; removed to Omaha in 1863, where he was city engineer for several years; in 1868 removed to Council Bluffs, and engaged in the dry goods business, and in 1870 came to Sloan and engaged in the mercantile business with Beal & Evans. In 1873 he took charge of his present office.

Joseph Gravel, farmer and stock dealer, was born in Canada in 1843; came to the U. S. in 1856, and the next year located in Sioux City, where he was engaged in mercantile business for three years; then removed to Sergeant's Bluffs, and in 1870 removed to a farm near Sloan, and was the original owner of the town site of that place. He was appointed postmaster in 1866, and held the office two years, when he resigned. He is now engaged in stock raising on a farm of about one thousand acres.

Edwin Haakinson, shipper and dealer in live stock, was born in Norway in 1844; came to America in 1861, and settled in Winnebago county, Wis. In 1862 he enlisted in Co. C. 1st Wis. Heavy Art.; served three years, and was soon after the battle of Lookout Mountain taken sick with the small pox, and taken to the foot of the mt., and left to die; was there alone six days, survived and returned to the company, and was detailed to Gen. Lester's headbuarters as orderly. for six months; then was appointed mail carrier between Knoxville and Greenville, Tenn. When discharged he returned to Wis., and engaged in ship-building. In 1869 he removed to Sloan, and engaged in mercantile business until 1878, when he engaged in his present business. He owns 180 acres of land near this place, and about $30,000 worth of business property in Sioux City. He married Carrie Hansen, in 1869, and has three children—Emil H., Carl, and Herbert W. Has lost one child by death.

C. A. L. Olsen, dealer in general merchandise, was born in Norway. Dec. 1st, 1838; came to America in 1860, and settled in Milwaukee, Wis.; was employed on the lakes as a sailor. seven years; came to Iowa in 1869, and settled on a farm near Sloan, and engaged in his present business in 1881. In 1867 he married Alvildo Resmusen, and has seven children.

W. M. Parker, proprietor of the Parker House, was born in Oswego county, N. Y.; in 1837 removed to Adams county, Wis.; thence to Montana and engaged in mining; thence in 1867 went to Sioux City; thence in 1869 to Sergeant's Bluffs and to Sloan in 1880 and engaged in hoteling. He married Silpha Ladd in 1859, they have two children.

J. H. Scroggin, of the firm of J. H. Scroggin & Son, hardware dealers, was born in Tenn. in 1824; removed during childhood to Ill.; thence to Wis. in 1850; thence to Cass county, Ia. in 1872 and the next year to Sloan and bought a farm near the town and engaged in farming until he entered his present business, in Mar. 1881. He was married in 1848, and had ten children. The partner of the firm W. F., owns a farm near his father's; was married in 1877 and has two children.

MONONA COUNTY.

This county lies on the Missouri River, and is in the fifth tier from the northern and southern boundaries of the State. It is twenty-four miles north and south, by an average of nearly thirty miles east and west. in extent. and comprises sixteen full congressional townships, and some four or five that are fractional, embracing in all an area of about six hundred and eighty square miles. The Missouri River, which is the western boundary. runs in a southeasterly direction. making the southern boundary line some twelve miles shorter than the northern.

A considerable area of the county is of bottom, or valley lands, upwards of one hundred and sixty-five thousand acres being included in the great Missouri River bottom, through the western portion of the county. The ascent of these bottoms to the north is more rapid than that of the Missouri River, thus leaving a small portion of these valuable lands subject to overflows in high water seasons, and rendering them sufficiently dry and well drained for easy and successful cultivation.

The eastern portion of the county is a high and rolling prairie. well watered and drained by Willow Creek. Soldier and Maple Rivers, and their affluents, all of which are surrounded by wide, beautiful and exceedingly fertile valleys. The uplands abut abruptly on the bottoms along the east side of the Little Sioux, presenting the varied and peculiar features characteristic of the bluffs along the Missouri bottoms throughout their extent in the State. These bluffs are unusually uniform in elevation, the highest point being not less than three hundred feet above the sea level. The uplands in the immediate vicinity of the bluffs. are too broken and uneven to be practically adapted to agricultural uses, and are cut up with wooded ravines, while the valleys of the smaller streams. a few miles inland, are bordered by gentle acclivities which ascend from the sloping bottoms to the well rounded and gentle divides which intervene between the water courses.

Most of the streams in the eastern part of the county are bordered by beautiful bottom lands, varying from one-half to two miles in width, while the streams themselves are margined by grassy banks. with beds composed of mire and quicksand. The Little Sioux River, with several other streams, affords some good water powers for machinery, on which several mills have been established. while numerous other eligible locations still remaining will yet be properly and similarly utilized. Wells of excellent water are easily obtained in the valleys at depths varying from ten to twenty feet. while in the uplands it is often found necessary to sink through the bluff deposit to a depth of over one hundred feet before a permanent supply of water can be reached. Springs are found at frequent intervals issuing from the bluffs, and with the brooklets that are fed by them, as also with the larger streams, afford plenty of water for stock, which find excellent grazing on the uplands, while on the low-lands several varieties of native grasses furnish very nutritious hay. Several lakes of considerable size are found in the Missouri Valley, which are clear and inhabited with a variety of excellent fish. Some of these lakes have the appearance of having once formed a portion of the channel of the Missouri, which is now, however, several miles distant, with heavy cottonwood groves intervening.

The soil in the valleys is usually a deep black mold or fine loam, it is from six to fifteen feet in depth, and produces exceptionally large crops of corn, and other grains, and vegetables indigenous to the western slope. In the Missouri bottoms, low, sandy ridges are frequently met with, which are the remains of bars formed by the currents, when the river occupied the whole width of the valley from bluff to bluff on either side. The bottom deposits are quite variable in the character of their component parts, though the fine, dark loam constitutes by far the greater proportion of the surface soil. This is generally underlaid by sand and gravel, and sometimes by a deposit of clay containing large quantities of partially decayed wood, and other vegetable matter, which are frequently met with in sinking wells. Most of the upland is covered with a heavy coating of dark humus-charged loam, with subsoil of the light mulatto-colored bluff deposit. No sterile lnad is found in the county, for even that which is broken in the vicinity of the bluffs, is very fertile, and produces excellent crops of wheat, oats and other cereals, and in its native state produces very fine pasturage for stock.

The largest bodies of timber are the extensive groves of cottonwood, which border the banks of the Missouri, while more or less extensive groves of this and other kinds of timber are found on the Little Sioux, and many of the deep ravines running further back into the county are densely shaded with luxuriant forest growths. Like most of the counties on the Missouri slope in Iowa, Monona County has no stone or coal, while the bluff deposit furnishes an abundance of material for the manufacture of brick, which must be depended upon for the future supply of building material. The local supply of fuel, which all comes from the forests, though ample for the present wants, must become scarce in time, unless the future demand is anticipated by the cultivation of artificial groves.

So far as can be ascertained, the first white man to spend the winter in Monona County was Aaron Cook, who with some associates, passed the winter of 1851 here, engaged in herding cattle. The first permanent settler was Isaac Ashton, who, in 1852, located about two miles north of the present town of Onawa, where, in 1855, he laid out the town of Ashton. Philip Ashton, who was frozen to death in the winter of 1852, was the first white person to die in Monona County. Other settlers came in the summer of 1853, in which year Josiah Sumner located in the vicinity of On- awa, and Aaron Cook at Cook's Landing, on the Missouri River, seven miles southwest of Onawa. Among others who came prior to 1855, were C. E. Whiting, Robert Lindley, Timothy Elliott, J. E. Morrison, J. B. P. Day, and B. D. Holbrook. Several of the early settlers came from the eastern part of Iowa, while others were from Illinois and the Eastern States.

Among the early settlers of the county was Charles B. Thomp- son, a Mormon leader, who, with a number of followers, located on the Soldier River, in what is now called Spring Valley Town- ship, about fifteen miles southwest of the present town of Onawa.

They commenced their settlement in 1854. Thompson called the place Preparation, as he designed here to prepare his apostles for the "good time coming." As Thompson was an important man in the early history of Monona county, some account of him, and of the enterprise in which he was a leader, will be of interest. He had been a follower and disciple of Joe Smith at Nauvoo, but went to St. Louis in 1852, and organized a church. In the sum- mer of 1853, he sent some of his followers as commissioners to look for and select a location for his people in Iowa. They selected the valley of the Soldier in the south part of Monona county, all the land at that time being vacant.

In 1854 he brought some fifty or sixty families, and pre-empted several thousand acres of the best land to be found in the region. Some of the land he subsequently entered. Thompson regulated and controlled all the affairs of the colony, both temporal and spir- itual, pretending that he had authority to do so under the direc- tion of a spirit which he called Baneemy. Among other assump- tions, he pretended that he was the veritable Ephraim of the Scriptures, and directed his people to call him Father Ephraim. A strict compliance with his teachings divested his followers of all worldly care, and prepared them for the further essential doctrine of his religion, that in order to obtain the Kingdom, they must sacrifice all their earthly possessions. They accordingly conveyed to him all their lands and other property, including even their wearing apparel, and the right to their services.

Under this arrangement, "Father Ephraim" and Baneemyism progressed swimmingly, until the autumn of 1855, when a little rebellion occurred under the leadership of an Elder named Hugh Lytle, who, with some twenty of them, began a suit in the courts for the recovery of their property; but they failed, and the matter was subsequently compromised by the Lytle party receiving some of their property and withdrawing from the society.

The remainder adhered to Thompson without serious difficulty until the autumn of 1858. During the summer of that year, most

of the male adults of the society were absent in other States,
preaching the doctrines of Bancemyism to the Gentiles.   Thompson, who arrogated to himself the title of "Chief Steward of the
Lord," took advantage of their absence to convey all the realty to
his wife, Catharine Thompson, and to one Guy C. Barnum, reserving only forty acres as a homestead for himself.   His disciples,
hearing of this transaction, returned and immediately called on
"Father Ephraim" for restitution.   Being unable to obtain a satisfactory adjustment of the matter, they notified him that on a
stated day he would be expected to meet them in Preparation to
make settlement.

The "Chief Steward of the Lord," and " Assistant Steward of
the Lord " Barnum, had ̖not ̖sufficient courage to " face the
music," however, and postponed their visit to Preparation until
the day after the one appointed, doubtless thinking that the
angry crowd would have become dispersed by that time.   On the
way they were met, about a mile from the village, by a young woman who had not yet lost confidence' in "Father Ephraim" and
Bancemyism, and who informed them that the people were still congregated at Preparation, and would hang him on sight; which information had the effect on "Father Ephraim" it was well calculated to have, especially as at about that moment of time, men on
horseback were observed coming from Preparation at full speed,
and heading in all earnestness in the direction of the Chief Steward
and Assistant.   Springing from the wagon in which they were seated,
and unharnessing their horses, the two Stewards hurriedly sprang
upon the backs of the animals, and the chase, which ensued, was
of an exciting and highly interesting character.   After a lively
race of fifteen miles, across prairies and over creeks and ravines,
the "Father" and the "Assistant Father," arrived safely in
Onawa, where they were given protection by the citizens.

Thompson went from Onawa to St. Louis, and Barnum remained
in Onawa until the following spring, removing thence to Nebraska,
where he, in course of time, became a prominent citizen.   Thompson subsequently attempted to found another similar religious
society, but was unsuccessful, and next turned his attention to
publishing a book on the "Origin of the Black and Mixed Races,"
which book he pretended to translate largely from the Hebrew
and Greek languages, which, it is said, he in reality knew nothing
about.   The last heard of him by his former followers in Monona,
was to the effect that he was in Philadelphia in destitute circumstances.   After his flight from Preparation, his family was sent
to him at Onawa, his followers (?) dividing the personal property
among themselves, each taking such of his own property as he
could identify.   An action in chancery was immediately begun to
set aside the conveyances of real estate, which litigation lingered
in the courts for eight years, or until December, 1866, when the
conveyances were all declared to be fraudulent, and were set aside,

the Supreme Court of Iowa holding that Thompson held the property only as a trustee. The property was sold under an order of the court, and the proceeds were divided among the original contributors in ratio to the amount contributed by each. Of the sixty families brought to Monona by Thompson—to the settlement at Preparation —only three or four remain—to such an inglorious termination was Baneenyism destined to attain.

The proper name by which this peculiar sect sought to be known is said to have been the "Congregation of Jehovah's Presbytery of Zion," which was contracted to "Con-je-pre-zion," and hence the members came to be known as the "Conjeprezionites." Preparation was also familiarly known as Baneemy Town.

Monona county was organized in 1854. At the time of its organization, it had a population of 222; its population in 1860 was 832; in 1865 the population was 1,056; in 1870 it had reached 3,654, which was increased to 5,967 in 1875, and to 9,055 in 1880. Thirty-two votes were cast for Governor in the county in 1854; 134 votes were cast in 1857, and in 1859, Samuel J. Kirkwood and A. C. Dodge, Gubernatorial candidates, each received 105 votes in the county.

Charles B. Thompson was appointed the first County Judge. This was before the location of the county seat, so that the first county business was transacted at Preparation. In the autumn of 1854, the county seat was located by the commissioners appointed by the Legislature. They gave the place selected the name of Bloomfield, but there being another town of that name in the State, it was changed to Ashton. The county seat remained there until the spring of 1858, when it was removed to Onawa by a vote of the people. The following were the first county officers: Charles B. Thompson, County Judge; Guy C. Barnum, Treasurer; Hugh Lytle, Clerk; Homer C. Hoyt, Sheriff.

Monona county then embraced what is now the west range of townships of Crawford county, but the change was made in accordance with the votes of both counties in 1865. In 1860 a vote was taken on the question of the removal of the county seat from Onawa to Belvidere, and another vote was taken in 1862, on the removal to Arcola; both of which attempts, however, failed, and the location of the Sioux City & Pacific Railroad may be said to have, in all probability, finally settled the question.

The first newspaper was published by "Father Ephraim" Thompson at Preparation, and was called *Zion Harbinger and Weekly Messenger*. Thompson also published a monthly periodical. During the continuance of this paper, it flourished under several different names, such as the *Weekly News and Messenger* and the *Democratic Messenger*. This paper was started in 1854; in 1855, Thompson published a paper called the *Onawa Adventure*. In November, 1860, a paper was commenced at Onawa, by A. Dimmick and D. W. Butts, called the *Monona Cordon*. The next paper, the *West Iowa Gazette*, was started by Mr. Butts about the beginning of 1863, and was succeeded in 1865 by the *Monona County Gazette*, the first number of which was issued December 2d, 1865, F. M. Howdendobler and C. H. Aldridge being the publishers. The *People's Press* made its first appearance in Onawa in 1870.

The first frame house erected in the county was built at Preparation in the summer of 1853, of materials brought from Pottawattamie county. Thomas Lewis taught the first school in the county at Preparation in the same year. In 1854 the first lumber was sawed at Preparation. Amos Chase, at the same settlement, was the pioneer blacksmith. John S. Blackburn began the making of that very palatable article, corn meal, in 1857. In 1857, a frame school house was erected at Ashton.

The first officers of Ashton Township were: Lorenzo D. Driggs, J. B. Gard, Justices of the Peace; Josiah Sumner, Isaac Ashton, J. B. Gard, Trustees; Aaron Cook, Clerk; Lorenzo Driggs, Assessor; J. Sumner, M. Owens, Constables.

The present county officers of Monona county are: C. H. Aldridge, Clerk; James Walker, Sheriff; John K. McCasky, Auditor; G. H. Bryant, Treasurer; M. W. Bacon, Recorder; J. B. P. Day, Surveyor; J. G. Iddings, Superintendent of Schools; G. M. Scott, E. Wilber, Fred. McClausland, Board of Supervisors.

The Sioux City & Pacific Railroad traverses the county from north to south, along its western border. A branch of the Chicago & Northwestern enters Monona County at the northeast corner, and terminates at Mapleton Station. This line is, it is presumed to be built through the county, touching Onawa, and extended into Nebraska, crossing the Missouri at Decatur. Another line, running from a point in the western part of Crawford county, through Monona County, and passing on to Sioux City, is looked forward to. This line is expected to be built by the W. & St. P. company, and will pass about ten miles east of the county seat.

The towns of Monona County are: Whiting, situated in the northwestern part, on the Sioux City & Pacific; Mapleton, to the northwest; Soldier, to the southeast, and Onawa in the western part of the county.

ONAWA.

The prosperous and progressive town of Onawa, the county seat of Monona County, is located near the middle line of the county, north and south, and about eight miles east of the Missouri River, but only about four miles from the nearest point on the river to the southwest. The Monona Land Company laid out Onawa in 1857, including in its area about six hundred acres, with about six hundred additional acres of out-lots. The principal streets run east and west, and are one hundred and fifty feet in width, the other streets being eighty feet wide, with alleys sixteen feet wide. Two blocks were reserved in the northern part of the town for public parks.

S. S. Pearse built the first house in Onawa July 2d, 1857; the Onawa House was raised on the 4th of the same month, by J. E. Morrison. Among the first settlers were Judge C. E. Whiting, J. E. Morrison, Timothy Elliott, R. G. Fairchild and S. S. Pearse.

Surrounded by an excellent farming country, with plenty of timber within two or three miles, Onawa is certain to develop into a point of considerable importance. Since its incorporation, and the completion of the railroad, the population of the town has steadily increased. Onawa is thirty-seven miles from Sioux City, about sixty-five miles from Council Bluffs, and thirty-eight miles from Missouri Valley Junction.

Up to 1868, Onawa remained a sub-district of Franklin township district. A petition was presented in that year, praying for a special election to vote upon the question of the organization of an independent school district. This petition was granted, and the organization was effected February 22d, 1868. The members of the Board, for the first year, were: Charles Atkins, President; James Armstrong, Vice-President; F. M. Snow, Secretary; N. A. Whiting, Treasurer; R. G. Fairchild, L. D. Sittle and J. E. Selleck, Directors. The first school taught in the town was taught by A. R. Wright, now of Sioux City, in a little log school house, now on Main street, about the year 1857. There was a brick school house— 28x50 feet in dimensions, and one-story high, erected subsequently, which was successfully utilized until the building of the present edifice in 1874. The present public school building is a fine brick structure, 48x85 feet, and three-stories high. It contains six rooms. The building cost in the neighborhood of $20,-000. The present school officers are: Board of Education—J. K. McCaskey, President; S. B. Martin, Secretary; C. H. Holbrook, Treasurer; N. A. Whiting, B. D. Holbrook, G. E. Warner, J. E. Selleck, M. Vincent, members of the Board. The corps of teachers as composed at this writing, is as follows: W. H. Dempster, Principal; Belle M. Gilcrest, Assistant Principal; W. J. Maughlin, Annie C. Gillette, D. E. Smith, Flora J. Maughlin, Bessie Gray, teachers. Present enrollment, about 300. The school building is a model of architectural beauty and finish, the rooms are large, heated by means of furnaces, ventilated in accordance with the Ruttan system, and furnished with single and combination desks.

The Court House at Onawa was built by the Monona Land Company in 1858, and donated to the county. The building cost about $7,000.

A summarized history of Monona county's newspapers has been given hitherto. Room—or rather want of room—only suffices here to say that the *Monona County Gazette* was taken charge of in 1879 by W. A. Green alone, who ran the paper until 1870, when it subsequently passed into the ownership of the Gazette Publishing Company, with Mr. J. D. Ainsworth as the editor. In 1875, Ainsworth became sole proprietor, and has continued to hold the fort in a most commendable way. The *Gazette* is an eight-column folio, and has a circulation in excess of 800 copies.

The first railroad was completed to Onawa in November, 1867. The town gave the company the right of way, and lots, and cash to the amount of $8,000, besides donating twenty acres of land for depot grounds. Onawa has a reasonable prospect for a railroad from Mapleton during the present year.

The date of the platting of Onawa was the year 1857. The following persons composed the Monona Land Company: T. Elliott, J. E. Morrison, J. L. Merritt, C. E. Whiting, R. G. Fairchild, S. S. Pearse, A. B. Gard, W. S. Phillips, A. Dimmick; Judge Whiting being the President; T. Elliott, Treasurer; S. S. Pearse, Secretary.

The first Mayor of Onawa was Dr. R. Stebbins. Present municipal officers: H. E. Morrison, Mayor; T. P. Noble, Recorder; J. C. Pike, D. B. Kenyon, John Cleghorn, J. R. Thurston, T. C. Walton, Council.

The business interests of Onawa may be classified, with reasonable accuracy, as follows:

General stores, four; groceries, three; drug stores, two; millinery, three; harness, two; hardware, two; meat markets two; clothing, one; jewelry, one; agricultural implements, two; flour and feed, one; bank, one; barber shop, one; hotels, three; blacksmith shops, three; furniture, one; boots and shoes, two; livery, two; lumber, one; flouring mill, one; fancy goods, one; saloons, two.

CHURCHES AND SOCIETIES.

Congregational Church Society.—The Congregational Society was organized June 27th, 1858, by Rev. G. G. Rice, of Council Bluffs, and Rev. Reuben Gaylord, of Omaha. The first-named gentleman was the society's first pastor, and he was succeeded by the Rev. George L. Woodhull, who died October 1st, 1870, aged 28 years. Mr. Woodhull's successor was the present pastor, Rev. Charles N. Lyman, who assumed the charge January 1, 1871. The church edifice was erected in 1870, and was dedicated in December of that year. The cost was $6,000. Prior to the erection of this building, the society held its services in the Court House. The present membership of the society is fifty-five. A Sabbath School, with an average attendance of seventy-five pupils, is connected with the church. The superintendent of the school is the Rev. Charles N. Lyman.

Methodist Episcopal Church Society.—The Methodist Episcopal Society was organized October 9th, 1870, by Rev. J. F. Walker, who was the first pastor. The successive pastors were: Revs. L. H. Woodworth, A. L. Mattison, O. S. Bryan, J. B. Starkey, J. Warner, H. W. Jones, S. W. Owen, C. E. Chase, F. A. Burdick and A. J. Beebe, the latter being the present pastor. The edifice now in use was built in 1873, at a cost of $2,000. The society had previously held services in the public school house. The present membership is forty-three. The society has a parsonage, which was built in 1873, during Rev. Starkey's pastoral term. There is also a Sabbath School with about seventy-five pupils, the superintenaent of which is Miss D. E. Smith. The present Trustees of the society are: M. W. Bacon, S. W. Grow, L. D. Sittle, W. C. Marr and T. C. Walton.

Roman Catholic Church Society.—The Catholic Church Society at Onawa may be considered to date its existence from the building of its church edifice in the latter part of 1872. Mass had been celebrated there occasionally, as far back as 1866, and in 1867, when Bishop Hennessy assumed charge of the western part of the State, which, during the government of his predecessor, Bishop Smythe, had been administered by the late Bishop O'Gorman, of Omaha. Mass was celebrated prior to 1866, by priests of the Diocese of Nebraska, and particularly by Father Tracy, of old St. John's, who had charge from the Yellowstone to the Platte. Rev. B. C. Lenehan is the present pastor.

Monona Lodge No. 380, I. O. O. F.—This Lodge was organized June 7th, 1878, by Grand Master A. J. Morrison. The charter members were: E. W. Holbrook, H. W. Cady, L. H. Belknap, John Douglas, C. M. Ross, J. S. Baggs, D. L. Utterback, James Carmody, R. Horning and J. K. McCaskey. The first officers were: J. K. McCaskey, N. G.; J. Carmody, V. G.; J. Douglas, S.; E. W. Holbrook, T. The membership of the Lodge is twenty-eight. Present officers: P. T. Noble, N. G.; Geo. W. Penn, V. G.; L. D. Sittle, S.; W. M. Bacon, T. The meetings of the Lodge are held on every Saturday night of each week in the hall of the society over the bank.

Vesper Lodge No. 223, A. F. and A. M.—A dispensation was granted to this Lodge August 28th, 1867. The first officers were: F. W. Snow, W. M.; James Butts, S. W.; Truman Pierce, J. W.; Charles Atkins, S.; Fred McCouslan, T.; W. A. Grow, S. D.; M. A. Treeland, J. D.; John Baggs, Tyler. A charter was granted the Lodge June 3d, 1868. The charter members were F. W. Snow, James Butts, Truman Pierce and other wortny gentlemen. The present officers are: James Walker, W. M.; H. Douglas, S. W.; G. E. Warner, J. W.; J. D. Ainsworth, S.; R. Stebbins, F. S.; B. D. Holbrook, S. D.; D. Handle, J. D.; J. D. Giddings, S. S.; O. D. Bishop, J. S.; F. W. Snow, Tyler. The Lodge meets every Wednesday, on or after each full moon, in the hall over the bank. The membership of this society is thirty-eight, and it is in a flourishing condition.

Monona County Agricultural Association.—This association was organized in the spring of 1871, as a stock company. The first official board of directors was composed of the following-named gentlemen: C. E. Whiting, Fred McCausland, J. E. Morrison, M. A. Freeland, W. G. Kennedy, A. Dimmick and E. Peak. The first officers were: C. E. Whiting, President; M. A. Freeland, Vice-President; James Walker, Secretary; B. D. Holbrook, Treasurer. The association owns thirty-five acres of land situated about one mile north of Onawa, which land is enclosed with a good, substantial fence. Inside the enclosure is Floral Hall, an excellent building, with dimensions of 20x40 feet, as well as an additional "L," of 24x60 feet. There are also a fine Amphitheatre and good stables and cattle-sheds. A half-mile race-track is another improvement. All these are in good condition. The present board of directors is composed of W. T. Boyd, A. Oliver, J. D. Woodward, J. B. P. Day, R. G. Fairchild, C. E. Whiting and G. E. Warner. The present officers are: A. Oliver, President; J. B. P. Day, Vice-President; J. D. Ainsworth, Secretary; B. D. Holbrook, Treasurer. The society is in a very prosperous condition. Its last annual fair, the ninth, was held in September, 1881.

Monona County Old Settlers' Association.—This association was organized in August, 1879, by C. E. Whiting, R. Stebbins, T. R. Carratt, J. E. Morrison, Judge Oliver, F. H. Day and others. The first officers were: F. H. Day, President; C. E. Whiting, C. M. Scott, W. L. Ring, Vice-Presidents; James Walker, Secretary, R. Stebbens, T. R. Carratt, John Heisler, James Robinson, J. D. Woodward, Executive Committee. Present Officers: W. L. Ring, President; F. F. Roe, T. Elliott, G. M. Scott, Vice-Presidents; James Walker, Secretary and Treasurer; J. B. P. Day, C. E. Whiting, Judge Oliver, J. Cleghorn, Executive Committee. The present membership of the association is about 275.

MAPLETON.

This growing town was platted in the autumn of 1877, by the railroad company. The first hotel was built by A. P. Kennedy in 1877. The Maple River branch of the Chicago & Northwestern Railroad, was completed from Maple River Junction, the first train arriving in October, 1877. A branch of the C., M. & St. P. R. R. from Sioux City to Mapleton is now graded, and will ere long be placed in running order.

In September, 1877, J. Garrison built the first store in Mapleton. It was 10x12 feet in dimensions. The Messrs. Scott soon afterwards built the store they now occupy.

The first settlers in the village were: J. Garrison, W. F. Scott and brothers, W. F. McHenry and B. Whiting, who settled here in the autumn of 1877. The town was incorporated in 1878, with J. F. Scott as Mayor. The population is about 600.

The Mapleton Bank was organized October 3d, 1878, with B. Whiting, President; N. H. Bliss, Cashier, and with abundance of capital. It is a flourishing and substantial institution. At present, B. Whiting is the President, C. I. Whiting, Cashier.

The schools of Mapleton are graded, and in excellent condition. A handsome structure was erected in 1880-81, at a cost of $3,500. J. A. Wakefield is the Principal. About 100 pupils are enrolled.

An order of Odd Fellowship was organized Sept 11th, 1879, with five charter members. J. Hutton was the first N. G. The Lodge now has twenty-five members.

A Masonic order was organized in July, 1880, with ten charter members. The present membership is fifteen. J. D. Rice was the first Master of this Lodge.

The Presbyterian Church Society was organized July 31st, 1881, by Rev. A. K. Baird, assisted by Rev. J. C. Gilkerson, the present pastor, with a membership of seventeen. The church officers are one Elder and three Trustees.

The M. E. Church Society of Mapleton was organized by Rev. Thomas Cuthburt, during the year of 1880. The church edifice, a neat and durable brick building of the Gothic style, 32x50 feet in dimensions, was erected during the same year, at a cost of $2,300, and the following Trustees were appointed: W. E. Roberts, President; B. Whiting, Treasurer; George Adams, Secretary; A. W. Cobland, G. A. Smith, Trustees. The Society is small, but growing, was organized with a membership of six, and now numbers twenty. During the year, 1881, the Society built a parsonage at a cost of $800, the building being in every way highly creditable to the organization. There is, in this connection a Sabbath School, with an average attendance of eighty. W. E. Roberts is the Superintendent. Rev. H. P. Dudley is the present pastor.

The Baptist Church Society was organized in March, 1866, by Rev. George Scott. Its membership is thirty-eight. Rev. W. H. Dorward is the present pastor.

The Mapleton cornet band was organized in 1880, with ten members. A. I. Lanterman is the leader.

Mapleton's business and professional establishments are represented as follows: Four general stores, one newspaper—the *Mapleton Press*—one bank, four hotels, two livery stables, two hardware stores, three saloons, two blacksmiths, one boot and shoe store, one grocery, one millinery store, one harness shop, four physicians, two grain dealers, two lumber yards, one wagon factory, one furniture store, one farm machinery establishment, two meat markets, four dealers in live stock.

An article with the captivating caption, "Society in Mapleton," says: "Mapleton will compare favorably with older towns east or west as regards social privileges. Although a town of only eighteen months' growth, we here find many advantages that would be prized by those seeking homes in the West.

"Our people are mostly from the Eastern States, and are well informed, public spirited and up with the times. As yet we are without an organized church, but union services and Sunday school. are regularly held in the public hall, and there is a prospect that either a Presbyterian or Congregational society will soon be formed. The Methodist Episcopal church contemplate building a house of worship the coming summer.

"The 'Blue Ribbon' movement has reached Mapleton, and upward of 200 have signed the pledge. It is to be hoped that efforts that have been made in this direction will not be in vain.

"A literary society has been sustained during the past winter with considerable interest. Lectures, readings, concerts and other entertainments have not been wanting to afford amusement for the winter evenings. The many demands for money incident to carrying on the enterprise of a new town are met with cheerfulness and a ready response by our citizens and no laudable undertaking has yet failed for the lack of means.

"A tax has been levied in Maple Township and partly collected for the purpose of erecting a substantial school building, that will be the pride of our city. A mayor, six alderman, and other efficient officers manage municipal affairs; quiet and good order universally prevail in our midst.

"People looking for homes in Western Iowa should visit Mapleton before deciding on a permanent location."

The following is taken from editorial correspondence to the *Carroll* (Ia.) *Herald :* " Western Iowa is constantly furnishing examples of the sudden rise and rapid growth of new towns. The wild prairie of yesterday is frequently transformed into the busy and bustling center of trade to-day. One of the most notable of these instances is found in the history of Mapleton, from which place I write. The town was platted in the fall of 1877, and is consequently less than a year and a half old. The Maple River branch of the Northwestern road reached here about the middle of October, 1877. At that time there was no settlement worth mentioning. Now the town numbers five hundred inhabitants, and is growing steadily. The railroad, which leaves the main line sixty miles southeast, terminates at Mapleton. By virtue of this fact, the place enjoys exceptional advantages over other towns on the line. It is located near the beautiful Maple River in the far-famed Maple Valley, long noted as comprising within its limits the finest farming land in the west, but until recently not accessible by railroad. It will doubtless remain the terminal station for years to come, and its present prosperity cannot but increase in the future. Although Mapleton is young, it has none of the characteristics of a mushroom town. The buildings are extremely creditable and calculated for permanency. Many of the residences are handsome and attractive. The location of the town is excellent. It lies on high, but nearly level ground, sloping just enough to afford good drainage. The residence lots are all superior, and there is ample room for a large city. The land surrounding it is unexcelled for agricultural purposes, nearly every acre being tillable. The Maple River furnishes numerous water powers, there being three grist mills within five miles of the town."

WHITING.

Although comparatively young, in respect to many other Western Iowa towns, Whiting has made rapid strides since its first settlement. A complete representation of its more enterprising business establishments will be found among the biographical data hereunto appended.

MONONA COUNTY BIOGRAPHIES

ONAWA.

James Butts, M. D., was born in Genesee county, N. Y., in 1822; remained at home until twenty-one years of age; then began the study of medicine. He moved to Wis. in 1856, and engaged in the practice of medicine; was also postmaster while in that State. He removed to Kans. in 1860, traveled extensively through the west, settled at Onawa in 1866, and has practiced medicine there ever since. He opened a drug store in 1873, and after four years, sold it. He has been twice married; the first time in 1844, and to Lucy L. Crawford, in 1880.

I. Cummings, dealer in groceries and provisions, was born in N. Y. in 1844; removed to Fremont county, Ia., in 1855; thence to Chicago, Ill., in 1871, where he remained five years, and located in Onawa, Ia., in 1877. In 1881, engaged in the present business, by buying out J. R. Thurston.

John Douglas, jeweler and music dealer, was born in Scotland in 1851; came to America in 1872, and settled in Neb.; moved to Onawa in 1876, and engaged in his present business. He was married in 1876, and has two children—Mary, and an infant daughter.

W. J. Eva, harness manufacturer, was born in Wis. in 1847; removed to Worthington, Nobles county, Minn., in 1872; thence to Onawa, Ia., in 1876, and engaged in his present business in 1878. He was married in 1875 to Lucy Manning, and has three children.

B. D. & Chas. Holbrook, proprietors of the bank at Onawa, came from Pa. to this city in 1857, and engaged in the law, loan and real estate business, until 1865, when they opened the bank. H. E. Morrison is cashier of the bank.

A. G. Hurst, farmer and stock dealer, was born in Ind. in 1832; removed with parents in 1836 to Ill.; thence to Newton, Ia. In 1855 came to Ashton, near Onawa. He enlisted in March, 1862, in Co. K., 17th Ia., and re-enlisted as a veteran in the same company. He was taken prisoner with the rest of the regiment and confined at Andersonville one hundred and eighty-five days; was discharged at Davenport, Ia., June 16th, 1865, and returned to Monona county, and engaged in farming and dealing in stock. He was married in 1859, to Julia Brink, and has ten children.

W. H. Kelsey was born in N. Y. in 1841. He enlisted in Co. B, 64th N. Y. Vol., in 1861, was discharged in 1862; re-enlisted in the 13th N. Y. Heavy Art. as a veteran, and was again discharged in 1865. He was one of five brothers, who enlisted; two were killed and the others disabled in the service. He came to Onawa in 1865. He was married in 1877.

D. B. Kenyon, miller and grain dealer, was born in N. Y. in 1845; removed to Wis. in 1856, and from there to Onawa in 1872, and engaged in his present business. He was married in 1869 to N. F. Freeland. They have one son and two daughters.

C. G. Perkins, postmaster, and dealer in general merchandise, was born in Rockingham county, N. Y., in 1830; removed to Wis. in 1855, and engaged in farming. He enlisted in 1862 in Co. G, 19th Wis., and was discharged in 1865; then came to Onawa, and engaged in farming four years. He was then elected county recorder; resigned in 1872. He was a member of the 14th assembly in 1872-3; engaged in his present business in 1873. He was married in 1853 to R. S. Stearns, and has three children—C. W., Mary W. and Addie M.

P. Sawyer, proprietor of city blacksmith shop, was born in Oxford county, Me., in 1846. He enlisted in 1862, in Co. D, 28th Me. Vol.; was discharged in 1863, and went to Concord, Mass.; thence to Onawa in 1865. He was married in 1867, to M. T. Cunningham. They have four children—Edwin E., Altha M., Earl, and Margie.

John W. Somers, druggist, was born in N. C. in 1834; removed to Champaign county, Ill., in 1843 and was clerk of the courts for several years. He enlisted in 1862 in the 76th Ill. Vol. as a private; was promoted to commissary sergeant, then to first lieutenant, and regimental quarter-master; left the army in 1865, and returned to Ill. He engaged in the drug business in 1867 at Urbana, and in 1879 removed to Onawa, and again engaged in the drug business. He was married in 1858 to Sarah J. Fitzgerald. They have one son and one daughter.

Richard Stebbins. M. D., and druggist, was born in Springfield, Mass., in 1824. He was educated for a physician; removed to Council Bluffs in 1857, and engaged in the practice of medicine; remained there six months; removed to Onawa, and continued the practice of his profession, and engaged in the drug business in 1864. He was married in 1859 to Mary J. Billings, and has a son and a daughter.

J. R. Thurston, proprietor of the Onawa House, was born in Herkimer county, N. Y., in 1833; removed to Cass county, Ia., in 1856; thence to Onawa in 1860, and engaged in farming, until 1877, when he engaged in the mercantile business, which he sold in 1881, and engaged in his present business. He was married in 1855, and has five children.

T. C. Walton, proprietor of the Walton House, was born in Somerset county. Me., in 1829; removed to Wis., in 1854, and remained two years and returned to Me. In 1864 he again removed to Wis., settling in St. Croix county, and engaged in the drug business. In 1869 he came to Onawa, Ia., and in 1871 built the hotel he now occupies. He has been twice married, and has four children—Lona, Ida, Geo. and William.

Maj. George E. Warner. dealer in general merchandise, was born in Sullivan county, N. H., in 1843. He went to Boston, Mass., at the age of twelve to learn the dry goods business. In 1862 he enlisted in the 6th Mass. battery, and at the end of six months, entered the 10th U. S. colored corps as first lieutenant; was promoted to Major, and discharged in that rank in 1867; came to Onawa, Ia., and engaged in his present business. He was married in 1868 to Mollie E. Morrison, of Onawa, and has one child, a daughter.

N. A. Whiting, dealer in general hardware, was born in N. Y., in 1823; lived on a farm until eighteen years of age; then learned carriage making, in which business he was engaged for fifteen years in O. and Ala. He came to Onawa, Ia., in 1857, and the following year engaged in his present business. He was married in 1853, and has three children—Eva, Charles and Estella. Chas. is engaged in the banking business at Mapleton, Ia.

W. G. Woods, dealer in grain, enlisted in 1864 in Co. E, 48th Wis., and was discharged in 1865. He was married in 1873, to Matilda Barber, and has one son and one daughter—Arthur and Zellie.

MAPLETON.

J. Q. Adams, proprietor of the Mapleton dray line, was born in Franklin county, Me., in 1837; moved to Iowa in 1854. He moved to Onawa in 1858, and engaged in farming. He engaged in his present business in Mapleton, Jan. 25th, 1881.

G. H. Butler, of the firm of G. H. Butler & Co., furniture dealers, was born in Ind.; moved to Ia. in 1856, and engaged in milling. He moved to Monona county, Ia., in 1865, and engaged in farming, and in 1878, engaged in his present business.

J. R. Cameron, dealer in general merchandise and grain, is a native of Ohio; came to Ia. in 1852, and engaged in the land business. He came to Monona county in 1878, and engaged in the grain and land business, and, in 1880, added the mercantile business. He was agent for the railroad company for three years.

J. R. Chapman, dealer in lumber, coal and builders' supplies, is a native of N. Y.; moved to Ohio when young, and to Scott county, Ia., in 1860. He came to Mapleton, in 1877, and engaged in his present business.

J. Garrison, hardware dealer, was born in Ill.; moved to Iowa in 1873, and located in Calhoun county, and engaged in farming. He moved to Dunlap, and engaged in the mercantile business; thence to Mapleton, in the autumn of 1877, and built the first store in the place, and entered the mercantile business.

Porter Hamilton, of the firm of Hamilton Bros., dealers in farm machinery and lumber, was born in Ill.; moved to Cedar Rapids, Ia., in 1872; thence to Mapleton in the autumn of 1877, and engaged in his present business. During 1881, his sales of farm machinery amounted to $25,000.

Samuel Holliday, proprietor of the City billiard hall, was born in Muscatine county, Ia., in 1842, and engaged in farming, until entering his present business in 1880.

T. Martin, proprietor of blacksmith and wagon shop, is a native of Ill.; moved to Ia. in 1880, and engaged in his present business.

M. Morgan, of the firm of Butler & Morgan, grocers, was born in Scott county, Ia., in 1846. He enlisted in May, 1864, in the 44th Ia. regiment, and was discharged in autumn of the same year. He re-enlisted in Jan., 1865, in the 20th, Ia., Co. G; was transferred to the 29th Ia. regiment, and in Sept., 1865, returned to Iowa, and engaged in farming. He located at Mapleton in 1879, and entered his present business in Jan., 1881.

J. D. Rice, attorney at law; is a native of N. Y.; moved to Marshall, Ia., in 1874; thence to Mapleton in 1878, and engaged in the practice of the law. He is a member of the school board.

W. E. Roberts, agent for the C. & N. W. R. R., is a native of England; came to America when quite young, with parents, and settled in Wis.; moved to Tama county, Ia., in 1863. He afterwards moved to Battle Creek, as agent for the railroad company; thence to Mapleton in Nov., 1880.

W. F. Scott, of the firm of Scott Bros., dealers in general merchandise, is a native of W. Va.; moved to Clinton county, Ia., in

1864, and to Denison in 1871, and engaged in the mercantile business. He came to Mapleton in 1877, erected a large store building, and engaged in his present business. He was appointed postmaster in Dec., 1881, and is also express agent.

B. B. Snyder, proprietor of the Stowell House, is a native of Pa.; came to Logan, Ia., in 1876, and engaged in the hotel business. He erected one of the first hotels in Mapleton, and opened his present house in 1881, which is in charge of his son, James S. Snyder.

WHITING.

Cassady & Whiting, dealers in general merchandise, located in Whiting in June, 1880. Mr. Cassady is a native of O.; moved to Ia. in 1867, and settled near this place. W. C. Whiting is a native of Monona county, and has always resided in it.

Koon & Dimmick, dealers in general hardware, established business in Dec., 1881. Mr. Koon came to Mills county, Ia., in 1868, from Ill.; thence to Monona county in 1873. Mr. Dimmick is a native of Pa.; moved to Ashton, Ia., in 1856; thence to Whiting in 1881.

D. Rust, M. D., of the firm of Rust & Morley, druggists, was born in Ill.; moved to Fremont county, Ia., in 1876. He established his present business in Whiting in 1879, and in 1880 L. A. Morley became a partner. They do a general drug business, and deal in paints, oils, etc.

Lyman Whittier, the pioneer merchant of Whiting, was born in Essex county, Mass.; came to Ia. in 1870, and located at Missouri Valley and engaged in the mercantile business; removed to Whiting in 1873, and built the first store and started his present business. He enlisted in Oct., 1862, in the 1st battery of Mass. heavy artillery, and served until June 1865. Mr. W. traveled extensively through Europe during the year 1879. He was appointed postmaster of Whiting in 1873, and has held the office ever since.

A. G. Wight, dealer in general merchandise, was born in Ohio; moved to Ia. in 1865, and settled in Monona county in 1867. In 1875 he moved to Whiting and engaged in the hotel and livery business which he still continues, and in 1876 engaged in the mercantile business.

CHEROKEE COUNTY.

If there is any one class of men who deserve more than another to have their names perpetuated in history, it is, perhaps, the hardy pioneers who left their homes of comfort and luxury in the old Eastern States, and, voluntarily abandoning all the comforts of home an l civilized life, plunged boldly into the unknown and limitless prairies that spread out beyond the great Father of Waters, to explore the mysteries of this mighty region, and to open up new fields of industry for themselves and their posterity. To the historian, no more delightful task presents itself, than to recount their deeds of daring, to chronicle their persistent self-sacrificing efforts, to recite their marvelous achievements, to tell of the indomitable pluck, energy and determination that characterized their movements, and then to make the wonderful transformation all this has effected in one of the grandest countries the sun ever shown down upon. To the individual who visits this section to-day, these recitals seem like fairy tales. He cannot comprehend, as he sits in his elegant palace coach, and is whirled from one city and village to another, almost with the speed of the wind, or skims along the iron track through waving fields of the richest grain, that a few short years ago this section was tenanted only by wild animals and the equally wild and savage red-man; and his wonder is still further increased, as he notes, on every hand, the commodious and even elegant farm buildings, and sees the innumerable herds of fine cattle grazing on the nutritious grasses. The transition has indeed been wonderful, but probably nowhere more marked than in Cherokee County, where, a trifle over thirty-six years ago, no sign of civilization could meet the eye throughout its entire length and breadth. But a country of such surpassing beauty and unequalled richness could not always be given over to painted savages, albeit they alone had enjoyed its fair skies and beautiful scenery for so many years.

Cherokee County was formed in January, 1851, at which time most of her sister counties were located and their boundaries defined. In January, 1853, it was attached to the county of Wahkan—now Woodbury- for revenue, election and judicial purposes. At this time, however, it was a county in nothing but name; for its fertile prairies, beautiful rivers and clear, sparkling brooks had as yet failed to attract the attention of the "vanguard of civilization." Finally, in the Spring of 1856, Robert Perry, a hardy pioneer from the eastern part of the State, visited this section and stopped for a short time near what is now known as the city of

Cherokee. The solitude proved altogether too unattractive, and he soon took his departure for another and more thickly settled portion of the State.

In the early part of the same year, a number of hard-working, intelligent men in Milford, in the old commonwealth of Massachusetts, became fired with a desire to visit this wonderful Eldorado, about which they had heard so much, and if possible, to secure for themselves homes here. Under the leadership of Dr. Russell, a prominent citizen of Milford, a joint stock company, known as the "Milford Emigration Society," was formed, consisting of fifty-five members, twenty-four of whom were heads of families, the design being to find homes somewhere in Western Iowa. Just prior to the formation of this company, Carlton Corbett and Lemuel Parkhurst, both stalwart, daring young men, had been sent out by the citizens of Milford to explore this portion of the country, and select a suitable location for colonists. Twenty persons, under the auspices of the Milford Emigration Society, started on February 11th, 1856, for northwestern Iowa, intending to meet Corbett and Parkhurst at Sioux City, that being the objective point of the colony at that time.

On arriving at the mouth of the Big Sioux River, Messrs. Corbett and Parkhurst discovered, much to their disappointment, that others were in advance of them. Mr. Parkhurst remained here, but Mr. Corbett pushed on up the country for a distance of fifty miles above Sioux City. Not finding what he considered a desirable location, he again turned south with the determination of exploring Cherokee County, of which he had heard very favorable reports from Mr. Perry, who was then located at Sioux City. A thorough exploration of the county convinced Mr. Corbett that it was altogether the finest section of country he had yet visited. Hastening to Correctionville, he met the Milford colony, and had but little difficulty in inducing that party to locate here. They proceeded up the Little Sioux River, until they reached Cherokee County, where all were amazed at the magnificent panorama nature had spread out, seemingly for their benefit. The weary company arrived at a point on the Sioux, near the present site of Cherokee, on a beautiful May morning. The river danced and sparkled in the sunlight, as it dashed along its pebbly bed; the birds sang sweetly as they flitted from bough to bough, through the thick growth of timber that then skirted the high river banks at this point; the view on either hand was the most enchanting mortal eyes ever beheld, and to the weary wanderers, many hundred miles from home, and over one hundred miles from any settlement, it seemed that all nature was bidding them "welcome" to the peerless county of Cherokee.

On every side were moderately high bluffs, beyond which, stretching away for miles upon miles, was the rich rolling prairie-land, of which they had so long been in search. The entire company con sisted of twenty persons, some of whom are still living in the county. The colonists, among whom were G. W. Lebourveau, Carlton Corbett, B. W. Sawtell, Lysander Sawtell, Robert Hammond, Albert Simonds, Asa Slayton, were undaunted by the fact that there was no friendly roof to afford them shelter, and believing that a bright and prosperous future awaited them if only the necessary pluck and muscle were exercised, they immediately commenced the construction of a log house, 17 by 18 feet, near the present site of Mill Creek Mill, and for some time this small building, the first ever erected in Cherokee County, afforded shelter and a home to the entire colony. The two teams belonging to the colony were immediately put to work, and 150 acres were broken for a crop, of which about thirty acres were planted with corn. They also raised 200 bushels of excellent potatoes and a large quantity of small vegetables. During the season four more houses were built, one by G. W. Lebourveau, one by the Sawtell brothers, one by L. Parkhurst and one by William Holden, the two latter and Albert Phipps having joined the settlers later in the season. The postoffice and the nearest trading point were sixty miles from the settlement, and nearly all merchandise had to be hauled from Council Bluffs, 130 miles distant.

During the Summer, a village was planned; 320 acres were surveyed into town lots, and all the land adjoining the village plat was made into twenty-acre lots, though a few contained as many as sixty. The lands selected were principally west of the Little Sioux River, and south of Mill Creek, and located near the center of the county. An unusually severe winter followed, the snow at one time lying three feet deep on the level prairie, and the colonists suffered not a little.

On the 18th day of June, 1856, another colony from Hardin county, Iowa, consisting of G. W. Banister, John Banister, John Moore, Charles Moore, Alfred Moore, Jacob Miller, T. Lane, Marvin Alison and Martin Burns, arrived at this place, and immediately started a settlement seven miles below the Milford colony. Enoch Taylor and three others met with poor success in attempting to start another settlement in the northern part of the county. Cold weather was now coming on, and Mr. Corbett and L. Sawtell made a trip to Council Bluffs, with ox teams, to procure winter provisions for the colony.

Thus far the Cherokee colony had been favored with uninterrupted prosperity, but an Indian out-break in February, 1857, threatened for a time to overthrow all the bright hopes of the settlers. In this month a party of Sioux Indians passed down the river, but as they appeared very friendly to the Cherokee settlers, no uneasiness was felt. At Smithland, the whites took the arms away from the Indians, which so enraged the latter that they started back up the stream, vowing vengeance on all the whites they should meet. They entered every house on their way back, appropriating everything in the way of fire-arms they could lay their hands on. With the arms thus obtained they arrived at Cherokee, and scattered the settlers and captured their arms, provisions and other articles. Cattle were stolen, provisions seized, and the unfortunate settlers forced to cook them at the muzzle of a gun in the hands of an Indian who seemed more anxious to shoot than otherwise. The savages remained three days, during which there existed a regular reign of terror. On the night of the third day, Messrs. Lebourveau and Parkhurst returned from a trip to Sac City, and the Indians, thinking they had come from Smithland, and that the armed citizens of that place would follow, left the next morning in great haste. Hurrying to Spirit Lake, they massacred the entire colony, men, women and children.

When the horrible tale of the Spirit Lake massacre reached the Cherokee settlers, they became thoroughly alarmed, and by the advice of friends in other settlements, they abandoned their settlement entirely in the latter part of February, some going to Ashland, some to Smithland and others to Onawa.

As no further outbreak took place, the fears of the settlers gradually subsided, and in the following May most of the settlers returned and put in their crops.

The first school was taught during the summer in the old log house called the Cherokee House, by Mrs. Parkhurst, the funds for its support being sent from Milford, Massachusetts. Among those who attended that school, are Clara, George and Thomas Brown; John. Frank and Addie Phipps, all of whom were long residents of this county. Miss Phipps afterwards taught school herself in this county, and was considered one of the most successful teachers in the county.

Up to this time, Cherokee had remained attached to Woodbury County for judicial, election and revenue purposes. Sergeant's Bluffs was then the county seat of Woodbury County, and as all business for Cherokee County had to be transacted at that place, and as the distance was great, the inconvenience became so serious, that, in August, 1857, the county was completely organized, and its independent political life fully inaugurated by a special election. Twenty-three votes were cast, and the following officers elected: County Judge, A. P. Thayer; District Clerk, B. W. Sawtell; Prosecuting Attorney, C. Corbett; Recorder and Treasurer, G. W. Lebourveau; County Sheriff, S. W. Haynes; Coroner, G. W. Banister.

Early in 1858, the first tax was levied, amounting to twelve and a half mills on the dollar. The total valuation of property was $97,820. The first county warrant ever issued in Cherokee County was drawn October 2d, 1858, for $4.30, payable to D. N. Stoddard, on account of services as chainman on Road No. 1, to Plymouth County line, and is signed by A. P. Thayer, County Judge. The first bridge over the Sioux was built by Mr. Blair, he receiving therefor $1,600. To pay this, the people voted a seven-mill tax, fourteen votes being cast for the tax and one against it.

In the fall of 1857, a number of the colonists left, carrying with them dismal stories of the rigorous winters and terrible Indians, and from the year 1858 to the year 1863, there was but little cheering in the history of Cherokee County.

Isolated from all the privileges, comforts and conveniences of old communities, Cherokee County became a little world of its own, albeit a rather gloomy one. A land grant, made in 1856, had led the settlers to hope for an early completion of the Dubuque & Sioux City Railroad, but as time passed on without other prospects of the road being built, the hopes of the settlers were extinguished, and a general feeling of despondency took possession of all.

In the month of November, 1859, occurred the first marriage in the county, that of Carlton Corbett, and Miss Rosabella Cummings.

For three succeeding years but little occurred in the county worthy of record. In 1860, the population of the county was fifty-eight, but in 1863, this had decreased to fifteen. In 1862, the Indian outbreaks assumed such formidable proportions that the settlers were once more compelled to flee from their homes and seek safety at other and better protected places. Mr. Corbett returned in the fall, and he was followed by O. S. Wight, J. A. Brown, and Robert Perry, all of whom were accompanied by their families.

During the civil war, Cherokee County furnished more soldiers in proportion to her population than any other county in the Union. Among those who enlisted from this county were G. W. Lebourveau, Silas Parkhurst, Joel Davenport, and Albert Phipps. Eight in all entered the army for the Union, leaving but five men in the entire county.

In 1863, a court house was built at the cost of $1,900, and this building is yet being used by the county. In 1865, the first saw mill was erected on the site now occupied by the Bliss mill. This year the population of the county was but sixty-four, and the census of 1865 returned nine residents, with a population of fifty-two, twenty-nine males and twenty-three females. There were twenty-one horses and ninety-eight cattle, and only eighteen acres of spring wheat were sown, twenty-three acres of oats, seven of barley, and thirty-eight of potatoes.

For some years, prior to 1866, the settlement had a monthly mail, which was carried between Cherokee and Sioux City. During the year 1860, a weekly mail was established, which was considered a wonderful step in advance, and then for the first time the settlers began to realize that they were really a part and parcel of the civilized world. Early in this year, G. W. Lebourveau, G. W. Banister and Silas Parkhurst, three of the original settlers, returned to Cherokee county. The developments of the county from this time until the year 1869, was very slow, and but little worthy of record transpired. In 1868, the population numbered 227. The general election was held in the fall of this year, at which sixty-four votes were polled. Hon. Eli Johnson, of Cherokee, was elected to the State Legislature by a handsome majority. Mr. Johnson is at present a resident of Cherokee, where he is publishing a paper, the *Cherokee Free Press*. During this session of the Legislature, the preliminary survey for the Dubuque and Sioux City Railroad was run through Cherokee county, and the line established. The work of building the road was immediately commenced, and pushed forward with all possible vigor. In the Spring of 1869, immigration commenced to pour into the county, and it seemed, indeed, that an era of prosperity had at last been inaugurated. About this time a store was opened in the old village by a Mr. Foskett. He was soon followed by Mr. Van Eps. A saw mill was also erected in Pilot Township by Mr. Rodgers.

During the year work on the railroad progressed with great vigor, and in May, 1870, the road was completed, so as to admit of through trains, but as the road left the village of Cherokee about a mile to the east, an effectual stop was put to its growth. As soon as it was known exactly where the road would run, it was decided to establish a new town site, and in March, of this year, Carlton Corbett and G. W. Lebourveau laid out the new town of Cherokee in the immediate vicinity of the site selected for the depot. The citizens of the old town immediately removed their buildings to the new site, where all was bustle, life and activity. The spring was one of remarkable activity; immigrants flocked in by the hundreds, and busy industry soon converted the bleak prairie into a thriving, prosperous village; and, by December, there were at least ninety new buildings in the town. In June, of this year, there were in the county 1,244 cattle, 444 horses, thirty-six mules, thirty-nine sheep, and seventy swine. The entire valuation of all personal property was $79,979.55.

At the opening of the year 1871, the prospects for Cherokee County were brighter than ever before in her history. The many struggles of fifteen years to obtain a foot-hold had at last brought forth their legitimate fruit, and from this time forward, unparalleled prosperity has been the portion of Cherokee County.

New villages sprang into existence as if by magic, and the rich prairie land was soon dotted over with well tilled farms and good farm buildings. In 1870 the foundations were laid for the first building in Hazard, and in 1871, the first house was erected in Marcus, and Aurelia was started in 1877.

We have thus sketched in brief the more important points in the history of Cherokee County; have seen it transferred from a wild, unbroken prairie into one of the richest and most thickly settled countries in all the great Northwest; have noted the almost superhuman exertion necessary to accomplish this task; have chronicled the repeated failures, the renewed efforts and the final triumph. It is now proper to describe this, one of the most fertile and picturesque sections in all the great State of Iowa.

Cherokee County is situated in the third tier of counties south of the Minnesota line, and the second west of the Dakota line, lying between Plymouth and Buena Vista counties; is twenty-four miles square, and contains 368,640 acres of rich and fertile land. It is well watered by innumerable clear, sparkling brooks, springs and dashing rivers, the largest river, the Little Sioux, passing diagonally through the county, making its exit near the southwest corner. Every township in the county has a stream running through it, and all of these streams abound with fine fish. The Maple has its headwaters on the northeastern border of the county. Along the banks of the Little Sioux considerable timber is to be found. The general surface of the country is rolling; there are but few acres of the land too broken to be tilled, and Cherokee ranks among the best agriultural counties in the State. Its numerous valleys, formed by clear, running streams, have a soil especially adapted to the cultivation of cereals. For stock raising it is superior to most counties in the northwest, as its numerous running streams afford an abundance of pure water, and the nutritious grasses, which grow so luxuriantly, afford an excellent pasturage, and stock can be kept in good condition the entire year with but little trouble or expense. The climate is very similar to that of other counties in Northwestern Iowa—healthy and invigorating; extremes of heat and cold are the exception, and not the rule, mild weather generally characterizing the entire year. The air is dry and bracing, and lung diseases are almost unknown. The soil is a drift deposit, covered with a deep, rich vegetable mould. Along the streams, it is alluvial, and every-where capable of producing the most luxuriant vegetation. Cherokee County has 1,085 acres of natural timber, and 1,275 of artificial. The inhabitants embrace all nationalities, though the original stock from Massachusetts and other Eastern states is largely in the ascendancy.

In 1874, the population was estimated at 5,000, while in the same year 80,000 acres were under crop. In this year about 1,100 cars of wheat were shipped from the county, while the total assessable value of the property of the county footed up in round numbers to $1,600,000. In this year there were 1,200 farms in the county with an average cultivation of sixty-six acres, located in all the townships in the county. During the same year there were sixty-four schools in the county, the total value of the school houses being $32,241. Though statistics are unquestionably rather dry reading, in this case, at least, they show conclusively the rapid strides Cherokee County is making towards supremacy.

If the figures given above afford occasion for congratulation, those for 1881 are still more satisfactory. The taxable real estate of this county this year amounts in round numbers to $1,800,000; personal property, $375,000, based as near as possible on one-third their actual values. The bonded indebtedness of the county is $48,-300.

The educational interests, the criterion of a county's prosperity, are in a very flattering condition. There are ninety-two frame school buildings in the county, valued at about $50,000, while the value of the school apparatus is in round numbers $3,-000. One hundred and sixty-nine teachers are employed, and 3,-200 children are enrolled, the averaged attendance being 2,110. Of the general funds on hand, the last report has the following: School house fund, $4,500; contingent fund, $5,500; teachers' fund, nearly $12,000.

The present officials of the county are: Hon. H. C. Lewis, District Judge; Hon. J. R. Zuver, of Sioux City, Circuit Judge; R. L. Robie, Auditor; Eli Eshleman, Treasurer; E. Miller, Recorder; W. C. Bundy, Clerk of Courts; R. J. Smythe, Sheriff; Miss Ella M. Slater, Superintendent of Public Schools, and J. H. Davenport, Surveyor.

With all the advantages we have cited, land can be purchased in this county at from $5 to $15 per acre, according to location. As a general rule, the farmers of the county are devoting unusual attention to stock raising, not because grain cannot be grown successfully, but because stock pays better.

CHEROKEE.

The county seat of Cherokee county, much of whose history necessarily appears in the above detailed county history, is in every respect a handsome, substantial and growing city. It is located nearly midway between Fort Dodge and Sioux City, in the midst of a prosperous and fertile county. As a writer in a former similar work expresses it, "Cherokee has a surprisingly beautiful site, skirted on all sides by gentle bluffs, that swell just enough to shield it from the blasts of winter, yet not to impair the beauty of the landscape. Through the vale and to the south of the village the Sioux River winds its devious way in search of the great Missouri, where her crystalline waters are swallowed up in the current of mud. The banks of the Sioux are lined with timber, the first of any consequence that greets the eye of the traveler after leaving Fort Dodge. This greatly adds to the picturesqueness of the scene, and prepossesses the traveler in its favor.

Cherokee was located in August, 1870, a small number of buildings having been erected prior to that date, however, but of a character which admitted of their being moved to the future county seat. The facts as to the settlement upon the permanent location of the town appear elsewhere. The residence of E. Cowles is stated to be the first building moved from the "old town," in

March, 1870, and was the first dwelling in the new village; but the farm residence of G. W. Lebourveau, adjoining the village, was erected prior to that date. The growth of Cherokee has been rapid and healthy, and to-day it is deservedly ranked among the most substantially prosperous of Iowa's many prosperous villages.

The following as to the natural features of Cherokee and vicinity will prove of interest:

"Cherokee county lies wholly in one large valley, the highest point on its eastern border being 908 feet, and on its western border 877 feet; the city of Cherokee being the center of the depression is only 565 feet. Through the center of this valley from northeast to southwest flows the Little Sioux. This peculiarity, nowhere else found in the west, gives the surface of the country a slightly rolling appearance, and with gentle slopes to the river bed underlying the prairie proper about 100 feet. The valleys formed by the river being particularly rich, are very desirable. The soil is very loose and mellow, and never 'bakes,' and is much easier cultivated than the soil of the eastern states. It is what is particularly known as the 'bluff deposit,' varying in depth from two to three feet. Being slightly tinctured with sand, it matures crops rapidly. Read what eminent geologists say of it. Prof. Owen, in his Geological Survey, says: 'It is a silicious marl closely resembling the 'loess' deposit in the valley of the Rhine, famous the world over for its richness.' As far as known this deposit covers an area of nearly two hundred miles drained by the Missouri. Prof. White, in his Geological Survey of the State, says: 'The fortunate admixture of soil materials gives a warmth and mellowness to the soil, which is so favorable to the growth of crops that they are usually matured as early as they are upon more clayey soils of the southern part of the state, although the latter are more than 200 miles to the southward.' Impassable roads are never known. A few hours of sunshine after the most severe storm, make a road dry and passable for loads. The drainage is so good that 'muddy' roads are impossible. The county has a most perfect water system. Through the center of the county flows the Little Sioux; on the west Rock Creek and Willow Creek; on the north Mill Creek and Gray Creek, and on the east the Maple, while on the south is Silver Creek. All of these having more or less tributaries, give bountiful supplies of water for stock-raising and other purposes. In fact there is hardly a section of land but what there exists upon it flowing streams or living springs. Pure, healthy water is obtained everywhere at a depth of fifteen to thirty feet."

Not the least of the attractions which Cherokee affords, is her famous

MAGNETIC SPRING,

one of the most remarkable curiosities in nature, the essential particulars concerning which are as follows:

This spring was discovered in 1879, while prospecting for coal; when the depth of 200 feet was reached, a stream of crystalline water two inches in diameter flowed to the surface with a force that projected it several feet above the level of the ground.

The stream was so great that the prospector had to abandon his work. Unaware that he had tapped a spring superior in curative properties to any other in America, he felt disappointed and dispirited. Several weeks afterwards. in fastening an iron rod a quarter of an inch thick and ten feet long to a cord, with the intention of sinking the rod to the bottom in order to raise the sediment which had accumulated in the tube, to his astonishment the rod fastened itself to the iron piping, and so far from sinking it required considerable strength to detach it and bring it up.

This accidental discovery paved the way for future experiments, which resulted in demonstrating that the water of this spring was heavily charged with magnetism, so much so that by immersing a steel instrument in the waters it shortly becomes a perfect magnet, capable of suspending needles, nails, watch keys and iron substances of greater weight.

The sceptical at first said the magnetism was in the iron tubing, and that it had been charged artificially. but as the pipes were those purchased to conduct water by a hydraulic ram and re-purchased from a neighbor who knew nothing about the spring, the doubters had to give that theory up. It was next charged that any iron tube sunk in the earth to a great depth becomes charged with magnetism; that the magnetism was not in the water. This was disproven by scientific tests, viz: taking the water from the spring and immersing in it steel bars, tested by a galvanometer and pronounced free from electricity; after a short interval of time these were found charged with magnetism, capable of suspending other bodies of iron. The mechanical action of the water upon the iron, is too obvious to be denied, and so manifest that the most illiterate can readily see it. It requires no theoretic demonstration to convince the observer that it must have an effect upon living tissue which is well known to be an electrical conductor.

Invalids began drinking the water, and the results were at once of a highly favorable character. Dyspeptics were greatly benefited by their use, they afforded relief to every form of constipation, and their aerated qualities proved an antidote to acidity and distention of the stomach. A demand for bathing facilities was made on the proprietors, and the fame of these wonderful healing waters spread to every State of the Union. Letters of inquiry poured in, and the water became a standard article of export to hundreds of towns and cities.

Thus far the well had, by its inherent virtues. forced itself on the public, and the public in return. by their urgent demands, in a manner compelled the proprietors to fit up a bathing establish-

ment, which they have added to from time to time, until it now
has a sufficient capacity to meet all ordinary demands, while the
surroundings have been improved and beautified so as to make it a
really interesting spot.

Like most other institutions, it had to encounter opposition.
This mainly sprang from the jealousy of the profession, since the
many remarkable cures, and general improvement of chronic
sufferers, wholly due to a continued use of these waters, seemed a
rebuke to the ordinary methods of treatment, but opposition was
silenced by the voices of the many who drank health from this
magnetic fountain. Physicians found the waters had intrinsic,
health-giving qualities, and soon learned to recognize them among
the potent agencies in the cure of a long train of diseases.

For a considerable time the proprietors were reluctant to make a
heavy outlay for the benefit of invalids and health-seekers, as such
a course was entirely foreign to their original purpose—that of
finding coal—but the representations of the public were so continued and earnest, that all objections on this score were waived,
and the large investments made have been warmly seconded by an
appreciative public, whose liberal patronage is the safest guarantee
that the outlay has been wisely made.

The Bathing House is a commodious and well finished structure,
one story and a half high, with waiting rooms and ladies' parlor.
The bath rooms are neat and comfortable, and the baths are constructed on the most recent and approved plan, and heated by steam.
The ladies' rooms are reserved exclusively for their use, and are in
charge of polite and attentive female waiters. · The ladies' and
gentlemen's bathing departments are separated by a suite of rooms
insuring the most perfect guarantee that nothing need offend the
instincts of the most delicate.

The flow of water from the Spring is so great that an artificial
lake of over six acres in extent has been made, the waters of
which average four feet deep, and are almost transparent as the
air above them. One side of this lake washes the southern porch
of the bath house, and flocks of wild ducks have, for the past
year, been continually about the lake in their season: they have
become so tame that persons may approach them within a few
feet.

The grounds surrounding the Spring comprise sixty acres, have
been laid out by a skilled arborist and gardner, with a view to producing the best æsthetic effect, and have been planted with native
and ornamental trees and shrubbery, the lake being skirted by
choice varieties. Time alone is required to make this park one of
the handsomest and most interesting in the western states.

Another, and not the least interesting feature of this charming
spot, is a one-half mile race course, sixty feet wide, and as level as
a lake, one side bounded by the river bank, the other by the lake.
A better race-course or a prettier is not easily found. The pro-

prietors have spared no expense to improve and beautify the grounds, which have already earned the reputation of being the most inviting known at any western watering place. In addition to the new park, the proprietors have purchased an island in the Sioux river of about one hundred acres in extent, heavily wooded with timber of large and small growth. A little work could make this as romantic a retreat as river and forest can afford.

The waters of the Spring are so pure and free from inorganic matter that they keep perfectly sweet and pure for two or three weeks after being drawn. Those who have had them shipped for hundreds of miles have been astonished to find that even after being kept for a month, no sign of putrefaction was discernible, and that to the taste they were as pleasant as when drawn. This quality is of incalculable advantage for shipping purposes. Those who, from weakness, or any other cause, are unable to come to the Spring, can have the water shipped to them at reasonable rates, with the assurance that it will remain sweet and pure for a long time.

The boarding facilities at Cherokee are quite equal to those of any other city of sixteen hundred inhabitants. There are four good hotels, and several good boarding houses in the city. Fruits and every delicacy in its season may be had here abundantly. No one need have any hesitancy in coming to Cherokee on the ground of insufficient accommodation. The city has two excellent livery stables, with horses and vehicles in abundance, so that with driving, shooting and fishing the most pleasing and invigorating recreation may be had at all times and seasons. In fact the city of Cherokee is sufficiently metropolitan to afford an ample variety of sports, comforts and recreations.

There are in Cherokee Congregational, Presbyterian, Catholic, Methodist, Baptist, Advent, Episcopalian and Universalist church organizations. The first six have houses of worship. The church property of the county is in valuation perhaps not less than $20,-000. The officers of the Congregational church are: Pastor, J. B. Chase; Deacons, J. W. Coombs, J. P. Dickey, H. C. Kellogg; Clerk, W. C. Bundy; Treasurer, J. P. Dickey; Trustees, J. A. Risley, F. E. Whitmore, Richard Opie; Ushers, Richard Opie, E. F. Coombs; Sexton, Fred Boddy.

The Presbyterian church society was organized in 1870. Rev. Alexander M. Darley was the first pastor. The Union Sabbath School of Cherokee has a flourishing membership of more than sixty members. The Children of Zion church organization was perfected in the summer of 1880 by Bishop D. D. Patterson, of Grand Rapids, and hold regular services, with a flourishing Sunday School. The Baptist society dates its organization from the autumn of 1870. Services were first held in the old brick school house. Rev. A. W. Hilton was the first pastor. The church building was erected in 1873, and is 30x40 feet in dimensions.

Among the pastors at different times have been Revs. E. N. Jencks, W. H. Irwin, J. P. Cuffman, John Edminister, George H. Brown. An addition, 14x22, was made to the church edifice in 1881. The first sermon preached in Cherokee was delivered by Rev. Alexander Darley, of the Presbyterian denomination, in the store of H. A. Fife, in 1870.

On the 14th day of November in the same year, the first marriage license in the county was granted to C. Corbett and Rosabella Cummings. A school was taught during the summer in the old school house, by Mrs. Parkhurst, the funds to defray the necessary expenses being sent from Massachusetts.

For a young city, having by the recent census only 1,522 population; Cherokee has a large local trade, and does an extensive shipping business in grain and stock. Its magnitude may be inferred from the following:

BUSINESS SUMMARY.

Abstracts	3	Groceries	6
Agrl. Implements	4	Hardware	3
Attorneys (firms)	7	Harness makers	2
Bakeries	3	Hotels	4
Banks	3	Insurance agencies	15
Barbers	2	Jewelers	2
Blacksmiths	6	Livery stables	3
Books and stationery	3	Lumber	4
Boots and shoes (excl.)	3	Manuf. carrg's, wgn's, etc	1
Boot and shoemakers	4	Manuf. of sash, doors, blinds, etc	1
Brick yards	1	Meat markets	2
Carriages	2	Merchant tailors	1
Clothing, etc., (excl.)	2	Music	1
Contractors and builders	4	Milliners	2
Creameries	1	News depots	2
Coal and wood	5	Newspapers	3
Dentists	1	Photographers	1
Drugs	3	Physicians	6
Dry goods	1	Printers (job)	2
Elevators	4	Produce	1
Feed mills	1	Real estate and loans	7
Flouring mills	1	Restaurants	3
Furniture	1	Sewing machines	3
General merchandise	6	Stock	6
Grain	4		

Cherokee Lodge No. 322, I. O. G. T., was organized November 17th, 1879, with seventeen charter members. Its first officers were: W. E. Hitchcock, W. C.; A. C. Hobart, W. V. C.; Rev. R. C. Glass, Chaplain; H. H. Henry, Secretary; W. H. Hall, F. S.; J. Boles, Treasurer; David Lynn, M.; W. Stebbins, I. G.; E. N. Corbett, O. G.; C. P. Hobart, P. W. C. T.

The Masonic Lodge of Cherokee was instituted in 1871. Cherokee Lodge No. 188, I. O. O. F., was organized in February, 1870, with five charter members. Its present membership is forty-four. Its first officers were: C. E. Schofield, N. G.; G. W. McCoun, V. G.; J. C. Hubbard, Secretary; Z. P. Herrick, Treasurer. The following are the present officers: Thomas McCulla, N. G.; R. H. Gross, V. G.; D. W. Benway, Secretary; R. J. Smyth, Treasurer.

The Advent Church Society was organized in 1873, in Afton Township, with a membership of ten, and was moved to the town in the following year: In the summer of 1875, a very successful series of revival meetings was held, and the membership steadily increased, until the Society numbers nearly fifty. A church was provided in the autumn of 1875, and Elder J. Ridley was secured as regular pastor.

T. S. Steele & Son, bankers, of Cherokee, organized their business in 1874, starting in a small wooden building. Their present building was erected in 1879, is 24x40 feet, and two stories high. T. H. Steele is cashier, and is ably assisted by D. T. Steele.

Scribner, Burroughs & Co.'s bank was organized in 1871, under the firm name of Fulton & Scribner. Mr. Burroughs became interested June 12th, 1872, the business having been started in a small and unpretentious building. The present building was erected in 1875. The bank's surplus capital is now $100,000, its business having increased proportionately to its capital. Mr. Burroughs came to Cherokee from Adrian, Mich., locating permanently in Cherokee, after having successively lived at Salt Lake and other sections of the western country. Mr. Scribner is a native of Plattsburg. N. Y., and came to Cherokee in 1871. Mr. B. has a stock farm of 660 acres adjoining town, and keeps an average of about seven hundred cattle on his lands.

In 1874, Mr. Satterlee began the sinking of a coal shaft, and in the Spring of 1879, on Mr. Burrough's land, a depth of one hundred feet was reached, when, on penetrating a rocky stratum, flowing water, strongly impregnated with sulphur, was reached. At a further depth of fifty feet, another stratum containing magnesia was found, and at two hundred feet the magnetic water, which is fully described above was discovered. It is impossible to overstate the importance of this discovery to Cherokee.

March 22d, 1879, Kellogg & Herrick organized the Cherokee Butter and Cheese manufacturing Company. The building is 24x50 feet in dimensions, with an addition twenty feet square. The firm buys cream from about 1,000 cows. This industry bids fair to become a very important one.

The *Cherokee Times* was established October 21st, 1870, and is consequently now in its twelfth year. It is in every sense a highly creditable publication. Robert Buchanan is the editor and proprietor.

The *Iowa Free Press*, like the *Times*, is an eight-column folio, Robert Johnson and Will P. Goldie, editors and proprietors; both papers are well sustained, of good typographical appearance, and newsy.

The population of Cherokee may be set down as very nearly, if not quite, two thousand. Its educational advantages are exceptionally good. The public schools are on an unusually good footing, and a college is in contemplation, the opportunities for such an institution in Cherokee being apparent.

The future prospects of Cherokee as to railroads are good. Already two different companies are surveying through the southern part of the county, and strong talk of a road running northeast and southwest, following the Little Sioux river, connecting Omaha with St. Paul and Minneapolis by a more direct route, and giving the vast lumber regions a new and more direct outlet to the Southwest; also a new railroad is projected through Cherokee from Des Moines to the wheat fields of Dakota. These roads secured will make Cherokee a town of 10,000 inhabitants, and an excellent manufacturing point.

MARCUS.

The town of Marcus is a substantial place, whose personal interests will be found to be well represented in the biographies hereunto attached. The first building was erected in 1871. I. M. Jackson and A. H. Dwight were the first settlers. The first school was begun in 1873, and the first sermon in Marcus was preached in 1875, by Rev. W. F. Rose, Congregational minister. The church societies are well represented by the Catholic, Lutheran and Methodist denominations.

The Independent Order of Odd Fellows, which has a flourishing lodge in Marcus, had for its charter members I. Cask, S. W. Weaver, W. H. Skinner, M. I. Ames and R. W. Heath. Its active members are eleven. The lodge meets at S. W. Weaver's. A Masonic lodge is also one of the prominent features in this connection.

The Good Templars' Society has fifty-nine members, and holds its meetings in the school house. C. P. Kilburn is W. C.; Mrs. J. H. Sheldon, W. V. C.; T. W. P. Clough, P. W. C.; J. H. Sheldon, S.: Miss N. Cleglow, F. S.

The Presbyterian Church Society was organized during the past season, by Rev. George Knox, of Cherokee.

The population of Marcus is about 450, and is composed of a sturdy mixture of nationalities, German, English, Swedish, Scotch, etc.

The depot was built in the winter of 1869–70, and is 30x79 feet in dimensions. A grist mill with three run of stone, two elevators, warehouses and two hotels are among the important acquisitions to the town. The first white man to settle in the township is stated to have been H. Bowman, a native of Vermont. Mrs. Bowman is still living in Marcus. The first female settler was Mrs. W. E. Rose, who came in 1871. The first house was erected on section 36, by Mr. Bowman, in 1869, the first soil in the township being broken that year.

In 1874, the first regular election occurred, the depot building being used as a voting place. Fourteen votes were cast, that being the entire vote of the township. The first officers elected were as follows: R. Wilmot, J. M. Sheldon, E. Prunty, Trustees; W. E. Rose, Clerk; I. Bowman, Supervisor; A. H. Dwight, Elion Prunty, Justices of the Peace; E. Gearon, Constable; I. M. Jackson, Assessor. The first assessment was made in 1875, the number of families being fourteen; population forty-four; number of houses, nineteen; cattle, fifty; hogs, thirty-nine; acres improved, 620. The first person to locate in business in Marcus was I. M. Jackson. C. Parkin built his grain house in 1873. A store was opened by J. Hyndman in September. 1873. R. Wilmot opened the first hotel in July, 1874. The school house was built in the same year. The first car of stock was received by J. Clarkson in February, 1877.

Clarkson & Metcalf have a warehouse with a capacity of 15,000 bushels; L. Gund, of a capacity of 10,000 bushels.

The village of Marcus has doubled in population in the past year. The receipts at the depot for the twelve months just prior to this writing were $36,400. Five hundred and fifty-six cars were sent out from the town during the same time.

A public hall 22x50 feet, with ceiling twelve feet high, adds greatly to the convenience and advancement of the community. There is also a half-mile circular track in excellent condition. The population of the county is closely estimated at 10,000.

Among the noteworthy farms of this section is that of Theo. Groff, about a mile northeast of Marcus. Mr. Groff came to this part of the country about four years ago.

The first school in Marcus was taught in 1873-4, Miss Nina Sheldon being the teacher. Nine pupils were enrolled.

The first birth was that of Elsie Bowman in April, 1874; the first death, a brother of John Bird, Sr., in 1875; the first marriage, George Panctier and Miss Nina Sheldon, in 1878; the first grain brought to market, by I. Gorner in September. 1873; the first car of grain shipped, was in September, 1873, by C. Parkin.

There are more than one hundred pupils enrolled in the public schools of Marcus. There are three lumber yards in the town, each one of which is doing a thriving business. H. D. Dwight is the postmaster, and the office is very satisfactorily and systematically conducted. The business of the office has doubled within the last year.

CHEROKEE COUNTY BIOGRAPHIES.

CHEROKEE.

James Archer, dealer in lumber, grain and coal, established business July 12th, 1869; was born in Scotland in 1828; came to America in 1842, and located in Rockford, Ill.; from there he removed to Fayette county, Iowa; thence to Waverly, Iowa, where he was engaged in the lumber business three years. In 1869, he removed to Cherokee, and engaged in business as above. He has been a member of the town council, and has served several terms on the school board.

S. B. Allen, proprietor City Hotel, was born in Washington county, New York, in 1832; came west in 1868, and located in Buchanan county, Iowa, where he remained until the spring of 1881, when he removed to Cherokee and engaged in business as above.

C. Allison, senior member of the firm of Allison Brothers, dealers in dry goods, notions, boots and shoes, was born in Wisconsin in 1846; received his education at Madison, Wisconsin. He went to Nevada; where he was foreman of the Opher mine for several years; thence came back to Eldora, Ia., and in 1873 he came to Cherokee and established his present business.

H. Allison, junior member of the above firm, was born in Wis. in 1857. In 1869 he went to California, where he remained until he came to Cherokee. These gentlemen intend to erect a brick building, 30x100 feet, the coming spring.

N. T. Burroughs, of the firm of Scribner, Burroughs & Co., bankers, was born in Michigan in 1840; moved to Ia. in 1869, and engaged in the real estate business. In 1872 he entered business as above; is also extensively engaged in the raising of fine stock. Married Addie H. Phipps in 1873.

Thomas S. Brown, blacksmith, was born in Massachusetts in 1852; when he was four years of age he came to Cherokee, where he has since resided.

E. S. Block, dealer in clothing, hats, caps, and gent's furnishing goods, trunks, valises, etc., etc., was born in Bohemia in 1848; came to America, and engaged in the clothing business in New York City; from there he went to Arkansas; thence to Nebraska City, and after traveling throughout the west, he, in 1876, located in Cherokee, and engaged in business as above.

D. W. Benway, dealer in furniture of all kinds, established business in June, 1881. He was born in Massachusetts in 1849; from there he removed to Wisconsin; thence to Independence, Iowa. In 1877 he came to Cherokee, and for a time was proprietor of the City Hotel. In June, 1881, he engaged in business as above.

Charles Blaesser, barber, also dealer in tobacco and cigars, was born in Germany in 1845; came to America in 1866, and located at Milwaukee, Wis. In 1874 he removed to Cherokee and engaged in business as above. He married Regina Schmidt, of Wis. They have two children—Walter A. and Charles H.

Carlton Corbett, of the firm of Corbett & Whitmore, dealers in real estate, was born in Massachusetts, August 12th, 1831. In January, 1856, he came west and located in Cherokee; has held the office of county recorder and treasurer, and is one of the pioneers of Cherokee county.

John Collins, of the firm of Collins & Minor, was born in Kentucky in 1852; came to Clayton county, Iowa, when quite young, where he lived until 1875, when he came to Cherokee, and for a time was engaged in farming. He married Fannie F. Pearson. They have three daughters.

W. B. Chick, dealer in groceries, fruits and provisions, established business in 1872; was born in Maine in 1848; came to Michigan in 1868, and two years later he came to Cherokee. He enlisted in the first Maine light artillery, and served two years and three months. He has been three terms county auditor of Cherokee county.

J. H. Davenport, county surveyor of Cherokee county, was born in New York in 1838; came to Michigan in 1856, thence to this state, and in 1860 located at Cherokee. He was elected to his present office in 1866, and has held the office almost continuously since; has also been superintendent of schools of this county and served three years in the U. S. army in the Indian department.

Eli Eshleman, county treasurer of Cherokee county, was born in Pa. in 1829; came west in 1856, and settled in Ills., where he lived seventeen years; in 1872 he came to Cherokee and engaged in farming; was elected to his present position in 1879 and re-elected in the autumn of 1881. He married Amanda Fry, of Lancaster county, Pa. They have ten children—five sons and five daughters.

O. C. Ford, wholesale and retail grocer, and dealer in queensware, established business in 1876; was born in New York in 1841; came to Wisconsin in 1849, and in 1871 removed to Cherokee; for a time engaged in the insurance business, and was then employed as clerk in a hardware store, which he continued until he engaged in his present business.

J. S. Green, dealer in grain, groceries, queensware, fruits, etc., established business in 1879. Was born in St. Louis, Mo., in 1847, for fourteen years he traveled for Chicago and St. Louis wholesale houses. In 1879 he settled at Cherokee and engaged in business as above.

Robert Gick, dealer in stoves, hardware and farming tools of all kinds, established business in 1880. Was born on the Isle of Man, in 1845; came to America in 1870, and settled in Warren, county, Ill.; thence to Jasper county, Iowa, and in 1872 removed to Cherokee, where he has since resided.

W. S. Heymer, of the firm of Heymer Brothers, liverymen, was born in Essex county, New York, in 1847. He came west in 1878, and settled in Cherokee, and entered the employ of F. D. Yaw, in the livery business. He married Julia Canfield of this State. They have one son—Frank.

Thomas Heymer, of the firm of Heymer Bros., was born in N. Y. in 1846; his first location was in Dubuque county, Ia.; thence to Jackson county; thence to Cherokee. He served three years in the army in Co. I, Iowa volunteers.

George W. Hodgins, liveryman, established business in 1870. Was born in Vermont in 1826, his first location in Iowa was in Hardin county; thence to Marshalltown; thence to Bedford, and in 1870 he came to Cherokee and engaged in business as above. His son, Eugene D. Hodgins, was born in Missouri in 1859, and is now a partner in the above business.

Edwin Hughes, harness maker, established business October, 1881. Was born in Wales in 1852; came to America in 1870, and his first location was at Portland, Maine. From there he went to New York; thence to Ohio, and after making a trip to the Black Hills, returned to Cherokee and engaged in business as above. He married Sarah Mills, a native of England. They have one son and two daughters.

Robert Hall, of the firm of Robert Hall & Son, dealers in farm machinery and grain, was born in N. Y. in 1822; came to Ills. in 1857, and in 1871 he removed to Cherokee and engaged in business as above.

Jas. Henderson, dealer in real estate, established business in 1871; was born in Scotland in 1818, came to America in 1848 and settled in Clayton county, Iowa, and was engaged in farming. In 1868 he removed to Cherokee. He has been twice elected to the position of county treasurer; has also been a member of the city council.

C. E. P. Hobart, of the firm of Hobart & Snyder, dealers in grain and coal, was born in Vermont in 1819; from Vermont he went to Oshkosh, Wis.; and in 1870 he came to Cherokee and engaged in the lumber business. The following year he engaged in business as above.

William Jones, merchant tailor and dealer in ready-made clothing and gents' furnishing goods, was born in Wales in 1844; came to America in March, 1870, and located in Cherokee and engaged in business as above. Mr. Jones makes a specialty of making suits to order; he employs none but experienced workmen, and he has a reputation second to none in western Iowa.

George A. Johnson, dealer in general merchandise, established business in March, 1874; was born in Canada in 1842; he came to Michigan in 1864. In 1867 he returned to Canada, and in 1871 he came to Cherokee, Ia., and was employed as clerk until 1874, when he engaged in business as above. He married Eliza Head, of Canada. They have four children.

H. Kennedy, of the firm of H. Kennedy & Co., dealers in general merchandise, established business in 1875; also have a branch store in Peterson, Clay county. He was born in Ohio in 1830; came to Iowa with his parents in 1855. He next moved to Cherokee and engaged in business as above.

A. B. Knox, of the firm of Knox & Nicholson, proprietors of the N. Y. store, established in 1872, was born in Pa. in 1855; came to Cherokee, Ia., in 1879, and engaged in business. He married Lizzie Goheen, a native of Pa.

George W. Lebourveau was born in New Hampshire in 1828. In 1857 he came to Cherokee, and is one of the pioneers of this county; was the first treasurer and first recorder of this county, was also the first mayor of Cherokee, which position he held two terms. He is one of the original town proprietors. He enlisted in Co. I, 7th Ia. cavalry, and served three and a half years.

David Lynn, of the firm of Lynn & Bryant, proprietors of meat market, established business in 1881. He was born in Ohio in 1844; came to Jasper county, Iowa, in 1859; thence to Winneshiek county; thence to Jackson county, Ills.; thence to Cherokee. He served in Co. A. 2nd regiment, U. S. A., three years; married Annie E. Underhill. They have one daughter—Mary F.

E. R. Little, jeweler (repairing a specialty), established business in 1880. He was born in Ohio, November 4th, 1858, and received his education in Ohio, where he also learned the jewelry business. He moved to Grand Rapids, Mich., in 1879, and the following year removed to Cherokee and engaged in business as above.

George L. Moore, manufacturer and dealer in harness and saddles, established business in 1881; was born in Aurora, Ill., in 1857. He came to Cherokee in 1872, and engaged in the same business.

Arthur Molyneux, of the firm of Molyneux Bros., law and collecting agents, was born in Sullivan county, Penn., in 1856; graduated at Iowa City law school in the class of '81, and soon after located in Cherokee, and engaged in business as above.

R. D. Minor, of the firm of Collins & Minor, was born in Waukesha county, Wis., in 1853; came to Cherokee in 1871, and engaged in farming until he engaged in his present business.

E. Miller, county recorder, was born in Pa. in 1850; removed to Cedar county, Ia., in 1852, and to Cherokee in 1872, and engaged in farming; was elected to his present office in November, 1880; has served as town clerk, also assessor. He married Belle Stone, of Ohio. They have two children—Oretas and Orville.

Thomas McCulla, attorney at law, was born in Hamilton, Canada, in 1856; came to the United States when quite young, and located in N. Y.; afterwards moved to Muscatine, Ia., and there attended school; then entered the Baptist Institute at Wilton, after which he entered the university at Iowa City, graduating from the law department in the class of '79; came to Cherokee and opened office; makes a specialty of collections.

Chas. Nicholson, of the firm of Knox & Nicholson, was born in Sweden in 1855; came to America in 1871; settled in Mich.; then moved to Hampton, Ia.; thence to Cherokee, and became a partner in the above business, which was established in 1872, and is one of the largest mercantile houses in the city.

L. W. Newell, dealer in boots and shoes, was born in Ill. in 1855, and when seven years of age moved to Muscatine, Ia. He traveled for a Cincinnati house for two and one-half years, and in June, 1881, moved to Cherokee, and established his present business in Aug. of same year.

H. A. Olmsted, station agent for the I. C. R'y. company, was born in Mass. in 1848. He was appointed to his present office in 1871. He married Cornelia Jones, of Neb. They have three children.

E. L. Olmsted, was born in Mass. in 1851; came to Delaware county, Ia., in 1858. He was for five years in the employ of the C., & N. W. R. R. Co., as station agent and operator.

O. R. Olmstead & Son, are dealers in boots, shoes, overshoes, gaiters, etc. R. S. Olmstead, was born in Wayne county, Pa., in 1854, and the same year moved with his parents to Wis. He entered the employ of J. P. Dickey & Co., in 1876. He married Frances Brown, of Woodman, Wis.

Dr. W. H. Palmer, dentist, was born in N. Y. in 1855; was engaged in dentistry in Syracuse, N. Y., and in 1881 moved to Cherokee, Ia., and opened office the same year. He married Frances Campbell, of N. Y., in 1880.

T. Patton, of the firm of Robertson & Patton, dealers in lumber, grain, sash, doors, blinds, etc., was born in Ireland in 1844; came to America in 1864, and settled in Dubuque county, Ia.; thence to Delaware county, and in the autumn of 1870 came to Cherokee, and was one of the first settlers; was for some time in the employ of the railroad company; established his present business in 1876.

Joseph Reed, proprietor of the bakery and restaurant, was born in Pa. in 1829; removed to Ill. in 1864; thence to Ia. in 1875; located at Cherokee in 1881. He married Mary Tallman, a native of Pa. They have three sons and two daughters.

J. G. Reigel, blacksmith, repairer and manufacturer, was born in Germany in 1849; came to America in 1854, and located in Butler county, Pa.; removed to Hardin county, Ia.; thence to Missouri, and in 1876 came to Cherokee, Ia., and established his present business. He married Ellen L. Kenyon, and has one child—Effie M.

James Robertson, of the firm of Robertson & Patton, was born in Scotland in 1833; came to America in 1856, and settled in Canada; removed to Cedar county, Ia., in 1868; thence in the following year to Cherokee, and engaged in buying grain. His present business was established in 1876. He married Catherine Comrie, a native of Scotland, and has two sons and three daughters.

R. L. Robie, county auditor, was born in Vt. in 1850; removed to Tama county, Ia., in 1868; thence to Cherokee, and engaged in farming. He taught the grammar department of the public schools here one term; was appointed county superintendent of schools, and served during 1876, and was then appointed deputy clerk and treasurer. He was elected to his present office in 1881. He married Ella L. Fairfield, of Fond du Lac, Wis.

A. B. Ross, dealer in staple and fancy groceries, tobacco, cigars, crockery, glassware, queensware, etc., was born in Nova Scotia in 1843. He came to Cherokee, Ia., in 1870, and engaged in the above business in 1874.

S. F. Russell, manager of the Fountain House, was born in Venango county, Pa., in 1839; removed to Story county, Ia., in 1867, and two years later came to Cherokee and engaged in farming. In 1878 he took charge of a hotel at Meriden, where he continued two years; then engaged in his present position. He served in the army four and one-half years in Co. A, 10th Ill. Cav.; was promoted step by step until he reached first lieutenancy; received his discharge at San Antonio, Tex.

W. A. Sanford, cashier of Scribner, Burroughs & Co.'s bank, born in Norwich, N. Y., in 1854; removed with parents in 1860 to Decorah, Ia.; thence to Cherokee in 1875, and engaged in business as above.

Dr. Sherman, of the firm of Butler & Sherman, physicians and surgeons, was born in Pa. in 1846; moved west in 1862; graduated from the Keokuk medical college in the class of '73, and began the

19

practice of medicine in Cherokee the same year. He is also surgeon for the Ill. C. Ry. He married Nellie Terry, and has one
child—Annie.

E. B. Smith, of the firm of E. B. Smith & Co., furniture dealers
and undertakers, was born in Canada in 1851; came to the U. S.
in 1871, and located in Cherokee, Ia.; was engaged in various oc-
cupations for a time: then engaged in the above business, which
was established in 1870. He married Ida Brown, of Syracuse, N.
Y., and has two children—Homer and Frank.

A. H. Smith, jeweler and dealer in fine watches and jewelry,
(business established in 1872), was born in Canada in 1849; removed to Ill. in 1859, and located in DeKalb county; thence moved
to Calhoun county, Ia., and in June, 1869, moved to Marcus, and
the following year to Cherokee. He engaged in business in partnership with G. S. Brown, and afterwards became sole proprietor.

R. M. Smith, of the firm of H. Assman & Co., dealers in staple
and fancy groceries, was born in Pa. in 1838; removed to Sioux
City, Ia., in 1868; thence to Cherokee in 1872, and engaged in
farming until engaging in above business, which was established
in 1876. He served in the army in the 78th Pa. Inft.; was promoted to captain, major and the lieutenant colonel; received his
discharge at Nashville, Tenn. He married Maggie Stephens, of
Pa., and has four children—Leota, Leona, Roy and Meda.

M. Wakefield, attorney at law, will practice in all courts in the
state. He was born in Ill. in 1842; moved to Sioux City, Ia, in
1870, and the following year located in Cherokee; received his education at the Ill. State Normal University, from which he graduated in 1865; read law at Bloomington, Ill., and was admitted to
practice by the supreme court, Jan. 18th, 1869. He is mayor of
Cherokee, and has held minor offices in the city.

Walbridge & Moore, attorneys at law, land, loan and real estate
office. They have fifty thousand acres of wild land for sale, ranging in price from three to ten dollars per acre; also improved farms
for sale. Business was established in 1879.

Z. A. Wellman, postmaster, was born in N. Y. in 1826; studied
law and was admitted to the bar in 1849; came to Delaware county,
Ia., and engaged in the practice of his profession, which he continued for twenty years. During President Fillmore's administration, he was appointed postmaster, but his health failing him,
he engaged in farming, and in 1870 removed to Cherokee from
Benton county, and engaged in the drug business. In 1872 he
was appointed postmaster of this city, and has held the office ever
since.

L. M. White, of the firm of White Bros., proprietors of restaurant and bakery, and dealers in staple and fancy groceries, was born

in Bloomsburgh, Columbia county, Pa., in 1859; received his education at the State Normal School, at Bloomsburgh; removed to Cherokee in 1881, and established the above business in June of the same year.

J. C. Wilson, photographer, (copying and enlarging a specialty), was born in Ottawa, Canada, in 1848; moved to Ogdensburg, N. Y., in 1862, and came to Cherokee, Ia., in 1870, being one of its earliest settlers; has served as a member of the city council two years. He married Carrie L. Bates, of Durand, Ill., and has one child—Bessie M.

Ed. Williams, dealer in all kinds of grain, took charge of this business in 1879; was born in O., in 1847; moved to Cedar Falls, Ia., in 1854, and engaged in buying grain near that place. He married Carrie Maxwell, of Ia.

F. D. Yaw, liveryman, was born in N. Y. in 1836; removed to Delaware county, Ia., in 1861, and to Cherokee in 1876, and established his present business; has a large barn and can furnish good rigs at reasonable rates; also buys and sells horses on commission.

Geo. W. Young, of the firm of Geo. W. Young & Co., proprietors of the Washington House, was born in N. H., and was formerly connected with the Gulf City House, at Mobile, Ala. He perfectly understands the hotel business, keeps a house that is first-class in every particular, and will spare no pains to make it pleasant and comfortable for the traveling public. 'Bus to and from trains. The house is going to be remodeled soon, another story added, and also an addition 30x50 feet, and all modern improvements, bath rooms, etc.

MARCUS.

Joseph Beck, dealer in general hardware, established business in 1877. He was born in Germany in 1838; came to America in 1864, and engaged in wagon making and the hardware business in Jackson county, Ia., in 1872; removed to Marcus in 1877. He at present is town trustee of that place. He married Margaret Smith of Germany, in 1867. They have five children—Joseph, Kate, Bennie, Laura and George.

C. F. Collier, of the firm of C. F. Collier & Son, dealers in dry goods, groceries, clothing and furniture, (business established in 1876), was born in Mass. in 1830; moved to Vt. in 1839; thence to Illinois in 1853; thence to Dubuque, Ia., in 1862, and engaged in railroading. He married Lydia Dow in 1854, and has two children—Fred F. and Luther D. F. F. C. was born in Ill., in 1856; moved to Marcus in 1876, and engaged in the above business. He was elected city marshal in 1880.

John Ernster, of the firm of Ernster & Oleson, dealers in boots, hoes, clocks, jewelry and sewing machines, was born in Germany in 1851; came to America in 1861. He engaged in the boot and shoe business in Marcus in 1875, and in his present business and partnership in 1881.

J. H. Grey, of the firm of J. H. Grey & Co., real estate, loan and insurance office, dealers in lands in Cherokee, Plymouth, O'Brien and Sioux counties. Business was established in May, 1881. He was born in Darlington, Wis., in 1853; was engaged for a time in the real estate business in Neb.; removed to Iowa in 1881.

Louis Gund, president of the Marcus Bank, established business in 1881, with a cash capital of $15,000. He is also proprietor of a large grain elevator in Marcus. He was born in Germany in 1843; came to America in 1847 and settled in Ill.; moved to Ia. in 1867 and for a time was engaged in the hotel business; then engaged in the agricultural business at Blairtown, and came to this city in 1876. He married Margaret Schall, of Ia., in 1869, and has three children—Minnie C., Cora, and Wm. Louis.

P. J. Hiltgen, cashier of the Marcus Bank, was born in Germany in 1849; came to America in 1861 and settled in Minn.; moved to Ia. in 1877, and engaged in the mercantile business; was elected town clerk in 1878 and justice of the peace in 1879. He married Therisa Barud of N. Y., in 1874, and has one child—Lucy.

John Hyndman, dealer in dry goods, groceries, notions, boots, shoes and coal, is the pioneer merchant of Marcus; established business in 1873. He was born in Ireland in 1838; came to America and settled in Canada in 1853; began teaching school the same year, and continued in that occupation for more than ten years. He came to Iowa, and was elected secretary of the school board of Marcus, which office he held for two years.

J. Jungers, proprietor of the Marcus Hotel, was born in Belgium in 1832; came to America in 1853, and settled in Marcus in 1856, and engaged in the hotel business. He married Annie Pool, of Belgium. They have nine children—John, Lucy, Josephus, Barbara, Mary, Kate, Frank, Lena and Jennie.

John Metcalf, of the firm of Clarkson & Metcalf, land agents and dealers in grain and live stock, established business in 1875; was formerly engaged in the live stock business in Eldora; then in the millinery and live stock business in Alden; then came to Marcus. Mr. Clarkson is from Aurelia, where he was engaged in the mercantile business.

C. B. Oldfield, of the firm of J. H. Gray & Co., real estate dealers, was born in Worcestershire, Eng., in 1859; came to America in 1881, and located at Marcus.

Ole Oleson, of the firm of Ernester & Oleson, dealers in boots, shoes, clocks, jewelry and sewing machines, established business in 1881. He was born in Norway in 1856; came to America in 1877, and settled in Iowa county, Wis.; came to Iowa in 1880.

HARRISON COUNTY.

This county is one of the most populous, popular, and, at the same time, conservative counties of Iowa. It is rich, without being aggressive; secure, without being assertive; in other words, a fine body of land, owned by a fine class of people. Harrison county has a right to be proud of herself.

Lying on the Missouri River, in the fourth tier from the southern boundary, Harrison is one of the western border counties of the state; is twenty-four miles north and south by an average of about twenty-seven east and west, and contains a superficial area of nearly six hundred and sixty square miles.

Like most of the counties in Iowa bordering the Missouri River, Harrison county presents a greater variety of surface configuration than is found in the inland counties to the eastward. A number of streams, that are more or less fully described in the histories of adjoining counties, gain the Missouri bottoms within the limits of this county. issuing from the uplands through the bluffs, causing them to assume those strikingly picturesque and peculiar shapes characteristic of the scenery of the valley of the middle Missouri. Nearly every portion of the county is well watered and drained by clear, sparkling streams and brooklets, which flow diagonally across its territory in a general southwest direction. The principal of these water-courses are the Boyer, Soldier and Little Sioux Rivers, and Wilson, Pigeon and Mosquito Creeks, several of which are of considerable size, and afford along their course in this county a number of excellent mill sites, only a portion of which have been improved. The valley of the Boyer is a beautiful tract of alluvial land, from one-half to two miles in width, bounded on either hand by gently ascending slopes until it nears the Missouri bottoms, where the surroundings become more abrupt and bold. The course of the Little Sioux in this county is mostly through the bottoms, though where it merges from the uplands it is marked by bluffs of peculiar interest, whose tops are conical peaks, flanked by sharp-crested, spur-like ridges. One of the most beautiful valleys of this slope is that of the Soldier River, which is bordered by bluffs which are unrivaled in the variety and picturesque beauty of their scenery. The bottoms slope gently from the foot of the bluffs toward the river, and form well-defined terraces, which afford beautiful rural situations. The valleys of Pigeon and Mosquito Creeks, in the southeast, are margined by high sloping upland, and their beds occupied by tracts of rich alluvial lands, which are unsurpassed for beauty and fertility. The current of the Missouri River, which bounds this county on the west. is very rapid, with a deep, constantly changing channel, often cutting off whole sections

of land in one season. These bottoms are vast level plains, varying in width from four to ten miles, and are bordered on the east
by beautiful rounded bluffs, rising from one to three hundred feet
above the river level. They are traversed by low benches or undulations, which, running more or less parallel to the river, are intervened by low grounds that afford natural drainage channels,
that receive and confine within bounds much of the surplus waters
of the Missouri in seasons of freshets, which would otherwise flood
extensive tracts of the best land for agricultural purposes in the
West. A belt of cottonwood timber extends through the county
up and down the river, from one-half to six miles in width, inter-
spersed with elm, mulberry, walnut, willow, ash, etc. The cottonwood grows very large and tall. In passing over the bottoms
through the timber, a person will observe a streak of very heavy
cottonwood timber, and then of tall willow trees from a foot to
three and four feet each in circumference. The willow follows
the old bed of the river, and as soon as the channel changes and
leaves the bed dry it springs up rapidly, and when the bed of the
river is raised to a certain height,then cottonwood crowds in, and a
dense forest is soon made. The soil in the bottom is very rich and
deep, producing every kind of grain and vegetables in the greatest
abundance. Corn grows very large. The grass is said to be so
rich and luxuriant that cattle will keep fat on it even in winter
without cutting or curing. Many farmers in mild winters have
let their cattle range in the bottoms without any feed, pasturing
them on the grass and keeping them in good order. Water underlies the soil of the bottoms at the depth of fourteen feet, and
wherever you find water there you find quicksand. It is supposed
that the whole bottom, from the bluffs of the Nebraska side to the
bluffs in Iowa, has been one vast lake, and the Missouri River
running through it has filled it up and formed the bottom lands.
There is every indication of it. Every few rods along the bottoms
you will see evidence of where once has flowed the channel of the
river. The settlers on the bottoms say they are getting drier every
year, and less subject to inundation. The agent who located
swamp lands in 1857 relates that he rode for miles through water
where there is now fine, high and dry farming lands. The low
places along the bottoms are fast filling up, and where once were
ponds and marshes is now dry land with good farms upon them.
The Missouri bottoms will be at no distant day covered with the
finest farms in the Union.

There are quite a chain of lakelets commencing near the mouth
of the Little Sioux River and continuing along the bottoms. Some
of them are near the bluffs, others out in the bottoms and near the
river, while all have at one day been in the channel of the river or
are the old bed of the Missouri. Many of these little lakes have
fish in them; and are beautiful and nice little sheets of water. The
channels of the streams in the bottoms are, or have been, chang-

ing. The mouth of the Soldier River is one mile from where it was twelve years ago, and the Missouri also, at this point, is over a mile from where it was in 1855. The land in the old channel is as high as that of the surrounding country; no more subject to inundations, and is covered with a heavy growth of cottonwood. The lakelets, it is said, are fast filling up, and perhaps when the country becomes settled and cultivated will entirely dissapear. Persons digging wells frequently find logs, driftwood, bark, etc., several feet below the surface. A farmer digging a well recently, near what is known as Soldier's Lake, found a large pocket knife fourteen feet below the surface.

The soil in the uplands consist of the light colored deposits of the bluff formation, which does not differ materially from that in the bottoms, except that the silicious material of which it is largely composed is more finely comminuted, and has a less amount of vegetable matter or humus. As the soil of the uplands and bottoms was derived from the same source, it only differs in degree, that in the former reaching a depth of sixty or one hundred feet below the surface. It is said that dirt taken out of wells sixty feet deep seems to produce as well as that on the surface. The soil is easily cultivated, and produces all the grains and vegetables common to this latitude in great abundance. It does not cave; wells do not have to be walled, except for a few feet down from the top and at the waters' edge. The soil never bakes, but can be plowed without injury in wet weather. It stands both wet and dry weather remarkably. A failure of crops has never been known. The soil in the bottoms is more of a clay nature, and in wet weather is very sticky.

Harrison contains more timber than any other county on the Missouri slope, yet it is limited in extent, its distribution being governed by circumstances favorable to its preservation, and is consequently found in the deep shaded ravines that crowd up into the bluffs, and along the small streams which are confined to narrow valleys hemmed in by steep bluff ascents. But, as observation has repeatedly shown in all parts of the state, forests are not necessarily confined to the valleys and moister localities, and thrive as well in one location as another, when the devastation of the prairie fires are checked for a period of sufficient duration to allow the young trees a few years of unretarded growth. Hundreds of acres of prairie have been overgrown with thrifty groves of vigorous young timber within the memory of early settlers, which period extends back scarce a score of years. These tracts of young forests add a pleasing feature to the landscape in these beautiful undulating divides, as that near Magnolia, and Harris' grove south of Logan, attests. Fine groves are met with in the valleys of the Soldier and Little Sioux Rivers, while the banks of the Missouri throughout its course in this county are lined with a belt of fine forest growth.

Numerous orchards have been set out in the county, and apples, pears, quinces and grapes grow in abundance, and of excellent quality. Some peaches have been raised, while in the bottom lands the finest quality of wild grapes are found in great profusion. In 1867 over five hundred barrels of wine were made from these grapes and shipped to Chicago, besides large quantities which was used at home.

Limestone is found, the best and most extensive quarries being found near Logan, from which a considerable amount is annually shipped to Council Bluffs and other points. There are also two or three other quarries which have been worked to some extent in other parts of the county.

As a stock-raising and producing county, Harrison has had quite a reputation, the native grasses being very nutritious and affording excellent pasturage at nearly all seasons of the year. Fat cattle from this county have for years been famous in Chicago markets and command the highest prices.

Daniel Brown was the first white man who settled in the county, locating where the village of Calhoun now is, April 3, 1848. His nearest neighbor was twelve miles distant, his nearest mill twenty-two miles, and nearest post office Council Bluffs, twenty-five miles. He had to go to St. Joseph, Missouri, one hundred and fifty miles for provisions that season, and while he was gone the Indians came and robbed his family of provisions and all the necessary articles of comfort. When he returned he found his family destitute of food and clothing. Soon after his return the Indians stole all his horses, and all those of the other settlers in the county. He and his son followed them for several miles, trying to recapture them, but were unsuccessful. They fired a number of shots at the Indians. The Indians frequently killed his cattle and annoyed him a great deal during the first few years of his residence in the county. The following were also among the first settlers, Silas Condit, two brothers by the name of Chase, Charles Lepenta, James Hardy, Dr. Robert McGovern, Andrew Allen and Jacob Patee.

The county was organized in 1853, when Stephen King elected County Judge; P. G. Cooper, District Court Clerk; Chester Hamilton, Sheriff; William Cooper, Treasurer and Recorder; George White, Surveyor; and Jacob Huffman, Coroner. The first county court was held August 5, 1853, by Stephen King, Judge. First road petition presented was for the establishment of a road, commencing at the south line of the county, running thence to the residence of Daniel Brown, and thence to Magnolia. The first mortgage on record was made by Samuel Jack to James Jack, acknowledged by Frank Street, County Judge of Pottawattamie County. First deed on record was made by Ezra and Catharine Vincent, to Walter Barrenger, conveying the northeast of the southeast of section 8. township 79, range 48. The first wedding was celebrated June 9, 1853, Stephen King, County Judge, uniting in the holy bonds of wedlock, John Jones and Miss Elizabeth Outhouse. The second occurred on the 16th of the following August, when the same judge united Samuel McGaven and Miss Mary M. Harden. The total number of marriages since the organization up to January 1, 1868, was four hundred and ninety.

The first district court was held by Honorable S. H. Riddle in May, 1855, at which time the first cause on the docket was William Kennedy vs. D. Pate, while the total number were four civil and one criminal. The first grand jury were: Creed Saunders, James Garnett, John Conger, Chester Staley, H. Locklin, T. Meadus, P. R. Sharp, Thomas Sellers, S. A. Seaman, Solomon Barnett, John Deal, 1. H. Holton, D. E. Brainard, Silas Rue and Solomon Garnett. D. E. Brainard was appointed foreman. John Jeffary was the first person naturalized, and Thomas Thompson the second. The number of cases since the organization of the county up to November 25, 1867, were, civil, 749, and ninety-one criminal.

In the Fall of 1853 a party of Indians camped on Willow Creek. The settlers were afraid that they would commit some depredations, organized a company and went to drive them off. Among the number was a gentleman from Virginia, who had been a captain in the Virginia militia, and had brought his broad sword and regimentals with him, and was "decked out" in full dress, and took command. He boasted of his bravery and would show the bloody red skins a trick or two." The company set out on horseback, marching in gallant style, led by their brave and daring officer—in his own imagination. The bloody savages were to be exterminated, a brilliant victory to be obtained, and the troopers were to return home covered all over with glory. While marching along to the scene of conflict, they discovered the Indian encampment about a mile ahead across Willow Creek. They halted, commenced firing, and continued it for some time. The Indians hearing it, some half a dozen warriors got on their ponies and rode towards the troopers to see what was the matter. The latter seeing the warriors approaching, suddenly imagined that they would be surrounded, overpowered, slaughtered, and scalped, broke for their homes as fast as their horses could carry them. Many of the troopers were so badly scared that they did not know their own houses, but went on past them. The warriors seeing the fleeing troopers, raised a big laugh, and rode back to their encampment in safety.

For several years the Indians annoyed the settlers a great deal by stealing or begging. Companies were frequently organized to drive them off, and some times there would be some shooting, but no one was ever hurt. Mr. Brown states that in 1853 there was a large party of Indians encamped on the Boyer; he with twenty-six others went out to drive them off. They came near the encampment and formed in battle line. The chief and a half-breed got on their ponies and rode out to them. The chief proposed to

make a treaty with the whites, and it was made with the condition that the Indians should leave the county. There were 120
warriors with their women and children. The Indians left the
county.

In the Fall of 1853 quite a large party of Ottoe Indians were
encamped within eight miles of Magnolia. One evening the
settlers informed them that they had better leave or the Sioux
would attack them before morning. In the night a firing was
heard by the settlers. They went upon a high bluff to see what
was the matter, and sure enough the Sioux were pouring a heavy
fire into the encampment of the Ottoes. The latter were scream-
ing and yelling with all vengeance, and fled into the Missouri
bottoms. The next day the settlers attacked them and drove
them across the Missouri River. They swam the river on their
ponies. Harrison County seemed to have been a hunting ground
for the Indians, as no tribe resided in the county.

On Willow Creek, about six miles from Magnolia, there are old
ruins of some kind of a house that has the appearance of having
been built out of burnt brick.

MONDAMIN.

Mondamin, one of the heavy shipping points of the Lower Missouri Valley, is situated thirty-eight miles north of Council Bluffs
on the Sioux City & Pacific Railway. The oldest settlers on the
town-site is Capt. John Noyes, who with Clarke Ruffcorn, his son-
in-law, came here from the east and settled in the township in the
fall of 1856. The township at that time was a fraction of Raglan
township. It was subsequently named Morgan, which name it
still bears. Although Capt. Noyes is the oldest settler in Mondamin, he preceded Mr. E. J. Hagerman, the present postmaster,
but a few weeks. The former gentleman arrived by boat, while
Mr. Hagerman came by team. Both started from the same place
together and, but the difference in the time required for the journey intervened between their arrivals. Previous to the arrival of
Messrs. Noyes and Ruffcorn, there were but four settlers in the
township. Mr. David W. Fletcher, although there was no thought
of a town being located in the vicinity at that time, had just previous to the advent of the gentleman named established a general
merchandise store, and shortly after the arrival of Mr. Hagerman,
the two formed a partnership. With one exception, no other business house was erected in the place prior to its platting, in the
winter of 1867-8, when the railway was first laid through the town.
The exception noted was a general store erected by Capt. John
Noyes, some months after.

The postoffice was established in Mondamin in the summer of
the year 1868, and the D. W. Fletcher before-mentioned was
commissioned as postmaster. Mr. Fletcher held the position less

than a year, when he was succeeded by the present postmaster, Mr. Hagerman. As the salary attached to the office amounted to but twelve dollars per year there was not a great deal of wrangling over the appointment. The office at present, though having considerable business, is not a money-order office.

The town was platted in the winter of 1867-8 by John J. Blair and others of the Iowa Land Company. At first, when the railroad was built, no town was platted, the calculation being to locate the town some distance north of the present site. Measures to this end were actually taken, on account of the unwillingness of settlers to part with the required land. Some of the settlers, however, reconsidered matters, and the town was eventually located where it now stands. The site comprises 160 acres, though it is not all platted. Eighty acres of this land was sold to the owners of the town-site by Capt. Noyes, and the remainder by Messrs. Fletcher and George Morgareidge, in the fall and winter of 1868. Previous to the building of the railroad, no thought of a town in this particular locality was had.

The oldest building now on the town-site is the residence of Dr. T. H. Allison. This structure was erected in the fall of 1868.

Although the vicinity of Mondamin is not, strictly speaking, a wheat country, it has other resources of magnitude, and its trade in corn is not second to that of any town on the line of the Sioux City & Pacific railway, north of Missouri Valley Junction. This promises to continue, as a twenty-five-year resident of the county gave the assurance that in the time specified, there had never been a failure, and but few small crops. Mondamin has cribbing capacity for 100,000 bushels of this grain, and the number of bushels handled by dealers during the year closed was 200,000. The coming year promises an increase.

In addition to corn, cattle, hogs, wood and other country products, are exported in large quantities. One dealer of Mondamin paid nearly fifty thousand dollars last year for hogs alone.

Mondamin having reach about two hundred population, her enterprising citizens took measures at the October, 1881, term of the Circuit Court to file articles of incorporation, with a view of securing a village charter. In sequence thereto, an election to secure ratification by the citizens was had, and a mayor, clerk and five trustees were elected. Subsequently it was discovered that in accordance with the revised statutes, a sixth trustee would be necessary to give legality to the incorporation, and another election was held. The second election resulted in the re-election of the officers first chosen, and F. M. Dupray as an additional trustee. The full board was: E. J. Hagerman, Mayor; A. Spooner, Clerk; Byron Strode, Thomas Reagan, Z. T. Noyes, E. Jones, P. C. Spooner, F. M. Dupray, trustees. The first meeting of the board was held November 26th, 1881.

One of the most potential influences in the incorporation of the place, was *The Mondamin Independent*, a neat little six-column folio newspaper published weekly, the first number of which was issued August 13th, 1881, by W. H. Wonder, who, a year before, had established in Mondamin *The Musical Banner*, a four-page musical journal. Besides conducting these journals, the publisher practices his profession of teaching and publishing music, organizing musical conventions, etc. The results of the incorporation are beginning to make themselves apparent in the shape of new sidewalks, etc.

The general business of Mondamin, classified, is as follows: Three dry goods and grocery stores, two grocery and notion stores, one drug store, jewelry store, hotel, restaurant, two hardware and tin-shops, furniture store, blacksmith shop, wagon shop, two livery stables, shoe shop, stock shipper, three grain dealers, meat market, billiard hall and saloon, agricultural implement dealer, lumber yard, harness shop, carpenter shop, dealer in music books and sheet music. There is also a notary public and insurance agent. The bar has one representative here, and medicine three.

CHURCHES, SCHOOLS AND SOCIETIES.

Mondamin Congregational Church Society.—This society was organized with about thirty members, in the early part of 1876, by Rev. C. N. Lyman, of Onawa. Mr. Lyman still ministers to the spiritual wants of the congregation, and holds services in the school house once in two weeks. Although somewhat at a disadvantage for the present regarding a place of meeting, arrangements have been made for the erection of a suitable house of worship the coming spring, and over $700 have already been subscribed for the purpose. The society, owing to the departure from the vicinity of a number of its original members, is now not quite as large as it was at the outset, and at present has but about twenty-five members. The society has also a Sabbath school in connection therewith, of which P. C. Spooner is superintendent. The average attendance is about forty-five, and services are held every Sunday morning in the school house.

Methodist.—Although there is no organized Methodist society, of any branch, in Mondamin, there are a number of adherents to the doctrines of the Methodist Episcopal Church, and for their benefit services are held in the school house once in two weeks by Rev. H. J. Smith, of Little Sioux.

Other Religious Sects.—Although there are numerous representatives of other religious sects in this vicinity, particularly Universalists, there is no other organized society beyond the one mentioned. The sect particularized has occasionally been preached to by various itinerant brethren of their belief.

Mondamin Public Schools.—Although the town is incorporated, Mondamin, as yet, has not been made an independent school district, but the limits within the jurisdiction of the town school is known as Sub-District No. 1 of Morgan Township. It is believed, however, by those in a position to know, that the sub-district has sufficient population to warrant its admission as an independent district, and that this consummation will soon be attained. There are 100 pupils in the sub-district. The sub-district erected a one-room building, 30x40 feet in dimensions, in the fall of 1871, when the sub-district was first organized, but the increased attendance has necessitated the renting of another room. This difficulty, however, is soon to be met by a larger public edifice. The first sub-director was E. M. Harvey. The present one is E. J. Hagerman.

Mondamin Lodge No. 392, I. O. O. F.—This lodge was organized May 22d, 1879, with charter members as follows: F. M. Dupray, N. G.; E. Jones, V. G.; J. A. Yost, S.; A. W. Garrison, P. S.; F. W. Brooks, C. M. Gilmore, Byron Strode. Thomas Byers, B. J. Faylor, members. Six other members were also initiated the same evening, and of these several were immediately placed in officers' vacant chairs. The lodge was organized by D. G. M. J. C. Miliman, of Logan. The lodge at present contains thirty-four members, with the following officers: B. J. Faylor, N. G.; Benjamin Morrow, V. G.; J. A. Yost, S.; R. B. Hall, T.; F. M. Dupray, W.; B. Strode, C.; T. Morrow, R. S. N. G.; T. C. F. Brenneman, L. S. N. G.; C. Gilmore, O. G.; William Griffith, I. G.; A. Forrester, R. S. V. G.; E. Jones, L. S. V. G.; Anton Uhrig, R. S. S.; Z. T. Noyes, L. S. S. The lodge which is in a flourishing condition; meets in Noyes' hall every Saturday evening.

Mondamin Lyceum.—This society has just been organized with thirty members, and its history is yet to be made. The object is intellectual and social development. B. Strode is the President, and the Society holds its meetings in the schoolhouse on Friday night of each week.

Mondamin Chorus Choir.—This society consists of about fifteen members, and it is non-sectarian in character. The object is musical cultivation. The choir meets every week in the schoolhouse.

RIVER SIOUX.

This thriving place is located on the Sioux City & Pacific Railway, at or very near the junction of the Missouri and Little Sioux Rivers, on the south side of the latter stream. It contains a population of 225. The town, although unincorporated and small, is delightfully situated in the midst of heavy timber, of various kinds, and is one of the most progressive business places in the county. The town owes its origin to the advent of the Sioux City & Pacific Railroad, the authorities of which platted it in October, 1868. The original town site was a few hundred yards north of the present one, on the north side of the Little Sioux River. This location, however, was found to be too low for a town site, as it was subject to inundation, and the town was accordingly removed to its present location. This transfer was made in the summer of 1876. The new location showed the wisdom of those who chose it, as it is the highest point of land on the railway south of Sergeant's Bluffs. On the original town site there were but three settlers, Reuben Newton, depot agent, S. Chase, who lived there prior to the advent of the railroad, and E. J. Davis.

The land to which the town site was finally transferred was owned by Henry Herring, E. J. Davis and James Crabb and the undivided half of eighty acres, was by them given to the railway company with the understanding that the town should be removed thereto.

As before stated, the business of Little Sioux, in proportion to population and number of establishments, is quite large. The following are the various kinds of business, ennumerated: Two general merchandise stores, drug and grocery store, drug store, hardware store, three saloons, hotel, lumber yard, two saw-mills, blacksmith and wagon shop, grain and stock dealer, butcher shop.

The professions are represented in River Sioux by two physicians, two lawyers and one civil engineer.

As River Sioux is situated in the midst of a productive country, which is rapidly increasing in population, the shipments of various kinds of produce are necessarily quite large, and they are rapidly increasing in amount and value. At present they will aggregate from two to three car loads per day. The business of the station is ably handled by the agent, R. Newton, who is at present the oldest settler on the town site, he having removed thereto with the transfer of the town site. Although River Sioux cannot properly be described as a port of call for Missouri River steamers, vessels of this description have in previous years come up the Sioux as far as the town, and it is thought that a systematic course of dredging and widening of the channel would make it possible for this description of craft to come up at all stages of water. In justice to dissenting opinion, however, it must be stated that there are those who regard such a scheme as chimerical to the highest degree.

CHURCHES, SCHOOLS AND SOCIETIES.

Methodist Episcopal Church Society.—This society has no church building, but is composed of about thirty members. The congregation meets in the town hall. The society has been in existence only since the organization of the Little Sioux Circuit in 1876, and has no resident pastor, and it is now one of the appointments of the Little Sioux Circuit, of which Rev. H. J. Smith, of Little Sioux, is the minister. The erection of a church at no distant future is being discussed. Outside of the members of the society, there is a good attendance of non-members, and there is more than a probability that the society will soon see a church of its own. Be-

sides this society, there is no other organized religious body in River
Sioux, although occasional services have been held in the place by
the clergymen of other denominations.

Odd Fellows.—There is a lodge of Odd Fellows at River Sioux.
The lodge contains twenty-three members, and was organized in
January, 1879. The following is the list of elective officers first
installed: N. G., J. Simmons; V. G., J. Bowie; S., C. A. Demun;
T., S. Demmon. The present elective officers are: John Whiting,
N. G.; Henry Herring, V. G.; James Harmon, S.; John Henry, W.

Good Templars.—Although there is no temperance organization
in River Sioux, an effort is making looking towards the organization of a subordinate lodge of the Independent Order of Good
Templars.

Public Schools.—The school district, of which Sub-District No.
6 (River Sioux) is a part, is Little Sioux Township District, which
was organized in April, 1857. Sub-District No. 6 was organized
September 21, 1874, and Charles McEvers was elected the following
spring as sub-director. The present officers of the school township are: Samuel Ellis, President; Samuel Dewell, Secretary;
Charles Smith, Gilbert Smith, S. A. Page, Samuel Taylor and
George W. Rock. Sub-District No. 6, has at present a neat little
school-house 26x40 feet in dimensions, but as there are ninety
children of school age in the Sub-District, the space is inadequate
to its wants, and the coming season a larger structure will be
erected at a cost of $3,000. The school is under the supervision
of E. A. Baldwin, of Little Sioux, and is in a flourishing condition.
Although containing but one room, two departments have been
maintained until recently, but lack of space necessitated the dis-
continuance of one department. This state of affairs is to be
remedied hereafter. Upon the completion of the new school-
house, the District will be made Independent.

WOODBINE.

The first permanent settler in the vicinity of Woodbine was
Richard Musgrave, who arrived in 1852, from Council Bluffs. Mr.
Musgrave settled in the Twelve-mile Grove, two miles south of
town, where he still resides, engaged in farming. Mr. Musgrave
was one of a number of monogamous Mormons who came to western Iowa and located at the time of the migration of the original
church from Illinois and Missouri.

L. D. Butler was the second permanent settler in the vicinity.
He has never resided in the town proper, but has been in business
there most of the time since his arrival. Mr. Butler came to
Council Bluffs in 1849. At that time, this portion of Harrison
County was a wilderness, inhabited only by wild deer, elk, wolves,
etc. The only settlements that had been made anywhere near
were by the Mormons aforesaid, of whom Mr. Butler was one at

the time. In a stray excursion northward, Mr. Butler was struck by the beauty and fertility of the land in the neighborhood of what is now Woodbine, and in 1853 he came here and located near the town-site, occupying one of a number of abandoned Mormon dwellings until he could erect a suitable building. The building he put up was situated about one and one-half miles east of the present town. He then commenced farming. Mr. Butler built a grist and saw-mill at the point mentioned in the year 1855. This was the first mill erected in Harrison County.

Among other old settlers are Jacob Harshbarger, David Selleck, Dr. Cole, Henry Hushaw, G. W. Pugsley, John Jeffries, Matthew Hall and others whose names could not be readily obtained. These came between the years 1853-5.

The town was platted in the fall of 1866, by the Blair Town Lot and Land Company. This was the year of the completion of the Chicago and Northwestern Railway to this point. The Land Company purchased 1,200 acres of land for the use of the town, though but a comparatively small portion of it has been platted. The parties selling this tract to the Land Company were Matthew Winters, David E. Barnum, Hiram Wisener, W. F. Clark, G. M. Brown, I. McAtee, John Johnson and M. Kiger.

The town was incorporated in the latter part of 1877, and the first meeting of the town council was held on December 7th, 1877. The following was the composition of the first council: A. W. Curtiss, Mayor; C. C. Matter, Recorder; Joseph Clizbe, J. W. Vinacke, G. H. Kibler, C. W. Jeffries, C. D. Stevens, Trustees. The present officers are: J. V. Mallery, Mayor; Frank Folts, Recorder; Frank A. Butler, T. L, Canfield, J. C. McLain, H. B. Kling, S. L. Winter, O. D. Smith Trustees.

The money-order postoffice at Woodbine is a legitimate successor of an office established in 1858, eight years before the town was platted. The original office was located at the grist-mill of Mr. Butler, previously mentioned, some distance from the town-site. The intention of the settlers was to name the office Harrison City Postoffice; but the department at Washington did not care to issue papers with that name as there were already several Harrisons in Iowa, and it was thought an additional one would lead to confusion. The name Woodbine was finally suggested by Mrs. Butler, and it was accepted. The name was taken from the cottage in which Mrs. Butler resided, as a girl, in England. The first postmaster was Mr. Butler, who held the office for about ten years and for some time after its removal to its present site. The present postmaster is Lysander Crane, who has been in office about a year. The postoffice name was applied to the town by the platters of the same.

The first building erected on the town-site was Gallagher & Bros. saloon, which was built just before the railroad was graded to this point. The first residence was put up in 1866, by William A. Jones.

The next building erected was in 1866 by J. P. Moore. The house, the Woodbine House, is still standing, with additions, and was the first hotel in the place. Among other buildings erected about this time, were the residence and the hardware store of A. Cadwell, Sleight & Williams' agricultural implement warehouse, C. D. Stevens' grocery store, L. D. Buttler's general merchandise store, (the first in the place), McAtee's grocery store, Dr. Cole's drug store and several other smaller concerns.

Woodbine Lodge, No. 405, I. O. O. F., was instituted in April, 1880. Charter members: F. J. Porter, S. L. Winter, W. J. Callender, A. P. Lathrop, W. C. Sampson, George Musgrave, and others. First officers: F. J. Porter, N. G.; S. L. Winter, V. G.; W. J. Callender, Secretary; W. C. Sampson, Treasurer. Present officers: A. P. Lathrop, N. G.; George Musgrave, V. G.; H. B. Kling, R. S.; J. V. Mallory, P. S.; S. L. Winters, Treasurer. The Lodge has about forty members. Meetings are held in Odd Fellows' Hall Wednesday evenings of each week. The Lodge is in excellent working condition, and its membership is of as equally excellent a standard.

The Masonic fraternity is as well represented by men of standing and thorough-going qualities. Charter Oak Lodge, No. 401, A. F. & A. M., was instituted in 1880. Its charter members were: R. Yeisley, H. C. Harshbarger, F. J. Porter, J. R. Burkholder, C. D. Stevens, W. H. DeCou, Lysander Crane, P. A. DeCou, R. Jacobson, L. D. Butler, I. A. DeCou, J. S. Hall, G. Smith Stanton. First officers: Reuben Yeisley, W. M.; H. C. Harshbarger, S. W.; F. J. Porter, J. W.; G. Smith Stanton, Secretary. C. D. Stevens, Treasurer. Present Officers: Reuben Yeisley, W. M.; F. J. Porter, S. W.; H. H. Rathbun, J. W.; H. C. Harshbarger, Secretary; C. D. Stevens, Treasurer; J. R. Burkholder, S. D.; C. W. Mendenhall, J. D.; N. E. Cowles, Tyler. The membership is twenty-five. Meetings are held Saturday evenings on or before the full moon.

Woodbine has a circulating library of about 800 volumes. This library is owned and conducted by Geo. Musgrave, proprietor of the *Twiner*, at his office.

There are three church buildings, the Presbyterian, Methodist, Episcopal and Baptist. The religious interests of Woodbine are zealously cared for.

There is every advantage offered in an educational way. The school building is a handsome and roomy structure of four departments. C. C. Matter is the principal; Miss Hester Hillas teaches the Intermediate Department; Miss Etta Boies, the Second Primary; Miss Harriet Elkins, the First Primary. One hundred and fifty pupils are enrolled. The building was built in 1880, is of brick, two stories in hight, and cost about $5,000.

MODALE.

The location of this place is on the Sioux City & Pacific Railway, sixty-five miles south of Sioux City, and a li tle less than thirty-two miles north of Council Bluffs. Modale contains about 200 inhabitants, most of whom are native Americans. The village is not incorporated.

Modale was laid off by Benjamin Martin in 1872, under the the name of Martinsville, which is still the legal name of the place, in all deeds of town property it being thus designated. The name Modale, however, is the older name, and seems to be preferred by the citizens. The name had a somewhat singular origin. In the year 1858, the few settlers then living in the vicinity were desirous of securing a postoffice, and a petition was drawn up and sent to Washington asking that one be established. T. A. Dennis, who forwarded the document, also sent recommendations as to name and location. The name suggested was "Missouri Dale;" but the writing being somewhat illegible and the word "Missouri" being abbreviated to "Mo.," the postoffice authorities could make nothing of it but "Modale" and with that name the papers were filled out. This postoffice was located two miles and a half northwest of the present town. The postmaster was Stephen Hester. The office was shifted according to population several times before it reached its present location. The last move was in 1873. C. J. Cutler, the present postmaster, the oldest living settler on the town-site was the first postmaster. The name Modale was further fixed by the building of an addition called "Modale addition" after the town was platted, and by the railway company's giving the station the name of Modale.

At the time of the building of the railway through here, in the fall of 1868, the intention of the company was to make no regular station, but simply a station. This idea was carried out, and it was a number of years after before any but flagged trains stopped at Modale. But in course of time, as population and products increased, a station was found necessary and one was made, the enterprise of Mr. Martin and others providing the town site. The original plat, as laid out by Mr. Martin, contained but ten acres, but a year afterward thirty acres more were platted by that gentleman. About the same time Alonzo Beebe platted the Modale addition of six acres, which made the total number of acres in the town site forty-six. No more additions have been made since.

The oldest building on the town site is the old school house, which though still standing, is deserted and dilapidated. This building, size 26x30 feet, was the second school house in the district, and was erected in 1866. The first building erected after the town site was platted was the residence of A. M. Snyder, which was erected in 1874, and in which Mr. Snyder still lives. A number of other small residences were erected shortly afterward.

Among the early settlers of Modale are C. J. Cutler, before mentioned; B. F. Martin, son of the founder of the town, and A. M. Snyder, also previously mentioned. These all came about the time the town was platted. There were others, some of whom are dead, who were also early settlers of the immediate vicinity. Among the extreme old settlers of the vicinity, though not a resident of the town proper, is J. J. Anderson. He, however, is separated from the town by but a narrow lane. His house had been built for many years prior to the platting of the town. Mr. Anderson came to the township some time in the early '50's. Other old settlers in the township are Joseph Haskins and Joseph Bross, who both came to Taylor Township nearly thirty years ago. The priority of settlement was not ascertained.

The business of Modale, though not varied, is large in proportion to its population, and is constantly improving. The exports consist principally of corn, hogs, cattle and wood. The latter, regarding which no exact figures could be obtained, is shipped across the river into Nebraska. Modale has a large corn-cribbing capacity—at least 100,000 bushels, but double that amount of this cereal was shipped during 1881. Besides, a large quantity was purchased for home consumption. The shipments of cattle and hogs amounted to several hundred car loads of each, but as the cars in which the animals were shipped were sometimes partially filled at towns above before reaching Modale, it is not possible to give the exact number.

The situation of Modale is a beautiful one, and it was high enough to escape the heavy overflow of the Missouri in 1881. There is heavy timber near the town, and a number of citizens find profitable employment in clearing it. The people, like most of the people on the valley, are wholesouled and generous, and the vicinity presents many advantages to prospective settlers. The merchants carry stocks of goods far heavier than the town would at first sight seem to warrant, yet all seem to be thriving and doing good business.

Modale is not yet incorporated, though the subject of incorporation has received considerable attention.

The business of Modale, classified, is as follows: Two general merchandise stores, grocery store, hardware store, furniture store, millinery store, drug store, saloon, two hotels, butcher shop, two blacksmith shops, carpenter and wagon shop, weigh scales, two stock dealers, lumber and agricultural implement dealer, wood yard, lumber yard, harness and shoe-maker, and livery stable. Two physicians comprise the practicing professional men of the place.

CHURCHES, SCHOOLS AND SOCIETIES.

With these Modale is but moderately well supplied—in fact, of secret societies she has none, though there are a number of members of various orders in the vicinity. She has no church building be-

yond a Union church, built by a stock company at five dollars per
share, and in this the societies which exist in Modale hold their services. It is open to all denominations. This church was built in 1875
and it is 28x46 feet in dimensions. The cost was $1,200. Below
are given the church and other societies of Modale:

Methodist Church Society.—This society was organized in 1866,
by Rev. A. J. Andres, the society at that time containing but six
or eight members. The first services were held in the school
house. The society now numbers nearly fifty members, and the
services are held every other week in the Union Church. The
pastor is Rev. H. J. Smith, of the Little Sioux Circuit. This church
has a Sabbath School of sixty members, of which W. W. Morton is
the Superintendent. The school was established in 1876.

Christian Church Society.—This society has had a number of
ups and downs. It was first organized in 1861 by Rev. D. R. Dun
can, with twelve or fifteen members; but since then it has several
times fallen into a condition of decay, and has as many times been
reorganized. It now has between thirty and forty members and
seems to be in a flourishing condition. The services are held in
the Union Church. The present pastor is Rev. D. G. Mullis.

Modale Public School.—This school is not independent, but is
the school of Sub-District No. 3, Taylor Township. As elsewhere
announced, it was organized twenty years ago, when there were
but four families in the district. The first sub-director was
James Mackintosh. The growing demands of the community
have caused larger buildings to be erected twice, and the present
building is the third one erected by the Sub-District. The present
building was erected in the summer of 1881. It is a two-story
frame structure, 30x50 feet, and has two rooms, each of which
constitutes a department. The higher department is taught by
J. A. Bradley, and the lower by Miss Clara Vanderhoof. There
are 104 pupils in the Sub-District. Several unsuccessful moves
have been made in the direction of rendering the Sub-District independent.

Modale Band of Hope.—This is an independent body, which
was organized November 6th, 1881. Arrangements are now in
progress to secure for it a charter from the State Band of Hope,
thereby making it a subordinate band of that institution. The officers are: J. A. Bradley, Superintendent; W. W. Morton, Assistant Superintendent; Eva Martin, Secretary; Bessie Silsby, Treasurer; Eva Martin, Chorister; Pamelia Taylor, Organist. The band
meets every Sunday at 3 P. M. There are seventy members.

Modale Literary Society.—This society has just been organized
with J. A. Bradley as President. Meetings are to be held weekly
in the school-house. There are but a few members as yet.

DUNLAP.

The settlement of Dunlap began in the summer of 1867, the prior settlement, which was virtually its beginning, however, being the town of Olmstead, to which reference has been made hitherto. The Olmstead settlement was known as the Yankee settlement, as its founders and population—if the latter word is not too comprehensive for so small a town—were from New England.

Of this Olmstead settlement it may be said that Henry Olmstead, H. B. Lyman, Edward Brace, and Calvin Nay, came together in the autumn of 1855 from Connecticut; J. L. Roberts came in November of the same year. The same autumn witnessed the arrival of James Welch, who settled on what is known as the Sam. Ettinger farm, about thirteen miles south of Dunlap. During the same autumn E. P. Brown built a log house about one-half mile west of Galland's Grove, in Harrison Township. A man named Riley, a native of Connecticut, came the same autumn in search of health.

About the last of November, 1855, Olmstead, Riley and Roberts assembled on the townsite of Olmstead, and voted a township organization. Olmstead was Chairman of the meeting, Riley was the Clerk, and Roberts sustained the important role of "voter." Both Riley and Olmstead are now dead. Riley died in Connecticut; Olmstead was killed by a runaway team. The latter was the first County Supervisor for Harrison Township, L. Kellogg, the next, and was succeeded by Roberts, whose term of office included the year during which the settlement of Dunlap was begun.

Like the "paper towns" in Iowa and elsewhere, Olmstead was not doomed to anything but a transitory existence. The establishment of the line of the C. & N. W. Railroad elsewhere than had been expected terminated the existence of a number of towns, and Olmstead was among the number.

Dunlap is located on section 3, township 81, range 41, and was platted by the Cedar Rapids Land Company in 1867. The town was incorporated in the spring of 1871. Its first officers were: L. G. Tubbs, Mayor; Frank Griffin, Recorder; S. M. Williams, W. C. Chapman, B. F. Carpenter, W. P. Webster, J. R. Wheeler, Trustees; Samuel Baird, Marshal; S. J. Patterson, Treasurer; William Magden, Solicitor; William Sears, Street Commissioner; H. W. Cotton, Assessor.

The following are the present town officers: F. W. Olmstead, Mayor; D. T. Stubbs, Recorder; O. P. Simmons, G. W. Chamberlin, John Noonan, Charles Gager, G. P. Moorhead, E. R. Cadwell, Council; E. K. Burch, Solicitor; J. B. Patterson, Treasurer; W. Van Slyke, Marshal. Board of Education: S. J. Patterson, President; R. R. Ballard, Secretary; J. A. Nay, M. Barrett, M. Roberts, H. W. Gleason, W. C. Chapman, J. Van Scoy.

302HISTORY OF IOWA.

Dunlap Bank, a prosperous and substantial institution, was organized in 1871, the firm at first being Clark, Kellogg & Thompson, and afterwards Kellogg, Morehead & Thompson. The present firm are Kellogg, Morehead, Satterlee & Patterson. L. Kellogg is president, S. L. Amsden Cashier, David Stubbs Assistant Cashier. The bank building, a handsome brick structure, was erected in 1879.

The town was named by the Railroad Company in honor of one of its officials. Its population, according to the census of 1880, is 1,418: its present population is fully 1,500.

Among the leading industries may be mentioned 1. Scholfield's flouring mill, which was erected in the summer of 1871. This mill is about five-eighths of a mile west of Dunlap, is 32x66 feet in dimensions, and three stories high, has four run of stones, and a capacity of sixty barrels per day. This mill has all the machinery for making the patent flour; but is mainly employed in doing custom work, a very large amount of which comes to it. Mr. Scholfield also owns a grain elevator at Denison.

His mill office and residence are connected by telephone. Mr. S. has a farm of three hundred acres connected with the mill, and is extensively engaged in hog raising. He is also the owner and editor of the *Dunlap Reporter*. This paper was started in 1871 by Geo. R. Brainerd, who was succeeded by G. W. Thompson. Mr. Thompson ran the paper about two years, part of the time in connection with James Ainsworth. Thompson sold to L. F. Cook, who ran it until May, 1880, when Mr. Scholfield purchased a half-interest. In May, 1881, Mr. Scholfield purchased Cook's interest and assumed entire control. He has changed the paper from an eight-column folio to a five-column quarto, and greatly enlarged its scope, paying very particular attention to the wants of the farming community, as well as to those of the home circle and the fireside. In this undertaking he is meeting with success. L. Ballou is the local editor.

There are three brickyards, of which James Van Scoy, Aaron Van Scoy, and Joseph Wood are proprietors. These yards furnish brick of the first quality at very low prices.

The business of the town in general may be classified as follows: Hotels, 3; general merchandise, 4; groceries, 5; hardware and farm implements, 3; bakery, 1; drug and book stores, 3; livery stables, 2; clothing, 1; furniture, 2; jewelers, 2; wagon and blacksmith shops, 2; blacksmith, 2; harness, 2; boot and shoe store, 1; meat markets, 2; confectioners, 3; barber shops, 2; grain elevators, 2; lumber yards, 2, agricultural implements and machinery, 1; art gallery, 1; cigar factory, 1; billiard rooms, 2; attorneys, 5; physicians, 6.

The Railway Eating House and Hotel, leased and conducted by Chapman & Castle, is liberally patronized by the traveling public. The building is large and roomy, and the accommodations excellent in every respect.

The postoffice of Dunlap was established in 1867, a Mr. Willard
being the first postmaster. He was succeeded by B. F. Carpenter,
and he in turn by Dr. D. Satterlee. The office was made a money
order office July 17th, 1872. Dr. Satterlee is the proprietor (in connection with his office) of a well conducted and arranged book and
drug establishment.

All in all, Dunlap is not only a thriving town, but, to the unprejudiced observer, a town destined to grow steadily in importance. It has, moreover, a substantial and beautiful appearance,
situated as it is, on a " bench " overlooking the rich and fertile
Boyer Valley, and equipped, as it is, with many handsome and substantial buildings.

CHURCHES, SCHOOLS AND SOCIETIES.

The Baptist Church Society.—Organized in August, 1872, by
Rev. E. G. O. Groat. F. W. Foster was the pastor in April, 1880,
and was succeeded by Rev. A. G. Delano, the present pastor, in
December, 1881. The church building was erected in 1878, and
cost $1,800. The membership is twenty-five. Wm. II. Garrett is the
Sabbath School Superintendent. Present officers: G. W.
Chamberlin, J. N. Chapman, Deacons; J. M. Baber, Clerk; J. N.
Chapman, W. II. Garrett, Col. Brown, Trustees.

The Catholic Society of Dunlap.—First held services in 1871, under the charge of Rev. Father McMahon, of Council Bluffs. The
building of the church was begun in 1872, and completed in 1878.
The edifice is of brick and about 46 feet by 70 feet in dimensions.
There is also a brick parsonage attached, which latter was finished
in 1881. Rev. Father Lynch is the present pastor, and took
charge of the society in 1876. There are between 200 and 300
communicants. The parish includes Missouri Valley, Magnolia,
Logan and Woodbine. The church was dedicated in 1880, and is
called St. Patrick's Church.

Congregational Society.—Rev. H. S. Mills is the present pastor
of this flourishing society. Among the first members who participated in the organization are L. Kellogg and wife, Theodore
Kellogg and wife, II. B. Lyman and wife, and J. L. Roberts and
wife. A church building was erected in 1876, in which services
are at present held. Previous to that time services were held for a
number of years in an old building, on what is known as "Gospel
Hill." The present church edifice was erected at an expense of
$4,000, and is among the finest in the city. There is a parsonage
near the church building. · The present membership is over 100.
M. P. Brace is Superintendent of the Sabbath School, which has
an attendance of 100 pupils.

M. E. Church Society.—Rev. Fletcher Brown is the present
pastor. The society was organized in 1869, and has now a membership of about 100. The church edifice was erected at an ex-

pense of $5.000. Z. T. Dunham is President of the Board of Trustees, and M. S. Bowman, Secretary and Treasurer. R. N. Blair is Superintendent of the Sabbath School, which is in a flourishing condition, and has an attendance of 115 pupils.

Dunlap Lodge, Iowa Legon of Honor, No. 117.—Meetings are held on the first and third Wednesday evenings of each month. This Lodge was instituted in August, 1881, with fifteen charter members. Its first officers were Charles Reiher, President pro tem; Dr. A. H. Hazlette, V. P.; L. A. Sherman, T. S.; Dr. S. J. Patterson, Treasurer; L. Ballou, Secretary. The present officers are T. B. Beach, President; T. E. Miller, V. P.; the remaining officers same as above. The present membership is about twenty-five, and meetings are held in Odd Fellows Hall.

Hospitable Lodge No. 244, A. F. and A. M.—Instituted under dispensation in August, 1868. Charter members and first officers: Dr. D. Satterlee, W. M.; Daniel Smith, S. W.; A. N. Warren, J. W.—E. W. Davis, Charles M. Robins, Thomas Rue and C. H. Wing. Present officers: Dr. D. Satterlee, W. M.; J. A. May, S. W.; O. Colburn, J. W.; A. D. Jones, Treasurer; W. J. Williams, Secretary; A. M. Warren, S. D.; I. Colborn, J. D. The present membership is about fifty. Meetings are held in Masonic Hall, Tuesday evenings on or before the full moon of each month.

Golden Rule No. 178, I. O. O. F.—Instituted Sept. 4th, 1869. Charter members: G. W. Thompson, W. W. Granville, P. Soules, E. W. Holbrook and Fred Kemp. First officers: G. W. Thompson, N. G.; P. Soules, V. G.; H. W. Colton, Secretary; W. W. Granville, Treasurer. Present officers: J. H. Read, N. G.; P. W. Tyler, V. G.; W. T. Howard, R. S.; S. R. Lindsey, P. S.; Z. W. Pease, Treasurer. Membership eighty-five. Meetings are held in Odd Fellows Hall in Commercial block Thursday evenings of each week.

The Band of Hope.—Organized in 1877. Present officers: Mrs. L. A. Nay, President; L. G. Tyler, Secretary; Miss Edith Pike, Treasurer; Miss Eva Waitley, Assistant Secretary. This organization is an anti-tobacco, profanity and liquor association, and has a membership of about seventy-five. Meetings are held the first Tuesday evenings of each month. Entertainments are given weekly, and consist of music, speaking, etc. Every third Sunday in each month regular exercises are held. They are non-sectarion in their character, and are held Fridays in the Congregational Church alternating on Sunday between the M. E. and Baptist Churches. This Society is in a flourishing condition.

The Ladies' Christian Temperance Union, is also one of the effective means for the promotion of its object in Dunlap.

The Young Peoples' Library Association.—This society was organized in 1879 and began with five or six members. It has now about seventy members. The present officers are: Frank Miers, President; Mrs. H. M. Mills, V. P.; Charles Strong, Secretary;

Chas. Waitley, Librarian. The prayer room of the Congregational church is used for library purposes. There are already about 200 well selected volumes in the library. The membership fee is fifty cents, with ten cents dues per month thereafter. No one can become a member of this organization but those between the ages of 16 and 30 years.

Guiding Star Encampment No. 68, I. O. O. F.—Instituted Feb'y 26th, 1874. Charter members: C. H. Tyler, G. W. Chamberlain, H. W. Colton, L. G. Tubbs, Hugh Ballard, Wm. Spendlove, A. K. Grow, R. B. Hillas, Z. W. Pease, G. W. Thompson. First officers: G. W. Thompson, C. P.; C. H. Tyler, H. P.; G. W. Chamberlain, S. W.; A. K. Grow, J. W.; Wm. Spendlove, S.; Z. W. Pease, Treasurer. Present officers: W. T. Hall, C. P.; Wm. Spendlove, H. P.; Samuel Ballard, Sec.; L. R. Lindsey, J. W.; J. Reed, S.; Z. H. Pease, Treasurer. Membership, about fifty. Meetings are held in Odd Fellows' Hall on the second and fourth Mondays of each month.

Knights of Pythias.—An order of this society is being organized with encouraging prospects for success.

A. O. H., Division No. 1, was organized in September 1880. Charter members: J. T. Noonan, M. J. Duggan, Ed. Lehan, Will. H. Page, W. Cavanagh, Peter Wall, James Malone, John Doherty, Richard Doherty. First officers: M. J. Duggan, County Delegate; J. T. Noonan, President; John Doherty, V. P.; W. Cavanagh, R. S.; W. H. Page, F. S.; Peter Wall, S. at A.; Thomas Noonan, Marshal. Present officers: S. T. Noonan, County Delegate; John Doherty, President; Jno. Brady, V. P.; W. Cavanagh, R. S.; Richard Doherty, F. S.; Michael Duggan, S. at A.; Thos. Noonan, Marshal. Membership, thirty-two. Meetings are held in Lahman's Hall on the first Sunday of each month.

Dunlap Cornet Band.—Organized in 1879, and has 10 members. A. S. Read is President, Henry Holden Secretary, H. W. Gleason Treasurer and Leader. The organization is a highly creditable one.

The Fire Department of the city was organized in the winter of 1879 and 1880, and has a chemical engine. There are about thirty active members, composing a most effective organization. J. A. Phillips is Chief, and B. W. Philbrook, Foreman.

Schools.—The first school taught was in 1857, by Louisa Cole, in an old building at the Olmstead settlement. There were but three pupils in attendance during the first term. The first school taught in the new Dunlap settlement was in 1868, in a building now occupied by J. L. Roberts as a residence. Mr. and Mrs. J. A. Ostrom were the teachers. Mrs. Ostrom is still living, and is yet a resident of Dunlap. Harris McKenney, of Harris' Grove, was the next teacher, and he, in turn, was again succeeded by Mr. Ostrom, who conducted the school, which was a private one, for several years. The first public school was taught by Mr. McKenney in

186. The first school house was erected in 1870. It is a two
story frame, and cost between $2,000 and $3,000. The present
structure, an elegant and commodious brick building, was erected
in 1880, at a cost of $13,000. It has six departments, presided over
by the following corps of teachers: I. A. Sabin, Principal; J. G.
Thompson, Higher Intermediate; Miss Jennie Barrett, Intermediate; Mrs. Sarah Kebler, Lower Intermediate; Miss R. M. Childs,
First Primary; Miss Stella Bang, Second Primary.

LITTLE SIOUX.

This town, which has as handsome a location as any on the
Missouri River bottom, or, in fact, in the State, is situated on the
south side of the Little Sioux River, about one mile east of River
Sioux and the Sioux City & Pacific Railway. The town dates back
to the year 1855, when forty acres of the present site were laid off
by S. W. Condit and T. B. Neeley. A short time afterward,
Messrs. Condit and Martin laid off forty acres more. Another
forty-acre tract was again platted in the year 1857. The parties
making the last addition were Joseph Jenks and Jasper Bonnly.
D. M. Gamet, merchant of Little Sioux, now the oldest settler on
the town site,—recorded the first plat. Mr. Gamet was at that
time Treasurer and Recorder at Magnolia, then the county seat;
but he shortly afterwards moved to Little Sioux, where he has
since remained. Mr. Gamet established the first general merchandise store in Little Sioux in 1857. He was also engaged in
the hotel business, his hotel being headquarters for the stages belonging to the line between Sioux City and Council Bluffs.
Although Mr. Gamet is at present the oldest settler on the town
site proper, and settled in Western Iowa in 1846, there were others
who made Little Sioux their place of residence prior to his advent.
Among these latter may be mentioned the Messrs. S. W. Condit,
T. B. Neeley, and Gabriel Cotton, the first and the last of whom
are deceased, and J. L. Perkins, whose reputation is international
in connection with the propagation of potatoes. Mr. Perkins,
who was born a pioneer, came here in the year 1853. He resides
at present but a few yards beyond the town limits. Moses German, now living outside the town limits, came in 1854. The S.
W. Condit, before mentioned, came in 1849. Jasper Bonnly came
here in 1856, and still farms near town. Avery Barber, now of
Nebraska, also came here about the same time. There are also
other old settlers residing in the neighborhood who came but a
short time subsequently. At the time Messrs. Condit, Neeley and
Cotton settled within the limits of what is now Little Sioux Township, Harrison County, though named, was not organized.

Though Little Sioux has been established for a long time, it
made no marked growth till within the past half-dozen years, and
most of the buildings are of recent erection. Notwithstanding

this fact, it would be difficult to find a handsomer or more enter-prising town of the same size in any portion of Iowa. This in spite of the fact that through a misapprehension in regard to mat-ters, the Sioux City & Pacific Railway left the town a mile distant from its track, and makes it dependent upon the station of River Sioux for its transportation facilities. Nevertheless, the citizens of Little Sioux are hopeful of a direct east and west line's running through the town at no far distant day. In case this hope should be realized, the 400 population of Little Sioux will be doubled within a very short time thereafter. The citizens are enterprising in the abstract, and though they missed one chance in securing a rail-road, they have in everything else been up to the times. One mark of this trait of character is the erection of a large iron bridge across the Little Sioux River at this point. This bridge was built ten or twelve years ago at an expenditure of about three thousand five hundred dollars. The bridge is 200 feet in length and consists of three spans.

The various business lines of Little Sioux, classified, are as fol-lows: Three general merchandise stores, two grocery stores, jew-elry and miscellaneous store, grocery and stationery store, shoema-ker shop, drug and grocery store, drug store, barber shop, hotel, two restaurants, livery stable, boot and shoe store, two furniture stores, meat market, blacksmith shop, blacksmith and wagon shop, grain and stock dealer, lumber and hardware dealer, agricultural implements, warehouse, saw and grist mill and milliner shop.

The professional men are two clergymen, one lawyer, and three physicians. The postoffice, which was established in the early his-tory of the place, is presided over by T. J. Lanyon. It is like that of River Sioux, not a money-order office. In addition to the branches of business already given, several insurance companies are repre-sented by local agents.

The exact shipments of grain and other produce from this point, cannot well be definitely ascertained, but they are quite considera-ble, and are constantly increasing.

The stocks of goods carried by the merchants of Little Sioux are quite large, and in several cases would be creditable to a town of 1,500 inhabitants.

CHURCHES, SCHOOLS AND SOCIETIES.

Reorganized Church of Jesus Christ of Latter Day Saints.—This sect, monagamous Mormons, is in point of numbers, better repre-sented than any other church in Little Sioux, and many of the leading business men of the place are connected therewith. This congregation represents a section of that portion of the Mormon Church which separated from the original Mormon Society under the leadership of Brigham Young. Joseph Smith, Jr., son of the founder of the Mormon Churches, is at the head of the reorganized branch, which numbers some 15,000 adherents. The headquarters of this branch are at Lamoni, Decatur county. The society has had an existence in Little Sioux for twenty years, and the congregation at present numbers about 140. The society has a church which was erected in 1876, at a cost of several thousand dollars. The size of the structure is 24x50 feet. The presiding Elder for this branch is D. M. Gamet, who holds services every Sabbath.

Roman Catholic Church Society.—The Catholics of the neighborhood have hitherto been without either church building or church society, and have been compelled to go elsewhere to enjoy the benefits of their form of worship. Although still lacking a society, the Catholics of the neighborhood have just finished a church building 26x40 feet in dimensions, and a society is in process of formation. The only Catholic service, as far as is known, ever held in Little Sioux proper, was on the Sunday preceding the opening of the church, January 29, 1882. This service was held in the house of M. Murray, and conducted by Rev. Father Michael Lynch, who will preside over the new church in addition to the previous charges of Dunlap, Missouri Valley, and Magnolia. The congregation of the new church consists of about twenty families, or 100 people, and services will be held once in four weeks.

Methodist Episcopal Church Society.—The first sermon preached in Harrison County under the auspices of this society, perhaps of any society, was in June, 1852, at Harris' Grove, by Rev. William Simpson; but the first sermon preached in the immediate vicinity of Little Sioux, was in 1865, by Rev. J. M. Rusk, who, when the county was divided into two circuits in 1857, assumed charge of the Western Circuit, and continued as its pastor for two years. The first class formed in Little Sioux was in March, 1864, from which time the society began its growth. The first regular preacher, who officiated at Little Sioux, was Rev. J. W. Adair. The Little Sioux Circuit was detached from the Magnolia Circuit in 1876, and as it now stands it consists of Little Sioux, Soldier Valley, River Sioux and Mondamin. The present pastor, who resides in Little Sioux, is Rev. H. J. Smith. The Little Sioux Society owns a building about thirty feet in dimensions. There are twenty-four members, and a good attendance of non-members. Services are held once in two weeks.

Universalist Church Society.—This society was organized in the latter part of 1870, by Rev. E. Vedder, of Dunlap. Mr. Vedder held the position of pastor but a short time, when he was forced to resign on account of ill-health. He was succeded by Rev. James Hoyt, of Belle Plaine, who continues to hold services once in four weeks. The society has no church buildings, and its meetings are held in the public hall. A movement has been inaugurated, however, for the erection of a church edifice. The membership is from thirty to thirty-five.

Union Sabbath School.—Although there is no denominational Sabbath School in Little Sioux, there was organized some time ago

a Union Sabbath School with an attendance of thirty-five. R. C.
West is the present Superintendent.

Little Sioux Lodge, A. F. & A. M.—This body was organized in 1878
with the following officers: H. M. Huff, W. M.; P. B. Terry, S.
W.; A. Gleason, J. W.; B. F. Croasdale, S.; S. J. Smith, Tr.; G.
F. Straight, S. D.; E. A. Baldwin, J. D.; N. F. Hillard, T. The
present officers are: N. F. Hillard, W. M.; F. C. Scofield, S. W.;
C. Ellis, J. W.; B. F. Croasdale. S.; S. J. Smith, Tr.; W. L.
Woodward, S. D.; Isaac Hunt, J. D.; T. J. Lanyon, T.

Public School.—The public school of Little Sioux is a graded
one, and comprises three departments, grammar, intermediate and
primary. The Principal, Thomas Macfarlane, has charge of the
first named department; the Intermediate is under the care of Miss
Alice Smith,and Mrs. C. Donaldson is teacher of the Lower department. The school district is the Independent District of Little
Sioux. It was organized from Township District No. 1, July 31st,
1879. The first school officers for the district were Michael Murray, President; L. S. G. Sillsbee, Secretary; A. M. Ellis, Treasurer.
The present officers are: Michael Murray, President; I. W. Bassett. Secretary; C. E. Cobb, Treasurer. There are 175 pupils in
the district. The school house is a two-story structure,30x65 feet.
with four rooms, though but three of the rooms are in use. Another teacher, however, is to be engaged the coming year.

Little Sioux Home Literary Society.—This society is devoted to
intellectual and social improvement. It has been in existence but
a short time, and as yet is not very firmly established. The society meets every other Friday, in the public hall.

MISSOURI VALLEY.

Missouri Valley, as do others of Harrison County's more important towns, dates its beginning from the first appearance of the
iron horse. The town is located at the junction of the Boyer
Valley with the Missouri Valley in the southern part of Harrison
county, at the base of the high bluffs on the north, and on the
margin of the Boyer Valley on the south, extending some two
miles, and of the Missouri bottoms on the west, some seven miles
wide, to the Missouri river, thus giving a large and extended plain
on the south, which, for beauty and fertility, is unsurpassed by
any part of Iowa. The town was located by the Chicago & Northwestern R. R. Co. January 16th, 1868, an election was held to
determine whether Missouri Valley should, or should not be incorporated. This important question was this time decided in the
negative by an adverse vote of 21. Missouri Valley is the junction of the Chicago & Northwestern, Sioux City & Pacific, and the
Nebraska Division of the Sioux City & Pacific railroads. The
shops and general offices of the latter company are located here,
and the officers of the company, who have their offices in this city
are as follows:

J. S. Wattles, Superintendent; C. F. McCoy, Assistant Superintendent; J. E. Ainsworth, Chief Engineer; K. C. Morehouse, General Freight Agent; J. R. Buchanan, General Passenger Agent; P. E. Robinson, Assistant Passenger Agent; P. C. Hills, Traffic Auditor; A. T. Potter, Train Master; B. F. Hageman, Train Dispatcher; T. B. Seeley, Train Dispatcher; Chas. Foster, Master Mechanic; Wm. Wells, jr., General Agent; F. M. Marsh, Road-Master; P. W. Brown, Store Keeper.

There are also located here the general repair shops, locomotive, car, paint and boiler shops of this road. The repair shops were started in 1868, and now give employment to about one hundred men. The general office building was erected in 1878 and affords room for all the above named offices. It is two stories high and is 32 ft. by 68 ft. in dimensions. The Sioux City & Pacific and Chicago & Northwestern companies, have, in connection with each other a freight house 24 ft. by 60 ft. in dimensions.

There is also an eating house, owned jointly by the two companies, which is leased and operated by John F. Cheney & Co., of Sioux City. All the offices of the S. C. & P. are connected by telephone and speaking tubes and furnished with elevators.

The town takes its name from the fact that it is the point of intersection of the Boyer and Missouri river valleys, the valleys of which at this point expand into a broad plain, several miles in width, and which comprises one of the finest agricultural districts in Western Iowa. It is one of the most important towns in Harrison county, and is provided with direct communication with Omaha and Council Bluffs on the west, Sioux City on the north, St. Louis and Kansas City on the south, and with the east by the great railways terminating on the Missouri River. The general character of the country surrounding this enterprising and progressive town is undulating or rolling, but not to so great a degree as to impair its utility for agricultural purposes. The soil is rich and fertile and produces an abundance of cereals. The raising of live stock is a very important feature of this township's industries.

Missouri Valley claims a population of 2,000, but it is also said that the census of 1880 was inadequately taken, and that the population given by that census 1,407, was much below the mark. The town is located at the base of the bluffs that skirt the valley of the Missouri River, from the summits of which a grand landscape is presented to the view. The dark bluffs dwarfed by distance that form the margin of the Nebraska shore can be seen for miles up and down, and compose a scene worthy of the contemplation of an artist's eye, and, with the added picture of the prosperous town in the distance, forms a spectacle, which, not only pleases the senses, but delights the practical eye.

Missouri Valley was finally incorporated in 1869, and is located upon Section 15, Township 78, Range 44. The Chicago & Northwestern Railroad was built to the present site of the town in the autumn of 1867, and the building of the town was commenced almost immediately afterwards, the town-site being platted by the railroad company during the winter of 1867-8. Among the first settlers may be mentioned Henry Warner, and Smith & Cogswell, who opened a business establishment during that winter. W. C. Ellis, who came during the spring of 1868 and started a general merchandise store.

The old town of St. Johns, two miles south of Missouri Valley on the other side of the Boyer river, was abandoned in consequence of the location of the latter place, and nearly all the residents of St. John removed to the new town that winter and the following spring, among them, John B. Lahman, who established a harness shop, Harris & McGavren, who established a hardware store and Ellis & Bro. who engaged in general merchandising. The American House, now the well known Commercial Hotel, was built in the spring and summer of 1868. The old town of St. Johns dates its settlement from the year 1857, when the town was laid out and platted by Geo. H. Cotton. The company which planned the town was composed of Dr. McMahon, J. C. Purple, C. Vorhees, Dr. Robt. McGavren, G. H. McGavren, John Deal and E. W. Bennett. There were several good business establishments, hotels, etc., and the town of St. Johns was prosperous up to the establishment of Missouri Valley. Dr. G. H. McGavren moved from St. Johns to the Valley in the summer of 1869. By that time St. Johns was nearly deserted, and Missouri Valley, its successor, was just entering upon a vigorous and substantial growth. Shortly after Dr. McGavren's removal to the new town, he opened a drug store.

Several newspaper experiments have been essayed in the Valley from time to time, with variable success, and ultimate failure, save in the case of the *Missouri Valley Times*, formerly the *Harrisonian*, and founded by Judge D. M. Harris, who, with his son, Robert H., continues to publish this prosperous and excellent paper.

The business houses of Missouri Valley, briefly classified, are as follows:

Physicians, 3; newspaper office, 1; drug stores, 2; bakery, 1; harness and saddlery store, 2; boots and shoes, 2; tailors, 2; groceries, 5; hardware, 2; saloons, 5; cigar stores, 1; gun store, 1; general merchandise, 6; hotels, 3; barber shops, 2; livery barns, 3; billiard parlors, 1; furniture, 1; bank, 1; wagon factory, 1; carpenter shops, 3; grain offices, 2; attorneys, 3.

CHURCHES, SCHOOLS AND SOCIETIES.

Missouri Valley has five church societies and three church edifices. An additional church edifice will be erected during the coming spring. These, with her excellent schools and other societies calculated to advance her interests, combine to make a community affording exceptional religious, intellectual and social advantages.

The Methodist Episcopal Church building was erected in 1869. The membership is large and increasing, and the society in a condition of encouraging prosperity. These remarks apply equally to the other church organizations of the Valley. Rev. W. W. Carhart is the pastor of the Methodist Episcopal Society. The Presbyterian Society erected their building in 1868. Rev. O. C. Weller is the pastor. Rev. Father Lynch is pastor of the Catholic Society, whose place of worship was erected in 1869. At the date of present writing, the Baptist Society is not supplied by a regular pastor. This society, however, has suitable grounds already purchased, upon which an appropriate edifice will be erected during the approaching spring. Rev. Mr. Hoyt is in charge of the Universalist Society, whose services are held in the Town Hall. C. W. Harris is Superintendent of the Methodist Sunday school; W. H. Campbell, Superintendent of the Presbyterian Sunday School.

A short distance up the bluffs, overlooking the town, stands the Public School building, an imposing brick structure, in the modern style of architecture, provided with all the improvements which the later spirit of educational progress can suggest, and affording unusual advantages. This costly structure is, indeed, a great credit to the community, and is, in itself, a sufficient commentary upon the enlightened liberality of Missouri Valley's enterprising citizens. The corner stone was laid, with appropriate public ceremonies, on the 17th day of August, 1871. Nearly four hundred pupils are enrolled. There are six departments, the following being the efficient corps of teachers: E. N. Coleman, Principal; Miss L. A. Ferguson, Assistant; W. R. Kirkham, Grammar School; Miss Annie Legan, Intermediate; Miss Hattie N. Legan, First Primary; Miss Estella Mattox, Second Primary. The members the Board of Education are: F. M. Marsh, A. Edgecomb, W. W. Hume, W. H. Ramsver, Joseph Harker. D. M. Harris is President of the Board, F. M. Dance, Secretary, and M. Holbrook, Treasurer.

Valley Lodge No. 232, A. F. & A. M.—Instituted in 1868. First officers: Robert McGavren, W. M.; W. C. Ellis, S. W.; P. D. Mickel, J. W. The Lodge has about ninety members. Meetings were first held in the second story of Fatchman's restaurant, and after several changes, the Lodge permanently located in the second story of Bump & Smith's brick building, corner of Fifth and Erie streets, in a handsomely furnished hall, which is also used as a place of meeting by the other lodges of the town. Valley Lodge is in a prosperous and flourishing condition, a statement which may as appropriately be made with reference to the other lodges of Missouri Valley. The following are the present officers: F. M. Dance, W. M.; C. J. Carlisle, S. W.; G. H. Carleton, J. W.; Thomas Weston, S. D.; George Barnes, J. D.; C. S. Hoar, Secretary; J. H. Crowder, Treasurer.

Valley Chapter No. 26, O. E. S. Instituted July 8th, 1878. Charter members: Mary E. Boies, M. M. Harris, Annie Davis, Ella Davis, Carrie Todd, Jennie Manchester, Mary M. Chapman, Belle Ransom, J. J. Legan, Louisa Miller, Laura A. Mann, Annie Schultz, Martha Pelan, Effie Mickel, Mollie Mathews, Viola Palmer, Annie Janes, Hattie N. Legan, Lizzie Butler. First officers: E. J. Chapman, W. P.; Mary E. Boies, W. M.; C. C. Lahman, A. M. Present officers: Mrs. C. C. Lahman, W. M.; D. M. Harris, W. P.; Mrs. Carrie Todd, Treasurer; Mrs. D. Burgess, Secretary; Mrs. J. W. Axtell, W. A. M. The membership is forty-six.

Triune Chapter No. 81, R. A. M.—This Chapter was organized under dispensation granted March 27th, 1876; its charter was granted October 4th, 1876. The petitioners for the charter were: William Pelan, H. P.; Robert McGavren, K.; E. J. Chapman, S.; C. W. Turton, Secretary; Theodore Mann, C. H.; T. W. Merritt, P. S.; J. T. Sharp, R. A. C.

Missouri Valley Lodge No. 170, I. O. O. F. Instituted October 21st, 1869. First officers: D. M. Harris, N. G.; William Compton, V. G.; T. E. Dubois, Secretary; James Laughery, Treasurer. Present officers: G. W. Burbank, N. G.; A. Edgecomb, V. G.; G. T. Hopkins, Secretary; D. M. Harris, P. S.; James Laughery, Treasurer. The membership is fifty-two.

Lilian Lodge No. 20, Daughters of Rebekah.—Instituted October 20th, 1875. Charter members: Robert McGavren, J. K. McGavren, F. M. Dance, William Compton, John S. Goss, James Laughery, James Ferrill, Reuben Palmer, D. M. Harris, G. W. McGavren, A. M. Cross, E. A. Boies, E. R. McGavren, Mary E. Boies, Martha Compton, Mary S. Goss, Rhoda Ferrill, Lizzie Laughery, Martha M. Harris, Ellen Cross. Present officers: G. W. Burbank, N. G.; Mary E. Boies, V. G.; G. T. Hopkins, Secretary; Mrs. William Compton, Treasurer.

Anchor Lodge No. 66, K. of P. Instituted December 19th, 1881, by A. E. Mennez, D. D. G. C. Charter members: D. J. Adlum, M. I. Bailey, F. Carlisle, W. M. Carlisle, T. O. Carlisle, E. N. Coleman, E. C. Connors, W. W. Cook, N. S. Dahl. F. Dodson, W. H. Fensler, O. B. Fredericks, W. M. Harmon, G. F. Hopkins, F. Johnson, A. S. B. King, C. W. McGavren, Neil McLeod, J. E. Marsh, T. P. Oden, W. R. O'Neal, W. H. Ramsyer, W. H. Ransom, L. Shauble, H. N. Warren. First and present officers: C. W. McGavren, P. C.; L. Shauble, C. C.; A. S. B. King, V. C.; G. T. Hopkins, P.; J. E. Marsh, K. of R. & S.; E. N. Coleman, M. of F.; W. H. Ramsyer, M. of E.; H. N. Warren, M. at A.; N. S. Dahl, I. G.; T. B. Oden, O. G. W. R. O'Neal, T. O. Carlisle and W. M. Harmon are Trustees.

Missouri Valley Lodge, No. 175, I. O. G. T. Instituted in 1869. This Lodge has had a somewhat varied existence, having been re-organized at several different times. There are at present about fifty members. Meetings are held in the Town Hall. The

21

present officers are: Mrs. Annie Schultz. W. C. T.; Miss Jennie
Gump. R. H. S.; Miss Emma E. Harris, L. H. S.; Miss Estella
Mattox. W. V. T.; Chas. B. Wilson, R. S.: C. S. Hoar. F. S.: Miss
L. A. Ferguson, W. T.; Miss Donna Goltry. W. C.; Harry
Stonesifer. W. M.; Miss Tennie Harris, W. D. M.; John Kane, W.
I. G.; Wid Lucas. W. O. G.; Miss Kittie E. Clark. Organist.

Women's Christian Temperance Union.—Organized in 1880.
Present officers: Mrs. S. C. Hileman, President; Mrs. E. J.
Ferguson, Mrs. H. C. Warner, Mrs. S. L. Berkley, Mrs. S. A.
Rogers, Mrs. D. Fenner, Vice-Presidents; Mrs. G. E. Wilson,
Treasurer; Mrs. E. A. Livingston. Secretary.

Public Library.—The Missouri Valley Public Library Association was organized in September, 1881, and has established already
a library of about one thousand volumes, which number is constantly increasing. The library is located on the corner of Erie
and Sixth streets. Mrs. Anna Schultz is the President; Mrs. C.
H. Foster, Treasurer; D. M. Harris and M. Holbrook, Finance
Committee.

Building and Loan Association.—The Missouri Valley Building and Loan Association was organized in October, 1880. About
$5,000 of capital was loaned the first year. D. M. Harris, is Presi-
dent: G. H. Carleton, Vice President: W. H. Bradley, Secretary:
M. Holbrook, Treasurer.

Harrison County Agricultural Society.—Organized in 1858, and
held their twenty-third annual fair at Missouri Valley, October
4th, 5th, and 6th, 1881. The present officers of the Society are:
Phineas Cadwell, President; H. B. Cox, Vice President; J. K.
McGavren, Secretary; F. M. Dance, Treasurer. The fair grounds
are located about one-half mile west of town, and contain forty
acres finely set out in growing trees. There is a good one-mile
track and substantial buildings have been erected; the grounds are
fenced in, and advantageously situated, with reference to stock and
other shipments, immediately on the line of the railroads, and also
upon the bank of Willow Creek, thus insuring a good water supply. Six thousand pepole are estimated to have visited the fair of
1881 in a single day.

LOGAN.

The county seat of Harrison County, is in every respect creditable
to the popular will which elected it to that position of official dis-
tinction and importance. Logan is located on the east bank of
the Boyer River, and occupies about one hundred and sixty acres
of land on a "bench," about seventy-five feet above the bed of the
Boyer. After leaving the "bench," the elevated land is timbered
for from one-quarter to one-half a mile, and gradually opens to a
section of prairie country of beautiful aspect, and dotted with improved and well cultivated farms. There is also a good and well
improved section of farming country to the east.

The town, as did Missouri Valley, Woodbine and Dunlap, grew out of the location of the line of the Chicago & Northwestern Railroad, and began its existence in the summer of 1867. It is located on section 19, township 79, range 42, and section 24, township 79, range 43. The Court House is upon, or very nearly upon, the division line of these two ranges.

A word here is in order as to the original town proprietor, Henry Reel, or "Uncle Henry Reel," as he is termed by his fellow townsmen. Mr. Reel was born in Montgomery County, Va., in 1803. Although stricken in years, he still retains considerable vitality, and is mentally as keen as in his younger days. From Virginia he moved to Ohio, and about the year 1824, he again moved to Putnam County, Indiana, where for forty years he resided. In 1853, he came to Harrison County, to where Logan now stands. At one time he had more than 1,040 acres of land in a body, in and around the present town-site of Logan. The coming of the railroad was what caused the location of Logan. It was the only available station between Missouri Valley and Woodbine, and although Mr. Reel was at first opposed to the location of a town upon his premises, he finally yielded to the march of events, and, with an engineer in the employ of the railroad company, laid out the future county seat. Subsequently a company bought an addition, and laid out the remainder of the town. The members of this company were: T. M. C. Logan, P. J. Rudasill, —— Mc-Curley, A. L. Harvey and G. S. Bacon. John Reed and Cutler Williamson are largely interested in town property.

Among the earliest settlers were: Judge Davis, George White. C. C. Cole, P. J. Rudasill, and A. W. Clyde, who came in 1867. There were others, whose names the writer did not obtain.

C. C. Cole established the first dry goods store, and was followed next in the mercantile business by P. J. Rudasill. George White built the first hotel. G. F. Waterman established the first drug store.

Logan was incorporated in 1876. The first town officers were: John V. Evans, Mayor and Treasurer; E. R. Cadwell, Recorder; George Musgrave, Marshal; J. A. Lusk, N. Palmer, Simon Mills, A. J. Norman, Lewis Walters, Councilmen. The present officers of Logan are: William Cadwell, Mayor; D. M. Hardy, Recorder; D. Kerkendall, Marshal; G. B. Seekel, J. W. Stocker, George Guilford, J. W. Reed, G. B. Cadwell, Fred. Kimpel, Councilmen.

The Logan Postoffice was established in December, 1867. John Reel was the first Postmaster. He was succeeded by C. C. Cole. William Giddings, the present Postmaster, was appointed May 12th, 1875. The office was made a money-order office July 1st, 1877.

The Huron County Flag, the first paper published in Harrison County, was published at Calhoun, Isaac Parrish being the editor —in 1858. Within less than a year it was taken to Magnolia, and Capt. William M. Hill became the editor. The Flag was subsequently removed to Missouri.

The Magnolia Republican was started in 1858, Geo. R. Brainard being the editor and proprietor. Brainard was succeeded by Henry Ford, and the latter by W. F. Benjamin. The *Republican* was continued until 1865, when it was changed to the *Western Star* by Hon. Joe H. Smith. The *Star* continued until 1871, the various editors being Hon. Joe. H. Smith, H. C. Cutler, Musgrave & Cook, G. F. Waterman, George Musgrave. The paper was then removed to Logan, where it was published for more than two years, when it was moved to Harlan.

The Huron County Courier was moved to Magnolia in 1875, from Canton, Ill., by Alpheus Davison, and from Magnolia to Logan in 1876. In August, 1880, Henry Reel purchased the *Courier*. A. J. Hard was the editor and manager for one year, when D. S. P. Michael succeeded him. Mr. Michael is both manager and editor, Mr. Reel still being the proprietor. The *Courier* is a handsomely printed eight-column folio, and well deserves the favor which is bestowed upon it by the public.

One of the valuable features of Logan is the stone quarry belonging to Mr. James McCoid, and located just across the Boyer River from town. This quarry was discovered about nine years ago. The upper stratum is about nine feet and eight inches below the surface. The stone is limestone, and is of excellent quality for building purposes. Beneath this are eighteen inches of yellow clay; then eighteen inches of black slate. Under that is large, blue rock, eighteen inches in thickness, which has been used as material for foundations, but which, however, Mr. McCoid states, is not durable. Beneath this are eighteen inches of yellow clay, under which there is layer after layer of a rock which very closely resembles granite, and is from six to eighteen inches thick. Numerous shipments of rock are made from this quarry to other points. It is stated to be the only paying quarry in Harrison county.

There is a public square of from three to four acres, planted in trees, and located between Fourth and Fifth Avenues and Sixth and Seventh streets.

A Driving Park Association is about to be organized, the grounds to be located on the farm of A. Whyte, adjoining town.

J. A. Lusk built a portion of the Lusk House in 1869. Additions have been made, until now it is one of the most commodious, as well best managed hotels in Western Iowa.

The town is well supplied with lawyers and physicians, has two banks—the Harrison County Bank and P. Cadwell & Co's.—a flouring mill, two hotels, and quite a number of first-class business establishments.

Brick-making is carried on quite extensively at Logan. Large shipments are made to other points, the brick being of the best quality.

The population of Logan is perhaps about 1,000, and is steadily increasing. The town has a durable appearance, is neat and attractive, and is keeping in every respect even pace with the rapid strides that are being made by her sister towns of Western Iowa.

CHURCHES, SCHOOLS AND SOCIETIES.

Logan Baptist Church Society. Organized in 1868, by Rev. George Scott, of New York, at that time living at Denison. The pastors in order have been: Rev. George Scott, J. E. Rockwood, E. G. O. Groat, B. F. Goldsby, J. E. Rockwood, Geo. Scott, J. E. Saunders, E. G. O. Groat, which latter is the present pastor. The membership is seventy-five. The church building was erected in 1869 at a cost of about $2,000, and has a seating capacity of two hundred. The parsonage was erected in 1876. There is a good Sabbath school, with about fifty pupils. J. E. Massy is the Superintendent. From this church soil other similar societies have grown. This was the first Baptist Society organized in Harrison County, holding meetings at Magnolia, Woodbine and Logan alternately. Meetings at Logan were first held over Rudasill, Wood & Low's store. P. J. Rudasill was a prime mover in the organization of the Baptist Society, and was indefatigable in promoting its interests. Rev. Mr. Groat has charge of the society at Magnolia, which has sixteen members.

First Presbyterian Society.—Organized August 29th, 1869, by Rev. George K. Carroll, of Council Bluffs, Synodical Missionary. The first pastor was Rev. T. K. Hedges, who was succeeded by Rev. J. B. Welty. Rev. Carroll is the present pastor. The erection of the church building was begun in the autumn of 1877, and the building was completed in the summer of 1878, at a total cost of $4,000. It will seat three hundred people, and is a very handsome structure. Rev. T. H. Cleland, of Council Bluffs, preached the dedicatory sermon, and was assisted by Rev. T. K. Hedges. The membership is about seventy. There is also a Sabbath School with an attendance of seventy. C. N. Cadwell is the Superintendent.

There is a Universalist Society presided over by Rev. J. M. Hoyt, of Belle Plaine. Services are held once in every two weeks in the church building owned by Henry Reel's.

The Adventists also have a society, the particulars concerning which are at this writing inaccessible.

Henry Reel erected a church building in 1878, in which services are held by the Old Regular—or as this sect is commonly known, the "Hardshell"—Baptists. Services are held regularly once a month. There is no regular pastor and no organized society.

The members of the Board of Education are: John V. Evans, G. B. Seckel, President; J. W. Barnhart, D. S. P. Michael, James Sorrey, A. K. Grow. George W. Wilson is the Secretary, and J. W. Reed, Treasurer. The school building, which was erected several years ago, is a very handsome and costly brick structure, and contains five departments. Prof. S. G. Rogers is the Principal; Sarah Gallagher, Grammar Department; Belle Wood, Intermediate; Clara Hedges, First Primary; Clara M. Evans, Second Primary. The enrollment is about three hundred pupils.

Boyer Valley Lodge No. 149, A. O. U. W.—Instituted January 31st, 1878. Charter members: John V. Evans, A. L. Harvey, J. B. McArthur, Fred. Kimpel, C. N. Hull, E. R. Cadwell, John H. Smith, C. L. Hyde, J. N. Young, S. I. King, W. W. Smith, A. J. Miller, E. P. Cadwell, W. H. Moore. First officers: Jno. V. Evans, P. M. W.; C. N. Hull, M. W.; Fred. Kimpel, Foreman; E. R. Cadwell, Overseer; J. B. McArthur, Recorder; C. L. Hyde, Financier; A. L. Harvey, Receiver; J. N. Young, Guide; John H. Smith, I. W.; E. R. Cadwell, O. W.; John V. Evans, J. W. Rudd, E. R. Cadwell, Trustees. Present officers: R. G. Brown, P. M. W.; D. Stewart, M. W.; James Ervin, Foreman; William Burnett, Overseer; George Kelly, Recorder; Fred. Kimpel, Financier; D. M. Harvey, Receiver; C. L. Hyde, Guide; J. B. McArthur, I. W.; John V. Evans, O. W. J. B. McArthur is Representative to the Grand Codge for 1882; John V. Evans, D. D. G. M. W. for the Fourth Judicial District of Iowa, and has held the office ever since the organization of the Lodge. The Lodge's condition is a prosperous one. It was the first Lodge of A. O. U. W. organized in the Fourth Judicial District of Iowa. Meetings are held every Tuesday evening in Odd Fellows' Hall.

Logan Lodge No. 219, I. O. G. T.—Instituted November 14th, 1877, with thirty-five charter members. First Officers: Frank Rugg, W. C. T.; Mary E. Wilson, W. V. T.; Belle Clevenger, C.; J. H. Giddings, S.; Adelia Fuller, A. S.; L. Harrington, F. S.; · James Harrington, Treasurer; A. B. Rogers, W. M.; James Copeland, D. M.; Nancy M. Wilson, I. G.; O. J. McKenney, O. G.; Wells R. Wheeler, R. H. S.; Lottie Noyes, L. H. S.; Isaac P. Hill, P. W. C. T. Present officers: Frank Stearns, W. C. T.; Mrs. K. Berry, W. V. T.; Lottie Cadwell, S.; Ben Wade Stearns, A. S.; C. A. Harvey, F. S.; Myra Grow, W. T.; Mrs. W. C. Cadwell, W. C.; F. H. Laporte, W. M.; Fannie Barnhart, I. G.; Willis Clevenger, O. G.; W. C. Cadwell, P. W. C. T.; Tillie Grow, Lodge Deputy. The membership is about fifty. Meetings are held every Wednesday evening in the hall over Stockwell's grocery.

There is also a Woman's Christian Temperance Union.

Chrysolite Lodge, A. F. & A. M.—Working under dispensation. Organized November 30th, 1881. Its officers are: Stephen King, W. M.; A. W. Ford, S. W.; A. L. Harvey, J. W.; J. W. Barnhart, Secretary; William Giddings, Treasurer; S. I. King, S. D.; J. V. Evans, J. D.; J. W. Stocker, S. S.; A. B. Milliman, J. S.; J. W. Stewart, Tyler. The membership is about twenty-five.

Logan Lodge No. 355, I. O. O. F.—Instituted in June, 1876. Charter members: T. M. C. Logan, J. C. Milliman. Fred. Kimpel, J. N. Young, W. H. Eaton, J. E. Townsend. First officers: J. C. Milliman, N. G.; Fred. Kimpel, V. G.; W. H. Eaton, Secretary; T. M. C. Logan, Treasurer. Present officers: W. C. Cadwell, N. G.; J. V. Evans, V. G.; C. L. Hyde, Secretary; J. E. Massey, P. S.; T. J. Roberts. Treasurer. Membership, twenty-two.

Columbia Encampment No. 101, I. O. O. F.—Instituted in 1880. Charter members: T. M. C. Logan, A. K. Grow, J. C. Milliman, Almor Stern, L. D. Parker, G. W. Smith, J. V. Evans, J. N. Young, Fred. Kimpel, C. L. Hyde. First officers: A. K. Grow, C. P.; T. M. C. Logan, H. P.; J. V. Evans, S. W.; J. C. Milliman, J. W.; Almor Stern, Scribe; C. L. Hyde, Treasurer. Present officers: J. V. Evans, C. P.; A. Stern, H. P.; J. W. Barnhart, S. W.; C. L. Hyde, J. W.; W. C. Cadwell, Scribe; J. N. Young, Treasurer. Membership, about thirty.

MISCELLANEOUS COUNTY DETAILS.

There was a considerable settlement in 1855, which was largely added to in 1857, and still more largely in 1860. Amos Chase came in 1851, as did also S. W. Condit, both of whom are now deceased. These, with H. M. Huff and C. W. Oden, were among the earliest settlers near Little Sioux. A pioneer settler in the same locality was also T. B. Neeley (the first representative to the State Legislature). Mr. Neely was a well-informed man of sterling and peculiar qualities, and, it is said, walked to Iowa City, at that time the State Capitol, carrying his shoes slung over a staff upon his shoulder.

Of Jacob Pate, who settled near Sandy Point, on the Missouri bottoms, on the western side, it is related that his particular characteristic was a steady determination to "keep ahead of the keers." He said he always had kept ahead of the cars, and he always meant to do so. But railroads finally came in upon Jacob from both the East and the West, and the old man had to succumb to the inevitable. He died a few years ago.

In Harris Grove and vicinity there were the McKinneys (Michael and John). Michael died about the year 1860, and John in the winter of 1880, the latter at Logan. Both had large families and considerable property. William Dakan came to Harris Grove at a very early day. He settled first near St. Johns, and soon afterwards moved to Harris Grove, where he is still living. Pearson Vore came to Harris Grove in 1856, and has been a continuous resident of that locality ever since. He is now about 81 years of age, and has had the misfortune in the later years of his useful life to lose his sight. James B. McCurley came to Harris Grove about the year 1853, moved to Logan about the time the town was organized, and is still living there. Judge Dow and family, who came in 1853, moved subsequently from Harris Grove to about eight miles below Denison, to what is now called in honor of the Judge, Dow City. John Rogers, with his family, came to Harris Grove in 1856. His grandson, Prof. S. G. Rogers, is now Principal of the Logan Public Schools. J. T. Stern, a venerable and sagacious settler, whom it was the historian's misfortune to be unable to see, settled at Harris Grove in 1857. He has resided on the same farm from that date continuously to the present time, and is 67 years of age. Almor Stern, son of J. T. Stern, came to Logan in 1878, and was elected Auditor of Harrison County in that year, to fill the vacancy caused by the death of W. H. Eaton, who had been Auditor for eight years prior to that time, and who was the first person elected to that office in the county.

There are thirty and thirty-three one-hundredths miles of the Chicago & Northwestern Railroad in Harrison County; thirty-two and forty-eight hundreths of the Sioux City & Pacific, and about one-half mile of the Milwaukee road in the southeast corner. The C. & N. W. came down the Boyer Valley in 1866; the Sioux City & Pacific was built about the same time, and commenced running in 1867. From that time forward there was a steady growth. The population at that time was 7,000; now it is nearly, if not quite 20,000. The census of 1870 gave only about 8,000. the population having nearly tripled within the past ten years.

Among the pioneers of Union Grove are: Samuel Wood, who came in about the year 1852, and has lived there ever since; Samuel Dibbles who first came about twenty-four years ago; Father Smith, now Postmaster of Union Grove, who came nearly twenty years ago; Jason Whitinger, William Cox, and the Smith family, who have lived there for twenty-five years. The Dobson family were also old settlers, but subsequently moved to Crawford County.

A full list of the first county officers, with the exception of the Board of Supervisors, is as follows: D. M. Gamet, Recorder; W. V. Cooper. Clerk of the Courts; Stephen King, County Judge; H. C. Harshbarger, Auditor (appointed in 1868); J. Z. Hunt, Surveyor; J. H. Smith, County Superintendent; C. M. Hamilton, Sheriff.

The present county officers are; I. P. Hill, Treasurer; A. K. Grow, Recorder; C. L. Hyde, Clerk of the Courts; Wiley Middleton. Sheriff; J. D. Hornby, County Superintendent; A. J. Miller, County Superintendent elect; Logan Crawford, Surveyor; Almor Stern, Auditor; J. K. McGavren, Thomas Morrow, Allen Stoker, Board of Supervisors.

The settlement at Twelve-Mile Grove had for its pioneers Richard Musgrave, who came in 1852; the Meffords, in 1851. Robert Mefford was the head of the Mefford family. Matthew Hall and L. D. Butler are also old settlers. The latter now lives at Woodbine.

Col. Asher Service, a man of native force of character, and who was at one time a political power in the county, settled at Six-Mile Grove about the year 1850; Owen Thorp in 1852. James McCoid ran a store there twenty-two years ago.

The well known Olmstead settlement in Harrison Township will be found to be treated of in that part of the county's history devoted more particularly to the town of Dunlap. By many, Harrison Township is considered the banner township of the county, in respect to the surface of the land, which is there more level. Mill Creek enters the Boyer in that township, giving it an exceptional "lay of land." There is, indeed, a fine southern view from Dunlap down through that section of country.

A grist mill was built on Allen's Creek west of Magnolia in 1853 or '54. It was never operated, but was afterwards moved away. The first mill on the Willow Creek, about one mile east of Magnolia, was built in 1854 by a Mr. Chatburn. Jacob Huffman also built a mill on the Willow about two miles below Chatburn's. E. T. Hardin built a saw mill at Calhoun on the Willow, about two miles below the Huffman mill. The first flouring mill in the county was built by Henry Reel on the Boyer in sight of the present town of Logan—in July, 1855. This mill began operations October 1st, 1856. The next mill was started at Woodbine by L. D. Butler, and in 1858. Butler and Grow put up their flouring mill. All these pioneer mills were run by water power. A. K. Grow built a mill in 1867 on section 31, in Harrison township, about half-way between Woodbine and Dunlap. This mill was very rudely constructed, its exterior being anything but handsome in appearance, but the excellent quality of its flour was undoubted, and built up for its owner quite a reputation. This mill was subsequently washed away.

The mills in the county now are: I. Schofield's flouring mill at Dunlap; Dalley & Noyes' mill at Woodbine; Alfred Longman's mill at Logan; a steam mill at Missouri Valley; also one at Magnolia; one at Calhoun, at the place where Hardin put up his saw mill; one on the Soldier River, by Theodore Mahoney, and Schofield's at Little Sioux.

About six miles northwest of Logan, in Magnolia Township, is the town of Magnolia, on the southeast quarter of section 32, township 80, range 43. The county seat of Harrison County was located at Magnolia by A. D. Jones and A. Fletcher, on the 14th of March, 1853. G. H. White was the Surveyor. The report of the Commissioners and Surveyor was approved by P. G. Cooper, County Judge, December 13, 1853, his acknowledgment being taken before E. Todd, Justice of the Peace. The election which resulted in changing the county seat from Magnolia to Logan, was held in the autumn of 1875. The tussle for the prize was peculiarly interesting, protracted and exciting, but provoked so many animosities, that it would hardly be possible for the matter to be treated of at length here in what all would admit to be a strictly impartial manner.

Lots were first sold in Magnolia in November, 1853. Ex-Judge P. G. Cooper is still living, in Blair, Nebraska. Among other early settlers of Magnolia township were Judges Hardy and Brainard. The removing of the county seat has had a depressing effect upon Magnolia, which has since that time, to say the least, failed to make encouraging headway.

It will be noted that Harrison County, like many other Western communities, has had her full share of "paper towns."

Upon the removal of the county records to Logan, the old Logan House was rented, in which to keep them. As an inducement to secure the county seat, the citizens of Logan contributed $6,000, depositing this sum in bank before the election. The election was carried, however, by a very small majority. The Court House was built in Logan in 1876, and cost about $11,000.

The following is a list of Representatives to the State Legislature from Harrison County. The Representative for 1863 resided without the present limits of the county. The years of their election are given:

T. B. Neely, 1855; D. M. Harris, 1857; W. W. Fuller, 1861; — ——, 1863; L. R. Bolter, 1865; Jos. H. Smith, 1867; Stephen King, 1869; Geo. H. McGavren, 1871; P. Cadwell, 1873; L. R. Bolter, 1875; H. B. Lyman, 1877; Geo. Ritchison, 1879; L. R. Bolter, 1881.

HARRISON COUNTY BIOGRAPHIES.

MISSOURI VALLEY.

S. Altshuler, dealer in dry goods and clothing, came to Ia. in 1864, and located at Council Bluffs; established his present business in Missouri Valley in 1867. He has a fine store on the corner of Fourth and Erie streets, and carries a large stock of goods.

M. I. Bailey, attorney at law, established business in 1875. He was born in Delaware county, N. Y., in 1847; removed to Missouri Valley, Ia., in 1875, and engaged in the practice of law. He married C. L. Ames, a native of N. Y. Mr. B. is the present mayor of this city.

J. H. Ball, proprietor of billiard parlor—cor. 6th and Huron sts—is a native of Ind.; moved to Knoxville, Marion county, Ia., with parents in 1851. In 1862 he engaged in freighting in com-

J. T. Baldwin, foreman of the boiler shops at Missouri Valley, was born in Md. He was employed in the navy yards at Washington, D. C., until 1868, when he moved to Omaha, Neb., and was in the employ of the U. P. R. R.; came to this city in 1870, and assumed his present position.

pany with J. B. Beard, which he continued until 1865. He then traveled through the territories until he settled in Council Bluffs in 1869; moved to Missouri Valley in 1878, and engaged in his present business.

C. H. Barber. proprietor of the Palace billiard parlor, is a native of N. Y.; removed to Clinton, Ia., in 1878, and was in the employ of the Union Iron Works: thence to Missouri Valley in 1879, and was in the employ of the railroad companies until 1881, when he established his present business.

J. M. Berry, proprietor of the city livery, is a native of Ind.; came with parents to Harrison county, Ia., in 1855, was engaged in farming until 1879, when he came to Missouri Valley and engaged in his present business.

T. N. Berry. of the firm of Morgan & Berry, grocers, was born in Pottawattamie county, Ia., in 1855; moved with his parents to Harrison county in 1856. He located in Missouri Valley in 1879, and was engaged in the livery business until 1881, when he entered the above firm.

J. L. Berkley, of the firm of Grigsby & Berkley, dealers in general merchandise, is a native of Va.; moved to Magnolia, Harrison county, Ia., in 1872; thence to Missouri Valley in 1876, and engaged in milling until Oct., 1881, when he engaged in his present business, with W. E. Grigsby, a wealthy farmer of Harrison county.

E. A. Boies, dealer in general hardware, is a native of O.; moved to Magnolia, Harrison county, Ia., in 1867. and to Missouri Valley in 1869 and was employed as salesman and journeyman tinner in the hardware business. He engaged in the business for himself in 1877, sold out after two years, and resumed business again in May, 1881.

Mrs. A. E. Bresee, dealer in millinery and fancy goods, located in Crawford county, Ia. in 1877, and moved to Missouri Valley in 1879, and engaged in present business; carries a large and complete stock of goods, and does all branches of millinery work.

W. H. Bradley, jr., of the firm of Walker & Bradley, dealers in general merchandise, is a native of Canada; came to the U. S. in 1869, and located at Missouri Valley, Ia. He was employed as salesman in the mercantile business, until he entered his present business in 1878.

L. Brown, attorney at law, was born in Jackson county, O., in 1845; removed to Appanoose county. Ia.. where he lived until he moved to Missouri Valley. He is a graduate of the Iowa State University. He married Fanny G. Manning, a native of Iowa.

W. P. Bump, of the firm of Bump & Smith, dealers in general merchandise, was born in Addison county, Vt.. in 1811; moved to western N. Y. in 1831, and in 1836 he engaged in the mercantile business; continued there until 1856. when he removed to Rochelle, Ill.: thence to Missouri Valley in 1869, and engaged in his present business.

D. Burgess, proprietor of billiard parlor. was born in Courtland county, N. Y. He was employed for several years as conductor on the S. B. & N. Y.Ry.. also was telegraph operator for same road. He moved to Neb. in 1875, and engaged in the stock business; removed to Missouri Valley in 1877 and engaged in his present business, on the corner of Fifth and Erie sts.

C. J.. T. C. & W. M. Carlisle, of the firm of Carlisle Bros., wholesale and retail dealers in hardware, wagon stocks, pumps, agricultural implements, and sewing machines, are natives of O.; came to Missouri Valley, Ia., in 1872, and engaged in their present business.

W. M. Chenoweth, manufacturer of cigars, is a native of Pa.; came to Missouri Valley in 1879. and engaged in his present business. He employs five men in the busy season.

J. C. Caley, dealer in boots and shoes, was born in Cleveland, Ohio. He enlisted in Co. I, 29th O. Vol.. served one year, and in the spring of 1863 went to Montana; returned to Ohio in 1864, and two years later came to Missouri Valley, and built the first building in the town, excepting a few R. R. buildings. He is the pioneer boot and shoe dealer of the city.

Wm. Conner, engineer for the S. C. & P. transfer company, was born in Va. in 1842; moved to Ill. in 1849, and in 1859 engaged in steamboating on the Mississippi river. In 1866 he went to Quincy, Ill., and took charge of the machine shops for two years; then came to Missouri Valley and was employed in his present position. He has been absent one year since coming to this city, traveling on the Pacific coast.

Maj. J. F. Cheney, senior proprietor of the Merchants and Depot Hotels at Sioux City, Ia.. also of a Hotel at Blair, Neb., and the Union Hotel at Missouri Valley, was born in Grafton county, N. H. In 1861 he enlisted in the 1st Ill. Light Art. as a private, was soon promoted to first lieutenant, then to captain, then to major and when discharged at the close of the war was lieutenant colonel. He then opened the Nachusa house at Dixon, Ill., also a summer resort at Spring Lake, Mich.. called the Spring Lake house.   He moved to Sioux City and opened the Merchants Hotel, in 1880, and his other hotel soon after. Major C. is one of the oldest hotel men in the country, and all of his hotels will be found to be first class.

G. W. Coit, M. D., was born in N. J., in 1837; was assistant surgeon during the latter part of the war of the rebellion. He graduated from the Bellevue Hospital, M. Y. in March 1866, and came to Harrison county in Nov. of the same year, and located at St. Johns; the following February, removed to Missouri Valley. He has been government examining surgeon for Western Iowa ten years.

J. H. Crowder, postmaster, also dealer in books, jewelry and fancy goods, is a native of Ind.; removed to Harrison county in 1866. He enlisted in the war of the rebellion, in the 18th Ia. Reg.; was a member of the band. He was appointed postmaster in 1871, which office he has since held.

N. S. Dahl, jeweler, is a native of Denmark; came to America in 1873, and settled in Chicago. He engaged in the jewelry business in various parts of the west, until 1879, when he located in Missouri Valley and opened his present business.

F. L. Davis, insurance agent, was born in Western N. Y. He enlisted in 1861 in Co. E, 5th N. Y. Cav., was discharged in 1862 and returned to N. Y., and soon after was appointed deputy sheriff of Cattaraugus county. He came to Iowa in 1870 and located at River Sioux; in 1872 moved to Missouri Valley and engaged in the livery business; was also deputy sheriff for several years. In 1878 he engaged in his present business.

C. H. Davis, was born in Penobscot county, Me., in 1839; moved to Mass. in 1852 and went to sea as a cabin boy. At the breaking out of the war in 1861 he enlisted in the navy in Com. Farragut's fleet; was transferred to Com. Dahlgren's fleet in 1864. He left the navy at the close of the war and in 1866 moved to Council Bluffs, Ia., and was engaged as engineer on the Missouri river, until coming to Missouri Valley; is here employed by the S. C. & P. R. R. company.

F. M. Dance, attorney at law, was born in Wis. in 1838; moved to Missouri Valley, Ia., in 1868 and engaged in general law and real estate business. He graduated from the law department of the Ann Arbor University, in 1867.

C. H. Deur, lumber dealer, was born in N. Y.; moved with his parents in 1860 to Pottawattamie county, Ia.; thence to Missouri Valley in 1877 and engaged in his present business. He has always a good supply of hard and soft coal, builders' supplies, lime, hair, cement, etc.

M. S. Frick, of the firm of Frick & Snyder, dealers in general merchandise, is a native of Pa.; moved to Ia. in 1865 and to Harrison county in 1868, was engaged in contracting and building, then dealing in furniture, previous to engaging in his present business in the spring of 1881.

Geo. S. Green, of the firm of G. S. Green & Co., proprietors of the Commercial House, is a native of N. Y.; moved to Vinton, Ia. in 1860; thence to Missouri Valley in 1875 and was engaged in various business houses, also in the postoffice, until Nov., 1881, when he purchased the hotel and engaged in his present business.

L. Harker, dealer in stock, is one of the pioneers of Harrison county, Ia., came to this county in 1867 and located at St. Johns, and engaged in the grocery business. He moved to Missouri Valley the same year and continued the grocery business; is now buying and selling stock.

J. J. Hancock, tobacco dealer, was born in England in 1830; came to America in 1851, and located at London, Canada; removed to Buffalo, N. Y., in 1853, and engaged in the boot and shoe business. He removed to Dubuque, Ia., in 1858; thence to Sioux Falls, Dak., in 1871, where he resumed the boot and shoe business. In 1878 he was in the employ of the American Express Company. In 1879 he located in Missouri Valley.

Hon. D. M. Harris, senior member of the firm of Harris & Son, editors and proprietors of the Missouri Valley Times, was born in Dayton, Montgomery county, O., in 1821, and moved with parents to Ind. in 1824; thence to Maury county, Tenn. In 1854, he came to Audubon county, Ia., and engaged in farming and the real estate business, and there served three terms as county judge. He represented the 26th Iowa district during two sessions of the legislature. He next removed to Panora, Guthrie county, and engaged in the practice of law, also editing and publishing the Guthrie County Ledger. In 1868 he first came to Missouri Valley and established the Harrisonian, which he sold in 1872, the name of the paper being changed to the Missouri Valley Times. In the the same year he moved to Independence, Kas., and published the Kansas Democrat, returned to Missouri Valley in 1873, engaging in the mercantile business. His establishment was shortly afterwards destroyed by fire, and he located at Exira, which town he had previously "laid out," and began the publication of the Audubon County Defender. Soon afterwards he published the Cap-Sheaf, at Atlantic, Cass county, which he conducted until 1876, when he resumed the publication of the Times at Missouri Valley. He was married in 1842 to Martha M. White, of Tenn.; has six sons and four daughters. Mr. Harris was the democratic candidate for lieutenant governor of Ia., in 1866, and was twice a candidate for county representative from Harrison county. He has held a number of minor offices. Robert H. Harris is a son of Judge Harris, and junior member of the firm. He was born in Tenn., in 1854, and in 1874 was married to Frances Chapman, of Exira, Ia. They have two sons.

E. F. James, dealer in agricultural implements, pumps, windmills, etc., is a native of Pa., lived during youth in Ill.; moved to Missouri Valley, Ia., in 1868. He engaged in railroading, until 1873, when he engaged in his present business; is also proprietor of the James line of drays and express wagons.

J. B. Lucas, attorney at law, was born in Lucas county, Ia., in 1858; removed to Missouri Valley in 1875. He was admitted to the bar in Harrison county, and established office in Oct., 1881.

F. L. Mandevill, druggist, was born near Rochester, N. Y., in 1835; moved to Milwaukee, Wis., in 1842; thence to Missouri Valley in 1871 and engaged in his present business; carries a complete stock in the drug line.

Hon. G. H. McGavren, M. D., is a native of Pa.; came to Harrison county in 1854 and first located at St. Johns; removed to Missouri Valley in 1868. He was elected to the legislature in 1870, and is engaged in the practice of medicine with his son, Charles, who is a graduate of the Rush Medical College, at Chicago, Ill.

S. H. Morgan, of the firm of Morgan & Berry, grocers, was born in Ind.; moved to Lucas county, Iowa, in 1859. He enlisted in 1861, in Co. C, 13th Ia. Vol.; served until Sept., 1862; then returned to Lucas county and engaged in farming; removed to Harrison county in 1864 and settled in St. Johns and engaged in the drug business; removed to Missouri in 1868, and came back to Harrison county in 1877 and located at Missouri Valley and engaged in his present business.

Hans Newman was born in Sweden; came to America in 1870 and was in the employ of the S. C. & P. Ry., at Sioux City, until 1879 when he was appointed passenger conductor on the Nebraska division.

W. H. Ramseyer, superintendent of the car shops at Missouri Valley, was born in N. Y.; moved to Neb. in 1867 and engaged in the furniture business, and in 1869 came to this city and was employed by the S. C. & P. R. R. company as pattern maker. He was appointed superintendent in 1871.

A. H. Rockwell, contractor and builder, was born in Otsego county, N. Y.; moved to Missouri Valley, Ia., in May 1873. He has built most of the brick blocks and fine residences in the place.

L. Shaubel, foreman of the S. C. & P. R. R. company's paint shop, at Missouri Valley, was born in Pa.; moved to Chicago, Ill., in 1854 with parents, and was employed in the C. & N. W. R. R. paint shops, until, coming to this city in 1877 and accepting his present position.

S. B. Shields, dealer in general merchandise, was born in N. J. He came west in 1870, settled in Missouri Valley in 1872, and engaged in his present business.

S. B. Smith, proprietor of the City barber shop, is a native of Ark.; removed to Polk county, Ia., in 1862 and to Harrison county in 1881, and established his present business at Missouri Valley.

A. L. Tamisiea, harness maker and dealer, was born in Dubuque, Ia., in 1855; removed with parents in 1856 to Harrison county, Ia. He came to Missouri Valley in 1875, and engaged in the confectionery business. He engaged in his present business in 1879.

J. D. Tamisiea, dealer in groceries and provisions, is a native of N. Y.; moved to Dubuque, Ia., in 1853; thence to Harrison county in 1856; moved to Missouri Valley in 1877, and engaged in his present business.

S. A. Teal, manager of the railroad machine shops, at Missouri Valley, Ia., was born in Albany county, N. Y., in 1831. He was for a time engaged in the iron business at Zanesville, O.; moved to Chicago in 1853 and was employed as engineer for the C., B. & Q. R. R.; remained there four years; then came to Cass county, Ia.; thence to Council Bluffs, in 1861, and was engaged as manager of the iron works at that place; thence to this city in 1876 and engaged as manager of machine shops.

C. Williams, of the firm of Williams & Blenkiron, proprietors of meat market, was born in England in 1855; came to America in 1861 and settled with his parents in Cherokee, Ia.; removed to Missouri Valley in 1876 and engaged in his present business.

Horace N. Warren, dentist, was born in Council Bluffs, Ia., Aug. 24th, 1858; he studied dentistry with Dr. H. N. Urmy. He located permanently in Missouri Valley in 1880; makes professional visits to Logan every two months, and three times a year at Little Sioux and Magnolia. Although comparatively a newcomer, he has by his careful and skillful practice, established a very lucrative business.

LOGAN.

B. C. Adams, of the firm of Adams Bros., stock raisers and dealers, (farms in Jefferson township, three miles north of Logan), was born in Asthabula county, O.; moved to Ill.; thence to Wis., and in 1854 came to Harrison county. Ia. He was in the government service during the late war, as deputy provost marshal and enrolling officer. Was married in Denison, Ia., in 1858, to Almira P. Carrico, and has five children—three sons and two daughters.

John W. Barnhart, attorney at law, was born in Northumberland county. Pa., Nov. 30th, 1837; moved to Mich. in 1849. He graduated from Michigan University, at Ann Arbor, in 1864; read law with H. T. Severns, and was admitted to the bar in 1865; came to Iowa and located at Boonsboro, Boone county, and opened an office. He was mayor of that place three terms. In Feb., 1878, he removed to Logan; has been mayor of this city one term. He was married in Mich. to Susan M. Hicks, of Saratoga, N. Y., July 11th, 1865. They have four children—two sons and two daughters.

John A. Berry, attorney at law, was born in Md. He was a student of the Agricultural College in the senior class of '71; came west in 1874, and after spending some time in Montana, located at Logan. He engaged in teaching school and in various pursuits, until 1880, when he was admitted to the bar, and engaged in the practice of the law. His office is known as the Harrison County Collection Agency. He married Martha Burnett, of Mount Vernon, Ia., Nov. 7th, 1880, and has one child, a daughter.

Hon. L. R. Bolter represents Harrison county in the state legislature. He was born in O. in 1835; moved to Logan in 1863, and engaged in the practice of the law. He was elected to the legislature in 1865, '73, '75 and '81 on the democratic ticket. He was temporary speaker of the house in 1874. In 1855 he married Caroline J. Rhinehart, of Cass county, Mich. They have two sons and one daughter.

T. J. Buchanan, furniture dealer and undertaker, was born in Boone county, Ill., March 10th, 1856; removed to Rockford; thence to Harrison county, Ia., and engaged in farming three years in Union township. In Feb., 1881, he bought his present business of Rudd & Soper, and carries an elegant stock of goods. He married Alice A. Brownell, at Rockford, Ill., April 14th, 1876, and has one child, a daughter.

S. A. Broadwell, land and loan office, was born in Cincinnati, O., March 21st, 1848. In 1862, he joined the 34th O. Zouaves; was afterwards courier and messenger, and in 1864 returned to Cincinnati. He was employed by Tyler, Davidson & Co. until 1866, when he was appointed sutler of Jefferson Barracks, Mo., where he remained two years; then went to New Orleans, and ran a trading boat for about a year, and then engaged in the wholesale boot and shoe business in New Orleans. He then removed to Mobile, Ala., and engaged in the same business, and through sickness was obliged to discontinue and travel for a time. He next engaged in the land and loan business in Champaign, Ill., remaining there five years; removed thence to Logan, and opened his present office. He is a very popular man, and does an extensive business, owning and controlling four thousand acres and more of well improved lands, besides a large amount of stock. He is one of the leading members of the Masonic order in Ia., being Grand Warden of the Grand Commandery of the State of Iowa.

Hon. Phineas Cadwell, president of the Cadwell bank, was born in Madison county, N. Y., April 17th, 1824; moved to Racine, Wis., and engaged in farming; thence to Harrison county, Ia., in Aug., 1854; engaged in farming, until 1875, when he established

22

his present business. He also deals in real estate, loans, and insurance. He was elected to the legislature in 1871, on the republican ticket. He has been president of the county agricultural society twenty years, and on the state agricultural board as one of its directors eighteen years, and served four years as trustee of the state agricultural college at Ames, Ia. He married Harriet N. Fisk, Oct. 7th, 1845, and has three sons and two daughters.

E. P. Cadwell, of the firm of King & Cadwell, attorneys at law, land, loan and insurance office, was born in Racine, Wis., Dec. 21st, 1854; moved with his parents to Independence, Ia. Entered the Ames Agricultural College in 1871, graduated in 1875, was admitted to the bar in 1877, under Judge Bradley, of Marshalltown, Ia., and soon after opened an office in Logan. In the fall of 1877 he formed a partnership with Mr. Barnhart, and in Nov., 1881, with Mr. King. He owns a fine stock farm in Jefferson township, of 840 acres, well fitted with buildings and improvements, where he keeps about 400 head of cattle, besides horses hogs, etc., and has 440 acres of pasture land in Monona county. He married Hannah P. Lyman, of Messapotamia, O., in the autumn of 1877. They have one child, a daughter.

S. H. Cochran, attorney at law, was born in Carmine, Ills., in 1852; in 1874 he graduated at the Iowa State Law School, and engaged in the practice of law at Missouri Valley; removed to Logan in the fall of 1881; attends exclusively to trial business. In 1880 he was engaged in the prosecution of the Western Millers' Association cases, involving the constitutionality of the "Iowa Fish Way Laws," in which a decree was obtained, holding them void, and he was also successful in obtaining a decree annulling section 3,058 of the code as unconstitutional. In 1880 he was appointed one of the committee of examiners of the law class at Iowa City; was the youngest lawyer on the committee. In 1877 he was married to Mary E. Shimmins, a native of Wis., although of English parentage.

Oscar Coffey, of the firm of Coffey & George, proprietors of bakery, restaurant and grocery, was born in Pottawattamie county, Ia.; was engaged in farming until locating here in Aug., 1881, when he established present thriving business.

A. W. Clyde, of the firm of Smith & Clyde, attorneys at law, was born in Otsego county, N. Y.; moved to Mitchell county, Ia., in 1855, and was proprietor of the Mitchell County News, for five years. He then moved to Logan, and engaged in the practice of the law. He was married at Madison, Wis., in 1877, to Bessie Johnson, and has one child, a son.

Logan Crawford, county surveyor, was born Jan. 13th, 1822, in Union, Conn.; moved to Mayville, Wis., in the spring of 1847, and was employed on the Fond du Lac & Watertown R. R. He surveyed in 1851, and in the summer of 1852 was again employed by the Railroad Company as surveyor, under J. S. Sewell, engineer. Mr. S. was transferred to the C. & N. W. R. R. on the Ill. division, and sent for Mr. C. to assist. In 1854 he settled in Harrison county, and bought land near Calhoun; has suffered large losses from prairie fire. He enlisted in 1861 in the 5th Ia. Infantry; enlisted as a private; was promoted in 1863 to lieutenant; was engaged in the battle of Pittsburg Landing; was wounded at Corinth, Oct. 6th, 1863, and again at Atlanta, Ga.; was severely wounded by musket shot through the chest, and reported dead; was taken prisoner in that condition, and put in the hospital at Macon, Ga.; was transferred to Charlestown, S. C., and exchanged in December in 1864. He was elected surveyor in 1879, on the republican ticket, and re-elected in 1881; has been justice of the peace of Calhoun township two terms. He married Helen M. Rising, at Maysville, Wis. They have four children living.

Dr. P. R. Crosswait, of the firm of P. R. Crosswait & Co., dealers in dry goods, clothing, groceries and general merchandise, was born in Fulton county, Ill., July 12th, 1853; removed to Cass county, Ia., in 1856, and engaged in school teaching until the beginning of the late war, when he enlisted in the 1st Ia. Cav.; served three years west of the Missouri river; was in the battle of Prairie Grove and the taking of Little Rock, Ark. In Sept., 1864, he was mustered out of the service, and went to Rush Medical College, Chicago, and in 1865 settled in Harrison county, where he practiced twelve years; then went to Miami College, at Cincinnati, and graduated in the spring of 1877; then returned to this county and practiced two years in Logan, when he engaged in his present business. He is a member of the I. O. O. F. lodge and encampment, also of the A. O. U. W. lodge. He married Mary Murphy, of Magnolia, Ia.

William Elliott, farmer, La Grange township, owns 305 acres of land all fenced and a well improved stock farm. He was born in Durham, Eng.; came to America in 1846 and located in Pa.; removed to Ia. in 1862 and located on his present farm and has a fine herd of cattle. He married Anna Phillips, in Pa., in 1853. They have seven children. He is a member of the I. O. O. F.

John V. Evans, attorney at law, was born in Genesee county, N. Y., Jan. 8th, 1847; removed to Clinton county, Ia., in 1863; studied law with Geo. B. Young of De Witt, and was admitted to the bar in Clinton, Dec. 7th, 1870. He removed to Magnolia, Harrison county; thence to Logan at the time it became the county seat. He was county attorrey two years and mayor of Logan the first two terms; is a member of the I. O. O. F. lodge and encampment and a blue lodge mason. He married Clara M. King, June 16th, 1875. They have one child, a son.

Wm. Giddings, P. M. and druggist, also dealer in stationery, toys, etc., was born in McHenry county, Ill., Aug. 26th, 1845; removed to Council Bluffs in 1868 and was with DeHaven & Giddings, druggists. In 1869, came to Magnolia, Harrison county, and in 1872 came to Logan and engaged in his present business. In June, 1875, was appointed postmaster of Logan. He married Helen N. Nelson in Beloit, Wis. They have one child, a son.

W. B. Goodenough, shoemaker, was born in Lewis county, N. Y., May 17th, 1862; moved with parents in Nov., 1867, to Logan, Ia., and is engaged in the above business, with his father M. H. Goodenough, who was born in Lewis County, N. Y., and was engaged in shoe making, until he came to Logan, where he resumed same business. He served from 1863 to the close of the war, in 20th N. Y. Cav. He married Aug. 17th, 1856, to Emeline Dodge. They have three sons and two daughters.

A. K. Grow, county recorder, was born in Courtlandt county, N. Y., in 1862; removed to Washington county, Neb., in 1857; thence to Harrison county, Ia., in Nov., 1858, and settled in Boyer township and engaged in milling for three years; then built a mill which he ran until 1875, and sold to John & Wilson Williams. Was elected to his present office in 1876 on republican ticket. He married Eliza J. Baskin, a native of Pa. They have one son and six daughters.

G. W. Guilford, proprietor of meat market, was born in Orleans county, Vt., 1843; moved to Tama county, Ia., in 1860. He enlisted in 1861 in the 10th Ia. Vol. Inft., and served four years and two months; was in twenty-seven engagements; was wounded at the battle of Champion Hill, Miss.; was at the seige of Corinth and New Madrid, at the battle of Missouri Ridge and wounded twice. Was with Sherman in the march to the sea; discharged in 1865. Came to Harrison county in 1867; resided in Dunlap thirteen years; while there, was a member of the city council four years. Has lived in Logan two years; is now a member of the city council of that place. He married Mrs. Campbell, of Harlan, Ia. They have two sons and three daughters. He is a member of the G. A. R. post at this place.

A. L. Harvey, of the firm of Harvey & Ford, proprietors of the Harrison County Bank, was born in Madison county, N. Y., in July, 1826; removed to Rockland county in 1853; thence to Jasper county, Ia., in 1856, and the following year located at Magnolia, Harrison county. In 1860 he was elected county treasurer and recorder, the two offices being consolidated; was re-elected in 1862. He opened a land and loan office in 1864, and when Logan became the county seat removed there; in 1876 established the bank with J. C. Milliman, who sold his share in 1878 to Mr. Ford. Mr. H. was the first land agent and first notary public in the county, has sold about 25,000 acres of land during the last year (1881), owns a fine farm of 436 acres, four and one-half miles from Woodbine, besides about 200 acres in other parts of the county. Has been internal revenue assessor three years. Is a member of the A. F. and A. M. lodge, also of the I. O. O. F.

D. M. Hardy, deputy treasurer, was born in Glenwood, Ia., in 1851; removed with his parents to Harrison county, is son of Judge Hardy, one of the oldest settlers of this county and the first county judge. He is an extensive farmer, and one of the proprietors of Willow mill, the oldest mill in the county. Mr. Hardy is a member of the A. O. U. W. lodge, also of the I. O. O. F. He married Miss Severins, of Wis., in 1872. They have two sons and two daughters.

C. L. Hyde, clerk of the courts, was born in Otsego county, N. Y., in 1843; came to Ia. in 1856, and first located at Little Sioux, Harrison county; has been a resident of the county ever since. He was elected to his present office in 1876 on the republican ticket. He enlisted in 1862 in the 20th Wis. Inft.; was discharged after seven months, and then joined the 41st Wis. Inft. He married Mary Russell, and has three sons.

G. T. Kelley, attorney at law, was born in Johnson county, Ill., in 1846; moved to Mills county, Ia., in 1854, and to Harrison county in 1867. He graduated and was admitted to the bar at the Iowa State University, June 10th. 1876, and soon after opened a law office at Logan. He married Maria Allen, in Harrison county, in 1870, and has two children, a son and daughter.

Fred Kimpel, jeweler and barber, was born Mar. 16th, 1847, in Bavaria, Ger.; came to America in Sept., 1864; learned the barber trade in N. Y. In 1866 he removed to Scranton, Pa., and engaged in the barber business; removed to Dunlap, Ia., in 1869; thence in 1876, to Logan, and engaged in his present business; owns considerable real estate in this city. He is a member of the A. O. U. W., I. O. O. F., and A. F. & A. M. lodges. He married Mary Fisher, in Scranton, Pa. They have one son and three daughters.

S. I. King, of the firm of King & Cadwell, attorneys at law, was born Sept. 8th, 1848, in Saratoga county, N. Y.; came to Harrison county with his parents in 1852 and located at Six Mile Grove. He is the son of Judge S. King, who was one of the first settlers of this county and one of the commissioners who located the county seat at Magnolia, in 1854. Mr. King removed to Boyer Valley, and was engaged in teaching most of the time, from the age of fifteen until 1867, when he attended the State University, of Iowa City. He left in graduating year on account of serious illness. Again engaged in teaching school; in 1870 taught the high school of Magnolia. Then traveled for the wholesale dry goods house of Smith & Crittenden, Council Bluffs. He attended the Law School at Des Moines in 1875, graduated and was admitted to the bar in 1876, and opened an office in Logan; at the end of two months he removed to Magnolia and opened an office there; came back to Logan in 1879 and formed a partnership with E. P. Cadwell in Nov., 1881. He is a member of the A. F. & A. M., and A. O. U. W. lodges. He is also chairman of the republican central committee. He was married in 1874 to Abbie M. Mark, of Fredonia, N. Y.

Hon. Thomas M. C. Logan, senator elect of 34th district, was born in Rush county, Ind., Feb. 13th, 1830; moved to Richland county, Ill., in April 1857; thence to Cedar Rapids, Linn county; and from there to Harrison county. He has been engaged most of his life in farming and dealing in stock. He resides on his fine farm adjoining Logan. He was married Feb. 17th, 1851, to Charlotte Snodgrass, in La Porte, Ind., who died in Jan. 1867, leaving a son and daughter. He afterwards married at Cedar Rapids, Harriet Herbert. They have four sons and three daughters.

A. Longman, Jr., proprietor of the Logan Flouring Mills, was born in Derby, Eng., in 1848; came to America with his parents in 1851 and located in Holt county, Mo.; removed to Harris Grove, Harrison county, Ia., in 1852. The subject of this sketch graduated from Oskaloosa College in 1874. The mill was built in the winter of 1855–6 by Henry Reel, who sold it to Mr. McCoid, of whom Mr. L. purchased it in Sept., 1880, and has established an extensive business. He was married in Wis., to Miss Whitcomb, in 1877, who died leaving one child, a daughter.

James A. Lusk, proprietor of the Lusk House and livery and feed stable, established business in 1869. He was born in Morris county, N. Y., in 1824; removed to Mills county, Ia., in 1855; thence to Harrison county in 1863; was engaged in farming until he engaged in the hotel business. He married Minerva Roberts (deceased) in 1846, and afterwards Lydia B. Kelsey. They have four sons and one daughter.

Horace C. McCleary, M. D., was born in Warren county, Ia., in July 1859; received his education at the Simpson Centenary College, at Indianola, Ia., studied medicine in the medical department of the State University, at Iowa City, and graduated in 1881 from Rush Medical College, Chicago. He located in Logan, July 20th, 1881, succeeding Dr. Giddings. Although a new-comer he is already in the possession of a lucrative and increasing practice. He is a member of the I. O. O. F. Lodge.

Allen Middleton, deputy sheriff, was born in Washington county, Ia., in 1855; came to Harrison county in 1867.

Wiley Middleton, sheriff, was born in O.; removed to Washington county, Ia.; thence to Harrison county in 1867. He was elected to his present office in 1879. He married Julia A. Lockling, and has three sons and one daughter.

Wm. Palmer, farmer, was born in London, Ontario, Canada, in Oct., 1833; came to Whiteside county, Ill., with his parents in 1851, where he remained two years; then removed to Walworth county, Wis., where he remained seven years; then came to Harrison county. He has been married three times; his present wife was Sarah Streeter; were married in 1880. He has three sons and three daughters.

J. W. Reed, dealer in general merchandise, was born in Va. in 1847; moved to Harrison county, Ia., in 1868, and engaged in present business with P. J. Radisell in 1875; became sole proprietor in 1877. He has been a member of the town council several years. During the war of the rebellion he served in the 43rd West Va. Bat., Mosby's command. He was married in 1874 to Miss Low, of Atchinson county, Mo., who died in 1876, leaving one child, a daughter. He was again married in 1878 to Miss Williams, of Boone county, Ia. They have two children, daughters.

H. H. Roadifer, of the firm of Evans & Roadifer, attorneys at law, was admitted to the bar in La Salle county, Ill., June 4th, 1875, before the supreme court. He came to Logan in 1878, and engaged in the practice of law with Mr. Evans: has been Mayor of this city one term.

J. W. Rudd, farmer in Union tp., was born in 1838, in Va.; moved to Harrison county in 1870 with his father, Wm. T. Rudd, and located at Logan, where they engaged in furniture and undertaking business, which they continued eleven years; then sold to T. J. Buchanan. He was city councilman three years, and is a member of the A. O. U. W., I. O. O. F., and A. F. & A. M. lodges. He married Sarah C. Sprinkel, of Amsterdam, Va., and has two sons and two daughters.

Geo. B. Seekel, dealer in lumber, grain and agricultural implements, was born in Taunton, Mass., in Sept., 1823; the most of his younger days were spent in Providence, R. I. In 1856 he moved to Madison, Wis., and engaged in the grain business; went south in 1864 and remained two years, after which he engaged in the lumber trade in Chicago; after two years he went to St. Paul, Minn., having the management and general agency of the Singer sewing machine. In 1871 removed to Logan and engaged in his present business; has been a member of the city council, and president of the school board several years. He is a member of the I. O. O. F. and A. F. & A. M. lodges. He was married in Dec., 1847, to Martha M. Williams, of N. Y., and has one daughter.

Geo. Soper, dealer in hardware, was born in Rome, N. Y., July 14th, 1853; moved with parents to Clinton, Ia., in 1857, and came to Logan in July, 1878, and engaged in present business. He is a member of the I. O. O. F. lodge. He was married Aug. 26th, 1878, to Lena Dodson, of Stanwood, Ia. They have one child, a son.

Hon. Joseph H. Smith, of the firm of Smith & Clyde, attorneys
at law, was born in Beaver county, Pa.; moved to Harrison county,
Ia. in 1857, and engaged in the practice of law; formed a partnership with A. W. Clyde in 1879. He enlisted in 1862 in Co. C. 29th
Ia. Inft.; was second lieutenant. He was elected a member of the
legislature one term. He married Julia A. Warrick. a native of
Pa., and has five sons and one daughter.

Daniel Stewart, wagon maker, was born in Little Falls, Herkimer county, N. Y., Oct. 31st, 1833; moved to Logan in 1872 and
engaged in his present business. He served during the rebellion
in the 121st N. Y. Vol.; was in a number of important battles;
was wounded Oct. 19th, 1864, and in hospital at Baltimore; was discharged May. 16th, 1865. He is a member of the A.
O. U. W. and G. A. R. orders. He married Margaret M. Clarke, of
Herkimer county, N. Y., in July, 1861, and has one child a son.

John W. Stocker, grocer and dealer in corn and stock, was born
in Caledonia county, Vt., June 2nd, 1835; moved with parents to
Lowell, Mass., in 1843; thence to McHenry county, Ill., in 1854
and engaged in farming; thence to Henry county, Ia., and engaged in setting up woolen mills; thence to Buchanan county in
1857 and engaged in farming one year; then moved to Little Sioux.
He enlisted in Co. C, 29th Ia. Inft.; was in a number of important
battles; was regimental quartermaster and commanded his com
pany the last year and a half of his service; was some time in Rio
Grande, Tex., and returned home Sept. 2nd, 1865; moved to Woodbine and bought an interest in the woolen mill there; after six
months sold out and removed to Magnolia, then the county seat,
and was elected clerk of the courts in 1866 and re-elected in 1868.
In 1876 he located in Logan and engaged in the stock and grain
buying business and added the grocery business in 1879. He is a
member of the Masonic, I. O. O. F, and I. O. G. T. orders. He
married Susan B. Bonney, in 1862. They have three daughters.

J. T. Stern, farmer, was born in Chester county, Pa., in 1814;
moved to Ia. in 1857 and settled on his present farm, in La Grange
township, Harrison county, of 200 acres of well improved land,
forty acres of it good timber. He was reporter for the Government Signal Service, Washington, D. C., for twenty years. He
married Millicent B. Fletcher, of Lincolnshire, Eng., and has two
sons and one daughter. His son Almor is county auditor.

Almor Stern, county auditor, was born in Chester county, Pa.,
in 1854; came to Harrison with his parents in 1857; was employed
in farming, until he engaged as clerk in auditor's office; was elected
to his present office in 1878. He married Laura Mann, of Harrison county in 1880. They have one child, a son.

Thomas Turnbull, dealer in grain and farm machinery, was born
in Greene county, O., June 20th, 1841, was engaged in farming and

stock raising there until 1874, when he came to Des Moines, Ia., and engaged in pork packing and curing with Fayette Meek; removed to Harrison county in Nov., 1876, and engaged in his present business. He owns a well improved farm in Jefferson twp., of 120 acres. He was married June 25th, 1865, to Susan B. Thompson, in Greene county, O. They have four sons and three daughters.

E. G. Tyler, land, loan and abstract office, was born in Chittenden county, Vt., Feb. 15th. 1856; in 1866 moved to Hastings, Minn.; thence to Dunlap, Ia., in 1867. He graduated in 1878 from the Iowa Agricultural College, at Ames, Ia. In 1879 he opened the office in Logan. He is a member of the I. O. O. F.

J. L. Witt, M. D., was born March 4th. 1855, in Galesburg, Knox county, Ill. He graduated from the medical department of the State University, at Iowa City in 1878, and located in Logan the same year and engaged in the practice of his profession. He was married in Logan Nov. 30th, 1881, to Millie Vanderhoof.

John Williams was born in Fayette county, O., in 1827; moved with his parents to Noble county, Ind.; thence to Mason county, Ill.; thence to Jefferson twp., Harrison county, Ia., where he now resides. He owns a well improved farm of 650 acres. He makes a specialty of raising fine stock. He has some very fine horses and one thorough-bred stallion which was imported from France at a cost of $2,500. In fact we may say that Mr. Williams has one of the finest stock farms in Western Iowa. He was married in 1849 to Sarah Anderson, of Noble county, Ind. They have three sons and five daughters.

MONDAMIN.

Thomas H. Allison, M. D., was born in Pa.; began the practice of medicine in 1849; removed to Missouri in 1857; thence to Mills county, Iowa; thence to Florence, Neb., and in 1864 located at Council Bluffs, Ia. In 1881 he came to Mondamin, and openedan office.

Charles Burrows, agent for the S. C. & P. R. R. at Mondamin, is a native of Cincinnati, O. At the age of nineteen years, he removed to Danville, Ill. In 1862 he enlisted in Co. C, 124th Ill. Vol.; served until Sept., 1865, then returned to Ill. and engaged in telegraphy at Springfield; has been in the employ of several of the principal railroad companies in the states of Ill., Mo., Neb. and Ia. He was appointed agent at Mondamin in Dec., 1880; is also express agent and attorney at law.

John T. Coffman, farmer, was born in Greene county, Tenn., in 1828; removed with parents to Johnson county, Mo.; thence to that part of Lee county, Ia., then known as the Spanish land grant; thence located in the edge of Putnam county, Mo., which in 1838 became Appanoose county, Ia. He removed to Lewis, Cass county, in 1863, and in the spring of the year following went to Virginia City, Montana; returned in the autumn, and in the spring of 1865 moved to his present farm in Raglan township, Harrison county. He owns one thousand acres of land, and pays especial attention to stock raising. He is a member of the A. F. & A. M. lodge. In 1852 he was married to Matilda J. Croft, who died in 1854, leaving two children. In 1856 he married Susan Croft, and has seven children.

Frederick M. Dupray, proprietor of hotel and blacksmith shop, was born in Ohio in 1831; moved to Mich. in 1843, and the next year to Jackson county, Ia. In 1852 he removed to Minn., and resided at St. Peter until 1857, when he returned to Ia. He located at Mondamin in 1876, and engaged in his present business. He was elected justice of the peace in 1879.

Charles Gilmore, farmer, is a native of O.; came to Harrison county, Ia., in 1850; his family followed the next year. He owns a farm of 1,200 acres, near Mondamin. He is one of the oldest settlers of this county.

B. Johnston, M. D., came from O. to Harrison county, Ia., in 1855; returned to O. in 1861, and enlisted in Co. G, 53rd O. Vol. as assistant surgeon; was discharged in 1862, for physical disability; returned to O., where he remained until 1869, when he returned to Harrison county, Ia., and engaged in the practice of medicine at Mondamin.

L. Maunhart, harness maker, was born in Algiers, Germany, in 1853; came to America in 1873, and located at Joliet, Ill. He came to Mondamin, Ia., in 1878, and engaged in his present business; deals in all kinds of harness, saddles, and horse furnishings found in first-class shops.

L. H. Noyes, grain dealer, is a native of O., moved to Harrison county, Ia., in 1867, and engaged in farming. In 1875 he engaged in his present business.

James Noyes, grocer, a native of O.; settled in Harrison county, Ia., in 1866, and engaged in his present business at Mondamin in Dec., 1881, on the corner of Maple and Main streets.

Z. T. Noyes, dealer in general merchandise, was born in O. in 1849; moved to Harrison county in 1856, with his parents, and settled near the present site of Mondamin; moved into the town in 1869, and was for four years employed in his father's store, previous to engaging in his present business.

Thomas Regan, dealer in general merchandise, was born in Cork county, Ireland; came to America in 1854, and settled in Conn.; removed to Chicago, Ill., in 1865. In 1868 he removed to Jones county. Ia.; thence to Mondamin, Harrison county, in 1870, and engaged in wagon making, which he followed until 1879, and then engaged in his present business. His wife is the pioneer milliner of Mondamin, having established business in 1870. Their daughter Mary, was the first child born in the place.

L. Snyder, hardware dealer, was born in Strausberg, Germany, in 1838; came to America in 1871, and located at Joliet, Ill.; moved to Mondamin, Ia., in 1880, and engaged in his present business.

P. C. Spooner, hardware dealer, was born in Vt.; moved to N. Y. at an early age and engaged in milling. In 1871 he came to Mondamin, Ia., and engaged in the grain and hardware business. A. Spooner, manager of the above house, came to Mondamin in 1871, from Omaha, Neb., and is township clerk and city recorder.

James D. Stuart, druggist, was born in Council Bluffs, Ia., in 1860. He graduated from the State Pharmacy in 1880, and in April of the same year engaged in his present business at Mondamin.

Byron Strode, jeweler, was born in O. in 1850; moved to Jones county, Ia., in 1875, and the following year came to Mondamin, Harrison county, and engaged in his present business.

MODALE.

E. Brandriff, farmer, is a native of N. Y.: moved to Ia. in 1859 and located near Council Bluffs, and was engaged in freighting to Denver, Col., until 1864, when he moved to Harrison county, and engaged in farming near Modale.

W. W. Broadhead, proprietor of billiard hall, is a native of O.; moved to Modale, Ia., in 1877 and engaged in farming. In 1881 he engaged in his present business.

Levi Crouch, dealer in groceries, is a native of Mo.: moved to Mills county, Ia., in 1851; thence to Harrison county in 1867. He engaged in his present business in 1878.

R. Christian, M. D., was born in N. Y.; moved to Jefferson, Greene county, Ia., in 1867; graduated from the Hahnaman Medical College, of Chicago, Ill., in 1874, located at Modale in 1879 and engaged in the practice of medicine.

C. J. Cutler, merchant and postmaster, is a native of Pa.; moved to Neb., in 1856. He enlisted in 1862, in Co. H, 2d Neb. Cav., and was with Gen. Sully fourteen months, on the plains; returned to Neb. and engaged in freighting. In 1866 he removed to Council Bluffs, Ia., and engaged in the grocery business. The same year he came to Modale, and in 1874 established his present business; was appointed postmaster the following year.

J. W. Huff, M. D. and druggist, was born in Harrison county, in 1857; graduated from the Rush Medical College, of Chicago, Ill., in 1881. He located at Modale, and engaged in his present business in April, 1880.

F. H. Ludwig, farmer, is a native of Pa.; moved to O. in 1855; thence to Modale, Ia., in 1869. He built the first grain house at that place.

Job Ross, stock and grain dealer, was born in Ill., in 1831; moved to Harrison county, Ia., in 1854, and engaged in farming. In 1876 he moved to Modale and established the first hardware store in the place. In 1880 he engaged in his present business.

W. A. Sharpnack, dealer in general merchandise, is a native of W. Va., and a son of Henry Sharpnack, who was one of the first settlers of Harrison county. He came to this county in 1857 and engaged in farming, until 1878, when he engaged in his present business. He also deals in grain.

W. M. Sharpnack, dealer in hardware, is a native of Va.; came with his father, John Sharpnack, to Washington county, Ia., in 1850, and four years later came to Harrison county, and engaged in farming until 1880, when he moved to Modale and engaged in his present business.

LITTLE SIOUX.

J. W. Alton, dealer in general groceries, is a native of Ill.; came to Iowa in 1875 and engaged in farming near Little Sioux, and in 1877 he engaged in his present business. He enlisted in the war of the rebellion in 1862 in Co. A, 118th Ill. Vol., and was discharged at the close of the war.

H. H. Bonney, proprietor of hotel and livery stable at Little Sioux, is a native of Pa.; removed to this place in 1865, and engaged in the grocery business. He erected the hotel in 1878, which is a first class house in all its appointments.

Colonel A. Cochran, was born in Va.; located at Little Sioux in 1854; went to Denver and Central City, Col., in 1861, and engaged in mining and mercantile business, and after four years engaged in the land business at Council Bluffs, Ia. He owns large landed property near Little Sioux, Harrison county.

C. E. Cobb, dealer in hardware and lumber, is a native of N. Y.; moved to Iowa in 1856 and engaged in farming, near Little Sioux, Harrison county. In 1874 he engaged in his present business.

B. F. Croasdale, dealer in general merchandise, was born in Pa. in 1839; moved to Council Bluffs, Iowa, in 1864, and was employed as salesman in a mercantile house until 1866, when he came to Little Sioux and engaged in his present business.

C. David, dealer in furniture, was born near Montreal, Canada, in 1856; came to Little Sioux, Iowa, in 1879 with but ten cents, to start with; is now doing a good business, and is the owner of considerable fine real estate.

Clark Ellis, druggist, was born in Ohio, in 1843, and with his widowed mother, moved to Harrison county, Iowa, in 1853. He enlisted in 1862, in Co. C, 29th Ia. Inft.; returned to this county at the close of the war, and engaged for a time in farming, after which he established his present business. He graduated from the Iowa State Pharmacy in 1880. A. M. Ellis, an older brother, now engaged in the stock business at this place, is also an old settler of this county. He enlisted in Co. H, 15th Ia.

D. M. Gamet, dealer in general merchandise, was born in Otsego county, N. Y., in 1811; moved to Ill. in 1837; thence in 1846 to Council Bluffs; remained there two years, and then removed to Glenwood, Mills county, of which place he was one of the proprietors. In 1852 he settled at Magnolia, Harrison county, and was the first recorder and treasurer of the county. Five years later he removed to Little Sioux and engaged in his present business.

Geo. T. Hope, of the firm of Hope Bros., photographers and dealers in drugs and furniture, is a native of Green county, N. Y.; moved to Ill. in 1851, and with his brother Wm. H., engaged in farming. In 1870 they moved to Little Sioux, Ia., and engaged in the mercantile business. They established their present business in 1879.

M. Johnson, wine and liquor dealer, is a native of Pottawattamie county, Ia.; moved to Harrison county in 1854 and engaged in farming. In 1874 he went to Idaho and Montana, where he spent four years; returned and engaged in his present business at Little Sioux.

Thomas J. Lanyon, postmaster at Little Sioux, was born in Pa. in 1848; moved with his parents to Monona county, Ia., in 1858; thence to this place in 1865. In 1870 he was appointed postmaster, and about the same time engaged in the fancy grocery business.

Mrs. S. J. Long, milliner, was born in Ohio, moved to Ill., and in 1864 to Salt Lake City, where she remained two years, and then settled in Little Sioux. Her husband, P. R. Long, is a native of N. Y., and is engaged in bridge and house building at this place.

M. Murray, banker, stock raiser and dealer in general merchandise, was born in Scotland in 1840; came to America at the age of seventeen years, located at Little Sioux, and was in the employ of the mail service at fifteen dollars per month until 1862, when he removed to Denver, Col., and engaged in the stock and freight business. Six years later he returned to this place and engaged in his present business. He owns a fine stock farm of several hundred acres near town, on which still stands the little old log house that he arrived at in 1857, a penniless Scotch lad. It was the first building used for a store in Harrison county.

C. W. Oden, manager of the banking and mercantile business of M. Murray, was born in Ross county, O., in 1831; moved to Ia. in 1858, and platted the town of Harlan, Shelby county; remained there until 1862, when he enlisted in Co. C, 29th Ia. Vol. He was promoted quarter-master, which office he held until the close of the war. In 1866 he located at Little Sioux and engaged in farming; was secretary of the Harrison Co. Agricultural society for fourteen years; accepted his present position in 1876.

J. L. Perkins, farmer, was born in O., in 1834; moved to Jackson county, Ia., in 1844; thence to Harrison county in 1850, and three years later located at Little Sioux. He devotes his special attention to the raising of fine varieties of potatoes. He raised over three hundred kinds in 1876. Bliss & Sons, of N. Y., offered a premium of one hundred dollars to the one raising the most potatoes from one pound of seed. Mr. P. raised 1,666¾ lbs. from one lb., winning the first and also the second premiums. As the offer was open to the world, therefore Mr. Perkins is universally pronounced the Potato King. One hundred of his potatoes averaged two pounds apiece.

Jeff. Smith, harness maker, was born in Ill.; moved to Ia. in 1868, and located at Sioux City. In 1874 he removed to Little Sioux and engaged in his present business. He deals in all kinds of single and double harness, saddles, robes, whips, etc.

J. A. Stockwell, blacksmith, is a native of Ind.; moved to Ia. in 1855, and settled in Harrison county; was one of the original proprietors of California Junction. He moved to Little Sioux in 1877, and engaged in his present business.

Reuben Wallace, M. D., was born in Mass. in 1812. He began the practice of medicine in 1845, at North Adams, Mass. In 1849 removed to St. Lawrence county, N. Y., where he remained until 1857, when he came west. At the close of the war he settled in Harrison county, and engaged in the practice of his profession.

J. S. Whiting, proprietor of billiard parlor, is a native of Mass.; moved to Wis. in 1854; thence in 1859 to Colorado, where he engaged in mining; from there he went back to Oregon and Idaho, and then back to Mass., where he remained one year, and in 1866 came to Ia. In 1875 he removed to Salt Lake City, Utah., and engaged in the bottling business. A year later he settled at Little Sioux, and engaged in his present business.

WOODBINE.

L. D. Butler, lumber dealer and farmer, was born in Ky. in 1826; removed to Clay county, Mo., in 1837 with par. nts. In 1846 was sent to England as a Mormon missionary, was gone two years, and in 1849 located at Council Bluffs; removed to Harrison county in 1853 and engaged in farming. He built the first grist mill in the county, which he sold to Dally & Clark. He engaged in the mercantile business in 1856, near the mill; moved the business to Woodbine in 1867 and was burned out the same year. He engaged in the lumber business in the spring of 1881. He owns a farm in Lincoln township of 880 acres, 160 acres in Douglas township and 200 acres in Boyer township. He has been Postmaster in Harrison county twenty years. He severed connection with the Mormon church twenty-five years ago. He was married in 1849 at Birmingham. Eng., to Anna Binnall. and has ten children.

Orrin DeWitt Cole, druggist, was born near Woodbine in 1859. His parents came to this county in 1856, and engaged in farming. The business was established in 1870, under firm name of J. S. Cole & Son, his father since retiring from the business.

N. L. Cole, furniture dealer and undertaker, was born in Indianapolis. Ind., in 1841; came to Harrison county with parents. He enlisted in the 6th Ia. Cav.; was engaged against the Indians in Neb. and Dak.; was injured while building a fort at Sioux Falls, Dak., Aug. 13th, 1865, and discharged in Oct. of the same year. He was married in Sept. 1867, to Libbie Irne. He was engaged in farming until May, 1881; bought furniture stock and building of W. Canfield. John S. Cole, father of the subject of this sketch was one of the first settlers of this county. He was a practicing physician. He was also a member of the county board five terms. Died Aug. 2nd, 1881.

L. H. Crane, deputy postmaster and grocer, was born in Rochester, Minn., in April, 1860; removed with parents to Jeddo. Harrison county, Ia., in 1862; the next year they moved to a farm two miles from Woodbine. He is a graduate of Miller's Mercantile College, of Keokuk, Ia. In 1879 he moved to Woodbine and engaged in business with his father, who was appointed postmaster in March, 1881.

W. D. Cromie, dealer in general merchandise, clothing and grain; was born June 29th, 1851, in Cecil county, Md.; moved with parents to Harrison county, Ia., in 1867. He graduated from Bailey's Commercial College, at Keokuk, Ia., in Feb., 1874. In 1875 located at Woodbine; held the office of postmaster for six years. He was married in 1877 to Florence Daly, and has one child, a son.

Joseph W. Dally, of the firm of Dally & Noyes, proprietors of the Woodbine flouring mills, was born in O. in 1829. He went to Cal. in 1852, and in 1855 settled in Hamilton county, Ia. He removed to Harrison county in 1859, and engaged in mercantile business at Magnolia. He built the Woodbine woolen mills near this place, which he ran six years, and in 1871 built the flouring mills. He is a member of the I. O. O. F., and A. F. & A. M. orders. In 1855 he was married to Miss Goodrich, of Indianapolis, Ind., who died in 1865. He afterwards married Nancy La Ferre, in Harrison county, and has four sons and six daughters.

J. H. Farnsworth, farmer, was born in O. in 1834; moved to Council Bluffs, Ia., in 1854; thence to Harrison county the same year and engaged in farming, near Woodbine. In 1864 he established the Woodbine nursery, which he recently sold to Pugsley Bros. He was married in 1855 to Olive A. Howorth. They have seven children.

George Garner, proprietor of Woodbine barber shop and temperance billiard hall, was born near Council Bluffs, Ia., in April, 1855. in 1861 removed with parents to Raglan Tp., Harrison county, and in Dec., 1881, he bought out the fixtures of O. Elkins, and keeps a strictly temperance hall, with lunch bar in connection.

H. C. Harshbarger, dealer in groceries, was born in Spencer county, Ind., in 1840; removed with parents to Mahaska county, Ia., in 1848, and to Harrison county in 1856, locating near present town of Woodbine. In 1861 he enlisted in Co. I, Neb. Inft.; was in several prominent battles, and in 1865 was discharged and returned to Harrison county. In 1865, he was elected county auditor, and county recorder in 1866, and in 1870 engaged in the mercantile business, which he continued for three years; then engaged in farming for six years, and in 1881 sold his farm and engaged in his present business. He still owns 240 acres of good farming land in the county. He was postmaster of this city three and one-half years, is a member of A. F. & A. M. order. He was married to Emily Mundy, in 1865, who died in 1870, and in 1872 he was married to Nettie Edgerton.

Sylvester B. Kibler, senior member of the firm of Kibler Bros. & Winter, dealers in general merchandise, was born in Portage county, O., in 1846; moved to Harrison county, Ia., with parents in 1853. He engaged in present business with his brother G. H. and in Aug., 1880, they took into the firm Mr. Winter. They have one of the finest buildings in the county, built in 1878, and carry a very large and complete stock of goods; are also agents for the Mason & Hamlin organs and the American sewing machine. S. B. Kibler was married in 1873, to Caroline Ellison.

A. P. Lathrop, harnessmaker, was born in Hastings, Ontario, Canada, in 1849; removed to Ill. in 1856 and learned his trade at

Morrison. He was in business in Syracuse, Otto county, Neb., two years; moved to Dunlap, Ia. in 1874, and was engaged in business with Mr. Howard of that place, four years, and removed to Woodbine in 1878. He was marshal of Dunlap two years; is member of encampment, I. O. O. F., and A. F. & A. M. orders. He was married in Shelby county, to Flora McGarvey, and has one child.

Charles F. Luce, land, loan, and collecting agent, was born in Wis. in 1860. He graduated from the Morgan Park Military Academy, in 1877; came to Harrison county, Ia., in same year locating at Woodbine engaging in lumber and grain business which he continued two years, and then engaged in stock business, which he still carries on in connection with the agency, which he established in 1881. Office in the new Boyer Bank building. He is a member of the I. O. O. F., order. In 1879 and 1880 he was deputy sheriff and jailor of Woodbine.

Capt. Wm. M. Magden, attorney at law, was born in Genesee county, N. Y., in 1818; he removed to Wayne county, Mich., and engaged in the manufacture of agricultural implements; afterwards studied law in the office of Morgan & Joslin, at Elgin, Ill., and with Gen. Baker, at Clinton, Ia., two years, and admitted to the bar in Clinton county, in Dec., 1859, Judge Dillon presiding. He practiced in that county until 1862 and enlisted in the 26th Ia. Inft., served three years, and was promoted to captain. He was in a number of prominent battles and was wounded in the right arm by a ball, in the right side by a bursting shell, and lost the ends of two fingers of the left hand. He was discharged in 1864, and returned to Clinton county; removed to Dunlap, Harrison county, in 1870, and soon after opened an office at Woodbine. He is a member of the A. F. & A. M. order. In 1855, he was married to Elizabeth Gates, at Elgin, Ill., and has ten children.

Geo. A. Mathews, of the firm of Mathews & Kling, dealers in lumber, grain and machinery, was born in Troy, Walworth county, Wis., in 1843. He was for twelve years engaged in the manufacture of brooms, at Stoughton, Wis. In 1877 he came to Woodbine, Ia., and engaged in present business, with L. M. Kellogg and Mr. Kling. The former sold his interest in the fall of 1881. Mr. M. was married in Troy, Wis., in 1867, to Mary E. Kling. They have two sons and one daughter.

John Mann, Jr., farmer, owns 240 acres in Allen township. He was born in Glasgow, Scotland, in 1853; came with parents to Woodbine, Ia., in 1871. His farm is well improved, and he makes stock raising his main object, and we may well say, has one of the finest stock farms in the county. He is a member of the I. O. O. F. lodge. He was married in April, 1881, to Candace L. Imley, of Magnolia, Ia.

E. P. Mendenhall, land, loan, tax-paying and insurance agent, was born in Guilford county, N. C., Oct. 28th, 1826; moved with

23

parents to Miami county. Ind., and in May, 1856, came to Harrison county, Ia., and engaged in farming on two hundred acres, one mile from the present town of Woodbine. He opened present land office in 1879. He was married in Miami county, Ind., to Mrs. Elizabeth Hunt, daughter of Captain Rector. They have two children.

Geo. Musgrave, publisher of the Woodbine Twiner, the county official paper, was born in Kendall, Westmoreland county, Eng., in 1837; came to America with parents in 1848; and settled in Harrison county, Ia., in 1851. He first began the printing business in St. Louis, afterwards at Council Bluffs, and then engaged in publishing the Western Star, at Magnolia, it being Harrison county's first paper; was republican in politics. In 1873 he moved his office to Logan, where he remained three years; and then sold to Geo. Ross, of Harlan, Shelby county, to which place the office was removed. Mr. Musgrave's next venture was at Tekamah, Neb.. where he published the Nebraska Advocate; finally sold out and located at Woodbine and established the Twiner, which has a subscription list of about nine hundred, and an office fitted in first-class manner.

W. C. Samson, M. D., was born in Batemantown, Knox county, O.; removed with parents to Licking county, O. In 1863 he enlisted in the 76th O. Vet. Vol., was through Gen. Sherman's campaign, march to the sea, etc., and a large number of the prominent battles; was discharged in July, 1865; returned to Ohio, and after visiting home, came to Ia., again returning to O. to attend the Medical College, at Cincinnati, from which he graduated in 1875. He then came to Cedar Rapids, Ia., and engaged in the practice of medicine with Dr. Yarnell, of that city. In the spring of 1876, removed to Woodbine and is now recognized as one of the leading physicians in the county. He was married April 4th, 1878, to Laura A. Pugsley, at Woodbine. They have one child. Dr. S. has been a member of the city council several years; is a charter member of the I. O. O. F. lodge.

Comstock Willey. farmer. was born in Asthabula county, O., in 1821; removed to Harrison county, Ia., in 1867, and located on present farm, in Boyer township; owns 170 acres of good farming land, well improved, with bearing vineyard of two hundred vines, and good young orchard. He has been justice of the peace five years: is a member of the A. F. & A. M. order. He was married in Asthabula county, O., to Rosanna Bell, and has four children.

Irving C. Wood, M. D., was born in 1857, in Franklin county, N. Y., attended the Delaware Institute, at Franklin, graduating in the literary course in 1875. He attended the Medical Department, of University, at N. Y. City, also Jefferson Medical College, at Philadelphia, Pa., where he received degree in 1880; the following spring took a practical course in operative surgery at the Philadelphia School of Anatomy, and was assistant surgeon at the Pa. hospital in out-patient surgical department one year. In July, 1881, he located at Woodbine, Ia.; office at Mr. Giddings' drug store. Dr. Wood, is already enjoying a lucrative practice. He is a member of the A. F. & A. M. order.

M. M. Vining, proprietor of Temperance billiard hall, was born in 1860, in Harrison county, Ia. He is a son of Richard Vining, one of the oldest settlers of the county. He established business in Dec., 1881; keeps for sale confectionery and cigars, but no intoxicants of any kind.

Reuben Yeisley, architect, contractor, and builder, was born in Pa. in 1836; located in Harrison county in 1858, settled at Little Sioux and worked at his trade; in 1862 was elected drainage commissioner, and in the fall of 1863, was elected recorder and treasurer of county, and at the expiration of the term, was employed by the railroad company buying rights of way and land for the company. In 1867 he engaged in mercantile business, at Magnolia, and sold out in 1870, and engaged in manufacturing woolen goods, and milling, near Woodbine; sold to Noyes & Adams in 1874, and engaged in his present business. He is a member of the A. F. & A. M. order. He was married in 1861, at Little Sioux to Effie H. Schoefield, and has one son and three daughters.

DUNLAP.

Samuel Baird, proprietor of Baird's livery stable, established in 1869, was born in 1847; removed with parents to Pa.; thence to Cumberland, Md., and in 1861 to Galesburg. Ill., when he engaged with his father and brother in the coal business. In 1863 he enlisted in the 139th Ill. Inft., and afterwards enlisted in the 8th Ill. Cav.; was discharged in 1865, and returned to Galesburg, and was employed in the flouring mills until 1869, when he moved to Dunlap and engaged in his present business. He was elected justice of the peace in 1877, which office he still holds; was mayor of Dunlap in 1877, and the first marshal of the city; is at present district deputy grand marshal of the Odd Fellows lodge. He was married in 1865, at Henderson, Ill., to Miss Sears, and has one son and two daughters.

Geo. D. Bryan, stock dealer and shipper, was born in Howard county, Ia., in 1857; moved with parents to Burritt, Ill.; thence in 1869 to Dunlap, Ia. In 1875 he was employed in Jackson's hardware store; in 1877 engaged in the stock business with his brother, T. J., as partner. They bought and shipped from Col. and Wyoming, as also in this vicinity. They also raised thoroughbred cattle. In Dec., 1880, they shipped a car load to Chicago which averaged 2,080 lbs. Geo. D. B. is now sole proprietor of the business at Dunlap. He is a member of the I. O. O. F. order.

E. K. Burch, attorney at law, was born in 1852, in Steuben
county, Ind.; removed with his parents to Hillsdale, Mich., where
he attended the Hillsdale Baptist College for five years; graduated
from the law department of the Union University of Albany, N.
Y., in 1876, and the same year was admitted to the bar, at the general term of the supreme court. He commenced practice in Dunlap, Ia., in Jan., 1879. He was admitted to the circuit court in
the fall of 1878. He is a member of the I. O. O. F. order. He
was married in Sept., 1880, at Denison, to M. S. Kuhn.

W. H. Bush, of the firm of Lowell & Bush, harness makers and
dealers in all kinds of horse furnishings, was born in 1849, in Morris
county, N. J.; moved to Des Moines, Ia., in 1869; there learned
the mason's trade with Morris & Naphey, and moved to Denison,
Ia., in 1873; worked at the trade until 1881, when he formed his
present partnership. They keep two men employed, and in the
spring of 1882 will move business to larger building.

G. W. Chamberlain, of the firm of Chamberlain & Lyman, dealers in groceries and queensware, was born in Feb., 1838, at Grand
Detour, Ill. He enlisted in the 75th Ill. Inft., and was discharged
in 1863, on account of lung disease; returned to Ill., and in 1868
came to Dunlap, Ia., and opened a restaurant, which he sold in
1874; remained out of business two years: then engaged in his
present business with Geo. Baker, who sold to H. Gleason, and he
to Mr. Lyman in 1881. He was town recorder two years, and member of the city council. He was married in Sterling, Ill., to Mary
Ellmaker, who engaged in the millinery business in 1869, which
she still continues, carrying a large and complete stock of goods,
at her location on Upper Ia. avenue.

Thomas M. Clements, grain dealer, was born in Sheffield, Ill.,
June 6th, 1865; moved with parents to Geneseo, Ill.; thence to
Greenwood. He attended the High school at Chicago two years;
came to Dunlap, Ia., in 1879, and formed a partnership with F. E.
Pike in the grain and agricultural implement business: sold his
interest in agricultural implement business to Mr. Pike in Feb.,
1881; bought Mr. P.'s interest in the elevator in Dec., 1881, and
now occupies what is known as the old Grange elevator.

E. J. Cronkleton, of the firm of Cronkleton & Warren, contractors and builders, was born in Delaware county, O., in 1835;
learned his trade at Columbus, and in 1856 moved to Lyons, Ia.,
and the next year moved to Davenport. In 1861 he enlisted in
the 2nd Ia. Cav. He was in a number of important battles, and
was taken prisoner at Ripley, Miss., in July, 1864, and imprisoned
at Cahaba, Ala.; was released at the close of the war and discharged
in 1865, at Davenport. In the spring of 1866 he went to Montana; returned in the fall, and located at Fort Dodge; in the summer of 1867 came to Dunlap and established his present business.
He married Julia O'Hare at Boone, Ia., and has four children.

M. C. Dally, of the firm of Patterson, Dally & Co., dealers in general merchandise, was born in Hamilton county, Ia., in 1857; came to Harrison county with parents in 1859. He was book-keeper for Mitchell & Laub, for three and one-half years previous to engaging in his present business.

Frank P. Eaton, painter and auctioneer, was born in Concord, N. H., in 1844; removed with his parents to Cass county, Mich. In 1862 enlisted in Co. I, 4th Mich. Cav.; was in several important battles; was discharged in Sept., 1864, on account of injuries re-ceived from being thrown from a horse; returned to Mich. and be-came a member of the firm of Eaton Bros. & Co., carriage and wagon manufacturers, at Dowagiac. In 1867, he engaged in traveling for a Chicago house, which he continued until 1871; then settled at Dunlap, Ia., and engaged in farming in Harrison township for three years, and in 1874 was appointed deputy sheriff, under J. J. Peck; was also constable, marshal and street commis-sioner of Dunlap. He is a member of J. G. Shattuck's detective association of Dubuque, Ia. He was married Dec. 17th, 1868, to Florence Thomas, at Dowagiac. Mich. He is a member of the I. O. O. F. lodge.

D. B. Erisman, wholesale dealer and manufacturer of cigars and tobacco, factory No. 220; was born in Lancaster, Penn., in 1844. He learned his trade there, and then established business in Lincoln, Neb., which he continued four and one-half years, and in July, 1881, established his present business in Dunlap, Ia. Keeps three men employed, and has a fine trade.

S. D. Fox, of the firm of Fox & Dabelstein, dealers in an l manu-facturers of boots and shoes, was born in Manchester, Eng., in 1847; learned his trade, and in 1869 came to America; located at Sylvania, O., where he engaged in boot and shoe making. In 1874 he removed to Bolton City, Col., and engaged in business; the next year came to Dunlap, Ia., and engaged in his present business and partnership. In 1875 he was married at Grand Rapids, Mich., to Miss Dabelstein, and has three children.

A. H. Hazlett, M. D., was born in Richland county, O., in 1837; attended the Hayesville Academy, and in 1857 removed to Toledo, Ia., where he studied medicine with Dr. Baldy. In 1861 he en-listed in the 14th Ia. Inft.; was in a number of important battles; was promoted to first lieutenant, and discharged in 1865; returned to Ia. and located in Johnson county. He resumed the study of medicine, and engaged in teaching school until 1872, when he went to Iowa City and attended the medical department of the Iowa University, and the next year attended the Eclectic Medical In-stitute at Cincinnati, O., from which he graduated in 1874. He engaged in the practice of his profession at Grand Junction, Ia., until, 1878, when he moved to Dunlap, where he has established a large practice. In Sept., 1866, he was married to Miss Kibler, of Johnson county, Iowa.

R. B. Hillas, dealer in general merchandise, was born in Vt. in 1836; moved to Detroit, Mich., at an early age. He enlisted in the 19th Ill. Inft.; was with the Army of the Cumberland, under Gens. Sherman and Thomas; was discharged in 1865; went to Chicago and was engaged in the house of J. V. Farwell & Co.; in 1876 removed to Dunlap, Ia., and engaged in his present business, which was the first business house established in the town. The establishment was destroyed by fire in 1873. His present store building was erected in 1878, is filled with a fine stock of goods, and has merchant tailoring in connection. He has been a member of the city council several years.

W. T. Howard, saddler and harnessmaker, was born in Mercer county, Pa., in 1846; moved to Fayette county, Ia., locating near West Union, in 1855, with his parents, who engaged in farming. In 1867 he removed to Kossuth county, and two years later to Denison, Crawford county; engaged for a time in teaching school at Dow City, and in 1870 removed to Dunlap, and engaged in his present business. He keeps three men employed, and does an extensive business. He has been mayor of the city, and is a member of the I. O. O. F. lodge and encampment. He was married in 1870, at Denison, to Mary E. Eaton, and has one child.

Walter Kavanaugh, proprietor of billiard hall and saloon, in basement of Lehan's Opera Block; established in 1879; entrance on first street, dealer in wines, beer, and cigars, and has two fine Brunswick & Balke tables.

E. W. Lyman, of the firm of Chamberlain & Lyman, dealers in groceries and queensware, was born in N. Y. in 1850; engaged in milling until 1870, when he removed to Dunlap, Ia., and was in the employ of the C. and N. W. Ry. until 1881, when he engaged in his present business. He is a member of the I. O. O. F. order. In 1874 he was married in Dunlap to Miss Lowry. They have three children.

Chas. Mackenzie, attorney at law, was born in N. Y. City in 1845; removed with his parents to Dubuque, Ia., in 1849; graduated from Beloit College, Wis., in 1862, and the same year enlisted in the 9th In. Vol. Inft.; was in several important battles, and was discharged in 1875. He was secretary of a government commission in New Mexico one year; returned to Dubuque and was engaged as principal of the public schools of that city for one and one-half years, and was associate editor of the Dubuque *Times* one year; studied law and was admitted to the bar in 1868; engaged in the practice of law, and in 1871 removed to Eldora; thence to Mason City, and in the spring of 1875 located at Sioux City and engaged in the practice of law with M. B. Davis, where he remained until Jan., 1881, when he removed to Dunlap.

C. D. Mitchell, of the firm of Mitchell & Thompson, dealers in general merchandise, was born in Athens, O., in 1842. In 1862 he enlisted in the 7th O. Cav.; was in a number of important engagements, and was promoted to captain and assistant adjutant general; was discharged July 4th, 1865, and returned to O., and in May, 1866, came to Harrison county and engaged in stock raising; in July, 1867, established his present business with H. C. Laub, of Denison; afterwards, Mr. L. retiring, he carried on the business alone, until forming his present partnership in Sept., 1879. They carry a large stock, occupying the three floors of their large store building. Mr. M. is a member of the A. F. & A. M. order.

J. T. Noonan, proprietor of the Dunlap meat market, was born in Va. in 1851; removed to Tenn. with parents, and in 1861 to Ky.; thence to Galway, Ireland; remained seven years; returned to America; lived in N. Y., N. J., and Tenn., and finally, in 1872, settled at Dunlap, Ia., and for two years engaged in farming; then was employed in the meat market of Dunham & Guilford, and in 1879 established his present business. He is a member of the city council; also the fire department; is president of the Ancient Order of Hibernians; was county delegate of that order in 1881, and is vice-president of the Dunlap land league.

J. B. Patterson, of the firm of Patterson, Dally & Co., was born in Highland county, O., in 1847; moved to Harrison county, Ia., 1867; was engaged in clerking for R. B. Hillas two years, then for Mitchell & Laub eight and one-half years, and June 26th, 1879, formed his present partnership. He enlisted in the late rebellion in 1863, in the 18th O. Inft.; was in several battles, and was discharged in the autumn of 1865. He was married in Oct., 1871, to Maggie Farren, and has three children.

H. E. Pease, proprietor of Sheltered Twin livery barn, was born in Mich. in 1845; went to Chicago in 1860, and was employed as newsboy on the C. and N. W. Ry. for about eighteen months; then as brakeman in Tenn. during the war; then promoted to conductor, and at the close of the war, located at Jefferson, Green county, Ia., and was engaged in running dray, express, mail and delivery wagons until 1868, when he removed to Dunlap and engaged in his present business. He has been deputy sheriff two terms; also constable, street commissioner, and marshal of this city. He is a member of the Legion of Honor beneficiary insurance society. He was married in Dunlap in 1871 to Julia Ford, and has one child.

Z. W. Pease, blacksmith and wagonmaker, was born in Blissfield, Mich., in 1842; learned his trade at Adrian, and in 1870 moved to Dunlap, Ia., and rented a shop and engaged in his present business, which has increased so that he bought the building in 1873, and in 1881 moved it back and erected in front a large two story shop with three forges; keeps three men constantly employed. He is a member of the I. O. O. F. lodge and encampment. In 1868 he married Lizzie Francisco, at Blissfield, Mich. They have one son and two daughters.

Dr. B. F. Philbrook, one of the oldest established dentists in the county, was born in Camden, Me., in 1853; removed with his parents to O., and received his education at the Ohio Weslyan University, at Delaware; moved to Ia., and engaged in the practice of dentistry with T. E. Weeks, of Council Bluffs; remained eighteen months, and in April, 1879; located at Dunlap. He has one of the best fitted offices in the west, with Johnson's dental engine, extension instrument, bracket, surgeon's case of liquid nitrous oxide gas, for th ' painless extraction of teeth, the pedal lever chair, with which any position can be obtained for the ease of the patient and operator. He fills appointments at Logan the first Tuesday in each month, and remains three days, and also goes to Woodbine one day each month. He is foreman of the fire department of Dunlap, and a member of the Royal Arcanum, beneficiary order. In Nov., 1879, he was married at Omaha, Neb., to Lucy Hartry.

Frank E. Pike, dealer in agricultural implements, was born in Erie county, N. Y., in 1851; moved with parents to Sterling, Ill., in 1856; thence removed to Boone, Ia., and was employed as brakeman on the C. & N. W. Ry., for nine months; then was promoted to conductor, in which position he continued until 1879, when he came to Dunlap and engaged in the grain and agricultural implement business in partnership with T. M. Clements. In Dec., 1880, he purchased Mr. C's. interest in the machinery business, and a year later sold his interest in the grain business to Mr. C. Mr. Pike handles the best goods in his line that are made, and keeps constantly on hand a large stock. He is a member of the beneficiary insurance society. He was married at Carroll, Ia., Jan. 1st, 1879, to Emma S. Town.

J. H. Read, of the firm of J. H. Read & Co., bakers, grocers and confectioners, was born in Kendall county, Ill., in May, 1855; removed with parents to Bureau county, and in 1868, came to Ia., and located in Cerro Gordo county; removed to Dunlap in 1878, and established his present business; has oyster and ice cream parlors in connection; has Vernon's patent steam coffee and peanut roaster, and keeps constantly on hand new-made candies. He is a member of the I. O. O. F., and A. F. & A. M. lodges. He was married at Dunlap in Aug., 1879, to Miss Zimmerman.

Issacher Scholfield, miller and proprietor of the Dunlap mills, was born in Delaware county, O., in 1833; moved with parents to Wis., and located near Milwaukee, where his father engaged in milling, mercantile business and farming, and he in attending the Quaker Academy in Belmont county, O.; and in 1853 engaged in land speculating in Marshall county, Ia., which he continued for three years; then entered into partnership with his brother, and built a mill one and one-half miles north of Le Grand on the Iowa river; this he sold in 1866, and built a mill on Timber Creek in Marshall county, which he sold in 1869, and came to Harrison county, locating permanently in 1871, and commenced building his present mill on the Boyer river. He has a fine stock farm, adjoining the mill, of two thousand acres, and one of the finest conservatories in the west. He is also proprietor of the Dunlap *Reporter*. He was married May 7th, 1857, at La Grange, Ia., to Mary H. Hanks, who is a cousin of President Abraham Lincoln. She is editress of that portion of the paper devoted to home decoration, by "Aunt Mary."

C. H. Sears, proprietor of meat market, was born Jan. 6th, 1852, in Knox county, Ill.; removed to Dunlap in 1869; was in the employ of S. M. Williams, and afterwards with Mitchell & Laub; then engaged in farming for six years, and in Dec., 1881, purchased his present market of B. J. Moore. In 1875, he was married in Ill. to Ida C. Hickman. They have three children.

L. A. Sherman, dealer in groceries, queensware, boots and shoes, was born in Fairfield, Vt., in 1854; moved with his parents to Texas in 1860, and in 1870 they came to Dunlap, and his father, J. H. Sherman, established the present business; in 1876 he became a partner with his father, and two years later bought him out; has been town treasurer one term, and is a member of the Iowa land league. In 1877, he was married at Elk Horn, Wis., to Fannie Sabine, and has one child, a daughter.

D. P. Simmons, of the firm of Simmons & Co., dealers in hardware and agricultural implements, was born in Courtlandt county, N. Y., in 1849; removed with parents to Beloit, Wis., in 1854, where he attended the Beloit College; then traveled for Northwestern Paper Co., of Chicago; then for Booth & Hinman, of Beloit, and in 1873 engaged in the boot and shoe business. In 1879, he removed to Dunlap, Ia., and bought out the stock of Mr. Jackson, and with T. S. Simmons, engaged in his present business. They handle goods from the leading manufactories, and employ a firstclass tinner. He is a member of the Morning Star lodge, number ten; also the A. F. & A. M. order. He is a member of the city council. In 1876 he was married at Rockford, Ill., to Alice Early, and has one child.

Geo. W. Thompson, of the firm of Mitchell & Thompson, was born Mar. 26th, 1842, in Whiteside county, Ill. He enlisted in Aug., 1862, in the 8th Ill. Cav.; was in several important battles, and in Dec., 1863, was transferred to the command of Co. C, U. S. colored troops; was discharged in Dec., 1865, and returned to Morrison, Ill., and engaged in the study of law; was admitted to the bar in Nov., 1866, and practiced there until the spring of 1869, when he came to Dunlap, Ia., where he continued the practice of law, until the organization of the Dunlap bank in 1871, of which he was a stockholder and cashier; remained in the banking business until Sept., 1879, when he formed his present partnership. He has been chairman of the county republican central committee, and a delegate to state conventions, and is well known as one of the county's leading republican politicians. He is a member of the A. F. & A. M., I. O. O. F., K. of P., and G. A. R. orders. Dec. 21st, 1865, he was married to Susan Forrer, and has five sons.

J. R. Wheeler, dealer in lumber and coal, was born in N. Y. in 1834; removed to Eau Claire, Wis., in 1854, and engaged in the lumber business. In 1861 he enlisted in the 16th Wis. Inft.; was wounded in the face by a bullet at Shiloh; carries two gun-shot wounds in his legs, and received injuries at Atlanta; was discharged in April, 1865; returned to Wis. and engaged in shipping lumber, and in Nov., 1866, established lumber yards at Denison and Woodbine, and the next year established a yard at Dunlap. He sold the first lumber sold in Crawford and Harrison counties. He established a yard at Blair, Neb., in 1868. He has been a member of the city council of Dunlap for several years. In 1875 he was married in Fremont county, Ia., to N. E. Tyler, and has one child, a son.

John Weed, contractor and builder, was born in O. in 1825; learned his trade at Orrville, and moved to Mich. In 1850, went to Cal., and in 1853 returned to Allegan county, Mich., and worked at his trade five years; then moved to Kane county, Ill.; engaged in farming until 1861, when he enlisted in the 8th Ill. Cav.; was in numerous engagements, and July 20th, 1865, was discharged, and returned to Ill., and worked at his trade until 1866, when he moved to Dunlap, Ia., there being at the time only one house where the city now stands. He was married in May, 1870, at Woodbine, to Martha Willey, and has three children.

Tilton & Weeks, proprietors of livery, feed and sale barn, have stable room for thirty horses; board private rigs, and keep fine rigs for hire. They came to Dunlap from Ogle county, Ill., in 1878, and engaged in farming until entering their present business in the spring of 1881.

MAGNOLIA.

Capt. George S. Bacon, farmer, was born in Cayuga county, N. Y., in Sept., 1825. He moved to Washington, D. C., where he attended the Columbia College; graduated in the regular course in 1849, and afterwards taught in the College. He moved to Fairmont, W. Va.; thence in 1856 to Harrison county, Ia., and located on the farm of one hundred and forty acres, where he now resides. On this farm is an extensive orchard of fifteen hundred bearing apple trees. He enlisted in 1862, was first lieutenant of Co. C., 29th Ia. Inft., until the death of Capt. Fuller, when he was appointed

Capt. He was in a number of important battles, and was wounded at Jenkins' Ferry, Ark., left on the field for dead, captured and held in prison thirteen months. He was exchanged in May, 1865, and returned with the last lot of prisoners. He was discharged in August of the same year. He has been treasurer of Harrison county two terms. In 1850 he married Mrs. Caroline Murphy, at Magnolia. They have two daughters.

RIVER SIOUX.

B. F. Bonney, dealer in groceries, is a native of Pa.; moved to Ia., in 1857; settled in Harrison county. and engaged in farming. He engaged in his present business in River Sioux in 1877.

James Bowie, dealer in drugs and groceries, was born in Ireland in 1821; came to America in 1840, and located in O. He removed to Little Sioux, Ia., in 1865, and in 1879 engaged in his present business at River Sioux.

Henry Herring, dealer in general merchandise, was born in Adams county, Pa.; moved to Ia. in 1857, and engaged in farming. In 1878 he engaged in his present business at River Sioux. He is also a dealer in hardware and lumber.

R. Newton, agent for the S. C. & P. Ry. at River Sioux, is a native of N. Y.; moved to Boone county, Ia.; in 1864; thence to Green county, and in 1868 settled in Harrison county. He was the first agent for this road, and billed the first freight on the road.

O'BRIEN COUNTY.

O'Brien County is the second from the west line and the second from the north line of the State, is twenty-four miles square, containing a superficial area of 576 square miles, and is divided into sixteen townships.

The largest stream is the Little Sioux River, which crosses the southeast corner. Henry Creek rises in the northeastern part of the county, draining several townships, while Waterman and Mill Creeks flow through the central and southern townships, and are all branches of the Little Sioux. Floyd River rises in several branches in the northwestern part of the county, affording drainage to several townships. The supply of timber is very limited, being mostly confined to groves on the Little Sioux, in the southeastern corner of the county, and is chiefly oak, hickory, maple, elm and cottonwood. When protected from the fires timber grows rapidly, and many of the settlers have promising groves of planted trees. The soil of this region is exceedingly productive, and in its wild state produces luxuriant crops of native grass, which is excellent for pasturage or hay. The bottom or table lands along the streams, are composed of a deep, rich vegetable mold, on a sub-soil resembling clay mixed with gravel. The soil of the upland prairies is the highly productive bluff deposit of this part of the State, with a vegetable coating, and produces in great perfection all kinds of grain and vegetables. The surface is generally undulating, and susceptible of easy cultivation. There are no exposures of rocks "in place," or in quarries, in the county, the only stone being the boulders that are found scattered over the surface, and are mostly granite, red-quartzite, with a few magnesian limestone. The material of the bluff formation is manufactured into very good bricks, and this, of course, is abundant. Excellent pure water is easily obtained in all places at a few feet below the surface. The great abundance of excellent wild grass and pure water renders this a fine region for stock-raising, especially where provision is made for winter shelter. In this, as well as other counties in this part of the State, settlers must plant trees to insure a future supply of fuel, and thus may soon obviate the necessity of depending upon coal shipped from other parts of the state.

The first white settlers in O'Brien County were H. H. Waterman and family, who on the 11th day of July, 1856, located on the northeast quarter of section 26, township 94, range 39. They removed here from Bremer County, Iowa, but were formerly from the State of New York.

The county was organized in 1860, the first election being held at the house of H. H. Waterman, where the following first county officers were chosen: J. C. Furber, County Judge; H. H. Waterman, Treasurer and Recorder; Archibald Murray, Clerk and County Surveyor. The first county seat was at a place called O'Brien, in the southeast corner of the county, where the principal settlement was made prior to the construction of the Sioux City & St. Paul Railroad. The first district court was held by Judge Henry Ford. The first religious meeting held in the county assembled at the home of pioneer Waterman, while Mrs. Waterman taught the first school at O'Brien. The first newspaper was the *O'Brien Pioneer*, commenced by B. F. McCormack and J. R. Pumphrey.

At the general election of 1872 a vote was taken on the question of the permanent location of the county seat, which resulted in favor of the geographical center of the county. Accordingly a town was laid out at that point, to which the name of Primghar was given. At the time the surveyors were engaged in the work of laying off the town plat, the persons present were Messrs. Pumphrey, Roberts, Inman, McCormack, Green. Hays, Albright and Rerick. The initials of these names in the order given form the word *Primghar*, and hence it was agreed that this should be the name of the new town. The first house on the town site was erected by J. R. Pumphrey for county purposes. The next was a house of public entertainment, erected by C. F. Albright.

Present County officers are: T. J. Alexander, Treasurer; J. L. E. Peck, Auditor; W. N. Strong, Clerk; H. Sprague, Recorder; D. Algyr, County Superintendent; W. C. Green, Sheriff; J. H. Smith, Surveyor; C. Longshore, Coroner.

Population of O'Brien County according to the census of 1880 was 4,156. Its population is now estimated at about 5,500. The towns in the County are: Primghar, situated in the center of the county; Sheldon, in the northwest corner; Sanborn, seven miles east of Sheldon, in the northern part of the county; Hartley, in the northeast part of the county, and O'Brien, in the southeast part of the county.

The Sioux City & St. Paul Railroad passes through the northeastern edge of the county, forming a junction at Sheldon with the Chicago, Milwaukee & St. Paul Railroad, which traverses the county east and west, passing through Sheldon. Sanborn and Hartley.

PRIMGHAR.

Primghar's closest railroad station is six miles, north, on the line of the C., M. & St. P., and its next nearest established station is Hosper, on the S. C. & St. P. R. R., some fourteen miles west.

Primghar has been the county seat since 1872. It is located at the center of the county on a high and well drained prairie, twenty-five miles from Cherokee, twenty-eight from Spencer, and twenty-eight from Sibley. The place is laid out with a public park, which has been planted with forest trees, and as it is surrounded by a region of great fertility, will doubtless continue a steady and a healthy growth. The town is in Summit Township.

The following humorous acrostic, descriptive of the origin of the name of the town, has been published heretofore:

P umphrey, the Treasurer, drives the first nail—
R oberts, the donor, is quick on his trail,
I nman dips slily his first letter in,
M cCormack adds M which makes the full Prim;
G reen, thinking of groceries, gives them a G,
H ayes drops them an H, without asking a fee,
A lbright, the joker, with his jokes all at par,
R erick brings up the rear, and crowns all PRIMGHAR.

W. C. Green built the first store in Primghar in 1872. The first dwelling was built by A. H. Willets. The population is about 200.

The present township officers are: J. Harris, T. G. Stewart, J. L. Rerick, Trustees; D. Algyr, Clerk; A. H. Willets, R. C. Tifft, Justices of the Peace; W. H. Willets, G. W. Ginger, Constables.

Summit Township's first teacher was Clara Healy, who taught school in a building erected in Highland, and used as a store and postoffice by Mr. Paine. This building was moved to Primghar and used for a Court House. Afterwards it was used for a drug store; then as a printing office. This building has since been moved to Sanborn by A. H. Willets.

The first paper printed in the county was conducted by L. B. Raymond & Co.

A school house was built in 1874, size 40x60 feet; two stories high, with two departments. It is a handsome and substantial building.

The members of the first Board of Education were: A. J. Edwards, President: J. T. Stearns, A. H. Willets. Present Board: W. W. Johnson, President; J. A. Smith, W. N. Strong, D. .W Inman, Treasurer; W. H. Willets, Secretary.

The cost of the school building was $3,200. S. Harris is the principal. Miss Ive Inman, Assistant. The total enrollment is 59 pupils.

The Court House was built in 1875, is 30x40 feet in dimensions with an addition, 10x14 feet; is two stories high, the upper part being used for the court room, and the first floor for offices. The cost was $5,000. The court yard is enclosed with a nice board fence, and the yard planted with a nice growth of soft maple trees.

The *Primghar Times* is a weekly paper, Schee & Achorn, proprietors. The first issue was January 12th, 1882. It is a seven-column folio, Republican in politics, and has a circulation of 600. Mr. Bundy is the editor.

There are in Primghar, a general store, hardware store, agricultural implement store, bank, meat market, lumber yard, newspaper, hotel, furniture store, drug store, blacksmith shop, grocery and saloon.

At the Methodist Episcopal Conference in Sioux City, held October, 1871, the Rock Rapids Mission was organized. This Mission took in the counties of Lyon, Sioux, Osceola and O'Brien. Rev. Ira Brashears was put in charge of this mission. At that time there were two societies in O'Brien County, with a membership of about twenty people. The M. E. Society in Primghar was organized in 1873. C. W. Clifton organized the first society in O'Brien County in 1871. Present officers of Primghar Society: T. J. Alexander, D. Bysom, Mr. Robinson, Trustees. Membership, twenty-four. The Sabbath School averages an attendance of sixty pupils. D. Bysom is the Superintendent. The church was built in 1880 at a cost of $1,300, is 26x50 feet in dimensions. There is also a parsonage.

Abiff Lodge No. 347, A. F. & A. M., was instituted in 1874. The charter was granted in 1875. Charter members: H. Day, A. H. Willets. Geo. W. Schee. D. H. Wheeler, E. C. Foskett, J. T. Stearns, J. C. Doling. W. Pursel, C. W. Inman, W. H. Brown, M. Dimon, A. B. Husted, S. J. Jordan. First officers: H. Day, W. M.; A. H. Willets, S. W.; G. W. Schee. J. W.; D. H. Wheeler, Treasurer; E. C. Foskett, Secretary; J. T. Stearns. S. D.; J. C. Doling. J. D. Present officers: A. H. Willets, W. M.; S. Harris. S. W.; D. Algyr, J. W.; E. C. Foskett, Secretary; T. J. Alexander, Treasurer. Membership, twenty. Meetings are held every Saturday on or before the full moon, in the Court House.

SHELDON.

This town was named after Israel Sheldon, who was a large stockholder in the Sioux City & St. Paul Railroad. Sheldon is 240 miles from St. Paul and fifty-eight miles from Sioux City. The country around Sheldon was settled several years before the town started. The railroad reached Sheldon July 3d, 1872. The first building was erected by S. C. Highly, for a saloon, in July, 1872; the second, by H. A. Fife, in the same year, and was used for a store. B. F. Bushnell and D. A. W. Perkins erected buildings the same year.

There have been two additions to the town, namely: Islinville and Hicksville. The population of the town is 1,200.

Sheldon is located at the crossing of the Iowa and Dakota Division of the C., M. & St. Paul Railway and the Sioux City and St. Paul Railway, and in the northwest part of O'Brien county, fifteen miles northwest of Primghar. The Main street runs east and west. This street slopes both east and west from the center of the town.

The depot was completed August 4th, 1872. The first dwelling was built by B. Jones in September, 1872; J. Wykoff followed in October of the same year. The first newspaper was the *Sheldon Mail*, by Raymond, January 1st, 1873. He was followed by Perkins, who was succeeded by J. F. Glover, the paper finally passing into the hands of its present editor and proprietor, F. T. Piper.

The first school was taught by Columbia Robinson in L. S. Bradley's lumber office. This building was also used for church purposes. The first general store was opened by B. E. Bushnell; the first marriage was that of Mr. and Mrs. Thomas DeLong, in January, 1873, at the Sheldon Hotel, H. C. Lane, Justice of the Peace, officiating; the first birth was a child born to Mrs. James Wykoff; the first death, a child of Patrick Walsh; the first postmaster was A. J. Buck: the first school house was built in 1873, and was taught by J. M. Webb.

Sheldon was laid out and platted by the Railroad Company in 1872. The town was incorporated in 1876. First officers: H. B Wyman, Mayor; L. F. Bennett, Recorder; J. M. Stephenson, S. W. Harrington, C. Allen, Geo. Boutelle, James Wykoff, Trustees; Geo. Hill, Marshal; E. F. Parkhurst, Assessor; H. C. Lane, Treasurer; R. Dodge, E. M. Brady, T. Holmes, G. Haskman, J. L. Kenney, Supervisors.

Present officers: James Wykoff, Mayor; F. H. Nash, Recorder; W. L. Ayres, Treasurer; F. W. Houck, Assessor; D. McKay, Marshal; Geo. Hills, Street Commissioner; J. A. Brown, S. C. Nash, J. Shinski, D. S. White, Jr., H. S. Islin, F. Frisbee, Councilmen.

The *Sheldon Mail*, previously mentioned, is a seven-column quarto; Republican; circulation, 960 copies. The *Sheldon News* is a weekly paper, started in June, 1879, with B. F. McCormack as editor and proprietor; it then changed to the hands of A. C. Satterlee & F. M. McCormack; then to A. W. Sleeper & Bro. Subsequently it was purchased by J. F. Ford, its present editor and proprietor. The *News* is a seven-column quarto; Republican; circulation, 700. While run by B. F. McCormack, the paper was independent in politics; under Satterlee it was Democratic, and under F. M. McCormack it was a Greenback organ.

The Sheldon Flouring Mill was built in 1879, is a frame structure, 60x70 feet, three stories high, and cost about $35,000; has six run of stone and four set of rollers; capacity, 200 barrels per day. The mill is furnished with the most modern machinery for manufacturing patent flour, and was built by J. H. Islin & Co. It is at present in the hands of Sleeper Bros.

There are in Sheldon, three general stores, two hardware stores, two drug stores, two boot and shoe stores, one grocery, one clothing store, two agricultural implement establishments, three blacksmith shops, two banks, three hotels, two meat markets, two saloons, two millinery stores, three grain elevators, one flouring mill, three restaurants, one barber shop, one merchant tailor, one jewelry store, two furniture stores, two newspapers, three lumber yards, two harness shops, two livery barns, two flour and feed stores, and two dray lines.

CHURCHES, SCHOOLS AND SOCIETIES.

Episcopal Society.—Organized in 1880 by J. H. and H. S. Islin and R. B. Arden. The first pastor was Rev. Hale Townsend, of Emmettsburg. First officers: D. C. Bothwell, H. S. Islin, and R. B. Arden. R. B. Arden is lay-leader. Services are held once each month. Lay-services are held three times each month, under charge of Bishop W. S. Perry, of Davenport. E. N. Toncey is Warden. There is a Ladies' Aid Society connected with this mission. This society has a building in course of erection, which will be completed during the coming spring. The building will be 46x 26 feet, and will have a steeple sixty feet high. The seating capacity will be ninety. The cost will be $2,000. This church is situated in Islinsville, one of the additions to the town. The lot was donated by the C., St. P., M. & O. Railroad in 1881. The membership is twenty. Services are at present held in the Congregational church. The present pastor is Rev. S. H. Johnston who came from England twenty-five years ago, and settled in Tennessee; then came to Sheldon, and took pastoral charge in 1881. He resides at Spencer, where he is in charge of "The Church in the House." The subscriptions for building were furnished principally by Eastern parties, Sheldon giving generously according to her ability.

Congregational Society.—Organized in 1874, by Rev. Mr. Covey. The first pastor was Rev. Mr. Wiard, who was followed by Rev. J. A. Palmer. The present pastor is Rev. E. Southworth, who took charge in April, 1878. Membership, about forty. There is a Sabbath School also, with an attendance of about forty pupils. O. F. Young is the Superintendent. The church edifice was erected in 1874, size 30x50 feet; seating capacity, 160; plain frame building, cost over $2,000. First officers: H. P. Holyoke, M. G. McClellan, W. C. Butterfield, Trustees. Services were held in the school house previous to the building of the church. Present officers: W. L. Ayres, M. J. McClellan, A. W. Husted, Trustees; O. F. Young, Clerk; A. B. Nash, Treasurer.

Methodist Episcopal Society.—Organized in 1874; first pastor, Rev. J. B. Starkey; then in order following, Revs. W. B. Hastings, C. W. Bryan, W. M. Edgar. Present pastor, Rev. J. W. Lothian. Membership, about forty-two. There is a Sabbath School with an attendance of sixty pupils. F. H. Zander is the Superintendent. The church edifice was built in 1881, and dedicated September 4th, 1881. It is a very fine building, 40x60 feet, with a seating capacity of 275, and cost $4,500. The society held meetings in Husted's Hall previous to the erection of this building. Present officers: J. A. Brown, D. A. Elder, C. Hook, G. M. Graham, Trustees. There is a parsonage in connection. The Stewards are: F. Brown, D. W. Wellman, F. Potter.

24

Catholic Society.—Organized in the spring of 1880, by D. O'Donnell. P. Guinther, Rev. J. Smith and J. Shinski. Rev. Father Lenehan, of Sioux City, first had charge of this Society; then Rev. Father P. Lynch. Rev. John Riley is the present pastor. First officers: D. O'Donnell, P. Guinther, J. Shinski, Trustees. These Trustees procured a donation of three lots from the Sioux City & St. Paul Railroad Company in 1880. A building was erected in the winter of 1880 and 1881, 37x60 feet in dimensions. It is a frame building, seating 600 people. It has a gallery twenty feet wide extending across the south end of the building. The cost was $2,500. The society previously held services in the school house, also in the town hall. Membership, about sixty families. Present officers: W. Gavin, J. Shinski, P. Guinther, Trustees.

Independent School District.—Organized in 1876. It has a fine frame building, containing four departments, which cost $5,300. First Board of Education: C. Allen, J. C. Elliott, A. B. Nash, J. A. Brown. The first term of school in the independent district was held in 1877. The first teacher was G. S. Mann; Kate O'Donnell, Assistant. The building is furnished with the latest improved seats and apparatus. Present Board of Education: J. Wykoff, President; S. H. Ladd, E. A. Ward, Mrs. A. Morton, Mrs. O. E. Waggoner, Mrs. Geo. H. Boutelle, Directors; E. C. Brown, Treasurer; F. E. Wyman, Secretary. The present teachers are: W. S. Wilson, Principal; Sarah Clark, Assistant; Mrs. F. C. Marcussen, Mrs. A. C. Green. The present school building was erected in 1879 at a cost of building and furniture, of $5,300, is 40x60 feet in dimensions, two stories high, and has four rooms. The average attendance is 117.

Northwestern Agricultural Association.—Organized in February, 1880. First officers: Henry Hollenbeck, of Sioux County, President; R. F. Andrews, of Osceola County, Vice President; H. Cook, of Lyon County, Secretary; J. I. Hartendower, of O'Brien County, Treasurer. This society extends over the four above named counties. The first fair was held in September, 1880, at Sheldon. The fair grounds are located here. Present officers: J. S. Kenney, of O'Brien County, President; J. R. Cook, of Lyon County, Vice President; C. F. Wyatt, of Osceola County, Secretary; H. Hollenbeck, of O'Brien County, Treasurer; D. S. White, of O'Brien County, Deputy Treasurer. A fair is held once each year. Forty acres of land have been leased for ten years, and are enclosed with a good board fence eight feet high. There are a half-mile track, floral hall, sheds, etc., etc.

Mistletoe Lodge No 376, A. F. & A. M.—Instituted June 26th, 1876. Charter members: H. B. Wyman, E. M. Winslow, J. C. Elliot, J. A. Brown, S. W. Harrington, J. D. Bunce, E. A. Ward, J. A. Waggoner, R. Sturgeon, A. E. Frear, O. A. Borden, C. J. Dunham, W. J. Newell, W. N. Strong.

First officers: H. B. Wyman, W. M.; E. M. Winslow, S. W.; J. C. Elliot, J. W.; J. A. Brown, Treasurer: J. H. Greattrax, Secretary. Membership, thirty-three. Present officers: E. C. Brown, W. M.; E. F. Parkhurst, S. W.; E. M. Winslow, J. W.; B. Jones, Treasurer; A. M. Dougall, Secretary.

Meetings are held once each month on the Saturday on or before the full moon, in Husted's Hall. The Society is in a flourishing condition.

Locust Lodge No. 367, I. O. O. F.—Charter members: C. H. Cottell, J. Wykoff, W. C. Butterfield, D. Barmore, H. B. Wyman, O. E. Waggoner, Geo. Taylor, J. Morris, C. W. Green, G. Schee, J. H. Pumphrey, E. M. Brady. First officers: C. H. Cottell, N. G.; J. Wykoff, V. G.; H. Humphrey, R. S.; D. R. Barmore, Treasurer; W. C. Butterfield, P. S. Present officers: Geo. Berry, N. G.; L. S. Hackett, V. G.; James Wykoff, Treasurer; N. F. West, R. S.; W. C. Butterfield, P. S. Membership, thirty. Meetings are held Tuesday evenings of each week in Husted's Hall. The Lodge is in a prosperous condition.

Sheldon Cornet Band—Organized in 1876. F. C. Marcussen is the leader.

SANBORN.

The town of Sanborn was laid out and platted by the C., M. & St. P. Railway Company in 1878. The town has made a very rapid growth, being now a town of 800 inhabitants. Quite a number of the settlers of Sanborn are former residents of Primghar. The end of the division of the railroad is located here. Located here also are some of the best stock yards east of Milwaukee, as well as the railroad company's machine shops, employing quite a large number of men. There is also at Sanborn a large round house, with a vast amount of appurtenances. Thanksgiving Day of 1878, the workmen arrived, and commenced work on the depot, a building which is quite a credit to the town.

The first house was built by Frank Teabout, and was used as a grain warehouse; the first store was opened by S. W. Clark in February, 1879; Teabout & Valleau opened a store about the same time.

The postoffice was established in December, 1878, and was in operation early in January, 1879. The first and present Postmaster is Ira Brashears.

The town was incorporated in April, 1880. The first school house was built in May, 1879—size, 26x40 feet; cost, $800. The first teacher was Mrs. L. Crossan. The first Board of Education was: Ira Brashears, President; W. M. Woolworth, Thomas Burns, Directors; I. W. Daggett, Treasurer; J. H. Woods, Clerk. The present school house was built in 1881—size, 40x60 feet, two stories high, and has four departments. It was built at a cost of

$4,000, and is seated with the improved desks. &c. Sanborn became an independent district in 1881. The present Board of Education is: M. D. Comes, D. L. Crowley, Wm. Harker. The present teachers are: Prof. C. E. Foote, Principal; Jennie Mayne and Miss G. Davis, Assistants.

The M. E. Church was organized March 28th, 1879, by Rev. W. H. Drake, who was succeeded by Rev. J. A. Beebe, he by the present pastor, Rev. S. C. Bascom. During the year 1879, the building was erected and was dedicated June 20th, 1880. First officers: I. W. Daggett. T. J. Alexander, C. Tifft, Ira Brashears and Daniel Bryson, Board of Trustees. The cost of the church was $1,400. Present membership, fifteen. The Sabbath School has an average attendance of fifty-five. J. H. Wolf is the Superintendent. The size of the building is 28x48 feet. The seating capacity is 200. The present officers are the same as given above.

The Presbyterian Society was organized January 30th, 1881, by Rev. W. S. Peterson, of Dakota. First officers: D. Miller, Elder; J. S. Grear, Trustee. The first pastor was Rev. J. M. McComb, who is also the present pastor. The membership is twenty. Present officers: D. Miller, R. E.; C. E. Foote, D. Miller, L. D. Thomas, Trustees; H. Day, Treasurer, and Mrs. C. E. Foote, Secretary. Services are held in the new school house. The present pastor took charge May 1st, 1881. The Sabbath School has an average attendance of forty. C. J. Everhard is the Superintendent. There is a parsonage in connection, which was built in November, 1881.

Onyx Lodge, I. O. D., was instituted October 22d, 1881. First officers: Harley Day, W. M.; J. H. Douglas, S. W.; J. T. Parker, J. W.; A. G. Mittels, Secretary. Charter members: D. R. Phelps, T. D. White, P. Miller, J. A. Stocum, C. E. Foote, E. M. Brady, A. G. Willets, C. Broadstreet, W. H. Skinner, H. D. Chapin, Ira Brashears, J. E. Drake, C. P. Veilie, F. Teabout, N. L. F. Peck, A. E. Bates, J. Morrell. Membership, twenty-five. Meetings are held every Wednesday evening on or before the full moon. The Masons have a fine hall, which is also used by the I. O. O. F. The internal arrangement of the hall is as fine as can be found anywhere in the West. The hall is furnished in modern style, carpeted and hung with emblematic tapestry, and supplied with furniture that would adorn a wealthy lodge of that order.

The Order of the Eastern Star was instituted in January, 1882, Mrs. H. D. Perry is Worthy Matron, and Mrs. A. G. Willets, Secretary. The membership is about thirty.

Sanborn Lodge No. 434, I. O. O. F.—Instituted November, 29th, 1881, by Hon. S. P. Leland, D. D. G. M., and a large delegation of the order from Sibley and Sheldon. First officers: H. D. Chapin, N. G.; W. C. Green, V. G.; E. R. Wood, Recording Secretary; J. R. Pumphrey, Permanent Secretary; W. H. Skinner, Treasurer. Charter members: H. D. Chapin, William Roberts, E. R. Wood,

J. R. Pamphrey, W. H. Skinner, C. Tifft, H. Algyer, C. Green, R. Boyd, L. D. Thomas, T. White, A. H. Roden, J. Clancy, F. A. Turner and Mr. Powell. The Lodge meets every Saturday evening in Masonic Hall. Membership, about thirty.

The Sanborn Cornet Band was organized in the spring of 1881. Ed. Drake is the leader; has made various changes since its organization.

The O'Brien Pioneer Weekly, was established in December, 1871, by L. B. Raymond & Co.; was afterwards run by A. H. Willets; then Willets & Inman; then in the order named: Willets & Pumphrey, A. H. Willets & Son, A. G. Willets, Walker & Willets—its present proprietors being Willets & Perkins. It has always been Republican in politics. It is a six-column quarto; circulation, 750 copies. It is printed on a large steam power press in a good, commodious building.

Sanborn can boast of having the best town hall in the county. It was erected by Messrs. Roden & Linden, at the corner of Main and First streets, in 1881. It is a frame structure, 32x70 feet, with a flat roof. The lower rooms are occupied by Henry Roden, as a restaurant and billiard hall. The hall up-stairs is arranged with a ticket-office at the entrance, and has a commodious and well adapted stage. The building and appurtenances cost about $6,000

The Main street in Sanborn runs north and south, and is located on level ground. Sanborn is a good shipping point. The town has telephonic communication with Primghar. The business may be thus classified: General stores, 3; printing offices, 1; hardware, 2; saloons, 3; groceries, 2; agricultural implements, 2; furniture, 1; lumber, 3; jewelry, 1; blacksmiths, 2; drugs, 2; carpenters 4; bank, 1; land, loan and law, 4; flour and feed, 2; restaurant, 1; boot and shoe, 1; meat markets, 2; barber shop, 1; livery, 2; hotels, 3

HARTLEY.

Hartley is situated in the eastern part of O'Brien County, on the C., M. & St. Paul Railroad, eight miles from Sanborn and eighteen from Spencer. It was laid out and platted by J. S. Finister in October, 1880. The first house in the town was built by the Railroad Company, in 1879. The first store was built by J. S. Finister & W. S. Fuller in April, 1879. It was also used as a dwelling. Then came A. H. Miller, J. K. McAndrew, M. G. Silverthorn, and W. H. Eaton, all of whom built in the year 1879. H. E. Hoagland built in 1880. Hartley is a thriving town, and has a population of 185.

The first school was held in Finister's store in 1879 and 1880. The first teacher was O. M. Shonkwiler; first Board of Education: W. S. Fuller, W. H. Eaton, C. A. Feitkaw. The present school building was erected in the spring of 1880, is 26x36 in dimensions, and cost $1,200. The first teacher was Allen Crossan; first Board, the same as above. Present Board: C. A. Feitkaw, George Bowes. Present teacher: E. A. Thomas. Number of pupils enrolled, sixty-seven.

The Baptist Society was organized in December, 1880, by D. F. Johnson. Membership, about ten. This society is not supplied with any regular pastor, and has no building, but holds it prayer meetings in the school building occasionally.

Methodist Episcopal Church Society was organized in 1881 by A. S. R. Groom. who was the first pastor. The first and present officers are: Allen Crossan, Class Leader and Steward; Mr. Whitman and Mr. Dice, Trustees. R. Crosby is also at present a Trustee. Membership, about seventy-five. They have no church building, but meet in the school building. This society built a parsonage in 1881, under the directions of Rev. Groom, at a cost of $300.

Hartley Lodge, I. O. G. T.. was organized December 28th, 1881, by F. E. Anderson, of Algona. Charter members: J. K. McAndrew, D. F. Johnston, Allen Crossan, D. M. Gano, E. A. Thomas, H. E. Finister, James Johnston, George Bowes. W. Bowes, T. Shoemaker. First officers: D. S. Johnston, W. C. T.; E. A. Thomas, W. V. T.; E. Finister, W. M.; Allen Crossan, Recording Secretary; D. M. Gano, Financial Secretary; Will. Bowes, Treasurer; Geo. Bowes, Chaplain. Present officers: E. A. Thomas, W. C. T.; M. E. Silverthorn, W. V. T.; J. Jones, R. S.; R. Makins, F. S.; D. M. Gano, Treasurer: Allen Crossan, Chaplain; W. Bowes. W. M.; Mrs. D. F. Johnson. I. G.; Ed. Williams, O. G. Membership, about thirty. Meetings are held Thursday evening of each week in the school building.

The business houses of Hartley are classified as follows: General stores, two; hardware, one; hotels, three; blacksmith shops, two: wagon shops, one; meat markets, two; lumber dealers, two; saloons, one; agricultural implement dealers, one: livery barns, one.

O'BRIEN COUNTY BIOGRAPHIES.

SHELDON.

D. M. Baker, proprietor of the Leland House, was born in O. in 1849; moved with his parents to Iowa in 1850. He came to Sheldon in 1881 and took charge of the above named house. In 1870 he was married to Rachel M. Gilman, and has six children—Tena, Etta, Minnie, Arthur. Linda and Frank.

J. A. Brown. proprietor of the Sheldon House. was born in Orange county, Vt.; moved to Iowa in 1860. He enlisted in 1862 in Co. M. 3d O. Cav., and was discharged at the close of the war. He then located in Ill. and remained until 1867, when he went South and remained one year. He afterwards engaged in business in various parts of Iowa, and in 1871 settled in O'Brien. He moved to Sheldon in 1873, and engaged as above.

C. H. Bullis, of the firm of Barrett & Bullis, attorneys at law, was born near Rochester, N. Y., in 1847. He graduated from Yale College, in the class of '69, and from the Columbia Law School in 1872. In 1873 he moved to Iowa, and located at Sheldon, in the autumn of 1881.

Frank and Fred Frisbee, of the firm of Frisbee Bros., proprietors of the livery stable, are natives of Wisconsin; came to Iowa in 1871, and settled in O'Brien county. They located at Sheldon in 1876 and engaged in the livery and express business.

G. M. Graham, lumber dealer, came to Iowa in 1856. He enlisted in 1862 in Co. B, 28th Ia. Vol., and served until the close of the war, after which he went to Mich., and engaged in the lumber business. He returned to Iowa in the autumn of 1877, and located at Sheldon.

A. W. Husted, hardware dealer, came to Sheldon in 1873, and was a member of the firm of Husted & Son, dealers in general merchandise, until 1879, when he engaged in his present business, with G. H. Boutelle.

S. J. Hutchinson, boot and shoe dealer, was born in N. J. in 1835. He enlisted in 1862 in Co. D, 100th O. Vol.; was in several of the principal engagements, and was discharged in 1865. He came to Iowa and settled in Cedar county; thence to O'Brien county in 1871, where he engaged in farming until Oct., 1881, at which time he engaged as above.

Jones, Parkhurst & Co., proprietors of the Sheldon Bank, which was established in 1872 by Messrs. Jones and Parkhurst. Mr. Brown became a partner in 1879. They are also dealers in all kinds of farm machinery.

Henry Mandersheid, (saloon), was born in Germany in 1845; came to America when young, and settled in Jackson county, Ia. In 1872 he moved to LeMars; thence to Dakota. He returned to LeMars, where he lived until 1879, when he came to Sheldon and engaged in business as above. Mr. M. has been twice married. He was married to his second wife in Sept., 1881. She was Jennie Gusher. He has three children—Annie, Henry and John.

D. McKay, farmer and marshal of Sheldon, is a native of Canada; moved to Cherokee, Ia., in 1870; thence to Sheldon in 1872.

A. McDougall, freight and express agent, was born in Canada in 1848; moved to Wis. in 1866; thence to Ia. in 1868. He has been in the employ of the C., M. & St. P. R. R. Co., for twelve years. He deals at wholesale in hard and soft coal.

D. O'Donnell was born in Ireland in 1831; came to America in 1847 and settled in N. Y. He moved to Canada; thence to Wis.; and in 1875 came to Iowa. Mr. O'D. started from Sheldon with an ox team for the Black Hills in 1877, and made the trip in forty-four days. He was married in 1850, and has nine children—John C., Kate, Maggie, Mary, Julia, Nellie, Edward, Annie and George.

John C. O'Donnell, deputy sheriff of O'Brien county. He is engaged in blacksmithing. He was married in 1874 and has two children—Alice and Margaret.

James Parden, proprietor of sample room and billiard hall, was born near Rochester, N. Y., in 1837; moved to Sheldon, Ia., in 1875. He occupies for his business the first building erected in Sheldon.

L. O. Peterman, agent for the American Express Co., was born in Ind. in 1853; moved to Winona county, Minn.; thence to Shelnon in 1881.

Joseph Shinski, dealer in general merchandise, was born in N. Y. in 1842. He is the pioneer merchant of Sheldon, having established business in 1873. He was married in 1875 to Ellen M. Kelley, of Sioux City. They have two daughters—Maud and Maggie.

Henry Schultz, liquor dealer and proprietor of billiard hall, was born in Hanover, Ger., in 1846; came to America in 1866 and settled in Wis. He came to Iowa in 1870 and to Sheldon in 1876. He was married in 1876 to Katie Berbrein.

Rev. E. Southworth, pastor of the Congregational church, was born in Mich. in 1834. He attended the Hamilton College, N. Y., and the University of Mich., at Ann Arbor. In 1866 he graduated from the Theological College, of N. Y., and the same year entered the ministry. In 1871 he moved to Ia., then back to Wis., where he remained four years, and in 1878 came to Sheldon, Ia., and took charge of the church as above. He married Sarah H. Humphrey, and has three children—Mary E., Edward P. and C. DeForest.

W. H. Sleeper, banker, insurance and land agent, was born in N. J. in 1853. He was for a time engaged in the mercantile business at Mount Holley, in Philadelphia. In 1877 he came to Sheldon, Ia., and engaged in his present business, with his brother, A. W. Sleeper.

Charles Stinson, of the firm of J. M. Comstock & Co., dealers in general merchandise, was born in N. Y.; moved to Algona, Ia., in 1871, and there engaged in the mercantile business with Mr. Comstock. They established business as above in Aug., 1880.

S. M. Wagers, proprietor of the City restaurant, was born in O. in 1838; moved to Wis. in 1856. He enlisted in 1862 in Co. H,

7th Wis. Vol., and was discharged the same year, on account of physical disability. He came to Ia. in October, 1880. In 1863 he married Adelia Hayerman, and has two children Edward and Mary.

E. B. Wheeler, blacksmith, was born in Orleans county, Vt.; in 1868; moved to Cerro Gordo county, Ia., in 1868. He was one of the first settlers of Clear Lake. He came to Sheldon in 1880, and engaged in business as above.

D. S. White, Jr., dealer in general merchandise, was born in N. J., in 1853; removed to Omaha, Neb., in 1871, and was employed under the Superintendent of Indian affairs in Nebraska. In 1877 he came to Sheldon, Ia., and engaged as above. He was elected a member of the city council in 1880.

F. E. Wyman, proprietor of restaurant and dealer in fancy groceries, is a native of Mass.; moved to Wabasha county, Minn., in 1858. He enlisted in 1864 in Co. D, 140 Ill. Reg., and was discharged soon after. He came to Iowa in 1872.

James Wykoff, the pioneer lumber dealer of Sheldon, was born in Ontario county, N. Y., in 1843. He enlisted in Dec., 1863, in the 50th N. Y. Vol., and served until June, 1865. He moved to Minn. in 1866; thence to Ia. in 1868. He came to Sheldon in 1872, and engaged in business as above. His daughter, Inez, was the first child born in the city.

F. H. Zander, proprietor of the Chicago Clothing Store, came to Sheldon in Oct., 1880, from Chicago, where he had previously been engaged in business. This is the only exclusive clothing house in the city.

PRIMGHAR.

C. E. Achorn, of the firm of Schee & Achorn, bankers and land agents, was born in Me. in 1861; removed to Boston, Mass., with his parents in 1869; thence to Wis. in 1878, and the following year located at Primghar. He engaged in the above business with Geo. W. Schee, in 1881. He married Ada Alexander in Jan., 1882.

Charles F. Albright, farmer, was born in Pa. in 1839; removed to Muscatine county, Ia., in 1858; two years later he moved to Cedar county. He enlisted in the war of the rebellion, and served three years. He came to O'Brien county in 1871, and settled on homestead in the center of the county, adjoining what is now the town of Primghar. He erected the first hotel here in 1873. He was married in 1865, to Adah C. Mackelwain, and has two children.

T. J. Alexander, treasurer of O'Brien county, was born in Ind. in 1845; moved with parents to Wis. the same year, and to Warren county, Ia., in 1859. He came to O'Brien county in 1869, and settled on a homestead in Liberty township. He was elected to his present office in 1878, and moved to Primghar; has been re-elected each term since. He was married in 1867, to Martha Brown, and has three children.

David Algyer, county superintendent of schools, was born in Montgomery county, N. Y., in 1849; came to Clay county, Ia., in 1871, and settled on a homestead. In 1873 moved to O'Brien county, and located at Primghar in 1880. He was elected to his present office in 1881. He married Marie S. Gowen in 1874. They have three children.

Milt. H. Allen, attorney at law, was born in Winneshiek county, Ia., in 1859; removed with parents to Clay county in 1871. He came to O'Brien county in 1873, and engaged in the practice of law with O. M. Barrett, in 1879. He opened an office in Primghar in 1881.

J. G. Chrysler, of the firm of Pumphrey & Chrysler, dealers in general merchandise, was born in Canada in 1858; removed with parents to Jackson county, Ia., in 1866; thence to O'Brien county in 1871. He located at Primghar in 1875, and engaged in his present business in 1878. He married Ida Thomas in 1879, and has one child.

J. B. Dunn, attorney at law, was born in Ind. March 5th, 1844; moved to Greene county, Wis., with his parents in 1846. He enlisted in Sept., 1861, in the war of the rebellion, and served three years and nine months; then located in Warren county, Iowa; removed to Primghar in 1880, and engaged in the practice of the law. He married Maria Hiett, in Nov., 1865. They have seven children.

Stephen Harris, teacher, was born in Brunswick, Me., in 1842; moved with parents to Boston, Mass., in 1845. He went to sea in 1860, and in 1863 enlisted in the army, and served two years. He came to Iowa, in 1869, and settled on a homestead. He was elected superintendent in 1870, and county clerk in 1871. He moved to Primghar in 1874; was deputy treasurer for four years, and also engaged in the land business.

D. W. Inman, proprietor of the hotel at Primghar, was born in N. Y. in 1835; removed to Ill. in 1837; thence to Butler county, Iowa, in 1858. He enlisted in 1864 in the 9th Vol. Inft., and served until the close of the war, when he returned to Iowa, and settled in O'Brien county in 1866. In 1879 he went to Primghar and engaged in his present business.

W. W. Johnson, lumber dealer, was born in England in 1844, and the same year came to America with his parents, who settled in N. Y. In 1859 he moved to Cedar county, Iowa; thence to O'Brien county in 1871, and engaged in farming in Highland township. He moved to Primghar in 1881, and engaged in his present business.

Thomas Murray, farmer, was born in Iowa in 1861; came to O'Brien county with his parents in 1871, and settled on a homestead in Center township. He moved to Primghar in 1881.

J. L. E. Peck, county auditor, was born in London, Canada, Aug. 18th, 1852; moved with his parents to Page county, Iowa, where he resided until graduating from the Iowa State University in 1874, when he moved to Winneshiek county. He came to Primghar in 1877, and engaged in the practice of law. He was elected to his present office in 1879, and re-elected in 1881.

Geo. W. Schee, of the firm of Schee & Achorn, was born in Clark county, Mo., in 1849; moved to Oskaloosa, Ia., in 1861 with his parents. In 1871 he came to O'Brien county and engaged in farming in Carroll township. He moved to Primghar in 1876, and was elected county auditor, in which capacity he served two terms; then opened a land and law office, and became a member of the above firm in 1881. He married Lizzie Dunning, in 1877. They have two children.

J. A. Smith, county surveyor, was born in Pa. in Oct., 1847; removed to Iowa county, Ia., in 1869, and the following year came to O'Brien county and settled on a homestead in Center township. He moved to Primghar in 1881. He married Mary E. Foust, in 1870, and has five children.

Hubert Sprague, county recorder, was born in Ill., Jan. 1st, 1858; removed to Madison county, Ia., with parents in 1868; thence to O'Brien county, and engaged in farming. He served as deputy recorder two years, and was elected recorder in 1881. He was married in April, 1881, to Callie Green, of Clay county, Ia.

H. A. Thayer, of the firm of Thayer & Co., dealers in hardware, was born in N. Y., April 29th, 1855. He went to Neb. in 1874, and remained six months; then located in Blackhawk county, Ia.; came to Primghar in 1878; was engaged in clerking until entering his present business in 1881.

F. M. Tifft, proprietor of livery and sale stable, was born in Wis., Oct. 11th, 1857; removed with parents to O'Brien county, Ia., in 1870, settling on a homestead in Center township. He moved to Primghar in 1876, and in 1880 engaged in business as above. He was married to Ellen Robbins, Jan. 23rd, 1881. They have one child, a son.

Frank A. Turner, clerk, with Schee & Achorn, was born in Ill., Oct. 13th, 1856; moved with parents to Butler county, Ia., in 1859. He attended the college at Mt. Vernon from 1874 to 1876. Came to Primghar in 1880, and was employed in the Primghar Exchange Bank, where he still remains.

HARTLEY.

A. B. Chrysler, of the firm of Pumphrey & Chrysler, dealers in general merchandise, was born in Canada in 1848; removed to Jackson county, Iowa, in 1865; thence to O'Brien county in 1870, and engaged in farming in Liberty township. He came to Hartley in 1880, and engaged in business as above. He was married in 1875, and has three children.

Allen Crossan, of the firm of Crossan & Gano, hardware dealers, was born in Scotland in Jan., 1848; came to America with his parents in 1852, and settled in Ohio; moved to Hardin county, Iowa, in 1865, and in 1870, settled on a homestead in O'Brien county. He graduated from the Normal School at Albion, Ia., in 1877, and in 1880 engaged in his present business.

W. S. Fuller, of the firm of Shonkwiler & Co., dealers in lumber and stock, was born in Ill. in 1844; moved with his parents to Wis. in 1846; thence back to Ill. in 1857, where he remained until 1867; then removed to Grundy county, Ia., and in 1871 came to O'Brien county, settling on a homestead. He moved to Hartley in 1879, and engaged in merchandising until entering the above firm. He was married in 1869 to Nancy Wilson, and has two children.

H. E. Finster, proprietor of the City Hotel, was born in Chicago, Ill., in 1848; removed to Mich. with his parents in 1854; remained there until 1864, and after traveling for some time, located at Independence, Ia., and engaged in marble cutting. He came to Hartley in 1880, and engaged in business as above. He was married in 1870, and has three children.

David M. Gano, of the firm of Crossan & Gano, was born in Ohio in 1840; removed with his parents to Ind. in 1846; thence to Wis. the following year. In 1870, he came to O'Brien county and settled on a homestead, and engaged in farming until 1880, when he moved to Hartley and built the second house in the town. He was married in 1865, to S. Chamberlain, and has two sons and five daughters.

H. E. Hoagland, lumber dealer, was born in Mich. in 1844; removed to O'Brien county, Ia., in 1870, and settled on a homestead in Liberty township. In 1878 he came to Hartley, and engaged in the lumber business with O. M. Shonkwiler. He was married in 1864, and has two children.

D. F. Johnston, contractor, was born in New Brunswick, in 1832; removed with his parents to Canada, and in 1855 came to Delaware county, Ia. He moved to Buena Vista county in 1873; thence to Hartley in the summer of 1881, and is in the employ of the railroad company. He was married in March, 1856, to Hepzebah Joyce. They have seven children.

F. E. Matott, proprietor of billiard hall, was born in Vt., in 1848, and the following year his parents moved to Ind., where he resided until 1871; then came to O'Brien county, and engaged in farming in Center township. He came to Hartley in 1881, and engaged in business as above. He married Emma L. Kiefer, in 1879. They have one daughter.

J. K. McAndrew, proprietor of Our House, was born in Milwaukee, Wis., in 1850; removed to Clayton county, Ia., with parents, where he remained until 1870, when he came to O'Brien and settled on a homestead in Grant township. In 1879, he moved to Hartley, and engaged in the stock and grain business, and shipped the first car-load from the town. He married Mary E. Biggs, in 1875, and has one child, a daughter.

O. M. Shonkwiler, lumber and stock dealer, was born in Ill. Dec. 31st, 1853; moved to O'Brien county, in May, 1876, and engaged in farming in Center township. He moved to Hartley in 1881, and engaged in the lumber business with Messrs. Hoagland & Fuller. He married Della Griffith, in Oct., 1877, and has two children.

E. A. Thomas, principal of the Hartley schools, was born in Jo Daviess county, Ill.; moved with parents to Mt. Carroll, in 1866, where he remained until 1875. He came to Hartley in Oct., 1881, and engaged in teaching.

E. D. Williams, butcher, was born in Wales in 1831; came to America in 1850 and located in Mich.; two years later moved to Wis.; thence to Hartley, Ia., in 1880, and engaged in his present business. He was married in 1857, and has nine children.

SANBORN.

E. F. Bacon, of the firm of Bacon & Son, dealers in general merchandise, was born in Wis.; removed with his parents in 1864 to Waverly, Ia., and came to Sanborn in 1880 and established business as above.

Wm. W. Barnes, proprietor of the Sanborn House, came to Ia. in 1869, and engaged in farming in Grant township, O'Brien county; removed to Primghar in 1876, and engaged in the hotel business; thence to Sanborn in 1878 and opened his present hotel.

E. M. Brady, the pioneer hardware merchant of Sanborn, is a native of Ohio; came to Iowa in 1874, and engaged in the mercantile business; removed to Sanborn in 1879 and established his present business.

Cal. Broadstreet, of the firm of Broadstreet & Boies, attorneys at law, was born in Ulster county, N. Y., in 1851; removed to Buchanan county, Ia., in 1857. He graduated from the Iowa State University in 1878. He began the practice of law in Sanborn in Oct., 1879. W. B. Boies, of the above law firm, was born in

Boone county, Ill., in 1873. He graduated from the Iowa Law School in 1880, located in Sanborn in Dec., 1881, and began the practice of his profession.

A. W. Creed, dealer in flour and feed, came from Ohio to Iowa in 1869, and engaged in the mercantile business; thence to Sanborn in 1880, and engaged in the hotel business; sold out in the fall of 1881, and engaged in his present business.

Harley Day, attorney at law, was born in St. Lawrence county, N. Y., Mar. 27th, 1841. He served in the 106th Reg. N. Y. Vol., as lieutenant of Co. K, for three years. Part of that time was spent in rebel prisons. After the war he came to Iowa and located in Butler county; removed to Buchanan county; thence to O'Brien county in 1871, and settled on a homestead. He was admitted to the bar in that county in 1876, and engaged in the law and land business at Primghar. In 1880 he removed to Sanborn. He married Margaret Braden, in 1867. They have one child.

I. W. Dagett, banker, was born in Franklin county, Maine, in 1851; removed to Franklin county, Ia., in 1865, and engaged in teaching school; thence to Primghar in 1875, and engaged in the practice of law, and in 1877 entered the banking and real estate business, and removed to Sanborn in 1879, and engaged as above.

Robert Elliott, merchant tailor, Sanborn, Iowa.

C. J. Everhard, dealer in furniture, was born in O.; removed to Sanborn in June, 1881, and engaged in his present business. He is the inventor of the patent barrel painting machine, which is now extensively used by the Standard Oil company.

Richard Finlay, M. D., is a native of Canada; moved to Cincinnati, O., in 1863; graduated from the Ohio Medical College in the class of '80. He came to Sanborn in July, 1881, and began the practice of medicine.

W. C. Green, Sheriff of O'Brien county, was born in Jackson county, Ind., in 1842; removed to Carroll county, Ill., in 1849; thence to Whiteside county, and engaged in the dry goods business. He moved to O'Brien county in 1869, and engaged in the mercantile business in the town of O'Brien. He platted the town of Primghar, in 1872, and moved there in 1873, and in 1879 removed to Sanborn.

J. L. Green, of the firm of Harkner & Green, bankers, was born in O.; moved to Wis. in 1847. In 1865 he moved to Marshall county, Ia., and engaged in the mercantile business. He established the Maple Valley Bank in 1878, and in 1880 came to Sanborn.

J. Grant, proprietor of the City restaurant, is a native of Scotland; came to America in 1879, and located in Sanborn Oct. 1st, 1881.

L. C. Green, of the firm of Green & Patch, proprietors of the livery barn, was born in Ill. in 1850; came to O'Brien county, Ia., in 1869, and engaged in the mercantile business with his brother, W. C. Green. He moved to Primghar; thence to Ponca, Neb., where he engaged in the livery business. He came to Sanborn in 1878, and engaged as above.

W. H. Gunsul, farmer and dealer in blooded horses, was born in New York, lived a number of years in Ill., and came to Sanborn in 1881.

W. J. Hovey, attorney at law, was born in Boston, Mass., in 1857; removed with parents to Buchanan county, Ia., in 1865. He removed to Sanborn in 1881, and began the practice of law.

Frank D. Jenkins, proprietor of the Jenkins House, located in Sanborn in 1880. The Hotel is opposite the depot, is convenient for the traveling public, and they will receive first-class entertainment.

W. T. Jones, the pioneer merchant of Sanborn, was born in Missouri in 1853; moved to Allamakee county, Ia., in 1855, and engaged in farming. In 1879 he removed to this place.

J. Limback, proprietor of the Key City restaurant, was born in N. Y.; came to Sanborn in Dec., 1881.

Charles H. Perry, druggist, was born in N. Y. in 1857; removed to Bremer county, Ia., with his parents in 1858, and to Sanborn in 1880, and engaged in his present business. He is about to remove his stock to his large new building, next to the Pioneer office.

J. R. Pumphrey, dealer in general merchandise, and one of the proprietors of the Sanborn Tribune, was born in Ohio in 1845. He enlisted in the 1st W. Va. L. Artillery; was quarter master's sergeant. He served three years, and was taken prisoner at New Creek by Gen. Rosser, held five months at Libby prison, and exchanged at the close of the war. He came to Sioux City in 1867, and was engaged in the county treasurer's and auditor's offices; removed to O'Brien county, and was elected county treasurer in 1871; also founded the O'Brien Pioneer, which he published three years. In 1873 he removed to Primghar, and engaged in the banking and mercantile business; thence to Sanborn in 1881, and engaged in his present business. His father located in Richmond, Va., in 1860; was paymaster in the U. S. A. during the late war, and was lost from a steamer between St. Louis and Island Number Ten in 1864, while on his way south to pay Gen. Grant's army at Vicksburg.

P. H. Roden, restaurateur, was born in Germany in 1838; came to America in 1861, and enlisted in Co. B, 37th O. regiment, and served until 1863. He engaged in the cooper business in Appleton, Wis.; removed to Cherokee, Ia., in 1869, and engaged in farming; thence to Sanborn in the spring of 1881.

J. P. Selig, proprietor of the Star restaurant, was born in West Va. in 1856; moved to Iowa in 1871, and settled near Sheldon; removed to Sheldon in 1879, and established the City restaurant; came to Sanborn in 1881, and engaged in his present business.

Charles Smith, M. D., was born in Middlesex county, Mass. In 1861 he enlisted as bugler in Gen. Sickles' brigade, and served until 1863. After the war he located at Washington, D. C., and was employed in the treasury department as messenger to Secretary McCullough. He graduated from the National Medical College in 1876, and engaged in the practice of medicine in Washington, D. C.; remained eighteen months, and then removed to Sanborn.

G. D. Williams, manager for the Oshkosh lumber company at Sanborn; established in 1881; dealers in all kinds of builders' supplies and fencing material. The only first-class lumber yard in town.

OSCEOLA COUNTY.

Osceola County is in the northern tier, and second from the western boundary of the State, and contains 392 square miles, or 250,880 acres. It is watered and drained by the east fork of Rock River, Ocheydan, Otter and several smaller creeks. These streams meander through valleys of great fertility, producing luxuriant crops of excellent grass. The soil is generally a dark loam, with a slight mixture of clay on the table lands, and a small quantity of sand and vegetable mould in the valleys. Osceola is emphatically a prairie county, composed of a gently undulating surface, sufficiently rolling to break the monotonous sameness of the level plain, with a rich inexhaustible soil, yielding an abundance of crops. There is but little timber in the county, though it is sufficiently plenty for fuel. Stock raising here, as in adjoining counties, is an imporant and lucrative industry. Though one of the younger counties, it is fast taking rank with the larger and more populous ones in the northwest quarter of the State. The schools in the county are in a flourishing condition, every township and sub-district having a school house. There are at present forty-five frame school houses in the county, and during the year 1881, according to the report of the State Superintendent, $11,300 were expended for school purposes, and according to the census taken during the same year by the secretaries of the various sub-districts, there were 746 children of school age, of whom 602 were enrolled as attendants upon the public schools. Schools are in session, on an average, six months in the year.

Capt. E. Huff was the first white man who settled in the county, coming in the fall of 1870, and locating on Otter Creek, in the southwestern part of the county. He did not remain over winter, but returned to his claim the following spring, 1871. He was accompanied by C. M. Brooks, D. L. McCausland, W. W. Webb, F. Stiles, M. J. Campbell and A. M. Culver, all of whom located claims. All the vacant lands were soon taken up, either by homesteading or pre-empting. The county was organized in 1871, having been previously attached to Woodbury County for revenue and judicial purposes, the latter connection being still maintained. The first election for county officers was held October 10th, at the house of A. M. Culver, when the following officers were elected: F. M. Robinson, Auditor; A. M. Culver, Treasurer; C. M. Brooks, Clerk of Courts, D. L. McCausland, Recorder; Frank Stiles, Sheriff; Delila Stiles, Superintendent of Schools; John Beaumont, Drainage Commissioner, and J. H. Winsherr, George Spaulding and H. R. Fenton, Board of Supervisors.

25

The present officers are: R. S. Hall, Treasurer; W. M. Moore, Auditor: H. N. Moore, Deputy Auditor; Alice C. Hill, Recorder; J. S. Davisson, Clerk of Courts; H. N. Moore, Deputy Clerk of Courts; J. R. Elliott. County Superintendent; J. B. Lent. Sheriff; M. J. Campbell. Surveyor; W. H. Burkhutf. Coroner; G. S. Downend, Robert Stamm, H. C. Allen. Wm. Mowthorpe. W. Boor, Board of Supervisors.

The population of the county, as given by the census of 1880, was 2,219. but as there has been an uninterrupted tide of immigration to the county since, its present population is fully 3,000.

The Sioux City & St. Paul Railroad enters the county near the center of section 9, in township 100, range 41, about 3½ miles west of the center of the north line of the county, and takes a diagonal course across the county. leaving it near the center of the south line of section 33, township 98, range 42, about 9½ miles west of the center of the south line of the county. The road-bed was graded through the county during the summer of 1871. The track was laid early in the summer of 1872. being completed through to LeMars in July, 1872, at which time the trains commenced running regularly.

SIBLEY.

Sibley, the most important as well as the oldest town in the county, was laid out and platted by the Sioux City & St. Paul Railroad Company in October, 1872, though several houses had been built on the town-site previous to its being platted, as early as 1871, the first belonging to F. M. Robinson, one of the pioneer settlers. The first business house was erected in the fall of 1871, by H. R. Rogers, who put in a stock of general merchandise.

The town was incorporated in 1876, and its first officers were: D. L. Riley, Mayor; C. E. Brown, H. S. Brown. H. S. Emmett, D. Cramer, G. S. Murphy, Trustees. The present city government is composed of D. L. Riley, Mayor; D. D. McCallum, Recorder; L. Shell, Treasurer; J. B. Lent, Assessor; W. P. Rhodes. Street Commissioner; C. M. Richards, Marshal; L. Shell, M. J. Campbell, H. C. Hungerford, E. Huff. N. Neill, H. S. Brown, Trustees.

The county seat was located at Sibley in 1872 by the following Commissioners appointed from adjoining counties, to-wit: Carson Rice, of Dickinson; C. W. Inman, of O'Brien; and J. S. Howell. of Lyon. The principal streets run east and west, most of the business houses being located thereon. Sibley's business establishments, briefly classified, are as follows:

Drug and groceries. 2; general stores, 3; millinery, 2; harness, 2; agricultural implements. 3; blacksmith shops, 3; wagon shops, 1; lumber yards. 3; meat markets, 2; shoe shops, 1; hotels, 3; billiard hall, 1; printing offices, 2; banks, 2; abstract and loan, 1; insurance, 6; barber shop. 1; grocery store. 1; hardware, 3; jewelry, 1; livery stable, 1; butter, wood and hide depot, 1; restaurant, 1; stationer, 1; furniture, 1; grist mill, 1; photograph galleries, 2; book store, 1; elevators, 2; law firms, 3; physicians, 2; dentist, 1.

The population of Sibley is now estimated at from 500 to 600, including East Sibley.

The *Sibley Gazette*, the first, and until 1881, the only newspaper published in the county, was established by L. A. Barker, and the first paper was issued in July, 1872. In May, 1873, it passed into the hands of Riley & Brown, who continued it for about three months, when they disposed of it to Craig & Glover. In July, 1874, Mr. Craig retired, the firm becoming Glover & Hauxhurst, they continuing it until the fall of 1875, when W. B. Reed purchased the interest of Mr. Glover, and they published it until March, 1876; when Hauxhurst retired, and Ira C. Edward assumed the management of the paper. Later in the year, the paper got back into the hands of its former proprietors, Messrs. Reed & Glover, but the partnership continued only a few months, Reed retiring. Glover remained as proprietor until the fall of 1877, when he sold out to George Carew, who conducted it until October, 1879, and then disposed of it to D. A. W. Perkins. Six months later, O. M. Foster purchased a half-interest in it, and the following April, he became sole proprietor. During the same month, however, he disposed of it to George Carew, who has continued its publication ever since. Notwithstanding the many changes in its proprietorship, usually so fatal to newspapers, it has been enlarged several times, and is now a seven-column quarto. The *Gazette* is Republican in politics, carefully edited, and a journal in every way creditable to the county. It has a circulation of about 400 copies.

September 29th, 1881, the *Sibley Tribune* made its appearance, with Charles E. Crosby as editor and proprietor. It is an eight-column folio, Republican in politics, ably edited, and devoted to local interests of Osceola county. It has a circulation of 400.

CHURCHES, SCHOOLS AND SOCIETIES.

The Congregational Church Society.—Organized in 1872, by Rev. B. A. Dean. He was succeeded by Rev. D. J. Baldwin, who continued in charge until 1881, when he in turn was succeeded by Rev. Thomas Pell, the present pastor. The church has a membership of forty. There is also a Sabbath School with an average attendance of forty pupils. C. M. Bailey is Superintendent. Rev. Mr. Pell also has charge of two societies in the country. The church building is located on two lots donated by the railroad company in 1874, and was erected in the fall of the same year at a cost of $1,800. It is a frame building, of semi-gothic style, 32 feet by 40 feet in dimensions, with a seating capacity of 200. It is nicely furnished and has a good organ. At the time of the dedication, November 29th, 1874, the building was entirely free of debt. There is also in connection with the church a comfortable parsonage. The present officers of the society are: O. Dunton, Clerk; Samuel Herbert, B. Wood and J. F. Glover, Trustees.

Baptist Church Society.—This society was partially organized in March, 1873, by Rev. W. Wood, of Cedar Falls, with a membership of twelve persons. A permanent organization was effected in February, 1876. The first officers were: T. O. Wilbern, A. Churchill, A. W. Mitchell, Deacons. The first pastor was Rev. T. H. Judson, followed by E. M. Heyburn, the present pastor, who took charge in 1880. Membership, forty. This society has no building of its own, but holds its services in the school house. The Sabbath School has an average attendance of twenty-five: T. O. Wilbern is the Superintendent; C. D. Wilbern, Secretary and Treasurer. Church officers: T. O. Wilbern, Deacon; C. D. Wilbern, Secretary, J. F. Glover, Trustee.

Methodist Episcopal Society.—Organized in April, 1872, at the house of A. M. Culver. The first quarterly conference of the Sibley Mission was held October 5th, 1872, by Rev. Aldrich. Rev. John Webb was appointed the first pastor, and was succeeded by Rev. Ira Brashears, September 20th, 1873. The church was served successfully, by Revs. W. W. Mallory, J. W. Rigby, J. W. Lothian and S. P. Marsh, the present pastor, who took charge in September, 1880. Membership, 120, including a class in the country. The first officers of the first class were: R. Stamm, Class Leader; L. Shell, William Thomas, E. Morrison, D. L. Riley, L. C. Chamberlain and S. C. Vanhorn, Stewards; J. P. Hauxhurst and B. Davis, local pastors; J. L. Robinson, M. J. Campbell, A. M. Culver, R. Stamm, L. Shell, D. L. Riley, H. K. Rogers, Trustees. Present officers: J. P. Hauxhurst, Class Leader; D. L. Riley, L. Shell, W. M. Moore, E. Huff and S. A. Wright, Stewards; D. L. Riley, R. Stamm, Levi Shell, S. A. Wright, W. M. Moore, Trustees; B. Davis, Local Deacon. The society has a flourishing Sabbath School with an attendance of seventy pupils; number of teachers, fifteen; S. P. Marsh, Superintendent. There is also a commodious parsonage in connection with the church. The M. E. church building is located on two lots just west of, and fronting eastward towards, the Court House Square. These lots were donated by the S. C. & St. P. Railroad Company, in the spring of 1873. The building is 32x50 feet. The building was commenced in the spring of 1873, but was not completed until September, 1874, when it was dedicated. It cost $2.200, and is well furnished.

Catholic Society.—Celebrated Mass in Sibley as early as 1873, Rev. Father B. C. Lenehan, of Sioux City, officiating. The society now comprises some sixty families, and services are regularly held every two weeks in the Court House. The society is now in charge of Father Thomas Riley, of Sheldon, who contemplates the erection of a substantial and commodious church building at an early day.

The Public School building is located on two lots fronting westward towards the Court House square, donated by the railroad company. The building is 22x36 feet, and was erected in May, 1872, at a cost of $3,500, and has a seating capacity of one hundred. W. A. Armine, assisted by Miss Flora Reeves, now has charge of the school, which has an average attendance of ninety pupils. The present Board of Education is composed of D. L. Riley, Levi Shell and T. O. Wilbern. The first school taught in the county was taught by Delila Stiles, who was also the first Superintendent of Schools, in 1871. Sibley remained a sub-district of Holman Township until 1878, when it became an independent district. The first School Board of the new district, was composed of C. M. Bailey, Levi Shell and A. W. Mitchell.

Broken Column Lodge No. 331, A. F. & A. M.—Instituted June 3d, 1874, with a membership of ten. The following are the charter members, and also first officers: R. J. Chase, W. M.; J. M. Jenkins, S. W.; J. Griffith, J. W.; D. G. Shell, Treasurer; G. S. Murphy, Secretary; J. C. Miller, S. D.; C. N. Sawyer, J. D.; W. H. Cooper, Tyler; B. F. Tabler, S. S.; S. H. Wescott, J. S. Present officers: J. B. Lent, W. M.; W. B. Humphrey, S. W.; W. H. Chambers, Treasurer; B. F. Tabler, Secretary; H. Littlechild, S. D.; Cline Bull, J. D.; W. Mead, Jr., Tyler; G. A. Pitman, S. S.; J. Q. Miller, J. S. The present membership, about forty. Meetings are held once each month in the Hall of the society over Wilbern's store. The society is in a flourishing condition, and has recently purchased a lot, upon which they contemplate erecting a new Hall at an early day.

Ocheydan Lodge No. 251, I. O. O. F.—Instituted in October, 1873. First officers: D. L. Riley, N. G.; F. M. Robinson, V. G.; C. M. Bailey, R. S.; C. H. Call, P. S.; W. M. Cram, Treasurer. Present officers: Cline Bull, N. G.; C. W. Jenkins, V. G.; J. S. Davisson, R. S.; D. D. McCallum, P. S.; A. W. Mitchell, Treasurer. Membership, fifty. Meetings are held every Monday evening in the hall over Wilbern's store. This society is in a prosperous condition, and will soon commence the erection of commodious quarters of their own.

Pioneer Agricultural Society.—Organized in 1872. The first officers were: L. G. Ireland, President; C. Dunton, Vice-President; E. Hogin, Secretary; F. M. Robinson, Treasurer; H. Jordan, J. F. Van Emburg and E. Huff, Directors. The society was incorporated and adopted constitution and by-laws in July, 1872. The first fair was held October 10th and 11th, 1872, in Court House Square. The present officers are: P. L. Piesley, President; J. W. Carson, Vice-President; S. A. Wright, Secretary; W. J. Miller, Treasurer; P. Proper, J. Cronk, G. S. Downend, J. Streit and H. Peters, Directors. The society is free of debt, with money in the treasury, and owns a tract of twenty-five acres one-half mile northwest of Sibley, enclosed by a substantial fence. On the grounds are a commodious floral hall, and a fine half-mile track. Fairs are held annually, and are largely attended.

Sibley Cornet Band.—Organized in 1873, and is a creditable organization. C. Armbright is the Leader.

The Court House is located on the most elevated portion of the townsite, and was erected in the fall of 1872, at a cost of about $5,000. The building is 36 feet by 36 feet, 20 feet high, and affords comfortable and commodious quarters for the county officials. The block on which the building is situated was the gift of the railroad company, who also generously set aside an additional block, centrally located, for a public park. The railroad depot at Sibley is 24 feet by 48 feet in dimensions, and is substantially built, as are all the buildings along the line of the Chicago, St. Paul, Minneapolis & Omaha Railroad. The company has acted most generously with the town of Sibley, and has, by its liberal donations of lots for school, church and court house purposes, done much towards the upbuilding of the town.

ASHTON.

Ashton, until recently called St. Gilman, is situated seven miles southwest of Sibley, on the line of the C., St. P., M. & O. Railroad. It is surrounded by an excellent agricultural district, and gives promise of becoming an important shipping town. It now has several general stores, a public school, two or three church societies, a good depot building and a grain warehouse.

OSCEOLA COUNTY BIOGRAPHIES.

SIBLEY.

Chas. A. Armbright, barber, was born in Germany; came to America in 1856; located in N. Y., and the same year enlisted in the 5th U. S. cavalry of the regular army. He was on duty in Texas, until the war of the rebellion, when he was ordered to Pa. for active service. He re-enlisted in 1863 as a veteran, and served until the close of the war. He came to Sibley in 1872, and engaged in his present business.

C. E. Brown and W. H. Chambers, of the firm of Brown & Chambers, dealers in general merchandise, are natives of Wis. They came to Sibley, in 1874, and engaged in their present business with a small capital; are now one of the leading firms in the county, and carry a complete stock of about $15,000.

J. Brooks, came from Ind. to Butler county, Ia., in 1852. He enlisted in 1862 in Co. H, Ia. Vol.; was in the service three years, fourteen months of which time he was a prisoner of war at Tyler, Texas. He was wounded at Fort Pillow, Tenn. At the close of the war he returned to Ia. In 1872 he located in Osceola county, and in Sibley two years later, and engaged in the nursery business. He has now retired from business.

J. S. Davisson, clerk of the courts, was born in Vt. in 1845. He came to Iowa and enlisted in Co. I, 9th Ia. Cav. in 1863; served until 1866; then returned to Iowa and settled in Washington county; removed to Osceola county in 1872, and to Sibley in 1880. and entered into business as a contractor and builder.

John H. Douglass, sheriff of Osceola county, was born in Scotland; came to America with his parents, and settled in Ill.; removed to Allamakee county, Ia., in 1856. He enlisted in 1862 in the U. S. regular army as drummer, and afterwards in the 1st Ia. Cav.; and served until the close of the war; then returned to Ia. He was engaged in various kinds of business, until 1872, when he was elected to his present office; is also engaged with the Iowa land company as superintendent of outside business, renting and looking after the interests of the firm in Osceola county. Mr. D. has the reputation of being one of the best criminal officers in the state.

J. F. Glover, attorney at law and land agent, was born in Union county, Pa., in 1845; moved with parents to Stephenson county, Ill., in 1846. In 1868 he enlisted in the 38th Wis. Vol. Inft.; was promoted to orderly sergeant, and commissioned second lieutenant. He graduated in the classical course, at the University of Wis., in 1871, and soon after located in Osceola county. In 1872 he was elected clerk of the courts, and in 1875 was elected to the state legislature, for the counties of Clay, Dickinson, Osceola and O'Brien. He was admitted to the bar in 1878. During his residence in Sbiley he was for several years engaged in editing the Sibley Gazette.

F. F. & H. S. Grant, of the firm of Grant Bros., dealers in general hardware, are natives of Wis.; came to Sibley, Ia., in Feb., 1881, and engaged in their present business. H. S. is business manager of the store at Sibley, and F. F. is the northwestern traveling agent for Grey, Burt & Kingman, of Chicago, Ill.

J. C. Hanon, proprietor of the Sibley House, is a native of Vt.; removed at an early age to Cincinnati, O. He followed railroading for a time; removed to Ia. in 1871, and in 1873 came to Sibley. He engaged in the hotel business in 1867, and has a first-class house and accommodations.

C. I. Hill, (deceased), late banker of Sibley, was born in O. in 1843; removed to Sioux City, Ia., in 1870; thence to Sibley in 1872, and engaged in the real estate and law business. He engaged in the banking business in 1876 which he continued two years. He retired from business on account of ill-health, and died in March, 1881, leaving a wife and one child—Eva. Mrs. Hill is a daughter of D. M. Sturges, of Vermillion, Dak.

Capt. E. Huff, land agent, came to Fremont county, Ia., from Ind. in 1856. He enlisted in 1861, in Co. A, 4th Ia. Cav., and served until the close of the war. He was taken prisoner in Dec., 1864, and confined in Andersonville prison for three months. After the war he returned to Ia., and in 1870 settled in O'Brien county; was the first settler of the county. He moved to Sibley in 1876, and was elected county recorder; served until 1880; then engaged in his present business.

H. C. Hungerford, county treasurer and lumber dealer, was born in N. Y. in 1846; came to Sibley, in 1874, and engaged in the lumber business. He was elected to his present office in 1876, and re-elected in 1878.

C. W. Jenkins, proprietor of the restaurant and news depot; came to Sibley in the spring of 1871, and engaged in his present business in the spring of 1876.

H. Jordan, attorney at law, was born in O. in 1843; came to Benton county, Ia., in 1855. He enlisted in 1862, in Co. H, 18th Ia. Inft., and served until the close of the war; then returned to Vinton, Benton county, Ia., and began the study of law. He began practicing law in 1868, and moved to Sibley in 1872; is the pioneer lawyer of Osceola county.

W. R. Lawrence, M. D., was born in Essex county, N. Y.; removed to Wis. in 1851. He enlisted in Co. C, 1st Wis. Vol., and served three years; was wounded at Perryville, Ky. After the war he went to Freeborn county, Minn., and engaged in teaching school. He graduated from the Normal School at Winona in 1866; came to Sibley in 1872, and engaged in the drug business. He graduated from the Northwestern Medical College, at Chicago, in 1878. He was elected county superintendent of schools in Osceola county in 1879, which office he still holds.

D. D. McCallum, attorney at law, was born in Canada in 1847; came to Clayton county, Ia., in 1859. He enlisted Feb. 1st, 1864, in Co. I, 27th Ia. Vol.; was afterwards transferred to the Twelfth Ia., and was on duty in Ala. during the reconstruction of that state under President Johnson's administration. He came to Sibley in the spring of 1872; was admitted to the bar in 1879, and engaged in the practice of the law.

A. W. Mitchell, of the firm of Mitchell & Walton, furniture dealers, was born in N. Y.; removed to Hudson, Wis., in 1855. He enlisted in 1861 in Co. G, 4th Wis. Inft.; served two years, and was discharged on account of ill health. He moved to Iowa

Falls, Ia., in 1865, and engaged in the furniture business; thence to Steamboat Rock, and in 1872 to Sibley; in 1873 he engaged in his present business.

W. M. Moore, county auditor, was born in Pa. in 1841; enlisted in 1861 in Co. E, Pa. Bucktail regiment; was taken prisoner in June, 1862, and held until Aug. of that year. He was wounded several times, and lost his right arm at Weldon R. R. terminus, in Aug., 1864, from a gun shot. He served through the war, and then returned to Pa. He came to Sibley in 1872, and was elected to his present office in 1873, which he has held ever since.

W. H. Morrison, jeweler, was born in Pa. in 1833; came to Ia. in 1855, settled in Allamakee county, and engaged in the jewelry business. He enlisted in 1862 in Co. E, 27th Ia. Vol., and served until the close of the war. He came to Osceola county in 1871, and settled four miles north of Sibley; moved into the city in 1881, and engaged in the jewelry business.

Hiram Neill, M. D., is a native of Canada; came with parents to Minn. in 1855, and settled in Hennepin county. He enlisted in 1863 in Co. A, 4th Minn. Vol. Inft.; served until 1865, and then returned to Minn., and began the study of medicine with Dr. Maddox, of St. Paul. He graduated from the Michigan University in 1871, and from the Bellevue Hospital of N. Y. City in 1870. He practiced medicine for a time in Minneapolis, Minn., and came to Sibley in 1875, where he has a very extensive practice.

W. L. Parker, druggist, is a native of Wis.; removed to Minn. in 1868; located at St. James in 1869, and engaged in the drug business. He removed to Sibley in 1873, and carries a very fine stock of drugs, paints, oils, fancy groceries, etc.

H. W. Phillips, farmer, is a native of N. Y.; came to Delaware county, Ia., in 1858, settled in Osceola county in 1872, and on his present farm on section 32, range 41, in 1879. He was the first man to try to raise sheep in the county, and is largely engaged in the tree and fruit culture.

Capt. D. L. Riley, mayor of Sibley, was born in St. Lawrence county, N. Y., in 1837; removed to Wis. in 1854. He enlisted in 1861 in Co. C, 2nd Wis. Cav., under Col. C. C. Washburne. He enlisted as a private, and came out captain of the company at the close of the war. He returned to Wis. and remained there until 1871, when he came to Osceola county and settled near where Sibley is now located. Mr. R. has held several town offices, and has been engaged in the lumber, coal and grain business since his residence in this place, which business he intends to resume at Spirit Lake in the spring of 1882.

H. K. Rogers, the pioneer merchant of Sibley, was born in O. in 1847; removed in 1870 to Salt Lake City, Utah, and engaged in the mercantile business, and in the autumn of 1871 came to Sibley,

Ia., and built the first building in the town for a store and dwelling, on lots eight and nine, Ninth street. He was afterwards burned out there, and moved to his present place of business on Third avenue and Eighth streets. Mr. R. carries a large and complete stock of merchandise.

L. Shell, lumber dealer, was born in Wis. in 1838; removed to Worthington, Minn., in 1872; thence to Sibley in the spring of 1873, and engaged in his present business, dealing in all kinds of builders' supplies and grain. He enlisted in Aug., 1862, in Co. K. 23rd Wis. Vol., and on account of wounds received at the battle of Vicksburg, May 22nd, 1863, was discharged in Dec., of the same year.

H. Walters, proprietor of the Pioneer House, was born in N. Y. in 1826; came to Iowa in 1856, and settled in Chickasaw county; removed to Osceola county in 1871, and entered a homestead on section 10, township 79, range 41. He engaged in the hotel business in 1874, it being the first hotel in Sibley. He enlisted in 1863 in the 4th Ia. Cav., and served until the close of the war; was wounded at Memphis, Tenn., by being thrown from his horse while on duty.

C. D. & T. O. Wilbern, dealers in general merchandise, came to Cherokee county, Ia., in 1868 and engaged in farming; removed to Sibley in 1873 and engaged in their present business. They were burned out in November of the same year, started again, and have continued ever since. T. O. enlisted in 1864 in Co. C., 153rd Ill. Vol., and was discharged in 1865.

S. A. Wright, deputy treasurer, was born in N. Y. in 1842. He enlisted in 1862 in Co. C. 112th N. Y. Inft. In 1868 he came to Iowa and engaged in the mercantile business; came to Sibley in 1872, and followed various business pursuits, until 1874, when he was elected county treasurer, which office he held until 1876, when he was succeeded by Mr. Hungerford.

PLYMOUTH COUNTY.

The thriving and fertile county of Plymouth is on the western boundary of the State, in the third tier from the north line. Its average length east and west is about thirty-five miles, and its width north and south twenty-four miles. It contains an area of about 840 square miles, or 537,000 acres. The principal streams are Floyd River, West Fork of Little Sioux River, West Branch of Floyd River, and Broken Kettle, Perry and Willow Creeks. Floyd River, the largest stream, crosses the county diagonally from northeast to southwest. It has many important tributaries, affording fine stock water and drainage to a large portion of the county. It also affords some water-power for mills. The West Fork of Little Sioux River crosses the southeast corner, draining and watering two or three townships. The entire county has a thorough system of natural drainage through small streams which course their way through all parts of it. The streams are clear, and never fail to furnish a supply of living water, as most of them are supplied by springs. There are no swamps or marshes.

The general character of the surface is rolling prairie, with some broken land in the western part of the county. The soil is the productive bluff deposit peculiar to the western part of the state. The valleys along the streams are not excelled in fertility of soil, and are adapted to all kinds of grain and vegetable crops. The uplands are not so well adapted to corn as the valleys, but produce fine crops of wheat and oats. The valleys of Big Sioux and Floyd Rivers present splendid belts of rich farming lands. The county is well adapted to grazing purposes, as there is a never-failing supply of pure, living water for stock, with an abundance of excellent pasturage.

The supply of native timber is quite limited, the principal groves being along the Big Sioux River, and a few small groves on Floyd and the West Fork of Little Sioux. Some of the early settlers have fine groves of planted trees, which will soon attain sufficient growth to furnish fuel for their owners. Some stone has been quarried in this county, but it is of little use as a building material. Some of it is burned into a fair article of lime. Material for brick is obtained in sufficient quantity.

The first settlements by whites in the county were made in the Summer of 1856, and were in the valleys of Big Sioux and Floyd Rivers. The following persons that year located in the valley of Big Sioux River: J. B. Pinckney, David Mills, Isaac T. Martin, Bratton Vidito, J. McGill, John Hipkins, James Dormichy and a

Mr. Guillhams. The settlement on Big Sioux River was commenced by Martin, Vidito, McGill and Hipkins, the last named having a family. They erected two houses, one for Hipkins and his family, and the other for the young men. In July they laid out a town, calling it Westfield. This was the first town laid out in the county, and its proprietors regarded it as the future metropolis of the Big Sioux Valley.

In 1856, A. C. Sheets, James B. Curry, E. S. Hungerford, Corydon Hall and Joel Phillips located in the valley of the Floyd River. The county was organized October 12th, 1858, by William Van-O'Linda as organizing sheriff. The election was held at the house of John Hipkins, on the Big Sioux River, and at the house of A. C. Sheets, on Floyd River. The following persons were elected county officers: William Van O'Linda, County Judge; Isaac T. Martin, Treasurer and Recorder; A. C. Sheets, Clerk of the District Court; David Mills, Sheriff; and A. E. Rea, County Superintendent of Schools. The same Fall a township election was held at Westfield, on the Big Sioux, when Isaac T. Martin was elected Township Clerk. There were sixteen votes cast at this election. The county judge held his office on Floyd River, in the middle of the eastern part of the county, while the treasurer and sheriff held theirs in the Big Sioux Valley.

The first place recognized as the county seat was called Melbourne, and was more a scattered settlement than a village, in the Floyd Valley. Here the business of the county court was transacted, and here the first district court was held by Judge A. W. Hubbard. Here also the first religious meetings were held by the German Methodists, and the first school taught by William Van O'Linda. Westfield, the rival of Melbourne for the honors of the county seat, was abandoned in the Spring of 1860, on account of large selections or entries of land made in that vicinity by half-breed Indians, which greatly retarded the settlement. The entries of land were made with half-breed script.

LE MARS.

Throughout all of Western Iowa the name of "Le Mars" is indissolubly connected with the idea of thrift, prosperity and enterprise. It is a growing little city, a prosperous one, and a pleasant one in which to live, as witness the unanimous opinion of all who have had occasion for knowledge in the premises. By a vote of 476 to 111, at a general election of 1872, Le Mars was made the county seat of Plymouth County. Its location is at the junction of the Illinois Central and the Sioux City & St. Paul Railroads, twenty-five miles northeast of Sioux City. The land upon which the city is located, originally belonged to Jerry Ladd, B. F. Betsworth and Mr. Marion. The location of the town-site was accomplished in the summer of 1869. The facts in connection with the selection of a name for the future city, are thus narrated: "Soon after its location the place was visited by John I. Blair and other railroad officers, accompanied by a party of ladies. Upon the latter Mr. Blair conferred the privilege of selecting a name for the prospective city. The initial letters of the Christian names of the ladies were combined so as to form the name Le Mars, and it was agreed that this should be the name of the new town."

The first business firm established in Le Mars was that of Blodgett & Foster, who were very closely followed by J. W. Young, John Gordon, Orson Bennett and C. H. Bennett. The first newspaper in the county, the Le Mars Sentinel, was started by J. C. Buchanan February 3d, 1871. Le Mars is surrounded by an extensive farming region, and is a shipping point of unusual importance.

The City Council of Le Mars for 1881, was composed of the following gentlemen: George E. Pew, Frank Miller, Arthur Brown, P. F. Dalton, John Perkee, A. Aldrich. C. P. Woodward was the Mayor; G. W. Argo, City Solicitor.

All branches of business are largely represented, and in no locality in Western Iowa will there be found greater inducements in the way of pecuniary, domestic or educational attractions than in the growing little city of Le Mars. An unusually creditable showing of LeMars' business and professional interests appears in the addenda of a biographical nature which are hereunto appended.

Among the important industries of Le Mars, may be mentioned the pork packing establishment of Roberts, Frost & Heaphy. The building, which is located in the northeastern part of the city, was erected in the latter part of 1881. It is a frame building, 20x60 feet in dimensions, and has a capacity of disposing of three hundred hogs per day. This building was erected at a cost of nearly $4,000. It is fitted up with the most approved apparatus, and is doing a thriving business.

Le Mars is also supplied with two large flouring mills. The mill owned by Burns, Treat & Co., was erected in the spring of 1876, is 36x80 feet in dimensions, three and a half stories high, with a basement. It was fitted up with good machinery, had a run of eight buhrs, and a capacity of one hundred barrels of flour per day. This building was remodeled in 1881, and refitted with the most modern improvements, having all the latest patterns of purifiers and smut-machines. It now has a run of six buhrs and ten rollers, with a capacity of two hundred barrels of flour per day. This mill ranks with the great Minneapolis flouring mills in regard to quality of patent and fancy flour, graham flour, and all kinds of feed, and their flour may be found in New York, Boston and Chicago.

The City Mills, operated by Gehlen Bros., were erected in 1870, by Peter Gehlen, at a cost of $50,000. This mill is a fine frame building, 50x100 feet, with four run of buhrs, and has a capacity of fifty barrels per day. It has all the modern improvements, and is turning out a first-class quality of flour. One hundred and fifty thousand bushels of wheat are handled by this mill each year.

CHURCHES, SCHOOLS AND SOCIETIES.

Congregational Society.—This Society was organized in 1870, under the supervision of M. R. Amsden and John Blodgett. The first minister was Rev. R. M. Sawyer, who was succeeded by Rev. D. D. Frost, and he by Rev. A. E. Arnold, the present pastor. The Society built a church in 1873, which is 24 by 60 feet in dimensions and cost $2,500. The Deacons at the present writing are, J. H. Springer. A. W. Gilbert and John Blodgett.

First German Erangelical Church.—Organized in 1878 by Rev. J. Heinsnieller, who officiated as the first pastor. Following him, was Rev. V. Griese. The following named persons participated in the organization: George Brendtstaedter, A. Kehrberg, Mr. Schaeffer, Mr. Mueller. This society held services in the Court House previous to the building of the church, which was erected in 1881. It is a frame building, 20 by 40 feet, will seat from 300 to 400 people, and cost $1,800. The church was dedicated December 25th, 1873. The members of this society now number about twenty-five. It has in connection a Sabbath School numbering thirty pupils, with J. G. Koenig as Superintendent. The present Trustees are, L. S. Staebler, G. M. Smith, Jacob Merryman, Albert Kehrberg, J. G. Koenig. Rev. F. Loehle is the present pastor.

German Methodist Episcopal Society.—Organized in October, 1873, by Rev. E. W. Henke, who was the first pastor. The succeeding pastors were: Revs. John Hank, S. Koener, C. Stellner, A. Biebichaiser, T. H. Wellimeyer, the latter being the present pastor. They have a large Sunday School in connection with the church, Prof. Wernli acting as Superintendent. The church building was formerly used as a public school building, was purchased by this society in 1875, and fitted for church purposes, the basement being used as a parsonage. In 1880 the building was enlarged, and is now 24 by 52 feet in dimensions. The total cost of this building was $2,450. The present Trustees are: Prof. J. Wernli, A. Trader, D. W. Held, H. Kluckbohn, F. Remer. The church membership is about 110 persons, and there is a large attendance upon the Sabbath School.

Parish of Grace Episcopal Society.—The first steps towards forming this Parish, were taken in the year 1872. A Mission was then constituted by Bishop Lee, then Bishop of Iowa. In 1873 Rev. R. Trewartha accepted a call to the Mission. In the following year the Mission was incorporated into the Diocese as a Parish. Some success was at first met with, and a small building was purchased and used as a church. After a time, however, Mr. Trewartha left, and the Parish fell out of the Diocesan records. In 1881. Rev. H. P. Marriett-Dodington, M. A., of Trinity College, Cambridge, England, came to Le Mars and set himself diligently to work to revive the church. By this time the town had largely increased. A large influx of Episcopalians had arrived from England. Services were first held at the house of Messrs. Close, Benson & Co., and were afterwards transferred to the Van Sickel Hall. A sufficient sum was raised to warrant the commencement of the building of a large church on the south side of town, at the cost of about $4,000. About June, 1881, Mr. Dodington returned to England, having first reconstituted the Parish. He was succeeded by the Rev. H. N. Cunningham, M. A., of Brasenose College, Buford, England. Under his direction the funds required for the church were raised, and the church was begun and finished. The society hope shortly to build a good parsonage close to the church, on one of the handsomest sites in the town. The Rector, Rev. H. N. Cunningham, who took classical honors at Buford, is founding a school, principally for boarders; terms, $30 to $50 per month. It is hoped that a permanent endowment may be raised in course of time, and that an assistant clergyman may be provided. When the weather is favorable, monthly services are held in Quorn and Portlandville, and an opening is sought in other towns in the neighborhood.

German Lutheran Society.—Organized in July, 1881, Rev. F. Bunger being the first and present pastor. The church building was erected in the same year, is 24x40 feet in dimensions, and cost $800. The membership is from thirty to forty persons. H. Dethlow and John Deuschle are the Trustees.

Methodist Episcopal Society.—Organized in 1870, by Rev. J. T. Walker. The church edifice was erected in 1872, by R. W. Thumburey.

St. Joseph's Catholic Parish.—Organized in 1872, by Messrs. Peter Gehlen, C. D. Hoffman and B. F. Manahan. The pulpit of this church was at first supplied by clergymen from Sioux City. Father Meis was the first stationed pastor, and was appointed in 1875. He is still in charge of the Parish. The membership includes about 300 families, about one-fourth of whom are English. The church edifice was erected in 1872. The main building was 40x35 feet in dimensions. In 1876, the building was remodeled and enlarged to 90x35 feet, with a wing 40x30 feet. The building is three stories in hight. The wing is used as a residence for the Sisters of Charity, of whom there are six, and for school purposes. A Parochial school was organized in connection with this Parish in 1878, with about fifty pupils, under the tutorship of Rev. Father Meis. In May, 1879, the Sisters of Charity took charge of this school, and it now has an attendance of 150 pupils. A rectory was built in 1879, which is 26x34 feet in dimensions. These buildings were erected at a total expense of $7,000. There are nineteen acres of land belonging to this Parish, eleven acres on which the buildings are located, and which are within the corporate limits

392   HISTORY OF IOWA.

of Le Mars; and eight acres, set apart for a cemetery, lying east of the former, and adjacent to the city limits. These grounds are enclosed by good fences, are beautifully located, and set out in evergreens, with other trees and shrubbery. They are tastefully laid out and pleasantly situated. The cemetery grounds were procured from Peter Gehlen for a consideration of $75; the church grounds, from the Cedar Rapids Railroad Company for a consideration of $90. Rev. Father Meis, the present Rector, also has charge of Prairie Creek, Hosper's and East Orange societies.

The Public Schools.—Le Mars has a fine three-story brick school building. Ten rooms are occupied by as many teachers, and there is an average regular attendance of 350 pupils. The school enumeration shows 771 pupils in the district. The High School prepares its pupils for the Freshman year in the best colleges of the East, and requires as many years for completion as the course of the State Normal School at Cedar Falls. Three years of German and an equal amount of Latin are thoroughly taught. The classes in mathematics are taken as far as Trigonometry. The usual quota of sciences, and a more than common literary discipline are among the advantages of the course here. Mr. A. N. Fellows, the Principal, is a graduate of the State University at Iowa City, and was previously connected with the schools of Morning Sun and Knoxville, in this State.

The first school of the independent district was organized in 1874, the first school house having been built in 1870. The present High School building was erected in 1876, is 58x62 feet in dimensions, with three stories and a basement. The first corps of teachers was: W. H. Stone, Principal; Ella H. Earl, Mary Gallagher, Etta M. Stebbens. The first Board of Education consisted of: A. W. Bennett, A. H. Lawrence, L. Greer, E. H. Betsworth, T. H. Tracy, M. B. Fritz; John Herron, Treasurer; F. W. Guernsey, Secretary. The present Board of Education is as follows: P. F. Dalton, President; C. P. Woodard, W. H. Dent, J. Long, C. D. Hoffman, George Pew.

The following are the names of the present teachers: A. N. Fellows, Principal; Mary Lynn, Hannah Gallagher, Carrie Byrne, Bertha Alline, Emma Wernli, Jennie Buchanan, Susie Sawyer, Mrs. F. W. Guernsey, Nellie Sweetland.

Plymouth Lodge No. 332, I. O. G. T.—Instituted in June, 1880. Charter members: William Wernli, William Wynet, Mrs. William Wynet, Mr. and Mrs. L. M. Garner, T. H. Dodson, J. G. Koenig, J. H. March, H. Thompson, George Smith, John Jones, Fannie Van Sickel, William Boyd, Mr. and Mrs. Samuel S. Williams, Thomas Griffin, Annie Wallace, Mrs. William Wernli, George Claypool. First officers: William Wernli, W. C. T.; Annie Wallace, W. V. T.; Thomas Griffin, C.; J. C. Jones, R. S.; Mrs. William Wynet, F. S.; J. G. Koenig, Treasurer; L. M. Garner, W. M.; C. C. Leidy, I. G.; T. H. Dodson, O. G. Present officers: T. H. Dodson. W. C. T.; Mary Carmine, W. V. T.; J. H. March, R. S.; Liza Morris, F. S.; Ernest Gauss, Treasurer; W. H. Briggs, C.; C. Thompson, M.; Mary Norris, I. G.; William Nipper, O. G. This Lodge now has fifty-six members in good standing. Meetings are held Friday evening of each week in Odd Fellows' Hall. New members are being continuously added.

Le Mars Lodge No. 255, I. O. O. F.—Instituted March 26th, 1873, by G. M. C. G. Kretchmer. Charter members: A. Black, S. S. Ambrose, J. C. Morris, J. W. Earl. W. W. Spalding. J. F. Fairfax, Charles Blind, R. M. Click, H. C. Curtis, R. M. Thornburg, J. C. Buchanan, S. V. Burg. First officers: J. W. Earl, N. G.; R. W. Click, V. G.; H. C. Curtis, R. S.; W. W. Spalding, P. S.; T. M. Porter. Treasurer. Present officers: J. S. Dunscomb, N. G.; H. B. Perry, V. G.; E. J. Pauley, Treasurer; J. F. Fairfax, R. S.; George Stanley, C. This Lodge now has a membership of seventy-six, and meets every Wednesday evening in its room over the Plymouth County Bank.

Juno Lodge No. 390, I. O. O. F.—This is a German Lodge, the work being done in that language. It was instituted February 20th, 1879, by D. D. G. M. T. J. Kinkaid, of Sioux City. Charter members: Gustave Haerling, John P. Nith. M. Krudwig, Charles Striegel, Charles Zink, J. C. Buchanan, John Kleeman. August Forner, George Hodam, Charles Reichert. A. B. Steiner. First officers: A. B. Steiner, N. G.; Matthew Krudwig, V. G.; J. P. Nith. Secretary; Gus Haerling, Treasurer. Present officers: C. G. Nobis, N. G.; Aug. Ihle, V. G.; Gustave Haerling. Secretary; J. D. Szetnick, Treasurer. Meetings are held every Thursday evening at Odd Fellows' Hall. The Lodge is regularly incorporated under the laws of the State of Iowa, and has at the present writing, twenty-six active members.

Giblem Lodge No. 322, A. F. & A. M.—Instituted December 26th, 1872. Charter members: William Rymers. D. W. Cook, S. Reeves, E. W. Burdick, W. S. Welliver. J. H. Mori E. H. Shaw, W. H. Wood, T. K. Bowman, David Gibbs. G. W. W. Pen, I. Struble, H. W. VanSickel, C. R. Smith. James Cai i N. Redmon. First officers: David Gibbs. W. M.; D. W. C. S. W.; William Rymers, J. W.; W. S. Welliver. Secre H. Shaw, Treasurer. Present officers: W. S. Welliver, \ . . : C. Adamson, S. W.; N. L. Greer. J. W.; N. Redmon, S. : George Powers. Treasurer. The Lodge has a membership t sixty, and is in a flourishing condition. Meetings are n Tuesday evening in each month on er before the full a i Masonic Hall, in Flint's Block. Main street.

Plymouth Lodge, Iowa Legion of Honor.—Instituted i - ber. 1880. Charter members: A. W. Durley. J. M. En H. Euseninger, F. W. Myers. J. F. N. Snydensticker. W. . J. C. Hebenstreit. D. W. Townsend, C. P. Woodard, Lawrence, C. B. Smith. J. A. Jones, J. G. Koenig, W.

Henry March, N. Richards, I. S. Struble, H. C. Curtis, G. W.
Powers, A. C. Stebbens, A. W. Moulton, F. J. Jenness. First
officers: A. W. Durley, President: H. C. Curtis, Vice-President;
D. W. Townsend, F. S.; W. H. Perry, R. S. Present officers:
D. W. Townsend, President; H. C. Curtis, Vice-President; J. M.
Emery, F. S.; W. H. Perry. R. S. The Trustees are, W. H. Dent.
Henry March and C. B. Smith. This Lodge has a membership of
twenty-four, and meets twice in each month over Steiner's book-
store. The whole number of members of this order in the State
is put down at 4,800. It is an incorporated life insurance society.
each member being insured to the amount of $2,000. The average
assessment is only forty cents to each member in case of death of
any one of the members of the order.

Plymouth County Agricultural Association. —Organized in 1872
by William Barrett, Andrew Black, A. E. Rea, B. F. Betsworth.
M. Hilbert, and others. The first officers were: A. E. Rea, President. and M. Hilbert, Secretary. The present officers are: C. P.
Woodard, President; Hon. R. Moreton, Vice-President; G. C.
Maclagan, Treasurer; M. Hilbert, Secretary. This society holds
two annual meetings, viz: the June racing meeting and the annual
agricultural fair in September of each year. The society has forty
acres of land adjoining the town plat, and within the corporate
limits of Le Mars. These grounds are enclosed partly with a fence.
and partly with a thick hedge. A fine amphitheater has been built
within the past year. There are also an excellent half-mile track
and a floral hall 40x60 feet in dimensions. Over $1,000 are annu-
ally paid in premiums by the Association, and in 1881 the citizens
of Le Mars paid $1.000 additional. Much interest is taken in
these annual exhibitions.

Le Mars High School Lyceum. — Organized in October, 1881. with
Prof. A. N. Fellows as President; Lizzie Sawyer, Vice-President;
C. A. Spring, Jr., Secretary: Clara Rounds. Treasurer; Carrie Gil-
bert, Organist. The officers at the present writing are: J. H.
March, President; Carrie Gilbert, Vice-President; Allen Campbell.
Secretary; Prof. A. N. Fellows, Treasurer. The membership is
about thirty, and meetings are held every Monday evening in the
LeMars High School building, the order of exercises consisting of
vocal and instrumental music. select readings, declamations, essays,
debates, etc.

LeMars Public Library Association. —Organized in 1876, by
Mrs. Wilkins and Miss Burroughs. Its first officers were: Mrs.
P. F. Dalton, President; Mrs. Wilkins, Secretary. Mrs. Wilkins
removing from LeMars, Mrs. C. P. Woodard was appointed Secretary in her place. The present officers are: Mrs. Dalton, President; Mrs. C. P. Woodard, Secretary; A. Aldrich, Librarian.
This Association had in its library, up to December 1st, 1881, 440
volumes. There was at that time in the treasury $150. The first
Librarian was David Gibbs, Jr., who was succeeded by W. F. Al-

lenson, and in order, T. H. Dodson and A. B. Steiner, who was
followed by Mr. Aldrich, in whose store the library is at present
kept. These gratifying results are due to the labors of the ladies
of LeMars.

LeMars Fire Company, Rescue No. 1.—This Company was organized in August, 1881, with A. Richman as President; D. D.
Hoffman, Treasurer; T. D. Hoffman, Foreman, and D. Padmore,
Secretary. The Company now has a membership of fifty-two, and
has at present one small engine. A 400-pound bell has been donated to the Company by R. W. Harrison.

PLYMOUTH COUNTY BIOGRAPHIES.

LE MARS.

Frank Amos, attorney at law, was born in W. Va. in 1840;
moved to Ia. in 1853, and settled in Jackson county; thence in
1869 to Le Mars. He was mustered into the service in 1862, in
the 31st Ia., acting as first lieutenant; was wounded at Atlanta,
Ga., in 1864, and discharged in 1865; was admitted to the bar the
same year. He was married to Martha Brown, of O., and has two
children- -B. F. and Talitha C.

J. E. Arendt, dealer in millinery, fancy dry goods and ladies'
furnishing goods, was born in Dubuque, Ia., in 1858. He was engaged in clerking from 1869 to 1878, when he established his present business at Le Mars.

Rev. A. L. Arnold was born in Adams, Mass., in 1838; removed
to Ill. in 1856. He graduated from the Chicago Theological Seminary in 1867, and was engaged in the ministry in Ill. until Feb.
1st, 1876, when he came to Le Mars and took charge of the Congregational Church, of that city. In 1869 he married Emma F.
Bourne, of Mass.

Fred Barrow, proprietor of the House of Lords, in connection
with the international club room, was born in England in 1840;
came to America in 1864, and settled in Dyersville, Ia.; then moved
to Dakota in 1874; located at LeMars in 1880. He was married
in 1867 to Sarah Ham, of Eng., and has four children—William,
Alice, John and Jessie.

Hon. William Barrett came to Plymouth county, Ia., from
Wis. in 1857, locating in Hungerford township. He was elected
county judge and served in 1861 and 1862. At the expiration of
two terms, was elected chairman of the first board of supervisors

for the county, and served until 1878, when he was chosen representative for the 70th district, and is again chairman of the board of supervisors. He has a fine large farm in Lincoln township, where he lives in the enjoyment of the luxuries of a farmers' life. He has the reputation of being not only a successful farmer, but also of being well versed in county politics, and it is a saying that when "Uncle Billy" figures in the election of a certain candidate, "He'll be elected."

Hon. G. P. Bennett, M. D., was born in Duchess county, N. Y., in 1834; moved to Ia. in 1861. Enlisted in 1862 in the 27th Ia. Vol., Co. K, as sergeant; was discharged in 1865. He moved to Dak. in 1866, was elected to the legislature in 1868, and served two years. He was appointed collector of internal revenue in 1869, and chief deputy collector in 1874, and served four years. He began the practice of medicine in 1877, and graduated from the Hahnemann Medical College, of Chicago, in 1881. He married Alma A. Wolcott, of Steuben county, N. Y., who is also a graduate from Hahnemann Medical College, of Chicago, in the class of '81, and is practicing medicine in connection with her husband, at LeMars. They have seven children—Frank L., Mary C., Alma L., Marian W., Addie D. E., Gilbert G., and Ernest B.

Blodgett & Hilbert, real estate and insurance agents; loans negotiated, collections made, lands sold, taxes paid and a general real estate business done; have abstracts of all lands and town lots in Plymouth county, made by Mr. Hilbert during an official term of six years as county recorder. They established their present business in 1876.

T. L. Bowman, of the firm of Guthrie & Bowman, dealers in real estate, established business at Carroll City, Carroll county, Ia., in 1871, and in LeMars, in 1877. They are also agents for the Ia. Railroad land company.

W. H. Briggs, of the firm of Gilbert & Briggs, dealers in harness, saddles, whips, etc. (successors to J. N. Lambert) was born in Canada in 1851; moved to Iowa in 1871, and engaged in his present business. This firm was established in 1881. He was married in 1874 to Miss Goldie, and has four children—Blanche, Harry, Beulah, and ———.

Paul L. Brick, M. D., was born in Prussia in 1846; came to America in 1864, and settled in Auburn, N. Y.; moved to Pa.; thence to Wis. and Ill.; to Burlington, Ia., in 1871, and to LeMars in 1879. He graduated from the Louisenstadt Medical College, of Berlin, Ger., in 1864. He was married in 1871 to Ida Holdzkom; and in 1877, was married to E. Sniffs, and has two children—Louis and Paul.

Dr. E. D. Brower, dentist, was born in Carroll county, O., Jan. 15th, 1858; moved to Ia. in 1872. He is a graduate from the dental department of the University of Michigan, class of '81.

M. Burg, of the firm of Burg & Hentges, dealers in general merchandise, was born in Germany in 1839; came to America in 1846, and settled in Caledonia, Minn. He established business in Le Mars in 1874. In 1880 he was married to Lizzie Dondlinger, a native of Germany. They have one child, Gregor.

Alexander Clark, dealer in dry goods and notions, was born in Ireland in 1844; came to America in 1864. Engaged in the linen business in 1876, and in 1881 engaged in the mercantile business in Le Mars. He was married in 1870 to Cassandra Lee, a native of Eng., and has three children—John A., Mary E. and James M.

Rev. Herbert Noel Cunningham was born in Hampshire, Eng., in 1851; passed through Haileyburg, then Brazenose, Oxford College, Eng., in 1871. He took his degree of D. A. in 1876 in classical honors, and the degree of M. A. in 1878. He then went to Haven as master; then to Oxford Military College in 1876, and the next year to Oxford Ministry College. In 1877 he took orders in the church of England. Held services in Staffordshire, Oxfordshire, Portsmouth and Hampshire. In 1880 was incumbent of St. George's, Tilihurst, near Reading. In 1881, he came to America and took charge of the Episcopal church, of Le Mars.

P. F. Dalton, president of the Plymouth County Bank, was born in Ireland in 1838; came to America in 1849, and settled in Livingston county, N. Y.; removed to Sandusky county, O., in 1854. In 1862 he enlisted in Co. G, O. Inft.; was appointed lieutenant, and served until the close of the war. In 1866 he located in Buchanan county, Ia., and in 1872 moved to Le Mars. The bank was established in 1874, with Joseph Wilson as president, and G. B. Van Sann as cashier. Mr. D. was married to Mary Few, a native of O., and has two sons.

W. H. Dent is president of the Le Mars Bank, which was established in 1872, by Rymer & Kent. In 1873 the firm was Proctor, Kent & Co.; in 1874, Wm. Rymer, and in 1875, W. H. Dent. He was born in Putnam county, Ill., in 1843, and moved west in 1875. He was elected a member of the school board of Le Mars in 1878. In 1871, he was married to Cora Cheiver, of Ill. They have two children—Hattie C. and Edith C.

J. G. Dietrich, proprietor of meat market, was born in Milwaukee, Wis., in 1850; engaged in the butcher business in 1864; moved to Fort Dodge, Ia., in 1871; thence the next year to Nebraska City, and in 1877 came to Le Mars and established his present business. He was married in 1871 to Miss Hodam, of Sioux City, and has four children - Minnie, Frank, Albert and Kate.

H. F. Dow, of the U. S. Clothing Co., dealers in clothing, hats, caps, boots, shoes, and gents' furnishing goods, was born in Sycamore, Ill., in 1852; was engaged in the clothing business at Colorado Springs, from 1878 to 1881, when he came to Le Mars, and established his present business. He married Mary McMorris, of Colorado. in 1881.

T. H. Dodson, dealer in groceries, queensware, notions, and gents' furnishing goods. was born in Sept., 1861, in Wis.; moved to Le Mars and engaged in the mercantile business in 1873.

A. M. Duns, county auditor of Plymouth county, was born in Germany in 1849; came to America in 1870 and engaged in the insurance business in Le Mars. He was elected town clerk and assessor in 1878. and to his present office in 1879. In 1873 he was married to Wynea Grade, of Ia. They have two children, Marcus and William.

J. M. Emery. postmaster, was born in Fairfield, Me., Jan. 1st, 1845; moved to Pa. in 1852. He enlisted in 1862 in the 3rd Pa. heavy artillery; was taken prisoner Feb. 1st, 1864, at Smithfield, Va., and confined in Andersonville fifty-three weeks, and was discharged June 1st, 1865, as paroled prisoner. He then engaged in the lumber business in Pa. In 1875 he settled at Le Mars and engaged in editing the Iowa Liberal. which was at that time a republican paper. In 1869 he was appointed postmaster. He was instrumental in organizing the Northwestern Iowa S. S. association, of which he was the president. in 1879. In 1865 he married Luella Clark, of Pa., and has two children—Mary L. and Clark.

W. H. Ensminger, M. D., was born in Lancaster, Pa., in 1842; moved to O. in 1864; thence to Ill. the next year, and in 1879 he came to Le Mars and engaged in the practice of his profession. He graduated from Jefferson Medical College, at Philadelphia, Pa., in 1871. In 1862 he enlisted in the 135th Pa. Vol., Co. E, and served one year. He married Sarah E. Patten, of Ill., in 1871. They have two children—Blanche and Gracie.

G. E. Eva, dealer in harness, saddles, whips, collars. etc.; also dealer in hides; was born in Dodgeville, Wis., in 1853; moved to Le Mars and established his present business in 1880. He married Clarissa Bastian, of Mineral Pt., Wis., in June, 1881.

N. C. Evans, of the firm of N. C. Evans & Co., dealers in dry goods, notions, and carpets, was born in Bellevue, Ia., in 1852; moved to Wis.; thence to Waverly, Ia., and to Le Mars, in Sept., 1878, and engaged in his present business. He married Lizzie Kegler, of Ia., in 1878. They have one child—Charley.

J. F. Fairfax. general house and carriage painter, established business in 1871. He was born in Boston, Mass., in 1848; moved to Wis. in 1866, and to Ia. in 1871. He was married in 1875 to Mary Merrick. of Ill.. and has two children—Nellie and Frank.

G. G. Gosting, photographer, was born in England in 1847; came to America while quite young. and settled in Cleveland, O.; moved to Delaware county, Ia., in 1858; thence to LeMars in 1876, and established his present business. He served in the 3d Ia. Inft. and was wounded at the battle of Shiloh; enlisted in 1861, and was discharged in 1864.

C. Gottschalk, attorney at law, office corner of Sixth and Main streets, LeMars, Ia.; will practice in all courts in this and adjoining counties.

Harder & Kemper, proprietors of the LeMars marble works, established business in 1881. Mr. Kemper was born in Ia. in 1853, and moved to LeMars, in 1881. Mr. Harder was born in N. Y. in 1842, and moved to Iowa in 1876.

J. F. Heeb, proprietor of restaurant and sample rooms, also dealer in ice and grain, was born in St. Louis in 1840; moved to Dubuque, Ia., in 1846; thence to LeMars in 1877, and established his present business. He was with Gen. Price in his last raid through Kan., in 1865, also in the battle at Westpert, Mo. In 1867 he was married to Susan Steermer, of Potosi, Wis. They have six children—Francis A., Joseph P., Eugene E., Mary, Estella E., and Arthur B.

John Herron, county treasurer of Plymouth county, was born in Ireland in 1834; came to America in 1850, and located at Madison, Wis., and engaged in the printing business. He removed to Mineral Pt.; thence in 1869 to Sioux City, Ia., and the same year to LeMars. He was elected to his present office in 1873. In 1874 he was married to Susan Gehlen, of Ia.

J. W. Hines, M. D., was born in Va. in 1828. He graduated from Emery and Henry College, Va., in 1857, and from the University of Va. in 1861, and engaged in the practice of medicine in 1865. He located at LeMars in 1880.

James Hopkins, sheriff of Plymouth county, was born in 1846 in Canada; moved to N. J. in 1852; thence to Ia. in 1856. He located at LeMars in 1873, and was elected to his present office in 1875. In 1871 he was married to Mary E. Murphy, and has four children—Thomas, James, Mary and Vivian.

I. M. Irmen, practical watchmaker, engraver, and manufacturing jeweler, also dealer in watches, clocks, silver plated ware, jewelry, etc.; fine watch repairing a specialty; established business in Oct., 1881, corner of Main and Sixth streets. He was born in Germany in 1855; came with his parents to America in 1857, and settled in Grant county, Wis.; moved to LeMars in 1881.

M. B. Kelley, county attorney, was born in Berkshire county, Mass., in 1859; moved to Mich. in 1871, and engaged in teaching school; afterwards studied law, and was admitted to the bar in 1880.

J. C. Kelley, attorney at law, was born in Canada in 1843; moved to Wis. in 1849; thence to Lyons, Ia., in June, 1860. In 1861 he enlisted in the 16th Ia. Vol.; lost his right arm in the battle of Pittsburg Landing, April 6th, 1862, and was discharged on the 25th of the following Aug. He attended the Notre Dame University, of Ind., from 1863 to 1865, and then went to Washington and graduated from Columbia College, as B. B. L. In 1870 he moved to Carroll county, Ia.; thence to Le Mars. In 1879 he married Ella C. Rilea, of Ia., and has two children—Maud and Jessie.

N. B. Kiser, dealer in boots and shoes, was born in Luxemburg, Germany, in 1833; came to America in 1854, and settled in Jackson county, Ia., in 1857. In 1875 he removed to Le Mars. He married Annie Kefel, a native of Germany, in 1856, and has seven children—Katie, Mary, Maggie, Tinnie, Lizzie. John and Peter.

J. G. Koenig, barber, was born in Germany in 1840; came to America in 1858, and engaged in the barber business in Baltimore; moved to Plymouth county, Ia., in 1871, and to Le Mars in 1879. In 1865 he married Mary E. Merryman, of Baltimore. They have six children—Carrie V., Jacob M., Theresa E., Ida C., Florence E., Herbert D. and J. G.

G. C. Maclagan, of the firm of Maclagan, Warren & Watson, proprietors of the Floyd meat market, was born in Scotland, in the city of Edinburgh, in 1852; came to America in 1880. Mr. Warren is a native of Ireland, and Mr. Watson, a native of Scotland. They are also proprietors of the Floyd feed and sale yard; stock sold at auction; established business in 1881.

Rev. Father Meis, of St. Joseph's Catholic parish, Le Mars, Ia., was born in Prussia, in 1835; came to America in 1867. He graduated from St. Francis Seminary, at Milwaukee, Wis., in 1875, and was ordained the same year.

C. A. Meyer, of the firm of McManus & Meyer, proprietors of the South Side meat market, was born in Germany in 1849; came to America in 1851, and located at Fond du Lac, Wis.; removed to Ia. in 1874, where he engaged in undertaking and carpentery, until he established the above business in Oct., 1881.

S. B. Mickley, proprietor of the Mickley House, was born in Pa., March 22nd, 1818; removed to N. Y. in 1835; thence to Ia. in 1866; settled in Bremer county, and engaged in the butcher business; thence to Le Mars. In 1842 he married Sarah Frantz, of N. Y. They have four children--Henry, Hudson, Emma and Cora.

Frank Miller, of the firm of Frank Miller & Co., dealers in groceries, fruits, queensware, willow ware, and notions, was born in Luxemburg, Ger., in 1842; came to America and settled in Dubuque, Ia., in 1865. He engaged in the mercantile business in Le Mars in 1876. He is a member of the city council. In 1871 he married Anna Beach, of Bavaria, Ger., and has five children—Argeline, Frank, Joseph, Louis and Nicholas.

J. W. Myers, cashier of the Plymouth County Bank, was born in Warren, Trumbull county, O., in 1832; moved to St. Paul, Minn. in 1854, where he resided eleven years; then removed to Independence, Ia., and came to Le Mars in 1878. He married Mary L. Kemberly, a native of Mich.

H. S. Payn, of the firm of Smith & Payn, real estate, law and insurance agents, was formerly engaged in farming in Plymouth county, Ia., and still owns a fine stock farm, situated two and one-half miles north of Le Mars.

J. F. Patterson, gun and locksmith, also dealer in rifles, shot guns, revolvers and all kinds of sporting supplies; was born in 1853, in O., was engaged formerly in telegraphing and merchandising; established his present business in 1878. In 1879 he married Abbie Noland, of Hazel Green, Wis., and has one child—Charley F.

W. H. Perry, dealer in coal, lime and cement, established business in 1880. He was born in Ill. in 1847; moved to Ia. in 1854. He enlisted in 1865 in the 44th Ia. Vol., under Col. Henderson, and was discharged the same year. In 1873, he married Leone Bond, of Buchanan county, Ia. They have two children—Maud and Bessie.

G. E. Pew, of the firm of Pew & La Rue, dealers in general hardware, also farm machinery, pumps, wagons, paints, and oils; was born in Wis. in 1850; moved to Le Mars in 1875, and engaged in the hardware business; is a member of the city council. He married Belle Burrows, of Dubuque, and has one child—George.

A. Reichman, dealer in dry goods, notions, ready-made clothing, gents' furnishing goods, hats, caps, groceries, crockery, glassware, etc.; was born in Germany in 1840; came to America in 1845, locating in Buffalo, N. Y.; moved to Dubuque, Ia., in 1864, and engaged in the grocery, flour and feed business. In 1877 he established his present business at Le Mars.

Geo. E. Richardson, real estate, loan, collection and insurance agent; makes improved farms and non-resident lands a specialty; taxes paid and abstracts furnished in Plymouth and Sioux counties. He was born in Springfield, Mass., in 1850; moved to Ill. in 1855; thence to Ia. in 1868, and was engaged in the produce business at Iowa Falls and Durango. He established his present business in 1879.

C. B. Smith, of the firm of Smith & Payn, real estate and collection agents, was born in N. Y. in 1847; moved to Ia. in 1873, and engaged in farming. In 1879 he engaged in his present business at LeMars.

H. S. Roberts, attorney at law, was born in 1859, in Joe Daviess county, Ill.; moved to Winfield, Kas., in 1879, and was admitted to the bar in 1881. He is also engaged in the real estate and loan business. Sept. 14th, 1880, he married Sarah Pooley, of Illinois.

F. A. Seaman & Co., dealers in musical instruments; special attention given to tuning and repairing organs and pianos. Although this firm was established as late as 1881, Mr. L. is an old and experienced hand at the business; having served an apprenticeship in tuning and repairing, and was connected with the business as early as 1860, in Dubuque, Ia., his former place of residence. He is therefore fully competent to distinguish between good and poor instruments, and will give his patrons a number one instrument at the lowest possible price.

J. H. Struble, attorney and collecting agent, was born in Newton, N. J., 1838; moved to Va.; thence to O.; was county treasurer of Tama county, Ia., from 1866 to 1870. He came to Le Mars 1872, and engaged in the law, loan and insurance business, in the firm of Struble Bros., and in 1880 retired from the firm and engaged in the law, loan, and collection business. He married Elizabeth C. Koehler, of N. J. They have two children—Louis W. and Florence E.

C. W. Trottnow, watchmaker and jeweler, was born in Prussia in 1849; came to America in 1856, and settled in Lee county, Ill.; moved to Neb. in 1868, came to Le Mars in 1879, and engaged in his present business. In 1873 he married Caroline Kalkman, a native of Switzerland, and has five children—Louis A., Mamie, Charles F., and ——

W. S. Welliver, clerk of the courts, was born in Greenwood, Pa., in 1847; moved to Ill. in 1856; thence to Le Mars, June 30th, 1872. He was elected clerk of the courts in Jan., 1879. In 1872 he married Isabel De Witt, of Wis., and has one child, Ralph L.

Prof. J. Wernli, superintendent of schools for Plymouth county, was elected to the office in 1880. He was formerly engaged as assistant principal of the Normal School at Plattville, Wis. He granted sixty first-grade and fifty-six second-grade certificates to teachers in this county during the past year.

L. A. Williams, baker and confectioner, was born in St. Paul, Minn., in 1857; moved to Ia. in 1878, and engaged in the bakery business at Storm Lake; came to Le Mars in 1880. He married Jennie Cummings, of Storm Lake, in 1880.

C. P. Woodard, mayor of Le Mars, and dealer in agricultural implements and real estate, was born in N. Y. in 1847; moved to Le Mars in 1873, and succeeded Blodgett & Flint in the agricultural implement business. He was elected president of the Plymouth county agricultural society in Jan., 1881, and mayor of the city in June of the same year. In 1873 he married C. T. Sheldon. They have one child, J. Sheldon.

SHELBY COUNTY.

The location of Shelby County is in the fourth tier from the southern boundary line of the State, and in the second east from the Missouri River. Shelby County is twenty-four miles square, and contains about 576 square miles. The general surface of the county is rolling, with deeply excavated valleys along the larger streams, while in some portions of the county it is quite rough and broken, with steep, precipitous hills and deeply cut valleys. The universally conceived idea of a prairie country is not wholly realized in Shelby County. A writer some years ago ventured the following imaginative bit of description, which for want of a better illustration, we here insert: "If the imagination of the reader will enable him to conceive what a tract of land would be. that had been in a liquid state, and had been so violently agitated that high waves ran from east to west, and these had suddenly received a transverse motion and solidified while the breakers were dashing in ponderous masses towards the skies, he will have a tolerably correct idea of the appearance of a large portion of the prairie in the northwestern portion of this county." Nevertheless, this is a very valuable agricultural section, the hillsides having an excellent soil, peculiarly adapted to the cultivation of fruit of all kinds, many considering it a decided advantage rather than a detriment to Shelby County.

The bottom lands usually slope towards the streams, and along the West Nishanabotany, which is one of the finest and most beautiful valleys in the State, average more than one mile in width, and are lined by narrow clumps of timber. All of the valleys in the county possess a soil of unsurpassed fertility, which, like most other portions of the county, is composed of a fine material known as the bluff deposit. The soil of the whole Northwestern Slope differs from that of the eastern and central portions of the State in that it has not the heavy sub-soil and under-stratum of clay. In Shelby County this peculiarity is quite noticeable, since, after a heavy shower or series of rain storms. plowing may be immediately resumed, the water which falls being soon absorbed by the earth. sinking rapidly away on account of the absence of clay to stop or impede its progress. The soil here is a rich, silicious loam, well adapted to the production of the usual western crops, with the single exception of the tame grasses. Corn, for which there is no better or more favorable soil than is found in these valleys, is probably the staple, while wheat. oats and other kinds of grains, as well as the different grasses and vegetables, grow to great perfection.

The county is thoroughly well watered, the West Nishnabotany River, which flows southward nearly through the middle of the county, receiving from the east the waters of the Middle Nishnabotany, Whitt's and Indian Creeks, while the western part of the county is drained by the affluents of the Missouri and Boyer Rivers, the most important of which are Silver, Mosquito, Pigeon and Picayune Creeks. Mill Creek is a small stream in the northwest, which flows into the Boyer in Harrison County, and on which is Garland's Grove, a fine body of native timber embracing nearly one thousand acres. Besides this, there are several fine groves bordering some of the other streams, which embrace the varieties commonly found throughout this section of the State, such as burr and red oak, white and red elm, butternut, hackberry, black walnut, ash, linn and ironwood; while there is often found a heavy growth of sumac, hazel, thornapple, blackberry, gooseberry and grape. Where now may be observed a little outlaying thicket of hazel and sumac—the pioneers of forest increase—a few years hence, unless arested by the devastating fires, groves of thrifty saplings will have sprung up, and thus, within a comparatively short time, by the repetition of this process, the beautiful prairie slopes will be converted into forest-clad ridges and sombre thicket-dells, as wild and uninviting to the agriculturist as the native forests of the middle States. The apparent scarcity of timber in this county is in reality no serious drawback to its rapid settlement, as building lumber can be easily obtained from the pineries of the north, and as these vast meadows of unbounded fertility hold out inducements to the settler such as no forest-clad region can boast.

The entire county is supposed to be underlaid by the upper coal measure, as the strata is known to exist in counties to the south and west, but is here concealed under the post teritary deposit not less than 250 feet beneath the surface. The supply of building material is limited, yet a fair quality of brick is made of the material of the bluff deposit. The only stone obtained for building are the boulders of the drift formation found scattered in various places.

Previous to any permanent settlements in the county, it was frequently visited by trappers and hunters, two men named Bowman and Berry being among the number. The county was organized in 1853, the following being the first county officers: James M. Butler, County Judge; V. Perkins, Clerk of the District Court; Andrew Foutz, Sheriff. The counties of Crawford and Carroll were at that time attached to Shelby for political, judicial and revenue purposes. Judge Samuel H. Riddle held the first session of the District Court for the three counties in the grocery of Solomon Hancock, at Galland's Grove. At this session the following attorneys were present: H. P. Bennett, of Glenwood; L. M. Cline, A. C. Ford and David Price, of Council Bluffs. At the election which made choice of the first county officers, only thirteen votes were polled.

About the time of the organization of the county, a town was laid out in the northwest corner township, to which the name of Shelbyville was given, and in 1854 this place was designated as the county seat, but the County Judge, being opposed to it, procured Hancock's grocery for holding the first court. The next term of the District Court was held, however, at Shelbyville. This was the first town laid out in the county, but is now known only in history, as the houses have all been removed to Harlan, and to the neighboring farms. Shelby County sent forty-seven soldiers into the war of the rebellion, though it had no organized company, the volunteers all joining organizations in the neighboring counties. Harlan, of which a lengthy description is given below, is the county seat, other settlements—more or less inconsiderable—in the county being Monteno, Mallory, Defiance, Westphalia, Kirkman, Shelby and Elk Horn.

HARLAN.

This thriving city, one of the best located and most prosperous on the western slope of Iowa, is situated in Harlan Township, Shelby County, and is the county seat. It is somewhat south of the geographical center of the county, but nevertheless, as a county seat, it is well placed. The exact location is just below the confluence of the middle and west branches of the Nishnabotany River, on the west side of the latter branch. The railway facilities of the place are furnished by the Harlan & Northern Branch of the Chicago, Rock Island & Pacific Railroad. This branch is thirteen miles in length, and runs from Avoca, on the main line, to Harlan. This line runs two mixed trains each way per day, and a large amount of produce is carried over the line. In addition to the railroad already existing, nearly the entire right of way for the building of an extension by the Chicago & Northwestern Railway Company from Kirkman to Harlan, seven miles, has been secured. The building of the line, however, seems to be surrounded by minor difficulties. The Iowa & Southwestern Railway, one of the Northwestern branch lines, now runs into Kirkman, and it is from this branch the proposed extension will, if present plans are carried out, be built. In addition to this, several other railway companies, among them the C., M. & St. P., give indications of probable future building in the same direction. In any event, the day appears not far distant when Harlan will have connection with eastern markets by one or two other routes than the branch line previously mentioned.

Harlan is a handsome place and handsomely situated on rising ground on the west side of the river. There are several slopes from the business portion of town, and the country is delightfully rolling for miles; therefore the drainage and water are excellent, and malarial complaints are almost unknown in the vicinity.

The city is laid out in a different manner from most northern cities, and but for its life and enterprise, which are apparent at first glance, would give one the impression of a Spanish or Mexican town. Though the city has numerous streets and considerable traffic in all directions, yet the main business portion of the place faces the center of the square of about one block in size, in the extreme center of which is enclosed the court-house. The arrangement throws the heavier portion of the trade of the place around a common center, and makes easy of access any business house. The buildings centering around the square are remarkably good for a new city, and many of them are large brick structures that would be a credit to a place three times the size of Harlan. The merchants all seem to be thriving, and heavy and well-selected stocks of goods are the rule. That the business men are well patronized is evidenced by the hundreds of teams that may be seen in the public square on any fine day during the busy season.

The business houses of Harlan may be summed up as follows: Eight general merchandise stores, four drug stores, three banks, representing an aggregate capital of $150,000 or more. boot and shoe store, book and news store, three grocery and crockery stores, two merchant tailor shops, two clothing and hat and cap stores, three hardware stores, two furniture and undertaking establishments, three milliners, three dress makers, four agricultural implement dealers, three lumber yards, four coal dealers, two jewelers, five land and loan agents, two brokers, five grain dealers, four stock dealers, three newspapers, two photographers, three barbers, three hotels, six restaurants, billiard hall and saloon, billiard hall, four saloons, two livery stables, four blacksmith shops, two blacksmith and wagon shops, five paint shops, ten contractors and builders of various descriptions, three harness makers, four boot and shoe makers, two bakers, two brickyards, each employing quite a number of men, two grist mills, one run by steam and the other by water, creamery, fence factory, three meat markets, nursery, two butter and egg dealers, house-mover, thirteen insurance agents. One of the blacksmith shops mentioned does considerable machine work. The professions are represented by eighteen attorneys, eleven physicians, two surveyors, dentist and three music teachers.

Harlan has also become metropolitan enough to maintain a telephone exchange. This has thirty-three subscribers, and good use is made of it. This institution was established about a year ago, with twenty or more subscribers, and the list, through good management, has been gradually increasing.

The population of Harlan, by the census of 1880, was 1,303, but the growth of the city has been very rapid since, and the number of residents now variously estimated at from 1,600 to 2,000. The latter figure has been estimated on the vote of last fall, and is probably not far from the correct one. The town is still growing

at a good rate, and numerous improvements are being made.
Among the most worthy of note of these is the brick opera house
being erected by J. M. Long, one of Shelby County's old citizens
and Harlan's enterprising men. The building will be a two-story
brick structure, 44x120 feet in dimensions. The lower story will
be divided into stores, and the upper story will be the opera
house proper. The cost will be something over $25,000. The
work of excavation for the foundation has been nearly completed,
and the opening of spring will see building commence. The
appointments of the structure will be first-class.

Harlan was named after Iowa's ex-senator of that name.

The survey of the original plat of Harlan was begun April 14th,
1858, by N. M. Kinney, surveyor. The plat comprised eighty
acres, and was surveyed for Dr. A. F. Ault. This original plat is
now known as "Old Harlan." Previous to this, Dr. Ault and others had platted a town on the opposite side of the Nishnabotany,
which town rejoiced in the euphonious name of "Simoda." Dis-
sensions occurred in the ranks of the proprietors of the site, and it
was this which led to the laying out of Harlan by Dr. Ault. On
July 15th, 1859, James M. Long platted an addition to Harlan of
160 acres. This addition now comprises the central portion of the
city. Mr. Long platted a second addition of eighty acres on September 16th, 1879. On January 15th, 1880, D. M. Wyland platted the portion of the town known as McDonald's addition. This
addition was bought by Wyland after McDonald had platted the
land and made arrangements for its recording; hence the reten-
tion of the name. On September 7th, 1880, Samuel L. Ganser and
D. Z. Ganser platted a small addition of fifteen lots. August 10th,
1881, another small addition known as Davis' addition, was platted by J. W. Davis. Wyland's addition of about sixty acres was
recorded by C. J. and D. M. Wyland on September 8th, 1881.
These numerous additions now give a space to the town plat of
about a section.

The first settler on the town site of Harlan was Isaac Plum, who
came about the time the town was laid out. Of the old settlers
living here at present, the second in length of residence is H. C.
Holcomb, Clerk of Courts. David Randall is another old settler,
as is also Peter Barnett. There were other settlers who came
prior to the advent of these gentlemen, but they have moved away.
Those named all came in the spring of 1858, as did Dr. Ault who
platted the town.

Harlan made no particular growth after the first two years until
the railroad was built· In fact, it is stated on good authority that
there were more people in the place in 1860 than there were in 1868.
The breaking out of the civil war took away a large number who
never returned, and various other causes also induced a heavy emigration. Since the advent of the railroad, however, the growth of the
city has been rapid and uniform, especially during the last two years.

The buildings of Harlan are mainly of recent construction; but there are one or two that date back almost to the time the original town plat was made. Among these is E. Bergstresser's dwelling house, which was the second dwelling erected in Harlan. This building was originally erected as a store in the spring of 1858. It has since been enlarged and remodeled. The next oldest building standing is William Errett's dwelling, erected by Isaac Plum in 1859. The Court House, though it had two predecessors, one of which was burned and the other turned into a tenement house, is also an old building. The last named structure, it must be stated, is a frame building of very indifferent character, and does not do an enterprising city like Harlan any great amount of credit. There is, however, a probability that a better building will be erected. This is greatly needed and will be hailed with gratitude by the majority of the people in Shelby County.

Harlan was incorporated in May, 1879, as a city of the second class. The first officers of the city were: Wm. Wyland, Mayor; Cyrus Beard, Recorder. The Trustees were, J. M. Long, Thomas Ledwich, D. M. Wyland, Peter Brazie, John Coenen, J. B. Stutsman. G. S. Rainbow was the first Marshal, and G. S. Gibbs the first City Treasurer. The present officers are: Thomas Ledwich, Mayor; Cyrus Beard, Recorder; D. M. Wyland. G. S. Gibbs, T. J. Robinson. John Coenen, J. B. Stutsman, E. J. Trowbridge, Trustees. L. D. Frost is City Treasurer; G. W. Watkins, Marshal; H. M. McGinnis, Street Commissioner.

The first postoffice established in the vicinity of Harlan was at the original town site, Simoda, in the summer of 1858. Samuel Dewell, at present postmaster at River Sioux, Harrison County, was the first appointed to the office. After some squabbling, the county seat was removed to Harlan in 1859, and the postoffice followed a few days after. The first postmaster, after the removal of the office to Harlan, was A. L. Harvey. ;Mr. Harvey was succeeded by D. H. Randall, still a resident of Harlan. At that time official red tape was not interwoven in the postoffice so closely as at present, and the mail, which was extremely small, was kept in a nail-keg or candle-box and stowed away in a corner. As occasion required, the box or keg was emptied out on the floor and the "boys" told to pitch in and sort the letters for themselves. The business of the office is now very large, and the candle-box system cannot well be continued. The present postmaster is B. I. Kinsey, who has held the office about fourteen years. The office was made a money order office July 1st, 1877.

The first mercantile business in Harlan was carried on by Dr. Ault, the founder of the town, who, about the time the town was platted, put in a small stock of general merchandise. The greater portion of the goods was carried in his arms by the Doctor from some neighboring town. This, though the first store in Harlan, did not pay well, and it was soon closed out.

The newspapers of Harlan are three in number and all are paying property. The date of the establishment of the first newspaper in Harlan or Shelby County is somewhat obscured by the dust of antiquity, but the "oldest inhabitant" sets down a paper known as the *Courier*, published at Shelby, as the first paper issued in the county. The publisher's name is not given. Several papers were started in Harlan before either of the present ones, but none of them "came to stay." In regard to those now in Harlan, we quote the following from a local writer:

The Harlan *Herald* was established in December, 1874, by Geo. Musgrave as a Republican journal, and has continued steadily on in that line to date. In 1875 George D. Ross purchased the office, and in 1876 he also bought the Shelby County *Record*, merged it into the *Herald*, continuing its publication until July 16th, 1877, when he sold the office and real estate to R. W. Robins. January 17th, 1880, C. R. Pratt, of Essex, Connecticut, bought a half-interest, sold out in December, 1880, to E. R. Parmelee, and March 1st, 1881, bought R. W. Robins' half interest. E. R. Parmelee came to Harlan in October, 1880. An interest in the office was recently purchased by a brother of Mr. Pratt, the firm now being Pratt Brothers.

Up to 1880 the paper was a seven-column quarto, when it was enlarged to nine columns, and served to a complete new dress, and an excellent cylinder power press ad led to the office. It is the largest paper ever published in the county, and has a large circulation. It is issued weekly, on Thursdays.

The Harlan *Tribune*, the first Democratic newspaper in Harlan, was established in June 1880, by U. S. Brown and A. D. Tinsley.

U. S. Brown commenced the newspaper business about thirteen years ago as editor of the Moberly *Daily*, at Moberly, Mo. From there he went to Lawrence, Kansas, as city editor of the Kansas *Daily Tribune*. About eight years ago he came to Iowa—first to Burlington as city editor of the *Gazette*; from there to Indianola, Warren county, as local editor of the Indianola *Tribune*. In January, 1879, he came to Harlan and engaged with George D. Ross as editor of the *Herald*, continuing about four months. In the latter part of May he commenced canvassing for the establishment of the *Tribune*, and succeeded in working up for it a liberal patronage. In March, 1881, he was elected city assessor.

The *Tribune* is now published by A. D. Tinsley.

The *Harlan Hub* was established in December, 1880, by Webb M. Oungst, who commenced the newspaper business about twelve years ago, at the case, in Grand Junction. He was afterwards employed by Mills & Co., of Des Moines, and with State Printer G. W. Edwards, and still later as foreman and local editor of the Creston *Gazette*, owning a half-interest therein. He came to Harlan, June 6th, 1879, and was foreman about two months in the *Tribune* office, and thereafter foreman in the *Herald* office, until he established the *Hub*. The *Hub*, like its contemporaries, is flourishing.

27

The stage facilities of Harlan are very adequate. Daily trips are made between Harlan and Kirkman, semi-weekly between Harlan and Denison, and tri-weekly between Harlan and Dunlap and intermediate points, weekly between Harlan and Logan. There is no trouble in obtaining transportation to almost any neighboring point on either of the railroads in this section of Iowa.

CHURCHES, SCHOOLS AND SOCIETIES.

Methodist Church Society.—This was the first religious society established in Harlan, and was organized in 1859 with one member, Aaron Bergstresser. The church was organized by Rev. J. J. Stewart, Presiding Elder. Harlan was formerly called Harlan Mission of the Council Bluffs District, Iowa Annual Conference. The records of the church are not in a very complete condition, but from them it is learned, that the first preacher to introduce worship in Shelby County, under the auspices of the M. E. church was Rev. H. A. Tarkington, not long before the establishment of the Harlan society. The first regular Methodist pastor appointed for Harlan was Rev. Kirtland Card, who came in the early part of 1859. The present pastor is Rev. D. C. Franklin, who is now serving his third year. The church edifice was erected in 1872. It is in size 30x50 feet, but a contract has been signed for enlarging the building. The church has in connection a flourishing Sabbath School of about 100 members. The school started shortly after the establishment of the church. The present Superintendent is J. M. True.

The Christian Church.—This society was organized February 18th, 1876, by Rev. C. W. Sherwood. The first regular pastor was Elder T. V. Berry, who was installed some time during the organization year. The society was organized with thirty-one members, but thirty-two names were sent in during the organization meeting, which made a total of sixty-three. The highest membership attained by the society was 122. The present membership, though over 100, is not quite up to this point. The church has a Sabbath School in connection, with an average attendance of about seventy. The school was started the same year. The present Superintendent is Mrs. M. Nance. The church building was erected in the early part of 1880. Previous meetings were held in the Court House and elsewhere. The size of the building is 34x56 feet. Prayer meetings are held on every Wednesday evening. The present pastor is Elder J. P. Lucas, who came in October, 1881.

Congregational Church Society.—A Congregational Society was organized in Harlan in July, 1871. There were seven members at the outset, but six more names were eventually added, making thirteen in all. This society, which had at no time a regular pastor, fell into decay. A small Presbyterian Society, which had also been organized in Harlan, was likewise in a poor condition, and in October, 1878, the society held a joint meeting with a view to reorganizing both societies as one. The result of the meeting was the disbanding of both societies, and the formation of a new one. A vote was taken as to the question of denominational precedence, and the result was a Congregational Society, which was organized November 10th, 1878. This society had twenty-three members. Prayer meetings were held on and after February 26th. 1879. The society was dependent on supplies for its preaching till July 1st, 1879, when Rev. J. G. Sabin was appointed regular pastor. The church is at present served by Rev. E. L. Sherman, who has been in charge since August, 1881. Meetings are at present held in the Court House, but a frame church, 32x50 feet, is in course of construction, and will be completed within a few weeks. There is also a Sabbath School of about 125 members, of which M. K. Campbell is Superintendent. This school has been in existence since July 6th, 1879. The church has at present sixty-two members, and is in a healthy condition.

Reorganized Church of Jesus Christ of Latter Day Saints.— The Harlan branch of this society was organized during the year 1872. The first regular pastor in Harlan was Elder Frank Reynolds, who came in 1872. The society was organized with fifteen members. Meetings have been usually held in the Court House, but now school houses in the suburbs are considerably used. The present pastor is Elder John Hardman. The present membership is forty-eight. It is still growing. The ladies of the society have organized for the purpose of raising a fund to be devoted to the erection of a church building. and a considerable sum of money has already been secured. It is expected that work will be commenced on a building the coming summer. The church has no Sabbath School, though one is being organized.

*Baptist Church Society.—*This society was organized in the year 1868. Rev. James Lambert was the first pastor. The first meetings of the society were held in the school house, but in the summer of 1870 a frame church 25x50 feet in dimensions, was erected. The present membership of the society is about 125, and it is in a prosperous condition. Rev. A. Jacobs is the minister.

*Independent School District of Harlan.—*This district was organized as an independent district in March, 1875. Previous to this it was a sub-district of Harlan township. The first School Directors were: H. C. Holcomb, J. W. Chatburn, F. A. Bayer. Since then the law has been changed so as to require six Directors. The Secretary and Treasurer are also independent of the Board. The following are the present members of the Board: N. W. Macy, President; C. J. Wyland, E. B. Moore, M. M. Bechtel, W. A. Gray, G. W. Cullison. F. A. Bayer is Secretary and O. P. Wyland Treasurer. The present school building is a four-room frame structure, built in 1875. Two other rooms are rented. Six teachers are employed. The Principal is A. K. Lind, and the subordinates W. K. Colburn, Mrs. M. E. McArthur, Miss A. George, Mrs.

M. E. Downey and Mrs. L. E. Waite. The present school facili-
tiesbeing inadequate, it was voted in March, 1881, to bond the
district for $18,000 and build a brick school house. This building
is now in course of construction. It will be three stories high
and contain nine rooms, furnished with all modern conveniences.
The building will be heated by steam. The number of pupils in
the district is now considerably over 400.

Parian Lodge No. 321, A. F. & A. M.—A dispensation was
granted this Lodge November 30th. 1872. The charter is dated
June 4th, 1873. The first elective officers were: John Fritz, W.
M.; W. J. Davis, S. W.; J. H. Louis, J. W.; H. S. Burke, T.;
Wm. Wyland, S. There were but twelve members when the Lodge
was started. The present elective officers are: P. B. Hunt, W.
M.; J. W. Chatburn, S. W.; W. W. Girton, J. W.; D. M. Wyland, T.; S. A. Burke, S. The membership at present is fifty, a
gain of seven since the annual report. The Lodge meets on the
Saturday on or before the full moon in each month. The place of
meeting is Masonic Hall, owned by the Lodge. The hall is 22x68
feet in dimensions and is well furnished.

Harlan Lodge No. 267, I. O. O. F.—This Lodge was instituted
February 26th, 1873, by D. D. G. M. Ben Newman, of Council
Bluffs. There were eleven charter members. The first elective
officers were: Samuel Potter. N. G.; N. Booth, V. G.; D. M.
Wyland, S.; W. S. Stutsman, T. The present officers are: W.
M. Oungst, N. G.; S. K. Pratt, V. G.; Wm. Bowlin, R. S.; O. F.
Graves, T.; A. K. Riley, P. S. The Lodge now has fifty-seven
members,and has of late received numerous accessions. The meet-
ings are held on every Friday night in Odd Fellows' Hall, Long's
Block. The Lodge Room is well fitted up, and one of the things
worthy of note in this connection is a handsome emblematic car-
pet. Application has been made for a charter for an Encampment.

V. A. S. Fraternity.—The Harlan section of this society, which
has for its object mutual insurance, was organized June 7th, 1880.
The first officers were: O. F. Graves, Rector; Riley Cass. Vice-
Rector; J. W. Beems, Scribe; G. W. Bumphrey, Usher; D. W.
Chase, Questor; S. F. Hurless, A. B. King, J. W. Cartlich, Cura-
tors; R. E. Floyd, Speculator. There were nineteen charter mem-
bers. The present officers are: James McArthur, Rector; A. B.
King. Vice-Rector; C. Will Fisher. Scribe; J. S. Ferguson,
Questor; E. G. Colburn, Usher; J. W. Beems. Speculator.

Harlan Lodge, Iowa Legion of Honor.—This Lodge was or-
ganized July 26th, 1881. There were twenty-six charter mem-
bers. The first officers were: J. W. Harrod. W. P.; G. W.
Cullison, V. P.; Thomas H. Smith, R. S.; W. H. Frazey, F. S.;
S. K. Pratt, T.; Rev. D. C. Franklin, C.; J. F. Huntzinger,
U.; E. R. Steinhilber. D.; S. W. Matters, M.; J. Dunlavy, W.
H. Axline, M. E's.; W. H. Carl, E. S. Burgin, C. A.
Mentzer, Trustees. The present officers are: G. W. Cullison, W.

P.; E. R. Steinhilber, V. P.; C. A. Mentzer. R. S.; T. J. Jones, F. S.; S. K. Pratt. T.: Thos. H. Smith. C.; J. F. Huntzinger, U.; Daniel Chase, D.: L. B. Tameseia, S.; Jas. McConnel, W. Carl, E. S. Burgin, Trustees.

Harlan Lodge No. 193, A. O. U. W.—This Lodge was organized June 12th, 1879, by J. J. Stuckly, of Des Moines. Meetings are held every Friday evening. The first officers were: W. W. Girton, M. W.; U. S. Brown, P. M. W.; B. I. Kinsey, F.; T. J. Robinson, O.; O. P. Wyland, F. R.; John R. Lehman, Fin.; E. B. Moore, Recr.; J. R. Wyerly, G.; J. F. Wyland, I. W.; C. Happe, O. W.; E. J. Trowbridge, E. S. Burgin, J. H. Waite, Trustees. There were twenty-eight charter members. The present officers are: O. S. Reynolds. P. M. W.; George E. Bennett, M. W.; S. H. Watters, R.; W. W. Girton, F.; L. P. Christianson. O.; O. P. Wyland, Rec.; C. Happe, G.; H. F. Locke, W.; T. J. Robinson, Trustee; E. A. Cobb, M. D., Med. Ex. The present membership of the Lodge is twenty-one.

Shelby County Agricultural Society.—This society was started about seven years ago by a few citizens, but it did not assume any particular prominence until within the past three or four years, and it was not a paying institution. The society started with but ten acres of land, whereas now it has forty. The fair grounds join the northeast portion of the town-site. The last two exhibitions have not only been well attended, but have more than paid expenses. Greater things are hoped for in the future. The grounds are provided with a good floral hall, an amphitheatre capable of holding 1,000 people, stabling for forty horses, good judges' stand, and one of the finest half-mile race-tracks in the State, all of which are enclosed by a tight board fence. In 1880, the society paid out $1,400 in premiums, and in 1881, $1.500. The present officers are T. Ledwich, President: C. C. Redfield, Secretary.

Utile Dulce Club.— This club which has been organized but a few weeks, has about thirty-five members. Its objects are physical and social improvement, D. M. Wyland is President. Meetings are held in Long's Hall every night in the week.

SHELBY COUNTY BIOGRAPHIES.

HARLAN.

W. E. Armstrong, barber, formerly of Humboldt, Humboldt county, Ia. (where he was engaged in business two years) came to Harlan in Dec., 1880, and established his present business on the west side of square; moved to his present room, which adjoins the City Hotel office, in Oct., 1881. He runs two chairs, keeping one man to assist.

William Baughn, farmer and stock dealer, was born in Washington, Fayette county, O., in Nov., 1857; moved with parents to Harrison county, Ia.; thence in 1866 to Council Bluffs, and to Shelby county in 1869, and engaged in farming until 1875, then engaged in the livery business at Harlan, which he continued about a year, sold to Elias Monroe, and returned to farming. In 1878 he engaged in the stock business. His office is in the Stock and Grain Exchange, on the southeast corner of the square.

Hiram Baughn, farmer, stock raiser and dealer, is one of the oldest settlers of Shelby county, Ia., and has a fine stock farm of 140 acres.

Merrills Barton, farmer, was born in Genesee county, N. Y., in 1823, and at four years of age moved with parents to Chautauqua county. In 1852 he moved to Waupaca county, Wis., where he engaged in farming until 1870, when he moved to Mitchell county, Ia., and the following year came to Shelby county, locating two miles east of Harlan. He owns a farm of 131 acres, where he resides, and another of 600 acres in Douglas township. They are both well improved stock farms. He was elected a member of the Board of Supervisors.

F. A. Bayer, M. D., was born in Dansville, N. Y., in 1840. In 1862 he enlisted in the 130th N. Y. Vol., was in several of the most important battles; was wounded at Opequan Creek, near Winchester, Va., and was discharged in 1864. He returned to N. Y.; afterwards entered the Medical College at Cincinnati, O.; from which he graduated in 1867, and moved to Benton county, Ia., and there engaged in the practice of medicine for four years. In 1872 he came to Harlan and opened his present office.

N. Booth, dealer in agricultural implements, wagons, carriages, etc.; came to Shelby county, Ia., in 1871, from Cal. He engaged in farming until 1881; then bought an interest in business of E. J. Trowbridge; afterwards purchased the entire business and premises on Upper Second street. He handles Deering's twine binders, N. C. Thompson's goods, of Rockford, Ill.; Moline Plow Co.'s goods, Norwegian Plow Co.'s goods, Davenport Co.'s goods, Courtland Wagon Co.'s goods, and is special agent for J. I. Case's machinery and Aultman & Taylor's threshing machines.

J. V. Brazie, stock raiser and farmer, was born in Schoharie county, N. Y., in April, 1853; in 1863 he moved with parents to Albany; thence the same year to Lapeer county, Mich. In 1864 he removed to Rochester, N. Y., and the year following to Butler county, Ia., and to Harlan in the spring of 1866. In 1847 he attended the University at Des Moines; engaged in teaching several terms, and in 1875 engaged in farming. In 1876, he purchased the livery stock of E. Monroe; conducted business until May, 1881; then sold to E. C. Swain, and continues farming, paying special attention to the raising of pure Berkshire and Poland China hogs.

M. M. Bechtell, grain dealer, was born in Hagerstown, Me., in 1822; remained there until 1843; then studied for the ministry at Pennsylvania College, from which he graduated in 1874; then took a course in the theological seminary at Gettysburg, Pa.; was licensed as a preacher in the Lutheran church, and ordained in 1853; moved to Somerset county the following year; continued preaching, and also engaged in the lumber business. In 1858 he moved to Cumberland county, Me., and continued the lumber trade; in 1865 was engaged in the oil trade in Pa., and the following year removed to Victor, Ia., and engaged in farming; thence to Mitchellville in 1873, and engaged in the grain business; the next year to Lennox, Taylor county, where he built a mill and remained four years; removed to Essex, Page county, and engaged in the mercantile business; thence to Harlan in 1879, and engaged in the hardware business, which he sold to Mr. Snively; then built elevator number two, and engaged in his present business.

Irving W. Beems, justice of the peace and insurance agent, was born in Muskingum county, O., in 1847; removed with parents to Jasper county, Ia., in 1856; was in the employ of the C. & R. I. railroad company several years, and in April, 1875, moved to Shelby county, and engaged in farming in Jackson township, until Sept., 1878, when he moved to Harlan, and engaged in the insurance business; is special agent for the Underwriters, of N. Y.; Gemania, of N. Y.; Westchester, of N. Y.; N. Y. City Fire Ins. Co.; American, of Philadelphia; Springfield Fire and Marine Ins. Co.; Iowa State, of Keokuk; and Hawkeye, of Des Moines. Office on the north side of public square. He was elected justice of the peace in 1881, on the republican ticket. He was married in 1868, in Jasper county, to Sarah E. Plummer, and has four children.

Charles Bergstresser, harness maker, was born in Snyder county, Pa., in 1847; moved with parents to Harlan in 1865. His father established the first harness shop in the county; he worked for his father two years; was employed by P. Louchor in Nov.,

1875; remained with him three years, and then purchased the business; keeps two men employed, and carries a full stock of everything in his line.

Henry S. Burk, justice of the peace and collecting agent, was born in Southeastern Ky., Sept. 23rd, 1816; moved to Decatur county, Ind., in 1827, where he resided until coming to Shelby county, Ia., in 1869; engaged in farming and gardening. In 1877 he was elected justice of the peace, which office he still holds.

S. A. Burk, attorney at law, was born in Decatur county, Ind., in 1853; came to Ia. with parents in 1869; received his education, at Moore's Hill College, Ind.; read law with Hon. Platt Wick, was admitted to practice in Mar., 1878, and became a partner with Mr. W., which partnership was dissolved in 1880, when Mr. Burk opened his present office in Harlan.

W. H. Carl, of the firm of Carl & Graves, dealers in furniture, and undertakers: was born in Wapello county, Ia., in 1849, learned carpentering, and in 1872 located at Harlan, and engaged in contracting and building in partnership with W. H. Griffith; in 1876 they bought out the furniture business of William Stanley. In Mar., 1880, Mr. Griffith sold his interest in the business to Mr. Graves. They have a fine business house, carry a large and complete stock of everything in their line, and in connection own a handsome hearse that cost $800. Mr. Carl is a member of the 1. O. O. F. In May, 1880, he was married at Harlan to Miss A. C. Bergstresser.

Riley Cass, proprietor of the Harlan steam carriage and wagon factory and blacksmith shop, was born in Chautauqua county, N. Y., in 1831; there learned his trade, and in 1853 moved to Van Buren county, Ia.; thence to Harlan in 1874, and established his present business in 1877, with a very small capital, in what is now his wood-work shop; added a blacksmith shop in 1879, and later in the same year added an engine room and polishing room; has a twelve-horse power, horizontal engine, also machinery for plow-work and sawing. He employs in his paint shop R. W. Straley, who is a painter and finisher of long experience. This factory has gained an extensive reputation for its fine work, having none but competent workmen employed. Mr. C. was married in 1856 to Sarah Brown, and has five children.

Hon. J. W. Chatburn, proprietor of the Harlan and the Shelby Mills, was born at Sabden, England, in 1821; served an apprenticeship there as millwright, and in 1845 came to America; was engaged in milling at Philadelphia, Pa., five years; removed in 1850 to Kanesville—now Council Bluffs—Ia.; remained two years; removed to Harrison county and took a claim near the present town of Magnolia; built a mill in 1853, which was the first mill north of the Boyer river; remained there until 1869; then moved to near the present town of Woodbine, and built what was afterwards known as Dunmire's mill. In 1867 he built the Harlan mill, which he still owns, and in connection has a flour, exchange, sale and feed store in Harlan, which is managed by J. Hersey. In 1878, Mr. Chatburn erected the Shelby steam mills, at Shelby, which are run by Thomas Chatburn. Mr. J. W. Chatburn was elected county judge of Harrison county for two years, and is a member of the county board.

Warren Closson, of the firm of Closson & Hardie, wholesale dealers and shippers of butter, eggs, etc., was born in Delaware county, O., in 1834. He served in the war of the rebellion, and at its close located in Ind., and in 1869 removed to Pella, Ia.; thence to Harlan in 1871; has been justice of the peace eight years; is a member of the I. O. O. F. and A. F. & A. M. orders; was mayor of this city in 1880, and in Nov., 1881, engaged in his present business with Mr. Hardie. He was married in 1862 at Fort Wayne, Ind., to Fannie Hardie, and has six children.

L. C. Cooper, barber, purchased his business in April, 1881, of Geo. Jackson, who established it in Jan., 1881. His shop is on the west side of square. It is well furnished. He has two chairs, and employs one man. Mr. C. was formerly in business at Avoca, Ia.

John Coenen, of the firm of Coenen & Luecke, proprietors of the one-price clothing store; dealers in clothing, hats, caps, gents furnishing goods, boots, shoes, etc., also have merchant tailoring in connection. He came from Marion county, Ia., to Harlan in 1878, and established a lumber yard; in 1880, built the corner block, also the brick store building occupied by the clothing store, and two business houses adjoining. He sold the lumber business to John Reid & Co. Mr. C. is vice-president of and a stock-holder in the Shelby county bank. H. Luecke came from Carroll county to Harlan in Dec., 1880; formed his present partnership in 1881.

Mr. Cullison, of the firm of Smith & Cullison, attorneys at law, graduated from the State Normal School, of Kirksville, Mo., in 1870; was conductor and principal of the Troy Normal School, from 1871 to 1875. He studied law with A. A. J. Allerton, of Kirksville, and was admitted to the bar in 1876; was associate principal of the Southern Iowa scientific institute, and superintendent of the city schools of Allerton, Wayne county, Ia.; thence came to Harlan and formed his present partnership in Jan., 1881.

J. W. DeSilva, attorney at law, was born in Gilboa, Schoharie county, N. Y., in 1834; attended the Gilboa Seminary, and in 1854 graduated from the Charlotteville Seminary; then began the study of law in the office of Hon. Lyman Tremaine, and was admitted to the bar in 1859; practiced for one year at Sullivan, and in 1869 came to Shelby county, Ia., locating at Old Harlan. His office is on Court street, opposite city building.

F. B. Eshelman, dentist, was born in Foreston. Ogle county, Ill.; began the study of dentistry with Dr. C. W. Chamberlain, of Lanark, Carroll county, Ia., in 1862; remained there until 1880; then located at Harlan, and formed a partnership with Dr. Frazey, whom he bought out in Oct., 1881. He has a fine, well furnished office, on the second floor of Long's block, of three rooms--reception room, operating room and labratory.

C. Will. Fisher, photographer, was born in 1849; came to Harlan in 1876, and established his present business, which was the first in the county. His close application to business, and the fine work produced, has gained him a reputation as an artist. Gallery on East Second street, one door south of Herald office. He is a member of the V. A. S., beneficiary society. In 1875 he was married at Andalusia, Ill., to Rachel M. Parker. They have three children.

Dr. L. D. Frost, druggist, was born in Morrow county, O., in Aug., 1834; removed to Guthrie county, Ia., in the fall of 1854; engaged in running the hotel and stage station at the old town of Morrisburg, and devoted much time to the study of medicine. The following year he removed to his present location, on the south side of the square, where he has a fine stock of drugs, groceries, confectionery, etc. He has an elegant private office, and fine library in connection. This was the first drug store in Shelby county. He was elected city treasurer in 1881. In 1854 he was married in Morrow county, O., to Lydia Babcock. He has an orchard of ten acres adjoining town, with one thousand bearing apple trees, and quantities of small fruit. This is the largest orchard in the county.

E. Gish, proprietor of the Central House, formerly known as the Swain House; was born in Va. in 1837; moved with parents to Green county, O., in 1847; thence, in 1856, to Jasper county, Ia., and engaged in farming, until 1864; then moved to Shelby county, bought two hundred acres of well improved land in Harlan township, and there engaged in farming until Apr., 1881, when he moved to Harlan and engaged in the hotel business. He has been engaged in this business before, and keeps a first-class house. He was married in 1867, at Bowman's Grove, Ia., to Marrietta Poling, and has two children.

G. S. Gibbs, dealer in general merchandise, was born in Ypsilanti City, Mich., in 1848; removed to Harlan, Ia., in 1869, and was in the employ of J. W. & E. W. Davis. They had at that time the only business house in the town. He remained with them five years, and was employed by J. B. Stutsman until 1876; and in partnership with J. Jackson established his present business July 1st, 1879. He purchased Mr. Jackson's interest, and now carries on the business alone; has a very fine stock, and does a lively business. Has a branch business at Irwin. which is conducted by W. W. Gibbs, under the firm name of W. W. Gibbs & Co. Mr. G. S. Gibbs has just completed a very fine brick residence in Harlan at a cost of $7,000. He was the first city treasurer of this place, and is at present a member of the council, also of the board of supervisors. Is a member of the A. F. & A. M. and I. O. O. F. lodges. He was married Jan., 1875, at Council Bluffs. to Della Baughn, daughter of Hon. Chas. Baughn. They have one son and one daughter.

J. T. Graham, of the firm of Graham & Munger, hardware dealers, came to Harlan, Ia.. in Dec., 1880 from Sharon, Mahaska county, where he was engaged in business three years. Jan. 1st, 1881, he bought a half-interest in the hardware store of E. J. Trowbridge, who sold the remainder to Mr. Munger June 18th, 1881. They have a full stock of everything in their line; keep two men employed, and a first-class tinner: have telephone connections.

O. F. Graves, of the firm of Carl & Graves, was born in Watertown, Jefferson county, N. Y., in 1848; there learned carpenter and joiner's trade; was for seven years engineer on the R. W. & O. Ry.; four years on the N. Y. & O. M. Ry.. and one year on the U. P. Ry. In 1875 he opened the sash, blind, and door factory of Graves & Van Doren, at Watertown. and in March. 1880, came to Harlan, Ia., and formed his present partnership. He is a member of the I. O. O. F. and V. A. S. orders.

S. W. Harmon, of the firm of Seeland & Harmon, proprietors of the temperance billiard hall, on East Market street. This firm has three Brunswick & Balke Co.'s billiard tables, and two pool tables. The room is fitted up in first-class style: keeps for sale cigars, cider and soda water.

Lucien Herbert, proprietor of saloon on west side of square, was born in Luxemburg. Ger.: is a graduate from the Luxemburg University, which he attended six years. graduating in 1878; came to the U. S. in 1879, and located at Wesphalia, Shelby county, Ia.; moved to Harlan in May, 1881.

J. A. Hardie, of the firm of Closson & Hardie, was born in Rockport, N. Y., in 1858; moved to Pella. Ia,. in 1869; was for four years foreman for R. P. Brown, at Grand Junction: has had nine years experience in present business. Their place of business is in the basement of Coenen's block.

Harry Howell, boot and shoe-maker. was born in Somerset. England, in 1848: came to America in 1868. first locating at N. Y. City: worked at trade there for six years: removed to Harlan, Ia., in the autumn of 1875; was in the employ of P. Louchor, harness, boot and shoe-maker, three years: then purchased the boot and shoe business; continued in the same place one year. and built his present place of business in 1879 in partnership with Charles Bergstresser. He is now doing a good business; keeps two men employed.

H. C. Holcomb, clerk of the courts, was born in 1823, in Essex county, N. Y.; moved to Kanesville, Ia., in 1853; was engaged in teaching school in Mills and Pottawattamie counties until 1858; then came to Harlan, which was just laid out, and erected the first house in the town, and engaged in carpentry, until 1859, when he was elected clerk of the courts; was re-elected in 1860, 1862 and 1864; was defeated in 1866, and re-elected in 1868 and 1870; was not a candidate for the next term, but was re-elected in 1878 and 1880. He was married in 1862 to Elizabeth A. McCoy, and has one son.

D. S. Irwin, attorney at law, came to Washington county, Ia., in 1865, from Pa. In the spring of 1870 he removed to Shelby county, and engaged in farming for several years, teaching school during the winters; was admitted to the bar at circuit court, at Harlan, in Mar., 1881, Judge Loofborow presiding; then engaged in the practice of law at Irwin, a new town on the Iowa Southern Ry. It was named after Mr. Irwin, having been laid out on his land. His office is in the postoffice building.

Hon. Thomas Ledwich, of the firm of Ledwich, Hunt & Long, dealers in lumber, coal, lime and cement; was born in Canada in 1841; came to the U. S. with parents, and located in N. Y. In the spring of 1861 he enlisted in the 2nd N. Y. Cav.; was wounded at the second battle of Bull Run. He was at the battle of Fredricksburg, the fall of Mobile, and several other important battles, and was discharged in 1865; remained in Ky. two years; then removed to Avoca, Ia., and in June, 1869, shipped the first car-load of lumber into that place that was ever received there, and opened a lumber yard. In 1871 he started the first newspaper of the place, called the Avoca Delta, which he sold after two years. He removed to Harlan in 1879, and formed his present partnership. Their office is on Market street; adjoining it is the door and sash room, and in connection they manufacture Fry's patent combination wood and wire fence, having the right for Shelby county. They keep four men employed, make sixty rods per day. Their large and well stocked lumber yard fronts Market and Court streets. Mr. Hunt was in business with Mr. L. at Avoca previous to coming to this place, and was the builder of the first steam mill there. Mr. Ledwich is president of the Shelby county fair association; has been president of the 'Botna Valley District Agricultural Society, he is mayor of the city, and has been a member of the council several years.

James M. Long, of the firm of Ledwich, Hunt & Long, came to Shelby county, Ia., in the spring of 1856, and located within three-fourths of a mile of the present town of Harlan; bought eight hundred acres of land in this and Harrison counties, and engaged in farming; two years later, the old town of Harlan was located, and in 1859 Mr. L. laid out the present town, which joins the old town on the south, and was called Long's addition. The same year the county seat was moved here from Shelbyville, and the year following he built the old court house; in 1870 he erected the Harlan House; six years later, the first brick business block in the town, on the north side of the square; in 1878, he built another business block on the southwest corner of the square, and the City Hotel, and a brick building in rear of the hotel used as a saloon; and now has in course of erection the new opera house, which is to be a first class opera house with all of the latest improvements. It will have three store-rooms on the ground floor, two in front and one in the rear. Besides these buildings, he owns a fine residence, livery barn, and other town and country property. In 1860 he was married at Jeddo, Harrison county, to Hattie McCoid.

Cyrus Mentzer, dealer in groceries and queensware, came to Harlan in the spring of 1880, from Marion, Linn county, Ia., where he was in business for eight years. He engaged in his present business with J. Jackson, and in the spring of 1881 bought Mr. J's. interest. He now employs three clerks, runs a delivery wagon for city trade, and carries one of the largest stocks of goods in his line in the city; store in Coenen's block, on the northeast corner of the square.

James E. Miller, harness maker, was born in Ky. in 1851; moved with parents to Mexico, thence to Audrian county, Mo., where he learned his trade; then came to Ottumwa, Ia., and worked with J. Taylor; afterwards to Des Moines, and was with F. Butler. In 1875 he came to Harlan, and was in the employ of E. E. Swain for two years, and after taking a trip to the Black Hills, took charge of the business for G. H. Walker, who sold to E. B. Gard in Sept., 1879. He continued in the business for Mr. G. until April 7th, 1880, when he purchased the business. He now keeps four men employed, and keeps constantly on hand a large and complete stock of harness, saddles, whips, etc.; also has a branch establishment at Irwin. He is a member of the A. O. U. W. order. Sept. 12th, 1878, he was married at Harlan to Hattie Brazie, and has two children.

Myerly, Sheller & Harrod, attorneys at law, land. loan. insurance and abstract office. The business was established in 1879, by R. E. Carruthers. Messrs. J. B. Myerly & Co. purchased the office Jan. 1st, 1880, D. B. Sheller joining in March of the same year, and Mr. Harrod in Jan., 1881, thus forming the present partnership. Mr. Myerly came to Harlan from Des Moines, and is a graduate from the Iowa City University; attends to the law practice of the firm. Mr. Sheller came from Dallas Center, where he was for several years in the Dallas Center bank; Mr. Harrod, is

from Shelby. this county. Mr. H. was elected county treasurer in
the fall of 1879, and at the expiration of the term became a partner in the present firm. They have an extensive and growing
business, are agents for the Hamburg American Packet Company,
Red Star Line, and American Steamship Company, for the sale of
emigrant tickets, and have a complete set of abstract books of this
county.

J. S. Murray, of the firm of J. S. Murray & Co., proprietors of
elevator No. 1. on the west side of the track of the Harlan branch
of the C., R. I. & P. Ry.; was born in Canada in 1837; came to the
U. S. in 1875, located at Avoca, Ia., and engaged in the grain
business; was proprietor of the Avoca elevator. He came to Harlan in 1878, built the elevator, and engaged in his present business. He has a branch business at Defiance, on a branch of the
C., M. & St. P. Ry., which is conducted by Miles & Miles. The
Avoca business was conducted by P. F. Murray until Sept., 1880,
when he came to Harlan, and became a member of the above firm.
They also handle Des Moines and Oskaloosa hard and soft coal.

J. W. Newby, dealer in agricultural implements, sewing machines, organs, etc., was born in N. C., in 1849; moved with his
parents to Carroll county. Ind.; thence to Mills county, Ia., in
1867, and to Shelby county the following year, locating one and
one-half miles east of Harlan, on what was known as the Baughn
farm. In 1875 he moved to Harlan, and established his present
business, which is now located on West Market street. He is
agent for the White. Domestic, and Household sewing machines,
and for Furst & Bradley's, Walter A. Wood's Wier Co.'s., and
Aultman, Miller & Co.'s goods. and for other leading manufactories. He has a branch establishment at Irwin.

Dallas F. Paul, county auditor, was born in Saratoga, N. Y., in
1846; moved to Mills county, Ia., in 1866, and engaged in farming
for ten years; then moved to Shelby county, and located in Cass
township, where he owns 728 acres of land, well improved for
stock purposes. He was elected to his present office in 1881.

Andrew Peterson, merchant tailor, was born in Denmark, in
1830, learned his trade and was engaged in business there; came
to America in Sept., 1873, and located at Troy, N. Y.; moved to
Schenectady, and was in the employ of Holtzman & Fritzmaurice,
as foreman in their tailoring department for two and one-half
years. In the fall of 1876 he came to Harlan and established his
present business.

R. M. Pomeroy, county treasurer, was born in Franklin county,
Pa., in 1849; moved to Louisa county, Ia., in 1872; was engaged in
business at Morning Sun, and three years later moved to Shelby,
Shelby county, and engaged in the mercantile business, which he
still owns. He is mayor of Shelby. He was elected county treasurer in 1881.

W. R. Parker, proprietor of billiard parlor and sample rooms, in rear of City Hotel, (formerly of Missouri Valley) established his present business in Nov., 1880. Has two Brunswick, Balke & Co.'s billiard tables, and one pool table.

H. C. & E. D. Potter, of the firm of Potter Bros., proprietors of the steam wagon, blacksmith and machine shop, on West Market street; came to Harlan, Ia., in Nov., 1878, from Whiteside county, Ill., and established his present business. They have a four-horse engine, and employ three blacksmiths and one woodworker. They make a specialty of building fine light buggies and track sulkies to order.

C. R. Pratt, of the firm of Pratt Bros., proprietors of the Harlan Herald, edits and conducts the paper. It was established in 1875 by Geo. Musgrave, is republican, and the official paper of the county, is thoroughly fitted for jobbing purposes; has a fine Campbell power press.

J. H. & E. W. Reynolds, of the firm of Reynolds Bros., contractors and builders, located at Harlan in 1879, shop on East Market street, where they employ two men, do wagon work in connection. They are from Keokuk, Ia., are thorough workmen, and capable of handling large contracts.

John Reed & Co., dealers in lumber, lime, cement, coal, and paints, were formerly of Rock Island, Ill., where they were engaged in the lumber business; came to Harlan in Dec., 1880, and purchased the business of Coenen & Fairchild, on Upper Third street. Mr. John Reed conducts the business at Harlan; they have a branch establishment at Kirkman.

Ramsey Bros., dealers in clothing, boots, shoes, and gents' furnishing goods; came to Harlan from Prairie City, Jasper county, Ia. The business was established in the spring of 1879, by Holdefer & Ramsey; the former sold his interest in Jan., 1882, to J. H. & J. W. Ramsey, who with their brother W. H. constitute the present firm. They carry an immense stock of goods, and do a flourishing business; store on north side of square. They have a branch house at Irwin, under the charge of J. W. Ramsey.

Frank and Albert Reynolds, of the firm of Reynolds & Co., photographers, formerly of Keokuk county, Ia.; learned their trade at Des Moines, and came to Harlan in the spring of 1879; established business in Sept., 1880. They occupy four rooms in Coenen's block, on the second floor. They make a specialty of copying and enlarging.

Alden K. Riley, attorney at law, loan and abstract office; was born in Schoharie county, N. Y., in 1852; began attendance at the Fort Edwards Institute, N. Y., in 1868, and graduated in 1872; then entered Princeton College, N. J., obtained a degree in 1876, and entered the law firm of Krum & Grant, at Schoharie; removed in the following year to Jefferson, Greene county, Ia.; there entered the law firm of Russel & Toliver, and was also professor of mathematics at the Jefferson Academy. In April, 1878, he came to Harlan, and opened an office. He is one of the stockholders and directors of the Shelby county bank, also attorney for the bank; office in Coenen's block, front room up-stairs. He is a member of the I. O. O. F. August 27th, 1878, he was married at Harlan to Betta M. Hard, and has one child, Alden K.

Geo. D. Ross, farmer and stock raiser, was born in Jefferson county, N. Y., in Dec., 1842. He enlisted at the commencement of the war in Co. G, 21st Wis. Inft.; was in a number of important battles; was wounded at Atlanta, Ga., necessitating the amputation of his right arm; was discharged in 1865. In May, 1872, he came to Harlan, purchased property and engaged in teaching school. In the fall of the same year he was elected clerk of the courts, and re-elected twice on the republican ticket. He established the first livery in the town, in the spring of 1873, which he sold after two years. He had the mail route between Harlan and Dunlap, and carried mail and express between Harlan and Avoca, for several years. In Aug., 1875, he bought the Herald printing office, of Geo. Musgrave, and in Feb., 1876, bought the Record printing office, combined them, and published the Herald until 1879; then bought farms joining town, one of eighty acres on the west, and 160 acres, one mile northeast of town. He also owns valuable town property.

John Rogers & Son, proprietors of restaurant and bakery, deal in staple and fancy groceries, confectionery, etc. They came to Harlan, in Dec., 1881, and purchased the stock and business of Lew Tamesiea on the east side of the square. They employ a first class baker and confectioner, keep day boarders and furnish lunches, ice cream, oysters, soda water, etc.

J. S. Snively, hardware dealer, came from Carroll county, Ill., where he had been engaged in teaching school, to Harlan, Ia., Oct. 1st, 1880, and established his present business, on the north side of the square. He carries a full stock of everything in his line; keeps three men employed; is the sole agent in the town for the Glidden barb wire.

Samuel Smith was born in Guernsey county, O., in 1836; removed to Guthrie county, Ia., in 1857, and engaged in farming. He engaged in freighting to Denver, Col., in 1861 and 1862; then returned to Guthrie county, where he remained until 1869; then came to Shelby county; engaged in teaching several years, and previous to the coming of the railroad to Harlan, ran freighting teams between there and Avoca.

Mr. Smith, of firm of Smith & Cullison, came to Harlan from Bloomfield, Davis county, Ia., where he studied law with M. H. Jones, was admitted to the bar in the spring of 1878, and came to this city the same year, and formed a partnership with P. C. Truman, which continued three years. Mr. T. then sold his interest to Mr. Cullison, in Jan., 1881, thus forming the above firm.

Joseph Stiles, attorney at law, and land loan and insurance agent, was born in O., in 1846; removed to Benton county, Ia., in 1853; thence to Western, Linn county, in 1856; there attended college, and in 1867 moved to Jefferson, Green county, where he engaged in teaching school. In 1873 he began the study of law, with Henderson & Howard. The following year he was admitted to the bar, in the district court, Judge Reed presiding. He was associated in practice with Judge Potter, of that place, one year; removed to Harlan in the autumn of 1875, and opened an office; was elected justice of the peace in 1877, which office he held two terms.

Steinhilber & Schnuettgen, dealers in furniture, and undertakers; established business April 1st, 1880. They command and occupy for the retail business the store building on Market street, having sales-room, work-shop and ware-room below, and on the second floor the finishing and undertaking rooms, in which they employ two men, a wood worker and finisher. Their factory on Third street employs from twenty to thirty men. They do a large wholesale business. E. R. Steinhilber was formerly engaged in the stock business in Davenport. Mr. Schnuettgen is by trade a fresco painter; worked several years in Philadelphia, Pa., and Milwaukee, Wis. He was employed on the Centennial buildings in Philadelphia.

E. C. Swain, proprietor of Swain's livery stables, was born in Ind. in 1848; removed to Ia. in 1857, locating in Guthrie county; the following year moved to Shelby county, and to Harlan in 1869. He engaged in the harness business for six years, and in 1878, bought an interest in the livery business of J. V. Brazie. The present barn was built by this firm in 1879, and in 1881, Mr. S. became sole proprietor; keeps sixteen horses and eight carriages for livery purposes.

J. B. Swain was born at Randolph, Ind., in 1825; moved to Dallas county, Ind., in 1854, and engaged in farming for two years; then moved to Denison, Crawford county, being one of the first to locate there; remained until the spring of 1859; then came to Shelby, and built a mill in Grove township, which he sold to Milton Lynch, in 1861. He again engaged in farming, until his removal to Dunlap, when it was first laid out, in 1867, and the following year opened a harness shop, which business he sold to his son, E. C. Swain. He purchased the Harlan House of J. M. Long, conducted it for five years, and in the spring of 1879 erected the Swain House, which he conducted until April, 1881, when he leased to E. Gish, and retired from active business. He was married in Wayne county, Ind., in 1846, to Irena Whitenger, and has three sons and five daughters.

28

D. O. Stuart. attorney at law, was born in Pa. in 1848; moved with parents to Va. in 1851; took a preparatory literary course at the university at Morgantown. He served one year as scout during the rebellion, and at the close of the war, removed to Warren county, Ia.; attended Simpson's Centenary College, at Indianola; graduated in 1872, obtaining the degree of B. A. He commenced reading law while at college, with Col. P. Gad Bryan, and was admitted at the Nov. term of the district court at Newton, Jasper county, in 1872; was admitted to practice in the supreme court in June, 1874, and to the U. S. circuit court in Oct., of the same year, at Des Moines. In the spring of 1877, he moved to Des Moines, and to Harlan in Aug., 1880. His office is in Long's block on the north side of the public square.

A. D. Tinsley, editor of the Harlan Tribune (established in 1879), was born in Wapello county, Ia., in 1854; removed to Harlan in 1875, engaged in joiner work with Kiley Cass, and taught school during the winter of 1875-6. In 1877 was assistant county treasurer under Thomas McDonald; in the fall of the same year, engaged in business with his brother Prior Tinsley, and in 1879, still retaining his interest in the store, he opened the Tribune office. He has since been chairman of the county democratic central committee. He has always been an active participant in the campaigns, and is recognized as one of the party leaders in the county. The Tribune has been a county official paper since its establ'shment, and a city official paper for some time; office on north side of the square. Nov. 10th, 1881, Mr. Tinsley was married to Cicily Chatburn, daughter of the Hon. J. W. Chatburn of Harlan.

G. W. Todd, M. D., was born at Bellevue, Huron county, O., in 1838; attended college at Granville three years, then the Cleveland Medical College, graduating in 1861, and obtaining a degree. He enlisted in the 55th O. Inft., Co. A, and was discharged in 1865; then came to Tabor, Fremont county, Ia., and engaged in the drug business; remained eight years, then moved to Montgomery county, Ia., and engaged in the practice of medicine at Milford. In the spring of 1878 he moved to Shelby, Shelby county, Ia., and to Harlan in 1881; where he formed a partnership with Dr. Cartlich, who located here in 1880.

Geo. H. Walker, was born in W. Va., in 1814; moved to Northern Ind., in 1834, and engaged in farming; was also engaged in the mercantile business at Benton, Elkhart county. In 1854 removed to Linn county, Ia., and engaged in farming until 1860, when he engaged in business at Mt. Vernon. In 1876 he moved to Harlan, and in June of that year established a mercantile house; retired from business in the autumn of 1881, still owning the property, besides other town property, and 420 acres of land in Thayer county, Neb. He was married in Ind., in 1842, to Celina Smith, and has four children.

A. G. Waynick, of the firm of Waynick & Hunter, grocers; was born in Monroe county, Ia., in 1852; moved with parents to Chariton, Lucas county, in 1854. In 1870 he went to Golden, Col., and two years later to Chicago, Ill.; thence, in 1874, to Burlington, Ia.; and two years later to Corning, where he engaged in the clothing business, until 1879, when he came to Harlan and established his present business, which he carried on alone until the spring of 1880. Mr. Hunter, of Corning, then bought an interest, but remains at Corning, Mr. W. conducting the business, which is in Long's block on the southeast corner of the square.

J. E. Weaver, attorney at law, was born in Henry county, Ind., in June, 1849; moved with his parents to Powsheik county, Ia., in 1859; entered the Iowa College, at Grinnell, Ia., in 1866, and in 1870 commenced the study of law with Emery & Lewis, of Montezuma; was admitted to the bar in 1873 by the district court, Judge E. S. Sampson presiding. In 1874 moved to Pella, where he practiced one year, and then came to Harlan, establishing his present business; office on the north side of square. He is a member of the A. F. & A. M. order.

Thomas R. Westrope, farmer, stock raiser and dealer, was born in Morgan county, Ill., in 1825; moved to La Fayette county, Wis., in 1850; thence to Montgomery county, Ia., where he owns sixteen hundred acres of well improved farming land, two hundred and fifty head of graded cattle and fifty head of pedigreed shorthorns. He came to Shelby county in the spring of 1881, and here owns 440 acres of land and 150 head of cattle; has 360 acres of well improved farm in Audubon county, and 260 acres in La Fayette county, Wis. He carries on all of these farms himself, keeping sixteen men constantly employed, besides extra help in cropping seasons. He is one of the most extensive farmers in western Ia. In 1848, he was married, in La Fayette county, Wis., to Sarah A. Huntsman. They have eight sons and two daughters.

D. M. Wyland, of the firm of J. C. & D. M. Wyland, was born in Elkhart county, Ind., in 1846; came to Shelby county, Ia., in 1861; in 1864 took charge of the treasurer's office under William Wyland, and the year following attended the university at Iowa City, remaining four years; returned to Harlan and was appointed clerk of the courts in 1869, which position he resigned in the spring of 1870, to accept one offered by the Council Bluffs savings bank; remained there until 1872; then formed a partnership with his present partner. He is a member of the city council, and of the A. F. & A. M. and I. O. O. F. orders. In Sept., 1878, he was married at South Bend, Ind., to Belle Keasey.

C. J. Wyland, of the firm of C. J. & D. M. Wyland, bankers, real estate, loan and insurance agents, was born in Ind. in 1836; came to Shelby county, Ia., in 1861, and engaged in farming in Harlan township; was elected treasurer of the county in 1871, on

the democratic ticket, and re-elected in 1873. In 1875, he, with
with D. M. Wyland, with whom he had previously been engaged
in the real estate, loan and insurance business, established the bank.
They occupied a frame building until 1880, when they erected the
present two-story building, of brick with stone front. The first
floor is used for the real estate, loan and insurance office and telephone exchange, of which J. C. has charge, and the second floor
by the bank, in charge of D. M. In 1864, the subject of this
sketch was married to Amanda H. Dunnington, at Harlan. They
have five children.

Hon. William Wyland, farmer, was born in O. in 1830; removed
to northern Ind. in 1832, with his parents, where he remained until 1856; then came to Shelby county, Ia., which at that time was
very sparsely settled, the inhabitants having to go to Kanesville—
now Council Bluffs—for mail and to do trading. He entered land,
and engaged in farming until 1859; was elected county treasurer
in 1857, and county judge in 1859; returned to farming in 1861,
and in 1873 engaged in the mercantile business in partnership with
Thos. Wood; closed out business in 1877, and returned to farming
in North Harlan.

Hon. Pratt Wicks, attorney at law and representative for the
74th district, was born in Manchester, Ind., in 1832; was admitted
to the bar in 1853, at a term of the circuit court at Shelbyville,
Ind., Hon. R. D. Logan presiding. The following year he began
the practice of law at Greenburg; was elected to the office of district attorney in 1856, and re-elected in 1858; was elected prosecuting attorney of the 4th judicial circuit in 1866; held the office
until 1869, and then resigned, on the division of the circuit, and
came to Harlan, Ia.; was elected to the 18th general assembly in
the autumn of 1879, and re-elected to the 19th general assembly
in 1881, on the republican ticket.

D. A. Williams, proprietor of the City Hotel, was born in Pittsburg, Pa., in 1846; removed with parents to Marshalltown, Ia., in
1857. He enlisted in 1863 in the 9th Ia. Cav.; was discharged in
1865, and assisted his father in the stock business; traveled through
the west in 1868, handling stock; was engaged in freighting to the
Winnebago Agency several years, and was in the stock business at
Missouri Valley, Ia., some time; also at St. Paul, Minn., Denver,
Col., and Texas. In 1875 he established a drug store in Council
Bluffs, Ia., which he sold in the summer of 1881 to Shephard Bros.
and then moved to Harlan Oct. 11th, 1881; he opened the City
Hotel, built and owned by J. M. Long, which is a fine building, well
furnished, has one of the finest sample rooms in the west for the
accomodation of commercial travelers, and has omnibus in connection.

J. J. Zimmerman, proprietor of livery, feed and sale barns, on
the west side of square, was born in Pa. in 1840; moved to Jones

county, Ia., in 1856, and engaged in farming; removed to Shelby county in 1876 and engaged in farming until March, 1880, when he engaged in the livery business at Old Harlan House barn. In Oct., 1881, he purchased Hurless' barn and stock, and now runs both barns; keeps eighteen horses for livery purposes, and nine carriages, has telephone connections.

CLAY COUNTY.

The county of Clay is twenty-four miles square, containing an area of 368,640 acres. It is located in the second tier from the third county from the west boundary of the State. The little Sioux River and its tributaries afford water and drainage in nearly all portions of the county. The stream, with its serpentine windings, has a length of not less than seventy miles within the limits of Clay County, and furnishes quite a number of good water powers. Its largest tributary is Ocheyedan Creek, which rises in Osceola County and, flowing in a southeasterly direction, empties into Little Sioux River near Spencer. Both these have broad, rich and beautiful valleys. Among other smaller streams are Willow, Prairie, Henry and Muddy Creeks. The eastern portion of the county has several small lakes, the most important of which are Lost Island Lake, Swan Lake, Pickerel Lake, Virgin Lake and Mud Lake. Fish abound in some of them.

The county has a very limited supply of native timber, but more than some of the other counties in this part of the state. The surface is undulating prairie, with scarcely any waste land, and the soil is exceedingly fertile. The staple productions are wheat, oats, corn, grass and the various root crops. The county is well adapted to grazing, on account of the abundance of nutritious wild grass and pure water.

The first settlement of whites in the county was made in July, 1856, by Ambrose S. Mead and Christian Kirchner with their families. The former built his cabin on section 34, township 94, range 38, and the latter on section 32 of the same township and range. John J. Bicknell had the honor of holding the plow that broke the first sod in the county, while Ambrose S. Mead was honored by driving the oxen. In the fall of 1856 there were several more families came in. to-wit: James Bicknell, Ezra Wilcox and two men named Gillett.

In the latter part of February. 1857, the Indians, on their way to Spirit Lake before the massacre, visited the infant settlement in this county, killed four head of cattle belonging to Mr. Kirchner, and drove away ten horses and five or six head of cattle belonging to Mr. Mead. Passing on to what is known as Gillett's Grove. they drove away forty head of cattle, four horses, and destroyed most of the personal property of the Gilletts. The five or six families in the county, in consequence of this raid, fled and were away several months. The first marriage was that of John A. Kirchner and Mary J. Bicknell. daughter of James Bicknell.

The first birth was that of Ella, a daughter of these parties. The first death was that of Clay Crego, infant son of Y. B. Crego. A barn erected by C. Kirchner was the first frame building in the county.

Clay County was, previous to its organization, a part of Woodbury County. In accordance with a petition of the majority of the legal voters of Clay County, presented to the Honorable County Court of Woodbury County, Judge John L. Campbell presiding, an election was ordered to be held by the said county on the 12th day of October, 1858, and the voters of Clay County were authorized to meet at the house of Ambrose S. Mead, for the purpose of perfecting an organization of Clay County, and voting for district, county and township officers, thus severing the ties between the independent county of Woodbury, and the independent county of Clay. James Bicknell, E. M. Wilcox, and Ambrose S. Mead were appointed to act as Judges of Election, and to make returns according to law; consequently, on the 28th of September, 1858, Ambrose S. Mead was qualified as one of the Judges of Election, with power to qualify the other Judges and Clerk of the same. There were eighteen ballots cast at this election. The first county officers were: F. M. Foreman, Treasurer and Recorder; E. M. Wilcox, Clerk; C. Kirchner, Sr., Coroner; J. Kindelspeyer, Drainage Commissioner; Ambrose S. Mead, County Superintendent; C. C. Smeltzer, County Judge. Present County officers: H. B. Wood, Auditor; H. Chamberlain, Clerk; P. E. Randall, Treasurer; S. W. Dubois, Recorder; P. W. Madden, Sheriff; M. M. Gilchrist, Superintendent of Schools; E. N. Jencks, County Surveyor; T. P. Bender, J. Goodwin, Reuben Somers, J. Dodge and H. Watts, being the Board of Supervisors, with T. P. Bender, Chairman. The population of the County, according the census of 1880, was 4,248; the present population may be safely estimated at 6,000.

At the time of the organization nearly all the settlers were in the southwest corner of the county, and Peterson was made the county seat. There was at this place a considerable body of timber and a good water power on the Little Sioux, on which John A. Kirchner erected a grist and saw mill.

SPENCER.

This is the county seat of Clay County. Spencer was platted by J. B. Edmunds, J. H. Hale and J. Calkins, in 1871. The second house in Spencer was erected by W. R. Lamberton, the first house being a log house which was built by J. W. Mastin upon the site where Spencer now stands, in 1866. B. P. Hough built a house in 1866; J. W. Mastin opened a stock of goods in his log house in 1869, this being the first store in Spencer. Perso & Bergin, and Tuttle & Smith, each opened a store in 1870. Horace Smith and Field Bros. also opened stores in 1871.

Spencer was incorporated in the spring of 1880. Its first offi-
cers were: W. C. Gilbraith, Mayor: Charles Penfield, Recorder;
J. Rood, C. M. Squire, T. P. Bender, M. P. W. Albee, M. E. Griffin,
E. E. Snow. City Council. Present officers: J. B. Edmunds,
Mayor; J. E. Steele, Recorder; I. F. Constant, Assessor: E. A.
Maker, Marshal; C. McKay, Treasurer; J. Rood, W. L. Bender,
J. C. McCoy, M. S. Green, A. C. Perine, J. P. Evans, City Council.
   The Spencer *Weekly Reporter* was first started in 1877, by J. F.
Ford, who was followed by A. T. McCargar; the Barnard Bros.
purchased it of McCargar January 1st, 1882. Its politics is Republican; it is a nine-column folio, and has a circulation of 1.250
copies, and is all printed at their office in Spencer. They have
a finely fitted office, situated on Main street, have a steam power
press, etc.
   The *Clay County News*, C. M. Whitman, editor and proprietor,
was established at Peterson in 1870, but was removed to Spencer
in 1871, under the management of J. F. Ford, now of the Sheldon
News. Ford sold to McCargar, who ran the paper some time,
subsequently transferring it to C. M. Gilbreath, who, in turn, disposed of it to C. M. Whitman, who took possession in 1880, and
has since continued in the management of the paper. It is a
seven-column quarto, having been enlarged by Whitman since he
took charge. It is the oldest paper in county.
   The *Owl*, a monthly paper, conducted by J. B. Edmunds, is
devoted to the land and immigration interests of Northwestern
Iowa. It was first issued in 1879, is a five-column folio, and is
gratitutiously circulated through many of the Eastern States.

CHURCHES, SCHOOLS AND SOCIETIES.

First Congregational Society— Organized March 14th, 1872, under
the charge of W. L. Coleman. First officers: E. Perine, P. M.
Moore, H. B. Coryell, Trustees: L. C. Bergin and P. M. Moore,
Deacons; A. W. Miller, Treasurer; L. C. Bergin, Clerk. The
church was organized with the following members: L. C. Bergin,
E. Perine, H. B. Coryell, C. Van Eps. C. Snyder, A. W. Miller, I.
Laughten, P. D. Graves, Helen Graves, P. M. Moore, Mary S.
Moore. Present membership, fifty-six. Rev. J. M. Cumings is
the present pastor. The church building was dedicated in February, 1875; size, 26x36 feet; is supplied with a church bell, the first
in the town, which was placed there by the church society under
the pastorate of Rev. J. M. Cummings in 1869. The cost of the
church was $2,754. A parsonage was built in 1880; size, 16x24
feet; cost, $435. There is a Sabbath School with ninety-three pupils;
Dr. McAllister, Superintendent; Clark Skinner, Treasurer. The
present officers of the church are: L. C. Bergin, P. M. Moore,
Deacons; Dr, McAllister. P. M. Moore, A. W. Miller, Trustees.

Methodist Church.—Spencer Circuit was formed in September, 1871, with Rev. Charles B. Winter as the first pastor. The first Board of Trustees were: John Hood, President; M. M. Peeso, Secretary; J. H. Hale, Treasurer; A. M. Calkins, W. W. Scott, R. Hough, H. B. Wood. The church was built in 1872, and dedicated June 18th, 1873, by Rev. J. W. Clinton, with a debt of $1,714, which was paid off by subscription. The first pastor was Rev. C. B. Winters, who was followed by F. M. Cooley, he by W. H. Drake; then in order by J. W. Lothian, Seymour Snyder, and E. C. Warren. The present pastor is Rev. P. H. Eighmy. The membership when first organized was 46, present membership, 115. The first church was destroyed by fire, and left the society in debt $600. It was rebuilt in 1880, during the pastorate of E. C. Warren, at a cost of $2,000, and the society is now free from debt. A parsonage was built in 1881 at a cost of $700; size, 16x24 feet. The Sunday School has seventy-five pupils; P. H. Eighmy, Superintendent; M. M. Peeso, Treasurer; Millie Hagrath, Secretary.

Baptist Church.—Organized January 7th, 1874, with David Skinner, Catherine Skinner, J. A. Bowman, W. H. Davis, S. Hayes, L. Chapin, J. J. Ayres and L. W. Miller, as members. First officers: D. Skinner, Deacon; L. F. Miller, Clerk; J. A. Bowman, Treasurer; D. Skinner, J. A. Bowman and W. H. Davis, Trustees. Present officers: D. Skinner, Deacon and Treasurer; G. C. Farr, Clerk; D. Skinner, W. M. Davis and William Desbrow, Trustees. First pastor, T. H. Judson, who was followed by A. V. Bloodgood. This society has no building of their own, and at present are not supplied with any pastor. There is a Sabbath School with forty-five pupils; G. C. Farr, Superintendent. This society has purchased two lots, upon which they propose soon to erect a church and parsonage.

Evening Shade Lodge No. 312, A. F. & A. M.—Instituted January 24th, 1872. Charter granted, June 8th, 1872. Charter members: S. Lacore, S. F. McDonald, A. Wright, J. W. Crist, S. B. Crist, E. J. Marvine, A. H. Wilber, William Harvey. A dispensation was granted by O. P. Waters, Grand Master. First officers, under dispensation: W. Harvey, W. M.; E. J. Marvine, S. W.; H. H. Wilber, J. W., who were also the first officers under the charter, with the addition of J. H. Hale, Treasurer; S. B. Crist, Secretary; J. W. Crist, S. D.; J. F. Ford, J. D.; J. H. Fend, Tyler. Present officers: W. C. Gilbreath, W. M.; M. P. W. Albee, S. W.; H. C. Brown, J. W.; J. F. Constant, Secretary; W. M. Davis, Treasurer; J. C. McCoy, S. D.; A. R. Claxton, J. D.; S. B. Taylor, Tyler. Membership about thirty. Meetings are held every Monday evening in each month, on or before the full moon. The Lodge has no hall of its own, but is in a very flourishing condition.

Spencer Lodge No. 247, I. O. O. F.—Instituted October 17th, 1872. Charter members: H. Smith, A. B. Kline, J. F. Ford, A. G. Hardin, W. I. Rood. First officers: A. S. Kline, N. G.; H.

Smith, V. G.; W. J. Rood, R. S. Present officers: A. F. Masterman, N. G.; P. E. Randall, V. G.; A. Hubbard, R. S.; H. Smith, Treasurer. Membership, fifty. Meetings are held Tuesday evening of each week in Mason's Hall. The Lodge is in a flourishing condition.

Spencer Temple of Honor No. 13.—Organized December 5th, 1881, by Grand W. C. T. Smith. Charter members: P. E. Randall, C. W. Whitman, M. Tuttle, P. Hodge, J. I. Garret, W. B. Davidson, Will Hodge, E. D. Sanders, M. C. Brainard, D. R. Hubbard, D. C. Skinner, and others. First and present officers: C. M. Whitman, W. C. T.; D. R. Hubbard, W. V. T.; P. E. Randall. F. R.; W. B. Davidson, Treasurer; M. C. Brainard, R. S.; P. Hodge, Usher; C. Skinner, Chaplain; membership, twenty; meet once each week (Monday evening), in the Court House. This is a temperance organization, and is doing effective work for the cause.

Spencer Lodge No. 201, A. O. U. W.—Instituted in August, 1879. First officers: A. T. McCarger, M. W.; W. C. Gilbreath, P. M. W.; C. P. Buckey, Rec.; I. F. Constant, Financier; W. L. Bender, Receiver; E. Pickering, O. S. W.; J. M. Haggarty, I. S. W.; J. P. Evans, Guide; M. P. W. Albee, Foreman; T. P. Bender, M. S. Green, M. E. Griffin, Trustees. Present officers: J. W. Andrew, M. W.; N. Tuttle, Receiver; M. E. Griffin, Recorder; I. F. Constant. Financier; P. E. Randall, Foreman; W. C. Gilbreath, O. W.; A. T. McCarger, I. W. Meetings are held once in two weeks.

Clay County Agricultural Board.—Organized in 1879. First officers: T. P. Bender, President; M. E. Griffin, Treasurer; W. C. Gilbreath, Secretary; Dr. C. McAllister. J. B. Edmunds, A. T. McCarger, James Godwin, Directors. Present officers: T. P. Bender, President; J. B. Edmunds, Treasurer; W. C. Gilbreath, Secretary; C. McAllister, A. T. McCarger, J. P. Evans, M. Hackett, R. Jackson, Directors. This society owns thirty acres of land, situated one-quarter of a mile northwest of town, and enclosed with a close board fence seven feet high. There is a nice amphitheater, which seats 400 people; a floral hall 24x36 feet; also sheds, stalls, pens, etc.; a Judge's stand, etc., and a good one-half mile track. Fairs are held once each year. The society is nearly free from debt. The total cost of the grounds and improvements was $3,000.

The first school-house in the town was built in 1869; C. Carver was the first teacher. Spencer became an independent district in 1874. Previous to this it was a part of Spencer Township District. The first Board of Education was: H. B. Wood, Secretary; H. Smith, Treasurer; M. Hines, President. The first teachers of the independent district were: Geo. Mann, Principal; Augusta Smith Assistant. The present school building was erected in the fall of 1879, at a cost of $4,000; cost of furnishing, $800; size, 48x58 feet.

The present Board is composed of the following gentlemen: T. P. Bender, President; A. W. Miller, J. C. McCoy, Ackley Hubbard. Present teachers: J. T. Lemar, Principal; Miss L. Parker, Miss E. Bean, Miss Cowan and Miss Olive Woodruff. The present enrollment of pupils is about 300.

The Court House was built by the citizens of Spencer in 1871. the county being given the use of it for three years. The county afterwards bought it. Its dimensions are 20x40 feet; cost $1,000. There is a prospect of a new Court House being soon erected.

The C., M. & St. P. Railroad was built to Spencer in 1878. There is a narrow gauge in course of construction to meet the Wabash, St. Louis & Pacific, from Des Moines through Spencer, and thence north through Dickinson County. The grading for this road is at present completed through the county of Clay.

The Chicago, Milwaukee & St. Paul Company have in course of construction a road from Spencer to Spirit Lake, most of the grading on which is completed. This road is expected to be completed through Clay County during the present year.

Spencer boasts of a creamery, which was established in 1878, by McPherson & Allen. They have a large building and steam power. This creamery is run on the cream-gathering plan, and uses cream from nearly every section of the county. It was operated in 1881 by Penfield, Allen & Co. The building is 20x50 feet in dimensions, two stories high, and cost about $3,000.

Spencer also has a plow factory, which does business on a small scale, but which it expects to largely increase in the near future.

The business establishments of Spencer may be thus classified: drugstores, two; harness, two; agricultural implements, three; billiard halls, three; hardware, three; shoe stores, two; saloons, two; bookstores, one; furniture, three; banks, three; general merchandise, ten; elevators, three; barber shops, two; merchant tailor, one; butter and egg packers, two; music dealers, one; livery, three; groceries, seven; lumber, four; hotels, three; restaurants, three; jewelry, one; meat markets, two; fruit store, one.

CLAY COUNTY BIOGRAPHIES.

SPENCER.

John B. Annett, shoemaker, was born in England; spent most of his younger days in Mass.; then moved to Ill., and in 1869 settled on a homestead in Spencer township, Clay county, Ia. He opened a shoemaker's shop on his farm in 1870, and in company with G. C. Farr, started a general store. He returned to Mass. in 1871, and again came to Spencer in 1877, and was employed by S. S. Birkson, with whom he still continues.

H. C. Brown, contractor and builder, was born in Indiana in 1848. He moved with his parents to Keokuk, Ia., where he remained until 1870; then came to Spencer and engaged as above. The first building he occupied in Spencer was a sod building.

H. Chamberlain, county clerk, was born in Vt. in 1849; moved with his parents to Ill. when six years of age; thence to Ia. in 1871. He was elected to the above named office in 1876, and is now serving his third term. He married Mary Ellis in 1875. They have two children.

William Carleton came to Iowa from Me. in 1851. and located in Marion county. He moved to Clay county in 1871; located at Spencer, and opened the first grocery store in the town. There were only four business houses in the town, and he, with his wife, lived for some time in a tent. He has been engaged in the grocery business since coming to the place until the first of the present year, 1882. Mr. Carleton spent several years as a sailor, and has visited various countries.

F. G. Daniels, proprietor of the Gregory House, was born in Herkimer county, N. Y., in 1838; moved to Chautauqua county in 1851. He was engaged as traveling salesman and collecting agent for a New York house for some years, and in 1862 engaged in business at Oil Creek, Pa. In 1871 he came to Iowa; was engaged in the patent right business for several years, and located at Spencer, in 1881. He married Mary F. Bennett, in 1871, and has one son.

J. B. Edmunds, banker and real estate dealer, was born in Mich. in 1845, removed with parents in 1850 to O.; thence to Minn. in 1851. He came to Spencer in 1870, and engaged in his present business. He was one of the original proprietors of the town. When he came here there was only one log house where the town now stands, and he has probably done more to build up the place than any other man. Mr. Edmunds published *The Owl*, a real estate paper devoted to the land interests of Clay county.

Thomas Eagan, proprietor of the City Hotel, was born in Ill. in 1854; removed with his parents during the same year to Wis., where he remained until 1881, when he came to Spencer, and engaged in his present business. He was married in 1874 to Catherine Reardon, and has four children.

Henry Green, railroad contractor, came to Iowa from N. Y. in 1852, and located in Allamakee county; thence to Clay county in 1871, and settled on a homestead. He moved to Spencer in 1880, and purchased the Spencer House, which he ran until Dec., 1881, then rented the hotel, and engaged in business as above.

S. H. Geddes, of the firm of Geddes & Goble, contractors and builders, came to Spencer from Bremer county, Ia., in 1878, and engaged in business as above. He conducted business alone until 1881, at which time J. J. Goble came to Spencer from Palo Alto county, and became a partner in the business.

Ackley Hubbard, attorney at law, came to Spencer. Ia., from N. Y. in 1869. He settled on a homestead and engaged in farming. In 1872, he was elected clerk, which office he held two terms. He was admitted to the bar in 1876, and has been engaged in the practice of the law ever since. He is also a member of the firm of Woodruff & Hubbard, furniture dealers. He has added to the city by putting into the market forty acres on the west side, which are now covered with some of the finest residences in the place.

T. B. Horton and S. T. Cruver, of the firm of Horton & Cruver, dealers in general merchandise, established business in Nov., 1880. They came to Spencer from Lake county, Ill., where they had been engaged in the same business. The business averages about $40,000 per annum.

E. E. Harris, painter, came to Spencer in 1874, from Ill. and engaged in the hotel business at the Metropolitan, now called Commercial. He afterwards opened the Central house now called the Gregory, after three years he rented the hotel and began working at his trade, that of painter. He worked at painting one year in the Black Hills. He is also agent for the Cedar Rapids Ins. Co.

D. R. Hubbard, special agent for the Cedar Rapids insurance company, was born in Floyd county, Ia., in 1858; moved with his parents to Clay county in 1869, when he settled on a homestead. He engaged in teaching school until 1878, when he engaged in his present business at Spencer. He married Rosa H. Feed in 1880.

W. C. Hubbard, agent for the Kimball organ, was born in Floyd county, Ia., in 1861; moved with parents to Clay county and settled on a homestead. He came to Spencer in 1880, and engaged in his present business with Arthur Hubbard. He now continues business alone.

W. S. Lloyd, proprietor of the eating house near the depot; came to Spencer in 1878, from Cedar Falls, Ia., and engaged in his present business. He furnishes warm meals at all hours, also rooms for travelers.

P. W. Madden, sheriff, was born in Pa. in 1845; moved with parents to Mahaska county, Ia., in 1852. He came to Clay county in 1871, and settled on a homestead in Lincoln township. He was elected to his office as above in the autumn of 1881.

E. A. Maker, dental surgeon, was born in Cincinnati, O., in 1842; moved to Ind. in 1860; there learned dentistry, and in 1865 moved to Grant county, Wis. In 1878, he came to Spencer, and opened the first dental office in the city. Dr. Maker is at present marshal of Spencer.

J. D. Powers, hardware dealer, came to Spencer in 1878 from Butler county, Ia., and engaged in his present business. He carries a stock worth from ten to twelve thousand dollars, and his sales average about $25,000 per annum. This is one of the finest hardware stores in Western Iowa.

P. E. Randall, county treasurer, was born in Lockport, N. Y., in 1843; moved with parents to Canada, where he remained five years, then moved to Wis. He came to Clay county in 1870, engaged in farming; after two years, came to Spencer and engaged as salesman. He was elected to his office as above in 1879, and re-elected in 1881. He was postmaster six years.

H. Smith, dealer in general merchandise, came to Spencer from Wis. in 1871, and engaged in his present business. There were only about fifty persons in the town when he came, and he was the third man to put in a stock of general merchandise. He started in the same building which he now occupies, which at that time was 30x20 feet, but which by reason of additions, is now eighty-two feet in length. He carries a stock worth from ten to twelve thousand dollars.

The Spencer Reporter was established in 1877 by J. F. Ford, and purchased by A. T. McCarger, in 1881, who sold it to the Barnard Bros. in Dec., 1881. It is a republican paper, all printed at home. They have the only steam-power press in the northwest, outside of Sioux City. They are prepared to do job work in all styles.

G. Thorine, business manager for the Eureka Furniture Company, established the business in 1878, as the Spencer Furniture Co. 1881, he sold to J. C. Lewis, who changed the name as above. Mr. Thorine was retained as manager.

H. H. Wade, contractor and builder, came to Clay county in 1869, and located on a homestead in Summit township, where he lived three years; then went to O. He returned to Clay county in

1880, and purchased a farm of the railroad company where he has since lived; engaged in business in Spencer as above. He has built some of the finest buildings in the city. He was married in 1876, and has two children.

C. M. Whitman, proprietor of the Clay County News, was born in Racine county, Wis., in 1852, learned his trade at Burlington, Wis.; came to Spencer, Ia., in 1880, and engaged in his present business. The News was the first paper in the county, having been established at Peterson in 1870 by J. F. Ford, who moved it to Spencer in 1871. It was purchased by Mr. McCarger, who sold it to W. C. Gilbreath, and was then purchased by its present owner. This paper is republican, and an advocate of temperance. Mr. Whitman was married in 1875; his wife died since coming to Iowa.

BUENA VISTA COUNTY,

Buena Vista County is the third from the west and the third from the north line of the State. It is twenty-four miles square, containing 368,640 acres. The Little Sioux River meanders through the northern portion of the county, watering three townships, and furnishing some valuable bodies of timber. It receives a tributary from the south, which waters two or three additional townships. Several other small streams pass through different parts, affording good water for stock, and surface drainage. In the southern part of the county is situated Storm Lake, a beautiful body of clear water, with steep banks, with fine undulating prairie farming lands stretching away in all directions, except on the north side, where the thriving town bearing the name of the lake is now located. There are other smaller lakes in the county. The surface of the county is generally rolling, with a soil as fertile as could be desired. It is adapted to all the cereals and root crops. In this part of the State generally, the supply of timber is limited. There are no stone quarries developed, but granite and limestone boulders are found on the prairies, along the streams, and about the borders of the lakes. Good brick are manufactured from clays found in the county, and from the "bluff deposit" which is characteristic of this part of the state. Many kinds of fish are found in the lakes and streams.

The government surveys were made in this county in 1855. The first permanent settlement was made in May, 1856, by Abner Bell, from New Jersey, at that time a bachelor, his brother-in-law, William R. Weaver and family, and John W. Tucker. They settled in the north part of the county at Sioux Rapids. Among the early settlers were Arthur T. Reeves, Moses Van Kirk, James H. Gleason, Lewis, Lindsey, and Metcalf. In March, 1857, occurred what is known in the annals of Iowa as Ink-pah-du-tah Raid, which culminated in the bloody massacre at Spirit Lake. Before reaching the lake the Indians passed up the Little Sioux River, driving away the stock and destroying the property of the settlers. The little colony at Sioux Rapids did not escape. The men were captured and guarded, and some of the women led away to the Indian camp, but the Indians committed no murders here. A few days after, the news of the terrible butchery at Spirit Lake came down the river, and Mr. Bell with a companion made his way across the prairie through the deep snow to Fort Dodge, to notify the people there of the massacre. This affair had the effect to check the settlement of this part of the state for several years.

Late in 1858, or early in 1859, a county organization was effected, the following being the county officers: Arthur T. Reeves, County Judge; William R. Weaver, Treasurer and Recorder; John W. Tucker, Clerk; and Abner Bell, Sheriff.

In 1860 the county seat was first located, by a commission appointed by Judge Hubbard, composed of D. C. Early, John Kindlespeyer and Sartel, on a tract known as the "Fuller Claim." At that time the place was occupied by William S. Lee, who executed to the county a bond for a deed to the northwest quarter of the northeast quarter of section 18, township 93, range 36. The tract was long known as "Prairieville, the County Seat of Buena Vista County," but no county buildings were ever erected upon it. Up to 1866 there were but few settlers in the county, and its affairs seem to have been badly managed. The early records of the county are very imperfect, and many of them are missing from the county. Up to this time the officials entered into large contracts for bridges and other improvements which were never made, although county warrants were issued in payment amounting to many thousands of dollars.

The county seat was removed from "Prairieville" to Sioux Rapids at an early date, 1869, when a Court House was erected. When the more southern part of the county became settled, the people of that part of the county continually agitated the question of removing the county seat from Sioux Rapids to Newell, a small town on the Illinois Central Railroad. In 1876, the Court House was burned at Sioux Rapids. This gave the people from the southern part of the county more grounds for having the county seat removed, and the people of Newell fought to have it there. The citizens of Storm Lake, as a matter of course, were opposed to this and with the combined efforts of Sioux Rapids, and their own, they kept the county seat from being located at Newell.

At an election held Oct. 5th, 1878, the people of Buena Vista County decided by a large majority to move the county seat from Sioux Rapids to Storm Lake. After eight years' effort this result was accomplished. At a meeting of the board, held January, 1878, the question was submitted between Storm Lake and Sioux Rapids, and the former gained the day. In the latter part of August, the citizens of Storm Lake decided to erect a building suitable for Court House purposes and donated the use of it to the county for a term of ten years, on condition that the county should use the same for Court House purposes. A company was formed for the erection of the building under the name of the Storm Lake Building Association. The building erected is 30x36 feet, two stories high, and rests upon a foundation of solid granite masonry. The first story is divided into four rooms which are used for county offices, the second story being occupied for a court room.

The present county officers are: Edgar E. Mack, Clerk of Courts; J. W. Warren, Auditor; George Espe, Treasurer; Daniel Smith,

29

Recorder; E. F. Farnsworth, Sheriff; Robert DeLoss, Surveyor; Thomas Whiteley, Coroner; Ira C. Harlan, Superintendent of Schools; L. E. Hay. S. Salerson, A. W. Seymore, Alden Pratt, James N. Hoskins, Board of Supervisors. The population of the county in 1880 was 7,557. It may now safely be estimated at over 8,000.

The soil in the northeastern diagonal half is a heavy, dark loam; and the southwest diagonal half is bluff deposit, or silicious marl; both kinds of soil being rich and productive, the eastern being more especially adapted to stock-raising and dairy products, and more level in its topography, while the west is more rolling and undulating, but none of it too much so for desirable tillage.

The Little Sioux River enters in 93 deg. 36 min., courses westward ten miles or over and back into Clay county, affording sites for two busy flouring mills in this county.

Coon River heads in Grass Lake, in 93 deg. 36 min., flows south and out into Sac County, through 90 deg. 36 min. Maple and Brook Creeks, and possibly one or two other streamlets additional, afford water for stock and channels for surface drainage.

The timber is limited, and yet sufficient, with its continuous growth, to supply domestic fuel; it is found along the banks and valley of the Little Sioux, and in artificial groves scattered over the county, representing the oaks, hard and soft maple, butternut, walnut, and a few other varieties.

The tide immigration into this part of Northwestern Iowa last year exceeded the aggregate of several preceding years, and was mainly of the more thrifty class, and many a broad acre was sold and broken up.

One of the most important features in farming in this northwestern country is flax culture upon new breaking, giving a liberal return, and aiding in subduing the land the first year.

STORM LAKE.

The first house in Storm Lake was moved into town and occupied by Barton & Hobbs as a law and real estate office. W. W. Sweetzer built the first dwelling house. T. L. Selkirk erected the first hotel.

There seems to be quite a difference of opinion as to how Storm Lake received its name. It is supposed to have been given it by an old trapper who trapped, upon its banks, on account of a very severe storm which occurred upon the lake. The town derived its name from the lake.

The first load of wheat bought in Storm Lake was purchased by Mr. Eddy, Oct. 20th, 1870. The amount was 100 bushels and the price paid was 75 cents per bushel. The grain was raised by D. B. Harrison.

The first child born in Storm Lake was that of Mrs. Wirrick August 11th, 1870.

The town was incorporated in April, 1873, under the code, S. W .Hobbs being the first Mayor, and T. S. Smith. W. II. McCune, J. M. Russell, J. A. Campbell and S. C. Highley Trustees; E. C. Cowles, Recorder.   The following are the present town officers: Mayor, Chas. Isbell; Recorder. Geo. H. Eastman; Attorneys, Robinson & Milchrist; Treasurer, L. E. Hay; Marshal, Street Commissioner and Sealer of Weights and Measures, Wm. Backer; Deputy Marshal and Night Watchman, J. E. Hall; Trustees, W. Brubacher, S. D. Eadie, J. B. Ames, W. C. Wilson, Jas. Harker and M. M. Cogswell. The regular meetings of the Council are held on the evening of the first Monday in each month.

The population of the town is now estimated to be about 1,500.

The Storm Lake *Pilot*, a weekly Republican paper. was established in 1870, the first issue being on October 26th. It was started by Vestal & Young. Young sold to E. I. Sutfin in 1881.   The paper is a seven-column quarto, and has a circulation of 1,000 copies. The paper, still conducted by Vestal &. Sutfin, is a first-class paper. The publishers have a first-class job office. and the paper is one of the best weekly papers in the Northwest.

The Storm Lake *Tribune* began its career March 24th, 1880, published by G. Rose, who sold it in October, 1881, to P. D. McAndrew, who is the present proprietor. It is Republican in politics,' is a six-column quarto, and has a circulation of 720 copies. Mr. Andrews also runs a nicely fitted job office.

Storm Lake has seen fit to protect itself against the ravages of fire by having a regularily organized fire company, with about seventy members, these equally divided between the engine company and the hook and ladder company. They are in possession of a fine engine and apparatus, and are regularly organized and uniformed. The department was organized in 1880. The citizens have built a large engine house, with a hall in the second story, and have a large fire-bell and plenty of good wells through the town, so they are well protected from fire.

Storm Lake boasts of as nice a postoffice as can be found in any town of its size in the west. In the year 1870 the postoffice of the town paid the postmaster the sum 812.50 per year. and now it pays a salary of 81,800. It has been a money-order office for several years, and is now rated third-class. The office occupies an entire room, is provided with all the modern conveniences, uses 670 boxes, of which 150 are the improved Yale lock. Col. W. L. Vestal, the present postmaster, has held the position of postmaster ever since the office was established with the exception of one year.

The Buena Vista Creamery is situated three-quarters of a mile north of Storm Lake. and was erected in the spring of 1881. Commenced operations June 1st, 1881. and ceased for the season November 1st, 1881. During the first five months were manufactured about 120,000 pounds of fine butter, all of which was

sold on the New York market, and quality pronounced equal to
the finest make of Elgin butter. The building is 66x70 feet, and
is arranged in the most complete and improved manner. The
motive power is a ten-horse power engine, and the capacity is
6,000 pounds of butter per day. All who have visited the creamery pronounce the plan of operations perfect. The creamery is
managed entirely on the "cream gathering" plan, and the success
of this system is practically assured. The interior arrangements
consist of receiving room, cream room, churning room, packing,
refrigerator room and ice-house 22x40 feet in dimensions, with a
capacity for 500 tons. W. B. Cromwell is manager.

The railroad was completed to Storm Lake in June, 1870.

Buena Vista County also has a branch of the Wabash Railroad
running through the northern part of the county. This county
also looks forward to a branch of the Chicago & Northwestern
Railway from Davenport to Sioux Falls, striking the county, as
the survey through is now in progress.

Storm Lake has a number of fine brick buildings. Two banks
are fine brick structures, and several of the mercantile houses are
built of brick. The streets are being graded, and the citizens
take great pride in keeping their city as clean and neat as possible.

The business houses may be classified as follows: General
stores, seven; clothing, one; groceries, one; boots and shoes, two;
banks, three; bakeries and restaurants, five; meat markets, three;
hotels, four; elevators, three; lumber and coal, three; millinery,
four; furniture, two; hardware, two; drugs, four; livery stables,
four; harness, two; cigar factory, one; jewelry, two; steam plow
factory; saloons, two; agricultural implements, five; photograph
gallery, one; barber shops, two; music and books, one; steam flouring mills; the usual number of blacksmith and wagon shops and
professional men

CHURCHES, SCHOOLS AND SOCIETIES.

Baptist Church Society.—The Baptist Church was organized
March 8th, 1871, with the following members: Mrs. V. Miller,
Mrs. Harrison, Mrs. Robinson and two daughters, J. K. Barns and
wife. Elder Norman Parks was the first pastor. He was suc-
ceeded by Wilcox, who in turn gave place to the present pastor,
Jesse Boswell. First officers: C. H. Yates, Deacon; Mrs. V.
Miller, Clerk. Present officers: C. C. Angier, Deacon; J. B.
Miller, Deacon; and C. L. Angier, Clerk. The present member-
ship is thirty-nine resident members. They have in connection a
Sabbath School of about forty pupils, with W. C. Wilson as
Superintendent. The church building was begun in 1873, but was
not dedicated until January 17th, 1875. It is a neat frame build-
ing 32x46 feet, and was erected at a cost of $2,000.

Methodist Episcopal Church Society.—This Society was organized in 1870 by Rev. Thomas Whiteley. This gentleman had

charge of a number of societies in this region of the country at that time and it was from his flock that the societies now of Storm Lake, Alta, Newell, and many other points sprang and became independent societies. The first pastor of the society in this place was Rev. Mr. Oswell. He was followed by Rev. Mr. Fry, who remained a short time and was succeeded by Thomas Whiteley, and the latter in turn by W. Whitfield, who was succeeded by C. Winters, he by Thomas Barr. Then came in succession Revs. Seymour Snyder, J. C. R. Leyton, T. M. Williams and the present pastor, W. F. Gleason, who took charge in 1881. The present officers of the church are M. Tolle, J. R. Lemon, W. L. Smith, D. Smith, J. G. McGregor, J. W. Berthards, E. L. Carrington, Thomas Whiteley, Trustees. This society has a membership of 120. It has a Sabbath School with an average attendance of 125 pupils, with J. R. Lemon as Superintendent. This church society was organized in a house that was moved into town and which is now occupied by A. Eadie. The church building was erected and dedicated in 1876. The dedication took place in October. It is a neat frame building 32x50 feet, and has a seating capacity of 300. It is nicely furnished and the building was lately supplied with a new bell. This building was erected at a cost of $3,500. The society has a neat parsonage in connection with the church.

German Methodist Episcopal Church Society.—This Society was organized December, 18th, 1875, by E. E. Schuette and G. Haefner. The first officers were: F. Petersmier, J. Buehler, R. C. Riekelfs, A. Hartman, C. Schaefer, Trustees. The first pastor was G. Haefner, who was followed by A. W. Henke, and he by the present pastor, C. F. Tramm. Present officers: R. C. Riekelfs, Geo. Witter, Jacob Brecher, Trustees. Present membership, ninety-eight. The society has a Sabbath School with an average attendance of twenty-five pupils. A fine frame building was erected in 1880 and was dedicated in January, 1881. The building is 22x44 feet, has a steeple, and cost $2,000. This society also has a neat little parsonage, built in 1881, which is 18x24 feet, one-and-a-half stories high, with a wing 18x18 feet. This building was erected at a cost of $1,200.

Congregational Church Society.—For several years it had been known that a considerable number of the members of the Congregational denomination had been making their homes in Storm Lake. But because a Presbyterian church had been previously established in the place, a large degree of hesitation was felt as to the expediency of organizing a Congregational church, and various attempts at union with the Presbyterians were projected. None of these, however, resulted satisfactorily, and in the summer of 1880 the conviction deepened that the interests of Evangelical Christian work demanded the organization of a Congregational church. The matter was canvassed somewhat during the early summer by Rev. Asa Countryman, of Newell, and farther during the autumn by

Rev. J. B. Chase of Cherokee. October 24th, at a called meeting, a paper was presented containing the names of twenty-six persons not connected with any religious organization in the town, who pledged themselves, if it were thought best, to enter into the organization of a Congregational church. On this pledge as a basis, knowing that several other persons in the community were favorable to the step, it was decided to organize, and the accompanying articles of faith and convenant were adopted, and a council consisting of the Sioux Association was called to review proceedings and if deemed best recognize the church. The council convened November 4th, according to invitation, reviewed the situation, endorsed the action of the church and formally extended the right hand of fellowship. Temporary arrangements were made for a house of worship, a Sabbath School and prayer-meeting were organized, and Rev. J. B. Chase, of Cherokee, consented to give as much of his time to the new enterprise as could be consistently spared from his other work. This society now has a membership of forty-two, and holds services in the Court House. It has a Sabbath School with an average attendance of 100 pupils. H. H. Smith is Superintendent. The first and present officers of this society are: G. Stetson, J. L. Dickerson and H. H. Smith, Deacons; E. E. Mack, Clerk and Treasurer; G. Stetson. H. C. Cutts and E. E. Mack, Trustees. Rev. A. S. Newcomb is the present pastor.

Catholic Church Society.—This society was organized in 1871, and was the first church organization in Storm Lake. It was organized by Rev. Father Malloy. The present pastor, Father Gaffney, the first and only resident pastor, took charge in November, 1878. The church building was erected in 1871 at a cost of $1,-300. There are about sixty-five families connected with the church at this place. There is also a Sabbath School in connection.

Universalist Church Society.—This society was organized March 27th, 1874. First officers: G. S. Robinson, W. L. Vestal and S. W. Hobbs, Trustees. First pastor, I. A. Everhart, he being succeeded by J. A. Hoyt, he by Karl Gerner, he by B. F. Snook. H. Whitney is the present incumbent. Present officers: S. W. Hobbs. William Guilford, J. A. Dean, Trustees. This society now has a membership of thirty-six, and a Sabbath School with an average attendance of fifty-four pupils. The school has a fine library containing 200 volumes. H. Whitney is the Superintendent. This society first held services in the Baptist Church. Up to this time the Baptist Society had a debt of about $600 upon the church building, and agreed to give the Universalist Society the use of the church for one-half of the time, the latter society to pay off one-half the standing debt. This lease was for five years. The Universalist Society erected a building in 1881. This is a frame structure, 30x50 feet, and cost about $4,000. This church is not only the largest but is the best furnished church in the city.

Presbyterian Church Society.—Organized December, 1870, with seven members, Rev. G. R. Carroll, missionary of the Presbyterian Board of Home Missions, officiating, S. D. Eadie, W. H. McCune, Elders. This Society has a nice frame building. Joshua Cooke is the present pastor.

Storm Lake Schools.—The first school taught in Storm Lake was taught in the house of S. D. Eadie, by Alma L. Gates. It was opened November 21st, 1870, with fifteen pupils in attendance. Storm Lake became an independent district in 1872. First school officers: J. I. Wirrick, President; G. W. Hobbs, Ed. Wirrick, J. O. Strong, Directors; E. I. Sutfin, Treasurer.

The first school house built in the town was erected in 1874, the first teacher being Maggie Ross. This building becoming too small to accommodate all the pupils, the town built a small frame building in 1875, which was used for primary purposes. These buildings becoming too small to accommodate the pupils, the town built an addition to the first building, which was of brick. This building was completed in 1880, and Storm Lake can now boast of one of the finest school buildings in the western part of the State. Present Board of Education: E. E. Mack, President; E. F. O'Neill, Secretary; Rev. J. Cooke, £. W. Benson, E. M. Fuller, W. H. Shoop, and S. W. Perrine, Directors. The present teachers are: Prof. A. A. Crary, Principal; Mrs. A. A. Crary, Miss S. A. Childs, Mrs. L. C. Lauder, and Miss L. Drips, assistants. The present enrollment of pupils is 318.

Storm Lake Lodge No. 221, A. O. U. W.—Instituted December 7th, 1880. First officers: J. A. Dean, P. M. W.; F. E. Cushman, M. W.; W. L. Vestal, Foreman: T. A. Strong, Overseer; C. W. Eccleston, Guide: E. E. Mack, Recorder; J. B. Ames, Financier; T. J. McCall, Receiver; T. A. Corbitt, I. W.; F. B. Brown, O. W.; W. Miller, S. B. Steiner and J. W. Gilbert, Trustees; J. N. Warren and W. H. Kerr, Medical Examiners. Present officers: H. C. Johnson, P. W. M.; E. E. Mack, M. W.; C. W. Seidel, Foreman; W. C. Wilson, Overseer; E. S. Donaho, Guide; C. W. Eccleston, Financier; J. T. McCall, Receiver; T. A. Corbett, I. W.; R. A. Benn, O. W.; Peter Schmitz, Wm. Miller, J. W. Gilbert, Trustees. Medical Examiners same as at first. This Lodge now has a membership of thirty-seven, and holds meetings once in two weeks. It is in a flourishing condition.

Storm Lake Lodge No. 221, I. O. O. F.—Instituted May 10th, 1871, by T. J. Kinkaid, of Sioux City, D. D. G. M. First officers: J. C. Spooner, N. G.; T. S. Smith, V. G.; J. L. Wilson, Secretary; L. J. Barton, Treasurer. Present officers: C. E. Cameron, N. G.; A. R. McCartney, V. G.; L. G. Malborne, Secretary; Wm. Miller, Treasurer. The present membership is about sixty. The Lodge holds meetings every Saturday night in Masonic Hall. There is also an encampment of this order, in a flourishing condition in connection with the Lodge.

Jewel Lodge No. 309, A. F. & A. M.—Instituted October 26th, 1871. Charter granted June, 1872. First officers under dispensation: J. E. Wirrick, W. M.; E. I. Sutfin, S. W.; E. Wirrick, J. W.; P. Schaller, Secretary; W. L. Vestal, Treasurer: D. B. Harrison, S. D.; E. S. Fanning, J. D.; N. Parks, Chaplain; E. W. Benson, Tyler. (The above named persons were the Charter Members.) Present officers: O. D. Pettel, W. M.; T. D. Higgs, S. W.; J. A. Dean, J. W.; S. W. Hobbs, Secretary; M. Tolle, Treasurer; B. F. Langdon, S. D.; Frank Webb, J. D.; M. Tolle, Chaplain; R. J. Fowler, Tyler. This Lodge now has a membership of forty-six, and meet the Thursday evening on or before each full moon in their hall, over the First National Bank. This Lodge is in a growing condition.

SIOUX RAPIDS.

Sioux Rapids was platted by D. C. Thomas and David Evans in 1869. The county seat of Buena Vista county was removed from Prairieville to this place in 1869, and, as was stated in Storm Lake items, was removed to Storm Lake in 1878. The Court House was burned at this place in 1876.

Tyford, Blake, Gilbert, and Hollinger are among the earliest settlers in this place. This town is not at this date incorporated, but steps have been taken to have it incorporated this spring. The town now has a population of about 400, and from the fact that the railroad is now completed to this point, it will rapidly increase in population, and incorporation will become a necessity.

The Sioux Rapids *Press*, a neat weekly, eight-column folio, made its first appearance May 25th, 1881. It now has a circulation of 740 copies. Is Republican in politics. W. S. Wescott is proprietor. It bids fair soon to rank with the leading newspapers of the county.

CHURCHES, SCHOOLS AND SOCIETIES.

Methodist Episcopal Church Society.—This was the first Methodist Society organized within the bounds of the charge known as the Spirit Lake Circuit. It was organized by Rev. Seymour Snyder with O. C. Potts as leader, in 1865. This society was organized about three miles from the present town of Sioux Rapids. In 1874 Rev. C. W. Wiley organized the first society in the present town. This society erected a church building, the first church in town, in 1877. This is a neat frame building, size 30x40 feet. The cost was $1.700. Rev. Seymour Snyder was the first pastor on this circuit, he being followed by Rev. Hawks, he by C. W. Clifton. Then followed Revs. Whiteley, Pitts, Ziegler, Fancher. C. W. Wiley, L. B. Keeling, Seymour Snyder, R. Fancher, O. H. P. Fauss and then the present incumbent. Rev. S. Snyder. First officers: D. C. Thomas, Lot Thomas, W. L. Pratt, M. Clemens,

Mrs. A. Tyers, J. M. Hoskins, Peter Dubois, Sr., E. Sands, J. R. Noel, Trustees; Mrs. A. Tyers, Mrs. C. M. Clemens, J. R. Noel, Stewards. Present officers: J. Frankenberger, S. Dubois, O. G. Taber, C. C. Awvell, A. E. Taber, L. Carter, Stewards; O. G. Brainard, P. Dubois, Sr., O. G. Taber and M. Hoskins, Trustees. This society has a membership of seventy-seven. There is a Sabbath School in connection, with an attendance of fifty pupils. Mrs. O. G. Brainard is Superintendent. This society has now in process of construction a parsonage 18x24 feet in dimensions, which will cost $400.

Baptist Church Society.—Was organized in 1881, by D. D. Proper. The first pastor was Rev. A. V. Bloodgood, he also being the present incumbent. First officers: W. A. Wilson, Clerk; P. W. Goodrich, Deacon. This society has a membership of eight, and holds services in the Congregational Church. There is also a Sabbath School with an average attendance of thirty pupils. W. A. Wilson is Superintendent.

Congregational Church Society.—Organized November 4th, 1875, its first officers being Henry Gleason and S. Warner, Deacons; H. S. Newcomb, Clerk; first pastor, Rev. J. W. Smith. The society has a membership of fourteen with A. M. Beaman as the present pastor. The society built a church in 1881, size 20x36 feet. This building was erected at a cost of $700. Present officers: Henry Gleason, S. S. Warner, Deacons, and H. S. Newcomb, Clerk.

Lutheran Church Societies.—There are two organizations of Lutherans in Sioux Rapids which were both organized in 1870, Rev. A. Johnson and Rev. G. Gulbrenson being the present pastors.

Sioux Rapids Public School.—Sioux Rapids became an independent school district in 1878, the first school being taught in 1869. The present school building was erected in 1870. The present teachers are Prof. J. S. McSparran and wife. The present enrollment of pupils is 100. The present School Board consists of S. S. Warner, Henry Jacobson and J. M. Hoskins.

Enterprise Lodge No. 332, A. F. & A. M.—Instituted 1874. The charter members were W. L. Pratt, D. C. Thomas, Lot Thomas, O. G. Brainard, Gus. Gilbert, T. M. Watts, E. Bailey, O. P. Warner, W. L. Pratt being the first W. M. Present officers: J. M. Hoskins, W. M.; C. L. Ward, S. W.; C. A. Anderson, J. W.; S. E. Harris, Treasurer; W. A. Jones, Secretary. This society now has a membership of twenty, and is in a flourishing condition.

Sioux Rapids' flouring mills are located on the Big Sioux River, which affords an immense water power. The mill was built in 1871, and has two run of stone, and one feed buhr. The mill has a capacity of fifty barrels per day. Wilson & Smith, the present proprietors, are making preparations to enlarge their mill for the manufacture of patent flour.

The business houses of Sioux Rapids may be classified as follows: General stores, three: hardware, two; drug store, jewelry store; harness, two; blacksmith shops, two; restaurants, three; hotels, two; lumber dealer; livery, two; furniture store: barber shop; postoffice, printing office, saloons, three; millinery; shoe shops, two; meat market, bank, and the usual quota of lawyers, doctors and land agents.

ALTA.

Alta was platted in 1872 by the Iowa Falls & Sioux City Land Company. It is situated on the Illinois Central Railroad, in the western part of Buena Vista County. The first house built in the town was erected by Mr. Tibbets, in 1870, and was occupied as a store. J. Morrisey and S. Furlong each built a dwelling about the same time. The town was incorporated under Code in 1879. First officers were: A. W. Seymour, Mayor; L. Wheelock, Jr., Recorder; A. Leander, Treasurer; C. T. Steever, Assessor; J. W. Slutz, P. M. Jencks, H. C. Kelso, A. F. S. Rokkan, Dr. R. B. Dando. F. O. Wiss, Trustees. Present officers: C. T. Steever, Mayor; W. H. Pierce. Recorder; A. Leander, Treasurer; R. B. Dando, A. F. A. Rokkan, D. Burke, H. C. Kelso, J. W. Slutz, G. Gerner, Councilmen; City Attorney, F. J. Stockwell.

The population of Alta is now estimated to be about 700. It has grown very rapidly, and being situated in an extremely fertile country, it is destined at no far distant future, to become an important point. It already does an immense business in shipments of grain and live stock.

The Alta *Advertiser* was started in September, 1876, as a monthly paper, but was changed to a weekly in June, 1877. It is independent in politics, and has a circulation of 660 copies. Its editor and proprietor is C. T. Steever, he having started the paper.

The business of Alta comprises: Three general stores, two drug stores; two grocery stores, boot and shoe store, two hardware stores, meat market, two lumber dealers, two agriculture implement dealers, bank, two furniture stores, clothing store, barber shop, two saloons, music store, two jewelry stores, restaurant, four blacksmiths, two elevators, grist mill.

CHURCHES, SCHOOLS AND SOCIETIES.

Methodist Episcopal Church Society.—Organized in 1870. The church building was erected in 1876 and was dedicated in November of that year. Rev. Henry Brown being the first pastor. He was succeeded by Rev. W. W. Brown and he by Rev. C. M. Bryan, and the latter by Rev. D. M. Beams. Rev. C. B. Winter, who took charge in September, 1881, is the present incumbent. First officers: H. Bennett, C. Schell, G. H. Richmond, J. L. Wilson, J. L. Bennett, Geo. G. Espe and W. S. Van Buskirk, Trustees. The present Board is the same as the first with the exception of S. Parker, instead of G. G. Espe. The society has eighty members, also a Sabbath School with an average attendance of eighty pupils. G. W. Wheat is Superintendent. The church building is a fine frame structure, 32x50 feet, with a seating capacity of 300 persons, and was erected at a cost of $2,500.

Swedish Lutheran Church Society.—This society was organized in 1875. It has never had any regular pastor up to this date. The present officers are: A. Banckson, Chas. Johnson, Geo. Johnson, A. Johnson, A. W. Johnson and L. Ljengqvist. H. Jacobson is acting as pastor for the church at present. The church has 160 members. There is a Sabbath School in connection, of which H. Jacobson is Superintendent. The church building was erected in 1881. It is a large frame structure, 32x60 feet, and 125 feet high, including steeple. It is nicely fitted up on the inside, and has a gallery extending across the north end of the room. This building was erected at a cost of $4,000.

Alta Public School.—The first school in Alta was taught by Mrs. E. P. Gilliam, in 1874, in A. Rokkan's house. Alta became an independent district in 1881. The first school building was built in 1876. The first School Board under the independent district was as follows: R. J. Macdonald, G. Gerner, R. H. Brown, T. O. Wiss, H. J. Poulson and S. B. Birdsall. S. Furlong was Treasurer, J. D. Adams, Secretary. This is also the present Board. G. W. Wheat has charge of the school at present, assisted by S. F. Keith and Miss A. Salisbury. They have a very comfortable building and a large enrollment of pupils.

Alta Lodge No. 383, I. O. O. F.—Instituted December 18th, 1878. The charter members were: A. W. Seymour, P. M. Jencks, J. I. Burkholder, H. C. Kelso, C. T. Steever, L. Wheelock and N. Anderson. First officers: A. W. Seymour, N. G.; P. M. Jencks, V. G.; L. Wheelock, Secretary; J. I. Burkholder, Treasurer. Present officers: L. Wheelock, N. G.; J. W. Bard, V. G.; W. H. Cox, Secretary; Geo. Steever, Treasurer. This Lodge has a membership of fifty-six and is in a very prosperous condition. It meets every Wednesday evening. The members have a room rented and fitted up in company with the Masonic order. The room is nicely carpeted and is well furnished.

Pomegranate Lodge No. 408, A. F. & A. M.—Dispensation was granted this Lodge November 30th, 1880, and a charter was received June 9th, 1881. The charter members were: C. T. Steever, R. J. Macdonald, G. Gerner, G. S. Kendall, S. G. Stout, J. H. Wadsworth, J. W. Slutz, B. S. Benson, Jr., G. W. Mathews, and S. B. Birdsall. The first officers were: C. T. Steevers, W. M.: R. J. Macdonald, S. W.; G. Gerner, J. W. Present officers: R. J. Macdonald, W. M.; G. Gerner. S. W.; S. B. Birdsall, J. W.; S. Furlong, Treasurer; W. H. Pierce, Secretary; W. Melville, S. D.; L. B. Collins, J. D.; J. Mathews, Tiler. This society meets once each month in the same hall with the Odd Fellows. There are twenty-four members. The Lodge is in a flourishing condition.

Summit Lodge No. 103, Iowa Legion of Honor.—This society was organized March 26th, 1881. Its first officers were: C. M. Beam, President; L. B. Collins, Secretary; J. S. Platt, Treasurer. Present officers: P. M. Jencks, President; T. E. Sprague, Secretary; C. M. Beam, Treasurer. The present membership is twenty, the organization having suffered the loss of two of its members.

NEWELL.

This town is situated on the Illinois Central Railroad, ninety-two miles from Sioux City and 234 miles from Dubuque. The town was laid out by the railroad company in July, 1870, but no lots were offered for sale until Nov., 1870. The first settlement was made in the town by E. G. Chandler, in 1869. The first house built in the town was that of W. R. Batton, in June, 1870. This was used as a boarding house. G. B. Sargent built the first store, the building being 22x42 feet, two stories high. The second story was used for church purposes and as a town hall. The first drug store was erected by E. W. Foy in 1870. G. W. Stevens erected a hotel the same year. Swezey & Stetson started the first lumber yard. G. B. Sargent was the first Postmaster.

The town was incorporated in 1878. The first officers were: L. H. Gordon, Mayor; Will White, Recorder; W. A. Waterman, Assessor; L. T. Swezey, O. H. Hazard, S. A. Parker, E. G. Chandler and W. A. Welch, Trustees. Present officers: Mayor, W. M. Borman; Recorder, L. S. Bunker; Marshal, William Conley; Treasurer, H. E. Harris; Street Commisioner, E. W. Stetson; Assessor, C. F. Chipman. Trustees: H. M. Redfield, Will Riddle, F. P. Mack, J. T. Redfield, L. F. Holbrook, Theo. Smith.

The Newell *Times* made its first issue August 24th, 1871. This was the first paper started in Newell, and was published by J. L. Long. It ceased to exist November 2d, 1872.

The next paper started at Newell was the *Newell Reporter*. This was established December 27th, 1872, with G. B. Sargent as proprietor, and H. R. Colman as editor. This paper sent out its last issue April 18th, 1873.

The Buena Vista County *Star* was the next journalistic venture in this place. It was started August 21st, 1873, with F. E. Raber as proprietor, and W. L. Raber as editor. This paper flourished for a short time, and then died.

The Newell *Mirror* then took up the line of march and made its first issue January 15th, 1875, with Will. White as editor and proprietor. This paper first started as a five-column folio, was enlarged to a four-column quarto, afterwards to a seven-column quarto. White sold it to B. C. Hill, who in turn sold it to James Miller. In March, 1880, Miller disposed of it to C. F. Overacker.

In December, 1880, Miller again took charge and rented it to C. Everett Lee, the latter purchasing the paper in July, 1881. It is now an eight-column folio, Republican in politics, and has an actual circulation of 480.

The Newell Creamery began operations in May, 1881. The proprietors have a building 20x30 feet, with two wings, one 10x20 feet and one 12x12 feet. The edifice is one story high. The creamery is supplied with a four and one-half-horse-power engine and all the modern appliances. It is run on the cream-gathering plan, by Norton & Welch, proprietors.

The Newell grist mill, L. F. Holbrook proprietor, is a steam mill with four run of stone, and manufactures four grades of flour—Superfine, Family, XXX, XXXX.

The business of Newell comprises: Four general stores, three drug stores, grocery store, two hotels, meat market, two restaurants, two millinery stores, harness shop, two lumber dealers, flour and feed store, four elevators, two agricultural implement dealers, three coal dealers, bank, news depot, furniture store, two jewelry stores, two barber shops, two shoe shops, two blacksmith shops, wagon shop, tailor shop, saloon.

The population of Newell is about 700.

CHURCHES, SCHOOLS AND SOCIETIES.

Methodist Episcopal Church Society.—This society was organized in 1872, by Rev. Woodford. The church building was erected in 1878. It is a frame building, 26x45 feet, and cost $2,400. The parsonage was built in 1875, at a cost of $500. This society has sixty-four members, with Rev. R. Fancher as pastor. There is a Sabbath School in connection, with an average attendance of seventy pupils. G. L. Dobson is Superintendent.

Congregational Church Society.—Organized in 1871, the first pastor being Rev. Griffin. The first officers were: E. W. Foy, H. A. Cushman, L. Gordon, J. L. Redfield and L. T. Swezey; Trustees. The present Trustees are: J. T. Redfield, S. A. Parker, E. Herrick, Mrs. J. T. Redfield. Rev. A. C. Countryman is the present pastor. This society has at present sixty members, with a Sabbath School in connection, with an average attendance of eighty pupils. D. C. Miller is Superintendent. The church edifice was erected in 1870. It is a large frame building, 28x44 feet, and was erected at a cost of $2,400. It is calculated to seat 200 persons.

Newell Public School.—Julia Lamreaux taught the first school in this place, in a school house situated one-fourth mile from the present town. Newell became an independent district March 28th, 1874. The first teachers under the independent district were: J. Davis and G. A. Childs. The first School Board was: A. D. Wilson, F. M. Cox, T. W. Lebo. Present Board: S. A. Parker, G. L. Dobson, H. M. Redfield; L. H. Gordon, Treasurer, and W. A.

Waterman. Secretary. The present teachers are: C. E. Rice, principal; Miss Nellie Dunphy, assistant. The school building, built in 1876, is a two-story brick structure, 28x38 feet, and was erected at a cost of $2,700. It contains two rooms.

Campaign Lodge No. 42, I. O. G. T.—Instituted January, 1882, by C. T. Griffith, of Maple Valley. Charter members: S. A. Parker, F. M. Maps and wife, L. H. Gordon and wife, Mrs. S. D. Driver, and others. First officers: L. H. Gordon, W. C. T.; Mrs. L. H. Gordon, W. V. T.; L. D. Winn, P. W. C. T.; Mr. Campton, W. C.; S. A. Parker, W. F.; Mrs. W. H. Scott, W. T.; O. A. Cate, W. S.; Mrs. O. A. Cate, A. S.; U. Metcalf, W. M.; Mrs. Metcalf, W. D. M. Present officers: L. H. Gordon, W. C. T.; Miss Nellie Dunphy, W. V. T.; O. A. Cate, P. W. C. T.; Mr. Campton, W. C.; J. Prayer, W. S.; Miss Welch, A. S.; Mrs. W. H. Stott, W. T.; U. Metcalf, W. M.; Mrs. Metcalf, W. D. M. This society meets Wednesday night in each week, in I. O. O. F. Hall. It has a membership of fifty, and is progressing finely.

Key Lodge No. 102, Iowa Legion of Honor.—Instituted March, 1881. It has a membership of twenty-two, with the following officers: L. H. Gordon, President; C. Dillon, Vice-President; F. P. Mack, Financial Secretary; H. M. Redfield, Recording Secretary; H. E. Harris, Treasurer; L. Longnecker, Usher.

Jewell Lodge No. 232, I. O. O. F.—Present officers: John Evans, N. G.; C. Everett Lee, V. G.; Wm. Borman, S.; L. T. Swezey, T. The Lodge now numbers twenty members. They meet every Saturday night in Swezey's Hall, which is a large room 25x60 feet, is carpeted and nicely furnished with all the furniture peculiar to the order.

The order of Free Masons are making preparations to perfect an organization of a lodge at this place.

BUENA VISTA COUNTY BIOGRAPHIES.

STORM LAKE.

E. W. Benson, of the firm of Benson & Son, dealers in all kinds of grain, flax, wool, seeds, live stock, etc., was born in O. in 1834; came west in 1854, located at Storm Lake, Ia., 1869, and engaged for a time in farming; then in grain buying. He served one year in the war of the rebellion in the 49th Wis. Vol. as corporal.

B. F. Benson, of the firm of Benson & Son, was born in Wis. in 1863; received his education in Storm Lake and Chicago, Ill., and Nov. 15th, 1881, associated himself with his father in the above firm.

D. D. Brown, of the firm of Brown & Morey, druggists, was born in Mass. in 1836; removed to Minn. in 1858; thence to Storm Lake in 1872, and is now engaged in the above business, which was established in 1876, by Cameron & Wagoner.

C. F. Barber, of the firm of Barber Boys, wholesale and retail dealers in carriages, buggies, spring wagons, etc.; also run a first-class livery barn in connection, the size of which is sixty by one hundred and twenty feet. C. F. B. was born in Freeport, Ill., in 1850; moved to Newell, Ia., in 1877; thence to Storm Lake in 1878, and engaged in business as above. He married May Ewing, of Freeport. They have two daughters—Mary and Ethel.

Robert Cummings, landlord of the City Hotel, was born in N. Y. in 1830; moved to Clinton county, Ia., in 1852. In 1872 he came to Storm Lake and engaged in farming. He served two terms as auditor of Buena Vista county, and is one of the representative men of the county. He engaged in the hotel business, Sept. 1st, 1881, and keeps a first-class house and polite attendants.

T. A. Corbett, manager for the Singer manufacturing company, for Buena Vista, Cherokee, Ida and Sac counties, was born in Ill. in 1849; moved to Cedar Rapids, Ia., in 1868. In 1880 he moved to Storm Lake, and engaged in business as above. He married Alice M. Demuth, of Cedar Rapids, and has one daughter—Aline.

E. Cameron, proprietor of the livery, feed and sale stable, was born in Buchanan county, Ia.; moved to Storm Lake in April, 1881, and engaged in the above business. He married Amelia C. Sanders, of Buchanan county, and has one child—Ada.

F. E. Cushman, dealer in staple and fancy groceries, fruits, confectionery, etc., was born in Niagara county, N. Y., in 1850; removed to Monroe, Wis., in 1855; thence to Eldora, Ia., and in 1880 to Storm Lake, and established his present business in May of the same year. He married Mary J. Metcalf, a native of Wis. They have one son and one daughter.

E. S. Donoho, carpenter and builder, was born in Delaware in 1849; moved to Troy, Ill., in 1870. In 1876 he came to Storm Lake, and engaged in business as above. He married Nancy C. Willoughby, of Ill., and has one daughter—Edna A.

James De Land, of the firm of Witt & De Land, proprietors of the Chicago bakery and restaurant, and dealers in confectionery, tobacco, cigars, etc., was born in Ohio in 1859; moved to Ill. with his parents in 1860. He moved to Storm Lake in 1877, and engaged in the above business in 1881.

J. O. Douglass, baker and dealer in confectionery, tobacco, cigars, staple and fancy groceries, etc., was born in Vermillion county, Ill., in 1852; moved to Decatur county, Ia., in 1855; thence to Vermillion, Dak.; came to Storm Lake in 1880, and engaged in business as above. He married Abbie Rhodes, and has one son, George G.

A. A. DeGraff, dealer in live stock, was born in Schenectady county, N. Y., in 1827; removed to Ill. in 1852: thence to Storm Lake in 1875 and engaged in his present business. He owns a fine farm near town. He married Caroline Rainbow, of Troy, N. Y., who died Feb. 22nd, 1880.

G. E. Ford, of the firm of Ford & Bro., dealers in general merchandise, was born in Vt. in 1850; moved to N. Y. City, and in 1874 to Waterloo, Ia.; two years later, he came to Storm Lake and established his present business, which occupies a fine store building, two stories high; employs five clerks, the sales averaging fifty thousand dollars per annum. He married Carrie Pettit, of Des Moines, Ia., and has one son and one daughter.

C. H. Fisk, proprietor of billiard hall and bowling alley: also deals in cigars, tobacco and confectionery. He was born in N. Y. in 1849; moved to Wis. in 1856; thence to Minn. In 1868 he came to Storm Lake and engaged in farming. He now owns 160 acres of land eight miles from this city, also property at Sioux Rapids. He has served in various town offices. He married Mary J. Alexander, of Ohio, and has one son—Ernest.

J. W. Gilbert, of the firm of Gilbert & Thomason, dealers in general merchandise, was born in Ia. in 1854; received his education in Clayton county, and in 1875 moved to Storm Lake, and was employed in clerking, until 1880, when he engaged in his present business, which occupies a fine brick store building of two stories and a basement. He married Katie King, of Sac county. They have one child, a son.

A. Grier, proprietor of the Farmers' hotel and restaurant, was born in Clinton, Pa., in 1851: removed to Freeport, Ill., in 1865, and in 1876 came to Storm Lake and engaged in farming, until 1880, when he established the above business, where can be had warm meals and lunches at all hours, and choice confectionery, oysters, etc. He married Jennie Nesbit, of Harrisburg, Pa., and has two children—Lizzie and Edith.

Hobbs & Sutfin, real estate and investment agents; agents for the Iowa railroad land company, the Iowa Falls & Sioux City railroad company, and the Iowa Falls & Sioux City town lot and land company. They have 200,000 acres of improved lands, with perfect titles, in Buena Vista county, Ia., which they offer to bona fide settlers on easy terms. Correspondence solicited.

Charles Isbell, dealer in grain, live stock, etc., was born in Ill. in 1846; was in the employ of the I. C. R. R. company as operator and agent for a number of years, then came to Storm Lake and engaged in his present business; was formerly in partnership with Mr. Benson. He served in the army during the late war four years, in Co. K, 52nd Ill. Inft. He is the present mayor of this city.

William J. Johnson, of the firm of Riekelfs & Co., plow manufacturers, was born in Delaware county. Ia., in 1861; came to Storm Lake in 1872. In Dec., 1881, he became a member of the above firm. He married Frederica Riekelfs, of Storm Lake.

L. C. Jones, of the firm of Jones & Fawkes, proprietors of the meat market and provision store, was born in Mass. in 1835; moved to Ogle county, Ill., in 1856. He came to Storm Lake in 1878. and engaged in farming. six miles from town. In Aug., 1881, he engaged in the butcher business, and since has added a complete line of groceries. He married Jane Wadsworth, of Ill. They have six children—Lettie J., Herbert R., Mittie V., Willie F., Charles C. and Grace E.

H. E. Kingsley, house, sign, carriage and ornamental painter, was born in Conn. in 1841; moved to Ill. in 1857; thence to Storm Lake in 1875; was engaged in farming for six years, after which he established business as above. Has held various public offices. He married Adella Tolman, of Ill. They have four children, Edgar W., George N., Fred L., and Maria A.

John R. Lemon, of the Buena Vista County Bank, was born in Ohio in 1836; moved to Freeport, Ill., and in 1874 came to Storm Lake. He established the above banking house in September of the same year, which is the oldest bank in the city. They do a general banking business, negotiate loans, etc. Correspondence: First National Bank, of Chicago; First National Bank, of Dubuque; First National Bank, of N. Y., and Preston, Kean & Co., of Chicago. Mr. Lemon has had a wide experience in the insurance business, having during his earlier life served as president and secretary of insurance companies.

William Miller, dealer in fancy groceries, tobacco, pipes, etc., was born in Germany in 1843; came to America in 1864 and settled in Clayton county, Ia. In 1872 he came to Storm Lake, and engaged in blacksmithing for three years. He then opened a restaurant and eating house, which he continued until engaged as above. He married Rosa Wise, of Germany, and has four children, Julia, Willie, Lottie and Eva.

R. R. Mann, of the firm of Warren & Mann, blacksmiths, was born in Plattville, Wis., in 1855; moved to Storm Lake in 1878, and engaged in the above business.

P. D. McAndrew is the editor and proprietor of the Storm Lake Tribune, a six-column quarto, with a circulation of thirty quires. The Tribune is republican in politics, and was established in Mar., 1880.

J. P. Morey, of the firm of Brown & Morey, was born in N. Y. in 1850; removed to Ill. in 1864; thence to La Fayette county, Wis.; came to Storm Lake in 1878. and became a partner in the above firm.

E. F. O'Neil, proprietor of the bakery near the depot, was born in Wis. in 1853, came to Sioux City, Ia., in 1870, and located at Storm Lake in 1876; married Cornelia Dutcher, of Wis., and has five children. He is the inventor of O'Neil's self-playing organ attachment, an invention that is attracting general attention. By its use the simplest as well as the most difficult music can be performed with absolute correctness. It can be attached to any keyboard instrument in an instant, and as quickly removed. The necessity of condensation in a work of this character alone prevents an extended description of this valuable invention. Mr. O'Neil was for several years city recorder of Storm Lake, and is a well-known and valuable citizen.

R. C. Rickelfs, of the firm of Rickelfs & Co., plow manufacturers and blacksmiths, was born in Germany in 1824; came to America in 1850, and settled in Ill., where he was employed as foreman in a large plow factory. He moved to Buena Vista county, Ia., and engaged in farming, until establishing the above named business in March, 1878. He married Tina Meints, of Ger. They have seven children.

W. S. Russell, of the firm of Langdon & Russell, dealers in general merchandise, was born in Wis.; moved to Fort Dodge, Ia., in 1866. In 1875 he came to Storm Lake, and in January, 1882, associated himself with B. F. Langdon, in the above business.

J. F. Roy, blacksmith, was born in Mass. in 1845; removed to Ill. in 1866, and in 1878 he came to Storm Lake, and engaged in his present business. He married Julia Murphy, a native of Mass. They have six children, Lucy, Mary, Clarence, Frank, Eugene and Albert.

J. Sampson, vice-president of the Iowa land and loan company, is connected with the Buena Vista county creamery, which began operations June 2, 1881, and has the capacity for making into butter the cream from five to ten thousand cows. From the time of commencing operations to Oct. 31st, of the same year, 113,290 pounds of butter were made. They have adopted the method of gathering the cream only, thus leaving the farmers the skin-milk, buying the cream by the inch, basing the prices on Chicago quotations. The churning is done by steam power, and the butter worked by a new power butter worker, therefore not necessitating the use of the hands in any stage of the manufacture. Any one wishing further information will receive it by addressing J. Sampson, Storm Lake, Ia.

John Scheler, proprietor of City meat market, was born in Germany in 1846; came to America in 1866, and located at Madison, Wis.; removed to Storm Lake and engaged in his present business in 1877. He married Mina Biggin, a native of Ger., in Sept., 1878.

Dr. J. H. Sherman, dentist, was born in Ind., in 1832. In 1862 he recruited Co. A, 85th Ind. Inft., of which he was captain, and served until the close of the war. In 1865 he located at Chillicothe, Mo., and engaged in the practice of dentistry; removed to Storm Lake in 1878. He was the first dentist to locate permanently in this city.

J. Y. Skeels, blacksmith, was born in England in 1856; came to America in 1866, and located in Woodford county, Ill.; removed to LaSalle county; thence to Storm Lake in 1880, and established his present business in May of the same year. He married Libbie M. Evans, a native of Ill., and has one child, Arthur E.

C. H. Springer, boot and shoe maker, was born in Me. in 1833; removed to Buena Vista county, Ia., in 1873, and engaged in farming, and in 1877 established his present business in Storm Lake. He still owns a farm of 240 acres in this vicinity; has been township trustee and school director several years. He married Octavia A. Currier, a native of Me. They have three children, Frank E., C. Percy and Ernest E.

T. S. Smith was born in N. Y. in 1814; removed to Ogle county, Ill., in 1847; moved to Buena Vista county, Ia., in 1869. He, with his sons, entered land, and then engaged in merchandising at the old town of Storm Lake; also engaged in the hotel business. He is the owner of the City Hotel property, which he built at the time he moved to this place; was a member of the city council during its first and second terms. He married Mary Caldwell, of N. Y. They have eight children, James S., Augustus, Mary C., Sarah, George B., Alfred J., Hattie D. and Libbie C.

A. L. Stetson, of the firm of A. L. Stetson & Co., dealers in general merchandise, was born in Farmington, Ill., in 1855; received his education at Boston and Lake Forest, and in 1878 came to Storm Lake, and engaged in the above business, which was established in March, 1879, and occupies a fine brick store building, of two stories and a basement.

Geo. Stetson, of the firm of A. L. Stetson & Co., was born in N. Y. in 1829; removed to Ill. in 1851, and engaged in merchandising and banking; came to Storm Lake in May, 1878, and is a member of the above firm; also operates 5,000 acres of land in this vicinity.

J. R. Sovereign, manager of W. C. Hockett's Keystone Marble Works, was born in Cassville, Wis., in 1854; moved to Cresco, Ia., in 1871; thence to Eldora; thence to Muscatine, and in 1880 to Storm Lake. He married Addie C. Saucer, and has three children, Stella, Clark and Plummer.

M. Tolle, dealer in general merchandise, was born in Columbus, O., in 1823. In 1850 he moved to California, and in the autumn of 1854 located in McLean county, Ill., where he resided until 1872, when he came to Storm Lake, and engaged in the grocery business, which he has since changed to the above. He married Helen Westervelt, of ¡Ohio.

H. O. Thomason. of the firm of Gilbert & Thomason, was born in LaSalle county, Ill., in 1859; came to Storm Lake in 1879, and was in the employ of Geo. E. Ford & Bro., until he engaged in his present business with J. W. Gilbert.

Vestal & Sutfin are the editors and proprietors of the Storm Lake Pilot, which was established in 1870, is a seven-column folio, republican in politics, has a circulation of eight hundred copies, and has never missed an issue since it was established. Terms. $2.00 per annum.

T. N Warren. of the firm of Warren & Mann, was born in De Witt, Ia., in 1850; moved to Storm Lake in 1881, and became a partner in the above firm.

C. Wilcox, M. D., was born in N. Y. in 1838; removed to Whiteside county, Ill., in 1855; thence to Jackson county, Ia., and after several changes of location, settled at Storm Lake in 1877. He was formerly connected in the ministry with the Baptist church: engaged in the practice of medicine in 1876. He married Amelia A. Ingham, of York, Ill., and has three children, Lucy J., Lizzie E. and Charles E.

George Witter, dealer in furniture and undertaking materials. occupies a two-story building twenty-one by seventy feet, and also owns the adjoining building, size 32x40 feet. He was born in Dubuque county, Ia., in 1851, and learned his trade at Dubuque and Galena, Ill. In 1878 he came to Storm Lake, and engaged in business as above. In 1878 he married Kate Bauman, of Dubuque county. They have lost, by death, one child, named Lora.

A. H. Witt, of the firm of Witt & DeLand, was born in Clark county. Ia. He moved to Madison county, and in 1879 came to Storm Lake. In 1881 he became a member of the above firm.

ALTA.

C. M. Bean, manager of .the Alta lumber yard, was born in Penobscot county, Me.; moved to Ia. in 1871, and settled in Mitchell county. In 1880 he came to Alta, and engaged in business as above. He carries a large and complete stock of lumber and builders' supplies.

D. Burke, of the firm of D. Burke & Co., millers, is a native of Mass.; moved to Dubuque, Ia., in 1836. He came to Alta in 1879. and established his present business. They have recently put in the patent rollers, and the mill has now a capacity of sixty barrels per day.

R. B. Dando, M. D., and furniture dealer, is a native of N. Y.; moved to Dubuque county, Ia., in 1838; thence to Alta in 1873, and engaged in the practice of medicine. The Doctor is the owner of some valuable patents. He engaged in the furniture business in 1881.

G. Gerner, dealer in general hardware, is a native of Pa.; came to Iowa in 1877, and engaged in farming near Alta. In 1880 he moved into the town, and engaged in business as above.

L. J. Harvey, M. D., is a native of Ohio. He began the practice of medicine is 1866; moved to Iowa in 1870, and opened office in Storm Lake. He came to Alta in Feb., 1882, and is already enjoying a lucrative practice.

Chester Hunt, dealer in sewing machines and musical merchandise, is a native of Pa.; moved to Story county, Ia., in 1861; thence to Buena Vista county in 1868. He built the first house in Nokomus township. In 1881 he came to Alta and engaged in business as above.

Dr. W. Kamp, jeweler, was one of the first to locate at Alta. He began the practice of medicine, and has since engaged in the jewelry business.

G. S. Kendall, proprietor of billiard hall, was born in Ill.; moved to Hamilton county, Ia., in 1855. In 1857 he came to Alta, and engaged in his present business.

R. J. Macdonald, of the firm of Macdonald & Prue, dealers in general merchandise, was born in Washington, D. C.; moved to Ind. in 1845; thence to Ill. in 1857; thence to Iowa. He soon after returned to Indiana, and was for several years employed by the Wood's Reaper Co., as traveling agent. In 1880 he came to Alta, and engaged in business as above.

William M. Reeder, furniture dealer, is a native of Ohio; in 1855 he settled in Johnson county, Ia., and engaged in contracting and building. In 1870 he moved to Storm Lake. His wife—now deceased—was the first white woman to locate there. He came to Alta in 1879, and engaged in business as above.

T. O. & C. J. Wiss, dealers in clothing, boots and shoes, also grain and stock, are natives of Sweden; came to America in 1869, and settled in Chicago, Ill. They moved to Iowa in 1875, and engaged in the hardware business. In Aug., 1881, they engaged in business as above.

NEWELL.

H. O. Austin, manager of J. H. James' harness shop at Newell. The firm carries a complete line of harness, saddles, whips, robes, blankets, etc. This is a branch of Mr. James' large establishment at Sac City, and was established in March, 1880, with Mr. Austin as manager.

Ball & Brooks, physicians and druggists, established drug business
Jan. 1st, 1882. They occupy and own a brick building, two stories
high, and carry a large stock of drugs, fancy and toilet articles,
stationery, cigars, etc. They employ W. J. Kilingbeck, who is a
registered pharmacist. Dr. J. H. Ball graduated from the Keokuk
Medical College in 1880, and engaged in the practice of medicine at
Newell. Dr. J. M. Brooks, also of Keokuk, commenced the practice of medicine in March, 1881. His office is over the store.

W. H. Borman, of the firm of Swezey & Borman, dealers in
lumber, lime, paint, etc., was born in Franklin county, O., in 1850.
In 1869 he came with his parents to Sac county, Ia., and the following year he pre-empted land in Buena Vista county, six miles
north of Newell. In 1876 he entered the employ of L. T. Swezey,
and in Jan., 1880, became a partner. Mr. B. conducts the above
business, which is situated near the depot. He was elected mayor
in 1881. Mr. Swezey is proprietor of an extensive hardware
establishment.

O. A. Cate, dealer in general merchandise, formerly of Sher-
brook, Quebec, Canada, came to Newell and engaged in his present
business in partnership with his brother, C. W. In Feb., 1882, he
became sole proprietor. His store is in Harris & Parker's block, on
Fulton street. He employs two salesmen.

William Conley, of the firm of Conley & Watt, proprietors of
the Newell livery, feed and sale barn, came to Newell in 1877 from
Sac county, where he had been engaged in farming for ten years.
He formed a partnership with L. S. Watt, and engaged in his present business. They occupy a barn on First street; have accommodations for sixty horses; keep for livery purposes eight teams and
nine buggies and carriages. They are proprietors of the hack line
between Newell and Sac City, and make daily trips, carrying the
mails. Mr. C. was appointed city marshal in March, 1881. Mr.
Watt came to Sac county in 1860 from Ohio. He was engaged in
farming until Aug., 1881.

C. Dillon, dealer in general hardware, came to Buena Vista county, Ia., in 1877, from Delaware county. He engaged in farming
for four years; then moved to Newell, and purchased the business
of L. T. Swezey. He owns the building he occupies on Fulton
st.; carries a complete stock of hardware, tinware, stoves, etc., and
employs one tinner.

Ellis Bros., proprietors of restaurant, confectionery, billiard parlor and barber shop; established business in Oct., 1881. They
came to Newell in May, 1874, from Green county, Wis., and engaged in farming, also contracting and building, previous to establishing their present business.

Hon. L. H. Gordon, dealer in lumber and coal, came to Newell,
Ia., from Dubuque where he had been engaged in manufacturing
doors, sash and blinds. He was burned out in August, 1870, and

the same year came to this city, and engaged in business as above.
He represented this district in the 17th general assembly, session
of 1877 and 1878.   He was the first mayor of Newell, and served
two years.

Harris & Parker, bankers, brokers and dealers in real estate.
The business was established in 1871, under the firm name of Condron & Harris.   In 1873, S. A. Parker purchased Mr. Condron's
interest, thus forming the present firm.   They own and occupy a
brick building, thoroughly fitted with fire proof vault, etc.   They
own valuable town property, and about 3,500 acres of real estate
throughout the county.   H. E. Harris came to Newell from N. H.
in 1871.   Mr. Parker moved from Quebec, Canada, to Newport,
Vt., thence to this city.

L. F. Holbrook, proprietor of the Northwestern flouring mills,
of Newell, Ia., was formerly of Vt.   He engaged in his present
business in 1878.   The mills were built by J. B. Thomas in 1871,
and were purchased by L. H. Gordon & Co., who sold to the present owner.   The mills have a forty-five horse power engine, and
a capacity of fifty barrels per day.

C. Everett Lee, proprietor of the Newell Mirror, which was established June 15th, 1875, by W. White, who sold it to B. C.
Hull in Dec., 1878.   It was afterwards purchased by J. N. Miller,
editor of the Sac Sun, who sold it to the present owner in July,
1881.   The Mirror is the county official paper, republican in politics, is an eight-column folio, and has a circulation of about five
hundred.   Mr. Lee was born in Schoharie county, N. Y., in 1846;
moved to Sac county, Ia., in 1862.   He served during the war of
the rebellion in the 10th Ia. Vol. Inft.   In 1876 he came to Newell, Buena Vista county.

Thomas Mankey, wagon-maker and blacksmith, came to Newell
from Mineral Pt., Wis., in Aug., 1879, and established business as
above.   He owns and occupies a building on Second st., and employs two men.

F. P. Mack, postmaster and dealer in stationery and news, came
to Newell in 1870 from Alden, Hardin county.   His wife is a
milliner, and carries a large and well selected stock of goods;
occupies same store-room with the postoffice.

Norton & Welch, dealers in general merchandise and grain, are
also proprietors of the Newell creamery.   J. T. Norton and John
R. Welch comprise the firm, which was established in 1878.   Their
mercantile business is in Union Block, and occupies a room twenty-
four by one hundred feet, which is well filled with general merchandise, and necessitates the employment of three salesmen.   The
creamery was established in 1881, and has a capacity for making
two thousand pounds of butter per day.

H. M. & J. T. Redfield, of the firm of Redfield Bros., dealers in grain, live stock, agricultural implements and coal, came from Oswego, N. Y., to Newell in 1872, and the following year established their present business. They own two elevators, with a combined capacity of ten thousand bushels; office and warehouse, on First st. They handle all the leading manufacturers' goods.

W. E. & G. H. Riddell, of the firm of Riddell Bros., dealers in general merchandise, established business in Aug., 1879, in the Swezey block, corner of Fulton and Second sts. They have a butter and egg packing department in the basement, and there employ one man. W. E. Riddell was formerly engaged in business at Manchester; G. H. was formerly with Field, Leiter & Co., of Chicago.

W. H. Stott. proprietor of the City meat market, was born in Philadelphia, Pa. He moved to Fairfax, Va.; remained one year; then returned to Pa., where he resided until 1868, when he moved to Iowa and located near Fonda, Calhoun county. In 1871 he came to Newell, and engaged in business as above; has also been engaged in the livery business here. He keeps a first-class market, and employs two men. Mr. S. has been marshal of Newell two years, and a member of the city council. During the war of the rebellion he served in the 110th Inft., and was twice wounded.

William Wart, of the firm of W. Wart & Son, dealers in general merchandise, came to Buena Vista county, Ia., in 1869, from N. Y. He purchased land, and has been actively engaged in farming ever since. He owns 440 acres of land. four miles east of Newell, which is well improved and stocked. He has been a member of the board of supervisors for several years. The store is in Union block, on the corner of Fulton & Second sts. They carry a large and well selected stock of goods. The business is conducted by T. A. Wart, the junior member of the firm.

CRAWFORD COUNTY.

The county of Crawford is twenty-four miles north and south by thirty east and west. It contains twenty Congressional townships, or a superficial area of 720 square miles, and lies on the Western Slope, the second county east from the Missouri River, in the fifth tier from the northern and southern boundaries of the State. It is well watered by running streams, the largest of which is the Boyer River, which traverses the county diagonally from northeast to southwest, entering five miles west of the northeast corner, and passing out three miles east of the southeast corner. East Boyer River, its most important tributary, enters Crawford from Carroll County, flows in a southwesterly direction, and unites with the main stream at Denison, a little southeast of the center of the county. Other important tributaries of the Boyer are Dunham's, Walnut, Ernst, Buss, Welsh, Paradise, Buffalo, Otter, Boone, Coon and Buck Creeks. The Nishnabotany River and Williams Creek, with their several branches, water the southeastern portion of the county. Soldier River, which crosses the northwestern corner, receives a large number of tributaries, among which may be mentioned Beaver Creek. A branch called East Soldier also passes through the northwestern part of the county, with a by no means inconsiderable tributary called Spillman Creek. Willow River waters a considerable portion of one township in the southwestern part of the county. All of the above streams are small, with the exception of the Boyer River, but all afford an abundance of water for stock throughout every season of the year. In a number of places fine springs are found, and good well water is obtained at moderate depths. The water of the running streams is excellent for drinking and domestic uses, and is usually clear and cold.

The finest groves of timber are on the Boyer and East Boyer Rivers, a number of groves being scattered along some of the smaller streams, however. The largest body of timber in the county is Mason's Grove, beginning about five miles northeast of Denison. This grove includes about 2,000 acres along the east side of the Boyer River. Dunham's Grove, on the East Boyer, six miles east of Denison, contains about 300 acres of timber, among which is a quantity of black walnut. In other parts of the county are groves of good timber, principally on or near the Boyer River. The timber lands of the county aggregate about sixteen sections, or 10,240 acres—about one acre of timber to each forty-five feet of prairie. The following varieties are included: Black oak, burr oak, black walnut, black and white hickory, linn, hack-

berry, soft maple, ash, elm, cottonwood, cherry, etc. The shrub-
beries are principally ash, sumac, hazel, pith-alder, etc., which generally grow in the valleys, or about the edges of the timber. There
is an abundance of walnuts, hickorynuts and hazelnuts.   Wild
fruits grow in abundance: there are plums, grapes, raspberries,
strawberries, gooseberries, cherries, crab apples, wild currants, and
occasionally blackberries. In consequence of the scarcity of native
timber, many of the farmers have planted groves of silverleaf maple, cottonwood, black walnut and box elder, all of which have
grown with astonishing rapidity; so much so that the former boundless expanse of prairie has within a few years become dotted with
beautiful groves, which ere long will re-arrange the nature of the
country, as they have already diversified and improved the landscape, affording, moreover, as great additions to the principle of
utility as they have already made in the direction of ornamentation.

The surface configuration of the county is rolling, the divides
separating the streams being bulky masses of earth which sweep
down into the valleys over beautiful declivities from the undulating
plains above. Near the headwaters of the streams the surface is
more rolling and broken than on the main divides, in a few places
being too uneven and precipitous for successful cultivation. The
soil is almost uniformly composed of the light colored, fine.
silicious material of the bluff deposit peculiar to the Missouri
Slope, is of great fertility, and is in places largely mixed with
sand. The Boyer Valley is probably unsurpassed in Iowa, is capable
of a cultivation which is being rapidly brought about, and which
when brought to the condition assured in the near future, will
present one of the most attractive farming portions of the State.
Compared with the size of the stream, the valley is wide, and has
a deep, rich soil, well adapted to the production of the finest crops
of corn, wheat, oats and other kinds of grain. Extending, as it
does, some thirty miles through the county, it embraces a large
area of land of unsurpassed fertility. It must not, however, be
understood that the upland prairies are sterile, as the greater portion of them is but little inferior to the bottom lands. The best
upland prairies are in the east, north and northwest portions. In
the smaller valleys and ravines extensive accumulations of black
soil or vegetable mould are often found, which probably came from
the washing of the ravines from the adjacent slopes, which bear
evidence of having been thus denuded of their coating of dark
humus. The enthusiastic lover of nature can scarcely picture a
more pleasing landscape than that afforded by the valleys of the
Boyer Rivers, viewed from the upland ridges at almost any point
along their courses, overlooking miles of their park-like valleys,
embellished with clumps of trees, well improved farms, orchards,
rural homes, and tasty villages.

Stone suitable for building purposes is not abundant, the only
quarry worked in the county being situated about four miles

southwest of Denison on a branch of Buck Creek. It is a species of limestone that answers for ordinary purposes. There are indications of the same formation in Spring Grove, Burnt Woods, and at other points in the county. Clay and sand suitable for the manufacture of brick, are sufficiently plenty, and a number of handsome brick structures have been erected in Denison and other localities. No veins of coal have been found as yet in this county, and it is probable that, if the productive or lower formation of the coal measure underlies the area embraced in Crawford County, it is at so great a depth beneath the surface as to render its development for the present impracticable.

The soil and climate are well adapted to the production of wheat, oats, rye, barley, corn, beans, peas, potatoes and other vegetables and grains indigenous to the Temperate Zone. The yield of spring wheat, which is the variety principally raised, has been from fifteen to forty-five bushels to the acre, with a probable average of about twenty-five bushels. Comparatively few farmers have engaged in the cultivation of tame grasses, but it has been fully demonstrated that timothy and blue grass will succeed well, while clover also does reasonably well, so far as it has been tried. There is a number of orchards in the county, which have been yielding for a number of years, and which give promise of assured success in the future. Much attention is being paid to fruit culture, which is destined to become one of the important industries of this section. Cherries, vines and all small fruit do well, growing luxuriantly and producing excellent varieties of fruit.

The Chicago & Northwestern Railroad enters Crawford County a little north of the center of the eastern boundary line, and running southwest down the valley of the Boyer, a distance of over thirty-one miles, makes its exit near the southwest corner. affording good communication with the eastern and western markets.

In May, 1849, Cornelius Dunham, of Jackson county, Iowa. brought Franklin Prentice and his wife to the county, and left them at the place known as Dunham's Grove, on East Boyer River, about six miles east of the present town of Denison. Mr. Prentice built a cabin for Dunham, who came with his family in the autumn of the same year, accompanied also by a man named Reuben Blake. This was the first settlement in Crawford County. The same year, Prentice took a claim at the mouth of Otter Creek, on Boyer River, near Mason's Grove. The next settlers were Jesse Mason and family, and George J. and Noah V. Johnson, all of whom came in June, 1850. and settled at Mason's Grove. In the autumn of this year, Levi Skinner and Calvin Horr settled at the same place. The next settler was Thomas Dobson, in the spring of 1851, who also settled in the vicinity of Mason's Grove. In the autumn of 1853, Edward Howorth. with his sons. Edward and Daniel, located at a place called Three Bee Tree Grove, in the southwest part of the county, not far from the present thriving town of Dunlap. In

1854, the settlement at Mason's Grove received the following additional members: Benjamin Dobson, A. R. Hunt, D. J. Fowler, Clark Winans, B. F. Wicks and E. W. Fowler.

During the same year Benjamin Dobson erected the first saw mill at this place, and the following persons located in other parts of the county: John Gilbreath, John R. Bassett, and Moses and Daniel Riddle, at Coon Grove, four miles south of the present town of Denison; Mathias Didra, at Buck Grove, in the southern part of the county: Charles Kennedy and Robert D. Butterworth, at Three Bee Tree Grove, and William H. Jordan, at Lost Grove, near the present town of Crawford, on the Chicago & Northwestern Railroad. John A. Dunham and Rufus Richardson came the same year. Those mentioned were all the settlers in the county up to 1855, during the spring of which year the following came: Reuben and John Vore, S. C. Dow, S. J. Comfort, Cyrus B. Whitmore, John Poordy, Isaac B. Goodrich, S. B. Greek, S. S. Sisley, John Sisley, Edward Van Vleet, James Slater and H. C. Laub. The last named settled at Mason's Grove, and the others in various places in the county. In 1856, there were but few additions to the settlers, the following, with their families, it is believed, comprising all: George C. King, William J. Todd, John B. Huckstep, Edwin Cadwell, Tracy Chapman, Morris McHenry, Esau McKim, and Joseph Brodgen, all of whom located at Mason's Grove; and R. B. Alexander, S. Bell, B. B. Bishop and William Wilkie, who settled in the southern and southwestern parts of the county. Hon. J. W. Denison came to the county in the autumn of 1855, and during that year and the next, selected a quantity of land for the Providence Western Land Company, and in September, 1856, commenced the settlement of the town of Denison. He brought with him Francis Reynolds and John B. Swain, who erected a steam saw and grist mill in the new town.

The first births in the county were David and George Jesse Mason, twin sons of Jesse and Eliza Ann Mason, born in 1852. The first marriage ceremonies took place at Mason's Grove, October 12th, 1853, at which time and place Rev. Thomas Dobson united in marriage George J. Johnson and Elizabeth Ann Mason, Noah V. Johnson and Jane Mason, Calvin Horr and Elizabeth Mowery. The first death was that of John A. Dunham, in the winter of 1854-5. The first entry of Government land was made August 21st, 1854, by John Gilbreath. The first school house erected was at Mason's Grove, in the autumn of 1856, in which Morris McHenry taught the first school, a term of three and one half months, commencing November 4th, 1856. The first sermon was preached Sunday, October 19th, 1856, by Rev. William Black, of the M. E. Church, and the same day, after the sermon, the first religious society was organized, with seven members, as follows: George C. King, Mrs. E. R. King, O. S. Wright, Tabitha Wright, John B. Huckstep, Martha A. Huckstep, and Rufus Richardson.

The first Sunday School was organized at Mason's Grove, under the auspices of the M. E. Church, with twenty pupils, on the 7th day of January, 1857, George C. King being the Superintendent. The first lawyer was S. J. Comfort, who was also the first acting Prosecuting Attorney. Dr. David McWilliams was the first physician.

Up to April, 1855, Crawford County was attached to Shelby for civil purposes. At the April election of that year the following county officers were elected: E. W. Fowler, County Judge; Thomas Dobson, Clerk; A. R. Hunt, Treasurer and Recorder; D. J. Fowler, Sheriff; Isaac B. Goodrich, School Fund Commissioner; Cyrus Whitmore, Prosecuting Attorney; Samuel Kennedy, Surveyor; L. S. Kinner, Coroner; John R. Bassett, Drainage Commissioner. At this time there was but one election precinct in the county, all the votes being cast at Coon Grove, in what is now Denison Township. New county officers were chosen at the following August election, at which time John R. Bassett was elected County Judge. Judge Bassett transacted his first official business September 3rd, 1855, on which date he acted upon a petition for a county road, refusing to grant the petition for reasons set forth in the records as follows:

"I set the road petition aside on these grounds: In the first place, I cannot find out that there were notices as the law prescribes in three public places in the county. Secondly, the notices not agreeing with the petition. Thirdly, and the greatest objection, is that there was no one offered to enter bonds for the security of the payment of the Commissioner, providing the road was not finally located. For these objections I hereby set the road aside and pronounce not in accordance with law."

On the 3d of December of this year, the Judge, Clerk and Recorder met and reported their accounts of moneys received from August 1st to December 1st, the Judge having received $5.75; Clerk, $3.00; Recorder, $8.70. Total, $17.45. They made an equal division of the amount and appropriated it toward the payment of their salaries. William L. Henderson, having been appointed surveyor and agent to select the swamp lands, made his report December 5th, 1855, and was allowed $150 for his services.

The first estate administered upon was that of Cyrus B. Whitmore, John Vore being appointed administrator. The location of county roads constituted a large proportion of the business of the County Judge. Judge Bassett continued to serve in this capacity up to the organization of the Supervisor system.

The following persons constituted the first Board of Supervisors: Thomas Dobson, Milford Township; Henry C. Laub, Denison Township; Daniel Howorth, Union Township. Daniel Howorth was President, and S. J. Comfort, Clerk of the Board.

The Court House at Denison was completed in the autumn of 1858. It is built of brick, 30x40 feet, and two stories high. The various county offices are in the lower story, and the upper story is used as a court-room and for various public meetings. The cost of the building was about $6,000. It is located in the center of the public square, a beautiful rolling track of ground, which is enclosed by a neat fence and planted with finely growing trees. Good bridges have been erected on all the principal roads over the streams.

About five miles below Denison, in the Boyer Valley, there is a semi-circular group of ancient artificial mounds. There are about nine of them, situated on a plateau or table rising above the lower bottom. They are about five feet above the general level of the ground. Another similar group is located on the second bottom at the mouth of Paradise Creek. Human remains have been found in some of them, showing that they were burial places.

Crawford County's present population is fully 15,000. There are 458,333 acres of land in this county, the valuation of which, for 1879, was $2,747,198; for 1880, $3,752,648; value of lots, $220,-590; of personal property, $458,214; of railroad property, $326,-646. The property valuation for the present year is not as yet obtainable, but there are certain indications of a most highly gratifying increase. There are thirty and one-half miles of railroad in the county, and two hundred miles of telegraph wire.

The present county officers of Crawford County are: A. D. Moloney, Auditor; G. W. Heston, Clerk of Courts; L. M. Cornwell, Treasurer; M. Smith, Recorder; J. D. Jones, Sheriff; E. M. Ainsworth, Superintendent of Schools; M. McHenry, Surveyor; A. McMartin, Chairman Board of Supervisors.

Crawford County's population in 1880 was 12,413; the total vote of the county for Governor at the election of 1881, was 2,136.

DENISON.

The county seat of Crawford County is situated a little south of the center of the county, at the junction of the Boyer and East Boyer Rivers. A portion of the town, rising upon the slopes adjacent to these streams, commands magnificent views of the valley of the Boyer, with its rapidly improving farms, the railroads, lines of telegraph, groves of timber, and other objects, adding variety and beauty to the scene. The railroad passes along the southern edge of the town, where it makes a bend directly southwest, leaving Denison well situated as a trading point for a large district of country unsurpassed in fertility. Its agricultural resources, when developed, cannot fail to make Denison a point of great importance. It is one hundred and fifteen miles from Des Moines, eighty from Fort Dodge, seventy-five from Council Bluffs, seventy-five from Sioux City, and forty-five from the Missouri River.

As stated in the general history of the county, the town was laid out in 1856, by J. W. Denison, from whom it derived its name, and at that time became the county seat. The town plat embraces about 700 acres, the general size of the lots being 50x150 feet, the principal streets being one hundred feet wide and the others eighty. Handsome and eligible blocks have been reserved for public parks and other public purposes. Quite a number of elegant residences and business blocks have been erected, which would reflect credit upon any city in Iowa.

Among the first settlers were Francis Reynolds and John B. Swain, who put up the first saw and grist mill in the place; R. W. Calkins, O. S. Gates, F. W. Vuescher, Jacob Whitinger, Morris McHenry, J. F. Seagrave and Eli Baer. Mary Louise Seagrave, born November 13th, 1856, was the first birth in the town, while the first death was that of a child of Francis Reynolds.

There is no reason to doubt that the population of Denison at the present time is fully, if not more than, two thousand. The town was incorporated in 1875. Its first town officers, after incorporation, were: A. F. Bond, Mayor; A. Carpenter, Recorder; J. L. McClellan, Marshal; L. Cornwell, Treasurer; C. H. DeWolf, C. F. Cassaday, John Seemann, Ward Matthews, W. J. Wagoner, Councilmen. The following are the present officers: R. Heffelfinger, Mayor; D. L. Boynton, Recorder; L. Cornwell, Treasurer; William Braddy, Marshal; C. Green, W. J. Wagoner, L. F. Carr, J. B. Romans, P. Miller, G. W. Heston, Councilmen; George A. Smith, Assessor.

Denison has two banks, the McHenry Bank, of which William A. McHenry is proprietor, and the Crawford County Bank, R. Heffelfinger, proprietor—both of which do a prosperous business.

The Germania Opera House, owned by the Germania Society, is a roomy and well built structure with a foundation of heavy masonry, cost from seven to eight thousand dollars, and is in every way creditable to the community.

The brickyard belonging to Cornelius Green manufactures on an average a half-million bricks per annum.

There are seven flouring mills in Crawford County, one at Dow City, one two miles southwest of Denison, one at Denison, one at Vail, one at West Side and two at Deloit.

The Luncy Bros. some time since inaugurated a series of enterprises, which reflect great credit, both upon themselves and the community. Their steam flouring mill was started in 1880, and has a capacity of about 1,000 bushels of wheat per week. This mill has three run of stone, and manufactures an excellent quality of flour. They have also in operation an extensive agricultural implement factory and foundry, from which they turn out plows, bells, shafting for mills, and, in fact, anything and everything in the line of first-class establishments of this kind.

Denison is in every respect, mechanically, professionally and in a business way, as well in the attractive as in the substantial elements of a progressive community, worthy to be the county seat of the rich and fertile county of Crawford.

The business establishments of Denison may be classified as follows: Six general merchandise establishments, three groceries, two furniture and cabinet making establishments, one boot and shoe store, two harness shops, one hardware store, two blacksmith shops, one wagon factory, one wagon and blacksmith shop, two hardware and agricultural implement stores, one agricultural implement depot, two restaurants, five hotels, four insurance agencies, one flouring mill, one brick-yard, one manufactory of agricultural implements, one foundry and machine shop, three millinery stores, one music store, two banks, four real estate agencies, three drug stores, two printing offices, one book store, one clothing store, two meat markets, one bakery, four stock and grain dealers, three lumber dealers, one creamery, two grain elevators, etc.

The *Crawford County Bulletin* was started in November, 1873, by Stephens & Daniells. A. B. Keith purchased Daniells' interest in April, 1874, and in June, 1876, became sole proprietor. The *Bulletin* is a nine-column folio, and has a circulation of 1,200 copies. It is the Democratic organ of Crawford county, and is ably conducted.

The first newspaper published in Crawford County was established October 1st, 1860, by J. W. Denison, and was named the *Boyer Valley Record*. It was a twenty-eight column sheet, Republican in politics, and continued about a year and a half. The next paper was the *Denison Review*, the first number of which appeared May 3d, 1867, under the management of Money & Stephens. In the autumn of 1868, Money disposed of his interest to R. W. McNeal. In 1874, the paper came into the possession of Hon. J. Fred. Meyers, who conducted it until the latter part of February of the present year. Under Mr. Myers' able management, the paper achieved an extensive reputation. His successors, the Messrs. Wrigley Bros., are gentlemen of capacity, and have already evinced an ability to fully maintain the *Review's* excellent reputation. Mr. Meyers has been Postmaster of Denison for a number of years, was formerly a resident of Washington, D. C., has an extensive acquaintance, and has occupied many positions of honor and trust. The *Review* is Republican in politics, and issues both English and German editions. It is a model of typographical neatness.

CHURCHES, SCHOOLS AND SOCIETIES.

First Baptist Church.—Organized in 1858, by Rev. J. W. Denison. The successive pastors were: Revs. George Scott, R. Dunlap, A. M. Duboc, J. B. Hawk, A. Robinson, the latter gentleman having present pastoral charge. The present membership is 120. The church building was erected in 1865, has a seating capacity of about 200, and cost, with the grounds, $7,000. It is located on the corner of Sweet and Chestnut streets. The present church officers are: J. D. Seagrave, S. W. Plimpton, Deacons: E. S. Plimpton, Clerk; Mrs. S. W. Plimpton, Treasurer; W. A. McHenry, J. R. Bassett, E. S. Plimpton, Trustees. The Sabbath School has an average attendance of about one hundred pupils. Its officers are E. S. Plimpton, J. D. Seagrave, Associate Superintendents; M. E. Jones, Treasurer; Nellie Strong, Secretary.

Methodist Episcopal Church.—The present pastor is Rev. D. Austin. This society has over one hundred members. Its present officers are: L. M. Shaw, C. Green, R. Heffelfinger, J. B. Romans, Trustees; H. C. Laub, Recording Steward; L. M. Shaw, Treasurer. The Sabbath School numbers about one hundred pupils; L. M. Shaw is the Superintendent. The church building was erected about the year 1865, at a cost of $1,800; its seating capacity is 350. Rev. William Black, the first pastor, was succeeded by the following: Revs. Mr. Glassner, Edwin Satterlee, M. D. Collins, W. E. Smith, Mr. Glanville, B. Shinn, Mr. Waynick, Mr. Fegtly, E. Sage, Asa Steeth, J. B. Wilson, Mr. Beck, and the present pastor.

Trinity Episcopal Parish.—Organized in 1875, by Rev. William Wright. Rev. C. S. Fackenthall is the present pastor. The membership is about thirty-five. The church building was erected in 1875, is 28x40 feet in dimensions, the total cost being not less than $3,000. Roger Hayne was the first Senior Warden, and Henry Gower, the first Junior Warden. At present J. G. Wyant is Senior Warden, William Rain, Junior Warden. The Society is free from debt. In July, 1877, the church building was blown from its foundations by a tornado, two other church buildings also being moved from their foundations on the same night, one of them, the Catholic church building, being occupied by the congregation, who were holding services at the time. Trinity Church is located in East Denison, on the south side of Broadway. The Sabbath School has about fifty members. J. P. Fitch is the Superintendent; Miss Gracie Myers, Secretary; Miss Blanche Stone, Treasurer.

The Catholic Church Society.—This Parish was organized by missionaries more than twenty years ago. The first pastor was Rev. Mr. Kelley, of Omaha. The church building was erected in 1872. It is a frame structure and cost $1,700. The congregation have made arrangements for the building of a fine brick structure during the coming season, the money for which has been already secured. The estimated cost is $4,000. Rev. M. C. Lenahan, of Vail, is the present pastor. Services are, for the present, held every alternate Sunday.

The German Lutheran Society.—Rev. G. Haar is the present pastor of this prosperous church organization. As stated elsewhere, the church edifice is a brick building formerly used as a school house. It is very neatly and comfortably furnished. The organization of the society dates back from eight to ten years.

81

The Presbyterian Society.—The present pastor of this society is the Rev. J. J. Franklin. The church edifice was erected in 1872, at a cost of $1,775. Although the membership is not so large as that of the Baptist or M. E. organizations, yet the society is in a substantial and encouraging condition.

The Public Schools.—Prior to the organization of the Denison independent school district, Tracy Chapman, Michael Riddle and A. D. Moloney, composed the Board of School Directors of a section of country embracing the entire county, with the exception of Union and Milford Townships. The first teacher of whom the writer has information was H. C. Laub, who was followed by I. T. Martin, John Funk and Miss Jennie Haskell. The first school house was a frame building, about 14x20 feet in dimensions, situated on the hill in East Denison. This building has long since ceased to be used for school purposes, and has been moved so many times as to make further trace of its whereabouts indefinite. A brick school house was next built, which is now used as a church building by the German Lutheran Society. The independent school district was organized about ten years since. The first Board of Education was composed of the following gentlemen: Dr. William Iseminger. Morris McHenry, E. S. Plimpton, W. J. Wagoner, and two others, whose names the writer was unable to learn. A. M. McNeal, an attorney now living in St. Louis, was the first teacher after the independent organization. He was followed by Rev. Mr. Gunnison, a Baptist minister, who was succeeded by a Methodist clergyman, whose name the writer was unable to learn. Z. T. Hawk was the first regular Principal of the Denison schools. He had three assistants. Under his management, the Denison schools first took definite form, were graded, and began the systematic and thorough development of which the citizens of the town are justly proud. There are now two school buildings. The first, a large brick structure of four departments and two stories in height, was erected in 1872, at a cost of $16,000, which figure, however, it is proper to add, is conceded to be altogether disproportionately large in comparison with the real value of the building. It is located in the western part of town, southwest of the Court House, and is known as the West Side building. The second school building was erected in 1877. It is a two-story frame, having two large rooms, is about 28x48 feet in dimensions, and cost in the neighborhood of $2,500. It is located near the center of town, and is known as the East School building. The total enrollment of the district, at the last enumeration, was 369 pupils: the average attendance is about 300. It is more than probable that another school building will be added during the present year. The present corps of teachers is as follows: Prof. M. Booth, Principal; Miss Nettie M. Dick, Grammar School, West; Miss Lillie Barr. First Primary. West; Miss Hattie McAhren, Second Primary, West; Miss Kittie Barr, First Primary, East; Mrs. Mary

Wade, Second Primary, East. The present Board of Education is as follows: C. Green, President; W. J. Wagoner, E. S. Plimpton, William Iseminger, Albert Palmer, John Seemann; C. F. Bond, Secretary; R. Heffelfinger, Treasurer.

Devotion Lodge No. 282, A. F. & A. M.—Instituted in 1869. Rev. B. Shinn was the first W. M.; C. H. DeWolf, the first S. W.; H. C. Laub, the first Secretary, and L. Cornwell, the first Treasurer. There were nine charter members. The present membership is fifty-five. Meetings are held Wednesday evenings of each month, on or before the full moon. For the present the Lodge meets in Masonic Hall, over H. C. Laub's place of business. A fine Lodge room is being fitted up in the McHenry block. This Lodge is in a condition of very gratifying prosperity. The following are the present officers: C. H. DeWolf, W. M.; G. W. Stephens, S. W.; M. Goldheim, J. W.; G. W. Heston, Secretary; W. J. Wagoner, Treasurer.

Denison Lodge No. 94, I. O. G. T.—Instituted in 1876. Meetings are held every Tuesday evening in Court House Hall. The membership is twenty-five. The present officers are: D. O. Johnson, W. C. T.; Mrs. H. J. Matthews, W. V. T.: Miss Hattie Harris, R. S.; Miss Hattie McAhren, L. S.; Mrs. E. S. Plimpton, Treasurer; Rev. A. Robinson, Chaplain.

Crawford Lodge, Iowa Legion of Honor.—Instituted in 1880. First officers: H. N. Wheeler, President; A. D. Wilson, Vice-President; N. J. Wheeler, F. S.; N. F. Smith, R. S.; N. Richards, Treasurer. Present officers: A. B. Keith, President; James Wygant, Vice-President; N. J. Wheeler, F. S.; M. E. Jones, R. S.; A. D. Wilson, Treasurer. The membership is fifty-two. Meetings are held on the first and third Thursday evenings of each month in Masonic Hall.

Root Post No. 58, G. A. R.—This Post was mustered in the autumn of 1881, with eighteen charter members, as follows: E. D. Partridge, Geo. W. Heston, W. A. Porter, A. J. Bond, R. L. Wilkinson, A. I. Phelps, S. W. Plimpton, Jr., R. W. Lownes, A. Simmons, Edward Miles, M. Smith, J. S. Gilbreath, W. H. Snow, B. W. Garlough, G. L. Wright, C. A. Lawton, H. S. Gulick, J. G. Vassar. The membership is thirty, and meetings are held on the second Friday evening of each month in Court House Hall. The following are the officers: Geo. W. Heston, Commander; G. L. Wright, S. V. C.; Jud. Bond, J. V. C.; I. T. Phelps, A.; S. W. Plimpton, C.; H. S. Gulick, Q. M.; E. D. Partridge, S.; R. W. Lownes, O. of D.; Benj. Garlough, S. M.

Denison Lodge No. 151, A. O. U. W.—Present officers: I. T. Roberts, M. W.; John Bayles, Foreman; S. W. Plimpton, O.; A. T. Weld, Recorder; D. H. Gill, Receiver; A. Anderson, Financier; D. O. Johnson, P. The Lodge has a membership of forty-four, and meets the first and third Friday evenings of each month in Masonic Hall.

Eureka Collegium No. 77, V. A. S. Fraternity.—Instituted in the autumn of 1881, with thirty-six charter members. First officers: William Familton, Rector; J. S. Nicholson, V. R.; G. A. Smith, S.; G. W. Heston, Q.; G. L. Wright, U.; L. J. Carter, Spec.; Dr. W. W. Holmes, M. E. Present officers: J. S. Nicholson, R.; Albert Palmer, V. R. The remaining officers the same as before. Meetings are for the present held at J. S. Nicholson's office, on the first Monday evening of each month.

W. C. T. U.—The Woman's Christian Temperance Union of Denison is in excellent working condition, and has done effective work for the cause of Temperance. Mrs. H. C. Laub is the President.

Denison Lecture Bureau.—This is an association whose object is to furnish the citizens of Denison intellectual entertainment by utilizing "home talent." Weekly lectures are given, which are largely attended, and which have been productive of highly beneficial results.

The Public Library.—Denison has a public library of quite respectable proportions. The library is temporarily located in the rear of A. Steel's furniture store. Mr. Steel is the Librarian.

Denison Cornet Band.—The Denison Cornet Band is composed of twelve members, and is quite a creditable organization. W. J. Wheeler, President; M. E. Jones, Secretary; F. Wahl, Treasurer; William Adams, Leader.

VAIL.

The prosperous and progressive community of Vail is located about six miles west of the eastern line of the county, and was laid out in the summer of 1871. The town-site is owned by the Blair Town Lot and Land Company, and by other parties, who have made additions thereto. The surrounding country, for a distance of twenty miles north and south, tributary to Vail, is of a most excellent quality.

Vail was incorporated in the spring of 1875. The first Mayor was Josiah McHenry, who was succeeded by the following in order: W. W. Anderton, Josiah McHenry, A. D. Young, F. B. Huckstep, the latter of whom is the present incumbent.

The following are the present town officers: F. B. Huckstep, Mayor; J. S. Nesbit, Recorder; E. Ryan, Treasurer; M. McGrath, Marshal; Thomas Ryan, Street Commissioner; J. P. Fitch, A. L. Strong, J. H. Barrett, E. Darling, E. B. Bannister, John Cousins, Councilmen.

Dr. James DeWolf, the present postmaster, and who came to Vail in the autumn of 1870, was the first *bona fide* settler of the town. He erected a store-building and warehouse where the post-office now stands. He also "broke" some land, and in return for a car-load of wheat raised thereon, obtained the first stock of goods that were placed on sale in the town. John Liddle started a blacksmith shop in Vail in 1871. During the winter of 1870-71, there was nobody on the present town-site of Vail, save Mr. De Wolf, his son John, and the trackhands employed upon the railroad.

The depot building was erected in the summer of 1871, but no agent was located therein until September, 1872. George Head was the first depot agent. In the summer of 1872, the following engaged in business at Vail: J. F. Powers, furniture; L. P. Mooney, general merchandise; E. B. Bannister, hardware; Mrs. E. B. Bannister, millinery.

The next year Greenough & Bullock, of Denison, established a branch drug store at Vail. Josiah McHenry built the first hotel in the autumn of 1872. Since 1873, there has been a steady and constant growth, until at the present time it is safe to estimate the population of the town at from seven to eight hundred.

A classified summary of the business establishments is as follows: General stores, four; grocery, one; hotels, two; livery, three; blacksmith shops, four; wagon shops, two; drug stores, three; shoe shops, three; paint shop, one; printing office, one; hardware, three; agricultural implement depots, three; grain elevators, three; flouring mill, one; lumber yards, two; butter and egg depot, one; restaurants, two; jewelry, one; banks, two; barber shop, one; insurance agencies, two; real estate and loan, three; lawyers, three; physicians, three; meat markets, two; stock dealers, two; machine shop, one; grain dealers, four; furniture, two; harness shops, two; brickyard, one; brewery, one; saloons, four; millinery stores, two; coal dealers, four.

G. A. W. Davison started the *Crawford County Observer* in May, 1878, and after conducting it about a year and a half, sold to J. Otto Engstrom. The paper was started as a six-column folio and was all printed at the home office; subsequently it was changed to an eight-column folio and published on the co-operative plan. In the spring of 1880, Engstrom sold the paper to Gregg & Roberts, the latter of whom became sole proprietor in the autumn of the same year, and continued to conduct it until his death, in the spring of 1881, when his father, J. H. Roberts, Sr., ran it for a short time, and then disposed of it to H. C. Ford. Mr. Davison repurchased the paper October 1st, 1881, and is the present editor and proprietor. The *Observer* is now a five-column quarto, is independent in politics, has a circulation of 500, and is one of Western Iowa's neatest and newsiest weekly publications.

John Short, of Boone County, started the Vail Flouring Mills in 1875. He was assisted by liberal subscriptions from the citizens in the establishment of the enterprise. The building is of three stories in addition to the basement, has four run of stone, and a steel buhr for grinding feed. It also has a grain sheller and elevator in connection. There are, besides, two more steam elevators in Vail, one owned by Benson & Wagner, of Chicago, the other by J. P. Fitch. The flouring mill is filled with the very best and latest improved machinery, and turns out a grade of flour of unusual excellence.

The Citizens' Bank is located in the postoffice building, and is conducted by J. H. DeWolf. The Traders' Bank, on the corner of Warren and Passaic streets, is owned by Messrs. Maynard & Price. Both banks are doing an extensive and prosperous business.

The postoffice at Vail was established in May, 1871; the first Postmaster was Martin Hale Smith, in whose name the office was conducted a year or more, when he was succeeded by Dr. James DeWolf, who has continued in office ever since. It was made a money order office in October, 1877.

CHURCHES, SCHOOLS AND SOCIETIES.

Methodist Episcopal Society.—This society has been organized a number of years, and is in a flourishing condition. The new church edifice, a neat and substantial structure, was dedicated Sunday, February 26th, of the present year, by Bishop Hurst. The building has a seating capacity of about 300. A largely attended Sabbath School has been organized, of which Mrs. A. A. Shesler is Superintendent; Miss Eva Gilman, Secretary; John J. Haas, Librarian.

Presbyterian Society.—The organization of this society was at an early date in the history of the town. The church building was begun in the autumn of 1877, and cost about $2,300. It was dedicated in May, 1878. The society was organized by Rev. Geo. R. Carroll, and Rev. W. H. Cuskey was the first minister in charge. Rev. S. C. Head is the present pastor. The church edifice is 30x 46 feet in dimensions. The erection of a parsonage at an early date is contemplated. The Sabbath School has an attendance of from sixty to seventy pupils. Dr. James De Wolf is the Superintendent.

Grace Episcopal Mission.—Organized January 3d, 1876, by Rev. F. T. Webb, of Council Bluffs. Services are for the present held in the M. E. Church edifice. The society will erect a suitable building during the current year. Rev. C. S. Fackenthall is the present pastor. The number of communicants is eighteen.

The Catholic Church Society.—This Parish has a large and constantly increasing membership. Unfortunately, the church edifice, a commodious frame structure, was blown down by a windstorm in the autumn of 1881. Nothing daunted, however, the congregation has formed plans for the erection of a new church building, which will be in every respect highly creditable, both to the members of the Parish and to the community in general. The proposed new building will be erected during the present year, will be of brick, and will probably cost from seven to eight thousand dollars. Rev. Father M. C. Lenahan is the present Rector of this Parish.

Swedish Lutheran Society.—At present this society, as an organization, may be said to be "without form and void," but matters are rapidly taking shape, and it is expected that during the present year a society of this denomination will be organized in Vail, there being many of this particular faith in the town and vicinity.

Vail Public Schools.—The independent school district of Vail was organized in the spring of 1879. The first Board of Directors were: J. P. Fitch, L. P. Mooney, E. Darling. E. M. Ainsworth was the first Principal, in which capacity he has been continued until the time of present writing. The first school in Vail was taught in the winter of 1871-2, the school house having been built during the previous summer. Miss Mary De Wolf, now Mrs. A. L. Strong, was the first teacher. She was succeeded by her brother, J. H. De Wolf. The first Sub-Director for this District was William Bennett, who was succeeded by Dr. De Wolf, and he by George Head. The present school house was erected in 1877, and has cost not less than $3,000. Its dimensions are 40x50 feet; it is two stories high, and has three departments. The present corps of teachers are: E. M. Ainsworth, Principal; Miss Mattie Snodgrass, Intermediate; Miss Mollie Snodgrass. Primary. The total enrollment is 195; the average attendance, 145. The present Board of Education is: J. P. Fitch, President; J. McHenry, L. P. Mooney, C. H. Britton, James McAndrews; J. S. Nesbit, Secretary; C. E. Price, Treasurer. Prof. E. M. Ainsworth, who has been engaged in teaching in Vail for the past seven years, having been elected County Superintendent of Schools, will retire in April of this year, and be succeeded by William Stephens. The Vail schools have an excellent reputation for thoroughness and efficiency.

Diamond Lodge, U. D., A. F. & A. M.—The first regular meeting was held January 3d, 1882. There were twenty-two charter members. The officers are as follows: E. Darling, W. M.; C. E. Price, S. W.; H. Robbins, J. W.; W. L. Leland, S. D.; C. Priest, J. D.; J. E. Edgar, Secretary; J. F. Long, Treasurer. The membership is twenty-two. Meetings are held in Odd Fellows' Hall Tuesday evenings of each month, on or before the full moon.

Vail Lodge No. 430, I. O. O. F.—Instituted August 22d, 1881. Charter members: W. L. Leland, J. B. King, T. W. Butler, E. B. Legg. H. Boyce, H. C. Ford, Joseph White, C. H. Britton, F. A. Deed. First officers: T. W. Butler, N. G.; C. H. Britton, V. G.; J. B. King, Secretary; E. B. Legg, Treasurer. Present officers: C. H. Britton, N. G.; J. F. Powers, V. G.; J. B. King, Secretary; J. E. Edgar, Treasurer. Meetings are held in Odd Fellows' Hall every Saturday evening. The membership is thirty-three. The Lodge is in a substantial and unusually encouraging condition.

Vail Collegium No. 78, V. A. S. Fraternity.—Instituted September 29th, 1881, with eleven charter members. First and present officers: E. Darling, R.; J. C. Butler. V. R.; F. B. Huckstep, S.; A. Z. Harmon. Q.; M. Fitzgerald, U.; T. J. Huffman, C.; Simon

Johnston, S. The membership is fourteen, and meetings are held the first Saturday evening of each month in Huckstep's law office.

DeSoto Lodge No. 63, K. of P.—Instituted November 10th, 1881. Charter members: E. M. Ainsworth, C. N. Clark, E. B. Legg, William Stephens, Simon Johnston, J. Cousins, H. C. Ford, C. C. Jewett, S. G. Hall, W. H. Brocklesby. First officers: C. N. Clark, P. C.; William Stephens, V. C.; E. M. Ainsworth, C. C.; C. C. Jewett, P.; S. G. Hall, K. of R. & S., J. Cousins, M. of F.; W. A. Brocklesby, M. of E.; C. G. Manchester, M. at A.; Simon Johnston, I. G. These officers continue the same as above. The present membership is seventeen, and meetings are held every alternate Friday evening in Odd Fellows' Hall.

W. C. T. U.—The Women's Christian Temperance Union of Vail was organized in 1880. Mrs. Dr. DeWolf is the President. This organization has been an effective agency in the promotion of the community's best interests.

Band of Hope.—Organized May 11th, 1880. Present officers: Mrs. J. F. Powers, Superintendent; Fred. Edgar, President; Fannie Moulton, Vice-President; Anna DeWolf, Secretary; Jennie Robbins, Treasurer. The membership is about forty.

Young People's Lyceum.—This society is composed of the pupils of the Grammar School. Weekly meetings are held, the objects being parliamentary drill, debates, etc.

Public School Library.—A Public School Library has been established, the funds for which were secured mainly by giving public entertainments. The District has levied a tax for the maintenance of the Library, and large additions will shortly be made.

Vail Silver Cornet Band.—Organized in 1876; William Stephens, President and Leader; Reginald Platt, Secretary; H. S. Keller, Treasurer. There are ten members. This band has an established reputation as one of the best bands in western Iowa.

WEST SIDE.

This is one of the brightest and most thriving towns along the line of the C. & N. W. R. R. It is located near the eastern line of the county, and has a large scope of country tributary to it—not only in Crawford County, but also in Carroll, Sac and Shelby Counties. In the language of a recent writer for one of the daily publications of the State, "We have nowhere seen more evidences of thrift and prosperity among the business men than at West Side; and no town in this section of the state has a more earnest, enthusiastic and energetic class of people. They are courteous to strangers, alive to their own interests, aware of their importance and generous in all matters of public interest.

"As a business point we doubt if any village of six hundred along this line of road surpasses West Side. Socially, it leads the van, and politically it has some of the strongest men in the West.

"The driving park association recently purchased several acres in the town-site, and will plant trees on the same this fall. The park contains one of the best half-mile tracks in the State."

West Side is located on section 24, township 84, range 37, six miles east of Vail, in West Side Township, and on the north side of the section. Payne's addition to West Side was made about the year 1878, and is located on section 13. The first addition to the town plat was made by the Blair Town Lot and Land Company. The town was laid out by the Blair Town Lot and Land Company. The first improvements were made in 1872, by M. Smith, present County Recorder of Crawford County, who in that year built the first residence in the place. There was, however, previous thereto a small house on the present town-site, for the accommodation of the section "boss."

Lampman & Wallace opened the first store in 1871. M. Smith and F. J. Gary engaged in the land, lumber and grain business in 1872 under the firm name of Smith & Gary. H. C. Newton was the first station agent. The business house of Carl Weidling, afterwards Weidling & Evers, was the first business house of importance in the town. E. House also was among the first to enter the mercantile business in West Side, the firm subsequently becoming House & Lamb.

West Side was incorporated March 11th, 1878, and has at the present time a population of about 600. The first town officers were: Carl Weidling, Mayor; L. L. Bond, Recorder; Henry Evers, Treasurer; E. M. Whipple, Marshal; James McClure, Street Commissioner; A. Waterman, M. Smith, W. L. Spottswood, F. J. Gary, P. J. King, Councilmen.

The following are the present officers: E. C. Haywood, Mayor; H. C. Ford, Recorder; C. D. Miller, Treasurer; H. B. Merrell, Marshal and Street Commissioner; A. Waterman, E. W. McCracken, P. J. King, I. B. Nelson, R. J. White, C. D. Miller, Councilmen.

The business establishments of West Side are represented as follows: Drug stores, two; hotels, two; general stores, four; livery, three; blacksmith shops, two; shoe shop, one; restaurants, two; wagon shop, one; printing offices, two; hardware stores, two; saloons, four; lumber yards, two; grain dealers, three; agricultural implements, three; banks, two; lawyers, two; physicians, four; stock dealers, two; millinery, one; meat market, one; harness shops, two; barber shop, one; flouring mill, one; corn sheller, one; news depot, one.

There are two banks, both of which do a thriving business, viz.: the West Side Bank, E. P. Gillette, Cashier; Exchange Bank, C. D. Miller, Cashier.

M. Smith was the first postmaster. He was succeeded by R. B. Taylor, whose successor was W. L. Spottswood, the present incumbent of the office. Mr. Spottswood received his appointment in 1879. The office was made a money-order office in 1875.

West Side has two newspapers, both of which are excellent exponents of the interests of their constituencies. The *West Side Enterprise* was established in March, 1880, by H. C. Ford, the present editor and proprietor. It is a six-column folio, is Republican in politics, and has a circulation of 500. Mr. Ford was formerly a resident of Wheatland, Iowa. The *West Side Dispatch* is a seven-column folio, Republican in politics, and was started April 19th, 1881. W. N. Becker, Jr., & Co., are the proprietors. Mr. Becker being the editor.

The West Side Flouring Mill was built by I. B. Nelson, the present proprietor. in 1878, the machinery being moved from Storey county. This mill is three-stories high, has a forty-horse engine, four run of stone, is furnished with the latest improved machinery, runs on full time, makes an excellent grade of flour, and has a capacity of one hundred barrels per day.

There is also a corn sheller at West Side, with a capacity of shelling one car-load per hour. Ralph Simpson is the manager.

CHURCHES, SCHOOLS AND SOCIETIES.

The M. E. Church Society.—The organization of this society was some time prior to the year in which the church edifice was built, which was in 1878, the total cost of the structure being about $3,600. The building will seat about 300 people, and the society is in a prosperous and growing condition.

The Public Schools.—The first school in West Side was taught in a carpenter shop in 1873. The first school house was built in 1874. It was 24x36 feet in dimensions. one story high, an addition of sixteen feet being afterwards made. The present school house was built in 1880, and is a large, two-story building of three departments. Prof. T. C. Branson is the Principal; Mrs. C. K. Ford and Miss Lottie Truesdal, Assistants. The school building is an imposing structure, in every way creditable to the community. The district was organized as an independent district in the spring of 1881. The total enrollment of pupils is 126. The following comprises the Board of Education: L. Schofield, President; R. B. Taylor, R. Wagoner, I. B. Nelson, Carl Weidling, S. T. Boynton; F. Knowles, Secretary; Henry Evers, Treasurer.

Setting Sun Lodge No. 349, A. F. & A. M.—Instituted 1875. with fifteen charter members. First officers: M. Smith, W. M.; Charles Levy, S. W.; B. E. Allen, J. W.; R. B. Taylor, Secretary; F. J. Gary, Treasurer; H. B. Allen, S. D.; S. A. Miller, J. D. Present officers: E. C. Haywood, W. M.; J. P. Fitch, S. W.; A. Johnson, J. W.; C. B. Winters, Secretary; Frank Brown, Treasurer. Membership, thirty-two. Meetings are held Saturday evening of each month, on or before the full moon.

: *Crawford Lodge No. 148, A. O. U. W.*—Instituted in 1877, with twenty charter members. First officers: E. P. Savage, P. M. W.; I. E. Blackman, M. W.; W. L. Spotswood, F.: Albert

Johnson, O.; N. A. Miller, R.; F. P. Wiseman, F.; F. Dean, S.;
M. L. Spotswood, G.; S. L. Perrin, I. W.; F. Brown, O. W. Present officers: W. L. Spotswood, P. M. W.; W. N. Becker, Jr.,
M. W.; I. B. Nelson, F.; T. McBride, O.; Carl Weidling, R.; A.
Johnson, F.; F. Brown, G.; C. P. Anderson, I. W.; George Curtis,
O. W. The membership is about thirty-five. Meetings are held
every Tuesday evening in Masonic Hall.

Kilpatrick Post No. 70, G. A. R.—Mustered February 14th,
1882, with nineteen charter members. Meetings are held twice a
month on Saturday evenings in Masonic Hall. The following are
the present officers: William Vickers, Post Commander; William
Johns, Senior Commander; S. D. Brown, Junior Commander; E.
P. Gillette, Quartermaster; A. Waterman, Surgeon; George Hieling, Chaplain; H. C. Ford, Adjutant; J. M. Locke, Officer of the
Day; R. B. Taylor, Officer of the Guard; W. T. Highberger,
Quartermaster's Sergeant; Isaac Patterson, Sergeant Major.

DOW CITY.

Dow City, or Dowville, as it was formerly called, was named in
honor of Judge S. E. Dow, the original town proprietor and first
settler, and is located on section 10, township 82, range 40, on the
Chicago & Northwestern Railroad, a little more than nine miles
southwest of Denison. Judge Dow, who is the Mayor of the
town, and as might well be supposed, in view of the circumstances,
one of its leading citizens, came from Harrison County and located
where Dow City now stands, in 1855. He still owns 1,860 acres
of land immediately surrounding the townsite, besides being a
large owner of town property.

Dowville was platted in 1869 by Judge S. E. Dow, and the Blair
Town Lot and Land Company, Dow donating a half-interest in
400 acres of the townsite to the Blair Company in consideration of
a railroad station being established at this point. A large addition
to the town was laid out in November, 1881, by Dow and the Blair
Company, who also donated a plat of ground, 300 by 540 feet in
dimensions, to the city for use as a public park, in consideration
of the city's agreeing to expend an amount agreed upon in improving and beautifying the same.

There was no building in Dowville until 1870. The depot was
built in December of that year. June 1st, 1870, Abner Graves
unloaded ten cars of lumber at Dowville, and immediately
engaged in the lumber business, the firm subsequently becoming Dow, Graves & Co., the grain and farm machinery business being added. About the same time Graves also erected his
present residence. During the season just ended, Graves disposed
of his interest in the above firm, whose title is now S. E. Dow & Son.

In March, 1879, Mr. Graves started the Dow City Bank, a flourishing financial institution, in a building which he erected for that
purpose.

Among others of the very earliest settlers were, L. E. Hardy.
who opened a general store; a Mr. Wiggins, blacksmith: W. C.
Hillas, general store: M. B. Lewis, drug store; William Cook, general store, in the building now occupied by T. J. Rasp & Co.; William Sullivan, saloon; Joseph McCole meat market; Albert Goddard, wagon and plow business; A. Manning, drayage; Bell &
Whalley, meat market; John Lewis, hotel; H. C. Bowring, livery.
Benjamin Heath, now with Dow & Son, was the first depot agent.
    The town was incorporated in November, 1878, at which time
the name was changed from Dowville to Dow City. The first municipal officers, under incorporation, were: S. E. Dow, Mayor: T.
J. Rasp, Recorder; Abner Graves, Treasurer; F. C. Platt, Attorney; H. E. Talcott, Marshal; Abner Graves, L. E. Hardy, W. B.
Hillas, Theo. Walker, W. B. Evans, Benjamin Heath, Trustees.
    The following are the present officers: S. E. Dow, Mayor; F.
L. Gilbert, Recorder; Abner Graves, Treasurer; F. C. Platt, Attorney; H. S. Jordan, Marshal; T. J. Rasp, J. J. Anthony, E. Goddard, Henry Bell, W. B. Evans, W. C. Hillas, Trustees.
    Sarah Gaetta Hardy, daughter of Mr. and Mrs. L. E. Hardy,
was the first child born in Dowville. She was born October 12th,
1870.
    The Dow City Flouring Mill is one of the most important in-
dustries of the place. It is located on the Boyer River, about 150
yards north of the depot, at the foot of Franklin Street. This
mill was built by T. W. Chatburn in 1875, who ran it about a
year, when the firm became Chatburn & Rule. Subsequently
Dow, Graves and Rule became proprietors, and at present the mill
is owned by Dow & Graves. The building is 42x52 feet in dimensions, is three-stories high, exclusive of the basement, has four run
of stone, and all the latest improved machinery for making the
patent and fancy grades of flour. The mill is complete in every
respect, and is as fine a mill, size being considered, as there is in
all the extent of country included in this work. Its capacity is
about seventy barrels of flour per day.
    The *Dow City Criterion* is a neat five-column quarto news-
paper, started in November, 1880. It is independent in politics,
and is in every way a creditable publication. F. Bangs is the editor: D. J. Butler and Stella M. Bangs, proprietors.
    The growth of Dow City has been a steady and sturdy one; its
location is picturesque and advantageous; the country surrounding is remarkably well adapted to farming and stock-raising, and
is already well improved. The buildings of Dow City are substantial and attractive.
    The following is a classified summary of the business establish-
ments: General merchandise, three; hardware, two; agricultural
implement depots, two; livery, two: hotels, two; drug-stores, two;
meat markets, two; harness, one; furniture, one: saloons, two:
lumber yards, two; grain dealers, two: blacksmith shops, three:

wagon shop, one; paint shop, one; barber shop, one; millinery and dressmaking, one; bank and land office, one: physicians, two; attorneys, two; insurance agency, one; printing office, one.

CHURCHES, SCHOOLS AND SOCIETIES.

The Baptist Church Society.—This society was organized in the winter of 1879, by Rev. Mr. Hawk, of Denison. Rev. F. W. Foster was the pastor until recently. At present the society has no regular pastor. The membership is about twenty. The church edifice was erected in the autumn of 1881. It is not yet completed. The estimated cost is $2,000. Its seating capacity is about 200.

The M. E. Church Society.—Organized in the winter of 1869. Rev. B. Shinn was the first pastor. He was succeeded, in the order named, by Revs. W. W. Glanville, Waynick, William Patterson, Wright, and C. Smith, the latter of whom is the present pastor. The church building was erected in 1879, at a total cost of $2,000. A parsonage was erected in 1877, at a cost of $600. The membership is about seventy-five. The Sabbath School has an attendance of about sixty pupils. George Rae is the Superintendent. The present church officers are: George Rae, T. Rae, M. M. McHenry, S. J. Comfort, S. S. Gibson, T. W. Parker, W. Whaley, John Rule, M. Wiggins, Trustees; S. J. Comfort, E. W. Pierce, Stewards; John Rule, Treasurer; L. E. Hardy, George Rae, Morris McHenry, Class Leaders. The church building has a seating capacity of 250, and is 32x48 feet in dimensions.

The Boyer Valley Branch of the Galland's Grove District of the Reorganized Church of Jesus Christ of Latter Day Saints of Dow City.—Organized in 1866. The present church edifice was, as is explained elsewhere, formerly the school house of Dow City and was purchased by the above society in 1879. The society has a membership of forty-one, all of whom, with the exception of six or eight, are converts to the reorganized church since about the year 1860. George Montague was the first Presiding Elder. The Presiding Elders since were in the order named, as follows: Aaron Hawley, George Montague, Absalom Kerkendall. Eber Benedict, C. E. Butterworth and John R. Rudd. the latter of whom is the present Presiding Elder. Charles E. Butterworth is at present the principal preacher for this society. The officers of the society are: John R. Rudd, Presiding Elder; Abel H. Rudd, Priest; C. M. Wilder, Teacher. The first preaching was in the year 1859-60, Elders McIntosh, William Blair and E. C. Briggs being the first ministers. As is elsewhere explained in the History, the reorganized church rejects the doctrine of polygamy. and abhor its practice. They preach the Bible with the Book of Mormon as concomitant and additional inspirational evidence.

The Public School.—As yet Dow City is not organized as an independent school district. The first school house was erected in 1872. It is a frame building, 24x36 feet in dimensions, and was subsequently sold to the Society of Latter Day Saints, being now used for church purposes. George Rae taught the first school in Dow City. The present school house was completed in 1878. It is a two-story building of four departments, and is 42x48 feet in dimensions. The School Directors in 1872 were: S. E. Dow, for the Dow City schools; J. V. McHenry. Thomas Binnell, John Pett, S. R. Huffman. The present Board is as follows: George Rae, for the Dow City schools; Thomas Binnell, Frank McHenry, E. Howorth, Martin Conroy, C. Fullerton: —— Brake is the Principal; Miss Nellie Morrill, Teacher of the Intermediate, and Miss Effie J. Kilbourne, teacher of the Primary Department. The enrollment is about 160; the average attendance, about 140 pupils.

Dow City Lodge No. 111, Iowa Legion of Honor.—Organized June 22d, 1881, with twenty-two charter members. The first officers were: J. J. Anthony, President; G. Hawley, V. P.; W. C. Pritchard, F. S.; W. H. Rule, R. S.; W. W. Cushman, Treasurer; Dr. W. Beatta, Medical Examiner; W. V. Whaley, C.; J. E. Rule, U.; N. H. Miles, D.; M. G. Wiggins, S.; E. V. Goddard, Benj. A. Heath, C. M. Wilder, Trustees. With the exception of M. G. Wiggins as F. S., William Sullivan, as Usher, M. B. Lewis, as Door-keeper, C. M. Wilder, Sentinel, and C. E. Butterworth as Trustee in place of C. M. Wilder, the present officers are the same as before. The present membership is eighteen. Meetings are held on the first and third Wednesday evenings of each month. The Lodge is in a substantial and encouraging condition.

The Township Library.—This library is located in Brake Bros.' furniture store, W. P. Brake being the Librarian. There are about 500 volumes in the library, which is recognized as an institution of great value, and which is being fostered by the citizens accordingly.

W. C. T. U.—The Woman's Christian Temperance Union of Dow City is one of the important and influential factors of the place, and has accomplished much in the promotion of the community's best interests. Among other results of the Union's efforts has been a series of instructive and entertaining public lectures. Mrs. C. Smith is the President; Miss Effie J. Kilbourne, Secretary; Mrs. Benj. A. Heath, Treasurer.

Dow City Cornet Band.—Organized in the winter of 1880-81. There are fourteen members. M. G. Wiggins is the President; C. H. Brooke, Secretary and Treasurer; Frank E. Wilder, Leader.

CRAWFORD COUNTY BIOGRAPHIES.

DENISON.

August Anderson, of the firm of Gregory & Anderson, was born in Sweden in 1849; was three years a sailor on the high seas. He came to Denison in the autumn of 1870, and was for seven years engaged as clerk for Sunough & Bullock. He married Matilda Kirnback, a native of Sweden, in May 1874. They have three children, Albert, Oscar K., and Carl Otto.

L. T. Carr, dealer in notions, stationery, and news—Main street, opposite court house—was born in Stark county, O., in Jan. 1846; removed to Ind.; thence to Ia. in 1869 and located in Denison in 1871 and engaged in clerking until 1875. He enlisted in the 1st Ind. heavy artillery; was mustered out at the close of the war. He was with Gen. Banks on the Red River expedition. He married Ellie Harriman, of Ind.

M. J. Cochran, wagon-maker, was born in Crawford county, Pa., in Feb., 1844; removed to Ia. in 1877 and engaged in business. He married Elizabeth Greeg, a native of Venango county, Pa., in1874. They have three children, Edward, Mary and Charles; have lost one, Lucy May, who died in 1877.

J. W. Cochran, blacksmith, was born in Crawford county, Pa., in July, 1847; removed to Crawford county, Ia., in 1869; was engaged for a time in farming, then learned his trade with John Little, of Vail. He married Catherine O'Neil, of Memphis, Tenn., in 1878. They have two children, Zella and George; have lost one, Louis.

Capt. B. F. Darling was born in Franklin county, Vt., in Sept., 1837; moved to N. H. in 1859; thence to Clinton county, Ia., where he enlisted in Co. A. 9th regiment of volunteer infantry; he was wounded at Pea Ridge, Mo., March 8th, 1862; was mustered out at the close of the war as captain. As a soldier he was conspicuous for bravery and fidelity. He was appointed clerk in 1881 to fill the vacant place of W. S. Wilson, deceased. He married Sarah Gibson, a native of England, in Jan., 1857, and has one child, A. W.; has lost one, Emma M., who died July 7th, 1862.

C. H. Evers, proprietor of the City Meat Market, one door west of McHenry's bank, was born in Holestein, Germany, in June, 1843; came to America in 1864, and settled in Denison in 1874 and engaged in his present business. In 1881 he erected a brick building with all the modern improvements for his business. He is also owner of the hotel known as the Farmers' House. He mar-

ried Wilhelmina Meiburg, a native of Germany, in 1861.   They
have seven children. Heinrich, Annie, Millie, Herman, Anyti, Edward and George.   Mr. E. is the owner of the right of sale of the
Champion force pump, in five counties.   He is one of the trustees
of the new German Opera Hall.

Edward Eaton, harness maker. Main street, was born in Ind.
in Nov., 1845; removed to O. in 1850, thence in 1854 to Fayette
county, Ia.   He enlisted in Co. F. 9th Ia. V. I.; was discharged in
July, 1865, and returned to Fayette county; removed to Crawford
county in 1870.   He married Louisa F. Gulick, a native of Ia., in
1876.

Wm. Familton, agent for the Iowa Land Company, was born in
Harrison county, O., Sept. 25th, 1825; removed to DeWitt, Ia., in
1852 and engaged in the land business.   He held the office of
sheriff and also was clerk of the court of Clinton county.   He enlisted in Co. F., 44th Ia. Vol. Inft., as captain, was mustered out
in 1864.   He came to Crawford county in May, 1871.   He was
married to Miss Gondy, of DeWitt, now deceased, who left six
children.   He took for his second wife Roena N. Horton, of
Denison.   He has one son.

Garrison & Roberts, attorneys and counsellors at law, Denison,
Iowa.

D. H. Gill, dentist, office room No. 1, in McHenry bank building.
He was born in Chester county, Pa., in Aug., 1844; removed with
his parents to Logan county, O., and then to Cedar county, Ia.,
in 1849, where his father is still living; engaged in the practice of
medicine.   In 1861 he enlisted in Co. G, 2d Ia. Cav.; was dis-
charged in 1865.   He first studied dentistry with Dr. Tabor, of
Cedar county, then with Dr. Tulloss, of Iowa City, then moved to
Independence; thence to Denison in 1877.   He married Ellen A.
Henry, of Buchanan county, in 1868.   They have four children,
Ethie, Percy, Alice and Annie.

H. W. Gregory, of the firm of Gregory & Anderson, druggists,
was born in Livingston, N. Y., in Aug., 1824.   Was engaged as
book-keeper for the Genesee River bank. then came west and was
engaged with the Horicon & Milwaukee R. R. as agent located in
Wis.; then went to Chicago and was in the employ of Stephens
Bros.; from thence he went to Wis., and purchased 140 acres of
land in Rock county: thence to Crawford county, Ia., and engaged in farming on 300 acres; sold out and engaged in his present business.   Has held the office of magistrate, also been secretary of school board.

E. D. Gould, farmer and stock dealer, section 17, East Boyer
township, was born in Lewis county,N. Y., in Nov.,1853; moved to
Ill. in 1861; thence to Crawford county, Ia., in 1872, and now owns
936 acres of land, with good house and the largest barn in the

county. The barn was erected in the autumn of 1881. He married Ella I. Morgan, a native of Buena Vista county, Ia., in 1870, and has two children, Captidona and Lodemia.

Geo. W. Heston, clerk of the court, was born in Philadelphia, Pa., in Apr., 1832. He enlisted in the 71st Reg. of Pa. Vol. Inft.; was taken prisoner and incarcerated at Richmond; afterwards was discharged and returned to Pa. He came to Ia. in 1870 and engaged in farming; was county surveyor four years. He married Lizzie B. Cann in 1856; she died in 1858, leaving one child, now Mrs. Mead, of Denison. In 1862 he married Sally J. Bender, of Philadelphia, Pa. They have four children. Mr. H. is a member of the A. F. & A. M.

Dr. W. W. Holmes, was born in Hardin county, O., in July 1843. He enlisted in the 15th O. Reg., and at the end of three months re-enlisted in the 123rd O. Inft.; was detailed as hospital steward, and discharged in 1863; then enlisted in the 135th O. Inft., and was mustered out at the close of the war. He studied medicine at Kenton, O., and graduated at the Miami Medical Institute in the spring of 1866; removed to Boone county, Ia., in 1869, and to Denison in 1874. He married Mary Ringer, of O., in 1868.

John F. Holst, proprietor of the City shoe store, two doors west of McHenry's bank building, was born in Germany in Oct., 1846. He took part in the Franco-German war, in 1870-71; came to America in 1872, and to Denison in 1874. His wife is a native of Germany. They have two children, John F. and Max.

F. O. Ivers, dealer in stoves and tinware, opposite Lamb's livery stable, was born in Holstein, Ger., in Oct., 1848; came to America in 1868 and located in Louisa county, Ia.; removed to Crawford county, Ia., in June, 1881. He married Dora Smith, who is a native of Ger., in 1876. They have two children, Ella and Mary.

Adelphus B. Keith, editor and proprietor of the Crawford County Bulletin, was born in Appleton, Me., in 1854; moved to Ill., and came to Crawford county, Iowa, in 1865; located in Denison in 1871. Married to Miss Carrie Bieber, of Denison, and has one son living. Mr. Keith headed the Iowa State democratic ticket, as candidate for secretary of state, in 1880. He is a graduate of the American Institute of Phrenology, of N. Y., is a student of unusual persistency, and has already achieved a more than local reputation as a lecturer on popular scientific topics.

Rudolph Knaul, druggist and dealer in fancy goods, was born in Berlin, Ger., in 1850; came to America in 1870 and located in Chicago; removed to Clinton, Ia., and came to Denison in 1878, and engaged in his present business. He married Maggie Au, of N. Y. City, and has two children, Mamie and Alice.

32

Thomas Luney, of the firm of Luney Bros., was born in Antrim, near Belfast, Ireland, Oct. 27th, 1817; came to America in 1865 and located at Pontiac, Ill., and engaged in farming; in 1868 he removed to Ia. He married Mary Smyth, a native of Ireland. They have had seven children.

Samuel Luney was born in Belfast, Ireland, July 7th, 1844; came to America with his parents in 1856; removed to Crawford county, Ia., in 1867. He is member of the firm of Luney Brothers, machinists and millers. He married Martha J. Hughes, a native of La Salle county, Ill. William Luney, Jr., member of the above firm, was born in Belfast, Ireland, in 1849.

W. A. McHenry (autobiography), banker, was born Mar. 6th, 1841, in Almond, Allegheny county, N. Y. His father, James McHenry, died the same year, leaving a family of thirteen children. W. A. being the youngest, lived with the oldest brother and sister at the old homestead until 1855 (his mother dying when he was but eight years old), when he went to Wis., where he worked on a farm summers and attended school winters. In the spring of 1860, he went to Ogle county, Ill., working on a farm until after the battle of Bull Run, in 1861. In response to his country's call, he enlisted as a private in Co. F. 8th Ill. Cav., re-enlisting as a veteran in the same regiment in Jan., 1864, and was mustered out of service as 1st sergeant at Benton Barracks, Mo., July 23rd, 1865. He then came to Denison and became a partner with his brother Morris in the real estate business, and also served under him in the county treasurer's office as deputy, until 1871, when the firm of McHenry Bros., in connection with their real estate business, established the first banking house in Crawford county. They occupied the upper story of a brick building on Main street, erected by Plimpton & McHenry as a general store, of which firm he was a partner eight years. In 1874 McHenry Bros., finding their present quarters inadequate to their growing business, erected on the corner of Main and Broadway their present commodious bank building, a fine two-story brick with terra cotta cornices and window trimmings, handsomely finished inside and furnished with fire-proof vaults and one of Hall's burglar-proof safes with a Sargent's time-lock attachment. The building complete cost $15,-000. In 1877, his brother, wishing to retire from active business, sold to him his interest and the name of McHenry Bros. was changed to the W. A. McHenry Bank and Land Office. In 1864 he was united in marriage to Miss Mary S. Sears, of Rockford, Ill., an accomplished lady, who preceded him to Denison one year, working in the county treasurer's office until the close of the war, thus lending her aid to establish one of the most successful business firms in southwestern Ia.

A. D. Molony, county auditor, was born in Queens county, Ireland, in 1818; came to the U. S. in 1836; was a resident of the eastern and southern states until 1861, when he came to Crawford county. He was appointed auditor in Apr., 1861. and elected to that office in the autumn, and has held the office ever since. He married Bridget Shaaran. a native of Ireland, and has four children.

·Fred. Nagel, proprietor of the saloon one door west of the Commercial house, was born in Wentdorf, Germany, in 1845; was engaged in the last war between France and Prussia; came to the U. S. in Oct., 1871, and soon after settled in Clinton county, Ia.; removed to Crawford county in 1878. He married Henlena C. Peterson, a native of Germany, in Dec., 1871. They have five children, William, Louis, Mary, Christina and Arthur.

S. Peterson, wagon maker, was born in Prussia, July 4th. 1846; came to America in 1871, and settled in Clinton county, Ia.; removed to Crawford county in 1879.

F. M. Penney, of the firm of Penney & Morgan, proprietors of the Peoples' One Price Cash Store, was born in Adams. Jefferson county, N. Y., June 16th, 1857; removed to Livingston county. Ill., where he was cashier of the Odell Mercantile bank for five years; then came to Denison.

John L. Richardson, deputy treasurer, was born in Chautauqua county, N. Y.. Sept. 6th, 1837; removed to Linn county, Ia., in 1861. He enlisted in the 20th Ia. Vol. Inft., and was engaged in the battles of Vicksburg, Fort Morgan, Blakely and Mobile. He was mustered out July 8th, 1865, and returned to Linn county: removed to Crawford county, June 6th, 1874, and engaged in farming, also teaching school. He has held the office of township clerk and assessor of Soldier township. He is a member of the A. F. & A. M. Lodge. He married Mary McArthur, of Linn county, Oct. 4th, 1867.

E. H. Smith. painter and glazier, was born in Morgan county. O., Jan. 28th, 1844; removed to Ia. in 1852, and settled in Clinton county. He enlisted in 1862, in Co. H, 26th Ia. Inft.; was in the Vicksburg campaign and Sherman's march to the sea. He married Miss S. R. Owens, of Ind., in 1864, and has four children, Emma, Belle, Louis and William.

Fred. Stoecks, dealer in millinery and fancy goods, was born in Germany, Apr., 25th, 1826; came to America in 1832 and located at Davenport, Ia.; removed to Denison in 1879. He married Matilda Schmitsch, in 1870, and has two children. Matilda and Harry.

John F. Stubbe, proprietor of the Denison Meat Market, cor. of Main and Broadway, was born in Holstein. Germany. July 26th, 1833; came to the U. S. in 1866 and located in Davenport. Ia.; removed to Moline, Ill., and learned his trade, then came to Denison in May. 1881. and engaged in his present business. In 1881 he married Matilda Achterberg, a native of Germany, but a resident of Davenport since the age of one year.

A. D. Wilson, of the firm of Wygant & Wilson, dealers in hardware, stoves and tinware, was born in Kane county. Ill., Jan. 5th, 1846; removed to Buchanan county, Ia.; thence to Crawford county; thence to Buena Vista county, where he remained eight years; thence back to Crawford county. He enlisted in May, 1863, in the 141st, Ill. Vol. He married Clara Wightman, a native of Canada, in 1868. They have four children, Harry, Lillie, Howard and Floyd.

VAIL.

E. M. Ainsworth, superintendent of schools for Crawford county, also dealer in drugs, notions and fancy goods, was born in Dodge county, Wis., in Sept., 1848; came to Ia. in 1868, and has been engaged in teaching in the public school of Vail for seven years, was elected to his present office in the autumn of 1881. He was married Sept. 1st, 1880, to Nellie Wightman, a native of Vt.

William W. Anderton, proprietor of the livery and feed stable and dealer in stock, was born in Lincolnshire, Eng., June 16th, 1813. He learned the printer's trade, served seven years, then published the People's Advocate, at Sheffield, Eng.; came to America in 1838 and located in Morgan county, Ill.; removed to Crawford county, Ia., in the autumn of 1857, and bought 160 acres of land near where Vail now stands; in 1872 he removed to Vail and has been mayor of the city two terms. He was married in Feb., 1836, at St. Peter's Church, Eng., to Eliza Authorton, a native of Sheffield, who died Feb. 13th, 1845. In Feb., 1846, he was married to Julia Cadwell, a native of Morgan county, Ill., who died April 26th, 1871. He has had six children, but three of whom are living, George H., Charles W., and John C.

E. B. Bannister, dealer in hardware, stoves, tinware and cutlery, was born in Naperville, Du Page county, Ill., in 1843. He enlisted in Co. B., 105th Ill. Vol. Inft., in 1862, and was appointed regimental postmaster; was in several battles and was discharged at Louisville, Ky., in 1863 and returned to Ill.; removed to Chicago, and in 1871 came to Denison, Crawford county, Ia., and to Vail in the fall of the same year and established his present business. He is a member of the town council. In the autumn of 1871 he was married to Jennie Gould, of Belvidere, Ill.

Morris Casey, of the firm of Casey & Casey, dealers in live stock, was born in Boston, Mass., in Jan., 1851; removed to'DeWitt, Ia., in 1854; thence to Crawford county in 1880. In Jan., 1877, he was married to Mary J. Barnes, a native of N. Y.

P. J. Casey, of the firm of Casey & Casey, dealers in live stock, was born in Ireland in 1843, came to America with parents and located at Davenport, Ia., in 1846; removed to St. Louis and engaged in business as an architect. In 1875 he came to Vail, Ia.

and established his present business. In 1866 he married Ella McSrath, a native of St. Louis. She died in 1871, and in 1877 he married Sarah Kelley, and has two children, Eddie and Susie.

J. W. Cousins, dealer in agricultural implements, was born in Lincolnshire, Eng., Aug. 26th, 1848; came to America and located in Clinton county, Ia., and engaged in farming. He established his present business at Vail, in 1880. He was married in 1869 to Anna Martin, a native of Clinton county, and has five children, Anna, Kate, William, Joseph and George.

J. J. Coughlin, blacksmith, was born in Canada, Jan. 1st, 1853; came to the states in 1874 and located at Dunlap, Ia., in 1875; thence to Vail in 1878.

Ed. Darling, M. D., was born in Franklin county, N. Y., in Mar., 1839; removed to Maquoketa, Ia., in 1848. He studied with Dr. J. H. Hollister, and then attended the Eclectic Institute at Cincinnati, O. He enlisted Aug. 12th, 1861, in the 9th, Ia. Vol. Inft., Co. A.; was appointed hospital steward; was in a number of prominent battles, and was discharged at Louisville, Ky., in 1865 and returned to Cincinnati, and graduated in 1866. He returned to Maquoketa and engaged in the drug business; removed to Vail in 1870. He married Addie Stephens, a native of O., in Jan., 1866.

G. Davison, publisher of the Observer, established that paper May 1st, 1875; he sold to Otto Engstrom, in Oct., 1879. Mr. E. sold to J. H. Roberts, Jr.. Mr. Roberts sold to H. C. Ford, and in May, 1881, Mr. Davison bought the paper again, and has continued to publish it ever since. He was born in Will county, Ill., in Feb., 1853; came to Ia. in 1865, and located at Lyons; thence removed to Marshalltown, and in 1868 to Boone, where he was employed in the Republican office for five years.

Hon. James De Wolf, M. D., postmaster, was born in Cavendish, Vt., in Feb., 1819; removed with his parents to Bradford county, Pa.; studied medicine with Dr. Barnes, of Le Raysville, and afterwards practiced with Dr. Horton, of Terryville. He removed to Carroll county, Ill., in 1852, and engaged in farming, was school commissioner, and represented his district in the state legislature. He removed to Cedar county, Ia., in the spring of 1865, and engaged in the land agency business; removed to Crawford county in 1871, and bought 560 acres of land and established a grocery business at Vail, which was the first business house at that place; has been justice of the peace. He married Anna, daughter of Maj. Horton, of Terrytown, Pa., in May, 1849. They have four children, Mary, John, George and Anna.

I. P. Fitch, dealer in lumber, grain and coal, was born in Rensselaer county, N. Y., July 24th, 1841; removed to N. Y. City, and in 1876 came to Crawford county, Ia., and engaged in

his present business; bought and sold about 200,000 bushels of
grain during the year 1881. He is a member of the board of
supervisors, and is S. W. of the A. F. & A. M. Lodge. He was
married Apr. 19th, 1863, to Lucia Sears, of Mass., and has six
children, Samuel, James D., Abbie E., Edward H., Julia L. and
Eilena.

M. Fitzgerald, M. D., was born in Chicago, Ill., in July, 1849,
enlisted in the Iron Brigade as a private, and was promoted to the
position of first lieutenant of company H. He was discharged as
captain. Sept. 15th, 1861, he re-enlisted; was imprisoned at Lex-
ington, exchanged and returned to service in W. V.; was wounded
at Winchester, Oct. 13th, 1864, and discharged Jan. 17th, 1865,
and returned to Chicago. He studied medicine in the office of Dr.
J. H. Taggert, and graduated from Rush Medical college in the
spring of 1873; engaged in practice in Whiteside county, Ill.
In Mar., 1877, he removed to Vail, Ia. He is a member of the
A. F. & A. M. In 1863 he was married to Ellen Quinn, a native
of Ill., who died in Aug., 1879, leaving one child, James W. He
married Ellen O'Connell, a native of Ia., in Apr., 1880.

G. C. Gerrick, wagon-maker, was born in Berlin, Ger., in Mar.,
1854; came to America in 1868, and settled in Chicago, Ill.; removed to Ia. in 1864. In 1879 he married Eila E. Thompson, a
native of Mich., and has one child, Nellie.

Perry Kemerling, of the firm of P. Kemerling & Bro., livery
and feed stable, was born in Henry county, Ill., in May 1856;
came to Ia. in 1874. He engaged in his present business in Vail
Nov. 24th, 1881. He married Fanny Bennett, a native of Henry
county, Ill., in Nov., 1874. They have two children, George M.
and Lucy Bell.

Miles Laughland, proprietor of the Board of Trade saloon, was
born in Kenosha, Wis., May 1st, 1854; came to Ia. Mar. 15th,
1862, and engaged in his present business at Vail, in 1881.

Rev. Father M. E. Lenihan was born in Dubuque, Ia., Oct.
5th, 1835; was educated at St. John's College at Prairie du Chien,
Wis.; then went to Canada and graduated from the Grand Seminary at Montreal, and was ordained priest Dec. 20th, 1879, and located at Lyons, Ia., where he remained two months and removed
to Vail, succeeding Father McGrath, who was called to Ireland.
Since residing here he has organized a Father Matthew Temperance society, and a good library. During the cyclone of Sept. 29th,
1881, the church was blown away. The congregation now contemplate building a fine brick edifice soon.

Henry Meyer, proprietor of the saloon and billiard hall, was born
in Germany, Oct. 4th, 1845; came to America in 1860 and located
at Chicago; removed to Clinton county, Ia., in 1873; thence to
Crawford county, in 1876, where he owns a fine farm of 440 acres.

He was married in 1869 to Doris Myer, a native of Germany. They have five children, Charlie, Caroline, Emma, Willie and Clara.

C. E. Rice, cashier of the Trader's bank, established in 1880, was born in Berkeley county, Va. June 5th, 1853; came to Ia. in 1873. He is treasurer of the school board and has been clerk of the town of Vail. He married Jennett Shaw, a native of Vt., Oct. 16th, 1881.

John Short, proprietor of the Vail Flouring Mills, capacity of sixty barrels of flour per day, also dealer in grain, lumber and coal, has the machinery for shelling and loading a car every half-hour. He was born in Edinburg, Scotland; came to America in 1850 and located in Canada; removed to Chicago in 1868, then came to Boone county, Ia., and built a mill; then came to Vail and built his present mill. He was married in Scotland to Margaret Mather, and has six children, Adam, Helen, Agnes, James M., Elizabeth and Maggie.

John Spire, blacksmith, was born in Lincolnshire, Eng., in Dec., 1838; came to America in 1866, and settled in Ill.; came to Crawford county in Mar., 1875. He was married Apr. 7th, 1850, to Mary A. Pocklington, a native of England. They have four children, George, Lena, Mary and Alfred.

A. L. Strong, dealer in general merchandise, was born in Canaan, Conn., in Feb., 1841. He enlisted in 1862 in the 37th Mass. Vol. Inft.; was wounded at the battle of the Wilderness, May 6th, 1864, and was discharged in June, 1865. He came to Ia. in 1872 and established his present business. He married Mary De Wolf, a native of Pa., in May, 1873. They have two children, Ella L. and Anna M. Mr. S. is a member of the town council of Vail.

John Thompson, miller, was born in Scotland, in Oct., 1848; came to America in 1860, and settled in Grundy county, Ill., and was employed as engineer, by A. K. Styles, of Gardner; then removed to Boone county, Ia.; thence to Crawford county in 1874 and has since been employed by John Short in the Vail mills. He was married in 1874 to Helen B. Short, a native of Canada. They have three children, Anna, George and John.

T. Weyener, baker and dealer in fancy groceries and confectionery, was born in Hamburg, Ger., in 1830; came to America in Sept. 1850, and located at Dubuque, and in 1875 came to Vail and opened a saloon and engaged in his present business in 1877. In May, 1838, he married Lena Fugenbachler, and has eight children living, lost two.

A. D. Young, dealer in lumber, grain and coal, was born in Scotland, in June, 1832; came to America in 1853, and settled in N. Y.; learned the carpenter's trade; removed to Canada; thence to Mo.; thence to Clarence, Cedar county, Ia., and engaged in the lumber business. In 1873 he came to Crawford county and bought 200 acres of land, and established his present business at Vail. He married Agnes Ferguson, a native of Scotland, in 1860. They have had four children, three of which died in 1877. Robert is engaged on the railroad.

WEST SIDE.

W. N. Becker, Jr., editor of the West Side Dispatch, established the paper in April, 1881. It is republican in politics, and already has a large circulation.

L. L. Bond, M. D., was born in Va.; moved to Wis. in 1848 with his parents. He began the study of medicine in 1865, and graduated from the Rush Medical College in the class of '70. He first began the practice of his profession in Clinton county, Ia., and in 1875 came to West Side.

Henry Greves, proprietor of livery stable and sample room, was born in Germany in 1849; came to America in 1869, and settled in Clinton county, Ia. He engaged in his present business at West Side in 1878.

C. Haldane, attorney at law, is a native of England; came to America in 1873 and located in Crawford county, Ia·, where he engaged extensively in farming. In 1877 he moved to Carroll, and began the practice of the law. Two years later, he opened an office at West Side.

E. C. Haywood, dealer in grain and stock, also agent for the Iowa Land Company, was born in England in 1841; came to America in 1852 and settled in Clinton county, Ia., where he engaged in farming, also dealing in stock and machinery. He came to West Side in 1875, and in 1881 engaged in business as above.

Albert Johnson, wagon-maker, is a native of Sweden; came to America in 1872 and engaged in wagon manufacturing, at Chicago. Came to Iowa in 1875 and engaged in present business; also has a branch establishment at Manning.

C. H. Langbehn, proprietor of Farmers' House and billiard hall, is a native of Germany; came to America in 1864 and settled in. Clinton county, Ia. In 1880 he came to West Side, and engaged in business as above.

E. D. Mereness, foreman in I. B. Nelson's flouring mill, is a native of N. Y.; moved to Mich. in 1864; afterwards went to Chicago, where he was employed in the Oriental flouring mills. In 1870 he went to the Pacific coast and remained six years, then located at West Side, and has since been employed as above.

C. E. Miller, banker, was born in Boone county, Ia., in 1855; moved with parents to Ill. in 1858 and returned to Ia. in 1874. He engaged in the drug business and studied medicine, which he practiced at Arcadia for three years. In 1878 he came to West Side and engaged in the drug business, until 1880, at which time he became proprietor of the Exchange Bank.

J. H. C. Peters, of the firm of Peters & Suhr, lumber dealers, was born in Holstein, Ger., in 1846; came to America in 1870 and settled in Clinton county, Ia. He was engaged for several years as carpenter and builder in Chicago and various places in Neb. and Ia. In March, 1881, he located at West Side and engaged in business as above.

John Rohwer, dealer in general merchandise, is a native of Germany; came to America in 1871 and settled in Clinton county, Ia.; came to West Side in 1875, and in 1880 engaged in business as above.

W. L. Spottswood, postmaster, was born in Pa.; moved to Clinton county, Ia., in 1866 and engaged in the harness business. He moved to Harrison county; thence, in 1875, to West Side, and engaged in harness making. Was appointed postmaster in 1877.

R. B. Taylor, of the firm of Taylor & Johnson, dealers in general hardware, is a native of Ill.; moved to Ames, Ia., in 1869, and engaged in the mercantile business. He came to West Side in 1874, engaged in the drug business, and is now a member of the above named firm.

Walz Bros., proprietors of the meat market, are natives of Germany. A. W. Walz came to America in 1869, and his brother came the next year. They located in O.; removed to Ill.; thence to Arcadia, Ia., and engaged in farming and stock raising; came to West Side in 1881, and engaged as above.

DOW CITY.

W. Beatty, M. D., is a native of Canada; came to Iowa in 1880 and located at Dow City; engaged in the practice of medicine. He is a graduate of Toronto University and graduated from Trinity College in the class of '80.

S. E. Dow, of the firm of Dow, Graves & Co., dealers in lumber, grain, stock and farm machinery, was born in N. H.; moved to Mich. in 1832 and engaged in the mercantile business. In 1852 he moved to Harrison county, Ia.; thence to Crawford county in 1855, and located near the present site of Dow City, In 1864 he moved into the city and engaged in stock and grain business.

W. C. Hillas, dealer in general merchandise, was born in St. Albans, Vt. He went to sea when quite young and followed sailing for eighteen years. In 1860, he went to California, where he remained ten years, and then located at Dunlap, Ia., where he engaged in business with his brother. He came to Dow City in 1875 and engaged in business as above. He has a very fine store and carries a large and complete stock.

M. B. Lewis, postmaster and druggist, is a native of Canada; came to the states in 1863 and located at Red Wing, Minn., in 1865. In 1874 he came to Dow City and engaged in the drug business. Was appointed postmaster in 1879.

W. H. Morton, proprietor of the Dow City House, is a native of Ohio; moved to Rock county, Wis., in 1853; thence to Freeport, Ill., where he engaged in milling. He next moved to Linn county, Ia., and came to Dow City in 1879 and engaged as above. He intends building a new hotel during the spring of 1882.

T. J. Rasp, of the firm of T. J. Rasp & Co., dealers in general merchandise, is a native of Canada; came to Iowa in 1848 and settled near Davenport. He came to Dow City in 1875 and was employed as book-keeper by Dow, Graves & Co., until engaging in business as above in 1881.

W. V. Whaley, of the firm of Whaley & Bell, proprietors of the meat market and provision store, is a native of Ohio; came to Dow City, Ia., in 1874 and engaged in the stock business. In 1879 he entered his present business.

C. M. Wilder, proprietor of restaurant, was born in Ohio; moved to Iowa in 1854 and settled in Clayton county. In 1865 he came to Dow City and engaged in teaching until 1881, when he engaged in business as above.

CARROLL COUNTY.

This county, which is twenty-four miles square, and contains sixteen congressional or land survey townships, is the third east of the Missouri River, and in the fifth tier of counties, both from the northern and southern boundary of the State.

Carroll is emphatically a prairie county, the entire portion being composed of a gently undulating surface sufficiently rolling to break the monotonous sameness of the level plain, while to the westward of the Middle Raccoon River, the surface is more broken and uneven, in many places rising into hills of considerable prominence. The great watershed dividing the waters which flow into the Mississippi from those which flow into the Missouri passes through this county, and at the highest point is 858 feet above Lake Michigan and 800 feet above the Mississippi River at Clinton. From this summit can be obtained a fine view of the surrounding country, extending in every direction as far as the eye can reach. On the east and on the southeast is seen in the distance the rich, fertile valley of the Raccoon River, on the south the unsurpassingly lovely country surrounding the Nishnabotny, and on the west the magnificent vale through which flows the Boyer. All of which in a clear summer's day afford scenery at once grand, beautiful and picturesque.

Being situated upon the great dividing ridge or watershed, this county is watered and drained mostly by small streams which flow both into the Mississippi and Missouri Rivers. The largest stream is the North Raccoon, which cuts across the northeast corner of the county, while the next two in importance are the Middle Raccoon and Brushy Fork, which take their rise in the watershed divide in the northwest, and flowing nearly parallel from four to six miles apart in a southeast direction, make their exit near the southeast corner of the county. Storm Creek, a tributary of the Middle Raccoon drains a large tract in the northern-central as does the Willow Creek in the eastern border. The North Raccoon is deeply excavated into the drift deposit, and its valley is bordered by rather steep acclivities from seventy to one hundred feet in height, while the Middle Raccoon is bordered on the west by high bluffs capped slopes, and on the east by drift hills, which gain the interior heights by more gradual ascents. Brushy Fork possesses a beautiful valley with gentle acclivities on either side, as does the East Nishnabotany and Boyer River and Whitted's Creek, which are on the west side of the watershed divide. The upper course of all of these streams are little more than diminutive prairie brooks, with gravelly beds, and clear, rapid currents, many of those having their headwaters in the great divide interlocking, as it were, being separated by a narrow crest as sharply defined as a gable ridge. Springs issue from the gravel deposits along these water courses, furnishing them with an abundant supply of limpid, pure water at all seasons of the year.   East of the Middle Raccoon River wells are easily obtained, while in the uplands west of that stream, those seeking water must go to a much greater depth, though the certainty of finding a never-failing supply is just as good.

In a shallow depression or plain below Carrolton, on the east side of the Middle Raccoon, several interesting spring mounds occur, which have excited much attention and are described as follows by Dr. White, in the Iowa State Geology: The plain is thirty or forty feet above the present level of the river, from which it is separated by a well-defined drift ridge, which, in places, rises into considerable knob-like eminences from one hundred to one hundred and fifty feet above the streams.   The plain, however, communicates with the valley both above and below, and was probably once the channel of the river.   The spring mounds are situated along an irregular line more or less in the middle of the depression; they are from four to six feet in height and as many yards in diameter, and are apparently entirely composed of vegetable matter, forming a peaty deposit which is largely mixed with the exuviæ of shells and other animal remains.   The crests of the mounds are covered with tall, rank flag or marsh grass, but upon the sides are usually two well marked bands of short herbage and moss encircling the mounds and separated by a narrow belt of tall grass. The deposit of the vegetation upon these places is exceedingly interesting, though the mounds themselves, doubtless, owe their origin to the existence of pools of water, indicating more or less accurately, the course of the former water channel, and which, being fed from higher sources, the tendency is what we observe—a gradual building up of a peaty formation.   The surface of the plain beyond the limits of the mounds is perfectly level, and the deposit consists of decayed vegetable matter mixed with sand forming a sandy muck."

Like that of Guthrie County, which lies on the great divide just southeast of Carroll, the soil of this county presents two well marked varieties: that on the east side of the Middle Raccoon being of the drift formation, is a gravelly loam of great strength and productiveness,while to the west of that stream the uplands are deeply enveloped in the bluff formation, which has imparted to the soil of this portion of the county its own peculiar characteristics.   Small groves of native timber are found on the principal streams; and in favorable locations, even upon the uplands, forests of young oaks are springing up.   Some two or three small patches are met with in the valley of Brushy Fork, and between Raccoon Rapids and Carrollton; on the Middle Raccoon more extensive tracts are covered with a fine growth of young timber.

No beds of coal have as yet been discovered; though it is not deemed improbable, says Dr. White, that the coal-measure formation underlies at least a portion of the county. The only specimens yet found have been discovered in digging wells and making other excavations, and are only small fragments associated with the loose material of the drift deposit. Peat is known to exist in several places in the county, some of which are of considerable extent, and should they be found to be free from sand and gravel, they will eventually become of some value as a resource for fuel. Good building stone is not found within the limits of Carroll County, the cretaceous sandstone being too friable to answer for ordinary building purposes, except some of the harder layers, which are employed in laying up rough under-pinnings, in walling wells, etc. Material for the manufacture of brick is found in abundance, yet care is necessary in selecting clay in the western portion of the county, in consequence of the prevalence of calcareous matter derived from the disintegration of the bluff deposits on the surface of the lower slopes. The lime thus mixed with the earth is converted into quicklime in the process of burning the brick, and on exposure to moisture the lime slakes and bursts the brick.

Enos Buttrick made the first settlement in Carroll County in 1854, on section 2, township 84, range 33. Buttrick came from Greene County. The first election was held at the house of Henry Coplin, on section 12, township 82. range 34, on the first Monday of August, 1855, when the following county officers were elected: A. J. Cain. County Judge; Levi Thompson. Clerk; James White, Treasurer and Recorder; Robert Lloyd. Surveyor; L. M. Curdy. Prosecuting Attorney; and J. Y. Anderson. Sheriff. The county was organized by S. L. Loomis, July 16th, 1855, under a commission from James Henderson. County Judge of Guthrie County. At this time the entire population was about 100.

Jane L. Hill taught the first school in Carroll County, at Carrolton, in the spring of 1856, and the first newspaper in the county was published at what is now Carroll City, by O. H. Manning, the present Lieutenant Governor of the State, in 1868. The paper was called the Carroll Enterprise. It was printed at Jefferson, Green County, and issued to subscribers from Carroll. An association of citizens subsequently purchased a printing press and material, and brought it to Carroll, with results as indicated in that part of the history of Carroll City which relates to the newspaperial enterprises of the town.

The Methodists organized the first religious society at Carrolton. The first District Court was held November 23d, 1858, Hon. M. F. Moore, District Judge. The first grand jury were Cornelius Higgins, Benj. Teller, Matthew Borders, Lafayette McCurdy, Crocket Ribble, Robert Morris, William Short, Robert Dickinson, Elijah Puckett, Cyrus Rhoads, James Colco, David Scott, David Frazier,

Samuel Lyon and Amos Bacon. James Coleo was appointed foreman. First case on docket was Nehemiah Powers and John Watson vs. Cornelius Higgins. Noah Titus was the first person
licensed to practice law in the county.

The first marriage license was granted September 16th, 1855, to
Joseph Ford and Sarah Ochempaugh. They were married September
23d, 1856, by A. J. Cain, County Judge. First estate administered
upon was Wesley H. Blizard's, May 3d, 1858. First administrator
appointed was James H. Coleo. The first deed was made by
Thomas Ford to Nancy Ford, for the east half of section 17, township 85, range 33, September 3d, 1855, and acknowledged by A.
J. Cain, County Judge.

The old Indian trail known as the War Path, or the dividing
line between the Sioux and Pottawattamie Indians' hunting
grounds, runs through townships 82, 83, 84, and 85, range 36, in
this county. It is plainly visible, and is as straight as an arrow.
It was a death penalty for an Indian of one tribe to cross the
path and be found hunting on the lands of the other.

An early settler relates that an old Indian chief told him there
was once a terrible Indian battle fought near Crescent Lake, about
one mile south of Carroll Center, between the Sioux and Pottawattamie Indians. There had been a feud for a long time existing
between the two tribes in regard to the infringement of the law
in relation to the hunting grounds by disloyal Indians. The Sioux
determined to exterminate the Pottawattamies. A large party of
the latter were encamped near Crescent Lake, in the grove of
timber. One morning a powerful party of the Sioux attacked
them, and a terrible and bloody battle ensued, resulting in the
death of all the Sioux warriors, and all but three of the Pottawattamies. The remains of the dead warriors were left to be eaten
by the wolves, or rot, and their bones to bleach on the prairie,
until the annual prairie fires consumed them.

The vote of Carroll county for Governor in the State election of
1881, was 2,219; its population, according to the census of 1880,
was 12,351. It is now, undoubtedly, a low estimate to place the
population of Carroll County at 15,000.

It will be seen by the above that Carroll County is not only,
with reference to its comparatively recent settlement, a populous
one, but also that it possesses all the requisite elements that insure permanent and progressive prosperity. Its towns and other
more especial features will be found to be described in detail as we
progress with the development of its history.

The present county officers of Carroll County are: Auditor, H.
E. Russell; Clerk of Courts, W. Lynch, Jr.; Treasurer, W. R.
Ruggles; Recorder, J. L. Messersmith; Sheriff, R. J. Hamilton;
Superintendent of Schools, C. C. Coleo; Surveyor, G. R. Bennett;
Chairman of Board of Supervisors, J. Thompson.

CARROLL CITY.

Whether or not first impressions are lasting, and whether or not first impressions are generally correct, are two questions which the writer cheerfully abandons to discussion by those who may be argumentatively inclined. In so far as Carroll City is concerned, it is certainly true that the general appearance of this thriving town can not fail to favorably impress all who visit it, and that this impression is more than confirmed by careful investigation. Probably no town of its population in Iowa has so many extensive and substantial business buildings as has Carroll City. A special correspondent of a leading Iowa journal, writing in the summer of 1880, has these things to say of Carroll City, to which, it may be prefaced, the brief lapse of time since then, has added many things of gratifying importance:

"It is seldom that the stranger has the pleasure of visiting a more interesting town than this, and when that privilege falls to his lot, there is but one sentiment to express and that is, astonishment—as so many evidences of thrift, prosperity, individual enterprise, social and business advancement, and the general harmony that seems to prevail in all matters of public benefit.

"A young city in the West is looked upon by eastern parties with a critical eye, and every advantage that a town possesses is carefully canvassed by those who contemplate locations for business enterprises, agricultural and stock pursuits, or manufacturing purposes. Carroll certainly possesses these, and many other advantages are to be made apparent in this work.

"So far as the country and railroad facilities are concerned, she has but few competitors in this section of the state. The surrounding country is of that nature which insures an everlasting and enviable local trade that can never be wholly cut off by rival towns; while the artificial strength given her by reason of the great trunk line that spans the vast territory on each side, and connects with competing lines in every direction, will be still more strengthened by the projected branch, extending from Carroll in a southwesterly direction through Shelby and Pottawattamie Counties, either to a direct connection with the great Union, Pacific Railway, or, what is better, to Kansas City and St. Louis, thus giving these people an outlet for their stock, grain and produce heretofore not enjoyed. At any rate the junction of these two lines, leading off through a most magnificent country, in different directions, bespeaks for Carroll a prosperity probably not anticipated by even her most sanguine business men."

Another equally impartial historian, writing at a date five years earlier than the above, observes: "This town which is the county seat and the most important town in the county, is very pleasantly situted on the line of the Chicago & Northwestern Railroad, a little north of the center of the county, and is surrounded by a fertile farming country. It was laid out in August, 1867, and has since had a steady and substantial growth; does a good retail business, and is the largest shipping point in the county. Good schools have been established; the leading religious denominations have organizations, and some of them commodious houses of worship. Being surrounded by a country having large agricultural resources, having good railroad facilities, and possessing a class of energetic, wideawake and experienced business men, who know how to make the best possible use of the advantages within their reach, Carroll is destined at no distant day to become one of the important towns in the western part of the State.

Carroll City was incorporated in 1869. O. H. Manning, William Gilley and a Mr. Tracy being the Commissioners of Incorporation.

The first municipal officers, under incorporation, were: I. N. Griffith, Mayor; B. B. Terry, Recorder; J. E. Griffith, Treasurer; Thomas Basler, Marshal; J. W. King, D. Wayne, F. E. Dennett, L. C. Bailey, William Boots, Councilmen. The present officers are: J. W. Scott, Mayor; A. E. Smith, Recorder; J. W. Hatton, Treasurer; Samuel Todd, Marshal and Street Commissioner; W. L. Culbertson, N. Beiter, Charles Hamilton, J. P. McAllister, James Thompson, L. F. Anderton, Councilmen.

I. N. Griffith opened the first general store, and Daniel Gifford the first furniture store, in 1868. The first grocery store was opened by D. Wayne.

The first child born was Carroll Kidder, or "Carrie," as she was generally called, daughter of Mr. and Mrs. A. L. Kidder. Mr. Kidder was the first Postmaster of Carroll. The family subsequently moved to Utah.

The Court House was built at Carroll City in 1869. It is a large two-story frame in the center of the public square. The Blair Town Lot and Land Company donated this square to the city. It is one of the most beautiful and eligibly located public squares in Western Iowa, and is thickly planted with finely growing trees. The Court House is well furnished with fire-proof vaults, but is in appearance the one blotch upon the beauty of an otherwise exceptionally attractive little city, and it is gratifying to note that there is a probability of its giving way for a more creditable structure at no distant time.

The population of Carroll City, according to the census of 1880, was 1,386; at present, there can not possibly be less than 1,700 inhabitants. The growth of the community, from the very nature of its surroundings, has been uninterrupted and permanent.

On the 25th of September, 1879 a disastrous fire destroyed two entire blocks of buildings and part of a third block. Nothing daunted by this weighty calamity, building was immediately resumed, and in the place of the "burnt district," massive and costly brick structures now attract the attention of the visitor.

The first number of the *Carroll Herald* was issued September 9th, 1868, and was conducted by J. F. H. Sugg for about two years. He was succeeded by E. R. Hastings as editor and O. H. Manning as proprietor. The paper was thus conducted about three years, when Mr. Hastings in connection with O. R. Gray, now of the Jefferson *Bee*, leased the office, under the firm name of Hastings & Gray. This firm subsequently purchased the establishment, and in April, 1877, Mr. Hastings became sole editor and proprietor. On the first day of January, 1882, Mr. Hastings leased a half-interest in the office to Ed. E. Adams, the firm now being Hastings & Adams. The paper is a seven-column quarto, and has a *bona fide* circulation of 1,100. The *Herald* is a model of typographical neatness, is conducted with unusual ability, and speaks volumes in each issue for the enterprise and prosperity of Carroll City and County.

The *Carroll Demokrat*, a German weekly newspaper, was established in May, 1874, by Bowman & Burkhardt. In 1876, H. W. Hagerman bought the office, and in March, 1879, the Demokrat Printing Association, a joint-stock company, purchased the establishment. The circulation of the paper is about 900. It is published every Friday, and is one of the neatest German publications in Iowa. Francis Florencourt is the editor, and B. T. Knieft the publisher.

The steam flouring mill, at Carroll City, has deservedly an extensive reputation. It is well and substantially built, is two stories high with a basement, and has the latest and best machinery. The mill was started in the spring of 1875, and is managed by Brooks & Baumhover.

There are two banks, each doing an extensive and profitable business, viz.: The Carroll County Bank, Patterson Bros., proprietors; Bank of Carroll, W. L. Culbertson, President; R. E. Coburn, Cashier. Both these banks occupy massive brick structures.

There were three brickyards in operation in the summer of 1881, all of which turned out brick of excellent quality.

The postoffice of Carroll City was established in 1868. A. L. Kidder was the first Postmaster. He was succeeded by John W. King, and in 1873, E. R. Hastings, the present Postmaster, was appointed to the office. Under the management of Postmaster Hastings it has become one of the neatest and best equipped postoffices in Western Iowa. It is located in the *Herald* building, a fine brick block erected by Mr. Hastings and L. Barbee. The office was made a money-order office in 1872.

The following is a classified summary of Carroll City's business establishments: General merchandise, eight; grocery stores, two; boots and shoes, two; clothing, two; hotels, six; restaurants, five; bakeries, two; hardware, four; agricultural implement depots, five; grain warehouses, two; stock dealers, three; livery barns, two; flouring mill, one; millinery stores, three; jewelry, three; drug stores, three; grain elevators, two; banks, two; real estate agencies, five; insurance agencies, six; blacksmith shops, four; barber shops, two; lumber yards, two; coal dealers, three; wagon-shop, one; loan agencies, eight; merchant tailor, one; printing offices, two; brick-yards, three; architects, one; paint shop, one; shoe-shops, three; saloons, six. There are thirteen attorneys-at-law and seven physicians.

CHURCHES, SCHOOLS AND SOCIETIES.

The First Baptist Church of Carroll.--The church organization was effected March 31st, 1878. The society was incorporated January 6th, 1879, under the name of "The Society of the First Baptist Church of Carroll." Rev. E. B. Potter was the First pastor, Rev. Edgar Hatfield second, and Rev. J. E. Sanders, the present incumbent, third. The present membership is fifty-four. The church edifice was built in 1873 by a Congregational church society, and was the first Protestant church edifice erected in the county. It was occupied by that society 'until 1877, when negotiations took place between it and the Presbyterian church society, resulting in the dissolution or disbanding of the Congregational church organization. The edifice was purchased by the Baptist society in 1878, and has been occupied by it ever since. Extensive repairs were made on the building in 1880. At the beginning of the Baptist organization there but nine members. The first regular services were held in July, 1879; the Sabbath School was organized at the same time. The present church officers are: Rev. J. E. Sanders, Pastor; Daniel Brainard, Alexander Dunphy, Deacons; H. S. Fisher, Clerk; W. L. Brockman, H. S. Fisher, Alexander Dunphy, Trustees; G. N. Dowd, Treasurer. The officers of the Sabbath School are: H. S. Fisher, Superintendent; Alexander Dunphy, Assistant Superintendent; Ada Elliott, Secretary and Organist; Lillie Hart, Librarian. The Sabbath School has a membership of seventy-five.

St. Joseph's Catholic Parish.--The present church edifice, which is beautifully situated on elevated ground, succeeded in 1877 a small structure in a lower part of the city. Services were held in the former building, from time to time only, by Rev. Father Kempker, who also had charge of the Missions at Mt. Carmel, Roselle, Arcadia and Westphalia. In 1876, Father Pape succeeded Father Kempker, and resided at Carroll. He selected the present grounds, and built the new church. In 1880, he was succeeded by the present incumbent, Father John Urbany, under whose directions both the new school house and St. Anthony's Institute were built. The Rector's residence, north of the church, was begun in 1879, and completed in 1880. The church cost about $4,500, and the residence about $1,600. The Parish numbers among its membership about 120 families, both English and German. Rev. Father Urbany took charge of the Parish in January, 1880, and in the summer of the same year, made preparations for a parochial school, which was completed late in the autumn, and opened under the management of the Sisters of St. Francis, from La Crosse, Wisconsin, with an average attendance of from 125 to 130. In the summer following, a handsome and expensive building, called St. Anthony's Institute, for the higher education of young ladies, was erected, south of the church and school, in the center of the block previously reserved for the purpose. St. Anthony's Institute is also conducted by the Sisters of St. Francis. Both educational structures are of brick. The four buildings, residence. church, etc., give a fine appearance to the southern part of Carroll City.

The M. E. Church Society.—This society dates its organization from about the year 1868. Its present membership is nearly one hundred. The church edifice. was erected in 1873, cost about $3,000 and will seat 250 persons. Rev. Samuel Jones is the present pastor. The Sabbath School has an attendance of about one hundred pupils. H. W. Macomber is the Superintendent. The church officers are: J. E. Archer, William Oldham, F. M. Howard, J. E. Thompson, Stewards; II. W. Macomber, J. E. Thompson, William Oldham, C. A. McCune, J. R. Atkinson, A. E. Smith, John Silbaugh, Trustees.

Presbyterian Church Society.—Rev. Mr. Elliott was the first pastor of this society, which was organized as long ago as 1867. There is a neat and commodious church edifice. Rev. T. S. Bailey is the present pastor.

Carroll City Public Schools.—The first school house was built in 1869. It was a frame structure, 40x60 feet in dimensions, two stories high, and contained two departments. The present building is a fine two-story brick structure, erected in 1880 at a total cost of about $14,000. The following is the present corps of teachers: J. M. Paul, Principal; G. W. Wattles, Grammar Department; Miss Grace Brainard, Intermediate; Miss Cora Shober, Second Primary; Miss R. M. Armstrong, Primary. There is a total enrollment of 255 pupils, with an average attendance of 220. The Board of Education is as follows: A. E. Smith, William Lynch, W. W. Macomber, N. Beiter, J. W. Scott, II. C. Stephens. J. W. Scott is President of the Board; R. E. Coburn, Secretary; W. L. Culbertson, Treasurer. The citizens of Carroll are justly proud of the unusual educational advantages the community affords.

Carroll Lodge No. 279, I. O. O. F.—Instituted April 16th. 1872, with twelve charter members. H. E. Cole was the first Noble Grand. This Lodge has a membership of forty-four, and holds its meetings every Saturday evening in Odd Fellows', Hall. The following are the present officers: S. P. Hart, N. G.; C. Henderson, V. G.; W. L. Culbertson, Secretary; E. II. Brooks, Treasurer.

Ellsworth Encampment No. 72, I. O. O. F.—Instituted in October, 1874. Charter members: J. W. Hatton, J. B. Cook, W. A. Moore, J. W. King. W. L. Culbertson, W. F. Steigerwalt, S.

M. Moore. First officers: W. L. Culbertson, C. P.; J. W. King, H. P.; W. F. Steigerwalt, S. W.; H. E. Cole, J. W.; J. W. Hatton. Scribe; S. M. Moore, Treasurer. Present officers: A. E. Smith, C. P.; J. W. King, H. P.; N. W. Ranger, S. W.; J. W. Hatton, J. W. and Treasurer; W. L. Culbertson, Scribe. The membership is twenty-one. Meetings are held on the first and third Monday evenings of each month.

Carroll Lodge No. 198, A. O. U. W.—Instituted in July, 1879. Charter members: James Thompson, C. L. Bailey, S. M. Towne, E. R. Hastings, Dr. Lane, S. Hoyt, C. A. Sawtelle, J. D. Lawrence, A. W. Morford, A. A. Wider, C. Henderson, F. Snydan, J. Nockles, D. A. Holmes. First officers: C. L. Bailey, M. W.; James Thompson, P. M. W.; F. Snydan, S.; D. A. Holmes, F. S.; J. Nockles, T.; C. Henderson, O.; J. D. Lawrence, F.; A. W. Morford, W.; A. A. Wider, G. Present officers: J. Thompson, M. W.; C. L. Bailey, P. M. W.; J. D. Lawrence, F.; C. Henderson, O.; F. Snydan, S.; J. Nockles, T.; A. A. Wider, G.; H. Fisher, W. Membership, twenty-two. Meetings are held every alternate Friday evening in the office of C. L. Bailey.

Jeff. C. Davis Post No. 44, G. A. R.—This post was mustered in September, 1881. The membership is sixty-five. Meetings are held every alternate Thursday evening in Joyce's Hall. The officers of the Post are as follows: J. V. Cook, Commander; D. A. Cadworth, S. V. C.; C. L. Bailey, J. V. C.; William Lynch, Adjutant; W. L. Culbertson, Quartermaster; J. W. Hatton. Surgeon.

Signet Lodge No. 264, A. F. & A. M.—This was the second Lodge of the order instituted in Carroll County. The Lodge was organized in August, 1869. The charter members were: J. F. H. Sugg, John K. Deal, Wm. Gilley, L. C. Bailey, J. E. Griffith, I. N. Griffith, Daniel Wayne, F. E. Dennett, R. Hogland. First officers: J. F. H. Sugg, W. M.; J. E. Griffith, S. W.; Wm. Gilley, J. W.; F. E. Dennett, Secretary; John K. Deal, Treasurer. Present officers: J. W. Gerstine, W. M.; R. B. Coburn, S. W.; John Kelly, J. W.; John W. King, Secretary; H. W. Macomber, Treasurer. The present number of members is forty-seven. The Masons and Odd Fellows bought a lot and erected a two-story brick building on the north side of Fifth Street. The lower story is leased for a dry goods store. The second story, 22x80 feet, is used by the aforesaid fraternities.

ARCADIA.

Arcadia is from nine to ten miles west of Carroll City, and is latterly taking on a new growth, which promises to place it among the front rank of Western Iowa towns. It has always been a place of sure promise and certain growth, but with its recent honors of incorporation "blushingly thick" upon it, the town has taken the initiative steps in the direction of more rapid progress.

It is beautifully located, and in every respect adapted to the conditions of permanent advancement. Its exact location is upon section 16, township 84, range 36. As usual, along the line of the Chicago & Northwestern, the Blair Town Lot and Land Company was its sponsor.

J. N. Voris was the original town proprietor, and laid out Arcadia in 1871. He subsequently sold the townsite to the company named above. Mr. Voris is still a resident of Arcadia.

The town is at the summit of the "divide," and is the most elevated town topographically in the state.

The first settlement of Arcadia was in the spring of 1871, when Mr. J. N. Voris built the first house. At this time Warren, Washington, Arcadia and Wheatland townships were unorganized, being attached to Carroll. Mr. Voris was a resident of California, and while passing through Iowa, eastward, was attracted by the singular beauty of Carroll County. Soon after, he returned from New York and purchased four thousand acres of land, including the site of Arcadia. This point was the summit or water divide in western Iowa, and trains doubled up and side-tracked here. Mr. Voris laid out the town and named it Arcadia, which took the place of the old railroad name of "Tip-Top." Immigration began pouring in, the town and county grew rapidly, and to-day the bright anticipations of the early settlers have been realized.

Low Lamson, now a resident of Chicago, came to Arcadia in 1870, with Mr. Voris. In the same year D. J. McDougall settled in the southeastern part of Arcadia Township. He came to Arcadia and taught the village school in the winter of 1873-4, after which he located there permanently, engaging in the grain and stock business, in which he still continues. Henry Carpenter built the first store, and is the present Postmaster of Arcadia. Mr. Carpenter came in 1871. James Carroll, a well known grain and lumber dealer, located at Arcadia in 1873. The changing events of time have brought about the removal of a number of other pioneers, whose names would otherwise be included.

L. S. Stowe, a well known and enterprising citizen, opened the first drug store in Arcadia, in the spring of 1874, which establishment has ever since continued to prosper under his proprietorship. His brother Michael was also one of the first merchants of the place, having opened a general store in the autumn of 1874.

The firm of Weidling, Evers & Moore, of which B. H. Moore is the active manager, was established in 1877, and began an extensive trade in general merchandise, farm machinery, etc. In 1879, this firm erected a brick building, twenty-four by eighty feet, with a cellar extending throughout its dimensions, and thus formed the nucleus of a business which would be quite creditable to a town of many times the population of Arcadia.

Arcadia was incorporated in the autumn of 1881, the following being the officers in pursuance of the incorporation: D. J. Mc-

Dougall, Mayor: F. A. Charles, Recorder; D. H. Moore, Treasurer;
E. H. Agnew, Marshal; D. H. Moore, G. E. Hawk, C. H. West-
brook, Claus Erp, Henry Ewaldt, Councilmen.

The population of Arcadia, according to the census of 1880, was
about 450; the present population claimed, is 600.

In addition to the earlier settlers named above, were John
Locke, now of West Side, and Henry Neiman, furniture dealer,
with others, whom want of space forbids us to particularize.

In 1880, a disastrous fire visited Arcadia, destroying nearly the
whole business portion of the town, and leaving but two stores un-
harmed, viz.: Weilding, Evers & Moore's and John L. McQuaid's.
The work of re-building was immediately commenced, and the
buildings destroyed were nearly replaced during the autumn of the
same year.

The following is a classification of Arcadia's business enterprises: Drug and book store, one; drug and grocery store, one;
general merchandise, four; hotels, three; livery, one, bank, one;
blacksmith shops, three; barber shop, one; millinery, two; meat
market, one: hardware, two; shoe shops, two; tailor, one; restaurants, two; furniture, one; undertaker, one; lumber yards, two:
agricultural implement depots, four; grain dealers, four; stock
dealers, two; real estate and loan agencies, one; insurance agencies,
two; job printing office, one; harness shop, one; wagon shops,
two; brewery, one; coal yards, three; lawyers, two; physicians,
two.

Arcadia Postoffice was established in 1872, with I. N. Voris as
Postmaster. H. C. Norton succeeded Mr. Voris, and Henry Carpenter, the present postmaster, was appointed to the office in 1874.
He was succeeded two years afterwards, however, by J. B. Benson, but was again appointed in 1881. The office was made a
money-order office in 1878.

The Arcadia Bank was established in November, 1881, and does
a thriving business. Louis R. Curran is the manager.

CHURCHES, SCHOOLS AND SOCIETIES.

The Presbyterian Church Society.— Organized in the spring of
1879, by Rev. T. S. Bailey, of Carroll. Rev. Mr. Eldfeldt is the
present pastor. The church building was erected in 1879, is about
fifty by twenty-four feet in dimensions, and cost $1,400. The
membership is about twenty-five. A Union Sabbath School is
conducted by the Presbyterian and Methodist Episcopal Societies,
of which Henry Carpenter is the Superintendent.

*St. John's Catholic Parish.—*In the spring of 1874, Rev. John
Kempker, of Mt. Carmel, organized a Catholic Mission at Arcadia,
services being held until the autumn of that year in James Carroll's
warehouse, north of the railroad depot. In the autumn of 1874, a
church edifice was built, which is 30x65 feet in dimensions. It is
the intention of the congregation to erect a church edifice, begin-

ning in the autumn of the present year. The proposed new structure will probably be 45x120 feet in dimensions, will be built of brick, and will cost from ten to twelve thousand dollars. Rev. Father Pape, now of Dubuque, succeeded Father Kempker, and Father Urbany, of Carroll City, came next. The Arcadia mission became a Parish August 15th, 1881, and Rev. Father J. B. Fendrich, the present Rector, was placed in charge of the growing congregation. The membership represents about 150 families, or a total of between 700 and 800 communicants. The parishioners are principally German, with a good representation of Irish, and services are held both in the German and English languages.

The M. E. Church Society.—Organized in 1873, by Rev. Mr. Vail. The succeeding pastors were: Rev. Mr. Brady, Mr. Eckels, C. V. Martin, J. W. Lewis, John Jefferson, and John Elliott, the latter of whom is the present pastor. The church membership is about twenty-five. The society has no church building as yet.

The German Lutheran Church.—Organized in 1877. The church building was erected in the spring of 1881, and is thirty by forty feet in dimensions. It cost about $1,200, and will seat 200 persons. There are about twenty families represented in the society. Rev. Mr. Gulge was the first pastor. He was succeeded by Rev. Mr. Schug, and the latter by the present pastor, Rev. Mr. Meineke.

The Public Schools.—The first school in Arcadia was taught in the winter of 1872-3, by a Mr. Hildebrand, who was succeeded by a Mr. Deal. D. S. McDougall was the next teacher, in the winter of 1873-4. The first school building was a one-story frame, which was enlarged in the summer of 1881, and is now a large building of three departments. An election to determine the question as to the organization of an independent district is to be held in March of the current year. The total enrollment is 130; average attendance, about seventy-five. The present corps of teachers is as follows: O. L. Bronson, Principal; Miss Minnie Sherman, Intermediate; Miss Lizzie Carroll, Primary.

St. John's Parochial School.—This school was organized in the latter part of February, 1882. Miss Annie Middendorf is the teacher. At present there is but one department. An additional department will be shortly made. The attendance of pupils will be from fifty to sixty in number.

German Lutheran School.—This school was established in the winter of 1881-2, has a goodly membership, and is taught by the resident pastor of the German Lutheran Church.

Arcadia Literary Society.—This society was begun in the winter of 1881. Meetings are held every Friday evening during the appropriate season, in the school house. The membership is about forty.

GLIDDEN.

The town of Glidden is picturesque attractive, prosperous and progressive. It is situated in the eastern part of Carroll County, and is surrounded by a country that for fertility of soil is not surpassed in Western Iowa. The country naturally tributary to Glidden, has a radius of not less than twenty-five miles, and the merchants of Glidden are exceedingly well pleased with their location. The town is well drained, and having good roads reaching out out in every direction, and an inexhaustible soil, there is no reason why Glidden should not become one of the most important towns in Western Iowa.

Glidden's artificial strength is principally derived from that great trunk line, the Chicago & Northwestern Railway, the management of which does not dictate a policy detrimental to the interests of towns along its line of road, but, on the contrary offers the best shipping facilities and the lowest rates possible. As a natural consequence hundreds of cattle, horses and hogs are brought here from every direction to be shipped over the road that seems to have adopted the motto "live and let live." At no distant day the people of Glidden anticipate a cross road connecting with north and south lines, which will give them competing advantages of a superior nature.

From an esthetic point of view is this beautiful town, environed with pretty suburban farms, groves and orchards, embellished in every quarter with elegant houses, tasteful lawns, many columns of forest trees that are fast turning the streets and avenues into arcades of living green. One meets evidences of social refinement on every hand. The city schools are in splendid condition and happily are its special pride.

As a business point Glidden is in the front rank of Iowa's enterprising towns. Its merchants do a thriving business, on a scale of unusual magnitude.

The population of Glidden is not less than 700, and its increase is continuous and uninterrupted. The town was laid out in 1866, and is a shipping point for a large district of country.

The following is a classified summary of the business establishments: General stores, five; grocery stores, two; confectionery, etc., three; hotels, two; blacksmith shops, two; wagon shop, one; barber shop, one; hardware, two; agricultural implement depots, three; lumber yards, two; coal dealers, two; grain dealers, four; grain warehouse, one; insurance agencies, one; real estate agencies, two; printing office, one; shoemakers, two; saloons, three; furniture, two; drug stores, three; jewelry, one; bank, one; millinery, three; livery, two; stock dealers, two; artist, one.

The Glidden Steam Flouring Mills were started about three years ago. The building is three stories high, and the quality of flour manufactured has justly achieved a most desirable reputation. The firm name is Messmore & Co.

The *Glidden Express* was started in 1875, with E. Tabor as editor and proprietor. Subsequently I. S. Russell became editor and proprietor. The paper is a five-column quarto, and is now called the *Glidden Sentinel*. The *Glidden News Boy* was started in 1881, by Cappie Holmes, editor and proprietor. It is a five-column quarto, independent in politics. Cappie Holmes is a son of Principal Holmes, of the Glidden Public Schools.

The Glidden Bank, of which G. H. Stalford is the proprietor, is a staunch and progressive institution, doing a large and increasing business.

CHURCHES, SCHOOLS AND SOCIETIES.

The Presbyterian Church Society.--This society has a handsome edifice, which was erected in 1874, at a cost of $1,200. The building is nicely furnished. The society dates its organization from 1870. Services were held in the school house prior to the erection of the church building.

The M. E. Church Society.—This society erected its present and commodious edifice in 1877, at a cost of about $1,200. Services were held in the Presbyterian church prior to the erection of the society's present building.

The Public Schools.—The independent school district of Glidden was organized in 1875. The first school building in the town was erected in 1869, or thereabouts, and was subsequently sold to G. H. Stalford. It is now used for business purposes, with a public hall in the upper story. The present school house was built in 1877, the total cost, improvements included, being from seven to eight thousand dollars. There are four departments, besides a large hall on the third floor, which will seat from three to four hundred persons. This building is of frame, with brick veneering, and is located in the east side of town, with a commanding situation.

Philo Lodge No. 391, I. O. O. F.--This Lodge was instituted in 1874, with about twenty charter members. Meetings are held every Tuesday evening in Odd Fellows' Hall. The following are the present officers: G. W. McNaught, N. G.; James Campbell, V. G.; T. R. Rich, Secretary; Geo. T. Chambers. Treasurer.

Haqqi Lodge, 369, A. F. & A. M.—This Lodge meets every Saturday evening of each month, on or before the full moon. D. N. Smith is W. M.; A. J. Morrill, Secretary.

Hope Stone Lodge No. 78, R. A. M.—Meetings are held every Tuesday evening of each month on or before the full moon. N. D. Thurman is H. P.; P. H. Hawkins, Secretary. The various secret organizations of Glidden are all in a condition of gratifying prosperity.

CARROLL COUNTY BIOGRAPHIES.

CARROLL CITY.

L. T. Anderson, harness manufacturer, is a native of Denmark; came to America in 1867 and located in Story county, Ia.; moved to Hamilton county; thence to Carroll county in 1878 and engaged in present business; deals in all kinds of harness and horse furnishings.

W. Artz, dealer in grain and stock, is a native of Ill.; moved to Carroll county in 1870, and engaged in mercantile business in Carroll in 1871, which he continued until engaging in present business. He has been treasurer of the county.

Wm. H. Bunch, barber, was born in Ill. in 1848; moved to Carroll, Ia., in 1881 and established his present business.

R. D. Backus, dentist, was born in Madison county, N. Y.; in 1860, he moved with parents to Ia.; came to Carroll in 1880 and established business; has a very fine office.

Thos. F. Barbee, attorney at law, is a native of Ky.; moved to Rock Island, Ill., and in 1878 came to Carroll, Ia., and opened his present law business.

N. Beiter, proprietor of meat market, is a native of Germany; came to America in 1866 and settled in Pa.; thence moved to Cedar county, Ia., in 1870, and to Carroll in 1874 and engaged in present business.

J. L. Bowdish, insurance agent, is a native of Ill.; came to Carroll in 1873; is justice of the peace, also notary public. He erected a fine brick block in 1881, now occupied by a clothing store.

E. H. Brooks, of the firm of Brooks & Baumhover, proprietors of the Carroll Steam Mills, was born in N. Y.; moved to Ill. in 1858; thence to Clinton, Ia.; and came to Carroll in 1870 and engaged in lumber business, until Aug., 1877, when he engaged in milling. The mill has a capacity of fifty barrels of flour per day and employs eight men.

Col. John B. Cook, dealer in agricultural implements, is a native of Mass. He served in the army during the late war, after which he settled in the South. He moved to Carroll, Ia., in 1871 and engaged in his present business.

Joseph M. Drees, attorney at law, was born in Boston, Mass., in 1849; removed to Dubuque, Ia., in 1858; thence to Carroll in 1873. He studied law with O. H. Manning, lieutenant governor, and was admitted to the bar in Sept., 1879. He is also engaged in the insurance business and is agent for a German line of steamers.

H. T. Emeis, M. D., is a native of Ill.; moved to Scott county, Ia. in 1856. He graduated from the Cincinnati Medical College in 1868, and came to Carroll in May, 1881.

H. F. Flinn, jeweler, is a native of Ill.; moved to Gilman, Washington county, Ia., in 1876; thence to Carroll in the autumn of the same year, and engaged in his present business.

W. E. Folkens, proprietor of the City Billiard Hall, is a native of Germany; came to America in 1858 and settled in Ill.; thence to Ia. in 1869 and located in Grundy county, and came to Carroll in 1874, and engaged in his present businesss in 1878.

I. W. Griffith, dealer in general merchandise, was born in Va. in 1813; moved to O. when quite young, and in 1844 came to Ia. and settled in Henry county, near Mt. Pleasant, and engaged in farming. He removed to Mahaska county; thence to Marshall county, where he engaged in milling. He subsequently came to Carroll and established the first store in the new town.

Wm. Gilley, is a native of Pa.; moved to O. with parents. He moved to Iowa City, Ia., in 1854 and to Carroll county in April, 1856, and engaged in farming; moved into Carroll in 1868; was county treasurer at that time. He has been engaged in banking and mercantile pursuits until a few years since, when he retired from business.

J. W. Gustine, M. D., was born in Pa. in 1822. He began the practice of medicine in Pittsburg in 1848, and moved to Iowa in 1854; two years later he located in Guthrie county, where he engaged in the practice of medicine, until 1875 then he moved to Carroll and opened an office.

P. M. Guthrie, dealer in real estate, was born in County Clare, Ireland; came to America in 1848, and located in Mich. and engaged in railroad contracting until 1854, when he moved to Dubuque, Ia.; thence to Carroll in 1869 and engaged in present business. He is agent for the Iowa Land Co.

R. J. Hamilton, sheriff of Carroll county, was born in Clinton county, Ia., in 1845; lived on a farm until coming to Carroll county in 1875, where he engaged in blacksmithing. He was elected to his present office in Oct., 1881.

C. Henderson, proprietor of the dray line, is a native of Ill.; moved to Carroll in 1872 and engaged in his present business.

H. C. Haywood, merchant and postmaster, at Elba, Carroll county, was born in Addison county, Vt.; moved with parents to Scott county, Ia., in 1850; thence to Carroll county and engaged in farming until appointed postmaster in 1878.

F. J. Kriebs, M. D., was born in Clayton county, Ia.; graduated from Rush Medical College, Chicago, in the class of 1881, and began the practice of medicine at Carroll the same year, and is early in the enjoyment of a good practice.

Louis Keckevoet, dealer in general merchandise, is a native of Germany; came to America in 1864 and settled in Ind.; removed to Dubuque. Ia., in 1870 and came to Carroll in 1875 and engaged in present business; he also has a general store at Hillsdale, this county.

Wm. Lynch, clerk of the courts of Carroll county, was born in Scotland in 1841; came to America with his parents and settled in N. Y.; removed to Pa. thence to Ia. in 1850. He enlisted in 1862, and was soon afterwards appointed hospital steward of the 31st Mo. regiment, and served until the close of the war. He then located at Carthage, Ill., and engaged in the drug business; remained there until 1869, then removed to Carroll and again engaged in the drug business. He was elected to his present office in 1875, and has held it ever since.

F. M. Leibfried, deputy county treasurer. is a native of Md.; removed to Wis. in 1850; thence to Carroll. Ia., in 1879. He was appointed deputy treasurer by Mr. Artz, and re-appointed by Wm. Ruggles in 1882.

S. M. Moore, dealer in general groceries and confectionery, is a native of Ind.; came to Ia. in 1869 and engaged in farming in Carroll county until 1875, then engaged in his present business.

M. Miller, druggist. is a native of Germany; came to America in 1857, and located at Dubuque, Iowa, and engaged as traveling agent for Honick & Walls, of Sioux City. He engaged in his present business at Carroll, in 1881, is wholesale and retail dealer in drugs and liquors.

J. L. Messersmith, recorder of Carroll county, is a native of Pa.; moved to Carroll in 1875 and engaged in wagon making. He was elected to his present office in 1876, and has been re-elected every term since.

F. M. Powers, of the firm of Powers & Powers, attorneys-at-law, is a native of N. Y. City: moved with parents to Blackhawk county, Ia., in 1857, graduated from the Iowa law school in 1877, and began the practice of law at Independence. He came to Carroll in 1880, and opened an office. The firm also do a loan and real estate business. J. M. Powers, of the above firm, was born in Cincinnati, O., removed with parents to Blackhawk county, Ia., in 1857. He graduated from the Iowa Law School in 1879, and has since been in partnership with his brother.

Geo. W. Paine, attorney at law, also does abstract, loan and insurance business. He was born in Duchess county, N. Y., in 1828. He first engaged in the practice of law at Poughkeepsie, in 1849; moved to New York City in 1860, and practiced there until opening an office in Carroll, Ia., in 1872.

J. A. Rohner, photographer, was born in Erie county, N. Y.; moved to Fremont, O., in 1867; thence to Chicago, Ill., two years later, and was employed there and in other cities in the west in the photograph business, until 1878, when he located at Carroll, Ia., and engaged in business. He was burned out in 1879, and was absent for a year; returned in 1881 and engaged in present business.

Abram Raught, proprietor of the Commercial House, was born in St. Lawrence county, N. Y.; moved to Neb. in 1873 and engaged in the hotel business; returned to N. Y., afterwards moved to Knoxville, Ia.; thence to Carroll and opened his present house, which is situated near the depot, and is a first-class house.

S. S. Sprague, proprietor of meat market, was born in Pittsburg, Mass.; moved to Ill. in 1856; thence to Carroll, Ia., in 1870 and engaged in present business.

August Stark, insurance agent, is a native of Germany; came to America in 1861 and enlisted in Co. G, 57th, Ill. Vol., was with Gen. Sherman in his march to the sea, and various; other places. He served until Aug. 15th, 1865, and then settled in Ill. and engaged in farming; in 1875 came to Carroll, Ia., and engaged in present business; was burned out in 1879, but started business again soon after.

C. B. Smith, agent for the C. & N. W. R. R. Co., at Carroll, Ia., is a native of New York; when quite young moved to Wheaton, Ill. He entered the employ of the above company and in 1871 was located at West Side, Ia. He came to this city in 1881.

J. E. Thompson, dealer in groceries, is a native of O.; moved to Scott county, Ia., in 1851, and engaged in farming. In 1876 came to Carroll and engaged in his present business, as wholesale and retail dealer in groceries and queensware.

J. W. Thomas, cashier of the Carroll County bank, is a native of England; came to America in 1873, settled in Ia. and engaged in farming until 1876, when he assumed his present position. The bank changed hands in 1881, but Mr. Thomas was retained as cashier.

R. R. Woodring & Co., wholesale and retail dealers in furniture, also manufacturersr This firm is composed of R. R. Woodring, I. N. Force and D. Burkhart. They do an extensive business in their line, and are one of the leading furniture firms in Carroll county.

A. L. Wright, M. D., is a native of Wis.; graduated from Rush Medical College, Chicago, in 1874. He located at Carroll, Ia., the same year, and has established a large and lucrative practice.

ARCADIA.

F. A. Charles, attorney at law, was born in Ill.; moved to Ia. in 1865 and located at Iowa City, in 1876 he engaged in the practice of law in Jackson county and in 1877 came to Arcadia. Was elected City Attorney in 1881.

Peter Clausen, proprietor of billiard hall, is a native of Germany. He came to Arcadia, Ia., in 1874, and engaged in his present business.

Henry Carpenter, postmaster, was born in N. Y.; moved to Ill. when quite young and in Aug., 1862 enlisted in Co. H, 105th Ill. Reg. He served until the close of the war, then returned to Ill. He came to Arcadia and built the first store building in the place. In 1874 he was appointed postmaster; he resigned in 1876 and was re-appointed in 1881.

Erp Bros., dealers in general merchandise, are natives of Germany; came to America in 1873 and settled in Iowa in 1875. They established their present business in 1881. Carry a large stock of general merchandise, and boots and shoes, also deal in coal and grain.

Henry Ewoldt, proprietor of Ewoldt's hall and sample room, was born in Holstein, Ger.; came to America in 1864 and settled in Scott county, Ia. In 1877 he engaged in his present business in Arcadia.

Thomas Fay, proprietor of saloon, is a native of Ill.; moved to Clinton county, Ia., in 1867; thence to Arcadia in 1877 and engaged in saloon business.

E. S. Lovely, general hardware dealer, is a native of Canada; moved to Carroll county, Ia., in 1873 and engaged in farming, until 1878, then went to Omaha, Neb., and entered the Western Business College; remained one and one-half years, then located at Arcadia, Ia., and engaged in the drug business. He subsequently engaged in business as above.

Henry Lahann, proprietor of the shooting gallery and saloon, is a native of Germany; came to America in 1856 and settled in Clinton county, Ia. He came to Arcadia in 1880 and engaged in his present business.

D. H. Mohr, of the firm of Weidling, Evers & Mohr, is a native of Denmark; came to America in 1853 and settled in Davenport, Ia. In 1867 he engaged in the mercantile business at Wheatland. Afterwards came to Arcadia and entered the above named firm.

H. W. Pruter, dealer in dry goods and groceries, was born in Germany in 1860; came to America in 1875 and located at West Side, Ia. He engaged in farming for two years and then returned to his native country. In 1878 he came again to Iowa, and settled in Arcadia. In 1881 he engaged in business as above.

Henning Petersen, proprietor of saloon and billiard hall, was born in Germany in 1827; came to America in 1865 and settled in Clinton county, Ia.; removed to Pottawattamie county; thence to Arcadia. Established present business in 1873.

L. S. Stoll, druggist, was born in Strasburg, France, in 1847; came to America in 1855 and settled in Dubuque county, Ia. He engaged in clerking in a drug store at the age of fifteen. In 1870 he engaged in business for himself at Dyersville, and four years later came to Arcadia, where he established business as above. He is also a practicing physician.

Frank Weber, proprietor of meat market, was born in Prussia in 1848; came to America in 1873 and located at Portage, Wis. He moved to Carroll county, Ia., in 1875 and two years later came to Arcadia and engaged in the meat business.

GLIDDEN.

L. A. Cushman, barber, was born in DeWitt, Clinton county, Ia.; moved to Glidden, in 1881 and established his present business.

T. A. Cochran, collection and real estate agent, is a native of O.; moved to Polk county, Ia., in 1854; thence to Green county and in 1864 to Carroll county and engaged in teaching school. Moved to Glidden in 1878 and opened an office.

J. Coder, of the firm of Dickey & Coder, dealers in general merchandise, is a native of O.; moved to Carroll county, Ia., in 1868 and engaged in farming and teaching school until 1878, then entered present firm.

Thos. Elwood, M. D., was born in N. Y. City; moved to Dallas county, Ia., in 1858. He enlisted in 1862 in the 39th Ia. regiment; went to Corinth, Miss., as hospital steward, and remained until the close of the war; returned to Ia. and settled in Carroll county, and began the practice of medicine; was elected county probate judge in 1867, which office he held three years, and county recorder from 1866 to 1868.

W. E. Foster, of the firm of Foster Bros., druggists, is a native of O.; moved to Glidden, Ia., in 1877 and engaged in the drug business in 1880.

N. G. Guild, proprietor of the Glidden House, was born in N. Y. in 1833; moved to Red Wing, Minn., in 1862 and engaged in farming and stock raising; thence to Glidden, Ia., in 1876 and engaged in present business.

H. H. Gates, M. D., was born in Rutland county, Vt.; moved to Ia. in 1855 and settled in Scott county; removed to Jones county later. He entered the army as hospital steward; was promoted to the position of surgeon of the 31st Ia. Reg. in 1863 and served until the close of the war, then returned to Jones county and in 1869 moved to Glidden and engaged in the practice of medicine.

C. I. Huiman. of the firm of Huiman & Beach. attorneys at law. is a native of O.; came to Boone county. Ia., in 1853 and engaged in school teaching. He served as superintendent of schools one term and graded the schools of Glidden. He graduated from Grinell College, Ia., and begun the practice of law in 1876 with present partner; they also do insurance and collection business.

J. A. Holmes, principal of the Glidden schools, is a native of N. Y.; moved to Glidden, Ia., in 1880 and engaged in his present occupation. He also deals in stationery, books and confectionery.

The *Glidden News-Boy*, a weekly newspaper published by Coppie Holmes, was established in 1880, when Coppie was but twelve years old. At first it was a four-page paper six by nine inches in size. but it has steadily increased in size and patronage and now (in 1882) it is a six-column quarto. The publisher does all the work upon the paper and considerable job work besides. He has put the receipts for advertising. etc., into the office and can now do good job work. He is the youngest publisher of a regular newspaper in Ia. and perhaps in the world; the newspaper press have given him many flattering notices.

C. O. Hood, M. D., is a native of Ind.; graduated from the medical department of the Butler University in the class of '79, and located at Glidden in 1880 and engaged in the practice of medicine.

G. W. Parsons, proprietor of barber shop and news depot. is a native of O.; located at Glidden, Ia.. in 1878 and engaged in his present business.

W. E. Potter, of the firm of Potter & Armitage. hardware dealers. was born in Oneida county, N. Y.; removed to the eastern part of Ia. in 1858, thence to Glidden in 1868 and engaged in farming; engaged in his present business in 1879; J. P. Armitage became a partner in 1880.

O. G. Prill, of the firm of Prill Bros., dealers in general groceries, is a native of Ind.; came to Ia. in 1875 and engaged in the above business in Nov., 1881.

F. G. Rust, insurance agent, is a native of Wis.; moved to Ia. in 1881, and settled in Glidden and engaged in his present business.

I. R. Sale, M. D., was born in Ind., he studied medicine there several years; he then graduated from the Kentucky School of Medicine in 1881 and came to Glidden in Dec. of the same year and took charge of the established practice of Dr. Dunkle.

R. E. Spurrier, druggist and station agent, is a native of O.: moved to Iowa county. Ia., in 1853, thence to Glidden in 1880 and took charge of the station and purchased the drug business of M. S. Dunkle, M. D.

D. N. Smith, dealer in lumber and coal, is a native of Carroll county, N. H. He enlisted in 1861 in the U. S. sharpshooters, served three years in Va. and then returned to N. H.; moved to Ill. in 1877 and the following year to Glidden, Ia., and engaged in his present business.

Geo. H. Stalford, banker, is a native of Pa.; came to Ia. in the spring of 1869 and engaged in farming, returned to Pa. in 1870 and remained three years; thence to Ia. again and engaged in the lumber and grain business; engaged in the banking business in Feb., 1877.

SAC COUNTY.

The population of this county by the census of 1880 was 9,300, but it is now estimated at over 11,000. This increase is partially due to a narrow gauge railway (a branch of the Wabash) which is in process of construction, and which will run across the county, passing through Sac City, thus giving additional shipping and traveling facilities to the people of the county. Depot grounds for the road have been laid out near the court house in the city named.

As stated elsewhere a complete list of the county officers from date of the organization of the county to present date is not obtainable, but the following are the present officers: Treasurer, Philip Schaller; Auditor, A. D. Peck; Sheriff, H. L. Willson; Clerk of Courts, Chas. E. Lane; Recorder, N. B. Flack; Superintendent of Schools, H. T. Martin; Surveyor, Chas. Pettis; Supervisors, Wm. Hawks, Chairman; H. Reinhart, Peirce Coy.

The general history of Sac County can probably be presented in no better shape than as we give it in the following extract from a well-written article, published in the *Sac Sun*, of Sac City, December 24th, 1880:

"The immense emigration from the Eastern and East Central States which has for the past two or three years rapidly settled up the lands of Kansas and Nebraska, has during the past two years been diverted to a great extent to the more certainly productive agricultural lands of Northwestern Iowa. Many more of these home-seekers might have been induced to settle in this section had the Iowa people and the Iowa government sooner awakened to the fact that so many thousands of good citizens were passing through Iowa to lands farther from market, and by no means so valuable as those which Iowa had to offer, and all because the Kansas and Nebraska lands were assiduously advertised, while those of Iowa lay undefended under the slanders mentioned in the appended letter. The General Assembly, however, to remedy this evil, appointed Hon. Geo. D. Perkins, of the Sioux City *Journal*, to the office of Commissioner of Immigration for Iowa, and appropriated a considerable sum for the promotion of immigration to this State. Read what Governor Campbell says:

NEWTON, IOWA, June 15th, 1880.

Hon. Geo. D. Perkins, Commissioner of Immigration for Iowa:

DEAR SIR: Your invitation to the immigration convention at Sheldon, June 22d, received on my return home from an extended trip east. I fully realize the importance of the convention, and the great interests to be considered, and I assure you my hearty sympathy goes out toward any effort that will tend to direct public attention to your beautiful country and fertile soil, and point the tens of thousands of homeless ones to that fair country that offers such splendid advantages for permanent homes and prosperous futures. During my visit east I had occasion to "talk up" northwestern Iowa in several localities, and I found:

1. A total ignorance of the fact that so large a territory in Iowa lies open yet to settlement, the impression having obtained that a State with over a million and a half of population must be well settled up.

2. I found the 'old grasshopper still sitting on the sweet potato vine,' in the prejudices of many, and it was only a work of a moment to convince them that the 'grasshopper' was long since a 'dead issue' in any portion of Iowa.

3. The terrible storms and daily hurricanes of wind were held up before me, and I told them they were more a native of Missouri or even of Ohio, than of northwest Iowa, and that the settlement of our State, the planting of groves, etc., had very materially ameliorated the climate.

These are only a few of the objections urged, but among the most weighty, and I name them that you may see the objections that obtain in various quarters. There are tens of thousands in the east who would be glad to find homes in Northwestern Iowa, were they fully acquainted with the true condition of affairs, climate, soil, prices of land, terms, etc. , With thanks for your invitation, and regret that I cannot be present. I am your well-wisher and friend,

FRANK T. CAMPBELL.

"This sketch is intended principally as a pen-picture of Sac County as it now is, and will include a short outline of its history and a few incidents of the life of the early settlers.

" The soil of Sac County is a deep black loam, and in its nature is purely a vegetable decomposition. Its depth is from eighteen inches to five or six feet. In some parts of the county the surface is almost perfectly level for long distances, but in general it is of the genuine 'rolling prairie' description. The inexhaustibility of the soil is shown by the fact that farms which have been under cultivation for from twenty to twenty-five years are now as fertile and productive as ever. More than that—the land may be plowed here when it is so wet that it is almost impossible to do work, and *it will never bake.*

"As regards the productiveness of Sac County, perhaps as effective a way of showing whether the detractors of Northwestern Iowa, mentioned in Governor Campbell's letter, are right or wrong, will be to give to our readers the benefit of some of the observations of the Hon. Eugene Criss, a pioneer and resident of Sac County for more than a quarter of a century. Judge

Criss says that his average yield of corn in his twenty-five years' residence has been from forty to fifty bushels to the acre, and the highest yield he has ever had was sixty-five bushels. Average yield of oats, forty to fifty; highest yield, seventy-six bushels. Average yield of wheat, fifteen to eighteen; highest yield, thirty bushels. This is his personal experience, and with fair cultivation only—no fancy farming; that he knows of at least two of his neighbors who have raised as high as forty bushels of wheat to the acre. Others, too, have raised, in more than one neighborhood in the county, from seventy to eighty bushels of corn per acre, and, it is said, without more than ordinary tillage. The principal agricultural products of Sac County and this section generally are corn, wheat, oats, flax, barley, rye and grass. Timothy, clover and blue grass grow readily and will make Sac, at an early day, one of the leading stock and dairy counties of Iowa. And Iowa is, with rapid strides, coming to the head of all the States in dairy products. We will put Judge Criss on the stand again in regard to the advantages for stock raising.

"We have stated that the tame grasses grow rapidly. Besides that fact, it is also true that the Kentucky blue grass is rapidly coming 'of itself' in places where it has never been sown. Along fences, along paths made by cattle through the brush and in pastures, in spots where the timber and underbrush have been cleared, in door-yards and other places, in some mysterious way that sweetest and best of feed for stock is making its appearance. It is a matter which the present writer does not understand, but it is a good thing, and we are glad to see that this section is so fortunate. Grass is always sufficiently high to turn out stock at a date varying in the different years from April 1st to April 30th. And now we produce Judge Criss's testimony. The Judge is a Virginian by birth, but has had some years' experience in farming in Maryland. After his many years' experience in the two States, it is his firm belief that both cattle and horses do better 'running out' during the winter months in this part of Iowa than they do in Maryland. This, our readers will observe, is not guess-work or the dictum of a traveler or chance observer, but the carefully considered verdict of *experience*.

The location of Sac County is on the Great Divide, as the watershed between the Missouri and the Mississippi is called. It is in the west northwestern part of Iowa, being the fourth county from the northern line of the State, the sixth from the southern, the third from the Missouri River, and the tenth from the Mississippi. Sac City, the center of the government, and not far from the geographical center, is about fifty miles by wagon road west from Fort Dodge and about eighty-five miles east from Sioux City.

Sac County's only railway communication with the busy world outside is by means of branches of the Chicago & Northwestern Railroad. These branches are the Maple River Railroad and the

Sac City & Wall Lake Railroad. The former has two stations in the County—Odebolt and Wall Lake. The latter has, as yet, no other stations than its *termini*—Sac City and Wall Lake, which are twelve miles apart. Another station is now being put in which will be better entitled to the latter name than the town which now bears it, being situated on the shores of the Lake, while the present station of Wall Lake is some four miles distant. It seems to us that the present town will be obliged, in honor, to resign its name in favor of the baby town not yet christened. Sac City is situated twenty-eight and eight-tenths miles from Maple River Junction, on the main line (Chicago & Council Bluffs) of the Chicago & Northwestern Railway, and just thirty-three miles from Carroll, the nearest town of any consequence in direct railway communication. Both these branches have been built within the past three years, and a large part of the present.

[The additional station on the Sac City & Wall Lake Railroad was eventually christened Fletcher. An account of it will be found in the proper place.]

"Sac County contains sixteen congressional townships, west of the Des Moines River. It contains 369,640 acres, nearly all of which is desirable land for either grain or stock farms, and the larger part available for either or both combined. The larger part of these lands are railway property and these can be purchased by home-seekers, who will occupy them at once, on the most liberal terms. Many of the private holders are also selling on nearly if not quite as easy terms as the railway land company. And as to the grasshopper and tornado bugbears, it is perfectly safe to say that the farmers of Ohio and Indiana are as much annoyed by them, and have as much prospect for annoyance from them, as the Sac county grower of grain and stock. Sum up these advantages, and the reader will readily see why the population has been rapidly on the increase ever since the opening of railway communication. Let those who have doubts give the county a visit and they will hesitate no longer. Sac county has not even the drawback so common to these fertile counties of Northwestern Iowa. What this is, is too well understood by the early settlers who located in Northwestern Iowa before there were railways to deliver coal at every man's door. Many counties in this section had little or no timber—Ida County, for instance, had less than a thousand acres within its borders. Sac County had many thousands of acres of oak, black walnut, hickory, ash, elm, maple, box alder, cottonwood, linn (basswood), and many other varieties native to the soil. The Coon River, which traverses the east part of the county, lies buried in woods for almost its entire course. Cordwood is delivered in Sac City at from $4 to $5 per cord according to quality. The timber culture laws of the State—relieving land from tax for ten years in consideration of the culture of a certain portion of forest trees—have also caused so extensive a growth of forest that there is

probably more timber now in the county than before the first axe
was struck on the banks of of the classic Coon.

" The early settlers of Sac, though they had the advantage of
being able to try fruit-raising under the protection of a considerable belt of timber, had small faith in the county as adapted to the
growth of fruits. Consequently it was not until some ten or
twelve years after the settlement of the county began that any attention was given to this important branch of the industries of the
county. When proper attention was given to the matter, it was
speedily demonstrated that Sac County was *well* fitted for fruit
growing, and there are now many orchards, vineyards and fruit
gardens dotting the fair surface of Sac-shire. Apples, grapes,
plums, cherries, strawberries, raspberries, blackberries, currants,
gooseberries, etc., grow rapidly and yield surely and abundantly,
and the quality is unsurpassed anywhere. We are informed that
pears are also successfully grown in parts of the county. In the
line of vegetables there is nothing usually grown in a temperate
climate which will not grow here and that in extraordinary perfection. This section is the garden of Iowa, as Iowa is the Garden State of the Union. The dry, pure air of our unexcelled
climate gives to trees and plants a healthy growth, and the fruits
and vegetables are solid and delicately flavored and tinted, as far
excelling the coarse flavor and blowzy coloring given to the same
fruits by the hot and humid air of California and Oregon as the
apple excels the pumpkin. You say the California fruit is larger
than ours! Oh, well, the pumpkin is larger than the apple; but
the pumpkin requires a good deal of cooking and spicing before it
is eatable, and if you get a California apple you had better use that
for cooking also. But our northern Iowa apples are of medium
size, of the finest flavor and will keep longer than any apple grown
in a warm climate. Therefore the Iowa apple is in the near future
the apple of commerce. and it is not unlikely that the principal future industry of Iowa, may be fruit-frowing. Apples are not the
only fruit which the Iowa soil and climate give a finer flavor than
elsewhere. Nowhere does the Concord grape come to such perfection as in Iowa. And although our fruits and vegetables do
not rival those of the Pacific coast in size, they are unsurpassed even
in that minor particular by those of any other section in the Mississippi Valley or any section on the Atlantic slope.

" The first settlement was made by Otho Williams, who came
from Michigan in the autumn of 1854, with his family, and took up
a claim in the timber near Grant City, in the southeastern part of
the county. He and his family were the first white inhabitants
of Sac county, but during the two succeeding years quite a number of settlers made their homes either in the same neighborhood
or in the vicinity of Sac City, and Otho Williams, at the end of
about two years. complained that ' folks are gittin' too thick
'round yer,' and he and his family ' folded their tent like the

Arab, and silently stole away.' · In other words, they sold their claim and disappeared in the direction of the setting sun. No one knows where they went. If they still live and preserve their aversion to near neighbors, they must be somewhere in the Rocky Mountain region. In the spring of 1855, Leonard Austin, F. M. Cory, Wm. Wine and David Metcalf, with their families, W. M. Montgomery, with his mother and sister, and S. W. Wagoner and Henry A. Evans, single men, took up claims in the county. On the 5th of August Eugene Criss and family arrived in the county, and located near Sac City. A few days later William H. Hobbs located in the same neighborhood. During the fall the population of Sac County was augmented by the arrival and settlement of John Condron, Joseph Lane, Joseph Williams and S. L. Watt, with their respective families. This, so far as we can learn, is a complete list of the population of the county up to the close of 1855.

" In the spring of 1858, the settlers in Congressional townships 87, 88 and 89, in range 36, now forming the townships of Wall Lake, Jackson and Delaware, thought that there was good reason to fear that all vacant land in those townships would be bid in by speculators at the annual land sale at Sioux City, thus preventing its immediate settlement. Nearly all the settlers, though not ready at that time to buy, wanted some of this land for their own use. They therefore met together and arranged matters, and when the day of sale came, the room in which the sale was held was packed full of settlers, and no others could make their way in. No bids were made, and the land was thus kept open for pre-emption.

" The first mill in the county was built by Wm. Lane, on the Coon River, near Grant City, late in the fall of 1856. That winter was so very severe that it has ever since been known as the ' hard winter,' but nevertheless, corn was hauled to the mill from Sac City and vicinity on hand-sleds. Many families ground their own corn in coffee mills. Provisions, flour, etc., were generally brought from Des Moines.

" In 1856, Sac County, which had previously been attached to Greene County for all administrative purposes, was granted a separate jurisdiction. S. L. Watt was the first County Judge—and the County Judge of those days was an autocrat, performing the functions of the present Board of Supervisors and County Auditor, and also, in part, those of the Judge of the Circuit Court. H. C. Crawford was first County Clerk, and F. M. Cory was first Treasurer and Recorder."

SAC CITY.

The population of Sac City is now estimated to be 800. The place is one of the most flourishing in this section of Iowa.

The present town officers are: Mayor, John Alexander; Recorder, Charles L. Early; Trustees. R. H. Lamoreux, Phil. Schaller, P. H. Hankins, N. B. Flack, Jos. H. James.

In 1856 Sac City was laid out on land belonging to Hon. Eugene Criss, and was selected as the seat of government for the county. It is situated on the Coon River, about five or six miles northeast of the center of the county. The business part of town lies on level ground, on the first rise from the bottom lands along the river, while the residences are principally on higher ground, overlooking the business streets.

The townsite is handsome and picturesque. In fact, it would be difficult to find in our prairie country a more beautiful location for a town. The Coon River, lined by a narrow strip of bottom land, half encircles the town. Native forest trees are scattered over the whole town site, so that even the later comers may have enough shade around their homes to take away the disagreeable bareness usually belonging to a new residence in a prairie country. It would be difficult for even the most fastidious to find fault with the appearance of Sac City, taking its age and size into consideration.

Sac City was incorporated in 1865, and Judge Criss, the founder of the town, was, quite appropriately, its first Mayor. The town is, in every respect, in a prosperous condition—growing rapidly and gaining every season in handsome and permanent buildings, and last, though not least, it is out of debt and has money in its treasury.

Judge Criss built the first house in Sac City. It was a log house and was built in 1855 and is still standing.

The Sac City Creamery was established in 1879. It was formerly situated one and one-half miles from town. The proprietor, G. M. Parker, has subsequently built a fine brick building 24x40 feet, with ice-house 20x32 feet, steam power engine and wash-room 16x30 feet, erected in 1882. The creamery is to be supplied with all the modern improved machinery. The cost of construction was about $5,000. It is to be run on the cream-gathering plan. The new creamery is to be known in future as the Pearl Creamery, and will begin operations in April, 1882.

The classification of business in Sac City is as follows: General stores, three; groceries, three; dry goods, one; boots and shoes, one; clothing, one; fancy goods, one; millinery, three; hardware, two; drugs, three; meat markets, two; blacksmiths, three; wagon-makers, two; banks, two; furniture, two; photograph gallery, one; restaurant, one; hotels, two; physicians, four; attorneys, four;

harness, two; livery, two; shoemakers, two; tailor, one; lumber and coal, two; elevators, three; cigar factory, one; mattress factory, one; stock dealers, three; saloons, four; iron foundry, one.

The Court House is 84x56 feet, solidly and handsomely built in brick, with limestone foundations and is one of the best county buildings in the northwest. It cost $30,000. The first floor is fitted up for the county officers, with vaults for the county records, etc. The upper story has the court-room, jury-rooms, etc. With the court-room fitted up for a session of court there are about 400 sittings, but in use as a hall for lectures or political speaking, there is sitting room for 600 people. The basement is only partly in use. One room is fitted up with floor, stove, chairs, tables, etc., and is in use as a jail. A cage of boiler iron, containing two cells, fills about half the room and makes the jail a pretty secure one.

On Coon River, adjoining the town, and only a quarter of a mile from the Court House, are the City Mills, the property of Hon. Eugene Criss. The mills have three run of stone (including one for the manufacture of patent flour), and are run by water power. Judge Criss, in 1857, built a steam saw mill, and in 1862 dammed the Coon and used the water-power for his saw mill. The building of railroads, and the consequent cheap transportation of pine lumber, made the saw mill no longer a necessity, and in 1872 the conversion of the Sac City Mill into a flouring mill was completed and in December of that year the first "grists" were ground. Since that time it has been the leading mill, and one of the most important institutions of Sac County, as well as a source of profit to its proprietor.

Sac City has a very pleasantly situated cemetery, just at the north edge of town, and on the bank of the Coon River, but about ten feet above high water mark. It has quite a number of native oak trees, and some of the burial lots have had considerable care bestowed upon them.

Sac City, has but one newspaper, and has been able to give it a fair living support. As a rule, it is the fault of the community if the local newspaper is a poor one. Give it a better patronage and it will be improved. It takes money to make any kind of business "go." The *Sac Sun* was first issued July 11th, 1871, as a seven-column folio, and was enlarged July 1st, 1878, to an eight-column folio, its present size. It is, and always has been, Republican in politics. Always among the handsomest papers in the State, typographically the *Sun* has also been always carefully edited and with special attention to those matters which are the life of a country newspaper. Mr. James N. Miller has been the editor and the publisher during its whole existence, and the *Sun* itself is the best evidence of his qualifications for that position.

Sac City had two newspapers for about six weeks near the close of the year 1877. Kelly & Yarham issued the first number of the *Reporter* at Sac City on the 22d of October of that year, but removed it to Odebolt on the 6th of December.

CHURCHES, SCHOOLS AND SOCIETIES.

M. E. Church Society.—The M. E. Church of Sac City was
the first church building erected in the town. It was built in
1873, and is a frame structure 30x50 feet. The building is located
on the corner of Ninth and Main streets. and cost $3,000. The
present pastor is Rev. Robert Smylie. The Society has a membership of sixty. There is a Sabbath School in connection, with
an average attendance of fifty pupils. A. D. Peck is Superintendent, J. L. Comstock Assistant Superintendent, Mrs. C. L.
Lane, Treasurer, and Miss Winnie Lane Secretary.

The Presbyterian Church Society.—The Presbyterian Society
of Sac City was organized in 1875. The present officers are J. N.
Miller, H. M. Conner, Elders; J. T. Bushnell was the first pastor,
then came Rev. Baxter. A. S. Foster is the present incumbent.
The church has a membership of thirty-three. There is also a
Sabbath School with an average attendance of fifty pupils. J. N.
Miller is Superintendent. The church has an elegant brick church
building, erected in 1875, and dedicated the following year. It is
34x56 feet on the ground. and contains about 300 sittings.

Sac City Lodge No. 323, I. O. O. F.—Instituted November 5th,
1878. The charter members were V. M. Crummett, H. W. Cran-
dall, G. N. Pratt, W. H. Hobbs, J. H. Thomas. John Dobson. H.
W. Mix, C. Wadell, D. Sargent, D. F. Gifford, M. Peyton. First
officers: M. Peyton, N. G.; D. Sargent, Secretary; D. F. Gifford,
V. G.; W. H. Hobbs, Treasurer. Present officers: D. F. Gifford,
N. G.; Martin Glass, V. G.; J. Koder, Secretary; M. Peyton,
Treasurer. This lodge has a membership of thirty and meets every Thursday evening in Masonic Hall. The Lodge is in a flourishing condition.

Occidental Lodge A. F. & A. M.—Instituted August, 1865; char-
ter granted June, 1866. Charter members: D. C. Early, J. Wil-
liams, W. V. Lagourgue, G. H. Wright, J. W. Fiberghien, T. M.
Cory. First officers: D. C. Early, W. M.; J. Williams, S. W.;
G. H. Wright, J. W.; W. V. Lagourgue, Treasurer; F. M. Cory,
Secretary. Present officers: P. Schaller, W. M.; C. E. Lane, S.
W.; J. H. Thomas. J. W.; W. M. Allen, Treasurer; C. E. Read,
Secretary. Present membership, seventy-two. The Lodge meets
the Saturday night on or before each full moon, in their hall.

Rose Croix Commandery No. 38, K. T.—Was instituted Dec.,
1881. The charter members were: D. C. Early, P. H. Hawkins,
E. R. Duffie, W. H. Hobbs, M. Childs, B. W. Trout, R. T. Shearer,
M. M. Gray, H. S. Briggs and Sidney Smith. First officers: D.
C. Early, E. C.; E. R. Duffie, Glo.; R. T. Shearer, C. G. The
present officers are: D. C. Early, E. C.: Phil. Schaller. Glo.; Levi
Davis, C. G.; W. H. Hobbs, S. W.: M. Childs, J. W.; Sidney
Smith. Secretary: C. L. Early, Treasurer. The present member-
ship is thirty. This society meets the second Tuesday in each
month. It is in a flourishing condition.

Darius Chapter No. 50, R. A. M.—Was instituted February 1st, 1871. The charter members were: Wm. McKay, W. H. Hobbs, E. R. Duffie, E. R. Chase, S. S. Armstrong, J. Orr, and Oliver Birt. First officers: E. R. Chase, H. P.; J. E. Armstrong, K.; E. R. Duffie, S. The present officers are: Levi Davis, H. P.; D. C. Early, K.; J. E. Armstrong, S.; R. H. Lamoreux, Treasurer; Sidney Smith Secretary. Present membership, seventy. The Lodge meets on the Monday evening on or before the full moon in each month.

Sac Collegium, V. A. S., No. 75.—Instituted August 21st, 1881. First officers: A. D. Peck, Rector; Geo. Schaller, Scribe. Present officers: A. D. Peck, Rector; Frank C. Knights, Scribe. The membership is twenty-one. Meet the first Friday in each month.

Sac City Public School.—Sac City became an independent school district in April, 1876. The first school house was built in 1855. The present teachers are: D. J. McDaid, Principal; Mrs. G. M. Parker, Miss Lizzie Baxter, Assistants. Present school board: A. D. Peck, President; D. C. Early, E. Criss, Phil. Schaller. W. H. Hobbs, Directors; C. E. Lane, Secretary; R. H. Lamoreux, Treasurer. The first officers were: B. W. Trout, Levi Davis, H. Baxter. The public school building in Sac City is a fine brick edifice, with a stone foundation, built in 1871 at a cost of $14,000. It contains three rooms, the whole upper story being devoted to the high school department, while the intermediate and primary departments are accommodated on the first floor. The building is well built and handsomely furnished, and is well ventilated, comfortable and more than ordinarily well lighted. The schools are in the best order, well disciplined and progressing most satisfactorily in the various branches of study.

ODEBOLT.

This town is situated in the western part of Sac County on a branch of the Chicago & Northwestern Railway. It was laid out by the Blair Town Lot and Land Company in 1877. M. H. Henipen is not only the first business man of Odebolt, but is one of the earliest settlers, having been engaged in selling supplies to the laborers before the town was laid out or the railroad completed. The first house erected in the town was built by W. Van Duesen, and served both as a store and dwelling. He was soon followed by Geo. McKibbin, and James Ross. The railroad was completed to this town in 1877. The first regular train reached this point November 19th, 1877.

H. T. Martin is among the early settlers of Odebolt. He organized the first Sabbath School in December, 1877, and was the first commissioned Notary Public in the place.

The depot was built in 1877. J. T. Martin was appointed the first depot agent, and Miss Emma Martin was first telegraph operator.

The town of Odebolt was incorporated in March. 1879, James Ross being the first Mayor, and J. M. Zane, Recorder; J. Flanders, J. Ketterer, E. Geist, C. Dalbkymer, C. B. Hatfield, and J. Bowles served as Councilmen. James Ross still holds the position of Mayor, W. V. Sindt, Recorder; J. Flanders, J. Ketterer, E. Geist, H. Rheberger, J. W. Fairbanks and C. S. Lee, are the present Councilmen.

The population of Odebolt is now estimated at 1,200 souls.

The Odebolt Reporter was started in Sac City in 1877, by W. W. Yarham, and was moved to Odebolt the same year. Frank Kelley purchased the paper from Yarham. It was afterwards bought by Taylor & Mann, and still later was purchased by A. J. Mann. G. A. Kikok afterwards purchased the paper and sold it to F. L. Dennis in April, 1881. This paper is republican in politics, is an eight-column quarto, and has a circulation of 600.

The Odebolt Observer is a neat six-column quarto weekly paper. It was started in July, 1880, by Martin & Bennett. Bennett soon bought Martin's interest, and is now the sole proprietor. This paper is Democratic, and has a circulation of 500 copies.

The Central Western Iowa District Fair Association.—This comprises the counties of Sac. Ida and Crawford, and was organized August 1st, 1881, with W. W. Field as President. P. Coy, W. Van Duesen, H. C. Wheeler, A. D. Peck, I. S. Bailey, E. P. Masser; E. A. Bennett and S. Peterson as Vice-Presidents; F. L. Dennis, Secretary; W. J. Summerville, Treasurer. This society owns twenty-five acres of land, situated one-half mile northeast of the town, and will hold their first fair in the fall of 1882.

Odebolt Fire Company.—The Hook and Ladder Company was organized in the spring of 1880, and consists of forty members, all uniformed. J. Mattes, Foreman; E. E. Hamlin, Secretary; W. V. Sindt, Treasurer; Dave W. Flack, Assistant Foreman.

Odebolt boasts of a flax mill which was established in 1880 by Winslow & Son. This is a large frame building with steam power. John Dement is the present proprietor.

Odebolt has the finest public hall in Sac County. It was erected in 1881, by John Wright. It is a brick structure, 50x90 feet with five hundred sittings.

The business of Odebolt may be classified as follows: Seven general stores, three groceries, two harness shops, two hardware stores, three drug stores. two jewelry stores, two furniture stores, three restaurants, two banks, three hotels, three elevators, three lumber yards, four agricultural implement dealers, three livery stables, four blacksmith shops, two wagon shops, three millinery stores, three barber shops, two meat markets, one photograph gallery, two printing offices, one ready-made clothing house, one exclusive dry goods store, three saloons, postoffice.

CHURCHES, SCHOOLS AND SOCIETIES.

Methodist Episcopal Church Society.—Was organized in 1877. This society organized with only three or four members. Rev. Mr. Faus, acting as first pastor, was succeeded by Rev. W. W. Brown, he by Rev. D. M. Beams, he by Rev. R. S. Fysh. The present incumbent is Rev. William Preston. This society now has a membership of thirty-two. It has a Sabbath School with an average attendance of seventy pupils. R. M. McDowell is Superintendent. The society has no church building but holds services in the Masonic Hall. The present officers are: E. Geist, A. B. Smith, M. D. Fox, J. Bowker, J. W. Savage, Trustees; J. L. Brown and E. Geist, Stewards. There is a parsonage which was erected in 1877 at a cost of $450, and a lot upon which is contemplated the erection of a church building this year.

The Catholic Church Society.—Was organized in the spring of 1879, by Rev. Father Pape. The first officers were: M. B. Lynch, Treasurer; J. Conradi, L. Suntz, J. Miller committee. The Rev. Father Norton is the present pastor. The present officers are H. J. Muxen, Secretary and Treasurer; H. Wester and N. Thies, committee. The society now numbers about fifty families. They have a fine frame building 40x60 feet erected in 1879, at a cost of $1,300. This was the first church building in Odebolt.

Presbyterian Church Society.—Was organized in 1879, by Rev. Fullenweider. The first and present officers are: John Bruce, James Taylor, C. W. Sutton, G. W. McKibbon, W. Van Duesen, Trustees, and W. Matthews and W. Simpson, Elders. Rev. Fullenweider was succeeded by Wm. Porter, he by Rev. Gilkerson. S. N. Vail is the present incumbent. This society numbers sixty. There is in connection a Sabbath School with an average attendance of sixty pupils, with C. W. Sutton as Superintendent. There is also a good, substantial frame structure 30x50 feet, with 250 sittings, which was dedicated in May, 1881. The cost of building was $3,300.

Odebolt Public School.—This school became an independent district in April, 1880. The first school taught in Odebolt was taught by Jacob Gable. The first school board consisted of W. W. Stanfield, Z. G. Sparkes, H. Hansen, J. Flanders and J. Ketterer, Trustees; Wm. Graham, Secretary; J. T. Martin, Treasurer. The present officers are the same, except in place of J. Ketterer, who has been succeeded by John Wilson. Mr. Taggert is the Treasurer at present. C. Messer is the Principal of the school, and Anna Beckman and Mrs. Emma Gill, assistants. The enrollment is 220 pupils, with an average attendance of 150. They have a neat frame building containing three rooms, which was erected in 1880 at a cost of $3,000.

Wheeler Lodge No. 398, A. F. & A. M.— Instituted October, 1879, and worked under dispensation until June, 1880, when their

charter was received. The charter members and first officers were:
J. M. Zane, W. M.; W. A. Helsell, S. W.; H. T. Martin, J. W.;
Frank Burleigh, Treasurer; F. A. Cobb, Secretary. H. C. Wheeler,
W. W. Field, Geo. Belt, and Mr. Douglas were among the charter
members. The present officers are: E. P. Messer, W. M.; W. A.
Helsell, S. W.; J. M. Zane, J. W.; C. W. Sutton, S. D.; E. Geist,
J. D.; Wm. Graham, Secretary; Frank Burleigh, Treasurer. The
society has a membership of thirty, and is in a flourishing con-
dition. This society meet once each month in their hall.

Harmony Collegium No. 5, V. A. S.—Was instituted Decem-
ber 3d, 1881. The charter members were: F. L. Dennis, Aaron
Young, A. G. Errenborn, C. D. Boardman, W. E. Mill, C. A.
Stoops, D. A. Watterman, C. R. Dingman, J. A. Gibson, H. B.
Preston, J. H. Wagner, H. F. Wanncke, Irwin Austin, W. Jacob,
E. Schmidt, H. Anderson, L. Halboth, George Halboth, A. B.
Cooley. The first and present officers are: F. L. Dennis, Rector;
Aaron Young, Vice-Rector; A. G. Errenborn, Scribe; C. D.
Boardman, Questor; W. E. Mill, Usher; C. A. Stoops, Speculator;
D. A. Watterman, C. R. Dingman and J. A. Gibson, Curators. The
society has about twenty-five members, and holds meetings once
each month.

Odebolt Lodge, A. O. U. W., No. 217.—Instituted May 25th,
1880. The first officers were: J. W. Dubbs, P. M. W.; J. W.
Burnside, M. W.; C. S. Lee, Foreman; W. Van Duesen. Recorder;
C. B. Francisco, Financier; H. Hansen, Receiver; T. M. Keever,
Guide; J. E. Emspohr, O. W.; A. E. Matthews, J. W.; A. Groman,
and C. D. Boardman, Medical Examiners. The present officers
are: W. Van Duesen, M. W.; F. L. Dennis. Foreman; Ed. Colvin,
Overseer; G. M. Tagget, Recorder; C. D. Boardman, P. M. W.; J.
Mattes, Guide; C. H. Babcock. Receiver; L. Olney, O. W.; C. B.
Francisco, Financier. There is a membership of about forty, and
the Lodge meets once in two weeks.

WALL LAKE.

Wall Lake is situated in Sac County, on the Maple River Railroad, seventeen miles from the Junction. This town is three
miles south of the Lake. It is situated on a beautiful plateau,
which slopes gently from the summit of the surrounding hills,
which form a part of the great watershed that passes entirely
through the state. To the south and west is a beautiful sheet of
water, containing a surface area of three square miles. This inland sea is frequently termed the "goose pond."

The town of Wall Lake was laid out and platted by the Blair
Town Lot and Land Company in 1877. The town plat consists of
two additions containing 300 lots. Perhaps it would be of interest to our readers to relate a coincidence between Storm Lake
and Wall Lake. The first lot in Storm Lake was sold the same

day of the month, the same hour in the day and for the same
money, as was the first lot in Wall Lake just seven years afterwards.

Wall Lake is surrounded with a splendid farming country. The
soil is a rich black loam. Splendid water can be easily obtained.
The population of Wall Lake may be fairly estimated at 400. Arrangements are now being made to erect a large steam grist mill
in this town, which will add much to its interests.

April 1st, 1877, Mr. Donaldson erected the first building for the
purpose of a saloon, the building material being brought across the
country from Storm Lake. The next actual settler was O. A. Anderson, who came April 15th, 1877. Mr. Peck completed his residence July 2d, 1877. P. A. Elpstrand opened a boot and shoe
shop, July 7th. 1877. F. Rohm, of Alta, opened the first blacksmith shop. The first religious services held in Wall Lake were
held at the residence of Mr. Palmer. on Sunday evening, August
15th, 1877, by Rev. W. P Griffin. On the 20th of July work was
begun on the depot, which was completed August 15th, 1877. The
first lot was sold to D. Wayne & Co., cf Carroll. who erected a fine
warehouse and purchased the first load of wheat sold at Wall Lake
of a Mr. North, at 75 cents per bushel. September 10th, 1877.
Wayne & Co. shipped the first car load of wheat. The first lumber yard was started by Wilcox Bros., in August, 1877. September 19th, 1877, G. M. Parker received and sold the first goods in
Wall Lake. August 7th, 1877, the first child was born in Wall
Lake to Mrs. O. A. Anderson. April 2d, 1878, the first death occurred in the family of C. E. Wentworth. April 21st. 1878. a de-
structive tornado passed through the city and vicinity. Seven
buildings near, and two in the town were entirely destroyed, eight
more being considerably damaged. The amount of damage done
was $30,000.

The first telephone was constructed February 11th. 1878, between
J. C. Fletcher's and C. E. Wentworth's places of business. Ehlers and Wentworth did the scientific part of the work.

Wall Lake was incorporated in March. 1881. A. D. Herrig was
elected first Mayor, W. L. Ehlers, Recorder; D. M. Bingman. Geo.
Burgan, F. E. Cheney, H. Mohr, H. J. Simpson and T. E. Wilcox
served as Trustees. These are the present municipal council.

The Wall Lake Journal, a neat. seven-column folio weekly
paper, was started August 29th, 1878, by F. L. Dennis, as a six-column quarto. Cook & Gregg purchased the paper April 1st, 1881,
and ran it as a five-column quarto. T. J. Newburg took charge,
October 1st, 1881. J. L. Kroesen, the present editor and proprietor, purchased the paper December 1st, 1881. Mr. Kroesen
runs a neat job office in connection with his paper, which is Republican in politics and has a circulation of 600.

The business of Wall Lake may be classified as follows: General
stores, three; hardware. two; restaurants three; hotels, two;

lumber yards, two; agricultural implements, four; livery stable, one; harness shops, one; elevator, one; grain dealers, three; saloons, three; furniture store, one; shoe shop, one; millinery stores, two; bank, one; barber shop, one; post-office; drug store, one; meat market, one; blacksmith shops, three; wagon shops, two; printing office, one.

CHURCHES, SCHOOLS AND SOCIETIES.

There are several different religious sects represented in Wall Lake, but there is no regularly organized society. Steps are being taken to organize a society soon. A building for public worship is in contemplation.

Wall Lake Public School.—Wall Lake is an independent school district and has been so for several years. The school building is a neat, frame structure, erected in the summer of 1879. It is 22x 36 feet and cost $750. This building is insufficient to accommodate the large attendance of pupils, and the Masonic Lodge room is used for one department. Emma M. Flanders and Allie Border are the teachers.

Lake Lodge, No. 390, A. F. & A. M.—Dispensation granted June 4th, 1878. Charter granted June 4th, 1879. The charter members were C. N. Levey, H. B. Allen, D. M. Bingman, L. J. Gifford, F. W. Weed, A. D. Herrig, B. E. Allen, C. M. Smith, W. D. Forbes and Wm. Throssel. The Lodge's first officers were C. N. Levey, W. M.; H. B. Allen, S. W.; D. M. Bingman, J. W.; A. D. Herrig, Secretary, and B. E. Allen, Treasurer. The present officers of the Lodge are: C. N. Levey, W. M.; W. L. Ehlers, S. W.; H. B. Allen, J. W.; P. L. Edson, Secretary, and T. E. Wilcox, Treasurer. This Lodge has a membership of thirty-two and is in a flourishing condition. Meetings are held every Wednesday evening on or before each full moon.

Fire Department.—The Wall Lake Hook and Ladder Company was organized September 25th, 1878. It has erected a large engine house and purchased uniforms at a cost of $700. Wall Lake is as well protected from the fire fiend as any other town in Western Iowa.

FLETCHER.

The first settlement in Fletcher was made by Robert Throssel and son, in the spring of 1867. They were followed by Joseph Parkinson, Noah Borah, Wm. Johnston, Thomas Waddicor, and Geo. Trainer, who settled on the east and south of the lake. W. A. Robinson came in the year 1869, and settled on a farm three miles from the present town site. This town was laid out by J. C. Fletcher, in 1880. The town was named after him. The first house on the town site was moved from Wall Lake by W. H. Robinson in the fall of 1880. J. C. Fletcher and Harry Seevers opened the first store in Fletcher. Then followed C. E. Gard and A. J. Thompson. W. H. Robinson erected the first elevator in 1881. J. P. Therkleson opened a hardware store in 1881.

The town of Fletcher is situated in Wall Lake Township, Section 33, and is located on the west side of Wall Lake. This beautiful, placid sheet of water is about three miles in length, and one-fourth of a mile in width. It is said to have derived its name from the fact that the surrounding country is much lower than the surface of the Lake, which is surrounded by a wall of earth and gravel about four feet above the surface of the water. This Lake, in its onward course, does not extend in a direct line, but in such a manner as to form a kind of a horse-shoe shape. The water is as clear as crystal, and abounds in fish of different kinds, and is a most beautiful sight to behold. This location will, in no far distant future, become a beautiful summer resort.

The railroad was completed to this point in the fall of 1879. The depot was erected in the fall of 1880.

The first hotel was opened by W. H. Robinson in 1880, and was known as the Lake House. The first lumber yard was opened by H. L. Briggs. The first postmaster was W. A. Robinson, who was appointed in December, 1880. He is also the present postmaster.

The population of the town is now estimated at 300. This town contains: Three general stores, two hardware, one furniture, one lumber yard, one meat market, one hotel, two saloons, one barber, two elevators, two agricultural implement warehouses, two blacksmith shops, one wagon shop, one livery stable, one drug store, one boot and shoe store, one restaurant.

There is no regular organized religious sect in this place. The Baptists hold meetings every Sabbath; W. N. McKendrick serves in the capacity of pastor. This society contemplate building a church this spring, when it is hoped they will have a regular organization.

Fletcher School.—A school of twenty-four pupils, with Miss Anna Searle as teacher, is held in Fletcher. There is no school building.

34

SAC COUNTY BIOGRAPHIES.

SAC CITY.

William Allen was born in Richmond, Va., in 1822; moved to McHenry county. Ill., in 1844, and engaged in blacksmithing. He went to California in 1849, and remained seventeen years. Three years of the time he was engaged in mining, and the remainder on a ranch. The steamboat landing in Tehama county, Cal., on the Sacramento river, known as Allen's Landing, was named after Mr A., for the reason of his owning the land and a large wood-yard there. In 1868 he sold out and moved to Chicago, Ill., and engaged in business; removed to Fort Dodge, Ia., and was engaged in the mercantile business there for three years; then came to Sac City, and engaged in the same business, which he sold to George Parker in 1876. He owns considerable country and town property, and has retired from active business.

Thomas Alexander, farmer, was born in Coshocton county, O., in 1827; moved to Sac county, Ia., in 1861, and purchased land one mile north of Sac City. He has one of the finest farms in the county. He owns 314 acres of well improved land, a fine bearing orchard of about three acres, and fifty acres of good timber.

E. F. Baxter, station agent and conductor, was born at Sidney Plain, N. Y., in 1833; moved to Rockford, Ill., in 1851 and engaged in mercantile business. In 1861 he moved to Wheatland, Ia.; thence to Marshalltown, in 1874, and in September, 1879, came to Sac City and took charge of the depot. He makes two trips a day as conductor, and during his absence the depot is in charge of Frank L. Stayner, operator. Mr. Baxter is agent for the American express company.

A. T. Benton, M. D., was born in Johnson county, Indiana, in 1847; moved to Dallas county, Iowa, in 1852. He attended the Adel High School several years; entered the College of Physicians and Surgeons, at Keokuk in 1867 and graduated in 1869. He then engaged in practice at Adel, where he remained until July, 1871, then came to Sac City. Office at his residence, on the south side of public square.

Hon. Eugene Criss. farmer, stock-raiser, and proprietor of the City Mills, was born in Preston county, West Virginia, in 1822; removed to Davis county, Illinois, in 1840; thence to Sac county, Iowa, in 1854, locating on Coon river, where the present town of Sac City was shortly afterwards platted by Wagner Bros., Evans and himself. Mr. Criss built the first dwelling house in the town, which at that early day was considered a fine structure. The lumber for frames and the doors and windows was hauled from Dubuque, with ox teams, and this was for several years a tavern and stopping place for freighters and travelers. He began the erection of the City Saw Mills in 1866, which were not completed until eight years after, and during that time cut a race twenty-eight feet deep and two hundred feet in length, which gave a fall of nine feet. In 1872 he built the flouring mill, which is a three-story building and fitted with the best of machinery. He owns one thousand acres of land adjoining town, and feeds about six car-loads of cattle every winter. He owns an elevator and deals in grain in partnership with Mr. Hanger, who has charge of the business. Mr. Criss was county judge for several years and representative in the State legislature.

Childs Brothers, dealers in dry goods, groceries, hats, caps and furnishing goods, came from Fort Dodge, Ia., where they had been engaged in business for ten years, and established their present business in Nov., 1879, in Bank block. They carry a large and complete stock.

J. L. Criss, merchant, was born in Wis., in 1846; came with parents to Sac City, Ia., in 1856. He engaged in business at Grant City, remained one year, then moved to this city. He has a fine store, and carries a full stock of dry goods, groceries, boots, shoes, etc. He employs three clerks and does an extensive business. He has a branch store at Early, Ia., which is managed by F. Rodda.

Levi Davis, cashier of the Sac county bank, was born at Newcastle, Ind., in 1841; moved with parents to Solon, Ia., in September, 1855. He received a diploma from the State Normal School, of Iowa City, and in August of the same year moved to Sac City, where he taught school two years. He went to Marshalltown in 1865 and was principal of the schools there for a year, then was elected county superintendent of schools, which office he held two years in Marshall county. He came back to Sac City and taught in the city schools for two years; was elected clerk of the courts in 1870 and county recorder in 1872. He was admitted to the practice of law in 1870, at a session of the Sioux Rapids district court, Judge H. Ford presiding. He went to California in 1874 and was for one year principal of the schools at Martinez; returned to Sac county and became cashier of the Sac County Bank, of which he is one of the stockholders.

R. H. Derby, carpenter, contractor and cabinet maker, was born in Wyoming county, N. Y., in 1853, where he remained until 1873, then moved with his father to Sac City, Iowa, where they engaged in mercantile business. They sold business and together engaged in present business.

Hon. Ed. R. Duffie is a native of Copenhagen, Lewis county, New York, where he resided until he had come to years of manhood, and where he began the study of law. In 1866 Mr. Duffie was sent as agent for a citizen of New York to the State of Texas.

His mission was to establish the validity of the grant of certain
lands from the Republic of Texas to the aforesaid citizen of New
York. Mr. Duffie left Texas and went to St. Louis, where he
sought employment through an educational agency, and was
offered and accepted the principalship of the public school at
Andrew, Jackson county, Iowa. He came to Sac County in 1866,
and engaged in teaching. In the spring of 1867 he was admitted
to the bar. In the spring of 1868 he formed a partnership with
Hon. D. C. Early, and henceforth devoted himself to the practice
of his profession. In 1869 he was elected County Treasurer of
Sac County, and in the fall of 1872 was elected Representative in
the General Assembly. Mr. Duffie, in 1875, accepted the Republican nomination for District Judge, and was elected in the fall.*
Was married in 1867, at Maquoketa, Jackson County, Iowa.

Hon. D. Carr Early, president of the Sac County Bank, was
born in Ohio, in 1830; removed to Sac City, Ia., in 1856, where at
that time there was but one building besides a log school house.
He pre-empted land on which he lived a short time to secure it.
He was elected deputy treasurer and recorder in 1857, and was re-
elected the three subsequent elections. He was afterwards elected
county judge, holding the office one term, the office then being
dispensed with. He established a real estate business when first
coming to the county, and did a general banking business several
years previous to connection with present bank. He still does a
land, loan and insurance business in connection with banking.
The bank was incorporated in 1876.

S. M. Elwood, of the firm of Davis & Elwood, attorneys at law,
was born in Greensburg, Pa., in Sept., 1850; moved with parents
to Grinnell, Ia., where he attended the Iowa College. He graduated
from the Iowa City law school in the class of '73. He moved to
Sac City in the autumn of 1875, and engaged in practice with Capt.
Stanfield, now of Odebolt. He formed his present partnership in
1877. He attends strictly to trial business, and is considered one
of the most successful attorneys in the county. Mr. Davis attends
to the land, loan and insurance business of the firm.

N. B. Flack, recorder of Sac county, was born in N. Y. in 1841.
He enlisted Sept. 2d, 1862, at Lisbon, in the 142nd N. Y. Vol.;
was at the battle of Fort Fisher, and was subsequently wounded
in the leg. He was discharged June 16th, 1865, and returned to
N. Y. In Oct., 1866, he moved to Scott City, Mo., and engaged
in milling; remained four years, then returned to N. Y. He then
came to Sac county, Ia., and purchased land which he improved
and still owns. In May, 1870, he came to Sac City and was employed by Platt & Criss as book-keeper. He was elected recorder
in the fall of 1874, to fill a vacancy, and for the full term at the
next election on the republican ticket. He has been re-elected
each term since.

John M. Fox, hardware dealer, was born in France in 1836; came to America in 1850. He learned the tinners' trade in N. Y. city, and in 1862 moved to Waterloo, Ia.; thence to Winona, Minn., where he worked at his trade two years, and after visiting N. Y., located at Waverly, Ia., remaining there eight years. He came to Sac City in 1874 and engaged in his present business. He carries a large and complete stock of hardware and tinware. He is assisted in his business by his sons, John and George.

E. F. Gifford, barber, was born in Erie county, Pa., in 1854; came to Ia. in 1871, and located at Independence. He removed to Carroll, and in July, 1872, came to Sac City and engaged in present business. He owns the building, of which he occupies one-half of the lower floor for a barber shop, renting the other half for confectionery store. The upper story is fitted for photograph gallery. Mr. Gifford employs a first-class barber and runs two chairs.

D. F. Gifford, druggist, was born in Erie county, Pa., in 1832. In Oct., 1854, he moved to Buchanan county, Ia., and engaged in contracting and building, then furniture, then drug business. He moved to Sac county in 1867, remaining one and one-half years, then moved to Carroll, Carroll county, where he engaged in the furniture and drug business, building the first business house in the town. In 1874 he sold out and returned to Sac City, engaging in carpentry until entering the drug business in July, 1879. His store is on upper Main street. He carries a full stock of drugs, paints, oils, stationery and toilet goods. He is agent for the Chicago Singer sewing machine.

H. C. Graff, of the firm of Graff Bros. & Whipple, came to Sac City in 1880 from Emerson, Mills county, Ia., where he was engaged in the hardware business three years. In partnership with D. W. Graff and A. A. Whipple, he purchased the stock and business of Terwilleger Bros., and engaged in his present business. The business is conducted by H. C. Graff. They carry a full stock of hardware, tin and shelfware, stoves, etc., making specialties of builders' hardware and barb wire. They are special agents for the Glidden barbed wire, and also for Charter Oak stoves. They employ two tinners.

Charles D. Goldsmith, attorney at law, was born in Middletown, Orange county, N. Y., in 1842; moved to Webster City, Ia., in 1869, and there finished the study of law, with Jacob Skinner, and was admitted to practice the same year. In 1873 he moved to Newell, Buena Vista county, where he practiced seven years. He moved to Sac City in 1880, and opened an office in the Commercial Bank building. He attends strictly to trial business.

P. H. Hankins and J. Y. Campfield, of the firm of P. H. Hankins & Co., dealers in lumber, coal, lime and agricultural imple-

ments, established business in 1879. Their office and yards are on
the west side of the railroad track, near the depot. They are agents
for the Grand Detour goods, McCormick and Champion reapers
and other leading manufactures.

A. H. Hendrickson, proprietor of the Hendrickson House, was
born in Oswego county, N. Y., in Jan., 1836; moved to McHenry
county, Ill., in 1856, was engaged in the hotel business two years,
then in the stock business until 1868; then moved to Sac City, engaged in mercantile business for two years; then engaged in the
hotel business for a time, after which he farmed for two years. In
Feb., 1875, he purchased the hotel which he now owns. He enlarged the building in 1881 making it the largest hotel in the city.

Hon. W. H. Hobbs, banker and insurance and real estate agent,
was born in New York City in 1837; moved with parents to New
Orleans; thence in 1852 to La Fayette county, Wis., where he was
employed by Judge Criss, as clerk. He moved to Sac City, Ia., in
1855, and pre-empted 160 acres of land and engaged in farming.
In 1858 he was elected clerk of the courts, which office he held
two terms. He was elected auditor in 1866, which office he held
until 1871; then was elected county treasurer and held office for
three terms. He engaged in real estate business in 1873, with D.
C. Early, and in 1875, in partnership with Early & Davis, established the Sac County bank. He takes charge of the land and insurance business of the firm. He has a very fine residence in the
city and owns a half section of farm land three miles north of
town, and other city and country property.

D. Herrold and S. F. Lusher, of the firm of D. Herrold & Co.,
deal in groceries, queensware, provisions, etc. Their place of business is on the corner of Main street and public square. The business was established in 1875 by Mr. Lusher and the present firm
has existed since Nov., 1881. They do an extensive business and
intend extending their premises the coming season.

M. H. Herrold, merchant, was born in Athens county, O., in
1844; moved with parents to La Porte county, Ind., in 1851. He
followed farming until 1864, then came to Sac City, Ia., and engaged in present business. He carries a well selected stock of dry
goods, boots, shoes, furnishing goods and notions. He intends in
the near future to build a brick block, feeling the need of more
room for his rapidly increasing business.

Louis Hunefield, proprietor of blacksmith and plow works, was
born in the province of Lippe Detmold, Germany, in 1829; came
to the U. S. in 1849, and located at St. Louis, Mo., where he
worked at his trade one and one-half years, then moved to Dodge
county, Wis., where he worked at his trade nearly twenty-two
years. He came to Sac county in 1872, and engaged in farming
for a year and a half; then sold part of his farm, retaining eighty

acres, and moved to Sac City. He was in the employ of Mr. Fishman for about eight years, then purchased the business. He employs three men and does a large business.

Joseph H. James, harness dealer, was born in Iowa county, Wis., in 1856, learned his trade at Mineral Point, and in Feb., 1877, moved to Webster City, Ia. In June, 1879, he came to Sac City and purchased the business and stock of Lewis Vanderworker; has since purchased building and lot. He employs three men and carries a full stock of harness, saddles, robes, blankets, whips, etc. In the spring of 1880 he established a branch shop at Newell, Buena Vista county, which is the only one at that place.

Jones & Baxter, proprietors of the City livery, feed and sale barn, established business in 1878. They own and occupy the barn on the corner of Fifth and River Sts. Have stalls for forty-five horses, keep twenty horses and twelve buggies and carriages for livery purposes. This is the only livery barn in the city.

John Kessler, wagon maker, came to Sac City, Ia., from Kenosha, Wis., in 1872, and established his present business. He occupies a shop on the south side of the public square; manufactures wagons and buggies and does a general repair business.

F. H. Knights, of the firm of George Knights & Co., dealers in boots, shoes, hats, caps, gloves mittens and rubber goods, came to Sac City in Sept., 1881, from Dubuque, Ia., where he had been engaged in the jewelry business for three years, and established his present business in partnership with his father, George Knights. They have the county agency for the Crown sewing machine.

R. H. Lamoreux, postmaster and druggist, was born in Orange county, N. Y., in 1839; moved to Wausau, Wis., and engaged in the lumber business. He moved to Sac City, Ia., in 1868 and engaged in the grocery business, which he conducted nine months, then purchased a farm and for four years engaged in farming. In the winter of 1872 he engaged in clerking in the drug store of Eli Camp, and also took charge of the postoffice under J. E. Armstrong. He purchased the drug business and stock in the spring of 1875 and the following spring was commissioned postmaster. His drug store, which is elegantly fitted, contains a full line of drugs, stationery, books, paints, oils, toilet and fancy articles, etc. He is assisted by F. B. Knight, deputy postmaster, and is also a registered pharmacist.

Chas. E. Lane, clerk of the courts, was born in St. Lawrence county, N. Y., in 1874; moved with parents to St. Catherines, Canada West, in 1846; thence to Dyersville, Dubuque county, Ia., in 1856. He moved to Sac county in 1873; bought land and engaged in farming in Eden township until the autumn of 1878, at which time he was elected to his present office, on the republican ticket. He was re-elected in 1880.

A. B. Mason, attorney at law, was born in Tama county, Ia., in 1857. He attended the Toledo High School for several years and afterwards the Iowa College of Law, of Des Moines, from which he graduated in 1880. He came to Sac City the same year and opened a law office in Sac county bank block, on second floor, also does a land, loan and insurance business.

James N. Miller, editor and proprietor of the *Sac Sun*, is a native of Pa., and was for several years editor of the *Republican*, published at Waynesburg. In 1870 he came to Iowa and located at Eldora, Hardin county, remained only a short time, then came to Sac City, and established the *Sac Sun*, which has grown to importance and is the official paper of the county. In 1878 he built the new office which he now occupies. The paper is an eight-column folio, and has a circulation of eight hundred. Mr. Miller is prepared to do first-class job work of all kinds.

H. T. Martin, county superintendent of schools, was born in Putnam county, Ind., in 1839; moved with parents to Boone county, Ia., in 1853. He returned to Ind. in 1855, and attended the Cloverdale Seminary for two years; spent the following winter in Mo., and in 1858 returned to Boone county, Ia. He engaged in teaching school, and for twelve years taught in that county. He then entered the employ of the railroad company and was agent at Ontario, Story county, for eight years, and for four years at Odebolt, Sac county, where, in partnership with Mr. Bennett, the present editor, he established the Odebolt *Observer*. He was also engaged in the restaurant business ten months. In the fall of 1881 he was elected county superintendent, on the independent ticket.

George M. Parker, merchant, was born in Hartford, Ill., in 1847; moved with parents to Manchester, Ia., in 1851; thence to Delhi, where he received his education. He traveled for wholesale houses of Chicago and Dubuque for six years. In 1872 he engaged in business at Earlville, Ia., and two years later came to Sac City and established his present business. The store is in the Bank block. In 1881 he commenced the erection of a creamery, which is fitted with a ten-horse power engine, and will have a capacity of from 2,500 to 3,000 lbs. per day. This is the only creamery in the county; it will employ from fifteen to twenty teams, and from twenty to thirty men. Mr. P. has for two years previous conducted the business on a smaller scale.

A. D. Peck, county auditor, was born in Onondaga county, N. Y., in 1846. He graduated from the Syracuse High School in 1872 and the same year moved to Cedar Rapids, Ia. He came to Sac county in the spring of 1873 purchased land and engaged in farming until the autumn of 1877, when he was elected auditor and was re-elected in 1879 and 1881.

Asa Platt, stock dealer and farmer, was born in Middlesex county, Conn., in 1830; moved with parents to Chautauqua county, N. Y., in 1839; thence in 1848 to Erie county, Penn., and engaged in the lumber business. In 1856 he moved to Sac City, Ia., which had just been laid out and contained only two log cabins. He pre-empted land near town, one hundred acres of which he laid out in town lots, and nearly all of which he has since sold. He engaged in mercantile business in 1864, which he continued for twelve years. In 1874 he erected a fine brick and stone residence in the city, at a cost of ten thousand dollars. He carries on his farm and is extensively engaged in buying and shipping stock.

J. O. Platt, of the firm of Schaller & Platt, proprietors of meat market, was born at Saybrook, Conn., in Dec., 1836; removed with parents to Chautauqua county, N. Y., in 1839. In 1850 he moved to Erie county, Pa., was employed for a time in a meat market, and afterwards engaged in business for himself; sold out in 1866 and moved to Sac county, Ia. He engaged in farming until 1874 when he moved to Sac City and opened a meat market which he run three years then sold. He next engaged in the stock business for several years, and in Aug., 1881, bought an interest in his present business. Mr. P. has been a member of the board of supervisors.

A. S. Platt, senior member of the firm of Platt & Platt, dealers in clothing and furnishing goods, was born in Windsor county, Vt., in 1839; moved to Dubuque, Ia., in 1870 and was in the employ of the I. C. R. R. four years. He moved to Osage, Wis., and was for about six years a member of the firm of Simons & Platt, grocers. He came to Sac City, Ia., in Dec., 1880, and purchased business and stock of J. M. Woodard and engaged in his present business. In 1881 he took into partnership his nephew C. A. Platt.

C. E. Read, furniture dealer and undertaker, was born in March, Canada, Dec. 20th, 1826; moved to Toledo, O., in April, 1856; was engaged in the drug business four years; then moved to Huron county, Mich., where he was engaged in same business for three years. In Aug., 1865, he came to Sac City and engaged in contracting and building. He entered his present business in 1873; employs first-class cabinet-maker, and carries a fine stock of everything in his line.

E. M. Reynolds is business manager for C. Hatfield, furniture dealer and undertaker. This business was established in 1879, and contains a complete stock of furniture and undertakers' goods, and is the agency for the White, Wilson and Victor sewing machines, also for the Mason & Hamlin organs.

Philip Schaller, county treasurer, was born in Woerth, province of Alsace, Germany, in 1838; came to America and landed at N. Y. City in Apr., 1854, and in Dec. of the same year located at Dubuque, Ia., and engaged in wagon-making. He enlisted in

1862 at National, Ia., in the 27th Ia. Inft., was sent to Minn. among the Indians, and thence south; was with Gens. Sherman, Smith, Steele and Thomas in some of the principal battles; was mustered out at the close of the war, and returned to Clayton county, Ia. He purchased land in Sac county in 1868, returned to Clayton county and remained until 1870, then engaged in farming in Sac county, on 640 acres of land. He was agent for the Iowa Railroad Land company while living on the farm, and was afterwards transferred to Storm Lake, and held the agency for Buena Vista county until he was elected treasurer of Sac county in 1877, to which office he has been re-elected each successive term since. He is now land agent for this county, having been appointed in Jan., 1878. He has been a member of the board of supervisors of this county for five years. He organized a Farmers' Mutual Insurance Co. in 1874, and was elected as its President, which office he still holds. The insurance company has about $800,000, issued in policies and on property.

J. & W. C. Shull, of the firm of Shull Bros., dealers in lumber, lime, coal, hair, cement, etc., office on Main street, established business in 1880. They were formerly of Montgomery county, N. Y. J. Shull graduated from the Fairfield Seminary and entered the employ of Walter Shoemaker, lumber dealer, Chicago, Ill.; came to Sac City in 1880. W. C. Shull, previous to coming to this city, was engaged in the drug business at Little Falls, N. Y.; afterwards with D. R. Dyche & Co., druggists, Chicago; came to Sac City in May, 1881, and formed present partnership.

George A. Smith, watchmaker and jeweler, was born in Belvidere, Ill., in 1851; moved to Waverly, Bremer county, Ia., in 1855. He attended the high school, at Ypsilanti, Mich., from 1868 to 1872; returned to Bremer county and learned his trade. He moved to Sac City in Dec., 1874, and established his present business in the Commercial Bank block. He keeps a fine line of clocks, watches, jewelry, silverware and opticans' goods, and in connection carries a fine stock of stationery, books and newspapers.

Rev. Robert Smylie, pastor of the M. E. church, was born in Ontario, Canada, in 1849. He graduated from Victoria College, Coburg, in 1868; entered the ministry the following year and filled various pulpits in Ontario. He was ordained at Dunville, in 1873; in Oct., 1880, he came to Sac City, Ia., and took present charge.

George Stanley, proprietor of the Stanley House, came to Sac City in May, 1881, from Bloomington, Wis., where he had been engaged in the mercantile business for eleven years. He purchased his present hotel property, and after thoroughly renovating and refitting it, engaged in present business. He keeps a first-class house and runs a 'bus to and from trains.

B. W. Trout, deputy recorder, was born in LeRoy, Bradford county, Pa., in March, 1843. He enlisted in the 106th Pa. Vol., and was in several of the most important engagements of the war.

He was wounded at Gettysburg and also at Petersburg, June, 1864, where he was captured and confined in Libby Prison a few days; started for Macon, Ga., and escaped, was recaptured and taken to Lynchburg, Va., thence to Raleigh, N. C. He was paroled in March, 1865, and discharged the following April. He came to Sac City, Ia., in May, 1867, and engaged in farming one season; taught school the following winter, and continued teaching until 1871, when he was appointed deputy treasurer, which office he held until 1878, excepting during the year 1874. He then filled a vacancy as recorder, and was appointed deputy upon Mr. Flack's being elected recorder. Mrs. B. W. Trout, milliner, established business in Dec., 1880. She carries a full and elegant line of millinery and ladies' furnishing goods, and employs a first-class milliner trimmer.

Henry L. Willson, sheriff, was born in St. Lawrence county, N. Y., in 1841; moved with parents in 1851, to Dundas county, Canada West. In 1869 he moved to Clinton, Clinton county, Ia., and engaged in contracting and building; thence to Sac county in the autumn of 1875 and followed same business. He was elected to his present office in the autumn of 1881 and moved to Sac City in Jan., 1882.

Christopher Waddell, collection agent and auctioneer, was born in Oxford, Eng. He was for several years in the Royal Mail West India service, also East India service. In 1851 he came to America and located at York, Dane county, Wis.; was engaged in farming, also livery business. In 1872 came to Sac City and engaged in the livery business. He was elected sheriff in 1876 and re-elected in 1877 and 1879 on the Democratic ticket, the county being republican by a majority of nine hundred. This speaks well for Mr. W.'s popularity.

John L. Woodward, junior member and business manager of the firm of Condron & Woodward, dealers in grain and machinery, was born in Champaign county, O. He served during the war of the rebellion a short time, doing garrison duty, after which he bought land in Dallas county, Ia. He engaged in the grain business at Dallas Centre, which he continued for two years and in 1871 located at Sac City, where he engaged in the mercantile business. In 1880 established business as above. During 1881 the firm shipped one hundred cars of grain.

ODEBOLT.

F. R. Bennett is editor and proprietor of the Odebolt Observer, which was established in July, 1880, and is a six-column quarto paper. In 1847 he edited and published the Advertiser, at Rock Island, Ill., afterwards was connected with various papers in Clinton county, Ia. He came to Odebolt in 1880. This is the only democratic paper published in the county and it has a subscription list of about 500. Office on second floor of Schmitz block and is thoroughly fitted up as a job office. He employs three compositors.

C. D. Boardman, physician and druggist, was born at Potsdam, St. Lawrence county, N. Y., in 1854; moved with parents to Lyons, Clinton county, Ia.; there attended school, and in 1871 entered the Agricultural College, of Ames. He graduated in 1874 and in the winter of same year entered the Chicago Medical College, from which he graduated in the spring of 1877. The same year he opened an office at Monticello, Ia., also engaged in the drug business, in partnership with Dr. Mellett; at the end of one year Dr. Boardman became sole proprietor. In May, 1880, he moved the stock to Odebolt and established his present business.

J. C. Bodine, farmer and stock raiser, was born in N. Y. in 1835; in 1865 moved to Aurora, Ill., where he engaged in the stock business. He moved to Grinnell, Ia., in 1868; thence to Sac county, in 1874. He purchased in Cook township, where he now resides, a farm of 320 acres, which is well improved. He also owns another farm, containing 160 acres, which he rents. Mr. B. is one of the representative farmers of this county; has filled many offices of trust; in politics is a democrat.

S. H. Bowman, of the firm of S. H. Bowman & Co., dealers in lumber, coal, lime and mixed paints, was born in Baltimore, Md., in March, 1854. In 1873 he entered the Business College of Poughkeepsie, N. Y., from which he graduated in May, 1874. He went to Neb. in 1878, and was engaged in the lumber business at various towns. In March, 1880, he came to Odebolt, Ia., and established the above business; he is the senior member and business manager of the firm, which has branch yards at Ida Grove, Battle Creek and Danbury.

J. W. Burnside, dealer in dry goods, boots, shoes, notions, carpets, etc., was born in Steuben county, N. Y., in 1833; moved with parents to Crawford county, Ia., when quite young. He received his education at the Methodist University of Delaware, O., afterwards attended Bryant & Stratton's Commercial College, of Chicago, from which he graduated in 1854. He then engaged in the mercantile business at Garden Prairie, Ill. In the spring of 1862 he enlisted in the 95th, Ill. Inft.; remained in the service until 1866. During that time he was transferred from the volunteer service to the regular army. He was in several important engagements, was wounded at the seige of Vicksburg, also at Fort Du Risse. After leaving the army he located at Boone, Ia., and engaged in mercantile business. In 1878 came to Odebolt and engaged in business as above.

Frank L. Dennis, editor and proprietor of the Odebolt Observer, was born in Clinton county, Ia., in 1852. He learned his trade in the DeWitt Observer office; remained there until 1878, then moved to Wall Lake, Sac county, and established the Wall Lake Journal, which he sold in April, 1881. He came to Odebolt and purchased the Odebolt Reporter, which was first established at Sac City by W. W. Yarham, who moved it to this city in November, 1877. The office is in the basement of Wright's Opera Block and is fitted for a first-class news and job office. The paper is republican in politics, is a six-column quarto, with a subscription list of six hundred.

Henry Dockstader, proprietor of the Revere House, was born in Jefferson county, N. Y., in 1836; moved in 1842 to Tioga county, Pa.; thence to Jones county, Ia., in 1857. He there engaged in farming until 1872, then moved to Panora, Guthrie county, where he farmed until the autumn of 1881. He came to Odebolt and took charge of the Odebolt House, which he thoroughly renovated and refitted, changing the name to Revere. It is now a first-class hotel.

Alfred G. Erlenborn, dealer in general merchandise, was born at Mendota, Ill., in 1860. He received his education at the Jesuit College, of Chicago, Ill., from which he graduated in 1875. He entered the banking house of Erlenborn Bros., at Mendota, of which bank his father was the senior partner. In 1879 he went to Denver, Col., was there employed as bookkeeper in a wholesale grocery house. He returned to Iowa in 1881 and located at Odebolt. He engaged in the loan business and also as bookkeeper for Warneke. Afterwards engaged in business as above; also does a loan and insurance business; is assisted by his brothers, Otto and Julius and W. Pitschner.

C. E. George, of the firm of George & Coy, attorneys at law, was born at Alexandria, Grafton county, N. H., Dec. 20th, 1857. He received his education at the high school of Bristol, N. H., and the New London, N. H., and Newbury, Vt., Academies. He read law for two years with Hon. S. B. Page, at Woodville, Vt., and in 1879 graduated from the Vermont University, obtaining the degree of A. B. He also graduated from the law department of the Ann Arbor, Mich., University. He came to Odebolt, Ia., in March, 1880, and engaged in the practice of his profession. During the summer of the same year he formed a partnership as above. Dell Coy, of the above firm, was born in Kane county, Ill., Aug. 15th, 1857. He received his education at Wheaton College, Wheaton, Ill., and in 1878 entered the Union College of law, at Chicago, from which he graduated in 1880. Came to Odebolt the same year. They attend strictly to law, collection and insurance business, and although both young, have placed themselves in the foremost ranks of the profession.

A. Groman, M. D., was born in Lake county, Ind., in 1856. He received his preparatory education at Crown Point Seminary and studied medicine with his father, Dr. C. Groman. In the autumn of 1876 he entered the Homœopathic College, of Chicago, from which he graduated in March, 1878. He opened an office at Odebolt. Ia., in June of the same year. Office on second floor of Wright's Opera block; consultation room adjoining.

Henry Hanson, grain. seed and stock dealer, was born in Sweden; came to America in 1868 and landed in N. Y.; remained in that state until 1874, when he came to Sac county, Ia. He purchased land and farmed until 1877, then moved to Odebolt and engaged in present business. He owns a steam elevator fitted with all of the latest improved machinery, employs nine men in elevators and warehouses, two bookkeepers and C. B. Hatfield, grain and stock buyer.

W. A. Helsell, of the firm of Zane & Helsell, attorneys at law, was born in Millersburg, O., in 1855; moved with parents to Iowa in 1861. He graduated in the scientific course at the Ames Agricultural College in 1877 and in 1879 graduated from the law department of Simpson's Centenary College. He was admitted to the bar before the supreme court at Des Moines, June 9th, 1879; and in the July following formed a partnership as above. He attends to the law and trial business and Mr. Zane to the loan, insurance and abstract business of the firm. They have a complete set of abstract books.

Martin Keck, proprietor of restaurant, ice cream and oyster parlors, also dealer in fancy groceries, confectionery, cigars, tobacco, etc., came to Sac county, Ia., in 1878; engaged in farming, then came to Odebolt and established business as above.

J. H. Kitterer & Co., proprietors of the Pioneer hardware store, which was established in 1878 by W. Van Dusen, purchased the business in Aug., 1879. The firm is composed of J. H. Kitterer and Joseph Mattes; they are men of long experience in the hardware business, having previous to coming to this city been engaged in the same. They carry a stock estimated at $18,000, and do a driving business. They employ one clerk and three tinners. Make specialties of Glidden barbed wire, "Splendid" heating stoves, "Diamond" and "Acorn" cook stoves.

C. S. Lee, dealer in staple and fancy groceries, came to Denison, Ia., in 1869 from Philadelphia, Pa. In May, 1877, he moved to Odebolt, and opened a restaurant; two years later added a full stock of groceries. He has since closed out the restaurant and now attends strictly to his fast increasing grocery trade.

Joseph Mercer, dealer in agricultural implements, was born in Beaver county, Pa., March 1st, 1856; moved the same year with parents to De Kalb county, Ill. In June, 1880, he entered the employ of the Sandwich manufacturing company, at Sandwich, Ill.; traveled for them until Nov., 1881, when he located at Odebolt and engaged in business as above. He is agent for the goods

manufactured by the following named firms: Sandwich Co.,
Briggs & Enochs. Scandia Plow Co., of Rockford. Ill.. Vandiver
Co., of Quincy, Ill., Daly Harrow Co. and others.

E. A. Moody, painter and grainer. was born in Milwaukee. Wis.
in 1848; was educated at Notre Dame College, of South Bend.
Ind. In 1861 he enlisted in the regular army. and served during
the war of the rebellion. Was discharged in 1865; returned to Milwaukee and learned his trade. In 1868 he moved to Cincinnati.
O., where he remained one year, then went west, and after a time
located at Yankton, Dak. He returned to Milwaukee and soon
after moved to Cherokee. Ia.; was there engaged in business three
years. In Dec., 1878. he came to Odebolt and engaged in business. He does a good business and employs five men.

Frank A. Ress, insurance agent. came to Odebolt from Boone,
Ia., where he had resided for twenty-five years. He first engaged
in teaching school, and in Feb., 1880, established business as above.
His office is at the Mayor's office, over the City Drug Store. He
is agent for the Home Life Association, of Burlington. Iowa, for
three counties, Sac, Crawford and Carroll.

H. F. Warneke, dealer in grain and stock, came to Odebolt. Ia..
from Plattville, Wis., in 1879. He established a saloon, which he
continued until Aug., 1881. and in the Sept. following he established his present business. He has shipped since establishing
business to Jan. 1st, 1882, two hundred car loads. His warehouse has a capacity of ten thousand bushels; employs five men.

H. C. Wheeler, farmer and stock raiser. was born May 10th.
1835, at Hopkinton. N. H.; the following year moved with parents to Chicago, Ill. He there received his education and finished
at the Academy of Warrensville. In 1854 he went to San Francisco, Cal.; there engaged in the real estate business. and after two
years returned to Chicago. He remained two years and again
went to San Francisco. He became one of the first members of
the San Francisco Stock Exchange and remained there until 1864.
After spending one and one-half years traveling in Europe, he
came to Sac county, Ia., and invested in real estate and commenced extensive farming operations. He now owns a large tract
of land adjoining Odebolt on three sides. Also one thousand
acres in Plymouth county, and one thousand acres in Crawford
county. In 1877 he donated the right of way, town site and
$2,000 in cash to the railroad company. He laid out and owns
two additions to the town of about one hundred acres. He resides
in Wheeler township, three miles from the city; has three boarding
houses on the farm, employs forty men and fifty teams. He has a
herd of sixty head of Short Horn cattle and forty Clydesdale
horses and colts, besides other stock. He has spent considerable
time in making practical a steam plow for use on his farm; it in-

cludes ten plows in a frame. Mr. Wheeler is one of the directors of the State Fair Association. He owns valuable property in Chicago.

John Wright, banker, came from Cedar county, Ia., to Sac county in 1872. He purchased 1,000 acres of land in partnership with his brother, N. Wright, and engaged in farming until Nov., 1878, at which time he opened the bank, having previously erected the bank block, the front room of which is occupied by the bank and contains a fire-proof vault and a Marvin safe, with an electric time-lock. The rear room is occupied by George & Coy, attorneys. Mr. Wright does an extensive loan business in partnership with C. E. George. He has recently erected, on the corner of Second and Maple streets, a brick block, containing two store rooms below and two offices in front on second floor, and fine opera hall in rear. This hall is well fitted with stage, scenery, dressing rooms and well lighted. He also owns other valuable city property.

Wheelock & Rehterger, dealers in agricultural implements, on corner of Second and Maple sts., handle McCormick's goods, also goods from all the leading firms, including Cook's buggies and carriages. R. U. Wheelock has been in the employ of the McCormick Co. for fifteen years, and is a man of extensive experience with machinery. Mr. Rehterberger is by trade a blacksmith, and owns a shop in the rear of warehouse, on Maple street, where he employs two men. He does a large business, making a specialty of wagon and buggy work.

Winchell & Webster are grain dealers and proprietors of the Star store. The grain business was established in Oct., 1879. They have three flax and wheat warehouses on First st., with capacity of forty thousand bushels. They shipped during the year 1881 three hundred cars of grain. They also own a coal yard. The store, which is situated on First and Second sts.—the building running through from one to the other—is two stories high; the first is occupied by dry goods, groceries, queensware and clothing, the second by boots, shoes, carpets and gentlemen's furnishing goods. They carry an average stock of $20,000, and employ three clerks and a book-keeper. Messrs. Winchell & Webster were formerly of Chicago; the former was there engaged in a wholesale house, and the latter in the coal trade.

John M. Zane, of the firm of Zane & Helsell, attorneys at law, was born in Cumberland county, N. J., Oct. 16th, 1845. He received his education at Bridgeton. At an early age he moved to Philadelphia, Pa.; during the rebellion he was for two years a member of the U. S. quartermaster's department. In Sept., 1866, he went to Springfield, Ill., there read law in the office of Herndon & Zane. He taught school at intervals while reading law; in Feb., 1872, he moved to Jasper county, Ia., and in Dec., 1873, was admitted to the bar at Newton, under Judge L. C. Blanchard.

He began the practice of law at Prairie City. In 1874, on account of failing health, he went to Colorado and spent two years traveling in the Rocky Mountains; then returned to Prairie City, Ia. He came to Odebolt in 1877 and opened a law office, and in July of the following year formed his present partnership.

WALL LAKE.

H. B. Allen, postmaster of the firm of Allen & Jacobs, dealers in hardware and agricultural implements, was born in Clinton county, N. Y., in 1835; moved to Elgin, Ill., in 1855, and engaged in farming. In 1860 moved to De Kalb county, Ill. He enlisted in the 95th Ill. Vol. Inft., served three years. He was with Gen. Grant in the Vicksburg campaign, and was wounded, losing a portion of his right hand; was discharged in July, 1865. In 1867 he came to Sac county, Ia., and engaged in farming. He moved to Wall Lake in the autumn of 1874, and established present business. He was appointed postmaster in May, 1881. Mr. Jacobs, formerly of Benton county, Ia., became a member of the firm in Jan., 1882. They carry a large and complete stock of hardware. The agricultural warehouse is on the corner of Main and First sts. They handle goods from all the leading manufactories.

George Burgan, grain dealer and manager of D. Wayne & Co.'s business at Wall Lake, was born in Wayne county, O., in 1845; moved with parents to Muscatine, Ia. In 1862 he enlisted in the 35th Ia. Vol. Inft.; was at the sieges of Vicksburg, Nashville, Pleasant Hill; was up the Red river with Gen. Banks. He was discharged in 1865, and returned to Iowa. In 1867 he located in Carroll county and engaged in farming until 1874, when he engaged in the grain business. Office and warehouse on First st. They shipped during the year 1881 one hundred cars of grain.

Frank Chandler, dealer in hats, caps, boots, shoes, clothing, furnishing goods and groceries, was born in Maquoketa, Ia., in Sept., 1849, there resided until 1870, then moved to Lyons, Ia., as agent for the Northern and Diamond Joe packet lines, and after two years, became book-keeper for the Clinton Chair Co., after which he traveled for S. G. McGill, and later for H. C. & C. Durand, wholesale grocers, with whom he remained five years, then located at Wall Lake. Employs two clerks.

W. L. Ehlers, bookkeeper for Wilcox Bros., lumber dealers, was born in Oskaloosa, Ia., in Feb., 1866. In 1872 he entered the State University, at Iowa City. In the winter of 1876 he took charge of the poultry packing establishment of Beem, Turner & Co.; remained with them two years and moved to Wall Lake; entered the employ of J. C. Fletcher, dealer in general merchandise. He engaged as above in 1879.

J. Elliott, proprietor of the Eureka House, came to Wall Lake in Feb., 1882, from Ames, where he had resided for twenty years. The hotel is on the corner of Main and First streets, is well furnished and a first-class house.

J. J. Fones & Sons, grain dealers, formerly of Chicago, Ill., where they were engaged in the livery business several years; came to Wall Lake, Ia., in Jan., 1881, and purchased the elevator and business of G. W. Pitcher. Elevator has capacity of ten thousand bushels, and employs two men. During the year 1881 they shipped two hundred cars of grain. The business is conducted by J. J. Fones, Jr.; office on 1st street.

E. L. Pierce, dealer in hardware, tinware, stoves, etc., was born in Linn county, Ia., in Oct., 1850; received education at Mt. Vernon College, and engaged in farming until 1874, then moved to Cedar county and engaged in milling with Peet Bros. He remained there four years then moved to Wall Lake and engaged in present business in March, 1878. He makes specialties of Fuller, Warren & Co.'s stoves and the Glidden barbed wire.

C. F. Peck, dealer in general merchandise, was born in New London, Conn., in 1845; moved to Oneida, Ill., when thirteen years of age, and worked on a farm until Oct., 1863, then enlisted in the 8th Ill. Vol. Inft. and served until the close of the war. He returned to Ill. and remained three years; afterwards moved to Jefferson, Ia. He was engaged as carpenter until 1877, then engaged in mercantile business. He came to Wall Lake in 1880 and engaged in business as above; carries a fine stock of clothing, boots and shoes.

W. H. Peck, dealer in lumber, coal, lime, etc., was born in Onondaga county, N. Y., in 1854; received his education from the High School of Syracuse. In 1879 he moved to Sac county, Ia., and in the autumn of the same year purchased above business of H. J. Simpson. Office on Main street, near depot. He is assisted by F. M. Gregg.

C. L. Sherwood, agent for the Iowa Land company, was born in Berlin township, Delaware county, O., in June, 1817; remained there until 1854, and then moved to Clinton, Ia., where he engaged in farming. In 1873 he came to Sac county, purchased land in Clinton township, which he improved, and still owns, the farming being conducted by his sons. Mr. Sherwood was for several years postmaster at Wall Lake, also was postmaster in Clinton tp. before the office was abandoned. He became agent for the above company in 1873; office with W. H. Peck, lumber dealer. Mr. S. is one of the solid republicans of this county.

N. Wright, president of the bank of Wall Lake, was born in Cedar county, Ia., in 1846; resided there until the autumn of 1871, then purchased 320 acres of land in Sac county, on which he moved the spring following. He farmed until Feb., 1882, when he established the bank. Does a general banking business; this is the only established bank in Wall Lake. W. S. Bell, the cashier, is a gentleman of extensive experience in the banking business.

FLETCHER.

W. H. Ball, of the firm of W. H. Ball & Co., dealers in grain and seed, was born in Cedar county, Ia., in 1853. He was engaged in the grain business at Centerdale, Clinton county, for nine years. In 1880 came to Fletcher and was the first to locate business there.

D. C. Cook, M. D., of the firm of L. A. Chapman & Co., druggists, was born in N. Y. in May, 1850. He received preparatory education at Mt. Vernon, Ia., and graduated from the State University at Iowa City in March, 1873. He commenced the practice of medicine at Calamus. In Aug., 1881, he moved to Fletcher and formed present partnership. They carry a complete line of drugs, paints, oils, toilet articles, etc.

Albert Davis, station agent and proprietor of the Lake House, came to Sac county in March, 1877, from Clinton county, Ia. He purchased land in Wall Lake township. At the time of the tornado of April 21st of same year, he was living in a portion of his barn, which was entirely destroyed together with his household goods, his family happily escaping unhurt. He afterwards built a house 20x30 feet in dimensions and had just got settled in it when it was entirely destroyed by the tornado of Oct. 15th, of same year. In Dec., 1881, he moved to Fletcher and built the hotel. He carries a stock of confectionery, cigars and fancy groceries.

J. C. Fletcher, founder of the new town of Fletcher, was born in Franklin, Ind., in 1849; the same year moved with parents to Oskaloosa, Ia. He enlisted in 1864 in the 47th Ia. Inft., and served until the close of the war. He returned to Oskaloosa, and in 1873 moved to Sheffield where he engaged in business for two years, then moved to Wall Lake, where he engaged in the mercantile business. In Oct., 1880, he purchased the town site of Fletcher which he laid out in town lots and placed in the market, now it is a lively growing town and is situated near a beautiful lake. Mr. Fletcher formed a partnership in March, 1881, with H. W. Seevers, built a business house on Main street and engaged in the mercantile business. Mr. Seevers was born in Oskaloosa in 1859 and came to this place in the spring of 1880.

C. P. Hicks, of the firm of W. H. Ball & Co., was born in Philadelphia, Pa., in Oct., 1848. He graduated at the Bryant & Stratton College and was for several years in the employ of a commission house in Philadelphia, as bookkeeper and entry clerk. He moved to Cedar county, Ia., in 1874; thence to Sac county in Mar., 1881, purchased land near Fletcher and engaged in present business. From Aug., 1881, to Feb., 1882, they shipped sixty cars of grain.

Rev. William N. McKendrick, undertaker and dealer in furniture was born in Edinburg, Scotland, in 1832; came to America with parents and located in N. Y. In 1847 he moved to Western N. Y. He attended the Baptist College, of Montreal, Canada, for three years, and entered the University in 1859. He was ordained in Michigan, Sept. 20th, 1875. He located at Mapleton, Ia., in 1879, and was pastor of the Baptist church there for two years. He resigned in Sept., 1881; came to Fletcher, purchased property and engaged in present business. He is pastor here and preaches every Sabbath at the school house.

Charles Potts, farmer and land agent, was born in Ross county, O., in 1832. He served during the war of the rebellion in the 28th Ill. Vol. Inft., was wounded at Jackson, Miss. He came to Sac county in 1871 and purchased land on the north shore of Wall Lake. He owns one hundred acres of well improved land one and one-half miles east of Fletcher. He is agent for non-resident lands in this vicinity, also for the Acme pulverizing harrow and clod crusher.

J. O. Rich, proprietor of the livery, feed and sale stables, was formerly of Independence, Ia., where he was engaged as mason and plasterer for four years. In 1878 he moved to Sac county, purchased land in Wall Lake township, which he still owns. In Feb., 1882, he moved to Fletcher and erected a livery barn on Third st.

W. A. Robinson, postmaster and hardware merchant, was born in Vt. in 1815. He moved to Stockbridge, Mass., when quite young; in 1856 moved to Mercer county, Ill., and engaged in farming until 1869; then moved to Sac county, purchased land in Viola township, which he improved and still owns. He moved to Fletcher in Jan., 1882, and filled the office of postmaster, to which he was appointed in Dec., 1881. He erected building on Main st., which is occupied by postoffice and hardware stock. Mr. Robinson has filled many minor offices, was the first justice of the peace in Viola township. He has a notary public commission, and does a general collecting business, is agent for several insurance companies.

IDA COUNTY.

Ida County is in the fourth tier of counties from the northern boundary of the state, and is the second east of the Missouri River. It contains 432 square miles or 276,480 acres. The Maple River runs through the county from northeast to southwest. Its principal branches are the Odebolt and Elk, flowing in from the east, and Battle Creek from the west. Soldier River flows westward through the southern tier of townships. There are many smaller streams draining the county in all parts. The valleys of the streams are unsurpassed in fertility, and Maple Valley is especially noted for the beauty and fertility of its farming lands. Maple River, in this county, furnishes several mill sites. The general character of the surface is undulating or rolling prairie, though no portion is too broken for cultivation. The soil in the valleys is a dark mould, in many places from three to six feet deep. The uplands contain more clay, and are well adapted to the raising of wheat and all the cereal crops. This, like other counties in this part of the state, has but a limited supply of timber. We have it on authority of the county surveyor that this county has only about 1,000 acres of natural timber, about one-half of this being in Ida Grove, which is situated on Maple River in about the center of the county. It is mostly oak, walnut, linn, elm and hickory. The white or soft maple skirts the borders of the streams in many places.

Among the wild fruits, the plum, grape, gooseberry and strawberry are found. Stock-raising and dairying succeed well in this county, as it is unsurpassed for pasturage or hay. The wild grass known as the blue-joint predominates in the valleys, and in many places the yield of hay is as high as four tons per acre. Fine well water is found in almost any locality by digging to a moderate depth, rarely exceeding twenty-five feet. No regularly stratified rock formations appear at the surface. The only rocks obtained in the county are the boulders. An abundance of material suitable for the manufacture of brick is found in all parts of the county. The bluff deposit, which overspreads the entire county, has been successfully used for making brick of a good quality. The principal productions are wheat, oats, corn, rye and potatoes. All kinds of vegetables and root crops common to the latitude succeed well. The various kinds of small fruits are easily raised, as well as some varieties of cherries and apples.

The first authentic account of the early settlement of Ida county was that, in 1854, of Robert Townsley and Edward Smith, who built a cabin and raised a small crop of sod corn. During the same summer Samuel King settled about a mile further down the valley, and broke up a small farm. These, however, proved to be but transient settlers.

The first permanent settlement of whites in Ida County was made in Ida Grove, on Maple River, in 1856. The settlers were E. Comstock, from Michigan, and Judge John H. Morehead, whose family still resides at Ida Grove.

The county was organized in 1858. The first election was held at Ida Grove in August of that year, when the following officers were elected: John H. Moorehead, County Judge; J. S. Loveland, Treasurer and Recorder, and B. Warren, Clerk of the District Court. At this time the population of the county was only about forty persons. Since that the population has increased very rapidly and in 1880 was 4,382. The county has settled very fast within the past two years and 5,500 may now be considered a low estimate of population. The present county officers are: Isaac Bunn, Clerk of the Courts; Wm. Jones, Auditor; F. W. Tibbetts, Treasurer; T. S. Snell, County Surveyor; E. L. Worcester, Recorder; F. A. Eastman, Sheriff; Dr. A. T. Baker, Coroner; Mrs. A. H. Smith, Superintendent of Schools; J. G. Freeman, Chairman; John Bunn, James Taylor, Board of Supervisors.

The first child born in Ida County was Ida Grove Smith, daughter of Mr. and Mrs. E. Smith. The first death was a child of the same family. The remains were taken to Smithland, in Woodbury county, for interment. The first railroad, a branch of the Chicago & Northwestern, crossed into Ida County August 21st, 1877, and is now extended as far west as Mapleton, in Monona County. Ida County has fair prospects for another road through to Ida Grove soon—the same one that passes through Sac City and Sac County.

IDA GROVE.

The county seat of Ida county was, previous to arrival of the railroad, in the fall of 1877, situated on the north side of the railroad track and Odebolt River. After the appearance of the railroad at this place, a new town sprang up on the south side of the river, which was christened Ida Grove. This town is now the county seat, and is located on the northeast quarter of section 15, township 87, range 40. The village commands a fine view of the beautiful valley of Maple River. It is about twenty-eight miles from Denison, Crawford county.

Upon one of the high ridges near the village there was formerly an extensive Indian encampment, where the remains of buffalo, elk, deer, and other game are still scattered over the surface, or half embedded in the soil. The course of a deeply worn Indian trail is said to have been a great highway for the natives, who only a few years ago occupied this portion of the State.

The first postoffice established in the county was located at Ida, and for years this was the only one.

The old town of Ida was laid out in 1871 by S. W. Hobbs. The new town was laid out by the Blair Town and Lot Company in 1877, and is situated on the left bank of the Maple River, about five miles from the geographical center of the county. Isaac Bunn built the first house in Ida Grove. Selling that almost immediately, he erected the second, and still later the third house in the town. The first brick building was erected by Chaffee & Williams, in 1880, and is the one in which the *Pioneer* office is now located. Since then a number of massive brick structures have been erected, and the town is fast building up with large and substantial brick buildings.

The first child born in the town was Sarah, daughter of Mr. and Mrs. J. H. Macomber.

The first store was opened by Engstrom & Smith as a hardware store.

The town was incorporated April 26th, 1878. H. A. Miller was elected the first Mayor, and J. W. Reed. Recorder. The first Trustees were: T. S. Snell, W. P. Evans, J. O. Engstrom, Calvin Bailey, and L. Tinkle. The present town officers are: Frank Burns, Mayor; Frank W. Shearer, Recorder; A. L. Houser. J. E. Jurgenson, J. H. Stough, Trustees, and R. Johnston, Assessor.

The Ida County Pioneer was the first paper published in Ida Grove. During the winter of 1872, Robert Wilkinson, Frank Burns, C. P. Lund, C. C. Brown. Geo. E. Johnson, H. H. Lund, M. G. Aldrich, R. H. Campbell, W. J. Wagoner, W. P. Evans, W. Wilkinson, James F. Wilkinson, C. Hathaway, Isaac Bunn and E. B. West, formed themselves into a stock company for the purpose of purchasing material and publishing a newspaper at Ida. The necessary money was raised, and W. P. Evans took charge of the publishing. The first number, then as now, was called the *Ida County Pioneer*. and the first issue was on Thursday, March 3d, 1872, from the upper story of the Court House. The paper was a six-column folio. Republican in politics and began with a circulation of 150. It was printed in long primer type, upon an old poster press, known among older Iowa journalists as "Old Muley," the press upon which J. N. Dixon, the "blind editor." published his first paper. the *Indianola Journal*. It had also done service in the early days of Des Moines journalism on the *Iowa Statesman* and *State Register*. Immediately after the first sheet of the *Pioneer* was printed, it was taken by E. B. West, the County Auditor, down stairs and presented to the Board of Supervisors, who were then in session, and was made by them the official paper of the county. Within two or three months after the first issue of the paper. W. P. Evans purchased the shares of all the stockholders and became sole proprietor. On the 27th day of August, 1874, Evans sold the *Pioneer* to C. B. Chaffee and George T. Williams, who enlarged the paper to a seven-column folio. In the spring of 1876 Chaffee & Williams sold an "Amateur" press and purchased a large stock of job type and a new quarto-medium "Star" jobber, and in 1877 purchased a new Washington press. April 4th, 1878, the *Pioneer* was enlarged to an eight-column folio. In the spring of 1881, Chaffee & Williams sold the *Pioneer* to Theron Akin, who suppressed the paper. About the 1st of April, 1881, W. P. Evans re-established the *Pioneer*, purchasing a large office with four presses. The present proprietor continued the publication until December, 1881, when he leased it to Suiter & Simpson, two practical printers, who are. the present editors. It is one of the official papers of the county, is a seven-column quarto and has a circulation of 1,200.

The *Maple Valley Era* is a Republican paper, and was started by L. Stanfield and C. N. Clark, August 22d, 1877. This paper was started as a five-column quarto, but October 18th, 1877, it was enlarged to an eight-column folio. March 22d, 1879, L. Stanfield sold his interest to the junior partner, C. N. Clark, who changed the day of publication from Wednesday to Friday. Mr. Clark then added to the office a quarto-medium Gordon jobber, and a new invoice of type. In March, 1880, the paper was again enlarged, this time to a nine-column folio. July 1st, 1881, the publisher purchased a new power press, and enlarged the paper to a seven-column quarto. L. T. Chapin purchased a one-half interest in the *Era* January 1st, 1882, and it is now run under the firm name of Clark & Chapin. It is a Republican paper, and one of the official papers of the county. It has a circulation of 1,000 copies.

J. H. Moorehead was the first postmaster in Ida Grove, he having received his appointment in 1860. He was succeeded by W. P. Evans, who was appointed late in the year 1872. C. N. Clark is the present incumbent. It is a money-order office.

The first Court House of Ida County was built in the town of Ida in 1871, and was nearly completed before another building was begun on the town site. January 12th, 1877, the Court House was burned, together with most of the county records, and for three years afterwards the county offices were kept in small buildings rented by the county. During the latter part of the year 1879, the present Court House was built on a contract by which the county had the privilege of renting or buying at certain figures. The Clerk removed to the new building in December, 1879, and the other officers followed in January. The upper story is used for court purposes, and the lower part for various county offices. The county purchased the building in 1880. The population of the town may now be estimated to be from 1,200 to 1,500, and it is fast increasing.

The business of Ida Grove may be classified as follows: Six general stores, three grocery stores, one clothing store, one boot and shoe store, two restaurants. three drug stores, two banks, two fur-

niture stores, three hardware stores, four millinery stores, three
meat markets, two jewelry stores, three elevators, one grist mill,
four saloons, three hotels, three lumber yards, four agricultural
implement depots, five livery stables, four harness shops, two barber
shops, four blacksmith shops and four wagon shops, one plow
factory.

The Ida Creamery was established in the spring of 1882, and is
operated by Mauer Bros. They have a commodious brick building
20x32 feet, with a wing 14x30, which is frame. This creamery
has a capacity of 1,000 pounds per day. It is situated one-half
mile from the town and is operated on the cream-gathering plan.
Its internal arrangements are of the most modern plan.

CHURCHES, SCHOOLS AND SOCIETIES.

M. E. Church Society.—The Ida Circuit was originally part of
the Smithland Circuit, but was detached from this circuit in 1869,
and formed into the Maple River Circuit. In 1875, it was again
divided and called Ida Circuit. The first pastor who traveled this
section when within the bounds of the Smithland Circuit was
Rev. L. Taylor, who included in this work what is known as the
Sioux City District. Taylor was succeeded by Rev. Seymore
Snyder, and he by Rev. Adams, who in turn, was succeeded by
Rev. Barker, who was the last preacher on the circuit before it
was divided. Maple Circuit included a point on Soldier Creek,
Mapleton, Battle Creek and Ida Grove. Rev. L. H. Woodworth
was placed in charge, and was succeeded by J. P. Hauxhurst, who
was appointed to Ida Circuit in 1871. In September, 1872, Ida
Circuit was set off from the Maple Circuit, and Rev. Harrison
Bailey was appointed pastor, and was reappointed in 1873. He
was followed by Rev. L. H. Woodworth. In 1875, Mr. Bailey
was again appointed to this charge, and was succeeded by Rev.
W. B. Hastings. At the session of the annual conference, in
September, 1876, Ida was attached to Fort Dodge district, with
Rev. Edwin Hobbs as pastor. Ida was made a separate charge in
September, 1878. Rev. C. B. Winter afterwards took charge and
was followed by Rev. Henry Brown, who is the present pastor.
The church building, located on Moorehead Avenue, in Old Town,
is the pioneer of the houses of worship. It is 32x45 feet, and
contains 250 sittings. It was erected at a cost of $1,900. It was
dedicated in November, 1878. The parsonage was erected in the
fall of 1881. It is 16x26 feet, and cost $700. The church mem-
bership is about eighty. With the church is connected a Sabbath
School, with an average attendance of fifty pupils. H. B. Pierce
is Superintendent.

Baptist Church Society.—Organized August 16th, 1879, by D.
D. Proper. Rev. J. W. Daniels was the first pastor. He was
succeeded by Rev. C. E. McManis, who took charge in July, 1881,

and who is the present pastor. The officers of the church are: W.
H. Bliss and R. H. Dawson. Deacons; Albert Needham, Clerk; F.
R. Moorehead, Treasurer. The Society now numbers about forty
members, and has a Sabbath School with an average attendance
of fifty pupils, with D. H. Sanford as Superintendent. The
church was built in 1880. It is a large frame building, 30x50
feet, with a side vestibule 10x16 feet. The whole is surmounted
by a belfrey. The basement is fitted up to contain a robing room
and a baptistry. The building was erected under the supervision
of Rev. J. W. Daniels. The seating capacity is about 350, including gallery. It is of the Gothic style, furnished with handsome stained glass windows, and is quite an ornament to the town.

Presbyterian Church Society.—This society was organized in
1873, by George R. Carroll. Rev. A. E. Smith was the first pastor
and took charge in 1878. The present officers of the church are:
John A. Lytle. Alex. Hartly and F. Sampson, Elders. The society now numbers sixty-four members. There is a Sabbath School
with an average attendance of ninety pupils. H. W. Rule is the
Superintendent. The church was erected in 1880. It is a neat
frame building 30x50 feet, with a tower 8x8 feet, and 60 feet high,
and a recess back of the pulpit 5x9 feet. It contains 150 sittings,
and cost about $3,000.

Catholic Church Society.—Was organized about 1879, and has
a membership of about sixty families. Rev. Father Norton is the
pastor. The church was erected in 1879. It is a frame building
30x40 feet, an l has about 250 sittings, and cost $2,400.

Ida Grove Public School.—This is an independent school district. The school building is a fine structure, erected in 1881.
It contains six rooms and a basement, and is heated by two
furnaces. It was erected at a cost of 11,000. There are three
teachers employed, and an average attendance of 100 pupils. Prof.
O. E. Smith is the principal, Miss Bertha Barker and Retta Dawson assistants. The present school board are: I. Kennedy,
President; D. A. Grosvenor, E. L. Worcester, L. Tinkle, S. B.
Higgins and Isaac Bunn, Trustees; F. W. Shearer, Secretary.

Kane Lodge No. 377, A. F. & A. M.—This Lodge was instituted July 8th. 1876, and the charter was granted June 8th,
1877. The charter members were: Matt. M. Gray, W. M.; O.
Waterman, S. W.; Chas. Beers, J. W.; W. Vankirk, S. D.; E. S.
Bigelow, J. D.; T. S. Snell, Secretary; Calvin Bailey, Treasurer;
A. A. Stowell, Tiler. These were also the first officers. The
officers now are: S. B. Carr, W. M.; W. Vankirk. S. W.; G. F.
Barnes, J. W.; H. A. Worcester, Secretary; Noah Williams, Treasurer; W. J. Scott, J. D., and E. Whitcomb, Tiler. The Lodge
now has a membership of thirty-seven, and meets once in each
month. The Lodge contemplates building a hall this year.

Ida Grove Lodge No. 74, V. A. S.—Instituted August 23d,
1881, by Mr. Maltbie. The first officers are: S. B. Higgins,

Rector; D. N. Goodell, Scribe: J. C. Higgins, Questor; P. H. Hillman, Usher, and Mr. Machahan, Speculator. The Lodge numbers nineteen members and meets the first Wednesday in each month. The present officers are: P. H. Hillman, Rector; J. B. Williams, Scribe; Isaac Bunn, Questor; Harry Shamo, Usher, and Frank Wright, Speculator.

Ida County Agricultural Society.—Organized March, 1875. The society has thirty-five acres of grounds, situated three-fourths of a mile from town, and the best half-mile track in Ida County. The grounds are all enclosed with a close board fence, and have a nice floral hall, sheds, etc. This society holds its fairs annually.

BATTLE CREEK.

Battle Creek, which is situated on the Maple Valley Branch of the Chicago & Northwestern Railroad, about forty-five miles from the junction, is located in the centre of the beautiful Maple Valley, and was laid out by the Blair Town and Lot Company, in 1877, on lands purchased by the company from W. J. Wagoner, of Denison. Located as it is, it presents a fair appearance from all points on each side of the valley. The soil is fertile and productive, and the town is located in a rich farming country. The depot was built in 1877.

Frank E. Beckwith moved the first house into the town in 1879, which building was used as a boarding-house. Charles Havens built the first house constructed in the town and used it as a saloon. The first store was opened by John Nott in the spring of 1880. William Warner soon after opened a store. Sam. Warnock was the first to engage in the lumber business. John Nott was appointed the first postmaster and has held the position ever since. John Holcomb was among the earliest settlers and was the first to engage in the hotel business.

The town was incorporated in December, 1880, and A. Bassett was elected the first Mayor; W. Jones, Recorder, and J. M. Boles, John Nott, William Warner, W. H. James, Sam. Warnock, and Peter Amerman, Councilmen. The population of the town is now estimated to be between 400 and 500 people. The present town officers are: A. Bassett, Mayor; J. C. Walter, Recorder; A. V. McKown, Sam. Warnock, W. E. Churchill, John Nott, B. C. Bowman and Hugh Smith, Councilmen.

The business of Battle Creek may be classified thus: Three general stores, two drug stores, one harness shop, two meat markets, three hotels, one bank, one furniture store, two saloons, three lumber yards, three agricultural implement depots, two millinery stores, one elevator, one barber shop, two blacksmith shops, one wagon shop, one livery stable, one restaurant.

Battle Creek is situated in the heart of an excellent farming country, and is undoubtedly destined, if one may judge the future

by the past, to become one of the most important business points
in Western Iowa. Its growth has been rapid and vigorous, and
still continues, and all fair-minded people who have given the subject consideration, will coincide with us in the view given.

The *Battle Creek Times*, a neat seven-column folio weekly
paper, was started by Hugh Brannan, April 23d, 1880. Mr. B.
ran the paper but three months, when the material was bought by
S. Warnock and W. E. Roberts, who hired John Jones to run it.
It was afterwards leased to J. L. Kroesen, now of the Wall Lake
Journal. S. W. Young purchased the paper in the fall of 1881,
and is now editor and proprietor. It is Republican is politics, and
has a circulation of 550 copies.

CHURCHES, SCHOOLS AND SOCIETIES.

M. E. Church Society.—The M. E. Church Society of Battle
Creek was organized March, 1881. The first pastor was Rev. O.
L. Neville, who was succeeded by the present pastor, Rev. F. M.
Luce. The first officers were: H. Haworth, M. L. Branch, F. M.
Lewis, and A. B. McKown, and are still serving as officers of the
church. The society now numbers about twenty. It has a Sabbath School in connection, with an average attendance of forty
pupils. M. L. Branch is the Superintendent. The church building was erected in 1881-2, and was dedicated February 26th, 1882.
It is a neat frame structure, 26x40 feet, with a tower 10x10 feet
on the corners, surmounted with a belfrey, which contains a large
bell. It has about 200 sittings and cost $2,000.

Presbyterian Church Society.—Organized June 13th, 1879.
The first officers were: E. P. Smith, G. W. McWilliams, R.
Warnock, James Preston, and John S. Piffer. Rev. A. E. Smith
was the first pastor. The present officers are the same as the first.
The present pastor is J. C. Gilkerson. The church building was
completed in 1880. It is 26x40 feet, and cost $2,000.

Battle Creek Public School.—Wilson Jones taught the first
school in the town. The district is still a sub-district of Maple
Township. The present school building was moved from outside
the limits into the town, and formerly used as a town hall. It was
converted into a school building a few years ago. The present
school board of Maple Township consists of ten directors, one
from each sub-district. S. Beard is President, Wilson Jones is
the Secretary, and A. Stowell Treasurer. The Battle Creek school
numbers eighty-five pupils. Wilson Jones is principal, and Mrs.
E. Warner, assistant.

Samaritan Lodge, A. F. & A. M.—Dispensation was granted
March 21st, 1881. The first and present officers are: G. W.
Hoskins, W. M.; J. P. Creager, S. W.; W. E. Churchill, J. W.
The charter members were: P. K. Taylor, A. V. McKown, H.
Lampman, Wm. Warner, H. S. Squyer, J. C. Stoughton, A. R.

Graiser, A. C. Hoyt, J. L. Richardson, Smith Waite. The society meets once each month, and has a membership of about twenty. *Battle Creek Lodge No. 202, A. O. U. W.*—This Lodge was instituted August 15th, 1879. The charter members and first officers were: A. A. Stowell, Foreman; R. K. Cameron, P. M. W.; I. N. Goin, M. W.; C. W. Oxwood, O.; H. N. Davis, Rec.; W. Jones, Financier; A. L. Brockway, Rec.; P. K. Taylor, G.; A. A. Nauman, I. W.; B. Graiser, O. W. The present officers are: J. Nott, M. W.; W. Jones, P. M. W. and Rec.; R. A. McWilliams, Foreman; A. Lampman, O.; C. F. Sufeld, Rec.; J. I. Rogers, G.; J. F. Snyder, I. W.; A. Nauman; O. W. The society now numbers about fifteen members, and holds its meetings every Saturday night.

IDA COUNTY BIOGRAPHIES.

IDA GROVE.

A. T. Baker, M. D., was born in Jackson county, Ia., in 1847. He began the study of medicine at an early age, graduated from the Iowa State University in the class of '76. The same year he located at Webster City, where he soon built up a large and lucrative practice. He moved to Ida Grove in 1879, and is one of the leading physicians of the county.

Ed. H. Barnes, stock dealer, was born in St. Albans, N. Y.; moved to Manchester, Ia., in 1855; was there engaged in business for twelve years. He went to Waterloo, where he engaged in the hotel business; then went to Yankton, Dak. He built the telegraph line from there to Fort Sully. In 1871 he came to Ida county, Ia., and was elected sheriff in 1872.

L. G. Blair, photographer, was born in Ill.; moved to Wis. when quite young, and in 1876 moved to Denison, Ia. He came to Ida Grove in 1879, and established business. He has a branch establishment at Odebolt; is prepared to do first-class work at low prices.

O. J. Blodgett, attorney at law, is a native of N. Y.; moved to Warren county, Iowa, in 1868; was admitted to the bar in 1880, and located in Ida Grove in 1881; is now one of the leading attorneys of Ida county.

Isaac Bunn, clerk of the courts, is a native of England; came to America in 1851 and located at Cleveland, O.; removed to Dubuque, Ia., in 1856; thence to Ida Grove in 1871, where he engaged in wagon-making and blacksmithing. He was elected to his present office in 1874, and has been re-elected each term since.

L. T. Burd, attorney at law, was born in Pa.; moved to Ill. when quite young. He read law in the office of the Hon. J. W. McDill; came to Ida Grove in Jan., 1882, and opened an office.

Buxton & Clark, real estate, loan and insurance agents. The firm is composed of Will. B. Buxton and C. J. Clark; they were formerly engaged in mercantile business at this place; sold out and engaged as above in 1881. They also have a complete set of abstracts.

Clark & Hubbard, real estate, loan and insurance agents. Mr. Clark is a native of Wis.; moved to Butler county, Ia., in 1868, and engaged in farming. He engaged in the real estate and insurance business in 1876 and two years later moved to Ida Grove, where he engaged in business as above. George C. Hubbard became a member of the firm in Jan., 1882.

Matt. M. Gray, attorney at law, was born in Hancock county, Ill., in 1850; moved to Mo. and engaged in the practice of the law. In 1872 he came to Ida Grove; opened the first law office in the town, and in 1873 was elected county auditor, which office he held until 1876; then was obliged to resign on account of his large and increasing law business. He has been associated in business with Hon. R. T. Shearer.

G. H. Gingrick, of the firm of G. H. Gingrick & Co., dealers in general hardware, is a native of Ohio; came to Iowa in 1878. He moved to Ida Grove and engaged in present business with A. M. Gingrick, who is also a native of O.; came to Iowa county, Ia., in 1856 and to Ida Grove in 1880. They carry a large and well selected stock of hardware.

E. C. Heilman, of the firm of Heilman & Moorehead, physicians and surgeons, was born in Scott county, Ia. He graduated from the Ohio Medical College in the class of '77. G. C. Moorehead is a graduate of the Iowa State University, class of '79.

L. D. Ingman, of the firm of Dean & Ingman, dealers in dry goods, clothing and carpets, was born in Ohio; came to Cedar county, Ia., in 1859. He enlisted in 1861 in the 5th Ia. Inft., was discharged in 1864, and returned to Cedar county, where he engaged in the mercantile business. He came to Ida Grove in 1880, and engaged in business as above.

William Jones, county auditor, is a native of Wis.; came to Ida county, Ia., in 1876, and engaged in teaching until elected to his present office, in the autumn of 1881.

Arthur L. Moore, of the firm of G. A. Edmunds & Co., dealers in general merchandise, is a native of Va.; came west in 1870, and in 1875 located at Sioux City, and was employed in the wholesale department of the dry goods house of Tootle, Livingston & Co., for six years. He then established present business. They carry a stock of goods that would be a credit to a much larger city; also have a branch house at Correctionville, Ia.

J. H. Macomber, attorney at law, was born in Piscataquis county, Me. Was admitted to the bar and practiced law in his native state until 1876; he then moved to Ida Grove, where he opened an office and resumed the practice of law.

H. H. Moorehead, manager for the Green Bay Lumber Co., came to Ida county, Ia., in 1856. He engaged in the mercantile business in the spring of 1869, which business he continued until 1878. In 1880 he engaged as above.

H. H. Perry, proprietor of Ball's Hotel, is a native of Ill.; moved to Marshalltown, Ia., in 1868, and engaged in the mercantile business. In Dec., 1881, he became landlord of the above house. This hotel is a first-class house, has large sample rooms, and all the comforts required by travelers.

H. B. Pierce, deputy recorder, is a native of Ill.; moved with parents to Cedar county, Ia., in 1865. He moved to Carroll county in 1874, and engaged in school teaching; came to Ida Grove in 1878, where he was principal of the schools for three years. In 1881 was appointed deputy recorder.

E. A. Porter, proprietor of the Porter House, is a native of O.; moved to Guthrie county, Ia., in 1856, and engaged in the grain business. He came to Ida Grove in 1881, and opened the above named house, which was newly furnished. It is a first-class house with good sample rooms.

Patrick Scanlan, agent for the C. & N. W. R. R. Co. at Ida Grove, came to this place in 1881 and took charge of the above office; is also agent for the American Express Co.

William J. Scott, druggist, was born in Pa.; is a graduate of Girard College, of Philadelphia. He moved to Glidden, Ia., in 1877 and engaged in the drug business. In 1879 he came to Ida Grove, and engaged in present business.

F. W. Tibbetts, county treasurer, is a member of the firm of Tibbetts, Thompson & Co., dealers in grain and agricultural implements. He was born in N. H.; moved to Wis. in 1855; thence to Iowa in 1864 and engaged in farming. He came to Ida Grove in 1877 and engaged in business with his brother; the firm soon after became Tibbetts & Tuthill, afterwards became Tibbetts, Thompson & Co. He was elected to his present office in 1881.

L. Tinkle, dealer in general merchandise, is the pioneer merchant of Ida Grove. The business is conducted by B. F. Dugan. He is a native of Ohio; came to Iowa in 1868 and engaged in the mercantile business at Fort Dodge. He became bookkeeper and manager of the above house in 1878.

O. G. Tremaine, M. D., was born in Oconomowoc, Wis., in 1854; moved to Hamilton county, Ia., in 1867. He began the study of medicine in 1877 and graduated from the Hahnemann Medical College, of Chicago, in 1880. He located at Ida Grove in Oct., 1881, and engaged in the practice of medicine.

Dr. J. T. Walker, druggist, is a native of Ind.; moved to Iowa in 1854 and in 1867 engaged in the mercantile business with his father, in Linn county. He studied medicine and in 1872 graduated from the Rush Medical College, of Chicago. He opened an office at Vail, Crawford county, Ia. Came to Ida Grove in 1877 and is the pioneer druggist of the place.

A. P. Williams, real estate and insurance agent, was born in Ind.; moved to Benton County, Ia., in 1856. He has been engaged in business in Cedar Rapids and Omaha. Came to Ida Grove in 1881 and engaged in business as above.

BATTLE CREEK.

D. R. Archer, real estate dealer and proprietor of the Holcomb House, was born in Ind.; came to Ia. in 1880, and engaged in the real estate business; has sold since about twenty-five thousand acres of land, of which one-third has been to actual settlers.

B. C. Bowman, of the firm of S. H. Bowman & Co., lumber dealers, is a native of Md.; moved to Neb. in 1876; thence to Ia. in 1879 and engaged in the lumber business at Odebolt, Ida Grove, Danbury and Battle Creek.

W. E. Churchill, dealer in hardware and agricultural implements, was born in N. Y.; came to Clarence, Ia., in 1862, and was employed as salesman in a hardware store until 1871, when he engaged in business for himself. He moved to Battle Creek in 1878, and engaged in business as above.

C. P. Lund, dealer in agricultural implements and stock, was born in Denmark in 1834; came to America in 1861 and engaged in farming in Wis. In 1870 moved to Ida county, Ia., and in 1877 came to Battle Creek and engaged in stock and lumber business. In 1881 engaged in the above named business.

Jasper McArthur, farmer, was born in Linn county, Ia., in April, 1857; came to Crawford county in March, 1878, where he engaged in farming on 145 acres, section 1. His postoffice is Battle Creek. On Jan. 1st, 1879, he was married to Ella Page, of Linn county. They have one child.

G. W. McIntosh, furniture dealer, is a native of Wis.; came to Ia. in 1869, and engaged as carpenter and builder. He moved to Red Oak in 1873, and to Battle Creek in 1877. In 1881 he engaged in his present business.

John Nott, postmaster, was born in Wis. in 1847; moved to Ida, Ia., in 1874; thence to Willow Dale, near the present town of Battle Creek, and engaged in the mercantile business. He was appointed postmaster in 1876; the office was moved to Battle Creek in 1877; he also moved there, having sold his business, and is still in office.

APPENDIX.

Under this heading will be found historical and biographical matters that were received too late for insertion in their proper places:

AURELIA.

Aurelia, located in the eastern part of Cherokee County, on the line of the Illinois Central Railroad. was platted by the railroad company in 1870. It was incorporated in 1880. The first town officers, under incorporation, were: W. C. Marsh, Mayor; J. W. McMillan, Clerk; George Wharton, Treasurer; George Nelson, Marshal and Street Commissioner; W. P. Miller, R. C. Kleberger, W. F. Quirk, Alexander Frazer, G. A. Enright. W. H. Reynolds, Councilmen. Present town officers: A. Potter, Mayor; J. W. McMillan, Clerk; George Wharton, Treasurer: J. Fraser, Marshal: D. Watts, Street Commissioner; R. R. Whitney, C. R. Kleberger, H. Bisheal, William Natress, George Orswell, E. Daniels, Councilmen.

The first store in Aurelia was built by J. Clarkson in the autumn of 1869; the first dwelling, by R. R. Whitney, in 1870; the first child born was Carrie Aurelia Sampson, daughter of John and Naomi Sampson, born March 19th, 1874; the first train of cars arrived at Aurelia, in July, 1870; the first grain was shipped from Aurelia in the autumn of 1871, by R. R. Whitney.

The business establishments of Aurelia may be classified as follows: General stores, five; lumber yards, three; grocery stores, two; hardware, three; boot and shoe stores, two; harness shops, two; meat markets, two; livery barns, two; hotel, one; furniture store, one; photographer, one; millinery stores, two; coal dealers, four; blacksmith shops, two; wagon shop, one; drugstore, one; bank, one; printing office, one; saloons, two; bakery and restaurant, one; grain elevators, four; warehouses, two; veterinary surgeon. one; attorney, one; physician, one.

CHURCHES, SCHOOLS AND SOCIETIES.

The Methodist Church Society.—Organized October 31st, 1878, by Rev. Mr. Faus, with four members. Present membership, about one hundred. Rev. W. Parfitt, present pastor. The church edifice is 45x26 feet in dimensions, and was built at a cost of $1,600.

The Lutheran Church Society.—This society erected its church edifice in 1881. The church is 40x28 feet in dimensions. and cost $2,000. Twenty-five families are represented in the membership. Rev. Amen Johnson is the pastor.

Aurelia Public Schools.—The schools of Aurelia will be graded during spring of the present year, and the district properly organized as an independent one. A fine school building 48x42 feet is nearly completed. It will cost $3,500.

Iowa Legion of Honor —On the 27th of February, present year, a Lodge of the Iowa Legion of Honor was instituted at Aurelia. The Lodge was started with thirty-three charter members.

AURELIA BIOGRAPHIES.

J. R. Atwood, cashier of the Bank of Aurelia, is a native of Illinois; came to Iowa in July, 1881, and engaged in banking at Aurelia.

Oscar Chase, dealer in agricultural implements, is a native of N. Y.; came to Iowa in May, 1869, and settled in Cherokee county, on section twenty-eight, and built the first house in the township. In 1881, he moved to Aurelia, and engaged in present business.

Edward Daniels, dealer in meat and live stock, was born in Middlesex county, Mass. Moved to Boston, and engaged in Boylston Market; remained there twenty years; moved to Iowa and settled near Aurelia, in 1869; engaged in farming until 1878, when he came to Aurelia, and engaged in business as above.

S. A. Frisbie, dealer in grain and stock, was born in Essex county, N. Y.; moved to Iowa in 1875, and engaged in the mercantile business at Aurelia. In 1881 he engaged in business as above.

Alexander Fraser, grain dealer, is a native of Wis.; moved to Clayton county, Iowa, in 1859; thence to Aurelia in 1871, and engaged in his present business. He is one of the largest grain dealers in the county, and one of the representative citizens of Aurelia.

W. C. Marsh, manager of the mercantile house of Wharton & Bruskill, is a native of N. Y. In 1849 he moved to Wis., where he engaged in farming; thence in 1875 to Aurelia. He built the first hotel in the town, and in 1879 engaged in business as above.

W. H. Nolte, of the firm of Nolte & Davis, dealers in dry goods and groceries, was born in Ill.; came to Aurelia, Ia., in 1880, and engaged in present business. The firm have a fine store, and carry a large stock of goods.

D. G. Toenjes, dealer in staple and fancy groceries and queensware, is a native of Germany; came to America in 1874 and settled in Jones county, Ia. In 1881 he came to Aurelia, and engaged in business as above.

George Wharton, of the firm of Wharton & Bruskill, was born in Dubuque county, Iowa, in 1851. He graduated from the Dubuque High School in 1874; then entered the store of Crotes & Walters, where he remained one year; thence to Aurelia, and engaged in business as above.

R. R. Whitney, grain dealer, is a native of Canada; moved to McGregor, Ia., when there was but one house in the town. He engaged in farming until 1869; then came to Aurelia and engaged in the stock and grain business.

SPENCER BIOGRAPHIES.

T. P. Bender and W. L. Bender, of the firm of Bender Bros., dealers in grain and stock, came from Pa. to Spencer, Ia., in 1872 and engaged in mercantile business. They built an elevator during 1881 at a cost of $7,000. This elevator has a capacity of 15,000 bushels and is the largest elevator on the line of the road west of McGregor. T. P. Bender has a large stock farm near the city. They have paid for stock and grain during the year 1881, $150,000.

J. F. and C. A. Constant, of the firm of Constant Bros., dealers in boots, shoes and gentlemen's furnishing goods, established business in 1881. They carry a large and complete stock of goods.

Rev. P. H. Eighmy is pastor of the M. E. Church of Spencer, Ia. He has been very successful since coming to this city and through his efforts added forty members to his church.

W. C. Gilbreath, dealer in grain and stock, came to Spencer in 1878 from Williamsville, Ill. He first engaged in mercantile business with I. F. Constant, but afterwards was engaged in publishing the *Clay County News*. In 1881 he engaged in his present business. He was the first mayor of Spencer.

A. W. Miller, cashier of the Clay county bank, came to Clay county in 1868 and settled on a farm near Peterson. He moved to Spencer in 1871 and engaged in milling; he entered the banking business in 1876. The bank is on the corner of Main and Fourth streets; it occupies a brick block that was recently erected.

SIOUX CITY.

The Sioux National Bank of Sioux City, Iowa, with a capital of $200,000.00, is the largest bank in Western Iowa. Bills of exchange are bought and sold on principal cities in the United States and Great Britain. The bank has special facilities for issuing drafts on cities in France, Germany, Norway and Sweden. The White Star Line of Steamers is also represented. The Directors are: J. C. C. Hoskins, Wm. L. Joy, A. S. Garretson, Judge J. R. Zuver, Geo. Murphy, Alexander Elliott, D. P. Hale. Wm. L. Joy, President; A. S. Garretson, Cashier.

R. J. Chase. attorney at law, was born in Unity, Sullivan county, N. H., in 1840; removed with family to Nashua, N. H., when quite young; came west at 17 years of age and settled in Vernon county, Wis. After serving in the army during the rebellion, he returned to Madison, Wis., and began the practice of law; came west in 1873 and platted the town of Sibley, Osceola county, Iowa. Mr. Chase's name, unsolicited by him, was used by his friends in connection with the district judgeship in 1874, and he received a good vote in convention. In connection with O. J. Taylor, he opened his present office in the fall of the same year. The firm has a large practice in the higher courts.

STORM LAKE.

J. A. Dean, of Storm Lake, Buena Vista county, is President of the Iowa Land and Investment Co.; was cashier of the Storm Lake Bank. and is a Director of the first National Bank of Storm Lake. The first named company has a capital stock of $50.000, and is incorporated for the purpose of negotiating long-time loans on real estate security, and transacting a real estate and general agency business. The Storm Lake Bank was discontinued on the 3d day of January, 1882, and its business transferred to the First National Bank of Storm Lake, which has an authorized capital of $100,000. James Harker is the President; J. C. French, Cashier.

Erratum.--In the table of population by counties, that of Plymouth County should read 8,567 instead of 3,567.

www.ingramcontent.com/pod-product-compliance
Lightning Source LLC
Chambersburg PA
CBHW022126020426
42334CB00015B/777

9783741123429